The Memorial Book
for the Jewish Community of
Yurburg, Lithuania

Translation and Update
of

Sefer HaZikaron
LeKehilat Yurburg-Lita

ספר הזיכרון
לקהילת
יורבורג-ליטא

(Jurbarkas, in Lithuanian)

Editor of the Original Book: Zevulun Poran

Editor and Compiler of the English Edition: Joel Alpert

Published by JewishGen, Inc

An Affiliate of the Museum of Jewish Heritage
A Living Memorial to the Holocaust
New York

The Yurburg Yizkor Book

The Memorial Book for the Jewish Community of Yurburg, Lithuania
Translation and Update

Copyright © 2003 by Joel Alpert
All rights reserved.
First Printing: January 2013
Second Printing: January 2004, Tevet 5764
Third Printing: March 2019, Adar II 5779

Editor and Compiler of the English Edition: Joel Alpert
Assistant Editors of the English Edition: Josef Rosin and Fania Hilelson Jivotovsky
Layout: Joel Alpert
Cover Design: Nina Schwartz, Impulse Graphics LLC

Published by JewishGen, Inc.
An Affiliate of the Museum of Jewish Heritage
A Living Memorial to the Holocaust
36 Battery Place, New York, NY 10280

JewishGen, Inc. is not responsible for inaccuracies or omissions in the original work and makes no representations regarding the accuracy of this translation. Digital images of the original book's contents can be seen online at the New York Public Library website.

The mission of the JewishGen organization is to produce a translation of the original work, and we cannot verify the accuracy of statements or alter facts cited.

Printed in the United States of America by Lightning Source, Inc.

Library of Congress Control Number (LCCN): 2003108677
ISBN: 978-1-939561-81-7 (hard cover: 800 pages, alk. paper)

Cover Credits:
Front cover:. The Wooden Synagogue in Yurburg, from a 1926 postcard. Back Cover: Betar and Hechalutz youth groups working with Lithuanian farmers near Shaudina (across the river from Yurburg), 1937, preparing for kibbutz life in Israel and the Yurburg Jewish Cemetery, 2012.

Title of the original Yizkor Book

ספר הזיכרון
לקהילת יורבורג - ליטא

בעריכת : זבולון פורז

יצא לאור ע״י איגוד יוצאי-יורבורג בישראל
ירושלים, תשנ״א—1991

Translation of the title of the original Yizkor Book

The Memorial Book
for the Jewish Community of Yurburg, Lithuania

Editor: Zevulun Poran

Published by:
The Organization of Former Residents of Yurburg in Israel

1991 - Jerusalem

JewishGen and the Yizkor-Books- in-Print Project

This book has been published by the Yizkor Books in Print Project, as part of the Yizkor Book Project of JewishGen, Inc.

JewishGen, Inc. is a non-profit organization founded in 1987 as a resource for Jewish genealogy. Its website [www.jewishgen.org] serves as an international clearinghouse and resource center to assist individuals who are researching the history of their Jewish families and the places where they lived. JewishGen provides databases, facilitates discussion groups, and coordinates projects relating to Jewish genealogy and the history of the Jewish people. In 2003, JewishGen became an affiliate of the Museum of Jewish Heritage—A Living Memorial to the Holocaust in New York.

The JewishGen Yizkor Book Project was organized to make more widely known the existence of Yizkor (Memorial) Books written by survivors and former residents of various Jewish communities throughout the world. Later, volunteers connected to the different destroyed communities began cooperating to have these books translated from the original language—usually Hebrew or Yiddish—into English, thus enabling a wider audience to have access to the valuable information contained within them. As each chapter of these books was translated, it was posted on the JewishGen website and made available to the general public.

The Yizkor Books in Print Project began in 2011 as an initiative to print and publish Yizkor Books that had been fully translated, so that hard copies would be available for purchase by the descendants of these communities and also by scholars, universities, synagogues, libraries, and museums.

These Yizkor books have been produced almost entirely through the volunteer effort of researchers from around the world, assisted by donations from private individuals. The books are printed and sold at near cost, so as to make them as affordable as possible. Our goal is to make this important genre of Jewish literature and history available in English in book form, so that people can have the personal histories of their ancestral towns on their bookshelves for themselves and for their children and grandchildren.

JewishGen
Yizkor Book Project

This book is presented by the
Yizkor Books in Print Project
Project Coordinator: Joel Alpert

Part of the
Yizkor Books Project of JewishGen, Inc.
Project Manager: Lance Ackerfeld

These books have been produced solely through volunteer effort
of individuals from around the world. The books are printed and
sold at near cost, so as to make them as affordable as possible.

Our goal is to make this history and important genre of Jewish
literature available in English in book form so that people can have
the near-personal histories of their ancestral towns on their bookshelves for themselves and for their children and grandchildren.

Any donations to the Yizkor Books Project are appreciated.

Please send donations to:
Yizkor Book Project
JewishGen
36 Battery Place
New York, NY 10280

JewishGen, Inc. is an affiliate of the
Museum of Jewish Heritage
A Living Memorial to the Holocaust

Notes to the Reader:

We apologize ahead of time for the poor quality of images in the book. Often these images had been scanned from the original Yizkor book which were of poor quality to begin with, being copies of old photographs. Each transfer results in loss of quality. We have done the best we could, given the original material and the resources and technology at hand. Even though images often appear of higher quality on computer screens, that does not transfer to high quality images in print. A reader can view the original scans on the web sites listed below.

Also please note that all references within the text of the book to page numbers, refer to the page numbers of the original Yizkor Book.

The original book can be seen on-line at the Yiddish Book Center web site:

https://www.yiddishbookcenter.org/collections/yizkor-books/yzk-nybc313803/poran-zevulun-sefer-ha-zikaron-li-kehilat-yurburg-lita

In order to obtain a list of all Shoah victims from Yurburg (Jurbarkas), the reader should access the Yad Vashem web site listed below; one can also search for specific family names using family name option. These lists are continually updated by Yad Vashem, so it is worthwhile to periodically search these lists.

There is much valuable information available on this web site, including the Pages of Testimony, etc.

http://yvng.yadvashem.org

A list of this book and all books available in the Yizkor-Book-In-Print Project along with prices is available at:
http://www.jewishgen.org/Yizkor/ybip.html

To obtain a video copy of the 1927 Craine film of Yurburg for study or research from National Center for Jewish Film please contact the National Center for Jewish Film, Brandeis University MS053, Lown bldg 102, Waltham, MA 02454-9110, or contact jewishfilm@brandeis.edu or www.jewishfilm.org.

Geopolitical Information:

Jurbarkas, Lithuania: 55°04' North Latitude, 22°46' East Longitude

Alternate names: Jurbarkas [Lithuanian], Yurburg [Yiddish, Russian], Georgenburg [German], Jurbarka [Latvian], Jurbork [Polish], Jurgenburg, Jurborg, Jurburg, Yorburg, Yorvorig, Yurbarkas

Period	Town	District	Province	Country
Before WWI (c. 1900):	Jurbarkas	Rossieny	Kovno	Russian Empire
Between the wars (c. 1930):	Jurbarkas	Raseiniai		Lithuania
After WWII (c. 1950):	Jurbarkas			Soviet Union
Today (c. 2018):	Jurbarkas			Lithuania

Jewish population in 1900: 2350

Nearby Jewish Communities:

Šiaudinė 1 miles E

Sudargas 5 miles WSW

Skirsnemunė 6 miles ENE

Smalininkai 7 miles W

Gelgaudiškis 9 miles E

Šakiai 14 miles SE

Eržvilkas 14 miles N

Šimkaičiai 15 miles NE

Sadovo, Russia 20 miles WSW

Veliuona 20 miles E

Kudirkos Naumiestis 21 miles SSE

Griškabūdis 22 miles SE

Batakiai 22 miles NNW

Tauragė 23 miles WNW

Vidukle 24 miles NNE

Girkalnis 25 miles NE

Skaudvilė 25 miles NNW

Raseiniai 25 miles NNE

Nemakščiai 25 miles N

Kriūkai 26 miles E

Seredžius 26 miles E

Kybartai 29 miles S

Upyna 29 miles NNW

Chernyshevskoye, Russia 30 miles S

Virbalis 30 miles S

Pilviškiai 30 miles SE

Čekiškė 30 miles ENE

Lithuania showing location of Jurbarkas (Yurburg)

TABLE OF CONTENTS

CHAPTER 2: THE FAMILIES

APPENDIX: Additional Materials Collected and Added After Publication of the Hebrew Book

Preface for the Third Edition

There are several reasons for creating a third edition of the *Yurburg Yizkor Book.* There has been much activity at the Yurburg Jewish Cemetery since 2003 when the first edition was published and we want to include material on these activities.

The **Friends of the Yurburg Cemetery** as formed and in 2005 worked with the town of Jurbarkas to erect a new entrance to the cemetery. Then in 2007 students from the Dartmouth College Hillel erected a new fence around the cemetery and rehabilitated many headstones in the cemetery, and catalogued the headstones.

Recently a new memorial to the extinct Jewish community of Yurburg is being planned and erected. This was done at the initiation of the mayor, Skirmantas Mockevicius. He contacted the Israeli ambassador to Lithuania, Amir Mimon, who then engaged David Zundelovich, a noted sculptor, whose family origins are in Yurburg, now living in Israel. He and his daughter, Anna, and son David, are working together to create the "**Synagogue Square Memorial**."

We are taking the opportunity to add material at the beginning of the book to cover these two topics, yet leaving the original translation and appendix as they were in the second edition, and additionally print the book in a larger 11 inch by 8 ½ inch format, with a newly designed cover, so the book will be more attractive. We have also added an index that should help readers in finding references to their ancestors and family.

We hope you find this updated version equally informative as the first two editions.

Joel Alpert, editor of the English translation

Foreword for the Translation

This translation was the result of a number of chance happenings. One day, probably in about 1991, I decided to make a trip down the road to the American Jewish Historical Society located on the campus of Brandeis University in Waltham, Massachusetts to try to locate the town of my maternal grandparents. The only hint I had was that deep in my memory I recall them mentioning "Yurburg" or "Yurberik." I found a map of Lithuania at the library and poured over it for a long time without any success finding either of these names. Then as I recall, a friendly man approached me and asked if he could be of help. I told him I was searching for "Yurburg," He responded that that was the Yiddish name and the maps list the Lithuanian name which is "Jurbarkas," which he immediated pointed out on the map. It turned out that the friendly man was the head of the Library. How lucky I was.

Next advance was in 1993, when I found out about the new web site on Jewish genealogy called "Jewishgen.org" and I logged in inquiring about the town of Yurburg or Jurbarkas. I received an answer from a man named Warren Blatt, who informed me that a Yizkor or Memorial book of the town had just been published in 1991. That was good news, but it was written in Hebrew. Fortunately a friend of my wife was returning to Israel and offered to buy the book at the Association of Lithuanian Jews in Tel Aviv. In spite of my living in Israel in the 1970s for three years, my Hebrew was only at about a third grade level, it was not sufficient to read and understand the book.

In searching around the JewishGen web site, I discovered the Yizkor Book project, in which people from all over the world would cooperate to get these memorial books often written in Hebrew and Yiddish translated into English and placed on the web for all to be able to read. The process required raising money for translating the material, finding a translator and then sending the material to be posted on the Yizkor Books Project web site. I recall observing that many of the translation coordinators who undertook to manage this process for each book, were seeking funding from organizations. I instead decided to turn to my family members who were also descended from emigrants from Yurburg. Long story, shortened, over about 8 years, I raised about $9,000 from these family members, had the help of a cousin Regina Naividel who located a translator, Irene Emodi in Israel. By 2001 the book was fully translated and up on the web. A number of articles had been translated by others, but Irene Emodi did the bulk of the translation. See pages 27 for a list of all the translators and contributors to the translation. So the book was translated in 2001 and was placed on the web for all to see.

So how did the book get published? Shortly after the translation was posted on the web, my wife Nancy Lefkowitz, remarked that there was too much material to read on the web, so I had to get it published in book form! I had made the acquaintance of Professor Dov Levin, chair of the Oral History Department at the Hebrew University, who had told me that getting this kind of material translated and available to the English reading public was most important. So I turned to him and he provided me an phone audience with the CEO of the Jewish Publication Society. After a long discussion to explain my need to publish this book, I asked it the JPS could publish it. I was told that such a book would not be financially suitable, but there was now the "print-on-demand" industry that was suitable and that Lightning Source, Inc. was a reliable company for this pursuit. It turned out that I had raised all the money for the translation by myself and according to the agreement with JewishGen, I retained the copyright on the translation. So I signed up with the company and set a goal that if I sold 100 books, so that 100 families could hold the book in their hands and read about the environment that their ancestors left, then I could declare victory! A few years ago, I lost count at over 400 books sold.

Below is a Krelitz family photo taken in about 1927 in Yurburg, that I found among my uncle George Ellis's photos after he passed away. I have identified all the people, have met two of them, one in Israel and another in Germany. Several were Shoah victims. I posted this photo on the JewishGen KehilaLinks site for Yurburg that I created and manage. It was found by a second cousin in Mexico whom I did not know and he did not know of his Krelitz family in the US (see page 24 for this story).

In 2012, having retired, I was searching for some creative activity to keep myself intellectually active. I came upon the idea of using the production of this book to as a role model for publishing Yizkor books of other towns with which I had not connection. I proposed this to JewishGen and that led to the formation of the Yizkor-Books-In-Print Project that operates under the Yizkor Books Project. Now six years later, along with volunteers from all over the world, we have published 75 titles and sold over 6500 books. So the publication of the Yurburg Yizkor Book has lead to many many families being able to hold their ancestral town's history in their hands.

Joel Alpert
November, 2018

Krelitz family photo taken in about 1927 in Yurburg
Top row from the left: Leib Kreitz (Shoah victim), Meir Krelitz, Leib Zarnitsky, Max Zarnitsky (emigrated to Israel), Aaron Abramson (slave camp survivor, remained in Germany), Joseph Abramson, -----.
Bottom row from left, Rachel or Feiga Krelitz (Shoah victim), Elka Krelitz Zarnitsky, Masha Krelitz Abramson, ----

Yurburg descendants in May 2001 posing at the rock where all travelers were brought. From left on bottom: Duba Most Rosenberg (Kovno), Gary Schumann, Joel Alpert, Lottye Brodsky, Marc Schumann (kneeling), Esther Bejar-Sherman, Fania Hilelson Jivotovsky, friend of Fania, Itzhak Zarnitsky. On rock from left, Brenda Freshman, Nancy Lefkowitz, Michael Jivotovsky.

TABLE OF CONTENTS OF THE BOOK OF REMEMBRANCE OF THE COMMUNITY OF YURBURG, LITHUANIA

6   The Yurburg Yizkor Book

CHAPTER 2: THE FAMILIES

CHAPTER 7: SURVIVORS OF YURBURG PERPETUATE THE MEMORY OF THEIR COMMUNITY

APPENDIX: Additional Materials Collected and Added After Publication of the Original Hebrew Book

Dedication of the English Edition

This English edition is dedicated to the memory of all the Jews of Yurburg and to our ancestors who were brutally murdered during the Shoah. The cause of their death remains as inconceivable today, as it ever was, for they died for no other reason but for being Jews. This volume may be the only work in the English language dealing with the vanished Jewish Community of Yurburg. The story inexorably reflects the horrible crimes of the Shoah never to be forgotten, if the darkest page of the Jewish history is not to be repeated ever again.

This book is also dedicated to Mr. Jack Cossid (Chicago), originally Yankel Chossid of Yurburg. Jack Cossid left Yurburg in 1937 and immigrated to Chicago. I came across Jack Cossid's name while reading the original Hebrew Edition of the Yizkor book and contacted him. Jack knew my Krelitz, Eliashevitz and Naividel families whom I, being second generation American, have never had a chance to know. Over the years Jack has become a dear friend, and it is through Jack's vivid and poignant memories of the past that many of us have learned about the lives and tragedy of our lost families and the loss of the ancestral Yurburg, the home to so many Jewish families. I will always treasure Jack's special friendship and his contribution to this work.

Joel Alpert in Boston Massachusetts, on April 20, 2003

Ten years to the day that I first laid by eyes on this book, and now 60 years to the day of the Uprising in the Warsaw Ghetto.

Special Note: Just prior to the publication of this book, the archives of the Yurburg Emergency Relief Society, Inc. came to light. This group was formed after World War II to assist the survivors from Yurburg. It was headed by Pauline and Charles Jaffe and operated out of their home in Brooklyn, New York. Today these archives are in the possession of their children, Professor Marvin Jaffe and Taube Jaffe Fine. This material includes letters, inquiries about relatives, and receipts for packages from many Yurburgers in need after World War II. There was not enough time to summarize these archives for this publication, however it is hoped to do so in the future and also deposit the archives at some appropriate place.

Acknowledgments

The original book was written in Hebrew and Yiddish by Jewish residents and survivors from Yurburg who wanted to preserve the memory and knowledge of their beloved community that was permanently and irreversibly destroyed during the war. It was published in 1991 in Israel by the ***Organization of Former Residents of Yurburg,*** (a sub-group of the **Association of Lithuanian Jews in Israel**, 1 Shderot David Ha'Melekh, Tel Aviv, 64953, Israel, Phone: 03-696-4812 and FAX 03-695-4821). The book was written mostly in Hebrew, with some Yiddish and with a five page English summary. Consequently, most of the contents have not been available to the English speaking community. It was Joel Alpert's idea to have the Yurburg Yizkor Book translated, compiled and edited into a new volume and made accessible to the English-speaking public.

We would like to express our sincere appreciation to the late Shimon Shimonov, Chairman and Head of the Organization of Former Residents of Yurburg, for his encouragement and cooperation that led to the publication of this English edition. Special thanks are due to **Rachel Levin**, widow of David Levin, and representative of the ***Organization of Former Residents of Yurburg*** for her approval to publish this book in English.

The editor of this version of the Yizkor book would also like to thank the **Jewish Genealogy (JewishGen.org)** organization for their assistance, cooperation and encouragement. Through its **Yizkor Book Project**, the organization hosts web sites enabling distribution of translated Yizkor book materials contributed by volunteers. This large volume of literature presenting very special historic content became available to English speakers through the efforts of JewishGen. Without the JewishGen organization, especially Susan King and Joyce Field, the initial version of this translation would never have been available on the Internet. A special note of thanks is also due to all the work by all the Jewish genealogists, whose work directly or indirectly contributed to the body of knowledge that went into this book.

We express our special acknowledgements to the assistant editor Josef Rosin (Haifa, originally from Kybart, Lithuania) for his heroic editing efforts to properly translate and transliterate the proper Hebrew, Yiddish, and Lithuanian names and place names. Rules used by Josef Rosin in transliteration of proper names and places are given in: www.jewishgen.org/infofiles/yidtran.txt and cited below.

The editor wishes to also acknowledge the enthusiasm, assistance and encouragement of Professor Dov Levin of the Hebrew University. Professor

Levin, author of ***Pinkas Hakehillat Lita*** (co-author with Josef Rosin, written in Hebrew) and ***The Litvaks*** (in English), encouraged and inspired the editor by stating that the most important work that can be done today is to "spread the word of the history of the Lithuanian Jewish community and the Shoah to the English speaking world."

Funds for this volume were raised almost entirely by the extended Naividel-Krelitz-Ellis (Eliashevitz) families, whose origins go back to Yurburg. Other Yurburg descendants contributed as well. Regina Naividel, in Israel, located the primary translator, Irene Emodi, and coordinated these efforts with Joel Alpert. As the translation work was in progress, it was placed on the Yizkor Book Project of JewishGen on the Internet for all English readers to access. This effort began in 1993 and culminated in publication of this book in 2003.

All contributors, translators and participants are gratefully acknowledged and we express our sincere appreciation to all those who helped. Thanks also to Dr. Ellen Frankel, Editor and Chief of the Jewish Publication Society, who provided important advice about publishing and the new "publish-on-demand" option, which ultimately was used for this Yizkor book. Thanks also to Max Michelson for his corrections of the transliterated list of headstones from the Yurburg Cemetery.

Finally, I must thank my dear wife, Nancy Lefkowitz, who helped and encouraged me in numerous ways during this whole time of personal adventure into my family history. She is now as knowledgeable about Yurburg and my family history as I am.

Joel Alpert, Boston

Yurburg is located on the North side of Nieman River 75 miles (117 km) West of Vilna at 55° 5' Latitude and 22° 46' East Longitude. It is identified on maps of Lithuania by the Lithuanian name "Jurbarkas." <u>See map on inside of front cover.</u>

For additional material on Yurburg go to the ShtetLinks Page for Yurburg. https://kehilalinks.jewishgen.org/yurburg/yurburg.html

At the time of the publication of this book in 2018, photos from a trip to Yurburg were placed on the *World Wide Web (www)* at: http://yurburgfriends.com/LithTrip/Roll6/LithPhoto.html and at

http://yurburgfriends.com/LithTrip/Roll7/LithPhoto.html

For the whole collection of Nancy Lefkowitz's photos of the trip to Lithuania go to: http://yurburgfriends.com/LithTrip/Lithdir.html

The web address of these photos may change, so it is suggested that a search engine, such as GOOGLE, be used for "Lithuania Trip Photos" or "Yurburg" or "Lithuania Trip Photos by Nancy Lefkowitz."

Acknowledgments for the Photographs for this English Edition

Inclusion of new photographs provide a unique glimpse of Yurburg, and show images of our ancestral town - the way it looked then and what has become of it today, presenting two realities in sharp contrast, thus providing more insight into our past, and into the common Jewish destiny in Europe. The new photographs included in the English edition of the Yurburg Yizkor Book, were graciously donated by friends and family; we express our sincere appreciation to the following persons for their wonderful contributions:

- to Jack Cossid, of Chicago, who shared the wonderful images from his photo album of Yurburg and its residents;

- to Professor Antanas Buracas, of Vilna, who provided images of the Great Old Wooden Synagogue of Yurburg, taken by his uncle, the noted photographer Balys Buracas in the 1930s;

- to the late Gita Abramson Bereznitsky, who donated images of the memorial site of the Mass Murders at the Jewish Cemetery in Yurburg and many family photographs;

- to Ruta Puisyte of the Vilna Jewish Museum for supplying images of the Great Old Wooden Synagogue of Yurburg;

- to Ben Craine, for the use of his father's photographs of Yurburg, including the Great Old Wooden Synagogue taken in 1927 as well as for the many portraits of former residents of Yurburg in the United States;

- to Diana Berzaner Tobin for her family photographs from the late 1930s;

- to Fania Hilelson Jivotovsky for photographs of her family from Sudarg;

- to Max Sherman-Krelitz of Mexico City for the photographs in his mother's (Leah Sherman-Krelitz) collection, taken by Leah's brother Moshe Krelitz of Yurburg;

- to the late Helen Kizell Beiles for family photographs;

- to Leslie Bern for photographs from his mother's (Fannie Eliashevitz Rubenstein) family album;

- to the late Bernard Laden for his family photographs,

- to Faye Shrage Ullman for her mother's Helen Feinberg Shrage's family photographs;

- to Dr. Ze'ev Bernstein for his father's Boris Bernstein's photograph;

- to Rachel Levin for the photographs of her husband and brother-in-law, Khanan and David Levin;

- to Rachel Hes Greenstein for photographs of her family;

- to Sarah Zilber Alkoni for the photographs of her father, Mordechai Zilber;
- to Bilha Bass Lerental for many family photographs;
- to Ashley Levinsohn for photographs and documents of his aunt, Hadassa Levinsohn;
- to Dr. Leon Menzer, Marc Shumann and Nancy Lefkowitz for their photographs from the trip to Yurburg in May 2001;
- to Gerrard W. Rudmin for photographs of the Yurburg cemetery taken in 1998;
- to Peter M. Hills (Walton on Thames, Surrey, U.K.) for the 1907 Yurburg property map;
- to Henry Scherr for his photos of his model of the Wooden Synagogue of Yurburg.

Additional Note to the Readers

The initial contents for the original Yurburg Memorial book were first collected from former residents of Yurburg, mostly living in Israel, when the Yurburg committee circulated a questionnaire in 1982. Subsequently, additional written materials were collected, serving to enhance its very special content. All initial submissions were included in their entirety. As a reader, you will find events repeatedly described by several authors. This is primarily because each writer tells the story of Yurburg in his or her own words as was requested by the original editor. Regardless of the repetition, these are authentic recollections of the former residents who lived through the events described in the passages.

The reader is sure to find the description of the town, families, institutions and personalities particularly interesting. While eyewitness accounts of the destruction of the community during the Shoah are tragic and poignant, the survival of these witnesses must be seen as miraculous. These first person accounts are powerful, up close and very personal. We can hardly imagine what these people went through, much less how they managed to survive these atrocities. I believe more than ever, that by bringing this translation to publication for the English reading public, that we are keeping alive the memories of those who perished and their way of life. In many cases this document is the only written evidence in English of the existence of many of the victims. As a reader, I expect that you will find a fascinating picture of shtetl life and its residents - how it once truly was, but is no more. I hope that you gain as much insight and pleasure in your learning about this town as I did in the preparation of the material.

Joel Alpert, Editor of the English Edition

Preface

I wanted to create the English version of the Yurburg Yizkor Book for only one reason – Yurburg was the town of my grandparents and I wanted to understand where they, and by extension, where I came from. In short, I wanted to discover my own history. I first obtained the original Hebrew version in 1993, only two years after its publication in Hebrew, and realized that my Hebrew was not adequate to understand the book. I took it upon myself to have it translated not only for my own benefit, but also for all Yurburg descendants to be able to read and understand the special story of Yurburg. With the help of donations from family and other Yurburg descendants, the translation was completed in 2002.

Thanks to the unlimited possibilities offered by the Internet, collection of new materials became possible, and in the twelve years since the first publication of the Hebrew and Yiddish Yizkor book appeared, this book has been updated to include material not found in the original book. The Appendix broadens the history of the community and includes stories told by those who immigrated to Israel, Mexico and the United States. Several Yurburgers who made their home in the US and one who immigrated to Israel provide gripping new facts, while the story of a Yurburger who immigrated to Mexico is told along with the harrowing story of her remaining family's failed attempts to escape to safety from their doomed town. We provided translations of some of the most poignant letters written from Yurburg on the eve of the Shoah. Finally, we added an article on our dramatic return journey to Yurburg in 2001.

What makes this book so unique is that former residents of Yurburg, who loved their town, and their community, wrote it. The vibrant and warm Jewish community of 3000 built over hundreds of years did not just gradually dwindle out; it vanished - disappeared off the face of the earth in the first months of the war, through well-planned executions. The book contains eyewitness accounts of the murders in July-September 1941. It is based on first-hand experience of those that miraculously survived or left before the horrors began. The stories tell about the wonderful community and about the great people who built and created its institutions. Even though it was not written by professional writers, its authenticity is enthralling, and its contents are factual and transfixing.

It must be mentioned that the editor of the original Hebrew book, Zevulun Poran was well qualified to write this book. He was born in Yurburg, immigrated to Palestine, where he became a noted educator and wrote many books on education. Upon his retirement, he dedicated himself to the creation of the original Yizkor book in Hebrew. Unfortunately, Zevulun Poran and his associate, Shimon Shimonov, as well as most of the other great contributors have passed away. It is now up to us to carry on the memory of this community.

Another remarkable document is "Holocaust in Jurbarkas," the 1997 bachelor's thesis of a Lithuanian student Ms. Ruta Puisyte. It is included in the Appendix on page 570. Her work is remarkable, because it was written in Lithuanian in a country where the national atmosphere is not particularly conducive to this kind of research. She presently (in 2003) works for the Lithuanian State Jewish Museum in Vilnius. Her research is based on legal documents and the work of the late Chayim Jofe, and contains a list of names of nearly 700 Yurburg victims who were murdered. This thesis has been translated from Lithuanian into English by the associate editor of this book Josef Rosin of Haifa, Israel and can also be found on the web at:

http://www.shtetlinks.jewishgen.org/yurburg/bathesis.html

A third remarkable document is a 16 mm film, now archived at the National Center for Jewish Film at Brandeis University, in Waltham, Massachusetts. The film footage was taken in 1927, when an emigre from Yurburg, Ben H. Craine, returned to his native town to visit his family, and filmed his relatives and friends. It shows many fascinating street scenes, smiling family members and casual episodes of shtetl life. The film is a rare glimpse of daily life in a bustling *shtetl* before the Nazi invasion. What is even more incredible is that the film was forgotten and lost after the untimely death of the photographer in 1943; his son discovered the film in a locked cabinet in 1985 and eventually was able to grasp its immense significance and remarkable content. It has since been re-mastered and archived thanks to generous donations from the Krelitz, Ellis (Eliashevitz), Naividel, Feinberg and Rosin families. See page 662 for the details of this incredible story. Video (VHS) research copies are available from The National Center for Jewish Film at Brandeis University; see ordering information on the bottom of page 4.)

These three "documents" provide us with an enriching prospective of a small town hidden on the Western edge of Lithuania. We are fortunate to have these unique and captivating time capsules which together describe both the richness of our heritage and the unspeakable tragedy, that without exception, has relevance to every family and every person.

This is the story of our own Yurburg Jews and it reflects the history of all European Jews.

This is the story that must be told.

FORWARD

For the English Edition

By Joel Alpert, Editor and Compiler

I hope that my personal journey of discovery will encourage others to seek out their own family histories and gain a better appreciation of our collective past and a deeper understanding of our Jewish history and us. This Yizkor (Memorial) book is the only history book we have about the town of Yurburg in Lithuania. I would encourage readers of this book to contact their own family elders and collect more information that could be appended to later editions of this book. It is our call to duty to preserve the "memory" of our ancestral town, the town of Yurburg.

I was born in the United States in 1944, and all that happened during World War II was "pre-history" for me. I grew up knowing nothing of our family in Europe or of a town called Yurburg (Jurbarkas) in Lithuania. I believed that my family had been spared any losses in the Holocaust. I thought that the Holocaust only happened to other "unfortunate families."

Only when I started to ask questions in the late 1960s did I find out otherwise. In the summer of 1968, my sister Niki and I decided that our grandfather Harry Ellis (born Hillel Eliashevitz in Yurburg) should take us out to a nice dinner before we returned to college in the fall. Away from parental interference, we asked him about the old country and his family and started to draw a family tree. To our surprise, we learned that he and my grandmother each had brothers who had not come to America. Below their names on the family tree, we wrote, **"Large families lost during World War II."**

That evening we learned that our family had not been spared.

At that time we did not delve into research of the lost cousins. Maybe, it was because we were so overwhelmed by all the family connections and names that began to resurface. Our grandfather had given us a family tree that traced back the roots of his grandfather and included all his aunts, uncles, and first cousins. Back then, families were large (our mother had nearly 80 first cousins), and the town was fairly small. We also learned that our grandfather's father, Sholom Eliashevitz, was the town's flour miller, and members of our Grandmother Celia Krelitz's family were the town's bakers.

1991-Entering the Computer Age

I bought my first computer in 1991, and one of the first pieces of software that I purchased was a genealogy program. I was determined to make some sense of that huge, confusing 1968 family tree. Having entered all the known names and incidental data, I contacted and quizzed elderly relatives. When I got to the note on the old family tree, "Large families lost during World War II," I wondered: Who were these people? What were their names? Had their memories been obliterated? Why didn't I know about them? I started down a path of incredible twists and turns, but luck and perseverance eventually turned my way, and I found the answers that added much to my knowledge of the family history and affixed a whole new dimension to my life.

Encounter at the American Jewish Historical Society

One rainy Sunday in 1993, I went to the American Jewish Historical Society on the Brandeis University campus in Waltham, Massachusetts, to find out about the family town. I had a dim recollection of my recently deceased Uncle George Ellis mentioning the town of "Yurberik" in Lithuania, a town along a river. With that information, I examined a map of Lithuania but had no luck. However, with the help of knowledgeable staff, I discovered that the town was called Jurbarkas in Lithuanian and appears on the maps under that name. In Yiddish it was known as Yurberik or Yurburg. It is located on the banks of the Nieman River to the west of the city of Kaunas, called Kovno in Yiddish at that time.

Diary and Postcards

More answers in my quest came in 1993 when an 86-year-old cousin, Rosalin Krelitz, recalled that her mother had kept a Yiddish diary of a 1927 trip to Lithuania and Palestine. When I promised to get the diary translated, she sent it to me. In its pages I found two postcards and a photo of a cousin, Max Zarnitsky, who had immigrated to Palestine in 1927. One postcard showed the famous wooden synagogue of Yurburg, built in 1790, destroyed along with the entire Yurburg Jewish community in 1941, and the other one was a 1926 picture of the students in the Talmud Torah or Hebrew school. The cousin also sent along an old photo of a handsome couple, with a note in Hebrew on the back, "To my dear Uncle and Aunt from your nephew, *Moshe Krelitz.*" Neither my cousin nor I knew of a Moshe Krelitz; he was not on the family tree.

Jewish Genealogical Society of Greater Boston - Warren Blatt

The next break came when Warren Blatt, whom I met at the Jewish Genealogical Society of Greater Boston, heard of my interest in Yurburg. He immediately searched on the Internet and found that the **Library of Congress had recently acquired the Yurburg Yizkor (Memorial) Book**. A few days later I called the Library of Congress Yiddish and Hebrew section, and learned the names of the book's publisher and authors: the Organization of Former Residents of Yurburg in Israel. Incidentally, I had heard about this book from a distant relative, Fay Schrage Ullmann, daughter of Helen Feinberg (Fainberg) Schrage, originally from Yurburg. Fay said that her mother, Helen, had a book about Yurburg so meaningful to her that she would never lend it out. Later in 1993, an Israeli friend, Hadas Eyal, offered to buy the book for me on her upcoming trip to Israel, and she returned with the book a few weeks later.

Struggling with Hebrew in the Yurburg Yizkor Book

The **Yurburg Yizkor Book** contained over 500 pages, mostly in Hebrew, with a few pages in English. Initially, I was very excited that I finally had a source of information about the town, and there was hope that I would find out about the lost members of the family. However, although I lived in Israel for more than three years, my Hebrew was not at the level where I could comfortably translate the material. Nevertheless, I tried to read as much as possible, finding some names in the various lists throughout the book. **No one said it would be easy!**

Finding Yankel Chosid (aka Jack Cossid) - Real Progress

After floundering for two weeks, I finally focused on the "List of Yurburg Residents Abroad," which was written in English. I tried to call some of the people on the list and soon reached a Jack Cossid in Chicago. After reassuring him that I wasn't selling anything, I asked if he was the Jack Cossid from Yurberik. He said "yes." I told him that my grandparents were from the town. Then to prove it, I asked him if the names Eliashevitz and Krelitz meant anything to him. He replied, "The flour miller and the bakers!" **Bingo, we were connecting!** I later learned that Jack had been a good friend of *Moshe Krelitz* (the same mysterious name on the post card) whom we ultimately found out was a first cousin of my mother. Jack had left Yurburg in 1937 at the age of 19. Yurburg had been his world; four years after his departure, that world was wiped off the face of the earth. Now, more than fifty years later, Jack suddenly gets a phone call from a living relative! **He now had a connection to his past! And so did I!**

An Unbelievable Discovery

Later in the conversation, I mentioned videotape that had been circulating in the family. A distant cousin, Ben Craine, had immigrated to the US in 1903, about the same time as my grandparents, and had become a successful portrait photographer in Detroit. In 1927, he traveled back to his home in Yurburg with a 16-mm movie camera. His films had been transferred onto videotape, and copies were making their way across the country into the homes of relatives. When I mentioned the film to Jack, I got no response. **Silence!** Concerned, I asked Jack if he was still there. He replied that his back was full of goosebumps. He then told me that he remembered standing behind that cameraman in 1927, and he proceeded to describe scenes from the film. He was ten years old at the time, nearly 70 years earlier, and he remembered it in vivid detail. Incredible!

A few months later, I brought the videotape to Jack in Chicago. He identified many of my relatives and also his own brothers and a sister, who perished in the war. I videotaped Jack's reactions as he watched the film. Jack was overwhelmed, so was I, as I watched him return to his distant past, when everybody was so full of life, unaware that just a little over a decade later nothing would be left but memories of those who would survive. For Jack reconnecting to his past was a miracle and he said that from then on he would believe in them.

The Naividel Brothers of Yurburg

I mentioned to Jack that the maiden name of two of my great-grandmothers was "Naividel." Jack said that he knew of two Naividel brothers who were attornies, Lushka and Mota. Jack remembered that Lushka had married Basia Meisler, an ophthalmologist, and Mota was engaged to a woman named Karabelnik from Yurburg. Jack mentioned that there was also a sister, who ran a variety store in Yurburg. The youngest brother, Reuven, ran a bicycle shop. The youngest sister was the same age as Jack. The two sisters and Reuven and their families were all killed in the Holocaust.

Before the war, a Maccabi social group had been organized called the "Kvuzath Naividel," meaning the Naividel Group. In his photo album Jack had a picture of the group, which included Lushka, I asked Jack what happened to them. He said that he did not hear about them after the war and assumed that they had perished, as had nearly everyone from Yurburg.

Kvuzath Naividel, with Hillel Naividel sitting in center

[Photo not in original Yizkor Book, provided courtesy of Jack Cossid]

An Unbelievable Find on a Trip to Israel - Reconnecting Family after Ninety Years

In May 1994, I traveled to Israel, toured the country, and visited relatives. On the very last day of the trip, as I was talking to Shimon Shimonov of the Organization of Former Residents of Yurburg in Israel, I mentioned that my family names were Krelitz, Eliashevitz, and Naividel. He interrupted me to say that there was a Naividel from Yurburg living in Tel Aviv! Thrilled with this information, I asked for his phone number.

Later that afternoon, I called and spoke to Benny Naividel and explained that I thought we might be related, although I had no record of any Benny Naividel in my research. He replied that the only relatives that he knew of were his uncle's family. I told him that my great-great-grandfather was a Hillel Naividel from Yurburg. Excitedly, Benny answered that his uncle was named Hillel Naividel. I suggested that maybe we were, indeed, related and that his uncle might have been named after my great-great grandfather. Benny wanted to meet me. I told him that we were leaving the next morning at 4 am for the airport and there was no time to see him. He insisted! So we arranged to meet later that evening at the home of a cousin Itzhak Zarnitsky, son of Max, with whom we had maintained contact for over 70 years.

When Benny arrived and we started to explore the possible connections, he said that his father, Mordehai, and uncle, Hillel, were attorneys from Yurburg. I still made no connection. According to Benny, Mordehai and Hillel, Hillel's wife Basia, and their daughter Rachel were in Kovno when the Nazis invaded Lithuania. They fled East with the Russian army and spent the war years in Uzbekistan, near the Chinese border. Mordehai's wife and a young daughter were in Yurburg and were killed during the first week of the war by the Nazis and their Lithuanian sympathizers. After the war, Mordehai, and Hillel's family returned to Lithuania and lived in Vilna. Hillel eventually became the President of the Supreme Court and died in 1969 while he was still working as the President. Mordehai, whose attempt after the war to reach Palestine was foiled by the KGB, spent eight years in prison as a "Prisoner of Zion." In 1979, at age 76, he and his second wife and their son Benny immigrated to Israel. Mordehai died in Beer-Sheva in 1993. These were the only family members Benny knew.

When I mentioned my discussion with Jack Cossid about Motta and Lushka Naividel, Benny told me that "Motta" and "Lushka" are Yiddish nicknames for Mordehai and Hillel! Yitzhak, Benny, and I were stunned. My hair stood on end. My grandfather had mentioned to us the name of Benny's grandfather, Meir Eliezer Naividel, but not Hillel and Mordehai, since they were born after my grandfather left Yurburg in 1903, and he didn't know them. With Benny's confirmation that his grandfather's name was Meir Eliezer Naividel, there was no doubt that we were cousins meeting after a ninety-year separation of our families. It was truly remarkable. This connection has been very meaningful to **Benny, because he grew up with little family and always wanted a big one.**

Now he had one!

The Continuing Search for Family in Israel and the Yurburg Network

After our short and exciting meeting that night in Tel Aviv, I began a correspondence with Benny and his wife Regina. Benny was starting a new business, so he couldn't devote much time to the search for family. However, Regina, who came from a very small family from Germany, caught the bug of "finding family." She took my grandfather's 1968 family tree, tapped into the Israeli network of people from Yurburg, and managed to add over 125 people to the family tree, including a whole branch that my grandfather had forgotten to mention. She sent a 25-page typed letter documenting her finds.

Her discoveries were beyond my wildest dreams. Clearly the people in Israel from Yurburg had remained in touch with each other, just as my grandfather's generation had when they came to this country. I had heard numerous stories of that immigrant generation traveling throughout the US and contacting their "landsmen." The exodus from Yurburg to Israel was about 50 years more recent than my grandfather's exodus, so the ties are still alive. In fact, Benny had arrived just 15 years before, and there were other cousins, Bella Abramson Kaplan and Gita Abramson Bereznitsky, (daughters of the town photographer, N. Abramson) who had arrived in Israel from Lithuania as recently as 1990.

The Internet and JewishGen Become Players in the Adventure

I had been told by my 86 year old cousin, Rosalin Krelitz, that a very distant cousin, Frank Rosen, lived in Dallas. To the best of anyone's knowledge, he had no children. I didn't know how to locate him or his family, so I posted a message on the JewishGen Internet discussion group asking for help from researchers in Dallas. In response, Jackie Ziff searched the Dallas city directories and found his name in the 1930 and 1940 books. **End of story! Or so I thought.**

Two weeks later, I receive another e-mail message from Jackie Ziff. She had been having Shabbas dinner at the home of friends who were longtime Dallas residents and happened to ask if they had heard of Frank Rosen. Not only did they know of him, but also the hostess turned out to be his niece! Moreover, Frank had a daughter and a granddaughter. Since then, I have met the granddaughter, Loyce Gender Weitz, who filled me in on that branch of the family. This eventually led me to a cousin, Josef Rosin, a survivor living in Haifa, who has been instrumental in documenting the history of the numerous Jewish *Shtetlakh* in Lithuania. He with his good friend, Professor Dov Levin, of the Hebrew University co-authored the most authoritative history of Lithuanian Jewry: ***Pinkas HaKehillat Lita, Encyclopedia of Jewish Communities of Lithuania,*** 1996.

Josef Rosin and I have established a personal and a working relationship in which he reviewed the research material collected for the ***Pinkas HaKehillat Lita*** book, and wrote new material about the shtetls of Lithuania. I then processed the material so that it could be placed on the JewishGen Shtetlinks pages on the Internet. Now many people with Internet connections can read about the towns of their *Litvak* ancestors. Josef volunteered to edit this volume for proper transliterations and of proper names and places and is the assistant editor.

The ShtetLinks Yurburg Page Enters The Story

I have placed the information on Yurburg on the JewishGen ShtetLinks server for others to read. On one of those pages, I placed an entry about a branch of the family that immigrated to Mexico City before World War II and with whom all contact had been lost. I had sent letters that were never answered.

A dead end! Or so I thought. But on December 23, 1996, I received e-mail:

> Dear Joel,
>
> My name is Abraham Sherman and I am a nephew of Rivka Krelitz. I am originally from Mexico City but I am living in Houston, TX. My father is Max (Meyer) Sherman Krelitz, son of Leah Krelitz who was Rivka's sister. Leah went to Mexico City on vacation in 1937 to see Rivka and was told not to return because of the situation in Europe. You cannot imagine his excitement in finding the same family photo of his grandparents' family on the web (see below). We have pictures of the whole family and even the letters in Yiddish in which my grandmother was told not to return to Europe because of fear of future disaster (several are in the Appendix). I have no idea why my grandmother does not appear in the list of the Krelitz family but I can tell you my father was totally overcome by emotion to find out he has other living relatives as he was told everybody died in the Holocaust. We never knew of family in the US. My father is fluent in English and both of us are sincerely looking forward to hearing from you.
>
> *Abraham Sherman*

I have since exchanged visits with Max and his sister Esther and other cousins in Mexico City, reestablishing the broken family connection after seventy years. Jack Cossid eventually translated the Yiddish letters mentioned above into English. Reading and translating letters written between 1938 and 1941 by his old friends (one being Moshe Krelitz) who had been murdered 55 years earlier was a daunting task for Jack. They were describing events in the town just months before the horrible massacre of Jewish residents, expressing their fears of a Nazi invasion. The letters were filled with fear and apprehension, and it is clear that they knew what was in store for them. Jack was learning from this precious time capsule what had happened to friends and cousins at that time as though it were happening now. (Max tells his story and has included the translation of some of the Yiddish letters in the appendix.)

Meir and Esther Krelitz - Max Sherman Krelitz's Grandparents

Photo in Max Sherman's living room

Not only did I learn the names of our murdered cousins, but I had read letters filled with their innermost thoughts, their love, worries and fears, and obtained their photos (see Appendix).

My search was long and circuitous, but I now had answers to my questions. Our knowledge of the family that stayed behind in Yurburg was lost over the years, but slowly I was beginning to get a grasp of our history and the destiny that had befallen those in our family who never had a chance to get out. **I have come to believe that there are similar sagas in most American Jewish families, just waiting to be discovered.**

Jack's Dream

Once, Jack told me that he had a dream the previous night. He was driving down a street in Chicago and saw all these people that perished in the war. He asked his dear friend Moshe Krelitz how everyone was (knowing in the back of his mind that they had all been murdered). Moshe responded that they were "all well." **Jack cried. I cried with him.**

The Internet, JewishGen, and the ShtetLinks Project have been most helpful in my search for my family and its roots. It is clear that without the Internet, these personal connections and discoveries would not have been made. It is truly amazing that now, over sixty years after the Shoah, we are still discovering new information and new relatives. I am now convinced that there is yet more to come. **The only question is where and how!**

Postscript:

I often receive questions from people who are looking to find out more about their lost relatives from Yurburg. They find information on Yurburg posted on the Internet. I refer them to Jack Cossid, who spends hours on the telephone with them. He remembers the people he used to know in Yurburg and tells them about the family that was, but is no more. I have developed a deep love for Jack, my Landsman from Yurburg, who has brought to life the memory of our lost cousins. *Joel Alpert*, **Boston, Massachusetts, USA February 2003**

**Leah and Moshe Krelitz on the Nieman River in Yurburg
Photo not in the Original Yizkor Book**

The Translators
The page numbers refer to the original Hebrew text.

Jack Cossid   Table of Contents of Chapters 1 and 2

Irene Emodi   Pages 9-13, 16-67, 88 - 113, 91 - 90, 117-196,
                                     199-201, 203-220, 225-252, 258-289, 268-
                                     327, 337-348, 337-357, 359-367 373-451,
                                     457-459, 463-470, 475-477, 493, 510-511

Regina Borenstein Naividel   Pages 201, 483-491, 497-507

Yakov Sherman*   Pages 14-15, 256-257, 358, 368-70 358, 472,
                                     494, 513

Rosi Sherman-Gordon   Pages 68-70

Yosef Rosin and Max Sherman-Krelitz*,
                                     Pages 71-73

Yosef Rosin and Fania Hilelson Jivotovsky:
                                     Pages 74-78, 79-81, 85-87, 334-336, 450,
                                     454-455

Yosef Rosin and Sarah and Mordekhai Kopfstein:
                                     Pages 82-84

Dr. Ulrich Baumann: Page 422, Ulm Trial Testimony Transcript,
                                     translated directly from the German.

William Berton: Pages 197-198

Dina Kapshud: Pages 253-255

*Yakov's Grandmother, and Max's mother, Leah Krelitz-Sherman
emigrated from Yurburg in 1937. In memory of Leah's sisters, Feiga and
Rochel (Kravitz) and brothers Moshe and Leib and their spouses and
children who were murdered in the Shoah.

List of Contributors to
The Translation of the Yurburg Yizkor Book

Beilis Family of Canada: In memory of the Members of the Beilis and Kizel Families who were Victims of the Shoah

Janice Bern Manhoff Family: In Memory of the Members of the Naividel, Eliashevitz and Rosin Families who were Victims of the Shoah

Leslie Bern Family: In Memory of the Members of the Naividel, Eliashevitz and Rosin Families who were Victims of the Shoah

Sidney Ellis Family of Milwaukee, Wisconsin: In memory of the Members of the Eliashevitz and Krelitz Families Who Were Victims of the Shoah

Steven Koppel Family of Milwaukee, Wisconsin: In memory of the Members of the Eliashevitz and Krelitz Families who were Victims of the Shoah

Members of the American branch of the Krelitz Family: In Memory of the Members of the Naividel and Krelitz Families who were Victims of the Shoah

Aaron Laden Family: In Memory of the Members of the Naividel, Eliashevitz and Laden Families who were Victims of the Shoah

Ben Laden Family: In Memory of the Members of the Naividel, Eliashevitz and Laden Families who were Victims of the Shoah

Irving Leipziger (grandson of Yizkhak Laiptsiger - father of Eliezer Latptsiger), his wife and their daughters: In Memory of the Members of the Laiptsiger (Leipziger) Family who were Victims of the Shoah

Donald Levinsohn: In memory of the Levinsohn family.

Erwin Koppel Family: In Memory of the Members of the Eliashevitz and Krelitz Families of Yurburg who were Victims of the Shoah

Gary Schumann of Miami, Florida: In memory of the Members of the Krelitz Family who were Victims of the Shoah

Rules used to transliterate Hebrew and Yiddish names into English

ROMANIZATION, YIVO-STYLE
A simplified version of the romanization (transcription) developed by YIVO.

1. What follows is a simplified version of the romanization (transcription) convention developed by YIVO. It is easy to use, once you have gotten the hang of it--not a daunting task. The scheme is quite straightforward, and it provides a uniform way to write "any" Yiddish word in any Yiddish dialect; if you can say it, you can write it, and be sure that your readers will know just how you're saying it.

2. The first column gives the names of the Yiddish letters and letter-combinations; the second column gives their approximate sound equivalents, for the most part in English; be warned that some of the English examples will be interpreted differently by native speakers of English from various dialect regions. The third column illustrates the transcription with Yiddish words. (The letters in square brackets in the first column occur only in words derived from Hebrew or Aramaic; their transcription in the third column is preceded by [H].) Writers not familiar with the Yiddish alphabet can ignore the first column altogether.

3. Note that the consonants and most of the vowels are pronounced in much the way that some other European languages pronounce them. There are a few possible exceptions, arising out of dialectal differences. For example: the Yiddish word for "good" is ALWAYS spelled giml-vov-tes, and the table shows that the Standard pronunciation of the vov (except when it's at the end of a syllable) is like the u in English "put"; so the Standard pronunciation is /gut/, rhyming with English "put." But the dialects of many native speakers call for pronouncing this vov as /i/, and these speakers would say and transcribe the word as /git/; such variants are welcome on Mendele.

4. The diphthongs may require some thought at first; /ey/ romanizes the sound in "Hey!" or "grey"; /ay/ stands for the sound of the "ay" in "Mayan" or the "y" in "my"; and /oy/ transcribes the "oi" sound in "oil" or "noise" (so the familiar expression of complaint or pain or surprise is romanized /oy vey/, and the Standard Yiddish for "my mother" is written /mayn mame/.)

5. Note that the shtumer (silent) alef has no sound equivalent or transcription. In Yiddish, it is written at the beginning of words before the vowels and diphthongs pronounced /u/, /oy/, /i/, /ey/, and /ay/.

| LETTER NAME | APPROXIMATE SOUND EQUIVALENT | ROMANIZED (TRANSCRIBED) AS |
| ---------- ---------- | --------------------- | --------------------------------- |

VOWELS AND DIPHTHONGS
-------------------- -----------------

shtumer alef	(silent)	
pasekh alef	a as in father	a in gas 'street'
komets alef	o as in sort	o in yorn 'years'
	u as in hut	o in hot 'has'
vov	u as in put	u in un 'and'
	oo as in goo (syllable-final)	u in du 'you'
yud	[Between i as in fit and ee as in feet]	i in tish 'table'
	[closer to feet]	i in zi 'she'
tsvey yudn (2 yuds)	ey as in grey	ey in eynikl 'grandchild'
pasekh tsvey yudn	y as in sky	ay in fayer 'fire'
vov yud	oy as in boy	oy in moyl 'mouth'
ayen	e as in end	e in entfer 'answer'

CONSONANTS AND CONSONANT CLUSTERS
----

beys or beyz	b as in ball	b in brem 'eyebrow'
[veys or veyz]	v as in heavy	[H] v in mazl-tov' congratulations'
tsvey vovn (2 vovs)	"	v in vursht 'salami'
giml	g as in give	g in gornisht 'nothing'
daled	d as in done	d in dorf 'village'
hey	h as in hot	h in hungerik 'hungry'
zayen	z as in zebra	z in zumer 'summer'
[khes]	ch as in German "achtung"	[H] kh in bokher 'young man'
khof	"	kh in khapn 'to catch'
tes	t as in time	t in tuml 'noise'
[tof]	"	[H] t in toyre 'Torah'
yud (before a vowel)	y as in yet	y in yagdes 'berries'
[kof]	k as in kill	[H] k in kosher 'kosher'
kuf	"	k in kamf 'struggle'
lamed	l as in lake	l in luft 'air'
mem	m as in mark	m in mentsh 'person'
nun	n as in neck	n in nudnik 'bore'
samekh	s as in self	s in samet 'velvet'
[sin]	"	[H] s in soyne 'enemy'
[sof]	"	[H] s in toes 'error'
pey	p as in pack	p in ponim 'face'
fey	f as in fence	f in frish 'fresh'
tsadek	ts as in fruits	ts in nayntsik 'ninety'
reysh	r as in French "rue"*	r in royt 'red'
shin	sh as in show	sh in shande 'shame'
zayen shin	s as in measure	zh in zhuk 'beetle'
daled zayen shin	j as in jump	dzh in dzhez 'jazz'
tes shin	ch as in chair	tsh in kvetshn 'to squeeze'

* i.e., trilling either the tip of the tongue.

Some General Points (adapted from Zellig Bach, Mendele 4.102) Each letter (or letter combination) in the third column has a specific sound. Remember that the YIVO scheme is meant to be efficient, unambiguous and easy to use; unnecessary letters just confuse the reader.

So:
1. No double consonants; they don't tell you anything. Write: ale, alemen, bobe, feder, got [God], shabes, yidish (NOT alle, allemen, bobbe, fedder, gott, shabbes, yiddish).

2. Excise the puste (empty) h's, since they provide no additional information: No "h" after the stressed vowel in words of German origin. Write: amol, yor, geyn, shteyn (NOT amohl, yohr, gehn, shtehn). And no "h"s after the final vowel in words of Hebrew or Slavic origin; they don't add any information either. Write: khale, kale, khevre, metsie, take (NOT khaleh, kaleh, khevreh, metsieh, takeh).

3. Skip the shtume (silent) e's: Write: bisl, fargesn, gutn, lakhn, zisn, shtetl (NOT bisel, fargesen, guten, lakhen, zisen, shtetel).

[19Aug95]
Source: Mendele Yiddish Language and Literature Mailing List. V.4.170
Web site- http://sunsite.unc.edu/yiddish/mewais.html
Provider: Mark H. David (mhd@world.std.com)

Additional Comments on Translation of Hebrew and Yiddish Names:

It is very important that the reader become aware that with these above adapted rules, the usual Anglicized Hebrew/Yiddish names such as Chaim becomes Hayim, and Mordechai becomes Mordehai, Leipzger becomes Laiptsiger, Reizman becomes Raizman, Feinberg becomes Fainberg, and so on.

A Request to You, the Readers of this Yizkor Book:
If you have further information about the history of the town, or of your Yurburg family, please make contact, so that it may be incorporated into future editions of this book or new books on the town. Contact Joel Alpert, 13 Michael's Green, Woburn, MA, 01801 or by email: jalp@comcast.net Computer files are appreciated.

Pages 5 and 6, Originally in English, same as pages 515-519

THE BOOK OF REMEMBRANCE OF THE COMMUNITY OF YURBURG, LITHUANIA

Introduction and Forward

The book of Remembrance for the Jewish Community of Yurburg is presented with great respect for the survivors of the community and for their children and grandchildren to the last generation.

The Book of Remembrance is not a historical documentary of the Jewish people in Yurburg, but a collection of authentic testimonies of the survivors of this special community, which arose from the smoke of the Holocaust. The experiences and impressions of the life of the community have been kept alive in the memory of the writers since their youth, and constitute the nucleus of the book.

None of the authors, once residents of Yurburg, are professional writers, yet in their own styles and best individual efforts they have presented personal impressions of the modest lives of their fathers in the community's time of prosperity. Only very few managed to escape from the snare of the Nazis, and from these survivors we learned of the desperate position, and the despair brought on by the hopelessness of their situation, as hell's torment opened before their eyes.

The story of Yurburg is striking, yet very sad. For more than three months of cold- blooded murder, the sadistic beasts annihilated the community, cutting it back to the very roots. These visual memories are horrifying. This Jewish community, hundreds of years old, was blotted out by demonic cruelty under the skies of Lithuania. The "civilized" world calmly watched and condoned this horrible persecution, not only by not rising against, not crying out against and not protesting against it, but added to the crime, pouring salt on the wound by actually giving assistance to the murderers. The burden of shame on the whole world and on the neighbouring Christian-Lithuanians will last forever because of their hypocrisy and lack of conscience.

The frightening horror of Holocaust shakes every cord of heart and soul. As long as the earth stands it will not cease telling the story of these terrible deeds. How women and children were taken to death chambers ... how numerous groups of men died in mass graves in the old Jewish cemetery . . . how aged, weak and infirm people were buried anonymously somewhere between Yurburg and Rasein. Why ? Why ? Why ? Women were beaten, mothers humiliated, they and their innocent children on their last journey to the Shventshani forest, were shot to death while their babies wept in their arms, and then were dumped into their last resting places ... These terrible Holocaust stories bring hatred to the eyes of the survivors of the community and do not give peace to their souls.

In the Book of Remembrance the only personal testimony of the days of the Holocaust is that of a young woman and a man, who escaped from the grip of these human scum, and they tell us their awful story. A story of hell, is written in the book. From the history of these two survivors we learn of the people of the community, who were cruelly persecuted by these savage people.

We will remember the terrible stories of our beloved ones forever and revere the memory of these unfortunates as long as their descendants live. How desperately the unfortunate mother of the escaped girl cried out in the last moments of her life: "Revenge, main Tochter, revenge! But is revenge possible?" Our poet Chaim (Hayim) Nakhman (Nakhman) Bialik said:

"Revenge like that, revenge for the blood of a little child satan has not yet created!

We will not forget, we will remember the victims of the Nazi German murderers and their Lithuanian helpers. The blood of our beloved ones cries out from the earth and demands remembrance forever.

With thanks and appreciation we thus acknowledge the help of our dear friends who kindly made possible the publishing of the Book of Remembrance - and most of all that of our brother and beloved friend Shlomo (Sol) Goldstein, resident of Yurburg, a survivor of the Holocaust and only survivor of his family, who lives in the U. S. A., but whose heart and soul are in Zion. His great contribution made this publication possible.

It is our pleasure to express our thanks to Dr Alexander Ullman, a true Zionist and friend of Israel, the director of the Rochester Hospital, the husband of Feia (Feigele) - Faye Schrage Ullman, the daughter of Hannah Feinberg-Shraga (Helen Schrage) from Yurburg, who contributed handsomely toward the publication of the Book of Remembrance.

Also we want to thank former residents of Yurburg in the U. S. A., especially Diana (Daniella) from the Berzaner family, and her husband Morton Tobin for their contribution toward the publication of the book.

And finally our dear friends of The Society of Yurburg in Israel especially our friend Shoshanah Pulerevitz - who together helped with the material of the Book of Remembrance, thus enabling it to be published for our community - the community of Yurburg, not forgotten.

Shimon Shimonov (Shim'onov) Chairman of the Yurburg Society
Zevulun Poran   Editor of the book

Pages 7 and 8 Originally in English

THE CHAPTERS OF THE BOOK OF REMEMBRANCE

The Book of Remembrance, is presented to its readers, by the community of Yurburg, in Israel and abroad, and contains a wide range of testimonies describing the city and its surroundings, its family homes, its Jewish citizens, its important people and images, their material and spiritual culture, their way of life and their everyday experiences.

Therefore, in order to help the reader get a clear picture of the book, and a better understanding of the main events in it, we thought it right to divide the book into seven chapters or subjects; each chapter emphasizes part of the image and life of the community. All the chapters together compliment one another and give a complete picture of the city and its Jewish community.

THE FIRST CHAPTER - the city and its environment on the shores of the Nieman River - is made up of articles and written records of the city of Yurburg, its history, its pastoral view and the life of its Jewish residents there. Within the text, the reader feels the great love of those who were raised in the city, for the countryside, for the exceptionally beautiful views - the forests, the rivers, the parks, the bridges and particularly the great river Neiman, which was the source of life and the channel which linked the residents of the city with the rest of Lithuania. Also the city itself - Kovno Street, and the busy trade center.

THE SECOND CHAPTER - families in Yurburg - contains exciting small articles of the authors' families. We look into the intimacy of family life, and sense the security and happiness of the individual. From this we learn of the family, of their relationship toward one another, of their ordinary lives during weekdays, and particularly of the Sabbath and holidays. Within the frame of the family, destinies were sometimes decided - days of happiness and joy of life merge with the days of suffering and mourning. All within the family ...

THE THIRD CHAPTER - dignitaries and personalities - offers some interesting descriptions of important people, residents of Yurburg, whose work was influential in the community. A great number of them established the community, everyone according to his ability working for its good. Included were rabbis, writers, doctors, philanthropists, teachers, artists and others. They deserve that we remember their work. We are very sorry that this list is not complete. The one presented in the book was only found with great difficulty. All those others who would have been able to tell about the work of the notable people and the visionaries of the community, have passed away.

THE FOURTH CHAPTER - culture and the formation of the community - expresses the spiritual life of the Jews, "for man does not live by bread alone." The struggle of the physical existence does not preclude the concern for the spiritual life. Education and the passing on of experience was a prime concern of the community. Synagogues were open for prayer and for learning the Torah. Public life was active and colourful, and many were accomplished in the cultural arts.

IN THE FIFTH CHAPTER - the youth and their activity in Yurburg pride in the youth of the community is expressed. Sports and scouting played an important role in the young people's lives. The Zionist atmosphere had a great influence in establishing the image of the young generation, so much so that the majority of them joined the Pioneer Youth movements. The aspiration of going on to the pioneer training program in order to receive the Certificate of Aliyah to Israel was the driving force of the young generation. Love for Eretz Israel was great and the Zionist ideal occupied the mind of almost every member of the community.

THE SIXTH CHAPTER - destruction of the Jewish Yurburg - is a hair-raising chapter of the great tragedy, which took place in the last days of the Jewish Yurburg. As the Nazi commandos broke through to Yurburg, the sun went down on the community. During three months of great horror all Jews of Yurburg were viciously persecuted and most of them killed. Out of the whole wonderful community, only one or two managed to survive. *{Note added in October 2018: See New Appendix at end of the book for more recent information.}* The Jews of Yurburg were the first to be annihilated because they lived near the German border. The glory of men's lives were trodden into the dust under the boots of the murderous Nazi barbarians and their Lithuanian helpers, who lacked human decency and conscience. The blood which was spilled in the streets of the city and in the surrounding forests, the blood of these tortured and violated people, cries out to us -

"Remember your brothers and friends, remember them ! . . . "

THE SEVENTH AND LAST CHAPTER of the book - survivors of Yurburg perpetuate their community - tells of all that was left of the people, those who survived this hell, of the escape to Israel and abroad, and of those who are now fulfilling the will of those holy souls, through the documentation of their heritage and the story of their disaster told to future generations. The survivors of Yurburg, who found deliverance in our country, remember also that their fathers prayed and awaited redemption, full of faith and hope, but did not see it. Therefore, in order to perpetuate their memory, the Yurburg survivors established memorials in the land of their dreams, and they are:

In the Holocaust Museum which is on Mount Zion in Jerusalem we printed on the memory board the atrocities, which the Nazi attackers did to our community. We also planted a memorial forest for the members of our community in Modi'in, a forest which is a living monument forever; and there in the shade of the trees fathers will tell their sons the story of calamity, of torture, of the days of slaughter and destruction of the community of Yurburg.

May the precious memory of our loved ones remain in our hearts forever.

At the conclusion of this book, it is my pleasure to thank Professor Dov Levin, who contributed from his expert knowledge of the Holocaust and provided me with important archival material.

My appreciation goes to my dear wife Tziporah who has faithfully assisted me during all the drafts and revisions of this book.

Zevulun Poran The Editor

Translated in English by *Surko*

Typical formerly Jewish home in Yurburg - Belonged to Menzer Family
Photo taken in May 2001 by Dr. Leon Menzer [Not in original book]

TRANSLATED FROM PAGES 9 - 10

THE COMMUNITY OF YURBURG AMONG LITHUANIAN JEWRY - COMMON AND UNIQUE FEATURES

by Professor Dov Levin

When Lithuania became independent, at the end of World War I, there were about 160,000 Jews in "Kovnian Lithuania" without the Vilna region which was conquered by the Poles, in over 200 settlements, including the town of Yurburg, to which this book is dedicated. When we compare the facts in this book with those of the other communities of Lithuania, particularly about ten of them which were of similar size (about 2,000 people), Yurburg stands out mainly in the economic, cultural and moral sphere. This town was an important commercial and transportation center between East (Russia and Lithuania) and West (Germany and England) due to the ethnic variety of its inhabitants and mainly due to its location on the banks of the Nieman River and its proximity to East Prussia. Moreover, German culture and universal, secular values increasingly left their mark on the town. All these had a strong influence on the local Jews and on their quality of life; many of them made a living in transport, wholesale trade, export, customs clearance, etc.

Although the Yurburg community was one of the earliest communities in Lithuania (it already belonged to "The Lithuanian State Committee" in the Kedainiai region) and its old synagogue was world-famous, its glory was not in the orthodox-religious realm. Till this very day those who come from Yurburg are proud of the fact that Avraham Mapu made Yurburg his home and the source of his literary inspirations. In any case, the secular movement (Tenu'ath Hahaskalah) was stronger here than in most other communities nearby. Although many people practiced their Judaism in the traditional manner, at least outwardly, secularization was apparently much stronger here than in the neighboring towns of the Zamut (Zemaitija) region.

This trend also flourished in the field of education: from setting up study classes for the children of Israel on behalf of the Czarist Russian Government to the existence of a Hebrew Gymnasium named after Herzl - which were to be found only in about a dozen places in all of Lithuania!

Eventually Yurburg also became famous for the scope and impact of its Zionist activity. An impressive example of the community embracing national-Hebrew spirit may be found in the name of one of the two parks in town was called "Tel Aviv." Nevertheless, the Yurburg community formed an integral part of the Jewish community of Lithuania and a number of phenomena and characteristics of the other communities were to be found here too. This refers among other things, to the ongoing trend in recent generations of a decline in the Jewish population due to emigration to overseas countries, the effects of World War I and the move to large cities, as well as emigration to Israel, and other reasons. As in other parts of Lithuania, in the Jewish "Golden Age" a modern Jewish community was facilitated in Yurburg in the early twenties, due to the support of the Government via the "Ministry of Jewish Affairs" in Kovno. A few years later, when the fascist regime came to power in Lithuania in 1926, there was a strong regression in the autonomic status of the Jewish minority and a substantial number of the national institutions - including the communities - were dismantled. At the same time restrictions against Jews were increased all over Lithuania, including Yurburg, from suppression of Jewish trade (the reason for the liquidation of the Jewish trade company "Export Handel") to bloody outbursts and burning of Jewish property (Fainberg station in 1940).

During the Nazi occupation the German Police were responsible for the Jews of Yurburg, yet for several weeks local Lithuanians tormented their Jewish neighbors like beasts, and some of them even took part in murdering them. Except for a few exceptional cases, the Lithuanian farmers in the area handed over the Jews who hid with them for money or the likes. This is the reason why the few survivors from this town consist mainly of a few Jews who managed to flee to Russia or other places [in the first days of the Nazi invasion] from where they joined the Lithuanian division of the Red Army or the Partisans.

Even today there are many Lithuanian families who live in the homes of their Jewish neighbors and hold their properties under the motto " have you killed and also taken possession?" Furthermore, to the extent that descendants of the victims are still to be found [in Lithuania], they too have to support the newly independent Lithuania, and [in order to remain in Lithuania] evidently do not condemn the part the Lithuanians played in the murder and robbery of their Jewish neighbors.

The bitter destiny of all the Jews of Lithuania was shared by the community of Yurburg surveyed in this Book of Remembrance - one of many such books published in Israel about the Lithuanian communities - which were destroyed and are no longer. This book is important not only as documentation, remembrance and perpetuation, but also for the history of the Jews of Lithuania. We are grateful for this and express our thanks to the experienced editor, who used his professional knowledge together with his warm feelings for his town. We also wish to thank the devoted friends of the Society of Former Residents from Yurburg and its Chairman, who worked hard to publish this book, contributing in mind and matter.

Professor Dov Levin

Head of Oral History Department, Hebrew University, Jerusalem

First Night of the Year 5751 (1991)

The following pages are turned on the pages so that the images are as large and as visible as possible. All of the images other than the synagogue were not in the original Yizkor book. The images are as follows:

- Page 40: Yurburg Town Map Properties from 1907 with partial streets identification - see pages 736 and 737 for an enlarged version of this map with more complete labelling of streets, and pages 733-735 for the list of property owners

- Page 41: Elevated view of Yurburg, likely from the church steeple, looking south-west, with the town of Shaudine across the Nieman River (Courtesy of Jack Cossid)

- Page 42: Great Wooden Synagogue of Yurburg-from a post card brought back in 1927 by Sam and Rae (Krelitz) Ellis (Courtesy of Rosalin Krelitz)

- Page 43: Students of the Talmud Torah of Yurburg-from a post card brought back in 1927 by Sam and Rae (Krelitz) Ellis (Courtesy of Rosalin Krelitz) - identification of students provided on page 340.

- Page 44: Students of the Hebrew Reali Gymnasium of Yurburg, 1925-1926

- Page 45: Students of the Hebrew Gymnasium of Yurburg, 1926-1927

- Page 46: Third Graduating Class of the Hebrew Gymnasium of Yurburg 1929

Yurburg Town Map Properties – 1907

SYNAGOGA erbaut in 1790

JURBURG

Jurbarko žydų prad. mokykla.

יורבורגער יידישע פאלקס שולע.
פאלקס שולע, יורבורג

אגודת יורבורג

הכנס הראשון 5/2 1926

Chapter 1
THE CITY AND THE SETTING ON THE BANKS OF THE NIEMAN RIVER

זכור

TRANSLATION OF PAGE 13

MY YURBURG

By Shelomoh (Sol) Goldstein

Yurburg is all and everything to me. A world abounding with memories and recollections. A town that is a dream never hidden. Yurburg is always in my mind, it is large and beautiful, the most beautiful town in the world. My Yurburg is full of love for the people of Israel and the love of one person for another. My Yurburg is Torah and wisdom, culture and a source of income. Larger and richer towns than Yurburg did not have a Hebrew gymnasium (high school), yet Yurburg's gymnasium was open to everyone, rich and poor alike.

Every youngster with a quest for knowledge had an opportunity to study and acquire an education. And indeed, there were educated young people in Yurburg, wonderful youngsters, with a Zionist and pioneer outlook. And there were teachers at the gymnasium - not all of them born in Yurburg, with a higher education. They deserve to be remembered - people such as Eliezer Laiptsiger (Leipziger), the principal Tsevi Altman, the physician Dr. L. Gershtein, the engineer Dov Khen, Alexandrowitz and others. My Yurburg was a liberal town. "Live and let live." In Yurburg there was room for all the different directions of Judaism - orthodox, zionist, volkists-autonomists and communists. Everyone had freedom of action and freedom of speech. There was a Hebrew school and a Yiddish school; there was a Hebrew library and a Yiddish library; and there was luxurious synagogue and other synagogues, all well cared for. And the Jews prayed "Our eyes shall soon behold the return to Zion. This is the Yurburg I knew as a child, the Yurburg that flows in my blood. I love it with all my heart and soul. I long to see my Yurburg again - wander through its streets, its market, the yard of the gymnasium (high school) named "Herzl" and the "Tel Aviv Park"; to breathe fresh air, the air of my Yurburg. Twice I applied for an entry permit to visit Lithuania, and was refused both times. Now that the regime has changed, I shall probably be able to obtain it. And when I arrive at my Yurburg I shall look for the dear members of the community and if I fail to find them - for they are no longer - I shall lie down on their graves and cry for them. My Yurburg, my dear dear Yurburg - woe is to me . . . !

Shelomoh (Sol) Goldstein

Street Scene

YURBURG ON THE BANKS OF THE NIEMAN RIVER

Demographic Numbers

By I.D. Kamzon

Yurburg lies on the banks of the Nieman River and is surrounded by forests. Yurburg is near the settlements of Shaudine, (4 kilometers, 2 miles), Sudarg (8 kilometers, 5 miles), Skirstiman (10 km, 6 miles), Erzhvilky (21 km, 13 miles), Vilon (30 km, 18 miles), and Smalininken (9 km, 5 miles).

The towns of Pakalnishky (13 kilometers, 10 miles) and Gavry - Gaure (28 km, 16 miles), were Jewish settlements before World War I, but they were destroyed during the period of independent Lithuania after World War I.

In the town there were wide streets with sidewalks and two public gardens (one by the name of "Tel Aviv"). Yurburg is located on the banks of the Nieman River; the streams of the Mituva and the Imstra also flow past the town. The Nieman River was heavily traveled between Kovno and Germany; it provided trade connections with East Prussia. Most of the cargo boats and ships on the Memel-Kovno line were owned by Jews. The brisk trade activity provided a source of income to the people of Yurburg.

The Jewish community dates from the fourteenth century, but actual data exist only from the year 1776. In that year 2,833 Jews lived in Yurburg, out of a total population of 7,391 people. The town is mentioned in the rabbinical responsa "Maharam" - Rabbi Meir Ben Gedalyah from Lublin by the name of "Yurbrig." In 1831 when Yurburg became part of Lithuania with the third partition of Poland by the Russians, Ruben Rozenfeld, a resident of Yurburg, was charged of helping the enemy and hung.

In 1906, a fire broke out and 120 homes were destroyed.

Most Jews had to leave during World War I. In 1923 the Jewish community numbered 1887, out of a total population of 4,409. The number rose in 1930 to 3,000, about 700 families, but before the Holocaust, it had declined to 2,000, about 600 families. The Jews traded in lumbers, chickens, and fish, fruit and eggs, which were exported to Germany. Market days were Mondays and Thursdays. There were 24 fairs held during the year. In the center of the economy life was the Peoples Bank (Folksbank), which had 360 members in 1929. There was a mutual bank for loans and credit, the Komertz Bank, the private bank of the Shmaryahu Bernstein Family.

Jews emigrated to South Africa, Australia and America and some of them to Israel.

The Great Wooden Synagogue Built in 1790

TRANSLATION OF PAGE 15

JEWS OF YURBURG

By Y.D. Kamzon

Yurburg was a very important city, which comprised much of population of the Rasein district. It was only 10 kilometers (6 miles) from the German border. The Ashkenazi tradition was followed Yurburg. Torah was taught there at a very advanced level. Yurburg was known as a town of high levels of education. Most of the Jews there were engaged in trades and crafts. The boats of the Nieman were owned by the Jews, and were used for travelers to come to Yurburg, and to trade with Kovno, the closest large city near Yurburg.

The Jews of Yurburg were proud of their very famous wooden synagogue (see above), which had a lovely Holy Ark, Bimah (platform for the leader of prayer) and beautifully wood carved Eliyahu's chair (pictured in Chapter 4). There also was a "beit midrash." There also were Jews in the towns close to Yurburg, who would come to Yurburg. Before the Holocaust, a total of 2,000 Jews lived there. There were two public gardens, one named of "Tel Aviv," and a Hebrew gymnasium, named "Herzl."

On September 1941, all of the Jews of Yurburg were murdered and the synagogue was set on fire and destroyed.

TRANSLATION OF PAGES 16-17

ON THE BANKS OF THE NIEMAN

By Shimon Shimonov

I think I'm right in saying we grew up "on the river." Since I remember Yurburg, the town of my birth, it is connected with water, a lot of water and rivers.

The Nieman, which started somewhere near the swamps of Pinsk, curved until it reached Lithuania, its waters lowering in accordance with regional conditions - high near Vilki and low near Yurburg. Near Skirstiman the Nieman widens and reaches its peak in the northern part of Yurburg, while in the middle of the river there is a small island full of bushes and weeds and next to it a strip of soft sand which served as the town's "beach." This island served as a playing ground and we hid behind the bushes. We used to reach the island by swimming or by boat. We used to spend most of our summer holidays on the beach, and I remember that I also prepared for my high school graduation on the beach, combining memorizing the study material and resting.

The Nieman beach was called "Di Zarde," a name and term connected with the town's daily life, both in a positive and negative way. The curse "Arop di Zarde" was very popular among the "common people."

The Nieman was the main transport route from and to Yurburg. Twice a day the steamships would arrive or leave from Kovno and back. The trip took between 6 to 8 hours (up stream to Kovno) and less down stream (from Kovno). These boats served for the transportation of merchandise and people, while the merchandise had storerooms and a deck area, the people merely had cabins. At night the cabins were used for sleeping as well.

I remember the rush for the carriages, close to the time of departure or arrival, when the children ran behind them shouting at the top of their voices. The whole family would dress up in order to greet the guests and they would walk together to the pier, which served as a homeport for the steamships.

These vessels - the steamships - were usually owned by Jews, the Levinberg, Fainberg, Karabelnik families and others.

In addition, transport ships would often pass through the Nieman. They were called "Boidkes" by the people and they transported merchandise to Memel while the main part of the ship was deep into the water, and when they returned, empty, the main part floated on the water while the steamship towed along the "boidke" up stream.

Another means of transport were the rafts - made of tree trunks, chopped down in the forests along the Nieman, tied together and sailing down the river as one unit up to Memel, as export merchandise. As children, we used to swim in the river, and hold on to these rafts for a number of kilometers.

In spring, when the ice melted, we would go to the banks of the Nieman and enjoy watching the blocks of ice floating on it. Often large ice blocks would slide on to each other - especially after the Mituva bend - and cause a huge blockage, which would result in floods. Often these floods would inundate entire streets up to the town center. We often sailed in a boat up to the "Daitshe Gass," the German street, in order to buy bread at Sara's bakery shop called "De Rure" which was not flooded.

To the children the floods were a source of "entertainment," enabling them to play around in the water and sail on a boat or boards.

The inhabitants of the inundated streets suffered immensely. The water would flood the storerooms and cause serious damage. The government would allocate sums of money to compensate for the damage. I remember that my late father was always appointed by the authorities to head the committee for assessing the damage for payment of compensation.

When winter came, the Nieman would serve both as a skating area and as a path for public transport, when the buses, wheels covered in iron chains, would move on the frozen Nieman, which served as a replacement for the road.

In spite of all the joy and pleasure this route of transportation also claimed victims, and we distinctly remember the drowning of the three townspeople, prominent citizens.

The Mituva, the second largest river, was in fact a tributary of the Nieman River flowing from the north and passing through the "Lithuanian Park" until it flowed into the Nieman.

In the Holocaust the Germans "used" the Nieman's shore as a place for torturing the Jews, and we will speak about this later on.

In summer we sailed on the Mituva in boats with bars and we also bathed in the river. The third "river" - the Imstra - smaller than the previous one, blithely flowed along the Jewish park "Tel Aviv" and joined the Mituva. In the summer months its shallow waters were the place where the small children played, while in winter it became a place for ice-skating for the boys.

That is how the residents of Yurburg lived, they and their children, on rivers that became a source of living and of entertainment ... until the bitter end arrived for the town's Jews.

TRANSLATION OF PAGES 18-20

A UNIQUE TOWN

Translated from Yiddish and edited by A. Sarid

The following story is based on the story of Yakov Lerman, who was a teacher at the Hebrew gymnasium in Yurburg,. He knew the town and its inhabitants well, and was very fond of them, just like any other resident of Yurburg - whether he lived there for a long or a short time.

The town's name in Lithuanian was Jurbarkas. The Jews called it "Yurburg" or "Yurberik," a small town on the bank of the Nieman River, with a population of 6,000, 2,000 of them Jews.

The town was built along the right side of the Nieman River that flows into the Baltic Sea. Like all the other little towns - Vilon, Srednik, Vilki and others along the banks of the Nieman, Yurburg too made its living mainly from the river. However, Yurburg was the largest town in the area between Kovno and Yurburg, andit was the most beautiful and the richest. Some of the owners of the steamships that sailed along the river were residents of Yurburg. There were passenger compartments on these ships, and cargo compartments for transports from Kovno, with the downward stream, up to Memel (Klaipeda, in Lithuanian), in the Kurish bay. Along the way the steamships would stop at towns and villages along the Nieman, pick up and drop off passengers, and load and unload merchandise. The Yurburg shore served as a homeport for all the ships. The mouth of the Mituva river was a natural port for the ships.

At all these towns Jews were employed as porters, workmen, coachmen or in any other service. The transport of course contributed to the development of wholesale and retail trade in which many Jews were active and on which they made a living.

It is impossible to think of Yurburg without thinking of the Nieman. The river was the thread connecting Yurburg with the world. The German border was close by, 9-10 kilometers (6 miles) and here was the little German town of Smalininken (Smalininkai-currently in the Memel district of Lithuania), which was the source of living of many Jews who lived in Yurburg. It is well known that under such geographic conditions smuggling thrives, and the inhabitants on both sides of the border made a profit in this way. As the famous saying goes: "Yurburg you visited and from smuggling you profitted. . .?"

The proximity to the German border not only gave the Jews of Yurburg the advantage of good-quality woven fabrics, excellent leather products and all sorts of haberdashery - but also lent the town an up-to-date western European flavor. Thus, Yurburg was more influenced by a higher standard of culture than the other towns in Lithuania, by technological achievements and by influx of radical ideas. Many Yurburg residents would visit Germany. The town's youngsters would go to study in western countries and return with a broad education and reactionary social ideas which were strictly forbidden in Lithuania under the totalitarian Russian monarchic regime.

In the period of 1905-6, when Russia was in an upheaval and in the throngs of the socialist revolution, the Yurburg youth took part in the revolutionary actions and raised its flag. Masses of Jewish youngsters took part in the demonstrations on the outskirts of Yurburg, carrying a red flag and singing revolutionary songs. The older generation - the generation of the fathers - was embarrassed by the outbursts of its rebellious sons, looking for freedom, and feared for their fate and the future status of the Jews. As in other parts of Russia, in Lithuania too nobles owned the land. "Poritzes" (Polish estates where Jews would rent some of the lands) and wealthy landowners. Most farmers were poor, without land and in fact they were serfs, who tilled the land of the nobles, in return for a small living for their kin.

The little town of Yurburg and its surroundings belonged to an area ruled by the Russian prince (Kniaz) Vasilshchikov, a member of the Romanov family, which reigned over Russia for 300 years. Prince Vasilshchikov used to come to Yurburg and spend the summer months there; he used to live in his beautiful summer palace, surrounded by a well cared for park. In those months the Jews were of course not allowed to enter this park. However, during most of the months of the year the Jews too were allowed to enjoy the fresh air and beauty of the park. However, the Jews of Yurburg did not need the prince's park, for there was a beautiful landscape all around the town, plenty of water, trees, sun and fresh air. Moreover, when Lithuania eventually became independent (1918) and was liberated from the Russians, the Jews of Yurburg bought a spacious house surrounded by trees, a luscious green garden and they had their own park, which they called . . . . "Tel Aviv." The beautiful house was used for the Hebrew gymnasium (high school) which became the cultural center of the Jews of Yurburg, of which they were very proud (photographs in Chapter 4).

In addition to the Hebrew gymnasium there were two elementary schools in town - in Hebrew and in Yiddish; "Talmud Torah," modern, in the framework of "Tarbuth," two libraries - one called "Mendele" in Yiddish and the other - called "Brener" which contained Hebrew books. There were religious and secular institutions in the town too.

The Jews of Yurburg were proud of the old synagogue, which was believed to be built in 1790; Jewish artists designed the building and the Holy Ark, and they were much admired by those who saw them. Many people would come to Yurburg to see this original building and its expensive artifacts.

Jews lived in Yurburg for hundreds of years, they established good relations with the Lithuanians who lived there, and got along with them. The Jews of Yurburg were proud of their closeness to their German neighbors to the west and considered them cultural and enlightened, but they would soon be disappointed. When the "cultured" German invader entered Yurburg in World War II - Jewish Yurburg was wiped out within months and turned into ruins.

Palace of the Russian Prince -[Not in original Yizkor Book]
[Photo taken by Dr. Leon Menzer in May 2001]

Parade in front of Talmud Torah School in Yurburg
[Not in original Yizkor Book - from photo album of Jack Cossid]

Imstra River Scene
[Not in original Yizkor Book - Photo by Dr. Leon Menzer in May 2001]

Over the beautiful Mituva stream - May 2001 -
[Photo by Dr. Leon Menzer - Not in original book]

TRANSLATION OF PAGES 21-24

YURBURG - MY TOWN OF BIRTH

By Dov (Berl) Levinberg

I spent the first twenty-four years of my life in Yurburg, the town of my birth. My memories take me back to 1913, the year before the outbreak of World War I.

Yurburg was one of the beautiful little towns along the bank of the largest river in Lithuania, the Nieman. The town was a haven of green, surrounded by orchards, fields, parks and pine tree forests. However, Yurburg's main attraction was the beauty of its rivers: the Nieman on one side, the Mituva on the other side and in the middle the Imstra river, flowing in a narrow stream, hidden at the foot of the mountain.

The rivers flowed peacefully during all the months of the year. However, in April when the ice melted, there was an outburst of strong currents of water, which flowed over the bank and flooded broad areas. The water of the Nieman sometimes reached the streets of the town and caused heavy damage. Nevertheless, these floods had their blessing too. The turrets of water would bring along fresh soil that benefited the town's gardens.

There was a large park covering a vast area of 200 dunam (50 acres). It was divided into two - one side was open to the public and the other side was declared a closed area, for this is where the palace of Prince Vasilshchikov of the Romanov family, the Russian monarchy, was located.

At the end of the park stood the Russian-Pravoslavic church, owned by the Prince. Gold jewels, diamonds, precious objects and works of art were stored there.

Every Saturday evening prayers were held at the church. A wonderful chorus sang beautiful religious songs here, heard by visitors to the park who enjoyed the lovely melodies. Not far from the Prince's palace were the horses' stables as well as a small zoological garden with various wild animals.

Yurburg's Jewish population was composed of businessmen, shop owners, craftsmen, coachmen, porters, peddlers, workers etc. Some of the Jews were orthodox - "Mithnagdim" ("against" Hasidim) - and some of them were orthodox in the modern way. Yurburg's proximity to the German border - 9 km (6 miles) from the little German town of Smalininken was a window to the European life style.

Slowly the town's Jews adopted the western European lifestyle. They learned the German language and culture, wore clothes imported from Germany and bought German tools and products.

Most of the town's youth were intelligent and wanted to acquire knowledge and education. Up until World War I there was a Russian-Jewish school in town, Talmud Torah and a modern-style school. There also was a library in the town with a reading room for those who spoke Russian. In 1918, when Lithuania became independent, the situation changed. A Jewish gymnasium (high school) was founded in which the study language in the first year was Yiddish, and afterwards a Hebrew - science gymnasium, founded by the "Tarbut" chain of schools. There were two libraries in town - "Mendele" with Yiddish books and "Brener" with Hebrew books.

The town did not stand still. The youth was organized in associations and various circles, such as "Maccabi," the Scouts (Hashomer Hatsair), the Jewish Sports Club J.A.K. (Jewish Athletics Club), Khovevei Zion (Lovers of Zion), Tseirei Zion, Poalei Zion (Zionist Workers), circles of General Zionists, Revisionists etc. There were also cultural circles and a drama circle for theater lovers.

The typical Jew was a Zionist and assisted in raising funds for Eretz Yisrael, such as Keren Hakayemeth (Jewish National Fund), Keren Hayesod and Kapai (Fund of the Labor Party). There were righteous and philanthropic Jews, as witnessed by the various public welfare institutions which were usually called "companies" such as Bikur Kholim (Care for the Ill), Gemiluth Khesed (Small loans without interest), Hakhnasath Orkhim (Accommodation for Passersby), Tsedaka Gedolah (Charity for the Poor), Maoth Khitim (Money for buying Matsoth etc. for Pesakh), Khevrah Kadisha (Society of the Cemetery and Burying of the Dead) etc.

The Popular Bank (Folksbank) was very important - it was the branch of the Central Bank (Zentralbank) in Kovno and its task was to assist in the Jewish cooperation. The bank assisted by extending loans for small-scale trade, to businessmen and other Jews who required a loan in times of need.

It is noteworthy that there were homeowners who fulfilled the obligation of "giving anonymously" ("Matan Besether") and helped those who had become poor and required assistance. The needy asked for and received help, while one had to look for the poor.

The theater group arranged parties and performances a few times a year for the benefit of the needy, such as buying clothes for poor children, and supplying matzot and wine for Passover.

The obligation of Passover alms for the poor, for example, was faithfully observed.

One of the town's wealthy men, the late Yehudah Rabinowitz, founded the "Talmud Torah" for the poor children who received an orthodox and general education there, and were given a school uniform once a year.

I would like to mention my late father, Yisrael Levinberg, who was a well-known philanthropist and helped the needy and poor. In addition to being a "ba'al tsedakah" he also loved the people of Israel. He took an interest in people and inquired who had or had not and how it was possible to help the latter. All those who needed help, a loan or donation, would be given to him. He was a wealthy businessman, a steamship owner in Yurburg. Our home had a traditional-nationalist atmosphere and my father was known to support the Zionist cause, and therefore he was very respected in town.

The synagogues in town were as follows: a prayer house, a synagogue and small houses of prayer. The great synagogue was built in 1790 in the architectural style of the Middle Ages. The Holy Ark was made of wood and covered with carvings of various wild animals, birds and plants. The synagogue was famous in the Jewish world. Guests and tourists came to see the beautiful synagogue and its pictures were distributed all over the world.

There was no industry in Yurburg. On the other hand, Yurburg was an important center through which export goods passed from Lithuania to western Europe, mainly to Germany and Great Britain. The export products were: wood, linen, seeds, fodder, eggs, fruit, hides etc.

Import was also important: sugar, herring, salt, dried fruit, textiles, oil, plaster and chemical fertilizers.

The Nieman was an important factor in the development of the import-export business. Steamships and cargo ships sailed the river. Some of them carried passengers and others carried cargo from Yurburg to Kovno and back. Wooden barges sailed the river from Grodno through the Vilija and other rivers. Transport on the Nieman constituted an important source of employment for the people of the town - both Jews and Gentiles.

Some of the inhabitants owned steamships, which formed the basis for the town's economy.

Yurburg's tale is long, a town and a mother in Israel, a home for the hundred-year old Jewish community - a lively community looking towards the future. But all of a sudden it came to an end. Destruction came to Yurburg and the people of Israel.

The Jewish Yurburg was no more;

Til today it has its glory

But its Jews

Alas, they are no longer - they were destroyed and are no more . . .

Translated to Hebrew from Yiddish by E. Kopelov

TRANSLATION OF PAGES 25-32

MEMORIES FROM YURBURG- THE TOWN OF MY BIRTH

By Emanuel Kopelov

I had a dream. I return to the town of my childhood. Everyone there is still alive! It was not yet destroyed! The houses are standing and the Jewish inhabitants were not annihilated . . .

When did it happen? When?

My thoughts return to 1922. In that year my family and I returned to Yurburg from far-away Russia, from Panze, where we stayed as did most of the refugees of World War I.

Avraham-Yitskhak and Miriam Kopelov

Shortly after I was born in Yurburg, World War I broke out. My late mother was afraid to remain in town and insisted we leave until the situation calmed down. Thus we abandoned the apartment where we lived. My parents fled to Russia, as far away as Kaluga and on to Panze. All the furniture and equipment remained behind in our apartment in Yurburg, many Hebrew and Russian books, a piano etc. My parents took us and fled, leaving our belongings behind in the apartment, hoping they would find everything back upon their return.

The stay in Russia was extended, just like the war, and it was almost natural that the apartment could not wait for us. The belongings in the apartment also slowly started "to move" to other apartments in town.

When we returned, many good people had a pang of conscience, and somehow some of the belongings were returned, the piano among them. We also found a good part of the precious books that belonged to my late father, and they are still in my possession.

During the period of independent Lithuania, the Jewish community of Yurburg was well based. It was located on the bank of the Nieman, surrounded by forests and parks, covered in green and divided by two rivers - the Imstra and the Mituva. The Imstra - at the end of the Kovner-Gass (Kovno Street) flowed into the Mituva that bordered on the area beyond the town. There on the other side was the Kaliani forest and further on to Smalininken the Prussian border. The town's center was mainly populated by Jews: businessmen, teachers, builders, craftsmen and others.

The Lithuanians lived all around. In the 1930s the Lithuanians became nationalistic. The "Shaulists" organizations started to expand - in the early days it claimed to be a sports club and afterwards it turned into a club waging a nationalistic war against the Jews. In our time the Lithuanians were careful not to hurt the Jews, for they would be hit twice as hard in return. However, after a while the situation changed, as is well known.

As I said, the town was located on the bank of the Nieman, and this formed its character and its economy. Yurburg was a town through which the steamships passed which sailed on the Nieman from Memel to Kovno and from Yurburg to Kovno and back. A large part of the various goods imported from Germany passed through the town, as well as the export of wood to Memel and Tilzit. Many people in town were employed in the activity on the bank of the Nieman. We recall the steamship owners and the Jews who made a good living from them. The steamships would also bring many tourists from Kovno and its surroundings in spring and summer. They came to attend the sports festivities, which were held in Yurburg's parks. Even today one may meet Jews from Lithuania and find out they visited Yurburg on one of the trips to the festivities, and were enchanted by the lovely scenery and the beautiful girls of the town. . . .

There were two parks in town, one of the Hebrew gymnasium and the other in memory of the days of Prince (Kniaz) Vasilshchikov - a large park with remnants of the Prince's palace and many different buildings used by the Lithuanian gymnasium in our days. Various festivities would be held in this large park, evenings of dance, conventions etc.

The activity of the "Hekhalutz" youth movement also took place in the parks, the games, meetings etc.

On the other side of the park there was a forest leading to Smalininken, and the famous "Mushroom" forest, "Der Schwemel." The articles about the "Mushroom" told of many visitors, each of them carving their name on the "Mushroom" tree.

Life passed along slowly in town, only on market days did things become livelier. Then the town thronged with people; many farmers from the surrounding areas came to sell their wares, and also Jewish farmers from little towns in the area, who would bring along carts of apples and pears.

Everyone would gather in the area between the synagogues on Kovner Gass (Kovno Street). Everything was done directly, until some of the farmers would get drunk and start to become rowdy because they had drunk too much wine. This was the hour of triumph of Berale Malchik. The moment matters got out of hand, one did not call the Police. Berale was called to the street and he would catch two farmers by their neck and take them to the Police, return and catch the other hooligans. Berale was one of the town's porters - a group working mainly on the bank of the Nieman.

In the 1930s a new road was paved and a bridge was built over the Mituva, along the Raseiner gass (Rasein Street), and this facilitated traffic from the town in the direction of Smalininken, along the Prussian border. The road cut through the Kaliani forest.

It is along this road that the Germans arrived at the start of World War II. The road that in the good days was used by the inhabitants of Yurburg to go on outings and trips in the Kaliani forest, now became the Via Dolorosa - the path of suffering. In the war the Jews were chased into the Kaliani forest via this road and there many good people of the town were murdered and thrown into the pits they had to dig -men, women and children.

We shall remember them forever.

Construction of a bridge (likely over the Mituva).

[Photo not in original book. Photo taken by Ben Craine in 1927.]

When I think of my town, which I left in 1935, on my way to Israel, a host of pictures come to mind which are connected to its general and its human landscape.

As I mentioned before, Yurburg was a town surrounded by greenery. It was graced by two parks. Three rivers - the Nieman, Mituva and the little Imstra added to its beauty. The Nieman also defined its shores as it served as a line of transport between Kovno, the capital of Lithuania and its center of trade, and Memel (Klaipeda) on the shore of the bay called "Kurischer Haf." Lithuanian import and export were conducted along the shores of the Nieman and formed the basis of the inhabitants' economy.

However, the Nieman was not merely a water line for trade - not merely so prosaic.

We remember its shores not merely as a station of embarkation. We spent our summer holidays on its shores. We sailed on boats. We swam in its water on the other side and we dreamt our dreams, some of them came true and others were shelved.

Some of our best friends met their death in the shadows of the Nieman when they sailed to meetings of an underground communist cell existing in our town. One of them, Shemuel Abramson, was a gifted young man and a brilliant student. He was my best friend, in spite of the differences in our views.

We always had a very good time when the ice and snow melted and the Nieman overflowed and came close to the town's houses, although they were two kilometers away from the bank. In this period the steamships would sail to Kovno not from the distant shore, but from another side of Kovno street, from the Mituva, which also flooded and served as a small port, or from the other side near the bathhouse near the great synagogue.

We would go for a walk on the banks of the Nieman to see who had come and who was leaving. There were occasions when a steamship would sail in the dark of the evening to Kovno and the "captain" would become confused and sail the whole night without leaving Yurburg's "territorial waters"; only when dawn broke would the "captain" find that his steamship was still in the vicinity of Yurburg although it had sailed all night long.

Ah - the steamships - how nice it was to sail on them. And how many unforgettable moments are connected with these sailings - school outings and ordinary trips to Kovno. I sailed many times in all the directions of the Nieman on missions on behalf of my late father. I was well acquainted with the shores of the Nieman and the little town along its borders. I loved the special atmosphere of sailing back and forth to Kovno. I saw many things on these sailings and now that I am writing these pages they come back to mind.

Shemuel Abramson - Drown in Nieman River

Brother of Gita Abramson Bereznitzky

[Not in original Yizkor Book

Photo from collection of Rosalin Ellis Krelitz]

The activity on the banks of the Nieman occupied many of Yurburg's residents. Most steamship owners were Yurburg residents. Some families made a good living by transporting passengers on the Yurburg - Kovno line and towing barges from Smalininken to Kovno and back.

In addition to the steamship owners, who were Jewish, many clerks worked as treasurers on the steamships. Among the steamship owners I also remember a respectable Christian, called Afsanov, who was always seen in Yurburg, but he had a large estate with a dairy in Raudondvaris, not far from Yurburg. This man was fluent in Yiddish and used to speak in this language to his customers.

Among the wealthy steamship owners were Israel Levinberg and the late Karabelnik. Their steamships "Lietuva" and "Planta" were beautiful and comfortable, and they would transport passengers on the Yurburg - Kovno line. We would joke among ourselves that one-day the prow of the "Planta" would be given to one of the daughters of the Karabelnik family as a dowry. We had no idea then of what would happen to the town and its Jews within a few years.

In addition to the steamship owners and their clerks, who were but few, Jewish porters worked on the shore. This was a group of people, strong young men, who loaded on their shoulders many tons of merchandise arriving at the town.

The town's daily life was connected with the three rivers close to and within Yurburg. In fact, only two of them could be called rivers: the Nieman, of course, and the Mituva, the third - the smallest - like those we have here in Israel in the valleys, was almost dry during most days of the year, but its river bed was deep and two bridges were built to cross over it. This was the Imstra, which in a way divided Yurburg into two and by chance, or perhaps not by chance, there was a certain demographic division on the two sides of this river; on one side the predominantly Jewish part, and on the other side - the Christian part with its Jewish minority. By the way, some of the town's poor people lived on the other side of the Imstra, at the end of Kovno street.

We used the Mituva for excursions and rowing. We had good times on its two banks and the thick forest. On one side, the park with its broad lawns and visible and invisible paths, the ruins of the castle of Prince Vasilshchikov, lent the place majestic splendor, and the woods on the other side, which went on to the village of Kaliani on one side and almost up to Smalininken on the other side. The youngsters were attracted to the park, and they held outings and performances there.

This place brings to mind two characters, an artist and a craftsman, who worked here. A sophisticated workshop for frames was left here from the time of the Prince, with excellent machines (very advanced for those days) where an old locksmith worked.

He got it into his head to solve the problem of Perpetuum Mobile - The "Perpetual Motion Machine." We, children, would often visit his workshop and inquire about his progress. I remember a sort of machine he built with which he hoped to reach "Perpetual Motion." Had the Nazis not killed him, and not confiscated his tools and machines, he may still be standing there, trying to *reach eternity!* This, of course, is just a manner of speaking. The man was very old and he has certainly been buried deep under the earth for a long time.

The second one, an artist, was a sculptor. I forgot his surname. He was a Lithuanian. He lived in one of the beautiful houses at the end of the park. This house was also used for the offices of the Prince's family in the days of glory. I would go to this house from time to time and see small and large sculptures, very interesting.

Once he worked on a large sculpture, investing a lot of work in it. He finished it and when he was about to transfer it to have it cast in bronze, the sculpture collapsed and broke into pieces.

The two people I mentioned resembled each other in a way - the artist and the craftsman. Their ambition and their fate!

I have strayed to the town's periphery. Let us return to the park of our gymnasium. The "Tel Aviv" park. We were proud of the gymnasium. Here we were educated and absorbed the love for Eretz Yisrael, and here we were inspired to realize this love. At the gymnasium we became friends with all the good and precious sons of Yurburg who are with us here in Israel, and those who did not have the good fortune to come to Israel and who live abroad and are still thinking about aliyah.

Yurburg was a typical small Lithuanian town. It was remarkable for its lively, active, cultural Hebrew youth. They were happy young people. The "Tarbuth" elementary school and the gymnasium, also founded by "Tarbuth," were instrumental in forming the nature of the town's youth. The Zionist youth movements had many members in town: "Hashomer Hatsair," "Maccabi," "Hekhalutz," "Beitar" and others.

Yurburg was famous for its old synagogue, built in the previous century. A wooden building, gloriously rising up at the end of the market square, next to the large prayer house, the new one. Here too was the small synagogue, set up by the Fainberg family and called "Fainberg's Kloiz." All the synagogues were full of worshippers on the Sabbath and holidays. The main street looked beautiful on the Sabbath and holidays when it was almost entirely inhabited by Jews - the town's Jews would walk along, surrounded by their children, to and from the synagogue to their homes. That was the time when the Jews would leave behind all their worries, about making a living and about bringing up their children, and would turn to the synagogue to celebrate the Sabbath or a holiday.

There was a Rabbi in town, Rabbi Avraham Dimant, a learned Torah scholar, but unlucky, he was blessed with two daughters who were grown-up, yet no husband was found for them. One sat at home and took care of her father and mother. She was hardly seen in town. The other fell in love with the town's physician - however, her love went unanswered, and he was unaware of it. From time to time she would walk up and down the sidewalk in front of the doctor's home, hoping she would at least see his face. In the end, she lost her mind . . . .

There was a Dayan (religious judge) in the town too: Rabbi Hayim (Chaim)-Reuven Rubinstein. He may not have excelled in the Torah, but he had splendor. He assisted many of us in going on aliyah. All those who were supposed to go to Israel in fictitious marriages received the required documents from him.

There were many good people in town, and many stories may be told about them that have not been forgotten. Yes indeed, it was a beautiful town and we were fortunate to have been able to absorb the good things it had to offer.

We remember Yurburg as Zionist in nature. However, on the Jewish streets of Yurburg there was also a group of Yiddishists, the main nucleus of which was composed of the porters on the banks of the Nieman. They had social awareness and were deeply Jewish and stood out in public. In addition, there were a number of businessmen and clerks who also had "Folkist" inclinations and they formed the nucleus of the Yiddishist group, striving for "Do'ikait."

They set up the library called "Mendele" in Yurburg at the Rabinowitz home. This was a large library comprising the best of Yiddish literature. Many readers would come here and they would always find nearly every new book that was published.

The gymnasium, set up in Yurburg in 1921, started its activity by teaching in Yiddish. Its first principal, Mr. Efrat, was the son-in-law of the Zionist leader and the first Minister of Jewish affairs in the Lithuanian government - Dr. Shimshon Rosenbaum. Mr. Efrat was a staunch Yiddishist and together with the teacher, Mr. Lifshitz, who also was a Yiddishist, and joined the group of teachers at the gymnasium, they tried to preach Yiddishism, however to no avail. In the second year of the gymnasium's existence the public committee and the parents demanded that Hebrew be the language of teaching. And, with the assistance of the "Tarbuth" center in Kovno, the Hebrew Gymnasium was founded and existed. The teacher Lifshitz left Yurburg.

Mr. Efrat too left Yurburg and started to teach at Vilkomir. The group of students who had to pass on to the eighth grade moved away with him. The eighth grade did not exist in Yurburg yet. They finished their studies at Vilkomir. Mr. Efrat ended his Yiddishist career. He went to Israel and taught at the "Tikhon Khadash" (literally: New High School) school in Tel Aviv. He was very popular with his students and admired by his colleagues. He passed away at a ripe old age in Tel Aviv.

Indeed, Yurburg was known for its Zionist nature. The gymnasium and the school, with their teachers, placed their mark on the people and an excellent training kibbutz assisted them by pioneer youth movements, and later on. Hebrew was heard on the street. At that time Lithuanian was only spoken with the Lithuanians. The older people spoke Yiddish among themselves and **the young people conversed in Hebrew**.

We should also mention the Folksbank, which was the only Jewish banking institution in town. Its management would be replaced each year in elections, which took place at the general meeting. The discussions towards the general meeting would start a short while before it took place and would reach their peak during the meeting. Two parties contended - the Zionists and the Yiddishists. Discussions would usually end when the two groups would reach a compromise and conduct matters quietly and with mutual understanding.

In addition to the Yiddish library, "Mendele," the "Brener" library was founded, a library which had mainly Hebrew books. A lot of energy went into the establishment of this library, and the main initiators were the late Eliezer Laiptsiger (Leipziger) and my late mother Miriam Kopelov. A large lottery was held in order to raise the money required for buying the books. Many people helped to distribute the cards and buy items for the lottery.

One of the many items in the lottery was a large painting by the former principal of the gymnasium, engineer Khen. This painting was connected to his affair with the daughter of the gymnasium's janitor, a beautiful redhead, who was his beloved, and who served as a model for the beautiful painting.

Significant sums were raised in the lottery, which served for setting up the library for those interested in Hebrew and Hebrew books; the library was the center of Zionist activity. The "Hekhalutz" (pioneer) training kibbutz was another beautiful corner in Yurburg. A large number of the members of this kibbutz at the time managed to come to Israel. One may meet them in Kfer Masarik, Beth Zera, Kineret and other places.

Festive meetings would be held in Yurburg's parks, the park near the gymnasium, there was dancing and athletics, together with the sports organizations. Many people would come to Yurburg from Kovno. These tourists would arrive at the Nieman shore, would form into rows and march towards the town, accompanied by an orchestra led by conductor Mirsky, who issued his orders in a clear voice, keeping pace. As a matter of fact, he was in Israel and lived in Rehovot.

Such was beautiful Yurburg, which we shall always remember!

By Emanuel Koplov

The Big Park in which we loved to stroll.

TRANSLATION OF PAGES 33-42

THE YURBURG I KNEW

By Mordekhai (Mordechai) Zilber

In a few days I shall be 63 years old (written in January 1970). The years have gone by. Writing these lines, I don't want to scrutinize the days of my life that passed, but I mainly want to remember my little town, in the land of Lithuania. The people of my generation are slowly disappearing, and soon there will be no memory of those born in the little towns and no one will be left to remember them.

We remember those little towns and they are the best memories we have from those days. Indeed, the little towns are no longer. Hitler's "deluge" flooded them, destroyed them, desecrated their temples and dispersed their bones over the fields and forests of Lithuania.

Shall my humble pen be able to set up a memorial for the semblance and image of our little town on the shores of the Nieman? My town was destroyed by villains, the Germans and the Lithuanians. For hundreds of years they were our neighbors. We were like everyone else, we Jews, part of the Lithuanian landscape, we the sons of a southern Semitic tribe in the far North.

Yurburg in 1928 viewed from the East - photo not in original Yizkor Book. Photo is courtesy of Lior Alkoni and Sara Alkoni-Silver, grandson and daughter of Mordechai Zilber.

The name of my little town was Yurburg. The Jews called it Yurbrik. The little town was situated on the shores of the Nieman, 80 kilometers (50 miles) from the then capital Kovno. About 600 Jewish families lived in Yurburg and about 50 Christian families. Yurburg was situated in a small valley; on one side were the fields of the Lithuanian farmers and on the other side the Nieman was its border, its steely blue waters flowing along courageously and sometimes flooding its shores. Beyond the Nieman were dense forests and the farmers' homes covered in straw of the little Jewish village Shaudine (Saudine). On the side of this village was the estate of a Baron, its white houses could be seen from afar. The connection with the capital was via the Nieman on which steamships sailed with glorious names such as "Kestutis," named after one of the historic Lithuanian princes, "Lietuva" - Lithuania and "Tevyne" - fatherland.

The water of the Nieman flowed into the Baltic sea. But my little town was the last stop for the steamships, while the German border was merely 10 kilometers away. Rafts would sail on the Nieman as well, made of tree trunks, harvested in the Lithuanian forests.

The Jewish tradesmen would sail these rafts to Germany. "Good" Jews would sail on these rafts, praying and studying Talmud . . . thus a "good" Jew would stand next to the large steering wheel while his small prayer shawl flowed in the wind and he would study the Torah. And at night the stars would shine brightly and the dark shadows would move along silently on the water. Rafts from the world of imagination! These were Jews from the little towns of Vilki and Srednik. Jews, Torah scholars who chose hard and dangerous work to make a living. The Nieman was their source for making a living. Jewish fishermen, porters on the steamships, carriage owners who transported the "Passengers" to the little town, ticket vendors on the ships and visitors.

Yurburg in 1928 - photo not in original Yizkor Book. Photo is courtesy of Lior Alkoni and Sara Alkoni - Silver, grandson and daughter of Mordechai Zilber.

When you would come to our little town from the side of the Nieman, you would see the entire town in front of you. First of all you would see the sandy land, humble vegetable gardens planted with potatoes, and the Mituva river next to them, whose water flowed into the Nieman. The shrill voices of frogs would be heard in the water of the small lake in the "Zarda," before the town.

And here comes the town itself - a gray block of one-story wooden houses, while on one side the red bell towers proudly rise up and the red roof of the Lithuanian Catholic church, and on the other side - the high house with the three roofs of the synagogue.

Former home of Menzer family - with Duba Most Rosenberg and Fania Hilelson Jivotovsky [Photo on in original book - photo taken by Dr. Leon Menzer in May 2001]

In my dream, I am walking through my town, which is no longer, which was destroyed and burned down, while the bones of its martyrs were collected in the forest next to my little town and buried in a large mass grave in the cemetery, at the initiative and with the efforts of the few who were left behind.

Here comes the "street of the butchers" "Yatkever Gass," with its crooked doors and windows, as in the paintings of Chagal. The street is paved with cobblestones, and here too is the large bakery shop of Kraid [Ben Craine's mother's bakery....note added by Joel Alpert]. And the butchers, Jews who observe the Torah, who in the days of the high holidays would "lead" at the synagogue and the sounds of their prayers would lament the bitter fate . . . only the last and terrible fate, that of Hitler - may he burn in hell - the days of the Holocaust they could not lament and they were sent to their death as sheep to slaughter.

And from the "street of the butchers," through short alleys, we arrive at the main street of our town - "Kovner Gass" (Kovno Street), a street on which almost all the houses are two-story brick buildings. Most of the town's shops were on this street. (See pictures on pages 72 and 73.)

Kovno Street (from right to left: Shakhnovitz's Bookstore to Church)

Same scene as above - Kovno Street Looking West - May 2001

Note church in distance in both photos - Photo not in original Yizkor Book

**Kovno Street - Main Street in Yurburg - From Hotel Kamilis to the store
of Polovin Moshe Krelitz's building is third from left.**

**Same scene as above - Kovno Street Looking East - May 2001
Moshe Krelitz's Brick building is on the far left
Identified by Duba Most Rosenberg - photo not in original Yizkor Book**

I remember there were weaving workshops there, and a grocery store and a wholesaler and retailer, and there were pharmacies, three hairdressers, Lapinsky's beer agency, two shops for kitchenware and paint. And there was the large store for farming tools and agricultural machinery of Grinberg (Greenberg), who was one of the town's wealthy men and engaged in thriving business with the Lithuanian village. And further on the shop where hides were sold, and the large store for stationery and books of Shakhnowitz. And there were the two hotels of Motl Komel and Fainberg. And thus we arrive at the municipal market, which every Monday and Thursday would be full of horse carts and the noise of the villagers. Next to this market stand the town's two synagogues - the House of Prayer and the Great Synagogue.

Further on is Fainberg's hotel and the Lithuanian citizen's club, the large yard of the Fainberg brothers; four brothers in the family, owners of the lumber mill, the flower mill and the electricity plant which supplied the town's electricity, from 6 o'clock in the evening to midnight. The electricity allowed the town's two little movie houses to show movies and bring the inhabitants of Yurburg in touch with the beautiful world outside - to get to know Emil Yanings, Konrad Feidt, Pola Negri, Charley Chaplin, and all the other famous actors. If a successful movie was shown at one of the movie houses, the other was empty that evening. The town's youth loved the movies, which took them out of their isolation. The movie house was open on Friday evening, Saturday evening and Sunday. Movies at that time were still "silent"; the movie was accompanied on the violin by the Poliak Stashmitsky and an old spinster played the piano - it was said she had a philosophically profound view of life. The second movie house operated without musical accompaniment. The movie house owner was afraid to incur unnecessary expenses. The movie house's billboards, the "Affishes"(banners) painted in various colors were set up in a wooden frame next to Shakhnovitz's bookstore. The boards were painted by Levin, a nice young man, who would receive a few cents for this and a few free tickets.

The movies would stir up longings for the world outside, would entice people to leave the town and its boring life behind. There was always talk about emigration in town, and the imagination traveled around the globe. Distant countries were mentioned. And some boys and girls went on training courses organized by "Hekhalutz" and they would wait a few years in order to obtain one of the few available certificates to go to "Palestina." Mexico was mentioned, Argentina, Uruguay, Peru, and Chile. America, Canada and South Africa were not mentioned, as these countries were "locked with seven locks," and there was no hope of getting there.

These were the 1920s and they "excelled" in lack of purpose . . . , however, only part of the town's youth was lucky enough to be saved and arrive in one of those distant countries. It is presently possible to find people from Yurburg all over the world, even in far-away Australia. Thus part of the youth was saved from destruction in the days of the Holocaust.

Let's walk on along the roads of our town. The next street is Kalishu street, named after a neighborhood village. What is so special about this street? - Nothing at all, except for the fact that it is our street, the street of my family and my aunts Rocha and Friedel. This street starts at a two-story house where the Kizel family lived, a family all of whose members emigrated to distant Canada. One of the sons was my best friend, Rafael, or Rafelke Kizel. The others, the grown-ups, did business with the Lithuanian village, fodder, hides and linen. The younger ones studied at the Kovno gymnasium. The Kizel family was a large family blessed with many sons and daughters (see article in the Appendix, page 652).

Further on, on the same street, there were a few modest shops and the "Stadola" of the hotel owner Motl Komel. The "Stadola" was usually empty, but once, not in my time, it was used as a stable for the horses of the "Post." The post coaches would go in and out there. The coachmen would rest at the hotel, and the horses in the stables. Opposite the large horse stables was the small house of Khone "Der Zeigermakher," the only clock maker in town, a kind Jew, who adopted an orphan and took him into his home. All sort of clocks were ticking on the walls of his workroom. When Khone would repair a clock this would be in "Garantia" - the clock "ran" for a long time. Khone would also be called upon to repair the large wall clocks of the "Kniaz" palace, of Prince Vasilshchikov, at the end of town, in the large park.

Further on we stand in front of the large two-story home, a beautiful house, of Rabbi Yehudah Rabinowitz. This was the most beautiful and largest house of which the town was very proud. This house could easily have stood next to other houses even in Petersburg, Russia's capital. It was not only a home, but also a large yard with all sorts of structures. The yard was paved with stones, not like the other yards in town, which in fall and spring, when the snow melted, would be full of dirt and mud and puddles of water impossible to pass. The house was a luxurious residence with strong brown oak doors with bronze handles. The windows were high and shining. When I was a little boy, Yehudah Rabinowitz was no longer alive. I knew that Rabinowitz had built the "Talmud Torah," a large wooden building with an attic. And there was a large yard around it too, a place where the town's poor children could play.

Rabinowitz was the richest businessman in town, he traded in timber and he had business connections with Germany. His picture hang in the school's largest hall, where all the town's weddings were held. In one of the houses, green in color, lived Doctor Rabinowitz, the late Yehudah's son. He was the town's important physician, a bachelor, who was only interested in medicine. The town's carriages would arrive at his home filled with fresh straw and carpets in order to take the doctor to a patient in the village. On one of Dr. Rabinowitz's visits to "Shaudine," the little Jewish village on the other side of the Nieman, he suddenly felt ill. He said to one of the Jews: "go tell my family that I am not feeling well and that I am about to die." He arrived at his home very sick and died.

My late mother, blessed be her memory, sent me together with the other children of the town to recite psalms next to his body covered in black. Dr. Rabinowitz often treated me during his lifetime and he stitched the sole of my foot that I once injured. Dr. Rabinowitz was a doctor for all illnesses, a general physician, he would deliver babies, carry out surgery, and he was also a doctor of internal medicine, what is called a country doctor in America. Needless to say that he was a kind man who assisted the town's poor people and treated them free of charge.

In that same large yard stood a small house with an honorable neighbor, the famous gentile of the town who was the servant of the Rabinowitzes. He was a tall gentile, "a gentile and a half," a drunkard, whose main job it was to clean the yard and the front of the large house. The gentile never let go of the large broom he held in his hand. This gentile came of a distinguished lineage. Everyone knew that he was a "potshotni promestavni grazdanin", an honorable citizen by birth. This gentile did not go any further in life for he was a drunkard and had no relations with anyone; he lived on his own and was solitary. It was said about the gentile that he still had medals from the time of the Russian army, but no one had actually seen them.

All this happened in the days of the Czar, prior to World War I. Later on, when our family returned from Russia, after four years of World War I, the general picture in Yurburg had not changed. One of the sons lived at the Rabinowitz residence, an aristocratic Jew, who was also an important timber merchant, like his father, who did business with Germany. At the doctor's home there was another doctor already, not a member of the family. His name was Dr. Gershtein, a handsome man who was also the principal of the Hebrew gymnasium in our town.

Yosef Rabinowitz, the son, had a special carriage, on which one sat as on a horse, with the legs on both sides. In this carriage he would ride to his forests in the town's vicinity. He was married to one of the daughters of businessman Fein (the largest grocery wholesaler in), a great beauty.

Opposite the home of the Rabinowitzes, at the Beth laBanim (Home of the Sons) was a coffee shop, where the young and idle youngsters of the town would go on Saturdays to "kill" time. This was already in the early twenties. Usually they would come to this coffeehouse to play cards, look through the Russian newspaper "Ahu," a poor newspaper appearing in Lithuania. The youngsters broke away from their fathers' tradition. When a serious person would enter the coffeehouse they would steal away through the yard.

Down the road, further on, stood the home of Abramson, the photographer and typographer, which occupied a place of honor in one of the Rabinowitzes buildings. He was one of the two photographers in town, but he was the only typographer-printer.

As photographer he would determine the "pose," position of the head and hands of the person whose picture he was taking. After that he would decide when one had to "freeze," not to move or blink an eye, for photography was an art. It would take a very long time to take a picture, until the "client" managed to attain permanence on the "negative." Mr. Abramson had a permanent exhibition of the pictures next to the door of his home and here the "photographs" could be seen. As a printer, he would mainly print the wedding invitations of the town's inhabitants. [The photo on back cover of this book was taken by the photographer Natan David Abramson.]

Opposite the home of photographer and printer Abramson stood the house of Levitan, a respected citizen of the town, who was the owner of the "Apothekarski Magazin." In this "magazin" one could obtain cosmetics, as far as they were being used by the town's ladies. Usually iodine was purchased at the "magazin," alcohol, cotton wool and "Schlack Tropens," on Yom Kippur (Atonement Day) eve. To say the truth, there was another "Apothekarski Magazin" in the "Kovner Gass," the one belonging to Mr. Rikler.

Here we pass Rasein street, the "Raseiner Gass" and see the hotel of the Polish woman in the corner - the widow Bilman, who lived here with her two sons and daughter. Gentile visitors would stay here, preferring this hotel to the two Jewish ones.

Here we pass Rasein street, the "Raseiner Gass" and see the hotel of the Polish woman in the corner, the widow Bilman, who lived here with her two sons and daughter. Gentile visitors would stay here, preferring this hotel to the two Jewish ones.

Downstairs was the tavern with the large buffet. The few officials of the town council - the Head of Police and two policemen, would frequent the tavern. Rich farmers from the surrounding area would also come here on market day, to wet their throat and brush their tongue. The hotel owner and her sons did not look fondly upon the town's Jews. *They were Polish - and anti-Semitism was in their blood.* Nevertheless, when the Jewish actors would come to town, to perform Yiddish plays, they had to stay at the Polish woman's hotel, because of the large hall, where they could hold their rehearsals, the "Repetities."

The best Yiddish actors would come to Yurburg, they also performed in Kovno, the temporary capital. When they came to town it was a real celebration. The people in town loved theater. Middle-aged people still remembered the time when they themselves took part in the play " The Sacrifice of Isaac."

The actors of the *"Kadish ve Khash"* group performed the *musical "Malkele Soldat"* and *"Komedies"* with songs and dance. There were actors with a serious repertoire as well. When the actors were rehearsing for a musical they would ask the town's Kleizmer singers to join them…the Polish man with his violin, the one who played at the cinema and weddings, Mr. Fidler with the flute from the wedding band, who also had a fish store and who would lease fruit gardens in the summer, and the one with the big bass and another one. All of them together, in a joint effort, worked hard to produce the sweet melodies of "Malkele Soldat." The beautiful sounds could be heard from the windows of widow Bilman's hotel. A large crowd gathered outside and stood close to the windows, enjoying themselves tremendously. The theater!

Those were the happy moments provided by the theater. We were amateur actors ourselves in those days, and we performed plays for "Bikur Kholim" (sick fund), "Mekhabei Eish" (fire fighters),and "Gemiluth Khesed" (loan fund). We didn't care on whose behalf we were performing, the main thing was to act and act! And the pretext helped. We performed the "Khasia di Yethoime," "Yankel Der Schmid," "Mirele Efrat," "Moshke Khazer," "Di Spanische Inquizitie" etc. We rehearsed for weeks, took down clothes from the attic, decorations etc., and the good Fidler, the barber, would take care of our make-up, on condition we did not look in the mirror, so that we never knew what we really looked like after his make-up.

Drug Store in Yurburg - Photo by Ben Craine - 1927
[Not in original book]

On the other side of the street, opposite the house at the corner of the Bilman hotel, stood the house of Aunt Friedel and Aunt Roche. Aunt Roche was a sick woman and the goodhearted and generous Uncle Mendel supported her. Uncle Mendel was an industrialist from Kovno. He was a partner in the chocolate and candy factory that had the Hebrew name "Kadima." My uncle was a wealthy man.

In the house where my aunt lived was "the bakery of Leah" [probably Leah Krelitz... the mother of many Krelitz's who immigrated to the US....note added by Joel Alpert] who would bake bread and khaloth, "beigalakh and pletslakh" (challas, beigels and pretzels). The smell of her bakery was like a smell from heaven. Even today, when I pass a bakery, the wonderful smell of the bread calls to mind pleasant memories of "Leah's bakery," and then I nostalgically remember "Leah's bakery" in my little town. I remember that we used to bring the "khamin" (meat stew) to Leah's bakery, the "cholent" of Shabbath. On Shabbath, after our fathers returned from the synagogue, we would gather at the bakery. We boys and girls would not wait until everybody was there in order to open the oven just once "so as not to let the cholent grow cold" . . . and we, the children, would run very fast with the cholent over the snow, on a winter day, to bring it to our home while it was still hot.

And here comes our home, the home of my parents. A wooden house, square and covered by a tin roof. This roof was the cause of great financial efforts on our part. First of all we talked about the roof for months, for there was no money. However, we somehow managed to "scrape together" - "men hot zusamengekratzt" - money by loans and we covered the roof. We decided to use solid material, for once and for all, for a roof covered by wooden shingles, called "Shindeln" in Yiddish, did not last very long; it would rot and let the rain through.

At our home was our store too, the grocery store. In Russian the shop was called "Bakaleinaya Lavka," a store for colonial goods, perhaps because of the black pepper, the cinnamon, the tea and coffee, which were imported from colonial countries. Such a store was also called "Kalania Lavka" in town. Proceeds would depend on the farmers, who would come twice a week, on Mondays and Thursdays, to the municipal market. When they came they would fill our house with the smoke of "makhorke," cheap tobacco from their pipes. The young farm girls would coquettishly look into our mirror, arranging themselves . . . The farmers would sit together for hours, inhaling the strong tobacco, which they grew themselves, and would spit onto the floor. We used to hear the word "sake-pasake"- all over again, which meant "he said" in Lithuanian, farmers' gossip.

These market days were a burden to my good and compassionate mother, but there was nothing we could do, for they were customers.

On the other side of the road was the large Lithuanian cooperative store, which looked upon our customers with envy. This store was opened in accordance with the new Lithuanian policy to take business away from the Jews. But my father had had connections with the farmers for decades, and therefore they preferred his store to that of the cooperative. In cold winter days the farmers found a place for their belongings in our warm home, a corner to have something to eat and meet friends. Our large yard, behind the house, was used for the farmers' horses and carriages. A farmer who would dare to be unfaithful to us and was seen shopping at the cooperative was simply told to "go away"! After such a market day my mother, blessed be her memory, would work very hard to clean the house and get rid of the smell of the "makhorke" and turn the house into a Jewish home again. (By the way, my father's name was "Aba," and that is why the farmers called him "Abakitis," and they called mother "Abakeine"). We never felt there was any hatred against us on the part of the gentiles. We had many friends among the farmers. And I remember that when World War I broke out and the Jews were deported from Lithuania, a rich farmer came to our house, with a large carriage with two horses and transported all our furniture and everything else in our home to his estate. When we returned from Russia to Yurburg in 1919 the farmer returned everything to us, and nothing was missing. The farmer's name was Yurgis Tamoshaitis, blessed be his memory. Later on his sons became priests and officers in the Lithuanian army. Once he came to father and said furiously - a Jew called me "goy" (gentile) - should I be called a goy? He was very offended and kept saying "me?".."me?"! His sons, the priests and officers, would always come to our home when they were in town and express their feelings of friendship for our family.

At the corner of Kalishu street and "Daitsche Gass" - in the wooden house - was the town's post office. Before, during the reign of the Czar, this was the "Monopol," the place where the government liquor was sold. That is why the bottle of liquor was jokingly called "monopolka." I remember that on the eve of World War I, the Czar issued a decree to destroy all the liquor at the "Monopol." Policemen stood there and broke hundreds of bottles of liquor and threw the contents into the gutter. The gentiles in town looked sadly how this precious beverage was thrown into the gutters. They stood there muttering sadly " that is the war - what a tragedy!"

The Czarist regime was afraid the Cossacks, who were near the border, would "attack" the "monopol" and get drunk instead of "attacking" the enemy. And that is indeed what happened. When war broke out the Cossacks, who were in our vicinity, entered the shops in town and asked for sweets, tobacco, cigarettes, free of charge. Their requests were more like threats. My father, beloved be his memory, good-naturedly weighed candy for them and handed out cigarettes, to stress that not everything was licentious. Those were the defenders of "Mother Russia." These sturdy Cossacks, short men with a mane of hair, the splendid "chuprinot" and the red stripes on their trousers and hats who inspired awe and fear in the Jews and in general.

In the days of the Lithuanian regime the town's post office took the place of the "Monopol" of the days of the Russians. Towards evening many towns' people would go to the post office, as they had nothing else to do. This was called "picking up the mail." Even those who stood no chance of receiving any mail went there. It was a way of "killing" a few hours of boredom. The post office would be crowded and it was mainly a meeting place for the youngsters. The little window of the post office was still closed and in the meantime the latest news would be circulating about the world beyond the little town. Our town too, was full of news - and when the little post office window opened only a tenth of the people would receive mail. Afterwards everyone would happily go home.

That is the end of the story, which unfortunately was not completed . . . .

Herzliyah, January 1970

Boat on the River Mituva - Sport and Enjoyment

Flooding in Yurburg
[Not in the original Yizkor Book - from Jack Cossid's photo album]

TRANSLATION OF PAGES 43-44

OUR YURBURG

From a Former Residents of Yurburg Association Conference

By Bath-Sheva Ayalon-Shtok

What was the difference between our little town Yurburg and other towns? Naturally we only remember the good things, could it be that we are nostalgic? When one reaches a certain age one tends to look back longingly.

Am I really nostalgic? Would I like to be back there? Of course not, after all, that is why I immigrated to Israel.

My vision of Yurburg is that of a town of working people. Work was the essence of life. Some people were not so rich, others were richer, and all of them worked. No one in Yurburg asked for charity, except for the beggars who came to town and stayed at the "hekdesh" (sanctum) behind the synagogue. There was concern for others- "the people of Israel take care of each other"- this lofty principle was carefully observed.

Yurburg was a town with a high cultural level. No home was without books. People did not live in large, luxurious homes, but in most of them there was a shelf with books on it, holy books and secular books. The Jews loved to look at a book; the children studied at the "kheder" and graduated at least from primary school. Before compulsory education became the law of the land, the Jews of Yurburg themselves adopted the law of compulsory education.

The Lithuanian government set up a Lithuanian gymnasium in town. The Jews did not want to send their children to study there, and with great effort they set up their own Hebrew Gymnasium, where studies were held in Hebrew. Thanks to the nationalist-Hebrew education received by the students at the Hebrew Gymnasium, they were attracted to Zionism, and thus to aliyah to Eretz Yisrael.

There were also libraries in Yurburg, in Yiddish and Hebrew. Emanuel Kopelov's mother fought for the establishment of the Hebrew library. There was a popular and simple culture in our town.

Our forefathers established a splendid synagogue in Yurburg, decorated with beautiful ornaments, and a pulpit and Elyahu's chair; this old furniture, how lovely it was!

Where did our fathers find the means to set up all this, if not from their meager savings?

The Keren Kayemeth box (the "Blue Box") was to be found in each home next to the charity boxes of Rabbi Meir Ba'al Hanes and others. The students would empty the boxes, they would sell *"Shekalim"* towards the Zionist Congress. The grown-ups participated in the elections to the Zionist Congress and considered this an important event for the Jewish people.

In general, Yurburg was a very well organized town, for example there were organizations such as the *"Froien Ferein"* and women's organizations to assist the needy. Our mothers organized these associations; they also took care of brides, visited the sick etc.

The memories of my youth in Yurburg accompany me wherever I go. We are now going through a difficult period in Israel. In the daily press we read about murders, killings and robberies. It seems to me that there were no Jewish murderers or thieves in Yurburg ... I don't remember such a phenomenon.

That is what Yurburg was like. It is nice to remember our little town, where we grew up and which we loved with all our heart.

Givath Brener

Bridge across the Imstra

Bridge across the Instra in May 2001
Photo by Nancy Lefkowitz
[Photo not in original book]

YURBURG - MY UNFORGETTABLE TOWN

A Few Memories   **By Hinda Levinberg (Beker)**

A long time ago, decades ago, I left the town of my birth, Yurburg. However, when I think of it, it seems as if I left only yesterday, and all the memories reappear, pleasant and sweet memories of the years of my youth.

Yurburg, or Yurberik, as its Jewish inhabitants called it, was a beautiful town, not large, but compared to the other little towns in Lithuania, Yurburg was a town, a real metropolis. . . .

Yurburg was close to the German border, about ten kilometers east of the little town of Smalininken, in the Memel district (which was right across the border). The Jews of Yurburg had close business ties with Germany and they were suspected of being "smugglers", "Kontrabandisten" in Yiddish. The Yurburg residents would cross the border and arrive in Smalininken in torn and faded clothes, and return dressed in new festive attire.. . .

Yurburg was located on the banks of the Nieman River, which originated in the Pinsk swamps. From here the water of the Nieman flowed slowly to a two hundred to three hundred meters wide riverbed, until it flowed into the Kurish Bay, near Memel, on the Baltic sea.

Yurburg was divided into two parts by the rivers, which flowed into the Nieman. One of them was the Imstra, which divided the town into two parts west and east. The western part was called *Uzh'Imstra*, i.e. "beyond the Imstra." A wooden bridge was erected over the Imstra for the crossing of vehicles, at the end of Kovno street. Pedestrians used a few small bridges (Klatkes). In summer the inhabitants would stroll along the dusky paths, covered by tree branches and green bushes growing on both sides of the Imstra. In this shallow area water flowers and beautiful weeds grew. Ducks and geese frolicked in the waters of the Imstra to the joy of the little children, who chased them, their laughter rising up everywhere.

The Mituva was a real river, separating the town from the beautiful Kaliani woods to the west. The Mituva river flowed into the Nieman, and thereby formed a broad water harbor where the steamships would anchor during the freezing winter days. In summer it was very nice to bathe in the Mituva and sail on it in boats.

The youngsters would rent boats from the farmers and would go on excursions on its clear water in which the high tree branches were reflected, creating a mysterious atmosphere. We would sing romantic songs and accompany our singing with the mandolin. Even today my ears resound with the sentimental melodies we sang in those days.

Yurburg's pride was its main street, Kovno street (Kauno Gatve), built along the right side of the Nieman. It was a street full of traffic. Parallel to Kovno street are the Raseiniu Gatve and the German street. A few other narrower streets crossed these streets vertically, to the north and south. The southern area, such as Yatkever Gass, Bod Gass and others were densely populated.

Kovno street had a beautiful urban look. Its two- story buildings were made of brick, built in the Gothic style. All the town's streets were paved in stone. On Kovno street there were pavements made of wooden boards or tiny mosaics. Flower gardens graced the front of the buildings on Raseiniu street and German street.

The shop windows displayed all kinds of industrial products such as clothing, shoes, household utensils and foodstuffs. In the center of town there were banks, pharmacies, hotels, an electrical power plant and flourmills. There were workshops in town as well, bakeries, a candy factory etc. The economy was mainly based on the businesses connected with the steamships, which transported passengers and goods to Kovno and back to Yurburg. The Jews also exported farm produce, mainly to nearby Germany.

Yurburg's business center focused on the market square. The old synagogue, a wooden building constructed in 1790, stood out here in its special form and style. Inside the synagogue was the striking Holy Ark, the pulpit and Eliyahu's chair with their artistic ornaments carved in wood by unknown artists. The synagogue drew Jewish and non-Jewish tourists to Yurburg, from all over Lithuania and from abroad, who came to see the beautiful building and its artistic treasures. Not far from the synagogue stood the prayer house, a brick building used by worshippers and Torah scholars. For many years there was a "yeshivah" here and in the last years only a small yeshiva, in addition to the general studies.

The Jews of Yurburg took care to observe their forefathers' tradition. At the end of the town's streets they set up "eruvs" to carry their belongings on Sabbath. On Shabbat they observed the Shabbat rest, but some of them went for a stroll in the streets and parks. The youngsters played soccer.

Yurburg was a clean and quiet town. The Police insisted cleanliness be observed in the streets. Those who did not observe police instructions received a steep fine.

It was nice to live in Yurburg. The inhabitants loved their town and were proud of it.

On the other side of the Nieman River, opposite Yurburg, was a small town called Shaudine where only a few Jews lived. Some of them dealt in trade and were shop owners and others worked the land and grew poultry, sheep and cattle. There was no school at Shaudine, therefore the parents had to send their children to the schools in Yurburg. Each day the parents would transport the children on a boat or ferry to Yurburg. On the ferries horses too were transported tied to a carriage, and goods and animals. Only in winter when the Nieman was covered by a thick layer of ice was it easy for the town's inhabitants to cross the river. They lived in symbiosis with Yurburg and depended on it for their daily life, making daily use of its economic and cultural institutions. In winter Shaudine became an inseparable part of Yurburg, which in a way was its parent town.

The Summer of 1914.

Immediately after the Shavu'oth (Pentecost) holiday many Jews in Yurburg used to go to summer resorts (Datshas in Russian), mainly to Kaliani, a Lithuanian village in a pine forest. At these resorts the Jews would rest from work, relax and forget their daily worries. They would rent an apartment or room at the farmers' homes and spend the warm summer months here. They would bring along very few belongings (Bebikhes in Yiddish), only the strictly necessary, such as bed linen, cooking utensils, clothes, that was all.

Two carriage owners (Balegoles in Yiddish) were available to those going on summer holidays, the first was "Bore Kliatshe," and the other Yoshe Nukh. Each of them had a large carriage with thin horses.

The wealthy vacationers would rent carriages from Shlomke Hodes or Betsalel the coachman (*Tsalel der Furman*, in Yiddish) in order to reach the Klaiani village in comfort. Most vacationers were women and children. The men would join their families only on the weekend, and they would spend two to three days together in the forest.

The vacationers hoped to strengthen their lungs in the pine forests with the fresh and pure air. Many people in Lithuania, particularly in Yurburg, suffered from lung diseases, apparently caused by the cold and wet climate. Indeed, a government sanitarium was set up in Yurburg for lung patients.

The food at the summer resorts mainly consisted of dairy products, fresh milk, and straight from the cow's udders, white cheese and cream. Toibe, who sold beigels (Toibe die Beiglnitse, in Yiddish) would breathe deeply and bear the heavy burden of bringing fresh beigels to the vacationers.

-"What can I do, Kinderlach, what can I do?" - Toibe would say. I need the income, I have to make a living . . . and indeed there was work - for "man was born to toil." . . And Toibe would sigh deeply and continue to bring beigels and rolls each morning, to the delight of the vacationers.

How would we spend the time at the summer resort?

Very simple.

We would string a hammock between two pine trees, lie in it, swing along and inhale the fresh air. From time to time we would get off the hammock and take a look at the samovar, whether we had to add a few acorns (Shishkes in Yiddish) to warm the tea. Tea was the most important item on the summer resort's menu. All day long we drank tea, with or without biscuits and jam. That is how the Jewish women would spend their summer holidays, without a care in the world.

The older children and youth would stroll happily in the woods, gather mushrooms and black berries (Shwartse Yagdes in Yiddish). Each day the vacationers would go down to the Nieman, swim and sunbathe. After the swim they would rest and rest again, and that is how the day passed. In the evening they would listen to the sound of birds and drift off in dreams. Some vacationers brought along a record player to the woods and the sound of music would go up into the air of the forest and the echo would be heard all over.

The children would play games, dance and have fun till late in the evening.

Each year a woman from Yurburg would come to the Kaliani resort to spend the holiday there. This woman was "aguna" (deserted). Her husband had deserted her and she did not have any children. The woman would bring along a bag full of "tales" to the resort . . . arduous love letters from the days of her youth. The woman would read these letters to herself in a loud voice and recite them, so that the vacationers would come close and listen to her excited reading. Sometimes the reading of the letter would turn into a pathetic recital dramatic game. The vacationers stood around her and listened attentively to the reading of the arduous love letters, unfulfilled love, love full of disappointment. And some of the women who listened to her reading would shed a tear "how sad," how sad" they would say.

However, in general, the vacationers would enjoy themselves . . . for this was a free performance.. . .

In mid-summer the corn in the fields would grow ripe, and the farmers would start the harvest. The farmers would leave in groups to harvest the crop, the wheat and rye. The village women would follow them, make bundles and gather them to the barn. The farmers would help each other. The Lithuanians would call this joint effort "Talka".

In the evening, after the hours of hard work, the farmers would meet, eat and drink vodka . . . and when the intoxicating liquor would go to their head there would be fun . . . men and women would start to sing and dance to the sounds of the mouth organ (harmonicas). Thus they would no longer be tired and would frolic and dance till the wee hours of the morning

The Jewish vacationers would join in the farmers' fun, join the circle and sing and dance till late at night . . . .

Tu- o-na leh-tu-tu-to

Tu- o-na-leh-tu-tu to

The vacationers also used their stay at the farmer's villages for a "real purpose." . .

They would buy cherries from the farmers, berries and fruit in season, such as apples, pears, plums etc. They would cook the fruit on a primus stove, to prepare jams and all sorts of desserts ("aingemakhts", in Yiddish).

Thus the vacationers would prepare the jams which they would use all year round, as a supplement to tea or to offer to guests and also to spread on bread. When the vacationers returned home they took along tins of jams and other delicacies. This was an excellent way to spend the time.

But, as we all know, all good things come to an end. And so did the summer holidays. The vacationers spent two months in the woods, relaxed and had a good time. Now they had to go home, full of pleasant memories.

On Tishah beAv (Ninth of Av) all the vacationers were back home and observed the fast. The atmosphere of Tishah beAv, the day of the destruction of the Temple, was felt in every corner of the home and the Jewish street. On this sad day the Jews would go to the cemetery, recite "Yizkor" and remember their dear ones, parents and relatives.

And I remember that after the beautiful summer of 1914, suddenly days of concern and sorrow came.

There were rumors in town that war was about to break out. "War?" - "Yes, war." No one in town knew what the reason was for the war. Had it already broken out? Who would fire the first bullet and why? Everyone talked and guessed, but they did not really know what was going on. The rumors were baffling and the people were terrified. And there was a jester, the town's "politician" who explained the reasons for the war to the Jews, as follows: "A German soldier shot a dog of the Russian Czarina and killed it . . . "So, what do you think - is that not enough reason for war?" And then there was another Jew, also a "clever man," who said with certainty - "The war will be short because the "Fonke-ganev" (a word of abuse for the Russian soldier) will not fight for a long time for Nicolai (the Russian Czar). Why should he? Therefore the war will end soon."

Jokes apart and reality apart, indeed the reality was bitter. The Jews got more terrified by the minute. They are already recruiting to the army and what does one do at such a time? The Jews, as is well known, are always between the devil and the deep blue sea.

A day passed, two days, and people started to flee, to get away from the German border and also a forced "escape" to send the Jews away from the German border deep inside Russia.

Thus a new chapter started for the Jews of Yurburg. A long time passed before my dear Jewish neighbors returned and gathered to rebuild their town together and form a Jewish community, which became an example between the two World Wars. This went on till World War II broke out, when, as is known, the Jewish community of Yurburg was wiped out (1941) and no longer exists. . . .

I shall never forget my dear Yurburg, as long as I live.

Translated from Yiddish and edited by Paz

TRANSLATION OF PAGES 52 - 54

SIAUDINE (Shaudine) - A NEIGHBORING TOWN

By Meir Levyush

After World War I the Baltic states, including Lithuania, gained independence. Prior to independence, Lithuania was divided into two regions - Zemaitija and Aukstaitija. They had two different laws. While the Napoleon Codex prevailed in Aukstaitija, the Russian law prevailed in Zemaitija, up to Napoleon's time (1812).

The little town of Shaudine was situated in the Aukstaitija region, near the Nieman, the largest river in Lithuania. On the other side of the Nieman was Yurburg, in the Zemaitija region. Most Shaudine residents were hardworking Jews, who worked in small trade and tilled the land. In fact, the Jews of Shaudine acted as go-between between the Shaudine farmers and the merchants from Yurburg.

About 40 Jewish families lived in Shaudine in the past, about 220 people. A few other families also lived in town, who were of German origin, and the others were Lithuanians. There was only one small plant in the town, for combing and processing sheep wool destined for the weaving of threads, to enable the farmers to knit gloves, stockings, vests etc. in the long winter nights.

When the economic and cultural situation of the Lithuanians improved, nationalism started to raise its head among the Lithuanian leadership, and this was reflected by trying to remove Jewish merchants from their economic positions, thus affecting their economic situation.

For this and for other reasons people started to leave our town - some went on alyiah to Israel in the framework of "Hekhalutz" (Pioneers), others immigrated to the United States. When one family member emigrated to the U.S., his family and relatives would follow him. Thus it came about that many Jews from Shaudine were concentrated in one town - El Paso, Texas, and Arizona *(and New Mexico - noted added by J. Alpert).*

Shaudine, like most other towns in Lithuania, looked very poor. The houses were built of wooden logs and most of the roofs were covered in straw. Perhaps that accounted for the Lithuanian name for our town ("straw town") . The government did not invest any money in developing our little town or other towns for that matter.

The streets were not paved. In summer the sandy land was swampy and each carriage that passed through the street would leave clouds of dust behind it. In fall the rain would turn the streets into mud and the carriages would drown in the mud up to their axis.

The ferry on the Nieman River-pupils from Shaudine coming to school in Yurburg

On a motorboat across from Yurburg in the Nieman River traveling to Shaudine. From left to right is a fellow from Czechoslovakia, Lebka Frank, Simka Rochzo, Yudel Most, Meika Heskelovitz and Moshe Krelitz on top. Dated March 12, 1935. Photo not in original Yizkor book. From photo album of Jack Cossid. Photo by Moshe Krelitz.

After the rainy fall came the cold winter. The snow covered everything in a white blanket. The only means of transportation out of town was the winter coach drawn by two horses. The link with the little town of Shaki, about 20 kilometers (15 miles) away, took half an hour to an hour in winter and in fall, during the rainy season, it took three hours. To Kovno one would travel in sledges, along the frozen Nieman, and the connection with Yurburg was the easiest - one would cross the Nieman in a winter carriage or on foot and be there in no time.

The Shaudine residents waited for the coming of spring for many months. Spring was the most beautiful and nicest period of the year. When the first sun's rays appeared on the horizon everyone would be glad. The snow melted and the land would change. The ice on the Nieman melted too. Large blocks of ice started to move down the river. Sometimes these blocks of ice would stop somewhere, accumulate and together form a kind of huge and threatening ice dam. . . . at the same time the water of the Nieman would flow over the shore, inundate the town and cause serious damage to the population. After a while, sometimes after a couple of days, the ice dam would collapse and the "dam" would burst to let through the blocks of ice and the streaming water. Then life would return to normal and timber rafts would sail along the river for the German paper industry. The connection with Yurburg would be renewed. Again it would be possible to get to Yurburg by ferry. The students would now cross the Nieman each day on the ferry to attend Yurburg's institutions of education.

It is noteworthy that the parents were glad to see their sons and daughters make progress in their studies at the gymnasium (in Yurburg) and that they were proud of their achievements. In spite of their poverty, the parents in Shaudine would make great efforts to send their children to the gymnasium, even when tuition fees were high and beyond their capacity. Some parents did not merely provide studies at the gymnasium, but even sent their children to institutions of higher education, such as medical studies in Italy and at other universities. My family, the Lebiush family, sent my brother to study at the "Herzliyah" Gymnasium in Tel Aviv when he was merely thirteen years old. My sister studied at the nurses' school in Kovno. My sister and I studied at the gymnasium in Yurburg.

Zalman Lebiush, our relative, studied at the Kovno gymnasium and at the same time took part in the drama circle of "Habimah," which was guided by actors from Eretz Yisrael (the Land of Israel), such as Michael Gur, Rafael Tsevi, Miriam Bernstein-Cohen and others. When Zalman Lebiush went to Israel he became a famous actor and producer.

As a matter of fact, all the youngsters in Shaudine wanted to study at the gymnasium and the university and their parents made extreme efforts to send them there, even when at home they merely ate herring, dipping bread and boiled potatoes into the salt water in the barrel. That is what many parents ate during most of the days of the week. The most important aim was that their children would study and acquire learning and intelligence. The Shaudinians were very proud of the fact that one of their sons, Shimon Volovitzky, became the mayor of Kybartai, a large town on the German border. The fact that their sons and daughters became more educated was compensation for the hard work and suffering of the parents.

(Kybartai was not a large town and Shimon Volovitzky was never the mayor of the town, he was for some years a member in the Municipality Council - n.b. J. Rosin)

We should also mention the beautiful and impressive landscape around our town - lawns, orchards, grain fields and green forests. It was a typical rural landscape, with a pastoral atmosphere, heart-warming. But the Jews of Shaudine did not have time to enjoy the scenery, for they toiled from morning till night, and if they went out into the country they used their time to gather berries, mushrooms, weeds for soup and fruit in season - in order to prepare for winter. All those who went on an outing knew that at home a few hungry mouths were waiting for them and all "ownerless" food would fill the empty stomachs. Therefore each outing had a purpose and was not merely a pleasure trip.

We have spoken about the Jews in our little town of Shaudine. Jews lived there for hundreds of years with their dreams and their hopes. Jews in heart and soul, they prayed and believed. They worked hard to make a living, brought up their children and taught them religion and knowledge.

These were innocent Jews, with human values, they did not have the good fortune to enjoy the success of their offspring, and one sad day they were uprooted and were cruelly destroyed by the Nazis and their barbaric Lithuanian helpers.

Only few managed to go to Israel, before the Holocaust, and only one person remained in Shaudine after the Holocaust, who immigrated to Israel. Those born in Shaudine fondly remember the Jews of their town who are no longer.

Town of Shaudine Viewed from Across Nieman River from Yurburg
Photo not in original Yizkor book. From photo album of Jack Cossid.

YURBURG - REGIONAL TRADE CENTER

Yurburg was an important regional center for trade and transport. There were close trade ties with neighboring Germany. Merchants from Yurburg exported farm products to Germany, which greatly needed them, such as: linen, corn, eggs, butter, fruit, poultry, hides etc. The main export was timber used as raw material for the paper and celluloid industry. Herring was imported from Holland and Germany and coal from mines, and iron, steel and various machinery from Silesia.

Agents-commissioners handled the foreign trade relations, trading between the merchants in Yurburg and trading companies and the industrial plants abroad. Among the trade agents in Yurburg we remember Yitskhak (Itzik) Karnovsky and Shelomoh Khanes. The agents in Yurburg made a handsome profit through their trading. In the 1920s a large group of exporters operated in Yurburg, unparalleled in the other Lithuanian towns, which were far away from the German border and west-European countries. The exporters bought farming products from the traders who would go to the villages and buy direct from the farmers. An entire network of small and large traders served the export carried out by exporters who were greatly respected in Yurburg. Well-known exporters were Leib (Leon) Bernstein and Efraim Heselowitz, who, by the way, were related. They both had large warehouses for processing linen, combing, refining for export. Leib (Leon) Bernstein was an expert in the linen business, a man with vision and initiative, who inspired considerable confidence abroad. In his warehouses were machines and combs with iron teeth, which would comb and improve the quality of the linen. Tens of workers prepared the shipments, mainly to Germany and Great Britain, from which linen threads were made for the weaving of cloth. After a while Bernstein expanded the scope of his linen export business called "Semilinas." In recognition for his extensive activity L. Bernstein was elected to the government trade bureau - "Handels-Kamer" in Yiddish. He traveled abroad frequently and had trade relations with many countries in western Europe.

The government granted "Semlinas" the special right to deal in export, while this right was not granted to other exporters. However, this license was limited to the Shavl region only. This went on till the revolution when the U.S.S.R. entered Lithuania. (in 1940 -J.R.)

In addition to linen, the exporters in Yurburg also dealt in linen seeds, from which oil was produced. The linen seeds were carefully measured in a sieve (large volume) in order to send them in bags abroad. Thus large shipments of produce were sent abroad, mainly to Germany.

In 1921 an exporters company was established in Yurburg, after lengthy negotiations, in order to prevent competition among the export traders - the **EXPORT -HANDEL COMPANY**. The company also aimed at expanding the scope of trade activities and improve ways and means of export.

Michael Leshtz was elected Chairman of the **"Export-Handel,"** he was the most senior member. For efficiency sake the activities were divided into three sections, each specializing in a different field.

A. The linen and linen seed section - headed by Yehudah Leib (Alter) Petrikansky.

Members of the section: **Michael Leshtz**, Yakov-Shelomoh Vainberg (Weinberg), Hirsch Vainberg (Weinberg). **The produce** was sent for processing to Memel and from there to Manchester (Great Britain).

B. The harvest, eggs and hides section - headed by Yehudah (Yudel) Mintzer.

Members of the section: Kovalkovsky, Mordekhai (Mordechai) Levin, and Menakhem Levin. The farming produce was mainly sent to Hamburg (Germany); the hides of animals such as foxes, rabbits and martens were sent to Frenkel's factory in Shavl and in part abroad.

C. The timber section -headed by Yisrael Levinberg.

Members of the section: David Karabelnik, Ossip Rabinowitz, Hayim-Reuven Danilevitz, Ze'ev (Velvel) Levin. The produce was sent to Memel, Tilzit and Koenigsberg (Germany). Treasurer and Manager was Dov (Berel) Levinberg. Bookkeeper was Nakhum Triberg.

The company operated and expanded economic activity in Yurburg; it allowed many small traders and merchants to make a profit. The company saw its task as a blessing. Trade was in many millions of Litas (the official currency, 10 Litas equal one dollar).

At the end of 1928 the activity of the **"Export-Handel"** company came to an end, when the Lithuanian government decided to **nationalize all the import-export businesses**. Traders in Lithuania in general, and in Yurburg in particular, could not cope with this anti-Semitic decree and lost a lot of money, many of them became very poor. All the alternatives to export were useless. The cruel deprivation continued till the bitter end arrived for Lithuanian Jews in 1941.

In addition to the commercial activity of **"Export Handel"** at the time, traders from outside the company also dealt in export, like Shmeryahu (Shmerl) Poliak,who exported geese to the U.K. The shipments were carried out on rafts. The geese shipments were called "musical transport" in Yurburg, for the geese "sang" with their throaty voices, making a lot of noise .

Other traders sent turkeys to England before the Christian holidays, at the end of the year. Fruit was packed into crates. The winter apples were wrapped separately in paper before they were put into crates, which were sent to Germany. Many workers were employed in egg shipments, for each egg had to be checked separately in candle light or under electrical lighting whether it was fresh, did not have any cracks and did not have a drop of blood. The checked eggs, fit for shipment, were packed into special crates earmarked for export. Traders also dealt in pig-hair, which was combed and cleaned before being shipped abroad. Work was hard and full of dust. In the storeroom of one of the traders there were no windows and the doors were closed. The workers asked the trader to open the door a little to let the air in, but the trader refused, claiming the wind might blow away the pig hair; pig hair was much in demand abroad and was good business.

In the winter months, when export of farming produce, such as fruit etc. came to a halt, the traders dealt in wood and employed many workers. The trees had to be chopped, sent to the sawmill and prepared for spring, when the ice on the Nieman melted and it was possible to send the wood on rafts abroad. There were large forests in the surroundings of Yurburg that produced the wood that was in great demand abroad for the factories where paper and celluloid were produced. Many families made a living in Yurburg from the forests and the trees. This situation continued until the crisis that eliminated the livelihood of the traders in Yurburg and in Lithuania in general.

The Jews mainly made a living ("Parnoses," in Yiddish) on trade, groceries, mediation and crafts. The Jews were mainly occupied in "trivial deals" ("Wind-Gesheften" in Yiddish) on which they made a living, some better some worse.

The question arises whether Jews in Yurburg and in [Lithuania]general also tilled the land? The answer is no. Only a few took a small part in tilling the land. There were Jews in Yurburg who rented fruit and vegetable gardens in spring and summer, invested some work in them, sold the fruit and vegetables they produced and that was that.

A number of Jews in Yurburg should be mentioned who tilled an area of land they leased from the municipality, called Zarda ("Die Zarde" in Yiddish). This was an area of land from the shores of the Nieman to the town's buildings. The land of the Zarda was fertile and suitable for growing vegetables. Families who were thus occupied enjoyed their work and made a handsome profit.

In fall the rainwater was absorbed into the land of the Zarda and in winter the entire area was covered by snow. When the snow melted the water of the Nieman flooded the Zarda and enriched its land with organic materials, which benefited the gardens for the planting of vegetables in spring. This good earth would produce an abundance of vegetables, mainly potatoes. Thus the owners of the plots were rewarded for their hard work. Although the work was hard, those who tilled the plots and their family got attached to their land and thought of it as creation. However, they were unusual "farmers," and they were but few, unfortunately. The Jews who worked the land proved beyond any doubt that they were capable of being real farmers.

In general, Jews were not inclined to turn to farming as a source of livelihood. In addition to work on the Zarda, there were a few Jews who dealt in farming as a supplement to their profession earnings for the upkeep of their family. We know that Jews from the east of town kept one or two cows. In the morning, in summer, the cow-herders (non-Jewish) would come and collect the cows and take them out to pasture. In winter the Jews were assisted by herders who helped them take care of the cows in the small sheds. The cow-owners enjoyed fresh milk for their children and a little cheese and cream, but it was not possible to make a good living on this.

A small number of Jews had yards with small gardens for growing vegetables, and a small poultry-pen to provide fresh eggs. This was but a hint of farming, not more.

The Jews of Yurburg, as in all the towns of Lithuania were not close to the land and had to deal in trade and crafts - that was their destiny in the Diaspora.

"Heaven and earth" existed in all the towns of Lithuania, but in Yurburg there were both "heaven and earth" and the river Nieman. And on this river the steamships sailed. The majority of these ship owners were wealthy Jews, residents of Yurburg. Those we remember are Yisrael Levinberg, Rabinowitz, Fainberg, David Karabelnik and others. The steamships employed many Jews.

Yurburg without ships was unthinkable from the economic and social point of view. The Jews would get up to the sound of the whistles of the ships leaving and would go to bed with the whistles. These ships affected their entire life-style. Two kinds of steamships sailed on the Nieman - passenger ships (mainly) and ships transporting cargo and "towing" boats (Baidakes in Yiddish). The cargo ships would carry merchandise from Kovno to Memel, Tilzit and Koenigsberg. Yurburg was an important passageway. The cargo ships sailed day and night. On these ships the Yurburg merchants would send their wares abroad. The cargo ship owners made a good living, without being particularly noticed by the population. On the other hand, the steamships carrying passengers ("Pasazhiren" in Yiddish) were definitely noticed. Everyone needed the steamships. Some for business and others for cultural and social activities, to visit relatives, go on excursions etc. All the inhabitants of Yurburg were attracted to the large town of Kovno, and to Memel (Klaipeda). When the ships sailed to and from Kovno they would stop at a number of little towns on the shores of the Nieman. When the ships stopped, passengers could go down and it was possible to take on new passengers.

The steamships therefore were the Yurburg residents' most important means of transport. The train station was tens of kilometers away from Yurburg, on a difficult dirt road. That is why the Jews of Yurburg and the other small towns on the shores of the Nieman only used the ships, like the Christian Lithuanians, though many of these would travel in coaches.

The owners of large coaches in Yurburg would compete with the cargo ships by transporting goods to and from Kovno at an inexpensive rate. To those traveling to Memel the coachmen would offer a cheap trip to Smalininken, in order to travel on from there in the narrow train to Memel.

Due to the fact that the Yurburg residents traveled to Kovno on ships, the authorities did not pave a road to Kovno, which was the capital in the period between the two World Wars. The trip by boat to Kovno was sometimes a little tiring - upwards stream - 6-8 hours of sailing and back to Yurburg - down stream - merely 5-6 hours. The passengers usually enjoyed the trip. They usually sat on the deck of the ship watching the beautiful, pastoral landscape go by. When one had to travel to Kovno, one would leave on the ship late in the evening and arrive in Kovno early in the morning in order to do one's business; in the afternoon one would again board the ship and return to Yurburg in the evening. During their trip at night most passengers would doze in their seats in the passengers lounge or on the ship's deck.

However, wealthy passengers would rent a "cabin" - a small room with a bed. The youngsters loved the boat trip. Organized groups of hundreds of youth movement members would sail from Yurburg in order to meet their friends in Kovno. (The steamships transported 500-600 passengers and more). The Kovno youngsters would pay a return visit and enjoy Yurburg's splendor, its parks and forests. Some even say its beautiful girls. . . .

"Maccabi" and the sports club "I.A.K." would organize parties in Yurburg and invite their friends to Kovno to have a good time. The young guests would fill Yurburg's streets with joy and fun. From the center of town the youngsters would go to the parks on excursions, and dance to the sound of music, like the "Geguzines" of the Lithuanians. The meetings of the youngsters created a lively youthful atmosphere in town, an exciting experience, fondly remembered.

All the parties took place in the "Tel Aviv" park, particularly the party of "Maccabi," the national sports movement. To the youngsters the park was the symbol of the link with Eretz Yisrael (the Land of Israel). The guests were proud and happy that the Yurburg Jews were able to keep a beautiful park and Hebrew Gymnasium, named "Herzl."

No wonder that the Yurburg residents loved the Nieman and the ships. They recognized each ship from afar, knew its name - Laisve, Lietuva, Kestutis etc. The Nieman and the ships were not merely a source of living but also a source of greater social and cultural life.

Jews would go out onto the pier of the port in order to meet acquaintances, or to hear the news from Kovno because the Lithuanian radio did not mention what was happening in the Jewish world and *Eretz Yisrael* (the Land of Israel). The Jews hurried to the pier to buy a new newspaper from Kovno and take a look at its headlines in order to satisfy their curiosity. Kovno served as a bridge for the Jews of Yurburg and a cultural connection with the Jewish world. Without this cultural link Yurburg would become a provincial town, without life and vision. Yurburg also served as a kind of bridge and a link to the western world next to which it was situated (Prussia was just a few kilometers down the Nieman River from Yurburg ---- note added by Joel Alpert) and from which it drew its economic and cultural nourishment. Yurburg and Kovno were sister cities, close to each other, linked by trade and cultural ties.

The relations between the ship owners were usually good. However, from time to time, a quarrel broke out. And then the passengers would enjoy the situation. Each ship would compete with the other and announce a drop in the price of the ticket, and moreover, would promise a bonus, a glass of beer with a roll etc. In the days of the "competition" the number of passengers who traveled back and forth almost free of charge increased. The passengers enjoyed the fierce "competition," but the ship owners lost. Only after all the ship owners became exhausted and lost because of the "competition," they would return and unite, ashamed. After the lust for "competition" was defeated everything returned back to normal.

In the winter season, days of rain and storm, snow and cold, Yurburg changes its face. The temperature drops to 20 degrees C. below zero (-6 degrees F.) and lower. People stayed at home. The streets are empty. Yurburg is cut off from the world and becomes a kind of independent republic. The Nieman freezes and is covered in a thick layer of ice. The steam ships are gathered together at the mouth of the Mituva river, which serves as homeport in the winter days. The only transport is the winter coach (the sled). Everyone travels in winter coaches drawn by two horses with bells ringing. People wear sheepskin coats or warm clothes and winter hats which make it difficult to distinguish their faces. At first, this seems very romantic, but only on a short ride. On a long trip it becomes tedious. The ways to Kovno - as to anywhere else - are covered in a thick layer of snow and they constitute a welcome opportunity for the coachmen to transport people and make some money. There were coachmen who traveled to Kovno along the frozen Nieman, but this way too was too complicated.

What can one do? Winter comes and goes - man must get used to changing weather conditions. He has no choice.

However, there is no shadow without a light. It is in winter that the farmers often come to the market in order to sell and buy. When there is no work on the land, the farmer has more time, collects his merchandise and comes to the market. It is in winter that business is brisk - and the Jews enjoy the situation. Twice a week - Mondays and Thursdays, there are market days, full of people, a real fair in town. The Jews do good business in their shops and say happily "A Yerid in Shtettel, a mekhaye ...."

Life in winter slowly becomes a routine. Export continues - how is that? - There are coachmen and winter coaches. The merchants load the merchandise earmarked for export on the winter coaches and carry them to Smalininken, in Germany, a short trip - merely 9 to 10 kilometers (6 miles). From here there is no problem to transfer the merchandise from the winter coaches directly onto the railway wagons, traveling to Tilzit and Memel. This is a welcome solution both for the exporters and for the coachmen. Everyone makes a profit.

However, there are many Jews in Yurburg who are left without a way of making a living in the winter months and they have to find other sources. There is no choice, if they don't find what they want they have to make do with what there is; and thus they pass the winter, each year, until the much-awaited spring arrives.

The winter months are very long in the minds of the people. Therefore the Jews in Yurburg try to make the best of it and increase social and cultural activity. People are more willing to read a book and the librarians have a full time job. Newspapers are being read as well as journals; some people play chess, others play cards, whatever they fancy. The winter evenings start at four o'clock in the afternoon and everyone has to find something to do in the long evening.

Some people go to the movies and others to study circles. The local drama circle is active and presents plays in Yiddish. Usually an actor or singer are invited to a cultural evening to provide entertainment for the Jews of Yurburg and its surroundings. An important event took take place when a drama group from Kovno was invited. That was a real treat for theater lovers. By the way, all these events took place in Yiddish.

Moshe Krelitz, Friend and Leah Krelitz on sled in Yurburg

Photo by Moshe Krelitz

Photo not in original Yizkor Book - Courtesy of Max Sherman-Krelitz

In winter, when the inhabitants were cut off from Kovno, every cultural-artistic event would be welcomed in town. Many activities were devoted to social causes. Tickets were sold and the proceeds were given to local charity institutions. Sometimes a lottery was held. The parties also became active in winter, held lectures and debates - and if this was the year of the Zionist Congress - the debates were very lively. There were activities on behalf of the national funds as well. And if an emissary arrived from Eretz Yisrael (the Land of Israel) or a Zionist leader, this was an important and popular event in Yurburg. The youth movements also increased their activities in winter at their clubs. They played snowball and had a good time.

On days when it was not too cold and the sun would shine through, adults, children and youngsters would go for a walk in the surroundings. They would walk in the snowy forests, climb mountains and slide down the slopes. Others would visit friends in the Lithuanian villages, and were warmly received. The youngsters would skate on the frozen rivers, fall down and get up again to the laughter of the bystanders, it was good to be young in winter, as in all the other seasons.

Everything comes to an end, even the long winter. It gets less cold. The sunrays become warmer and warmer. The land slowly sheds its white "cloak" and becomes covered in green. Soon spring arrives with its colors and enchanting smells; it bursts into the yards and the homes. Life changes. Winter clothes are discarded and everyone gets ready to go about his business. Nature wakes up and so does man - towards the renewed life.

Spring is nice, very nice, but there are special "spring problems" too in Yurburg, sometimes they are very serious. As mentioned before, Yurburg has the Nieman, which is usually a blessing, but in spring it sometimes becomes a curse. What happens? This is the story - when the ice on the Nieman starts to melt and large blocks of ice flow along the stream they sometimes form a "traffic jam"; a kind of huge iceberg is created which blocks the giant stream of water and causes the Nieman to overflow. The water floods the streets that are close to the Nieman and enters the houses. The flood is expected in spring each year, but the inhabitants are sure that "this year it will not happen." However, it does happen. The flood causes tremendous damage to the people in the houses that are close to the Nieman and are flooded. Imagine you wake up one morning to find yourself in a room full of water; in the yard and the storerooms there is water too; destruction is extensive and so is the damage.

Within hours people are bereft of their belongings and many families are left without anything. Although the municipality helped defray in the heavy financial costs of the inhabitants and the community committee donates its part to the assistance fund, this does not solve the complicated problems each family faces when their home is destroyed. Sometimes the people themselves would get organized and set up their own assistance fund to repair the damage. The rescue action was praiseworthy but those who were affected did not forget the tragedy for a long time.

Luckily the catastrophic flood and destruction did not recur every year.

The only people to enjoy the flood were the children who sailed on planks and wooden boards through the streets and among the houses, happy and merry. However, the "financial disaster" and the broken hearts belonged to the parents.

After a few days of suffering the flood subsided. As suddenly as it had come, it disappeared. Sunrays brought a smile to the faces. Spring gradually healed the wounds and life returned to normal. The homes were renovated and optimism returned. Many days after the flood the Jews would still talk about it and tell grossly exaggerated tales. The flood was a popular subject among gossip tellers, chatterboxes, and fabricators, who told all sorts of stories about the flood and in general.

There was someone in Yurburg called Elia (Eliyahu) "Hamelagus" (the fabricator) who told the following story:

"It was at the time of Sylvester (Christian New Year) when he, Elie Barukh (Baruch), traveled on the winter coach drawn by two strong horses on the ice of the Nieman. All of a sudden the ice started to crack and explode and the carriage started to sink in the water.

Elia started to yell at the top of his voice: "Gevald! Help! Gevald Help!"

The farmers who were harvesting on the shore of the Nieman heard his cries. . . .

The farmers hurried to the river, climbed onto the ice and with their sickles they tugged and tugged and saved Elia and the winter coach with the horses . . . "

As far as the floods in spring were concerned, which brought destruction to many families in Yurburg, many entertaining stories were told, such as the following:

"One story-teller (Melagus) said that during the flood in Yurburg he saw a house rise and float on the water and on the chimney of the house stood a hen shrieking koo -koo-ree-koo, koo-koo-ree-koo

----

Stories and jokes, truth and imagination, seriousness and light-mindedness, tears and laughter - mingle in our stories, reflecting the nature of our life in Yurburg, our town.

Translated from Yiddish (into Hebrew) and edited - Paz

Along the beautiful Nieman River in May 2001
Photo by Nancy Lefkowitz]
[Not in original Yizkor Book]

Kovno Street looking East in winter or early spring possibly at the time of flooding. Foto Levinas.

Photo not in original Yizkor book - From photo album of Jack Cossid.

Yurburg under a blanket of snow

JEWISH OCCUPATIONS IN YURBURG *

The majority of the Jews in Yurburg dealt in the trades. Others were members of the free professions, clerks, craftsmen, etc. Unfortunately, we do not have the full list of the occupations of the Jews in Yurburg and we can only provide a partial list, as follows:

Exporters - traders

The "Export- Handel" company (see the list of its other members in Hinda Levinberg-Beker's articles). Shmeryahu (Shmerl) Poliak & Sons (Shelomoh and Avraham) - potatoes, fruit; David Yitskhak Beiman - the same;

Efraim Heselovitz - Linen, fodder, eggs and hides.

Importers-traders

Mendel Fainberg - agent of a German company for the import of salt and cement, supplier to small towns in the region;

Tsevi (Hirschel) Fain - cement and iron;

Neta Aharonovsky - the same;

Tsevi (Hirsch) Yozefovitch - petrol, beer, herring and dried fruit;
Yisrael Levinberg - coal from Silesia and herring;

Mordekhai (Mordechai) Greenberg - iron and agricultural machinery;
Tsadok Yozelit - salt and flour; Sheitel Levinson

Kretchmer - hides for shoemakers and shops.

Traders -peddlers - suppliers to exporters

Shakhna Heselkovitz
Eliezer Meirovitz
Yakov Meirovitz
Avraham (Ortchik) Fain
Kalman Friedland.

Meat traders - supply of meat to Kovno and abroad

Aba Kaplan and his sons Mosheh and Yakov-Ber
Nathan Kaplan, Aba Kaplan's brother

Hirsch Hess
Reuven Hess
Yakov Hess
Tuviyah Hess
Daniel Hess
Yisrael Mer.

Agriculture - small parcels of land

Leib Fainberg
Yosef Grinberg (Greenberg)
Shakhna Heselkovitz
Small gardens - adjacent to the houses.

Business owners

David Polovin - fabrics wholesale and retail;
Meir Polovin - the same;
Mordekhai (Mordechai) (Motl) Perlman - fabrics, the same;
Akiva Flier - fabrics, the same;
Alter Shimonov - iron and hardware business;
David and Berl Lapinsky - beverage agency of Wolf, Kovno;
Pinkhas Shakhnovitz - books and stationery;
Yasvonsky - Shakhnovitz (Shachnovitz)'s father in law - haberdashery and
children's games.

Banks and their managers

The Folksbank - the National Jewish bank, branch of the Central Bank in
Kovno. Board members: Yitskhak (Isaac) Fainberg, Simon Zundelevitz, Yosel
Rabinovitz.
The Komertz Bank - Lithuanian bank - its manager Shmeryahu (Shmerl)
Bernstein.

Physicians

Yitskhak Rabinovitz
Goldberg
Gershtein
Soltz
Karlinksy
Shimonov (dentist).
A. Kopelov (dentist).

Pharmacies

Bergovsky (Kolia and Sasha);
Mosheh Rikler - Magazin Apothekai (pharmacy)

* Supplementary information to Hinda Levinberg-Beker's article.

TRANSLATION OF PAGES 68 - 70

I Remember Yurburg

By Zevulun Poran

I remember my pretty little shtetl

Between the flowing clean waters

Between the marvelous and grand

From our more important dreams and our values

I remember the gardens and the fields

I see the mountains and the valleys

Where we spend our youthful years

I remember the shtetl and her streets

Illuminated and full of life

Where Jews use to live very happily

I can still see the synagogue and the Bet Hamidrash

The old Synagogue had the presence of God

And the Bet Hamidrash for prayers and to implore the Lord

I remember the old wood synagogue

The great pride of Yurburg

Our World famous synagogue with its carved wooden Holy Ark

That is my deep memory

I remember the teachings of the Torah

The High School, the elementary school and the Talmud Torah

I remember the scouts from Hashomer Hatsair

And the discussions concerning Zionism and the Sabbath walks

And who does not remember the Hakhsharah Kibbutz

     (Preparatory training for kibbutz life)

And the youngest ideals from the Khalutzim (pioneers)

I remember the library named Mendel

Where the readers were thirsty for knowledge

And the library named Brener

For the young students that knew Hebrew

I remember the young people who performed in the theater

That the theater artists expressed themselves in the performances

Everyone in the shtetl was happy

Everyone dances, sang songs and were carefree
That way the Zeides and Bubbes used to live the way the parents used to like

And strive to live life with happiness and joy
Until the difficult days came
Which were not prepared for the bleeding lines
They hit us, they killed us
One child shouted in a shutter and horror
In a terrified shout, they finished off the Jews of our shtetl
The end of the world
Oh Yurburg, Oh Yurburg, you are my shtetl, my life
What happened to you, what was the cause?
Wild bandits, killing like wild people
They hit, they killed, they buried them without funerals
You are now an empty town
There are no Jewish homes, no Jewish beds
Only bodies dispersed around the town
Only dry broken bones!
We will always remember Yurburg with bitter tears
And with deep memories will we miss you
Cursed is the modern Haman
Cursed is Hitler's name

TRANSLATION OF PAGE 71-73

My Shtetl Yurburg

By Shimon Shimonov

The town Yurburg (Jurbarkas in Lithuanian) on the shore of the Nieman River with its tributaries, the Mituva and the Imstra, is 100 km (62 miles) west of Kovno and 9 km (5 miles) to the east of Smalininken in Germany. Its long and wide streets were paved with stones and there are concrete sidewalks on both sides. Forests and fields surrounded Yurburg.

The Lithuanians had inherited a big and beautiful park, which had belonged to the Russian Duke Vasilshchikov. In the middle of the park sprawled a palace, surrounded by bushes and flowers. On both sides of the palace beautiful buildings could be seen. These buildings housed the state-supported high school attended by the Yurburg Lithuanian (non-Jewish) youngsters and others from the vicinity. On Sunday afternoons the Fire Brigade band would play dance music and the public would have a pleasant time. Though most of the public were members of the Shauliai (who were anti-semitic) nationalist quasi-military organization, Jews also participated in the entertainment, called in Lithuanian "Geguzhines."

One nice day Lithuanians decided to forbid the Jewish youth from participating in this entertainment. At the entrance of the park the Lithuanian extremists erected a sign: **"Entrance of Jews and dogs is prohibited."** This anti-semitic inscription was an insult to the Jewish population. Immediately a committee was formed, and it was decided to buy a nice garden with a big building. The garden was converted into a park and the building housed the Hebrew gymnasuim (high school) which served the Jewish population of Yurburg, Tavrig and other towns along the Nieman River. The Jewish Park was named "Tel-Aviv" in honor of the newly built town in Eretz-Yisrael. Jews appreciated the park; which was close to town and together with the high school the park formed an important cultural center. Every Sunday entertainment, concerts and sport were organized in the park.

In the mid-1930s 3,000 Jews lived in Yurburg. The community was concentrated in the center of the town. Lithuanians (non-Jews) lived in the surrounding areas of the town, but the Catholic Church stood at the end of the Kovno Street, the main street of the town. On Shabbath and Jewish holidays all the businesses were closed. Jews of Yurburg felt like they were living in a Jewish town, where Yiddish and also occasionally Hebrew were heard spoken in the streets.

Mondays and Thursdays were the market days. The plot of land between the old wooden Synagogue and the solidly built [brick - still standing in the 1990s - *n.b. JA*] Beth-Midrash served as market place for the Lithuanian peasants and the Jewish population. The Lithuanian peasants would sell agricultural products and the Jews would sell haberdashery and industrial goods.

The old wooden Synagogue, built in 1790, was famous in Lithuania and all over the world for its artistic woodcarvings of the *Aron-Ha Kodesh* (sacred ark), the *Bimah* (pulpit) and the Chair of Eliyahu. In Yurburg there were many learned men, doctors, lawyers, bankers etc. Well known rabbis also came from Yurburg, the last one was Avraham Dimant, a famous Rabbi, a *Dayan* (religious judge) was Hayim (Chaim)-Reuven Rubinshtein. There was also a cantor Alperovitz who would write tunes for the liturgical melodies for the Jewish High Holy Days.

In Yurburg there were two Jewish schools - the Yiddish school and the Hebrew School. The town also boasted a Hebrew High School and two libraries - The "Mendele" library (Yiddish books) and the "Brener" (Hebrew) Library.

Several youth organizations were formed in Yurburg- "HeKhalutz," "Maccabi," Jewish Scouts - "HaShomer HaTsair," "Betar." Thanks to "HeKhalutz" a large number of youth immigrated to Eretz-Yisrael. Jewish political parties were active in town. The Jewish "Folksbank," the "Commerce Bank" and social institutions like "Bikur Kholim" (Sick Fund), "Hakhnasath Kalah" (Fund for the Needy) and others were the famous Jewish institutions of Yurburg.

Jews made their living from different sources. In Yurburg there were steamship owners who employed a great number of staff. Other popular occupations were exporters, merchants, hotel owners, shopkeepers, artisans and workers.

When Hitler took over the rule in Germany it was immediately felt in Yurburg. The Lithuanian Shauliai and other anti-Semites became vocal. For many Jews it became difficult to make a living. Life was becoming harder with every passing day, and for young people the future became doubtful. Some of the youth went to Eretz-Yisrael or abroad and others left for Kovno.

On June 22, 1941, at five o'clock in the morning, parts of the Nazi-German army invaded Yurburg. Dark clouds enveloped the future of the Jewish population. Only a couple of the Jews survived, and the entire community perished. In the first "action" 350 men were murdered, among them 40 Lithuanian communists. The remaining men, women and children of the Jewish population were murdered and buried in a forest near Smalininken. [Note added: Many of the murderers were the Lithuanians themselves.]

In 1945 Yurburg was freed from the murderers, but unfortunately no Jews were left in Yurburg - only pain remains in our hearts forever.

TRANSLATION OF PAGE 74-78

Once There Was A Shtetl

By Motl-Mordekhai (Mordechai) Zilber

I am beginning my writing the same way my late father would start a story when I was a child "once upon a time there was ..."

This is a story that sounds like a dream.

Forty years have passed since I left Yurburg and I still see it in my eyes as if it was yesterday. I have traveled the world - Russia and France, Canada and USA and now- Israel, but I could never forget Yurburg, it has always been in my heart. Yurburg has always remained in the hearts of all the Yurburgers who were scattered all over the world.

I often think about Yurburg, I see it in my fantasies where I visit Yurburg often. I meet with the people; my friends and I recall events. I visit places and forget that Yurburg was in ashes after the Nazis and the Lithuanians burned down the town; I forget that the people of the town were taken by force and murdered. I want to forget all that and go back to the past, when Yurburg was alive and we were happy.

I see the town as I open the iron gates of Duke Vasilshchikov's park. The park is fenced in with a stone wall. The entrance is through an iron gate between three thick brick pillars. In front I see the ruins of the Duke's palace. The palace sprawls near the Mituva river and on the other side, in the forest near the meadow there still is a wooden mushroom, its cap is red, its stem is white and it is covered with many inscriptions of couples in love. The duke built it, apparently, as to protect couples from rain.

The duke would come here only in summer months, and nobody would be allowed to walk near the palace, except outside the property. There were two other buildings - both for the servants. Later the buildings would house the Lithuanian high school. The duke had everything he wished for his comfort - a greenhouse covered with glass, stables, workrooms and a beer brewery outside Yurburg.

The legend goes that one of the duke's ancestors was the lover of Queen Katharine II, like brothers Orlovs and others, after the love became cooler, she would "exile" her lovers, endow them with estates at the borders of the great Russian Empire. Our duke Vasilshchikov was one of those who were "exiled" to our town of Yurburg.

Before we leave the park we will see a small Pravoslavic church. It is a small church built for the duke and his family and for the servants. People said that the big stone in front was a meteorite, a body that fell from the sky.

The palace of Prince Vasilshchikov in the Big Park, 1917

Youth of Yurburg on a stroll in the Big Park in 1927

"The Big Mushroom"

Standing from the right: Yehudah Gertner, (Visitor), Michael Tarshish, and Avraham Altman. Sitting from the right: Yehoshua Glazer, Yeshayahu Segal, Zevulun Poran.

Now we are going back. On the right side of the building there are the two movie theaters of Yurburg. On the screen of the movie theaters we saw the films of Emil Janings, Marlene Dietrich, Konrad Vaidt, Paula Negri and sometimes performances of Ivan Mazhukhin.

The house of the Altmans was next to the movie theater. This was the house of the diva of Yurburg, Fanichka Altman. With her excellent voice she made her listeners fall in love with her.

And here is the Imstra, a small creek flowing into the Mituva and then into the Nieman. In summer a hen could cross the creek without wetting "hens feet," but in spring when the Nieman was full of ice tide would flood the areas around. Then in this part of the town people would use boats, like in Venice. Even the priest's garden was flooded.

Let us look at the side lane, which leads to the park. The house of the Levinsons is there and on the porch two boys are waiting- they are Tony and Izy Levinson (now in South Africa). They are waiting for their father who works in the "Taryba" (Town Council). On the left there is a narrow lane along the Imstra leading to Rasein Street. It passes along the priest's garden and house. A small wooden bridge crosses the Imstra. It is so good to stand on the bridge and look at the small fish in the waters of the Imstra. Tailor Chertok lives near the bridge, he suffers greatly from the floods.

The road right of the bridge leads to the Mituva where the steamships are mooring before winter comes.

Our way leads us to the Kovno Street, past a church fenced by a stone wall. The church has two high towers and looks like a big fortress. It is a praying house for the entire community. The rural population gathers here. When someone dies the body is brought to the church and photographer [Nissan] Abramson takes the last picture. The same happens when there is a wedding. [Photo on back cover of this book was by Nissan Abramson.]

The rural community of Yurburg is considered rich. It was said that the Jewish population of Yurburg participated in financing the construction of the church with the calculation that it will increase the living opportunities of the town.

In front of the church, to the right, a road leads to the Nieman River. If you have time, let us wait for a steamship coming from Kovno in the afternoon - may be it is the staemship "Laisve," or the "Lietuva" or may be the "Kestutis."

Afterwards it will be announced who arrived. 20 people and 3 Germans, they would say. Like Germans could not be counted among people.

The road leads us through the Kovno Street; opposite the church we see the house of the Leipzigers. Eliezer Leipziger, was a very talented person, a lawyer and later the director of the Hebrew high school. . He married Fani Krechmer. At the end he and his wife were murdered by the bloody animals. This was also the house of Freidale Leipziger, today a teacher in Kibbutz Afikim.

Over there is the house of the "Minzers," a fine Jewish family, with two beautiful daughters and one son who immigrated to Cuba. He is a tailor and I unfortunately forgot his name.

And then there is the second movie theater of Yurburg. Films are shown by Pola Skeltz and an older woman. Skeltz has several trades but makes a poor living. He plays music at Jewish weddings; he catches fish. When he plays at a Jewish wedding, he would play a "Krakowiak." He is an ardent Polish patriot and when he plays the "Krakowiak" he becomes very exited, sings in a high pitched voice and stomps with his feet. After the movie is over he goes to the boarding house at the Fainberg's. An old bachelor, who, people say, plays the violin in the middle of the night when nobody hears. I never saw anybody coming to his boarding house.

And here is the green house of the Aizenshtats, the brothers Aizenshtat. They were considered the "elite" of the town. Liova died young from Typhus. He was married with Betty Yozelit. A sister, Leana Aizenshtat, lives in Canada. Opposite the Aizenshtats is the great yard of the Fainbergs. They are four brothers and one sister. They are considered the rich people in town. They own a sawmill, a flourmill and the power station. We get electricity from 6 o'clock PM until 12 o'clock midnight. Before the power is switched off we hear a warning to the public: "Here, we are getting off..."

One of the Fainberg brothers, Meir, is in arts, he performeded very well in Russian and we enjoyed his performances more than once.

Motl Zilber

It's a pity that we didn't receive the end of his descriptions. Motl passed away. All his friends and relatives will never forget him.

Jacob Levinsohn's Goose Farm near Yurburg

[Not in original Yizkor Book - Courtesy of Ashley Levinsohn]

The Beautiful Town of Yurburg

By Ben Devorah

Several kilometers before reaching Yurburg [traveling west from Kovno] you can immediately feel the ambiance of Western Europe. The fields are more intensely cultivated and exploited. The behavior of the rural population is more cultural. The German border is already close and its smells German.

Yurburg makes a nice impression. Wide streets, many quite nice buildings, nice shops with pretty shop windows are adding to the impression of a big town. Also the landscape of Yurburg is pretty. On one side - the Nieman River and on the other side - the lively Imstra stream. This pleasing geographic situation helps the Yurburg population to make its living. The forests serve as rest and recreation areas. It's obvious why the Health Department has established in town one of its two centers and hospitals for respiratory desease. The marvelous park, that once belonged to the Russian Duke Vasilshchikov adds to the beauty of Yurburg. The backbone of the economic life of Yurburg is the Nieman River. Many Jewish families make their living from this big river. When the summer season arrives, life around Nieman becomes intense. The several tens of steamships, belonging to Yurburg citizens, sail without pause upstream and downstream on the Nieman River.

Rafts are floating by and the oarsmen buy their necessities here. Carts, harnessed with strong horses, are going to and from the riverbank carrying stones, timber and other goods brought by the steamships. Tens of meters of fish nets are put in the water by fishermen, whose lives are strongly linked with the Nieman. The Nieman is the very life source and the pride of Yurburg Jews.

The population of Yurburg is mixed. In addition to Lithuanians and Jews, there are large German and Russian colonies. They all have their priests, their churches and schools. For some time the mayor of Yurburg was a German. Yurburg is a clean and relaxed town. All state, municipal and Jewish institutions have suitable and more or less convenient offices. All Jewish schools in bigger towns than Yurburg could only wish to have such facilities like the Hebrew and the Yiddish schools here. The Hebrew high school has its own building with a big and beautiful park named "Tel-Aviv," where all the entertainment takes place.

Though the economic crisis has affected Yurburg as well, but it seems that the Jews don't loose hope for better days to come.

Yurburg is proud of its beautiful Beith-Midrash, but in particular they cherish their really interesting old synagogue. The Aron-Kodesh of the synagogue is a rare object of art in woodcarving. Also the Bimah is beautiful. The blind Shamash (caretaker) of the synagogue complained to me that the Bimah was carved by another artist, who was jealous of the person who built the Aron-Kodesh and for that he concealed the Aron-Kodesh with the Bimah.

The older generation of Yurburg has special sense of self-esteem. They are classy, nicely dressed folks, with felt hats and dark gray summer coats as they come on holidays to the synagogue. Yurburg has a large number of students, boys and girls, who are studying in Kovno and many others abroad.

Yurburg was never looking for public and political activity, for that it got a Jewish-democratic Kehilah (Community Committee) late. In Yurburg there are no extremists. The Zionists, the orthodox and the Yiddishists don't make much noise. It is characteristic for Yurburg to have a Gabbai of the old synagogue, Alter Shimonov, who also happens to be the dentist. He is a man with a modern outlook and manners, a sympathizer of Zionism, who goes to the Beth Midrash on Shabbat and every morning put on phylacteries and would not eat dinner before a "ma'ariv" prayer. On Friday evening you can see the wife of the dentist lighting candles. On the other side we can see an important personality living in Yurburg with a woman whom he married in a civil wedding.

The relations between the Jews and Lithuanians in Yurburg are generally friendly. The Jews and the Lithuanians are proud of the fact that Yurburg gave Lithuania several famous personalities. Jews of Yurburg became renowned scientists, writers, artists and philanthropists and Lithuanians became such stately people as professor Tamoshaitis, consul Sidrauskas, prosecutor Bila, lawyer and public worker Taliushis.

Many projects were planned to improve the economic situation of Yurburg, such as pavement of new roads, improvement of transportation and other projects that promised a better future.

But all these were pleasant dreams. For the Jews the future would be bitter. During three months - in the summer 1941 - Jewish Yurburg was annihilated by Nazi-German soldiers with the active help of cruel Lithuanians with whom Jews lived together for generations and where Jews established their homes on Lithuanian soil.

Jacob Levinsohn's Goose Farm near Yurburg
[Not in original Yizkor Book - Courtesy of Ashley Levinsohn]

The New Beith Midrash in the Center of the Town

(From the periodical "Funken" - edited by Z.P.)

Former Beith Midrash Building in May 2001 - Note that third floor expandeded - [Photo not in the original book - photo by Dr. Leon Menzer]

TRANSLATION OF PAGE 82-84

Yurburg Under Water

Adapted by Zevulun Poran

On Wednesday, the 17th of March 1937, at 1 pm, the section of the Nieman River adjacent to Yurburg awoke from its winter sleep. As happens each year, so this year too, curious people gather on the banks of the Nieman, happy to see the ice move and hoping that by Pesakh (Passover) a steamship will sail on the river. The Nieman flows at such speed that you can hear the ice blocks crashing. And so, standing there in circles and debating the subjects of ice, water, floods, they suddenly look back and see that the water is already creeping up behind them.

The flow continues relentlessly at full speed up to a blockage near Smaleninken, as a result of which the water level in Yurburg rises more and more. At 5 P.M. the municipal siren wails for help.

People start to run all were curious to see how the water is rushing into the town. Police, firemen and all citizens are on duty to fight the intruding water.

Slowly the market is flooded and water is even flowing into Kovno Street. At first the flow is slow, but then it increases in strength and volume.

Yatkever (Butcher) street begins to flood - a howl, a yell: "Help! Rescue! We are inundated!" Mothers with sleeping children in their arms call for a boat to take them to a dry patch, panic is great.

A Jewish woman stands in the water, her hair disheveled, complaining to her neighbors that her stove, which had been renovated just a year ago, is now disintegrating, and in another woman's flat the table and chairs are swimming.

Lots of people congregate in Kovno Street, half of which is already flooded. It is now late evening, electric lights are on, small boats sailing to and for. People are walking on the still-dry sidewalks, but for the young this is entertainment, just like Venice!

Nobody is thinking of going to bed. The time is 1 AM, 2 AM, 3 AM, and the water is still slowly flooding more and more areas.

The shop owners of Kovno street decide to move goods from lower shelves to the upper ones, thus packages of goods, appliances, cigarettes and textiles are lifted up. Some put the goods on chairs in order to have them at least a few inches above the surface of the water. People are standing on sidewalks about to be flooded and wait, maybe God will show mercy -

On the other side of Kovno Street the situation is also bad. Here is a boat with bedding; there is one evacuating children and old people from dangerous places, someone is running with a package on his shoulders, and someone else with a table. Policemen are patrolling the streets, helping victims and guarding against looting. It is 7 AM in the morning and the water level is still rising. The "padriads" (special bakeries for Matzah baking) ought to be baking Matzos for Pesakh, which is already imminent. What can be done? Peasants are coming to the market and stop, they are scared. The market place is inundated.

Jews are standing around, worried and waiting for a miracle. Waiting and waiting - and suddenly - a miracle! The water starts to recede. Yurburg citizens lift their heads and smile - but most of them immediately feel the painful aftermath and cry silently. What will be? What will be? A help committee is set up immediately, but the damage is great. Can the committee manage to relieve the damage?

The situation is bad. But during all previous years of flooding people get over it and this year too they will recover and start again. True, the damage is great. May be the committee will be able to help. We must hope - because it is forbidden to lose hope!

(Edited byZevulun Poran)

Springtime Flood in Yurburg

TRANSLATION OF PAGE 85-87

The Shtetl of Yurburg

The article "The town of Jurbarkas" was published in the Yiddish daily newspaper **"Folksblat"** on July 16, 1939, in the days of the deep crisis for Lithuanian Jews just before the outbreak of World War II. The anonymous author of this article, as it seems from its content, was one of the supporters of the Yiddishist anti-Zionist circles, as he criticizes the Jewish youth who are getting Zionist education, and are interested only in "Hakhsharah" (preparation for moving to Palestine) and certificates for Aliyah. The author is disappointed that these Jews are not concerned with strengthening the (local) "existence "---what "existence " in the Diaspora.   **(Z. Poran)**

The town Yurburg is located in Raseiniai district. It has long, beautiful, wide streets, with concrete sidewalks on both sides, nice houses; some of them built in brick. It is getting more modern and spread out. A new quarter of the town was built, and it is called the New Town- reaching villages nearby. In the New Town a park was planted, where a monument for Vytautas the Great was built. Near the park you can see the Yurburg stadium. In the old-town, as we call it now, the old buildings are being demolished.

This difficult situation affects the poor and they are becoming weaker. Some will not have a place to live because the rents are becoming higher and there are no opportunities to earn a living in Yurburg. They used to live in small affordable houses but Yurburg is becoming more modern but not through private undertakings. The builders are the state and the municipality.

The municipality built a slaughterhouse and is maintaining the streets. The government built a second floor for the Yurburg Lung Sanitarium. This was the only Sanitarium in Yurburg. A road was also constructed several kilometers long joining Klaipeda and Jurbarkas. Two concrete bridges were built over the rivers of "Imstra" and "Mituva."

The government also intends to build a harbor for the steamships.

Yurburg is like a valley between high mountains. Around Yurburg there are big areas with splendid forests and fields with hills and valleys. There are two parks - one is the Jewish Park named "Tel-Aviv" where trees and their branches look like in a dream, inviting passers-by to enter and smell their pleasant odors. The second park is the Lithuanian Park, well maintained and in a continuous process of maintenance. Once it belonged to a Russian duke, today it belongs to the Lithuanian high school. The park has tens of paths, one very small leading to the Mituva, which is winding between the park and the forest. One big path leads to a place behind the park where you can see all the Yurburg surroundings.

The third river is the Nieman running along shores of town. The steamship traffic connects Yurburg with the economic and political center of Kaunas.

When a newcomer arrives in Yurburg he is impressed with the beauty of nature around town. The town is home for 6,000 people, 2,000 Jews among them from different social classes: merchants, artisans, and shopkeepers. The town is facing an economic decline it has been affected by the big world crisis, and by the persistent phenomenon of Hitler politics, which slows trade with Germany.

Although Yurburg does not compare with other towns, there are people here too who learned to hate. These are the so-called Lithuanian patriots who consider only their own pockets. They have their own shops and call for boycott of the Jewish business.

Often we can hear anti-Semitic slogans not only from the simple folks but more from the youth and the "Intelligencia."

The only institution watching over the Jewish economic situation is the Folksbank, which gives out loans. But how can the loans help when there is nowhere to use the money? From the cultural standpoint our town is better off than the adjacent towns. It has a state high school, 4 elementary schools, (2 Lithuanian schools, 1 Hebrew School and 1 Yiddish School), a Hebrew high school, a Lithuanian agricultural school, 2 libraries named after Mendele and Brener.

Jewish children don't go to either the Lithuanian high school or the Lithuanian elementary school. Most of them attend meetings of "HeKhalutz" and "Betar." They care only about "Hakhsharah" and certificates, but not about the local Jewish Community.

We also have an advantage of having the famous Lithuanian sculptor H. Gribas live in the area; his monuments can be seen in many cities and towns of Lithuania. Yurburg citizens are proud of their town and are proud to show their town to visitors.

The first object of pride a Yurburger could show a newcomer is the ancient synagogue built in 1790 with its rare fixtures. The second object is the atelier (artist's studio) of the sculptor Gribas with its marvelous artistic works. The third thing to show would be the beauty of nature [in and surrounding the town].

There is a cinema in town with occasional shows of wonderful films. It still belongs to Jews. There is little industry in town. Nonetheless, there is a small furniture factory, which was awarded a medal at an exhibition abroad and a flourmill with a power station.

The economic and social situation of our town is very sad, but let us not be depressed. One hour before dawn it becomes very dark and there is a struggle between darkness and light where the light becomes the winner.

A Yurburger

**Postcard of Yurburg, likely taken from the top of the church steeple.
Photo not in original Yizkor book. From photo album of Jack Cossid.**

**Group standing with Beis Medresh behind them. From left, unidentified
man, Jack Cossid in center with hat, with Rochel Panamunsky to the left
and Dora Gittleman Krelitz's sister to the right.**

March 31, 1937 - Passover.

Photo not in original Yizkor book . From photo album of Jack Cossid.

TRANSLATION OF PAGES 88 - 113

YURBURG UNDER THE SOVIETS

(From the Lithuanian Encyclopedia)

(Note added by Joel Alpert: During this period [after World War II]
there were either no Jews or at most two Jewish families in Yurburg)

The town of Yurburg in the Soviet republic of Lithuania is surrounded by the Nieman and Mituva rivers.

The town is 12 kilometers (7 miles) away from the borders of the Kaliningrad (formerly Koenigsberg) district.

In 1959 - 4,422 inhabitants - situated on the right side of the Nieman on a low and sandy place. The area was 413 hectars.

Yurburg's old city was established close to the shore of the Nieman. The buildings in the center of town were built in the Gothic style. The streets of the new town were well planned. The main part of town was built on the left side of the Mituva; the small Imstra River crossed it in part. Development was started on the right side of the river during the years of the Soviet regime.

The shore of the Nieman includes a strip of soft sand over 1 kilometer. Not far from the town - the large Smalininkai - and Vesvilis (Veshvilis) forests. In the southern part of town there is a large factory for processing linen seeds (established in 1950).

[The town contained] a boat dock, the base of the Ministry of Transport, a butter factory (established in 1931), a saw mill, carpentry workshops, factories for production of blocks and tiles, a flour mill, bakery and the Nieman fisherman's harbor.

Now roads connect Yurburg to Kaunas (Kovno) and Klaipeda (Memel). Roads lead to Raseiniai (Rasein) and Skaudvile (Shkudvil). A ferry crosses the Nieman from Yurburg to the other side of the river and from there to Shaki. Steamships sail to Kaunas and Klaipeda.

Most streets used by buses are covered in asphalt -. On the site of the market, the entire center of town is presently covered in green.

On both sides of the Mituva is the park of the former Kniaz, from the 19th century. In 1950 a memorial statue was set up here to honor sculptor I. Gribas. At the end of the park is a cemetery for those who fell in the battles of World War II. There is a 100-bed hospital in town, built before World War I, and a hospital for tuberculosis patients. There is a 30-bed maternity ward at the hospital.

Culture and education - As early as in the 18th century a high school was established in town. In 1924-27 a pro-gymnasium existed in Yurburg - "Saule" (Sun) and from 1931 a national gymnasium. There is also an evening school for high school education (1946-53 - pro-gymnasium), a kindergarten for children, in 1947 a cultural center was set up, a cinema and 300-seats theater. A museum in memory of I. Gribas was established in 1956. From 1963 there is a regional newspaper called "Sviesa" (Shviesa) ("Light") in town. Before that there was a newspaper called the "Flag" (1949-62).

In the northern part of town was the "Bishpil" mountain, crossed by the Imstra, creating a deep valley. On top of the mountain was a lookout post from which the 5-meter (17 feet) high wall of the old castle could be seen. At the observation post remnants of an ancient culture could be seen. In excavations various archeological findings were uncovered, such as ceramic utensils, bows and arrows and other articles from the 12th and 14th century. Some of them were transferred to the history museum in Kaunas. On the shore of the Nieman, 3 kilometers (2 miles) from the mouth of the Mituva - there were 2 small hills called "Bishpiliukais," from which there was a good view of the surroundings. It is thought that the Georgenburg (Yurgenburg) fortress stood on these hills, mentioned in the German chronicles and used as one of the ancient crusader fortresses along the Nieman.

In 1259 or close to this year, the Lithuanians established the "Bishpil" mountain. In 1260 the Lithuanians led by Dorbas attacked the crusaders who retreated from Georgenburg.

In 1353 the crusaders returned and took over the fortress again. Battles continued here almost until the 15th century. In early 1403 the fortress was set on fire by Vytautas' army.

After the Zalgiris battle, where the crusaders were defeated, the place lost its strategic value. When the crusaders retreated, the place called Yurburg started to develop as a permanent settlement.

In 1422 when the borders of Lithuania were determined, Yurburg turned into a border point. In the first half of the 15th century a customs post was set up here as it was an important commercial point, and also because of the Nieman River, which was a passageway for goods from Kovno to Tilzit, Memel (Klaipda) and Koenigsberg.

The town started to grow quickly and mainly gained its commercial importance since the 16th century, when trees started to be harvested from in the surrounding forests for transport to Gdansk and Koenigsberg where boats were built.

In 1557 the first primary school was established. In 1611 the Magdenburg Law was accepted in Yurburg and when it had 3,000 inhabitants. Yurburg maintained its status as a commercial center until the 19th century. In 1862 goods passed through customs in Yurburg in the sum of about 10 million rubles. In those days railway tracks started to be laid and this affected Yurburg's importance as a commercial center.

In 1864 there were 320 families in Yurburg with 2,659 inhabitants; in 1880 3,000; in 1901 Yurburg served as a "transit station" for the "Iskra" underground newspaper edited by Y. Lenin, which was sent from Germany to Kovno. In 1906 a large part of the town burnt down. In 1915 the German army destroyed the town which at that time already had the status of district town. In 1923 there were 4409 inhabitants in Yurburg.

Small factories started to be established in town, such as a flourmill and windmill that supplied electricity, a sawmill and dairy. The branch of the Lithuanian bank was opened and the agricultural bank, in addition to small private and public banks (*).

Trade stores were also opened along with a hospital, schools, a library, orphanages and a home for the elderly. In 1928-33 illegal material of the Communist party continued to be transferred through Yurburg from Germany to Kovno.

In the period of the conservative regime rightist parties were active in Lithuania as well as the Communist party L.K.P.-L.K.J.S. A branch of the Red Cross was also active in town. From 1929 the sculptor I. Grivas lived and worked in Yurburg. He was murdered by the German conquerors in 1941 together with another 350 inhabitants [mostly Jews, n.b.] of Yurburg. During World War II Soviet soldiers fought heroic battles against the German fascists, such as Prolov, S.Sergejev, I.Tolstikov. They received the "Hero of the Soviet Union" medal. After World War II the town was rebuilt, its main streets were expanded. Many houses were built; public institutions set up, among them a new high school (1960) and a cinema - a new theater (1960). Yurburg lies on both sides of the road leading to Klaipda (Memel).

Translated into Hebrew by Shimon. Shimonov

(*) [Hebrew] Editor's note - At that time the Jewish Folksbank was also set up in Yurburg which served the Jewish population. According to Holocaust survivors who visited Yurburg in recent years the town developed at a fast pace, but there are hardly any Jews. Only one family lived in Yurburg, which returned to settle there, the last remnant of the lively Jewish center, which existed and is no more.

Unfortunately, the encyclopedia does not mention in of the bitter fact that in 1941 when the Nazis entered Yurburg - in June, July, August and September - that over 2,000 defenseless Jews were brutally murdered. These were men, women, children and old people. They were murdered with the active assistance of the fascist Lithuanian murderers who had been the Jews' neighbors for hundreds of years and had built and developed the town together and finally - as a reward for what they had done - the Jews were murdered without mercy.

TRANSLATION OF PAGES 91 - 90

THE LAND OF OUR FATHERS

Zevulun Poran

For hundreds of years our fathers and our fathers' fathers lived in the land of Lithuania.

The following pages are a description of the land, its Lithuanian inhabitants and their history. Of course the Jews too will be mentioned, for they found a refuge here in this country, and lived there for a period of history of hundreds of years. The Jews, together with the Lithuanians, developed their land, established towns and villages with exemplary Jewish communities. The excellent relations between the Jews and the Lithuanian people were upset in the years 1941-1945 and ended tragically and with bitter cruelty when the Nazis entered Lithuania.

More is to follow.

Lithuania is one of the three Baltic countries - Lithuania, Latvia and Estonia, on the shores of the Baltic Sea. Lithuania is the largest of them. It presently occupies an area of about 80,000 sq.m. Formerly this land went from the Baltic Sea to the Black Sea and occupied large areas of the land of Russia, Ukraine, Belarus, Poland and Prussia. At present Lithuania only controls areas that are mainly occupied by Lithuanians.

Lithuania is a flat country without high mountains rising above. This is how Yitskhak Katsenelson, the Yiddish poet describes it:

> **My Lithuania, my Lithuania,**
>
> **All of it a plain, all of it flat,**
>
> **A land without mountains;**
>
> **Highways run through it**
>
> **Roads pass along.**

During most of the year Lithuania is a gray country. Narrow horizons. Rain. Very hot in some months of the summer and cold in winter (20 degrees C. below zero and less, that is — 6 degrees F.).

There are hundreds of rivers and lakes in Lithuania. Moss weeds and algae cover the lakes. These lakes are called swamps (Pelkes). The bottom of the black swamp is turf (peat) (Torf) which is good for heating and fertilizing.

The soil of Lithuania is mainly clay and does not absorb water, which therefore remains on the surface and creates rivers and swamps. The land of Lithuania is in part "black soil," very fertile, yielding a rich crop. Most of the Lithuanian land is good for agriculture.

The crops are linen, wheat, rice, oats, barley and sugar beets. Vegetables and plants are also grown in Lithuania, suitable for woven materials, such as linen and canvas. Lithuania grows excellent soft linen and has linen seeds that are very good for producing oil. Potatoes are grown for food (common food!) and some of it for liquor and starch. The fruit orchards are also important and pears, plums, apples are grown.

Animals are raised in Lithuania as well, such as cows, horses, sheep, pigs, poultry and bees.

In spite of all these achievements, farming in Lithuania between the two World Wars was considered primitive compared to farming in Germany, where the land was ploughed with sophisticated agricultural machines and was of very high quality. In the period when Lithuania was under Russian control cooperatives and farms were set up.

Tilling the land was improved by the use of farming machines. Lithuania's main export was agricultural produce such as fodder, timber, dairy products, eggs, meat, etc.

There are no natural resources in Lithuania, except for peat. Names of towns such as Kazlu-Ruda and Visakio-Ruda indicate iron ore (Ruda!); in the past iron was extracted in a primitive way.

The forests were Lithuania's natural and blessed wealth. The forests in Lithuania cover 16% of its area of land, enhance its landscape, supply wood and improve the climate. The forest is varied and has both evergreen trees and trees with leaves.

The most well known trees in Lithuania are the **fir trees** (Yolke), mainly used for export for the paper industry. The **pine tree** - good for heating, building and furniture. The **birch tree** (Berioze) - good for the furniture and household utensils industry. The **elm trees** - a soft tree from which matches are produced at factories, and also boxes for packing merchandise. The **oak** tree - which was not present in large numbers and which was a strong wood from which furniture and tools was made.

There are other kinds of trees and bushes of which there are smaller quantities in the forests of Lithuania, adding color to the woods. The Lithuanian forests are full of all kinds of berries (Yagdes) and mushrooms, good for eating.

The evergreen trees in the Lithuanian forests are good for people's health. In the summer months people would go to the villages or rest homes near the pine tree forests which were used for rest and recreation and for recuperation, mainly for lung patients.

Industry in Lithuania was minor most of the time. It gained impetus only after World War II. Textiles were produced, leather, paper, building materials and furniture, farming machines, electrical appliances etc.

Docks were set up in Klaipeda (Memel) where ships were built and repaired. The Klaipeda (Memel) port was used for Lithuania's foreign trade.

Transport in Lithuania was by railway lines, roads and waterways.

The **population** in Lithuania numbered over 3 million inhabitants, 80% of them Lithuanians and the others - Russians, Poles and others; there was a small minority of Jews among them, Holocaust survivors. In the past the Jewish population constituted over 7%. Vilna is presently the capital of Lithuania (about 400,000 inhabitants), Kovno (about 300,000 inhabitants), Klaipda (about 150,000 inhabitants) and then, with a smaller number of inhabitants, Shavl, Ponivezh - each of them less than 100,000 inhabitants. The **Nieman** - NEMUNAS - is the father of the Lithuanian rivers. When speaking of Lithuania, it is impossible not to mention the Nieman, which is not simply a waterway, but a source of life and national pride. The Nieman originates in the region of Minsk, the capital of Belorussia. It is 960 kms. (600 miles) long. Near Grodna the Nieman is about 100 meters (330 feet) wide, 230 meters (700 feet) near Yurburg and 170 meters (500 feet) near Klaipeda, where it flows into the Kurian bay; many small rivers flow into the Nieman. The beautiful 725 kilometer long (450 miles) Viliya - Neris - joins it near Kovno. The Nieman captures the heart of those who see it, with the magic of its beautiful shore adorned with trees and shrubs, and many poets, who admired its beauty, devoted their best songs to it. The poetess Elisheva writes in her poem:

"On the shore of the Nieman":

> **On the shore of the Nieman**
>
> **Far away beyond the border, the water**
>
> **Flows on, heavy and slow.**
>
> **The gray sky is full of sorrow**
>
> **Silent grief - in the flowing waves.**
>
> **On they flow to the sea,**
>
> **Riding along the strong current**
>
> **Losing themselves in the waves.**

However, in addition to its poetic side, the Nieman was very important, as it served as the main route for the transport of merchandise abroad, such as trees and farming produce and industrial goods to Lithuania.

The Nieman also served as an important internal way of transport, linking Kovno with the Baltic Sea. Numerous boats, the steamships (called "Kitoriot" by the people and "Dampfer" in Yiddish) among them, sailed to Kovno and Klaipeda and from Klaipeda back to Kovno.

Yurburg was the middle stop on these sailing trips, especially as most ships belonged to the townspeople, most of them Jewish.

The link with the Baltic Sea is very important for Lithuania, for in this way it was possible to do business with the neighboring Baltic countries and with the people from Western Europe and America.

The Baltic Sea is also an important source of living for the many fishermen. The Baltic Sea is rich in all kinds of fish. Another important source of income for many, mainly Jews, was amber, the precious "bernstein," discharged by the sea and used as a creative material for making precious jewels.

The shores of the Baltic Sea were also used by the Lithuanians as beach resorts, such as Zandkrug, Schwartzort and Palangen (Palanga) a little town where the Jews would often come in summer in order to bathe in the sea and rest and find healing for their aches.

ORIGIN AND HISTORY OF THE LITHUANIANS

The Lithuanians, as all the people in Europe at present, are Aryans, of the Caucasian race, of the Indian-European group of people. The mother of the Lithuanian language is Sanskrit, the source of almost all the European languages.

In the distant past the Lithuanian tribes were pushed towards the north by tribes and peoples, mainly the Slavs; the Lithuanian tribes were forced to hold on to both sides of the Nieman River, a cold and muddy land, the present Lithuania.

The Lithuanians are slender, slightly above average height, have blue eyes, flax-colored hair, pale skin and long faces, rather similar to the Finnish and German type.

The tribes that settled on the heights were called Aukstaiciai, and the tribes that settled in the west were called Zemaiciai. There also was a Yotvingiai tribe, which settled near Grodna, but this tribe was pushed away and mingled with the inhabitants of the surrounding area.

The dialect of the Lithuanians, who settled on the heights, became the cultural-literary language of the Lithuanian people. The Lithuanians are already mentioned in the chronicles of the beginning of the 11th century. At the time they lived in tribes and were pagans. They lived in a primitive lifestyle, but the muddy land and the forests assisted them in times of war.

Mindaugas was the first king of the Lithuanians. He became Christian in 1251. He conquered areas of land in White Russia (Belorussia). After his death his sons inherited his kingdom.

Gediminas, the Great Prince of Lithuania (1316-1341) fought against the Poles and the German noblemen and won. In those days the Vilna-Vilnius capital was established. After his death, he was succeeded by his two sons - Algirdas and Kestutis (1345).

Algirdas fought against the Russians and even reached the Black Sea.

Kestutis fought against the German noblemen and freed the areas of Lithuania held by them including Kovno (1362). When Algirdas died he left the regions of Russia, Belorussia and Ukraine to his son **Jogaila**.

Yogaila revolted against Kestutis and killed him together with the German - Teutons in 1382. However, Kestutis' son, **Vytautas** renewed the war against Jogaila and won. Jogaila established relations with Poland, married Jadviga, the Queen of Poland, became a Christian and was crowned the King of Poland called Vladislav II. Vytautas became Jogaila's deputy (1392) and ruled over Lithuania.

Vladislav II granted the Polish Boyars and Lithuanian noblemen as well as the Christian priests special rights.

Vytautas was declared the Great Prince by the Boyars. In 1410 Polish and Lithuanian forces joined ranks and went to war against the Teutonic Germans, led by Vytautas, who defeated them in the **Greenwald-Tannenberg (Zalgiris)** battle.

Vytautas also fought against the Russians, conquered areas of land and established his rule there. He granted rights to tradesmen and intellectuals and invited them to come and settle in Lithuania. Among those who were invited to do so were also **Jewish and Karaite tradesmen.** Since that time Jewish settlement in Lithuania grew. Vytautas died in 1447. After his death the Poles did not observe the agreement with Vytautas. However, Russian pressure forced the Lithuanians to take the side of the Poles. The Lithuanian nobility mingled with the Polish "shlakhte" and the Polish language became the language of the Lithuanian nobility.

In 1569 the Polish and Lithuanian Seimas (parliaments) met in Lublin and decided to unite Lithuania and Poland - **the Lublin merger** -(Lublin Unija) the Lithuanians had no choice but to agree to this. The "Polish Republic" was set up with a joint parliament, in which the Poles outnumbered the Lithuanians by three. In the subsequent years Poland, including Lithuania came under Russian pressure. From time to time areas were handed over to Russian rule.

Lithuania under Russian rule. In 1795 Lithuania was annexed to Russia. The Russian Czars were also called the Great Princes of Lithuania. The official language in Lithuania was Russian and thus the policy of "Russification" of Lithuania started. Use of Lithuanian writing was forbidden. Lithuania became the **northwestern region of Russia.** However, the Lithuanian intelligentsia did not abide by the Russian decrees and started to strive for national revival. In 1883 a Lithuanian newspaper started to appear in Tilzit (Prussia), edited by the physician Jonas Basanavicius. The newspaper was sent in a clandestine way via Yurburg for distribution in Lithuania.

In 1905 during the days of the first revolution in Russia, Dr. Jonas Basanavicius convened a conference of Lithuanians in Vilna where it was decided to demand **national autonomy for Lithuania.**

In World War I (1914-1918) the Germans conquered Lithuania. In 1917 a national conference was held in Vilna where the "Council" (Taryba) was elected headed by Antanas Samtona. The council announced Lithuania's independence under German patronage and at the advice of the Germans crowned **Wilhelm Urch**, the Prince of Wuerttemberg, King of Lithuania. The King called himself Mindaugas II.

In 1918 the "Red Army" conquered Lithuania and a Soviet government was set up for Lithuania and Belorussia, However, under the pressure of the Lithuanians the Russians agreed to grant Lithuania the right to set up an independent state. Jews also participated in the negotiations in favor of Lithuania and exerted considerable influence. That is how **the independent state of Lithuania** was established on **16 February 1918**.

A short while later the Poles conquered Vilna and the dispute between Poland and Lithuania continued until World War II.

Klaipeda (Memel) was annexed to Lithuania, and here **"Seimik"** was established as an expression of partial autonomy. The regime in Lithuania was **democratic**. In the first years of Lithuania's existence the Jews had **"national autonomy."** The Jews felt they were full citizens in Lithuania. However, at the end of 1926 a military upheaval took place - Smetona became the President and Prof. Voldemaras, head of the nationalist movement, became the Prime Minister. The constitution was abolished and the **"Seimas"** (parliament) was dispersed.

In 1929 Voldemaras was displaced and his extremist-nationalist group was dismantled.

Antanas Smetona was in fact the sole ruler in Lithuania. The party supporting the President was the nationalist "Tautininkai" party.

In 1934 Lithuania signed the **Baltic agreement** with Latvia and Estonia. In 1938, when Lithuania existed for 20 years a new constitution was created, ensuring return to the parliamentarian rule in the country. A new government was formed, but before it started to function World War II broke out.

In 1939 Poland demanded Vilna be handed over and asked for diplomatic relations.

Lithuania had to agree to the Polish demands and the border to Poland was opened. In March that same year Lithuania also had to agree to the German demand to hand over rule over the Klaipeda (Memel) region.

1939 was the year of upheavals in Lithuania. On August 23, 1939 it was agreed in a German-Soviet agreement that Lithuania would be under German influence, but in that same year, in September 1939, it was decided by Germany and the Soviet Union that Lithuania become a state under Soviet influence.

On October 10, 1939 Vilna was returned to Lithuania including a 9000 square kilometers (an area equal to about 60 miles by 60 miles) area around the town.

On June 15, 1940 Lithuania was forced to form a regime that was friendly towards the Soviet Union. When the new government was formed, headed by I. Paleckis, the Red Army took over Lithuania. President Smetona fled, and the

Lithuanian leaders were exiled to Siberia. The parties were dismantled. A **popular Seimas** was elected, 99% of which were Communists. The Seimas unanimously decided that Lithuania would join the Soviet Union.

When war broke out between Germany and the Soviet Union on June 22, 1941 a revolution took place in Lithuania which made it easier for the Germans to conquer the land. The Germans declared an independent Lithuania but united it with all the Baltic countries and Belorussia into an area of land called **Ostland**, where they planned to settle Germans. Nevertheless, the Lithuanians took the side of the Germans, particularly in the help they extended in the extermination of Lithuanian Jews - till the end of the war.

In July 1944 the Red Army conquered Vilna and in August it took over Kovno. Klaipeda (Memel) was only conquered in January 1945. Lithuania was a **Soviet Republic,** member of the Soviet group of peoples - up to the present day.

Recently, under the influence of Gorbachev's "Glasnost" the Lithuanians are asking for more independence, though not yet for total separation. As to the future - who knows?

Lithuanian language -writing and literature. For hundreds of years there was no Lithuanian language writing and literature. After Lithuania's merger with Poland, Lithuanian "nobility" was influenced by the Polish "shlachte." In those days the Lithuanians did not write in their own language. However, oral literature had always flourished in Lithuania - folklore, popular songs, stories and tales. They sang songs to their children in the cradle, during work, at weddings, holidays and celebrations. The Lithuanian peasants also had their own folk-dances. Such a popular lyrical song was called "Daina."

The first book to be translated into Lithuanian was the book written by Father Martinas Mazhvidas (1747), and the first original book to be written in the Lithuanian language was by K. Donelaitis (1714-1780). The book's contents are songs about the peasants' work during the year's seasons.

At the same time there were Lithuanian authors and intellectuals - university graduates - who wrote in Polish and German. One of them was Adam Mickevitz (1798-1855) who wrote in Polish about subjects dealing with Lithuania. One of his books of poetry starts with the words: "Lithuania, my fatherland.. . "

Lithuanians claim that also the philosopher Emanuel Kant (1724-1804), who lived in Prussia, was a Lithuanian and even developed a Lithuanian grammar. A street in Kovno was called after him - Kanto Gatve.

After the Russian occupation (1795) Russian liberal and revolutionary literature influenced the Lithuanian authors.

In the years 1883-1886 the first underground newspaper called "Ausra" ("The Dawn") was published and this established the unified Lithuanian-literary language.

One of the famous Lithuanian authors, who laid the foundations of the new Lithuanian literature, was **Vincas Kudirka** (1858-1899). One of Kudirka's songs - "Lithuania our fatherland" - "Lietuva tevine musu" was chosen as Lithuania's national anthem.

The authoress Julija **Zemaite** (1845-1921) described the life of the peasants in the village. The most famous poet of the generation of national awakening - rather like our Bialik - was Maironis (1862-1932). **Kreve - Mickevicius** was also greatly admired (1882-1954).

Lithuanian literature flourished in independent Lithuania until it was conquered by the Soviet Union (1940). Even today Lithuanian authors and poets are influenced by the socialist realism common in the Soviet Union. The socio-cultural changes taking place in the Soviet Union at present will probably also influence the character and spirit of Lithuanian literature.

In conclusion we would like to add that the Jews also assisted in the development of the Lithuanian language (Avraham Kissin and others) and its literature. Yitskhak Meras, the Jewish-Lithuanian author, presently lives in Israel and writes in Lithuanian, which is translated into Hebrew.

JEWS IN LITHUANIA

When did the Jews arrive in Lithuania? There are no historic documents in this respect, but it is most likely that by the 10th century there were Jews in Lithuania, individuals as well as groups, who served as brokers and go-between in matters of trade. They established connections between tradesmen in southern Russia and the commercial towns on the shore of the Baltic Sea.

Jewish immigrants arrived in Lithuania in two ways. The first were immigrants from the Caucasus, Crimea (Ukraine) and southern Russia. The names of these Jews and their customs resembled those of the Russians. There were Jews who came from the other direction, in the days of the crusaders in the 10th to 13th centuries, from Western Europe, mainly from Germany. In the days of the crusaders the German Jews were persecuted and they had to emigrate to the north, that is how they arrived in Lithuania, where Christianity had not yet taken root. These Jews brought the Yiddish language along with them, other names and customs influenced by the Germans. Till now it is possible to distinguish between the two streams of immigration according to the color of their skin: the German Jews were light in coloring while the Russian Jews were dark skinned. The names were also different; those who came from Germany carried names such as Weissberg, Zucker, Sternberg, Grossman etc. Those who came from Russia were called Ansky, Kaplansky, Rabinov, Ritov etc. Most of them spoke Russian and a few of them Tatarit. After a couple of hundreds of years the two streams of immigration merged and became one division. There was no trace left of the differences. Over the years the merger created the Jewish type of the special "Litvak" character.

Jews who were not particularly fond of the Litvaks criticized them and their supporters blessed them. This is how the late Professor Klausner describes the two groups: "The Lithuanian, i.e. the Lithuanian Jew, is dry: mind wins over feeling. He is "Mithnaged" "refuser" and lacks the sparkle and enthusiasm of the "Hassid."

The Lithuanian is clever, sharp-witted and outwits the Polish Jew and the Podoli-Volini Jew and, needless to say, the German and western-European Jew; however, this cleverness has a certain element of guile, which the Lithuanian uses to cheat the Jews of Poland and the other countries. The Ashkenazi Jews said the Lithuanian Jew's fear of God was not deeply rooted and sincere and he was suspected of concealed heresy and of thinking lightly of religious customs and obligations.

That is how the Lithuanian was criticized, but even his enemies recognized his great attributes:

> "The Lithuanian Jew is a "Talmid Hakham," ("smart student") knows the Torah better than other Jews and takes his Torah with him wherever he goes. On his many wanderings, caused by his poverty, he spreads the word of the Bible. The learned scholars, rabbis, cantors and shamases (caretakers), all these Jews carrying out the religious duties and included in the name "kley kodesh" come from this group. The intellectuals and Hebrew authors come from Lithuania as well, and not only from eastern Europe, most of the "learned men" and Torah teachers come from Lithuania, and this applies to western Europe as well as to the United States."

JEWS IN THE DAYS OF THE KINGS OF LITHUANIA

Under the rule of King Gadiminas the Jews received a bill of rights ensuring protection of body and property as well as freedom of trade, craft and religious observation.

The great prince Vytautas brought Jews to Lithuania, tradesmen and craftsmen, when he fought against the Tatars of the Krim peninsula and southern Russia. At that time he also brought Karaites, a group that separated from the Jews, to Lithuania. Vytautas allowed this tribe to set up a Karaite community in Trakai (1399). This community exists still today.

In 1495 Alexander Jagelon threw the Jews out of Lithuania and confiscated their property. However, in 1503, after he was appointed King of Poland, he allowed them to return and their property was returned.

When Lithuania and Poland merged into one state, the Lithuanian "nobility" received the same rights as the Polish "shlakhte." The situation of the Jews did not improve.

In the 16th century the "**Committee of the Lithuanian State**" was created in which the main communities were represented by leaders ("Heads of State") and rabbis. The "Committee of the Lithuanian State" collected taxes for the requirements of the communities. In 1633 the Jews were granted a bill of rights.

Lithuania became known as a Torah center. Students from Poland and Russia came to the yeshivas there. However, the pogroms of Khmelnitzky - decrees of (1648-9) - destroyed and annihilated the Jews of Lithuania. In 1764 the "Committees of the Lithuanian State" were cancelled and a one-year levy of gold was imposed on every Jew, from the age of one year.

In 1795 the Russians conquered Lithuania and Russification of the population started. The Russians allowed the Jews to attend the general schools and encouraged them to work on the land and in industry.

Czar Nicholas I ordered the enlistment of Jewish youngsters [into the army] and children for 25 years (the "Cantonists"). The children were brought up in peasant homes in Siberia, in the spirit of Christianity, while they were totally cut off from their parents and the Jewish community. Army service was very long. This terrible decree divided the Jewish community, for the rich people found a way to set their children free while the poor Jews were forced to carry out their duty. The "recruitment" of the children was carried out by Jewish kidnappers who handed them over to the authorities.

When Czar Alexander II came to power in Russia he cancelled the "recruitment" of the children and allowed large traders and high-school graduates to settle in the large cities, outside the settlement area. The settlement area was also reduced. The Jews were ordered to live together in small towns. The Czar wanted to spread education among the Jews. And indeed, many of them studied and learned yet did not mingle with the people of the land. Education led the younger generation not only to study and get acquainted with the foreign culture, but also to develop their Jewish-Hebrew culture.

Learned scholars and authors writing in the Hebrew language sprung up from among the Jews. A Jewish printing house of the " Rom Widow and Brothers " was opened. A study center for rabbis and teachers was set up. Indeed, the youngsters made good use of the opportunity to study and gain an education. The custom of a " government appointed community rabbi" was established for purposes of registration etc. (a rabbi who was a graduate of a publicly accepted yeshiva).

Under the rule of Alexander III the situation of the Jews got worse and emigration to Western Europe and the U.S.A. increased. At that time Jews who did not believe in a solution by emigrating from one Diaspora to another set up the **"Khibath Zion"** (Love of Zion) movement, with the aim of emigrating to Eretz Yisrael (the Land of Israel) and establishing Hebrew settlements there.

The first aliyah (immigration) to Eretz Yisrael (the Land of Israel) started in 1882. The Jews of Lithuania were among the first to set up settlements for tilling the land. However, many good youngsters did not chose the way of "Khibath Zion" but devoted their energy and strength to underground activity against the Czarist regime.

In 1897 Dr. Herzl convened the representatives of Hovevey Zion (Lovers of Zion) cfrom all the countries to the Zionist Congress - the first Zionist Congress in Basel. After lengthy debates the Congress decided to establish the **World Zionist Federation**, with the following purpose: "Zionism strives to create a homeland for the people of Israel in the Land of Israel as ensured by general rule." Dr. (Theodore) Benjamin Ze'ev Herzl was elected President of the World Zionist Federation. At first, response to the Zionist Federation was poor, but from one congress to another activities increased, it gained momentum and created tools for building Jewish settlement in historic Eretz Yisrael (the Land of Israel). Lithuanian representatives fulfilled an important task in the congress and subsequent activities.

The second aliyah (1904-1914) was an immigration of unmarried working youngsters, unlike the first immigration, when families arrived with their own financial means.

The Jews of Lithuania showed great sympathy for the activities of the Zionist Federation. In 1903 Dr. Herzl returned from a visit to Russia and stopped in Vilna. He was enthusiastically received by all the Jews of the town.

In 1905 a revolution took place in Russia. The **"Duma" (Parliament)** was elected. The Jews hoped they would be able to participate in government and that their situation would improve. However, after a short while the "Duma" was dispersed and hopes abided.

In World War I (1914-1918) the Jews of the Kovno region were banished to Russia, among them Jews from Yurburg, and only when the war ended were they allowed to return to their homes in independent Lithuania. Vilna was conquered by the Poles and Kovno became the temporary capital. The Jewish population within the reduced borders of Lithuania numbered about 160,000 people, i.e. over 7% of the total population. In the first years of Lithuania's independence the Jews attained **national-cultural autonomy** and self-rule on matters pertaining to the Jews. However, even after the autonomy was canceled, the Jews were allowed to act in the cultural spheres. The primary schools were financed by the government, but did not finance the high schools. The schools in general educated their pupils in a Zionist spirit. And so did the religious schools ("Yavneh"), except for a number of Yiddishist schools. There were large yeshivas as well in Slabodka and Telsh, which were among the most famous in the world. There was a Hebrew Teachers College in Lithuania as well - "Tarbuth" - which was recognized by the government. Furthermore, there was a chair for Hebrew studies at the Lithuanian University in Kovno, headed by Dr. Kh.N. Shapira. A few daily newspapers appeared in Lithuania in Yiddish and Hebrew periodicals. There was a Hebrew drama studio as well and a Jewish theater. Hebrew Jewish student organizations were active at the university. Zionist parties - General Zionists, Youngsters of Zion, Z.S.I. Workers Movement, the Revisionists and Mizrakhi. There were sports clubs as well for the youngsters - Maccabi, V.A.K.and HeKhalutz and HeKhalutz Hatsair, the Scouts, HaShomer Hatsair, Beitar, HaMizrakhi youth movement etc.

In the last years the economic situation of the Jews deteriorated. The Government restricted the tradesmen and forbade them to deal in import-export business; many of them fell into poverty.

When Vilna was annexed to Lithuania, right before World War II, the Jewish population of Lithuania numbered about 250,000 people. The Soviet regime canceled Hebrew education and dismantled the Zionist parties and Zionist youth movements. Many Zionists and rich Jews and yeshivah students were exiled to Siberia.

The Holocaust in Lithuania started the moment the Nazi warriors [soldiers] entered Lithuania. Only few [Jews] managed to escape. Small communities were destroyed and wiped out by the Nazis and their Lithuanian helpers, starting in the first days of the invasion; their belongings stolen and their houses demolished. [The homes were actually left intact and occupied to this day by the local Lithuanians, n.b. Prof. Dov Levin.]

The nationalist Lithuanians organized themselves into "activist partisans" and helped the Nazis to destroy the small communities. Only three communities in fact existed for a longer period of time - Vilna, Kovno and Shavl, where ghettoes were set up for Jews in small areas. At Ponivezh and Keidan there were only labor camps. The Jews in the ghetto were forced to wear a yellow badge. The elderly, children and weak were executed in Kovno **at Fort VII and Fort IX** and in Vilna **at Ponar (Ponari).** The healthy people in the ghettoes were sent to forced labor in towns or labor camps. Many were sent to work in Estonia as well. The living and economic conditions were bad.

The Nazis appointed "Jewish councils" (Eltesten-Rat) at the ghettoes. In Vilna the council was headed by Yakov Gans, a former officer in the Lithuanian army and a teacher of Lithuanian at the Hebrew gymnasium in Yurburg. In Kovno Dr. Elkes headed the Eltesten-Rat and when he died advocate Leib Garfunkel replaced him.

[Dr. Elkes died in Dachau. Garfunkel was a member of the Eltesten Rat-- J.Rosin.]

Underground groups of Jewish youngsters were formed at the ghetto; they collected arms, went into the woods and operated there as partisans, in coordination with the Red Army. There were about 1,000 partisan fighters from Lithuania in the Rudnitski forest.

Thousands of youngsters, who fled to the Soviet Union, joined the Lithuanian division, which fought in the framework of the Red Army against the Nazis in order to free Lithuania.

When the Jewish survivors got together at the end of the war, it transpired that merely 10,000 had survived, and they were but a small percentage of the total former Jewish population of Lithuania. At present most of them live in Vilna and a few in Kovno. There are synagogues in these towns, but in the present situation there is no Jewish community life there as yet. A certain revival is taking place recently among the Jews. A few Jews come on visits to Israel. Although the gates of exit were opened in Lithuania, there is no significant movement of immigration to Israel for the time being.

HISTORY OF THE JEWS OF LITHUANIA

The Jews of Lithuania, who had lived in the land of Lithuania for hundreds of years, lived as in a kibbutz, separated from their neighbors, the country's citizens. The Jews observed their own way of life, which was founded on the Torah and religious duties. The Jews of Lithuania had a great and deeply rooted love of the Torah.

The man who personified the rule of Torah, in the mid-18th century, was **Rabbi Eliyahu Shelomoh-Zalman, called the "Gaon of Vilna"** (1720-1797). "The Gaon of Vilna" and his students, the "Prushim" considered Torah study a guarantee for the survival of the nation, although they did not deny that in order to understand Halakha it was essential to study science. The "Gaon of Vilna" was one of the greatest philosophers and spiritual leaders of the Jews in the new era. He headed the Mithnagdim-Prushim" who fought against Hassidism, because they considered it a deviation from the historical tradition of the Torah. The "Gaon of Vilna" encouraged the establishment of "yeshivoth" and "kolelim" for Torah study, which trained rabbis for the small and large Jewish communities. The most famous yeshivas in Lithuania were - Volozhin, Mir, Slabodka, Telsh etc. Rabbi Kook and Hayim (Chaim) Nakhman Bialik were among those who studied at Volozhin. In his poem "HaMathmid" Bialik expresses his love for the Torah and its studies at the yeshivah.

It is noteworthy that after the death of the "Gaon of Vilna" Rabbi Menakhem Mendel from Shklov came on alyiah to Israel at the head of a large group of Lithuanians and settled first in Safed and then in the old city of Jerusalem. That is how the alyiah of the "Prushim" was able to renew the Jewish-Ashkenazi settlement in Jerusalem.

In the 19th century the Musar (Ethics-Morality) movement was founded in Lithuania, at the initiative of Rabbi Yisrael Salanter (Lipkin) (1810-1882), who wanted to strengthen rabbinical Judaism by studying the Musar theory as a barrier against Khasidism and Haskalah.

Among the well-known rabbis in those days in Lithuania was the Rabbi of Kovno, the Gaon **Rabbi Yitskhak Elkhanan Spektor** (1817-1896), one of the greatest rabbis of his generation. Nahlat Yitskhak in Tel Aviv is named after him. Torah Judaism under the leadership of Rabbi Yitskhak Elkhanan occupied an important place in the Lithuanian community.

The Haskalah. In those days the "Berlin Haskalah" started to spread in the world and in the towns of Lithuania. The rabbis fought against this phenomenon and warned the Jews of Lithuania against the negative effects of this Haskalah that was foreign to the Jewish spirit. The rabbis warned about Jews assimilating with the indigenous population, for this practice was spreading among the German Jews. However, the gentile education, which was spreading in the towns of Lithuania was completely different from that in Germany. Not only did the Haskalah not lead to assimilation, but also it even strengthened the love for the Jewish people and its cultural values. Intellectuals rose up in Lithuania, educated people, authors and poets - such as - Adam Hacohen Levinson, Micha"l, Yalag (Yehudah Leib Gordon) and story-tellers such as Kalman Shulman, Avraham Mapu, Peretz Smolenskin, M.L. Lilienblum, and critics such as A. Kovner, Paperna and others. The Jews, who were educated at the universities, spread general culture among the people and raised its standard.

The life of the Jews in Lithuania was reflected in the work of many writers who were born or lived in Lithuania when they were young and absorbed the special Jewish experience. Examples are Isaac Meir Dick, Mendele Mokher Sefarim ("In Those Days"), Prof. Yosef Klauzner, Ben Avigdor, Y.H. Brener, G. Shofman, Zalman Shneur, Yitskhak Katzenelson, Yakov Cohen, Y.L. Baruch, David Shimoni, A.A. Kabak, H. Lansky, Avraham Kariv etc. And there were writers who wrote memoirs about Lithuania, such as A. A. Lisitzky, M. Vilkansky, Hirshbein, D. Tsherni, Z. Segalovitz, Bergelson, Tsevi (Zvi) Vislavsky, M. Ungerfeld and many many others.

The period between the two World Wars was a time of rejuvenation for Hebrew and Yiddish literature in Lithuania. From this time we remember authors, poets and translators such as Hayim Nakhman Shapira, the son of the Rabbi of Kovno, who was a lecturer of Hebrew literature and language at the Lithuanian university.

Dr. Yehoshua Friedman, Nathan Goren (Greenblat), Yisrael Kaplan, Isidor Eliashev (Ba'al Makhshavoth), Esther Elyashev, Noakh Yitskhak Gotlieb, Yakov Gotlieb, Tsevi Osherowitz, Yehoshua Latsman, Ella Grinstein-Kaplan, Eliezer Heiman, Noakh Stern, Daniel Ben Nakhum, Yakov David Kamzon, Meir Yelin, Yudika, Sarah Aizen, Yosef Gar, Aharon Goldblat etc. Most of them wrote in Hebrew and some of them in Hebrew and Yiddish, others wrote only in Yiddish.

In the thirties a group of Hebrew writers "Patakh" of the Shlonsky-Steinman school became known. Among them were Leah Goldberg, A.D. Shapira (Shapir Dr), Ari Glazman (among the first to perish in the Holocaust), Shimon Gans and others.

The following are the publications that appeared at different times in Hebrew: Hatsofe, Hed-Lita, Netivoth, Olameinu, and Galim, in educational paths edited by Dr. Avraham Kissin. This Week (orthodox), "Ziv," - Hashomer Hatsair- edited by Yakov Gotlieb (Amit) and Daniel Ben Nakhum.

Yiddish literary publications: Vispa, Shliakhen, Mir Alein, Toieren, Bleter, Ringen, Briken etc.

The daily newspapers - in Yiddish: "Yiddishe Shtime" edited by L. Garfunkel (first editor), Reuven Rubinstein; "Dos Wort" edited by Efraim Grinberg and Berl Cohen; "Folksblatt" edited by Dr. Mendel Sudarsky, Yudel Mark and Helena Khatskeles; "Yiddisher Leben" - Agudath Yisrael (short period). In 1940 the newspapers "Yiddishe Shtime" and "Folksblatt" turned into a newspaper called "Emes."

Painters and sculptors in Lithuania. We should mention artists born in small towns, whose creations became known in Lithuania and all over the world; they include Yitskhak Levitan (Kibart), Mark Antokolsky and Iliya Ginzburg, Victor Brener (Shavl), the sculptor Jacques Lipshitz, the painter and sculptor William Zerakh (Yurburg), the painter and sculptor Barukh Shatz (Vorna) - founder of "Betsalel"; Max Band (Neishtot), Arbitblat and Markus, the painter Yekhezkel Straikhman (Sapizhishok), who is now a famous painter in Israel, the painter Abramowitz (in Israel), the paintress Bluma Odes-Ronkin (Plungian), Zelifker, Yudel Pen (Ezhereni), the sculptress Gorshein (in Israel), Liuba Kansky-Shaltofer (in Israel) and many others, some of them perished in the Holocaust. We should also mention the name of Esther Lurie, the painter from the Kovno ghetto.

Hebrew and Yiddish theater. They loved theater in Lithuania. There was hardly a town without a drama circle. Performances were usually in Yiddish and at Hebrew schools in Hebrew. However, real theater at a Yiddish artistic level was not to be found in Lithuania.

Immediately after World War I (1919) Leonid Sokolov, producer and actor on the Russian stage, founded a drama group in Kovno, which performed a few successful plays in Yiddish and Russian. When Sokolov left Lithuania the group dismantled.

From that time on they limited themselves to performances held by theater artists who came from abroad, such as Sigmunt Turkov and Yonas Turkov, who would perform with the assistance of local actors. The performances took place on the stage of the people's house in Kovno and also in other towns.

From time to time reading-artists would also come, such as Hertz Grosbard and Eliyahu Goldenberg, who would read literary passages to the public. The "common people" would fill the hall and be satisfied with what they heard. It should be remembered that there was a regular state theater in Lithuania that performed in the Lithuanian language, attended by quite a few Jews, however, it did not have any Jewish actors.

The Hebrew Studio-A Play with Zalman Levyush, Hayah Sali't (Clara Petrikansky) and her husband the actor and writer Ari Glazman

The Hebrew Studio. The visits by single actors and theater groups from Eretz Yisrael (the Land of Israel) (Habimah, Ohel) prompted the Zionist-Hebrew public to set up a Hebrew studio in Kovno.

Indeed, in 1927 a public committee was set up that founded the Hebrew drama studio. Members of this committee were Nathan Goren (Grinblat), Nakhum Prakhyahu, Dr. Alexander Rosenfeld, Goldfarb, Dr. Jehoshua Friedman and Nathan Shapira. The "Tarbuth" center managed by Dov Lipetz sponsored and supported the establishment of the studio. The "studionists" who were accepted into the studio after meticulous examinations were Nathan Shapira, Rekhava'am Mogiliuker, Zalman Levyush, Hayah (Klara) Petrikansky - Glazman, Ari Glazman, Hayim (Chaim) Leikowitz, Khanokh Paz, Barukh Klas, AdinahYudelevitz, Arieh Volovitzky (Ankorion), Tsevi Osherovitz, David Milner, Mordekhai (Mordechai) Gilda, Khavivah Grinstein-Yizraeli, Nekhamah Meizel, Mrs. Sirkin, N. Gutman, S.Riak and others. Most of them were students at the Lithuanian University.

The studio's producer was Michael Gur, theater actor in Israel, who taught drama and acting. Later on Miriam Bernstein-Cohen joined him as diction teacher.

In 1928 the studio performed the **Peretz party** with 4 stories: "The Death of the Musician," "Venus and Shulamit," "That's The Way " and "Moon Stories. " It was a tremendous success. In 1929 the studio performed **"Scapin's pranks"** by Moliere, a grotesque play. The public and Jewish press in Lithuania loved the performance.

In 1930 the studio performed **"The Tower of Strength" (Migdal Oz) by Ramkhal (Lutsato).** Victor Alekseievitz Gromov, one of the greatest producers in Russia, produced the play, which was extremely successful. The next play was **"The Gold Chain"** by Peretz produced by Rafael Tsevi from the "Ohel." The public fell in love with the play.

When Rafael Tsevi left, some of the actors went to Eretz Yisrael as well, among them: Zalman Leviush, N. Gutman, Khanokh Paz, Barukh Klas, Nathan Shapira, Arieh Volovitky (Ankorion), Adinah Yudelevitz, Nekhamah Maizel and Khavivah Grinstein-Izraeli. In subsequent years the activities of the studio continued at a slower pace until the Red Army entered Lithuania, which resulted in an overthrow of the regime. Yiddish was the language used in Hebrew education in Lithuania and everything connected with it, but this too was merely a matter of time. In 1941, when the Nazis entered Lithuania, everything was turned upside down. The studio disappeared, as did its people, together with all the Jews in Lithuania.

Most of the studio members who had gone to Eretz Yisrael successfully integrated with the theater groups in Israel; Zalman Lebiush became one of the pillars of the Kameri Theater. Khanoch Paz and Barukh Klas spearheaded drama culture on the kibbutz stage. The activities of the studio in Lithuania were not in vein.

The Yoel Engel choir counted 40 singers. Its conductor was Shaul Blekharovitz. The singer and famous soloist was Yonah Varshavsky. The choir's program included oratorio, cantata and popular songs in Hebrew and Yiddish. The choir's performances in Kovno and country towns were an artistic cultural event for the Jewish population of Lithuania.

The choir was founded by the "Tarbuth" center and supported by the Kovno municipality and national educational department. The Jewish public as well as the non-Jews loved the choir.

HEBREW EDUCATION IN LITHUANIA

After World War I the Jews returned from exile in Russia and established new communities in independent Lithuania. In 1919 minority rights were recognized in Lithuania and the Jews gained national autonomy. A Ministry of Jewish Affairs was set up, headed by Dr. Menakhem Soloveichik (Solieli) and Shimshon Rozenbaum.

In those days of glory a broad chain of schools was established for Jewish children. About 60-70% of the schools belonged to the "Tarbuth" trend; i.e. they were Zionist secular schools in the Hebrew language. More than 30-40% of the schools belonged to two other trends. One of them - Agudath Israel - "Yavneh," where studies were conducted in Hebrew.

Nearly 15-20% of the schools belonged to the "Kultur-Lige" trend where all studies were conducted in Yiddish. These schools were supported by the anti-

Zionist "Folks-Partei" (the Folksists) and the "Liebhober fun Wissen" company.

The fact that at over 80% of the schools studies were conducted in Hebrew was quite wonderful, for this was neither the mother tongue nor the language spoken in the area. Nevertheless, the experience was successful in spite of all the problems. The Hebrew school thrived on ground imbibed with the spiritual tradition of Torah and Haskalah.

The Jewish kindergartens were private institutions and were not supported by the government.

The primary schools -first 4 years and then 6 years of study - were governmental. The government subsidized wages to the teachers, and local authorities, municipalities etc., subsidized maintenance expenses for the schools (buildings, janitors etc.).

The pro-gymnasium (5th and 6th grades) were private. The parent committees were in charge of their maintenance.

The gymnasium (14 years of study including kindergarten) was the backbone of Hebrew education in Lithuania. At 9 points of settlement there were 11 gymnasia, as follows: Kovno (5), Shavl, Ponivezh, Mariampol, Virbaln, Vilkovishk, Vilkomir, Rasein and Yurburg. These were private institutions at the expense of the parents committees. Representatives of the government education department signed diplomas.

The Yiddish trend had two gymnasia - one in Kovno (Komertz) and the other in Vilkomir.

"Yavneh" had 4 gymnasia. They too were private institutions, as the others. The "kheders" were dismantled by virtue of the compulsory education law. The "yeshivas" were private and existed in Slabodka (two large yeshivas and smaller ones in Telsh and Ponivezh). In addition to these schools there was a professional school in Kovno, "ORT," which was of a high level.

Teachers colleges. From 1921 the "Tarbuth" center conducted two-year teachers colleges. At first the teachers were "yeshivah" graduates and from 1927 high-school graduates.

A Hebrew college for kindergarten teachers was held in Riga (Latvia) and belonged jointly to the three Baltic countries. The "Yavneh" trend had a teachers and kindergarten teachers college in Telsh, and the Yiddish trend had an annual kindergarten teachers college in Kovno. The parents carried the heavy burden of the educational enterprise, but the Jews of Lithuania managed very well, and they deserve all the credit for this.

Public library. There was hardly a Jewish settlement in Lithuania without a public library or two libraries in Hebrew and Yiddish. There were over 110 libraries in Kovno and country towns and about 120 libraries next to the schools. The Hebrew readers were mainly youngsters, students of the Hebrew schools. There were quite a few readers among the older generation as well.

The residents of Kovno were proud of a large Hebrew library called "Avraham Mapu" with a spacious reading room next to it, where those who were interested could peruse Hebrew books or read Hebrew newspapers.

There was also a Yiddish library in Kovno of the "Liebhober fun Wissen" company. Most Hebrew books printed in Lithuania were test books and but a few were poetry books or novels. The "Tarbuth" center founded the "Ezra" cooperative, which sold books at reduced prices.

VISITS BY WRITERS, ARTISTS AND ZIONIST LEADERS

The visit of a writer, artist or Zionist leader was a festive occasion in Kovno and the country towns. The halls were hardly large enough to hold the numbers of interested people.

Among the stage artists were the visits by "Habimah," "Ohel" and actors who came separately, such as Refael Klatzkin, David Vardi and Khava Yoelith, Michael Gur, Miriam Bernstein Cohen, Amitai and others.

The national poet Hayim (Chaim) Nakhman Bialik visited Lithuania twice and admired the Hebrew schools and their pupils who spoke Hebrew just as well as native Israelis. The writers Shaul Chernikhovsky, Zalman Shneur, Eliezer Steinman and Yitskhak Lamdan, whose cultural origins were to be found in Lithuania, were most impressed by the Lithuanian Jews and their Hebrew-cultural level.

Among the Zionist leaders who visited Lithuania we shall mention M.M. Usishkin, David Ben Gurion, Zeev Jabotinsky, Nakhum Sokolov, Berl Katzenelson, Nathan Bistritzky, Leib Yaffe, Yekhiel Halperin, Alexander Goldschmidt and Tsevi Zohar.

Furthermore, there were emissaries who came to train the members of the youth movements and for fund raising for the building of Eretz Yisrael (the Land of Israel).

THE YOUTH MOVEMENTS

The Hebrew schools scored tremendous achievements in the field of education. However, these impressive achievements of the schools had a junior partner - the youth movement. The blessed activities of the youth movements, in Zionist education, complemented the ideological-educational activity of the schools. Study hours at the schools were limited and it was impossible to find time to instill Zionist values. This is where the youth movement stepped in and taught their members lofty ideals. The movement's activities took place in an educational environment - the club. At the youth clubs the vision of Eretz Yisrael was created and its establishment as a homeland for the people. The aim obliged the members to toil each day for its realization. That accounted for the activity on behalf of the Jewish National Fund, fundraising for the purchase of land to make the desert bloom.

That is why there was a "Blue Box" at home and that is why funds were raised for the realization of the Zionist dream.

An atmosphere of Eretz Yisrael was created at the youth clubs; the members spoke Hebrew and prepared themselves for training and going on alyiah to the pioneer village, the kibbutz. The story of the youth movement is a wonderful story, full of the majestic splendor of the boys and girls whose lives, regretfully, were lost too soon, following the tragic events of the Holocaust.

The following are the youth movements that were active in independent Lithuania between the two World Wars: **Hashomer Hatsair** (59 branches - 3200 members); **Hashomer Hatsair Hatsofi Khalutzi** (34 branches, 1350 members); **Hekhalutz Hatsair** (15 branches - 1000 members); **Beitar** (38 branches - 1500 members); **Gordonia** (32 branches - 700 members); **Hanoar Hatsiyoni** (4 branches - 155 members); **Noar Khalutzey Hamishmar** (129 members), **Noar Z.S.** (Eretz Yisrael Haovedeth) - details are missing.

Sports organizations: "Maccabi"; "Hapoel" and "Hakoakh"; I.A.K.-Yiddisher Atletik Klub.

Students organizations: Beitariah (90); **Herzliyah** (38); **Yardeniah** (80); **Al Hamishmar** (129 members); **Noar Z.S.** (Eretz Yisrael Haovedeth) - details are missing.

(The above data are derived from "The Book of Lithuanian Jewry" - according to registration from 1931).

LITHUANIAN JEWS' CONTRIBUTION TO ERETZ YISRAEL (THE LAND OF ISRAEL)

The Lithuanian Jews' love of Eretz Yisrael was deeply rooted and was reflected in study of the Torah, prayers and yearning for redemption. From the alyiah of the *HaGaon Reb Eliyahu (HaGaon MiVilna)*, students -the Mithnagdim-Prushim in the 18th century, the Lithuanian Jews' spiritual ties with Eretz Yisrael grew. Among the "Gaon" students were people of mind and matter, such as the Rivlin and Salomon families, who set up new neighborhoods around the old city of Jerusalem and agricultural settlements all over the country.

When many new immigrants had problems they set up a financial enterprise - the Rabbi Meir Ba'al Hanes fund - in support of the Jews in Eretz Yisrael.

Following the alyiah of the "Gaon" students, other immigrants started to come, initially very slowly, who decided to expand settlement of the country. These were the well-known Rabbis Kalisher, Alkalai and Shemuel Mohliver, from Lithuania, after whom kibbutz "Gan Shemuel" is named.

Before the Shivath Zion movement was formed, Eliezer Ben Yehudah (Perlman) came from Lithuania and he enthusiastically spread the Hebrew word. Young people, mostly students in Russia, founded Bilu - Beth Ya'akov

Lekhu veNelkha (Isiah II: 5), and they went to Eretz in order to make the desert bloom. Among these immigrants were also a Bilui from Kretingen in Lithuania, Huravin, among the founders of Gedera and its head.

Other Biluim spread out all over the country and devoted their efforts to settlement.

That is how the first alyiah started. About 10-15 agricultural settlements were established, many of them by Lithuanian immigrants assisted by Baron Edmund Rothschild.

When the Zionist Federation was founded by **Dr. Theodore (Benjamin Ze'ev) Herzl** at the first Zionist Congress in Basel (1897) influential representatives from Lithuania took part. One of them - a Jew from Erzhvilki near Yurburg - Prof. Tsevi Shapira made a practical proposal at the Congress to establish the "Jewish National Fund" for redemption of land and settlement. Herzl's faithful assistant, David Wolfson, is the man Herzl describes in his book "Altneuland" as its central character - the " Litvak."

After Herzl's death (1904) **the" Litvak," David Wolfson,** was elected second President of the World Zionist Federation (Kibbutz "Nir David" is named after him).

Many youngsters from Lithuania took part in the second alyiah (1904-1914) - the workers' alyiah - they were Hebrew workers and laid the foundations of a new way of life - the kibbutz - "Deganiah" (M. Busel). They also founded the Hashomer organization (Yisrael Shokhat, Alexander Zeid and others).

Later on, in the third alyiah (1918-1924), of the pioneers, the pioneers from Lithuania were among the founders of the "Gedud Ha'avodah," drained the swamps, paved the roads and settled in the Jezreel valley.

In the fourth alyiah (1924-1929) the Jews from Lithuania contributed towards the building of Tel Aviv and industrial development; by the way, the founder of Tel Aviv and its living spirit was Akiva-Arieh Weiss, from Lithuania. Then there was Avraham Krinitsi, among the founders of Ramat Gan, and its mayor for many years. Zerakh Barnet as well, was among the founders of Petakh Tikvah.

In the fifth alyiah (1929), the last before World War II, many wanted to go on alyiah from Lithuania, old and young, but the hostile mandate authorities prevented them from doing so. The few who came on alyiah were members of the pioneer youth movements, who went to till the land; they set up tens of "Khomah uMigdal" ("Tower and Stockade") settlements and guarded and protected in the days of the bloody clashes and in the World War against the Nazi enemy.

The Jews of Lithuania contributed and left their mark on all spheres of life and creation in Eretz Yisrael; on each clod of land that was redeemed, on each stone that was upturned, and each settlement that was erected.

When the State of Israel was born, only a small part of the Jews of Lithuania were fortunate enough to fulfill their dream. Those who came from Lithuania and settled in Israel, took place in the building and establishment of the State - its institutions, government, science, defense, law, economy, culture and education.

It is a great pity and to be regretted that many people from Lithuania who yearned to witness the creation of the State of Israel and to live there - did not have the good fortune to do so. May their memory live on forever, in the work and creation of the Lithuanian Jews in Israel.

Zevulun Poran

Center of Yurburg with Synagogue on upper right, Beis Midrish is white building. [Photo not in original book. From photo album of J. Cossid.]

Chapter 2
THE FAMILIES

239   Karabelnik Family - Hanna Karabelnik-Trainin
240   Rudenski Family - David-Mordekhai (Mordechai) Rudenski
241   Rabinovitz Family - Yakov Rabinovitz
242   Rochzo Family - Yisrael Rochzo
243   Raizman Family - Sarah Raizman-Yagolnitzer
245   Rikler Family - Aharon Rikler
246   Shmulovsky Family - Avraham Shmulovsky
247   Shtern-Fin Family - Erika Katz

Arnstein Family in 1911
Standing: Uncle(?), Israel, Jacob
Sitting Middle Row:Aunt(?),Tsvia, Dora
Sitting: Yudl, Moritz

Arnstein Family in 1934
Standing: Yudl,Dora,Moritz
Sitting from left: Parents,
Tsvia and Jacob (physician)

[These photos not in original book]
Photos Courtesy of Roy Thacker (Arnstein Family Descendant)

TRANSLATION OF PAGES 117 - 122

The Story of the Escape and Remnant of My Family

By Alizah Leipziger-Porath

I was born in Lithuania, in Yurburg, close to the German border. Merely 10 kilometers (6 miles) separated Yurburg from the little German town of Smalininken. Yurburg was built on the slopes of a modest mountain, on the northern shore of the Nieman River. Two streams, the Imstra and the Mituva, crossed the town and flowed into the Nieman - they made the landscape even more beautiful. The influence of the German town's proximity was felt and was very important to the culture of our daily life.

I loved Yurburg. I always pronounced the name of our town with great reverence and pride. I loved everything about it - the rivers, the lush greenery, the parks and fields, the pine forests with their flora and fauna. I even loved the reptiles and insects, and all the different kinds and colors of mushrooms. I was always enchanted by the view. There is no sight more beautiful than the river Nieman, flowing slowly along the rows of trees and shrubs on both sides. I remember that as children we used to sail the river on boats, a sort of green crown above our heads, sunrays peeping though the clouds and caressing our cheeks. . . The song of birds also warmed our hearts. A sweet smell of flowers growing in the fields filled the air. Oh, how lovely!

In winter the rivers froze and were covered by a thick layer of ice. We would skate on the ice and slide down the snow-covered hills in small snow sleds, our cheeks stinging from the cold. The air was cold and fresh and our hearts filled with a beautiful feeling. We had four seasons in Lithuania, our home country, and each season had its own charm. I remember that as a pupil at the Hebrew Gymnasium, I would always look at the beautiful landscape of Yurburg. After some time, when I had already left Yurburg and gone to stay at the *'Tarbuth"* Teachers College in Kovno, and also when I was a teacher in little Lithuanian towns, I would long for my town and be happy to return to it, spend my holidays there and enjoy the beautiful view, which I remembered so well from my childhood. True, when I taught at a certain town I saw beautiful views and enchanting greenery all around, but they did not capture my heart.

I was attracted to "my own landscape," felt particularly close to it, a certain intimacy that was different from the feelings I had in other places.

When I had a day off from my studies, I would get up early in order to stroll all by myself along the fields and forests that were damp from the night's dew, till I would arrive at the giant "mushroom tree" that would cast its shadow on a hot day over the tired pedestrians who had come a long way. In that early morning hour I could feel the world awakening and I was overcome by emotions.

I loved to gather mushrooms. I was an expert at distinguishing between the different kinds of mushrooms and called them by name. I was not in the habit of picking flowers, for it was a pity to see them wilt instead of enhancing the beauty of the landscape. When I returned home, after a tiring but pleasant walk, I would share my feelings with my friends. I remember their reaction - "you are a poet, or you will be a poet." I regret to say that their prophecy and that of my literature teachers did not come true. I continued to love nature and be enchanted by its beauty, but I kept my feelings to myself and did not put them on paper.

At the end of town there was a beautiful and well cared for park, crossed by the Mituva River. Next to this river stood a glorious palace built by the Russian Kniaz (prince) Vasilshchikov, where he and his family spent the summer months. In the other seasons of the year he lived in St. Petersburg. The prince and princess would organize splendid parties when they stayed at the palace to which many guests were invited, but no Jews . . ..

One day a luxurious carriage drawn by two big horses stopped next to our home, the home of my parents. In the carriage sat the prince's messengers, who had come to invite my mother, Devorah-Leah Laiptsiger (Leipziger), to the palace. My mother, who was a very gifted seamstress, was asked to sew dresses for the princess and her daughters.

One day my father, Yitskhak Leipziger, was also invited to come and paint all sorts of decorative paintings at the palace. My father had the soul of an artist. He knew how to paint ceiling and floor paintings in beautiful colors, true craftsmanship. He was quite famous. He was often invited to Germany to paint the walls of public buildings and the homes of the rich. He would work from morning till night, together with his assistants. My sisters my brother and we saw very little of him at home, especially in the peak years of his work, when he was still in good health. After a while, he contracted cancer and his health deteriorated by the day. In spite of this, he continued to work, when he could no longer leave his studio at home and would paint billboards, panels, walls and ceiling decorations with truly mathematical accuracy.

He developed a special technique with his intuition. The walls of our home were also covered in paintings he had created. He was a very gifted artist.

I remember a small violin hanging on the wall of my parents' bedroom. I had forgotten this for many years. Once, on one of those evenings when former residents of Yurburg gathered together, one of them came up to me and said - "do you know that your father made a violin and played it very well?" I did not know what to reply. I was astonished at myself for forgetting such an important detail - testimony to my father's musical talent. And my friend from Yurburg went on to praise my parents, brother and sisters.

I have never seen my parents sit still. My mother would sew till all hours of the night, for she had a lot of work. There was a very long queue waiting to be accepted by her. The "customers" would sometimes wait for months, although she had a number of assistants and apprentices who learned to sew with her.

My oldest sister, Rachel, worked together with my mother, and after my sister Hannah completed cutting and sewing courses in Kovno, she also joined my mother's sewing workshop and took a successful part in the work. It was the dream of every girl that when she would grow up my mother would sew her wedding dress. Indeed my mother, kind soul that she was, would try to accommodate all those who approached her. My mother invested exquisite taste in every task she had to carry out and did so with all her heart. Her customers were very fond of her; they would talk to her and cling to every word she said for my mother was a clever woman with a wonderful sense of humor. Gentiles too were among her customers and she received them very graciously.

The more I think about my mother, the more I admire her. One of the most sacred missions in my mother's life was to give a good education to her children; I studied at the "Kheder" and afterwards at the Russian school. At that time Lithuania was of course under Russian rule. The first letter I wrote in my life was in the Russian language. My mother also saw to it that I studied music, and sent me to study the piano. For a couple of years I studied with a piano teacher, although I was not particularly talented in music.

In August 1914 World War I broke out. The Germans invaded Yurburg and conquered it. My parents were somehow convinced that bad things would happen to us under German rule and decided to escape. "Where to?" - this they did not know. My grandfather - my mother's father Dov Berlowitz- came in a carriage drawn by one horse and all of us sat down in it, with all our belongings, and left for Erzhvilki, not far from Yurburg. We traveled by night and when dawn broke we arrived at the little town which was buried in mud. We were told that Tsevi-Herman Shapira, founder of the Keren Hakayemet, was born here, and the townspeople were very proud of this fact. The late Shapira was a well-known scientist in the line of mathematics, and was a professor at Heidelberg University in Germany. A building was put at our disposal in this little town; it was actually the frame of an unfinished building. However, even before we managed to remove our belongings and take a rest we already heard the approach of horses. These were horsemen of the German army . . . and in the meantime, in the uproar, my mother had disappeared - "where is mother?" - we asked, but she was gone. After two hours she returned with good news - she had found a Rabbi who agreed to teach my brother Eliezer who was two years older than me, Jewish studies - I, said my mother, would be taught by my sisters. My sister Rachel would teach me Russian and my sister Hannah would teach me mathematics. That is how my mother temporarily solved the problem that worried her most, namely our studies. As far as I remember we remained "stuck" in Erzhvilki, the little town with its two dozen families, for a whole year. From Erzhvilki we went to Raseiniai, which was a real town compared to Erzhvilki. In Raseiniai we had a relative, a woman who was a teacher by profession. As the schools were closed in those days, the teacher agreed to teach my brother Eliezer and me all the study material, until better days would come. My mother took care of the household.

After a while we went back to our home in Yurburg and everything returned to normal. Once again we had an orderly home. We were a happy family, but my mother always thought of others, the poor and needy. As I was the youngest of the family, my mother would send me every Friday on missions of "mathan besether" (anonymous donations) to the needy - khaloth (Sabbath bread) for the Sabbath for some, fish for others etc. - always with a warm heart and very generously. We had all we needed at home. In summer my mother would already prepare food for winter and in winter food for summer. The house was clean and well cared for; everything was in its place and in good taste.

My mother was a clever woman, always looking for more knowledge. She loved to read, read the daily paper in Yiddish in order to be up to date on what went on in the world, but did not forget to read the "romantic serial" in the paper; my mother was an ardent reader. She read all kinds of books and novels, but also read "Tzena u'rena" (special book for Jewish women) on the Sabbath. My mother was observant. She observed the Sabbath and kashruth rules. My father was even more observant in carrying out religious duties. In spite of the observant atmosphere at home, our home was open to the spirit of the time. How happy she was, my mother, when she heard that her son Eliezer, the lawyer, had been appointed Principal of the Hebrew Gymnasium in Yurburg, there was no end to her excitement; she always strove to enable her children to acquire an education and now her efforts had borne fruit.

On the Sabbath and religious holidays we would go for a walk in the large park, to enjoy a restful Sabbath and holiday in nature. On religious holidays we would receive guests at home and have a good time together. We always lived with others and among others, and never remained aloof.

One morning, very suddenly, the Nazi hooligans took over Yurburg, and the people of our town and the members of our family were doomed to die in all sorts of strange ways - as is well known. The Jews of Yurburg were murdered; they were led to the forests near Smalininken, and to the cemetery and other places where they died a cruel death.

In the first days of the Nazi invasion they left my mother and sister Hannah alive and ordered them to sew uniforms for the Germans; day and night they would sew, day and night, terrified. They sewed and sewed, until the bitter end.

I heard this terrible story after a while from my cousin Shelomoh Goldstein, the only survivor in my family.

There are not enough words to speak about my home in Yurburg, the town where I was born.

My family home is like a fairy tale in my mind that was destroyed and is no more.

Now everything has been wiped out, my whole family and the entire town, which I loved so much . . ., and I, the only one to remain, I am still alive.

I was fortunate enough to go to Israel. I built a home at kibbutz "Afikim" together with my beloved Yitskhak.

For many years I was a teacher in Israel to a generation that continues and lives on forever.

Afikim

Family of Alizah Leipziger-Porath

Members of my family: me and my sister Rachel, with Mother sitting, my brother Eliezer, my Father Yitzhak sitting, and my sister Hannah.

This is a photo of Zvi Leipziger, brother of Eliezar Leipziger and Elisa Porat. He had left Yurburg when the above photo was taken. Photo supplied by his granddaughter, Janice Hutton. Photo was not in the original Yizkor Book.

MEMORIES OF MY PARENTS HOME

By Bluma Heselkovitz-Feldman

A long time ago we had a garden in Yurburg, the town where I was born, a large garden with many fruit trees. On the other side of the garden there were parcels of land where vegetables were grown. From the early days of childhood I remember the garden; I can see the large trees, blooming in many colors in spring, full of fruit in summer, bare in fall and crowned with snow in winter. I was deeply conscious of the silence of the garden in summer, the whistling of the leaves in fall, the secret whispering sounds - all the occurrences of nature when the seasons changed- all this is deeply engraved on the memories of my early years.

I loved our home and garden. I knew all its paths and the hidden corners where I sometimes found refuge.

A large gate opens onto Kovno Street, the main street of our town, and leads to a dirt road, which led to our house at the end of the garden. It was a handsome country home, original in style. We did not inherit the house and garden around it from our ancestors.

I learned from what my parents told me that a German nobleman, called Rauwald, built it for himself and invested a fortune in it, to improve it inside and outside. However, somehow, things took their course, the house was up for sale, and my father - the late Shakhna - bought the house and all around it.

I felt extremely fortunate to live in this house, and especially to spend time in the lovely garden. My friends often paid us a visit; we used to stroll in the garden and had a good time in the corners of our estate. I almost forgot to mention our dog Sarik, who was tied to a rope and guarded our property. Thus we lived a country life inside a Jewish town.

My late mother, Zelda, worked in the corners of the garden, where we set aside parts of land for a vegetable garden, she bent over the flower beds, together with her maid, a foreign woman. My mother loved to work in the garden and spent many days and evenings in it, hot summer days and rainy and cold winter days. My mother came from the country and she found it difficult to get used to city life. As all Jewish women in those days, she was diligent and devoted to her family and household. However, above all, she loved to work in the vegetable garden, which was at the center of her life and also constituted a source of living. To us, children, she would repeatedly say: " in our time there were no schools and gymnasia, and we could not acquire an education and fill our heads with knowledge, but you can do so. Learn - "Lernt, Kinderlekh!" (I.e. you must study children). And indeed we studied, thanks to our mother, for we knew that she worked hard for our benefit and looked after us with devotion. Our father was occupied with his business affairs, and most days of the week he did not take part in the daily family life.

Thanks to mother, who took care of all our needs, we were able to make progress in our studies, even when an economic crisis befell the Jews of Lithuania in general and our family in particular. These were difficult days, days of need and distress for many people in Yurburg. The Lithuanian government started to impose trade restrictions on the Jews, so that many of them were left destitute.

In those days we were forced to rent a wing of our house to the principal of the Hebrew Gymnasium, Mr. Mordekhai (Mordechai) (Mordechai) Taikhman, and his family. My mother regretted this, for she was used to space and privacy, but we, children considered it a great honor to live close to such an important person as the principal of the Gymnasium.

On the other hand, my mother was very happy that the rent paid for our studies at the Gymnasium. My sister, Jafah (Yaffa), "*Sheine*" in Yiddish, who was a year older than I, and I studied together at the primary school and gymnasium. We loved each other very much and were very close. My mother was pleased to see her daughters make good progress in their studies.

Every achievement in our studies and every time we advanced to a higher grade, i.e. made progress in our studies, my mother was very happy and glad.

When the economic situation in Lithuania grew worse and the situation became desperate, the sources for covering the expenses involved in our studies at the gymnasium, which were very expensive, dried up and then my father decided to sell the house and garden, and move to a smaller and more modest home. My mother, who was extremely preoccupied with the continuation of our studies at the gymnasium, had no choice but to agree to sell the house. "Studies are more important," she said. My mother was deeply sorry to leave her home and garden, for which she had cared so diligently, and her sole consolation was that her daughters would study at the gymnasium and acquire a broad education, as was necessary at the time.

The days at the gymnasium were the happiest period of my life. I also took an interest in the social life at the gymnasium and liked it very much: lectures and parties, study circles and above all- reading books. Apparently my soul longed for solitude. The house, the garden, the abundant nature around us contributed to this.

In the framework of this story, I should also mention the activity of the "Hebrew Scouting" youth movement, as it was called at first, and later on "*Hashomer Hatsair (Young Watchmen)*." My sister Jafah and I belonged to the movement almost from its beginning. The movement brought us together. We were groups of youngsters who were linked by bonds of friendship. The movement educated us to do well, and here we acquired Zionist and humanistic values. For a while I was a madrikha (youth leader) of a group of "*khaverim*" (friends) some of whom went on aliyah to Eretz Yisrael, to live there and take part in its building. There have always been ups and downs in life, happy occasions and sad ones. And one day, all of a sudden, a terrible tragedy happened to us. It was a tragic event, which I shall never forget.

We had five children in our family - the oldest sister, Hayah, two sons, and again two daughters - Jafah and me, the youngest. My oldest brother was called Menakhem (Mendel in Yiddish) and the other was called Moshe. They were both healthy, strong young men, members of the "Maccabi" sports club in Yurburg. They were both successfully active in various branches of sports. Moshe was an excellent soccer player. He was a member of team A and was the best player in it; he was much admired on the soccer field. He was extraordinarily fast, flexible and knew how to outwit the opponent, an admired sportsman.

Maccabi was proud of him. He was the outstanding player on the team. One day a match took place between "Maccabi" and a Lithuanian soccer team. The game was full of tension and very fierce, as it was decisive as to who would be the champion team in town. Moshe remained cool; he was full of self-confidence and courage, as usual; he protected his goal and warded off the ball of the competing Lithuanian team; the goal of this team a constant threat during the game. The players of the Lithuanian team knew Moshe and were aware of his power and ability, therefore they were on the lookout for him all the time and bothered him. When Moshe burst through the opponent's goal - the Lithuanian players jumped on him, and one of them, a cruel young man, threw him to the floor and strangled him - - -

It was a terrible tragedy to our family. His friends at "Maccabi" were deeply shocked and all the Jews in Yurburg and Lithuania were very sad. The Jewish press in Lithuania gave extensive coverage to the obnoxious and unforgettable murder. This added a black page to the relations between the Jews of Yurburg and their Lithuanian neighbors. My mother was shattered by this terrible tragedy. She could hardly overcome the disaster. Her hair grew white and she was depressed. Although she continued to work in the vegetable garden, it was not the same as before. The "Maccabi" federation in Lithuania erected a tombstone on Moshe's grave, and many attended the unveiling ceremony. This is what was written on the tombstone:

> **Memorial Stone**
> **To the holy and innocent soul of**
> **Mosheh-Tsevi Heselkovitz**
>
> **Our heroic and modest friend**
> **Who was slain**
> **By a cruel hand**
> **For "Maccabi" and its honor**
> **And the splendor of his youth**
> **Was darkened forever**
> **On 20 Sivan 5686**
>
> **May his blood that was spilt**
> **Be the seal of "Maccabi" for faith and innocence**

For people and country
May God protect his soul
With the souls of our brothers
Who die for you
Always and ever

Gravestone of Moshe Heselkovitz, (the brother of Bluma and Sheine). "Maccabi" soccer player. From left: Moshe Krelitz, Yoske Miasnik, Headstone, Rochzo, Rozansky, Frank, Feivel Chossid, Hannah Magidovitz (Identification by Jack Cossid) Photo by Moshe Krelitz

When my sister Jafah and I finished our studies at the Hebrew Gymnasium in Yurburg, at the end of the twenties, we left our home and place of birth, carrying with us memories of joy mixed with sorrow.

I studied at the Lithuanian University in Kovno, and my sister Jafah - at the "Red Cross" medical institute, where she trained to be a nurse. We both strove to realize our dream to go to Eretz Yisrael. When we got married, we decided to go on aliyah. I was the first to go, and a year later (1935) my sister too emigrated, after finishing her training in the *"Hekhalutz"* movement.

My sister Jafah built her home in Pardes-Hanna and she is a nurse at the "Kupath Kholim" (General Health Fund) of the Histadruth (Workers Union); she brought up her children to be respectable people in the midst of a happy family.

I built my home in Tel Aviv, the large Hebrew city - the commercial and cultural center of the entire country. When my only daughter was three years old, I went to visit my family in Lithuania; I enjoyed the beautiful green landscape of summer, the fresh forests and rivers full of water.

However, I walked among the people as a stranger in the country where I had been born and raised. I asked myself: "what am I doing here?" And I quickly returned to my own home and country. My daughter presently has a son and daughter and we we have two grandchildren, one of them is an aspiring pilot in the IDF Airforce while I am writing these lines (1976).

The moment we left Lithuania we cut off the physical ties, but the family tie always linked us to it; we left parents behind, a married sister, a brother and quite a few relatives. When World War II broke out and Hitler's army invaded Lithuania, their destiny was as bitter as that of the other Jews in town; they were all murdered by the beasts, and their place of burial is unknown. My oldest sister had four daughters; all of them perished in the terrible Holocaust. The only one to be saved was my brother Mendel, who was an officer in the Soviet army when the Germans invaded Yurburg. He went to Russia with his unit and remained there till the end of the war. After many hardships he found his wife and only son in Tiflis in *Gruziya* (Russian Georgia), a war invalid. After the war my brother Mendel returned to Lithuania and lived there. He did not have the good fortune to come to Israel, as he had hoped and planned. He died and was buried in Vilna.

The dim sounds and views of Yurburg, which was a world full of experiences to us, are slowly vanishing, and here today we live our lives, which are entwined with the life of our country. **To us the development and achievements of our country are the revenge on the gentiles who inflicted the Holocaust on our town and all the Jews of Lithuania.**

As long as we live on this earth we shall never forget the cruelty and degradation of the Nazis and their Lithuanian helpers who destroyed our beloved community.

TRANSLATION OF PAGES 129 - 141

Me and My Family in Yurburg

By Shoshanah Petrikansky-Knishinsky

I have a bad conscience - and I feel guilty - for not having written many years ago about my life in Yurburg, where I was raised and grew up. Time takes its course. The personal and family events, the landscape and surroundings get blurred with the years that pass, and even the most striking personal memories of experiences disappear as if they had never taken place. I have to make an effort, therefore, to try to bring back the memory of some of the impressions that are still engraved on my brain and conscience.

It was therefore a very good idea of the "Association of Former Residents of Yurburg" to decide to publish this memorial book about wonderful Yurburg in order to remember and record our memories the town, its residents and life, the Jewish town that was and is no more.

My family - the Petrikansky family - was a large and well-known family in Yurburg, consisting of nine people - parents and seven children, four sons and three daughters.

My mother's name was Malkah and my father's name was Yehudah, although everyone called him Alter.

My sisters - Clara and the late Rachel. My name is Roza or Rozka, as my friends and acquaintances used to call me. In Israel I adapted as my name to the Hebrew name Shoshanah. The names of my brothers - Zevulun (Poran), may he have a long life, and Yakov, Moshe and Yitskhak, blessed be their memory. My mother, Malkah, was a woman of average height, with pale and fine features, soft-spoken and with a perpetual smile on her lips. I have never heard her raise her voice at her children. My father, on the other hand, was a strong man, dark-skinned, broad-shouldered, good-natured. His prime concern was to look after his family. He always wanted the best for us. My parents were a truly ideal couple. We were a close-knit and happy family. Everyone took care not only of himself but also of the others. We grew up in a warm atmosphere, pleasant and calm. We absorbed important and useful values from our parents, which molded our personality and served as a guiding light throughout our life. My parents were virtuous people, hospitable and gracious, and therefore our home was always full of guests and friends, who would come to ask for advise and assistance or merely for a friendly chat; usually boys and girls would come.

We lived in the center - on Kovno Street, the town's main street - named after the capital of Lithuania in those days. Our house stood opposite the main square near the great synagogue, which was famous all over Lithuania, and the prayer house. Many Jews from Lithuania and other countries would come to see the synagogue with its beautiful architecture, built in 1790, a wooden building which looked like an Indian pagoda. The special features of the building were the pulpit, holy ark, and Eliyahu's chair - made of wood carvings of animals, flowers, birds etc. *[photos of the pulpit and Eliyahu's chair can be found in the section on the synagogue on pages 321 to 329]*.

The surroundings of our home were not always quiet. Once or twice a week farmers from the area would come to the square on the other side of the street to sell their wares to the town's Jews. In those days the square was full of people and when the farmers would get drunk on alcohol, the "goyim" (gentiles) would be merry and the Jews had nothing to lose from the noise and uproar.

Let me speak about our home again - a striking building rising slightly above the area around it. A number of stairs led to the main entrance at the front of the house; there was another entrance as well, which led to the house through a moderately sized yard, with a stone floor and with a fence around it. We always had various kinds of flowerbeds in the yard, which had a wonderful smell in spring and summer. My mother took good care of these flowerbeds. The house was not particularly large and when guests would come to visit it was rather crowded.

The house included four living rooms and a large kitchen. One of the rooms was particularly large and it served as a reception room. The corridor on the side of the yard stairs led to the second floor. There was a corridor there with cupboards. An average-size room too, which was furnished and here the girls stayed. From the window of the room the square could be seen with its buildings and also-further away- the Nieman River and the area beyond it. I loved my room, where I would host my girlfriends, and where we would do our homework - and where we would, of course, talk, laugh and spend many wonderful hours together, the beautiful years of our youth.

Yurburg was known as a town of trade and crafts. As it was situated on the banks of the Nieman River, most of its merchandise was connected with business that had to do with the large river. Many tradesmen had steamships, called "Dampfer" in Yiddish.

Instead of a railway-track the Yurburg traders had a "Nieman track." The steamships would transport passengers and goods, mainly from Kovno, along the river, up to Yurburg and from Yurburg to Memel (Klaipeda) on the shores of the Baltic Sea, to the west of Lithuania. The Yurburg traders exported farming produce and imported industrial goods from Germany. The trip from Yurburg to Memel was very interesting. On one side of the Nieman there was a Lithuanian area and on the other side a German area with the large city of Tilzit and not far from there Koenigsberg, previously the capital of Prussia.

The parents of my friends Judith and Sheinke Levinberg owned steamships so did other Jews in Yurburg, as well as Christians who were partners in the ownership of the steamships. All the business activity on the steamships and around them was the economic basis of the Jews in Yurburg. As it was said: "the Jews of Yurburg live on the Nieman and make a living from the Nieman."

We, children, loved the Nieman and mainly loved to sail on the steamships. I remember the first day I sailed together with my parents to relatives in Kovno. It was wonderful. A lovely experience. The Jews from Kovno also liked to visit Yurburg on festive occasions and just for a rest.

My father was a businessman, but he was not directly connected with the steamship business. As my father dealt in linen and linen seeds (Zamen in Yiddish) destined for export, he too used the steamships for transporting the merchandise abroad. The linen and linen seeds business was a very important branch of export. Behind our house there was a large, long yard where my father had a plant for processing the linen. Yakov-Shelomoh Vainberg (Weinberg) was his partner. Many Lithuanian men and women worked at the lab.

In the same yard, at a certain distance from our home, Leib (Leon) Bernstein, my mother's brother lived with his wife, Vitel, and three daughters, Clara, Mikhalina and Dora. Uncle Bernstein was a large-scale linen trader. He exported linen to various countries in Western Europe and a famous businessman in Lithuanian economic circles. He was a member of the "Handels-Kammer" - the national trade council. He went on many trips abroad on business matters, made friends and was trusted by the businessmen there. He was very wealthy and expanded his business from time to time. When my uncle left Yurburg, together with his family, they went to live in Kovno. At that time an "economic revolution" took place in Lithuania.

 The government, in accordance with the new policy, transferred all business to the Lithuanians. This was a severe blow to the Jews. Their source of living was destroyed. However, Leon Bernstein was rather fortunate. All the linen business in the northern district of Lithuania was given to him. He therefore moved to Shavli, where he built a luxurious home and set up a plant for linen processing called "Semlinas." When business was restricted, my uncle transferred some of his business abroad. The government policy seriously affected the Jewish businessmen in Lithuania and in Yurburg. The life of the Jews in Yurburg became very hard. Entire families fell into poverty. My father was also seriously affected. For lack of choice my father left Yurburg and tried his luck in Poland, where the government policy did not affect the linen business of the Jews and they could export linen abroad. However, my father did not succeed in his business there, and he returned to Lithuania. Uncle Leon Bernstein was happy to let my father work at his "Semlinas" plant in Shavli and gave him an important managerial position. We then moved from Yurburg to Kovno. We were very sad to leave Yurburg, even though the last years of our stay in Yurburg were difficult from the economic point of view, as we were a large family. In spite of all the problems it was nice to live in Yurburg, absorb the atmosphere of its refreshing surroundings and its cultural and social experience. Were it not for the economic crisis that befell all of us, it would never have occurred to us to leave Yurburg.

To this very day I remember every corner of our home and the workdays and the holidays. My parents were not orthodox, but I would say they were observant, like most Jews in Yurburg. My mother conducted a traditional household and observed the rules of kashruth. On Sabbath there was a very nice atmosphere at home. On Friday my father would come home early from work in order to put on festive clothes and go to the synagogue, my younger brothers would usually join him. When my father returned from the synagogue he would say *"A gut-Shabes, A gut Shabes"* i.e. "have a good Sabbath." Then we would get ready for our meal. Everyone sat in his fixed place. The candles were burning on the table, the *Khaloth* (challas) were covered by an embroidered cloth and my father would bless the Khaloth in the traditional melody Then my mother would serve the "lokshen (noodle)" soup and then the meat with dressings and finally the stewed fruit dessert.

The next day we would go through the same ritual of the meal again, but the menu was more opulent. First of all wine and "kikhlakh" (cookies) would be served and then fish or liver, then soup and meat with "tsimes" and also "cholent," and dessert. By the end of the meal we would all be drowsy and quiet. And then father would say - "it is a pleasure to sleep on the Sabbath." The youngsters would not give in to the"minister of sleep" and slip out for an excursion or activities at the youth movement.

When I try to remember those days, I feel that all the family occasions of my youth were so beautiful and fascinating, and they left such a strong impression, that they are impossible to wipe from memory. Many things were forgotten, but the impression made by the holidays and Sabbath accompany me all my life.

The Herzl Hebrew Gymnasium where I, my brothers and sisters, studied, was situated in the "Tel Aviv Park" park, as it was called by the Jews of Yurburg. The park was not particularly large. There were splendid old trees in it, bushes and flowers. There were paths all along the park. There were charming romantic corners with benches where people could rest. The inhabitants of Yurburg loved to stroll in this park, for it was close to the center of town, where the Jews lived. Nevertheless, they did not forego the large park of the "goyim" (gentiles) either, which for a time they had scorned when a sign had been erected at the entrance to the park on which was written in bold letters: **"Jews and dogs not allowed to enter."**

All the Jews of Lithuania protested strongly against this outrage and the decree was canceled. That is why the Jews of Yurburg were more attracted to their own park, especially because here was the building of the gymnasium, which was a cultural center for the Jews. The students would also find various sports installations in the yard of the gymnasium, which caught their interest.

Mordekhai (Mordechai) Taikhman was the principal of the gymnasium in my time. He came from Vienna, and had west European manners. He was a nice man with a good sense of humor. On the other hand, he was very strict. He demanded much of himself and naturally of his students. When he started to manage the gymnasium he imposed down rules of discipline and behavior that restricted the pupils. We had to wear school uniform - and woe to the student who violated a rule. It was strictly forbidden to go to the movies before one of the teachers had seen the film and expressed his positive or negative opinion. As is well known, students are even more attracted to things that are forbidden.

My friends and I often dressed up and secretly slipped into the movies, when lights had gone out. We were terrified that our "crime" would be discovered. We sat bent over at the rear of the hall, shivering with fear. I remember the film *"Michael Strogoff"* was once shown, of which it was said in town that it was a good film, a thriller. The management of the gymnasium forbade us to see it. However, in a daring undercover act we did manage to see it. It was an excellent film, with a fascinating plot, which deeply affected us. We were moved to tears about the bitter end of Michael Strogoff who became blind.

The team of teachers at the gymnasium was quite large, however, unfortunately, I have forgotten the names of most of my teachers. I only remember the names of two teachers - one was called Kosotsky, an excellent teacher who taught literature in my class, and the other Eliezer Leipziger, born in Yurburg, who taught history. Eliezer Leipziger later on became the deputy-principal of the gymnasium, and in the last years its principal. He was a nice man and very popular with the students.

It was the custom at the gymnasium to hold a festive party for the students before the start of the holidays, and at the end of the school year the eighth and last grade would have to put on a performance for the parents and students. The teachers' council usually chose a play with a nationalistic and educational theme. Students from other classes would also take part in recitals, song and dance.

Often I was also invited to take part in the recitals at the party. I remember that I once recited a poem by H. N. Bialik.

One of the beautiful plays performed by the last grade at the gymnasium was "Captain Dreyfuss." My sister Clara took part in this play; she had the role of Lucia, Dreyfuss' wife. The performance was impressive. The students' parents were full of admiration for the educational contents and the beautiful Hebrew spoken by the students, as if it was their natural tongue. My sister Clara gave an outstanding performance, and her gift for playing drama was already apparent then. Indeed, after a while Clara took drama courses at the "Habimah" studio in Kovno, and was an excellent actress, who was supposed to join "Habimah" in Tel Aviv, but she did not have the good fortune to do so.

From time to time cultural, social and sports events were organized at the gymnasium. There was a relatively large Hebrew library there as well.

Management tried to buy almost every new book that appeared in Eretz Yisrael. Our choir sang all the new songs sung in Israel. All these activities strengthened our ties with Yisrael and everything going on there. Indeed, the atmosphere at the gymnasium was Zionist-pioneer and Israel.

We loved the gymnasium and we loved to have a good time there in all the seasons of the year. In the long winter months snow and ice covered the land of Lithuania. The management of the gymnasium therefore took care to prepare an ice rink in the yard. After classes we would come, in spite of the fierce cold, to skate on the ice. I remember that my brother Yakov taught me how to skate on ice. I often fell and hurt myself, but I did not give up until I learned to skate. We were full of joy then. Sometimes we would also build a snowman; roll snowballs and "fight" each other.

From time to time there were snowstorms and school would be closed down for a day or two. Then we would sit at home and look outside through a small peephole, which we had scraped in the glass of the window, which was covered by a thick layer of ice, looking like flowers. It was beautiful to see the snow-covered trees and the roofs covered in a white blanket, as if a white tablecloth had been spread over them. Only when spring arrived did everything come alive again. The trees bloomed in a host of colors, the birds sang merrily, and the insects appeared from their places of hiding to warm themselves in the brightly shining sun. The whole universe burst to life with all its fauna and flora, inspiring joy in the human heart.

In spring tension was in the air at school. The teachers increased their demands - they demanded repetitions, tests- until the end of the school year. Only then were we free of the burden placed on us during the year and particularly in the last few months.

There were difficult tests too in the Lithuanian language, literature and history. These tests were government-controlled, by the Ministry of Education. The holidays, therefore, were days free of the pressures of the past year. We were able to engage in any activity we chose.

In addition to trips in the parks and nearby forest, we would enjoy sailing in boats on the Mituva River and bathing in the Nieman. I, however, was particularly fond of reading. I loved to read, and exchanged books at the gymnasium library and the Hebrew library named after Brener. I used to read anything I could put my hands on - adventure books, novels and historical novels, such as Mapu's Love of Zion and Samaria's Guilt, Friedberg and others.

I must mention that there was a very lively public life in Yurburg. In addition to cultural activities there were sports activities as well. There were two sport organizations - "Maccabi" - a Zionist organization and Y.A.K. - Yiddisher Athletik Klub, i.e. national-Jewish athletics organization, an anti-Zionist organization opposed to Hebrew studies. In addition, there were movements such as the "Hebrew Scouts" - Hashomer Hatsair -to which my brothers belonged and in which they were active. This movement was very active on behalf of Keren Kayemeth. The other movement was the Beitar youth movement, which followed to the Zionist-Revisionist phylosophy.

It should also be mentioned that volunteer organizations were also active in Yurburg. They engaged in mutual assistance and various charities.

Yurburg was all and everything to us, a world full of social activity, where the Jews created a beautiful daily life together for their own generation and for those to follow, but all of a sudden the dream was destroyed.

During my studies at the gymnasium I had many friends. Together we passed the long period of eight study years. It was a long period in the life of each of us. We were a close-knit class with very good relations.

I was fond of most of my classmates, and I think they liked me too. I was always surrounded by a happy group of friends. However, at the gymnasium itself our life was not easy. There were subjects we did not like, such as chemistry and physics. Studies were mainly theoretical, for we did not have the tools to give substance to the study material. In other fields of study we also had to make great efforts. The teachers would give us a lot of homework; they surely had good intentions, but they had no mercy; they tried to raise the standard and give the gymnasium a good reputation. We did all we could to improve ourselves, knowing it was for our own benefit. In spite of all the tensions at school we found time to enjoy ourselves too. We went on many trips to the parks and forests near town. We talked about many different subjects. We dreamt about trips in the wide world, to get to know new countries and interesting people. We also gossiped endlessly and laughed and talked about the teachers, friends and acquaintances. Those were the best years of our life. We were openhearted, talked and dreamt about a bright future, like all teen-age girls are wont to do.

I used to do my homework with a couple of friends I had chosen. They were all nice, honest girls, but the one I admired most was Sonia Kretchmer. She did not look very impressive; was small and not very beautiful. Nevertheless, she had a lot of good sense and charm, clever eyes and a deep understanding of life. I also loved her modesty and goodheartedness. She always volunteered to help her friends when they needed encouragement or assistance.

In those days we were preoccupied by the question of what profession to chose. It was a hard question to answer. I was the only one who did not have any hesitations. I was convinced that I wanted to be a teacher, for I had always loved children.

Luckily I was able to implement my dream. I went on aliyah to Eretz Yisrael as a pioneer, at first I worked in the citrus groves, and after a number of years I became a teacher in Yisrael, after I had graduated from courses in education and teaching. I was a teacher and educator for twenty-eight years. Unfortunately, my dear friends did not realize the dreams of their youth; the murderous Nazi hooligans destroyed the light of their young lives. It is oh so hard for me to forget them all -and my heart bleeds for them.

After the holidays, after we had done everything possible to enjoy our freedom, we returned to school, as usual. However, before we even managed to get used to the customary round of studies, the Rosh Hashanah (New Year) and Yom Kippur (Atonement Day) holidays arrived, which made me sad. We started to feel the holiday atmosphere when the "Shanah Tovah" (Happy New Year) greeting cards were printed, and we started to receive blessings from friends. My father would take care to have the cards already printed at the beginning of the month of Elul and we would draw up a list and write the addresses on the envelopes. I felt sorry for the gentile mailman who carried heavy parcels of mail and was very tired and exhausted. However, he was rewarded for his ordeal. Every family gave him a small gift.

On Rosh Hashanah (New Year) eve, as on Pesakh (Passover) eve, we would put on new clothes, to be able to say the blessing "Blessed be the new." From the early morning hours, on holiday eve, the holiday was in the air. Everything was clean and shining. The holiday meal was ready on the stove in the kitchen. A tablecloth covered the table, with candles on it, sweet wine and fruit so that the new year would be " happy and sweet." My parents would pray at the Beth Hamidrash (prayer house). They had permanent, good and respectable seats at the *"Mizrakh"* (eastern side).

On the two days of Rosh Hashanah we enjoyed good food - fish, soups, meat and additions. The "Tsimes" - a potato, prunes and raisins dish - constituted an important part of the menu. The meal concluded with dessert of stewed fruit, etc. Before Yom Kippur we would observe the *"kapores"* (expiatory sacrifice), called "Shlogen Kapores." Mother bought a white cock for father for the *kapores* and a white hen for herself. The children would observe *kapores* with money donated to the poor. On Yom Kippur the parents and older children fasted. I started to fast from age twelve and to this very day I fast on Yom Kippur.

Towards evening, immediately after the "Ne'ila" (closing) prayer, the girls would set the table and welcome those coming from the Beth Hamidrash (prayer house). At first one would drink and eat fruit of the season. After a short rest the meal would be served.

One religious holiday followed in the footsteps of the other.

The high holidays were immediately followed by Sukkoth (Feast of Tabernacles), of which the children were particularly fond. My father built a sukah and the boys would help him, while the girls would decorate it.

We would hang colorful paper chains and small lanterns and pictures. Then we would cover the sukah with thatch bought from the farmers. A time for joy. Father would come, bless the wine and all of us with the "Moadim le Simkhah" blessing. How nice it was to sit in the sukah. The next day we would go to the

Beth Hamidrash (prayer house), hold the "lulav" (palm-branch) and smell the "ethrog" (citron), all the things that bring back memories from the past. Father would express the wish that we would have the good fortune to taste the fruit of Eretz Yisrael and see its orchards.

Often the weather would not be on our side; the autumn rain would come early, and then we were forced to eat the holiday meal inside. However, on days when the weather was good, it was nice to sit in the sukah, sing and have a good time. That is how the days of the holiday passed. However, as a rule, we were at the whims of the weather.

Once the Sukoth holiday passed, the days of gray weather came. Fall, rain and storm. School resumed and once again we marched to the gymnasium each day, our schoolbags on our back. The teachers tried to instill as much knowledge as possible in us. Thus we studied until the end of term at Chanukah (Feast of Lights). Pressure was heavy, as usual. To obtain a good mark we had to work very hard. However, the days passed quickly and the Chanukah holiday arrived. We were quite tired and longed for a rest. We prepared for the Chanukah festivities in class, performances, and recitals, songs - as if we lived at the time of the Maccabeans, took part in their heroism and victory.

At home preparations were under way to celebrate the eight days of Chanukah. The Chanukah menorah appeared, the symbol of the holiday, which mother polished beautifully. The orthodox lighted an oil menorah, but usually candles were lit. There was not a home without a Chanukah menorah. Passing through the streets of Yurburg in the early evening hours, one would see the candles shine through the windows. A host of little lights. Entering one of the homes, ours amongst them, one would find the children playing with the spinning- top, made of wood marked with the letters (in Hebrew for) *A.M.H.T.* (A Miracle Happened There).

Mother would prepare tasty potato pancakes, which we devoured. Our home was full of warmth and happiness. The "Chanukah gelt" (money) we received from our parents and friends added to our joy.

Yes, Chanukah was celebrated at home and in the entire town. The public festivities and parties in town were numerous. There was always an occasion to celebrate - and why not? The Jews celebrated in order to forget their daily worries, and after all, why not?

The holiday and celebrations passed. The weather changed from day to day. Rain and storm, snow storms and freezing cold. A new way of life. We put on a coat and went to the gymnasium. Life, however, goes on as usual. Only when the Nieman River freezes, a change occurs. Yurburg is cut off from the outside world. To reach Kovno one has to travel in a winter carriage, a two-day trip. There is no train and no road. Sometimes it is as if everything has been frozen. Not only the Nieman, but the world around us. However, the same routine recurs every year. One gets used to the idea that that is how it is. Winter passes and life returns to normal, and only when the ice melts and the river flows over, new problems arise - the floods that recur each year. We, children, love winter, we like to frolic in the snow, skate on the ice, and walk through the enchanting landscape created by the snow. However, even the long winter comes to an end - as a matter of fact, it ends with a festivity - Purim. After the cold days and tiring studies, spring comes and brings along the Purim holiday, which is so attractive and colorful to us, children.

On holiday eve we go to the Beth Midrash (Prayer House). We read the "Megilath Esther" (Scroll of Esther), the adults clap their hands and the children swing their rattlers around. All those who come to the Beth Hamidrash rejoice in the fall of Haman . . . a merry go-round. From the Beth Midrash we return home and enjoy the holiday meal, mainly composed of "Haman Tashen" ("Haman ears,") stuffed with poppy-seed, baked by my mother. On Purim we are allowed to sip a drink and it is even considered a duty to do so, therefore Purim is merry, we sing and make a lot of noise . . .

The days after the Purim holiday pass quickly. The weather improves from day to day. Nature puts on festive clothes. The white world turns green. However, there is no time for outings. Studies continue in full. The students anxiously await the Passover holidays, to take a break from their studies. However, until the holiday they have to prove themselves.

Time is short and there is much to be done. Both at the gymnasium and at home. Our home is turned upside down. It is being painted, scraped, cleaned and cleaned all over again. The Passover dishes are taken down from the attic and my mother works hard to clean them. The *"shikse"* (gentile maid) assists her. There is a lot to do and mother says "A Kleinikeit," as if it is easy to prepare for the coming holiday. Pesakh is almost there, and we, children, are not allowed to bring *"khametz"* (leaven bread) into the house. *"Khas vekhalilah"* ("woe and behold") says mother, *"khas vekhalilah* that *"khametz"* should be found at home. Finally the preparations are over and the holiday culminates in the "Seder," i.e. "Seder Pesakh." We put on festive new clothes. The girls help mother to set the table. First of all the table is covered in a white tablecloth, and after that bottles of wine are put on the table and a special beverage prepared by my mother which tastes of paradise . . . and thus the table is covered by plates and matzot (unleavened bread) and all sorts of other items, such as maror (bitter herbs), horse -radish, etc., etc.

When father and the children arrive from the Beth Hamidrash the festivity really starts, the "Pesakh Seder." Everyone has a "Hagadah." The youngest of the family - Yitskhak - asks the four queries in the traditional melody - and he is answered by all. Reading is done aloud, father is the conductor of the choir and the singing is heard outside the house, in our home and in the homes of others, the singing pierces the evening silence and merges into a giant choir. Thus the Jews celebrate the feast of freedom in the distant Diaspora, hoping and waiting for the good days to come, for true liberation - "Next year in Jerusalem."

Family of Shoshanah Petrikansky (Poran)-Knishinski

Malkah and Yehudah-Leib (Alter) Petrikansky, Parents of Zevulun (Poran) and Shoshanah Petrikansky

Summer arrives, we are about to end the school year, immediately after the Shavu'oth (Pentecost) holiday. And on Shavu'oth - the feast of the gift of the Torah - we eat dairy products, according to tradition. My mother always takes care to observe the traditional customs.

It is hard to believe, but studies have come to an end. We go on a long leave of two months. Some are happy, others less so. Everyone is rewarded. The reward is in accordance with the efforts the students invested. One thing is certain, every student has acquired knowledge and education in the course of the year.

As a matter of fact, we are all grateful to the gymnasium and proud of it. Not every town has a gymnasium. It is thanks to a group of enthusiastic parents that the gymnasium was established in Yurburg.

The initiators, many parents, made tremendous efforts to send their children to study at the gymnasium. The Jews of Yurburg deserve to be praised for this. Actually, Yurburg was not a densely populated Jewish town, merely 2000 people lived there, but the majority of the population in Yurburg were at a high cultural level. Perhaps this was due to the influence of western culture, which the Jews of Yurburg absorbed as they were close to the German border. Anyhow, there were quite a few Jews in Yurburg with a secular or religious education. Many of them studied abroad and acquired an education, and many others were self- taught.

It was nice to live in the cultural atmosphere of Yurburg, there was incentive to make progress in learning and acquire an education and knowledge. Many graduates of the gymnasium went on to study at the University of Kovno, among them my brother and sister who studied there. Some managed to complete their academic studies; others didn't, due to the terrible tragedy that befell the Jews of Lithuania, among them the Jews of Yurburg. Alas, our beautiful Yurburg ceased to exist.

I loved Yurburg, its streets and alleyways. I shall always remember it and its good people. I shall remember my friends whose candle was extinguished when they were merely youngsters. They were and are no longer. All the Jews of the town, men, women, the elderly and children were murdered. They died an anonymous death and the whereabouts of their graves are not known. . .

My dear family also perished. The loved ones did not separate in life or death. They all went together. Only me and my brother Zevulun (Poran) survived. Perhaps destiny had ordained us to go to Israel, and we find solace in the fact that we were able to contribute a bit of our ability and power to build a national home for the Jews, a home that is a state for the remnants of the people who return to their homeland to live there in safety.

As long as I live I shall always cherish the memory of my relatives, and all the Jews of Yurburg. Blessed be their memory.

Krelitz Family Shabbas in Yurburg about 1935
Leib, wife, three friends, Leah and Moshe Krelitz
[Photo not in original book - From Leah Krelitz-Sherman Photo Collection - photo by Moshe Krelitz]

TRANSLATION OF PAGES 142 - 148

YURBURG AND PEOPLE OF OUR CHILDHOOD

By Hannah Shraga (Helen Feinberg Shrage)

Many years have passed since the Holocaust, the terrible days of World War II.

Our bodies still feel the pain and our heart finds no rest. The wound does not heal and the anguished soul finds no peace. It is hard to imagine how an entire town full of people, an active Jewish community, suddenly fell silent. Grumbling voices, children's shouts and the sounds of mothers and fathers are no longer heard - it is as if they never existed. This Jewish town of Yurburg, our home for centuries, has turned into a heap of ruins. However, happy childhood memories, the dreams and hopes of youth, cannot be erased from the heart and mind. We will remember Yurburg and the people from Yurburg as long as we live and exist on this earth.

Today I am far, very far from Yurburg, but I still see it both in my dreams and when I am wide awake. I see its beautiful streets, clean and calm, and its flowing rivers - the great Nieman River, the pastoral Mituva, and the winding Imstra.

I imagine myself wandering around the town, passing the elementary school where I was a pupil, and remembering it used to be called "Talmud Torah." Now it is a modern school. Here was the young principal, Mr. Yisrael Bekin, a scholarly and friendly man. He taught us Hebrew, instilling in us the love of our national tongue and Eretz Yisrael, our age-old homeland. And I was also fond of Hebrew grammar and bible studies. At "Talmud Torah" there were no gymnastics or singing classes - but today there are.

And on I go, walking slowly along the quiet street, and in front of me I see the building of the Herzl Hebrew Gymnasium. A tall building, standing alone, different from its surroundings.

On one side the view is open, on the other side the building borders on a beautiful large park with many old trees, shady boulevards, rest corners and benches, romantic corners; this park was called "Tel Aviv" after Tel Aviv in Eretz Yisrael. Here is the area for assemblies, sports and gymnastics, which used to be called Gymnastica. I can still hear the deep Russian voice of teacher Kaplan who taught gymnastics according to the Swedish method. I remember the teachers, Dr. Efrath, the principal and mathematics teacher and Avraham Kosotsky who taught us Hebrew literature and history and Tsentkowsky with whom we had bible studies. I preferred the humanities to exact sciences, and I loved the dancing class at the Gymnasium, and so did my friends. I remember my classmates, the Perlman sisters, Dartvin, Clara Petrikansky, Miriam Shlomovitz - who were sitting next to me.

The Gymnasium left its national-Hebrew mark on us and gave us a Zionist outlook, taught us to love our country and the Hebrew language. This Zionist education is still the essence of my life abroad, after two generations.

When we were young, we made many excursions. Yurburg's enchanting surroundings enticed us to go outside. The large park, rowing on the Mituva, sailing on the steamships to Kovno and a host of interesting places.

Here, at a certain distance from the Gymnasium, was the clubhouse of the Hebrew Scouts. Today the clubhouse is deadly silent, but I remember it as a busy "ants' nest" full of the charm of youth, joy and happiness. Yes, our clubhouse! Here we organized our dreams and created a corner of Eretz Yisrael, a charming corner, a little noisy sometimes, but usually calm and serious. At the "kibbutzim" - group activities - we really learned not only to be scouts, but also general studies in accordance with the "steps plan." I remember the scouts' camps in the forest where we sometimes spent one or even three days.

We enjoyed life at the camp, we were really happy and did not want to return home. I was a member of the movement for four years and for two years I was a "kvutsa'ith," i.e. head of a group of girls younger than myself. I loved my girls and remember them - Leah Shtok, Frida Perlman, Rivkah Karabelnik, Hannah Braun and others. I liked the educational work and I was very busy preparing the subjects for discussion at the group.

When the scouts movement adopted the "HaShomer Hatsair" ideology, we had to educate the youngsters towards active Zionism, i.e. being pioneers, aliyah and kibbutz life in Israel. I had to prepare myself thoroughly for the lectures at the group. I remember I once lectured to the girls in my group about Hillel Tseitlin's (Zeitlin) doctrine. The head of the scouts unit, Hayim (Chaim) Sigar, a teacher at the school, listened to my lecture. He praised me, and in general was very nice to me. He appreciated me and maybe even loved me . . . he was a teacher and educator at the scouts unit, a very special person. He taught us religion but also enriched our experiences. He used to sing to us and play the mandolin. He was a very virtuous man, close to the "Musarnikim" of Rabbi Yisrael Slanter's college.

There was a group of older youngsters at the scouts unit to which I also belonged. Among them I remember Zevulun Poran, Dov Mintzer, Hannah Smolnik, Eliezer Shapira, Menakhem Pukhert, Rachel Karabelnik, Mosheh Raizman (Reizman), Frida Shakhnovitz and Bathsheva Shtok (Ayalon) who was very close to me and who I admired very much. At present Bath Sheva is a member of kibbutz Givath Brener. She visited me in the United States and I love to visit her when I am in Israel.

The scouts unit with its intensive activity in a way tore us away us from our parents' home, but this feeling is true only for when we were teenagers.

When we were young we loved our home and everything connected with it. We loved our parents and all the members of our family. I remember that our family was very close and there was a nice atmosphere at home, thanks to our parents who were devoted to us. We were a relatively large family. When we sat around our large dining table it was a pleasure to watch - father at the head of the table, mother next to him and the brothers and sisters - Yitskhak, Rafael, Tsevi, Pesia and Gedalyahu (Gedalia). We enjoyed mother's wonderful food and loved to listen to father's "zemirot" (songs). We were a good family; all of us loved our home.

I remember our home, which was quite large. We lived in a corner house on Kovno Street, next to the well-known well of the town. On the other side the house faced the Liatkower Gass, there were sheds in the yard. Up front we had a store for leather goods where mainly my mother, Sarah, worked while the children sometimes helped her. We loved our mother. She worked hard and never complained. Mother was a beautiful woman, not bent on pleasure. We always saw her busy and occupied. Nevertheless, she found time to help the needy, those who had no food or clothes. Mother paid attention to them and helped them as much as she could, to some she gave food, to others clothing. These good deeds gave mother much satisfaction. The needy appreciated mother's efforts and her kindness.

My father, Hayim (Chaim)-Meir, was a merchant. As most merchants in Yurburg he dealt in export to Germany. The shed at our home was for the sale of building materials and in particular, as far as I remember, wood boards for carpentry and construction.

Although father was a very busy man, he always found time for the needs of the home and for the children. He was a good man, and always thought of others. He helped the needy whenever he could.

As far as I remember the life of my family, it appears nice and beautiful to me in an ideal atmosphere. We felt especially good on the religious holidays. On these days we would forget the everyday problems, take off our daily clothes and put on holiday gear. The house also appeared to change. We felt the holiday atmosphere in every corner. I can't forget the holidays at our home and the deep impression they left on me. I remember that when the "High Holidays" approached, a hidden fear would rise up in me. Maybe this fear was the result of the atmosphere at home and around us. There was much activity towards the "High Holidays." I saw the Jews walk around sad and full of concern. Do you think it is easy, said the Jews, "a Kleinikeit," after all, the day of atonement is approaching, in our home too there was a special atmosphere on the "High Holidays," the days of reckoning. The same was true for the homes of our neighbors. The Jews felt a certain mutual forgiveness on these days and as if there were no rich and no poor - all were equal in the eyes of God. They went to the synagogue, prayed and were strengthened by their faith. That is how they behaved around us, and that is also how my father behaved. He took care to go to the synagogue and pray near the prayer desk where his name was engraved. My brothers stood next to him and prayed too.

Hannah Feinberg Family in 1931

[Original Photo supplied by Faye Shrage Ullmann]

Standing from left: Hannah Feinberg (Helen Feinberg Shrage), Pesia Feinberg, Gedalyah Feinberg; Sitting from left: Itil Berzaner, the mother Sarah Feinberg, Henia Feinberg; Girls from left: Raizel Berzaner, Miriam Berzaner

I also have memories of Purim. A short holiday, but full of joy and derision. "Homentashen" were prepared and "Shalakhmones" sent. The Scroll of Esther was read at the synagogue and the children made a lot of noise with their groggers. And at home- what joy!- there were Homentaschen and plenty of glasses of wine. I also remember Pesakh at our home. Mother was busy cleaning the house on holiday eve, seeing to it that -God forbid! -Not a grain of "khametz" was left, buying new clothes for the children and preparing the holiday meal, kasher lemehadrin. And here comes holiday eve, the "Pesakh Seder." Father is sitting at the head of the table on white cushions. He looks like a king and mother like a queen in her elegant clothes. The table is laid according to the rules. Father starts to read the Hagadah and everyone joins him. We drink four glasses of wine and eat "kneidlakh" ... after all, as the joke goes, that's what it is all about. That is how we celebrated the holidays at home, just like the other Jews in our town of Yurburg.

Berzaner Family [Original Photo supplied by Faye Shrage Ullmann]

**Sitting from left: Itil Berzaner (Mother); Mordehai Berzaner (Father)
Standing from left: Raizel (daughter); Dinah'le (daughter); Mita (Miriam-
daughter). Mita and Dinah'le immigrated to the USA - the rest were all
murdered.**

[This paragraph was not in the original Yizkor Book: Diana Berzaner
Tobin relates that she emigrated from Lithuania in May 1939, at age 9, with
her mother Itel and an older sister Miriam. Her mother went back, sensing the
impending war, to get the remaining sister, Raizel, and her husband Mordehai.
The war broke out; they were all caught and murdered along with all the Jews
of Yurburg. Diana has been told that the Jews were rounded up by the Nazis
with the help of the local Lithuanians and told that they'd go to work camps so
that they would take their most valuable possessions. They were taken to to
outskirts of town and murdered. Diana found out that her sister Raizel was
initially hidden in the town high school by a Christian friend, but was found
about a week later because someone told the Nazis. Diana says that at least her
parents went to their deaths knowing that at least two daughters would survive
and maybe a third would. Diana has tried to find out more through
International Red Cross.]

One day bad things happened at our home. The world, as we had known it,
suddenly turned dark. This is what happened. My dear father fell fatally ill and
passed away. Without father the home changed. The pillar of support was
missing. In addition to the pain and sorrow the main provider was gone.
Mother had to take care of us. She broke down under the pressure of the pain
and the concern for the family. I was forced to give "private lessons" to

children who had problems in their studies. Tuition fees at the Gymnasium were high and I had to help mother carry the heavy burden. It was not easy for me to study at the upper grades of the Gymnasium and at the same time teach in order to pay for tuition.

After a short while my two brothers immigrated to [Detroit, Michigan in] the United States. The family separated. My mother followed my brothers to America and so did I. The dream to go to Eretz Yisrael was set aside. I had to abandon it although I remained faithful to the Zionist ideals.

The other members of my family remained in Yurburg. They stuck to their roots in the town of their birth. And then the cruel war broke out which destroyed and brought disaster on the Jewish homes. The Jews of Yurburg were put to death without mercy by the Nazis and their Lithuanian collaborators. My family suffered the same fate as the rest of the community. They all died as martyrs and left nothing but their memories behind. And I truly remember them; they are with me at all times. Countless years abroad, far from the place of terror, have not blurred the pain and sorrow I feel. I remember them and will do so forever.

When I arrived in the United States, I did not forget my origins. I arrived here with the spiritual values I acquired at my beloved parents' home in Yurburg, at the Hebrew Gymnasium and the youth movement. These values helped me build a Jewish home abroad. I studied at the Teachers College and taught Hebrew to adults and youngsters. I learned the art of drawing, which I found very interesting and useful.

I married David Shraga who comes from Tavrig, Lithuania. He is no longer alive today. We had two sons, Reuven-Jonah and Hayim (Chaim)-Yehudah and a daughter, Tsipora (Feigele). My daughter married Alexander Ullman, a well-known physician and hospital director. A nice man, who loves Israel and Eretz Yisrael. The sons are active in management and business, and the daughter is a teacher of Hebrew and Jewish subjects at the school belonging to the synagogue. I brought up my children in the best Jewish tradition, and taught them to love the Jewish people and Eretz Yisrael.

My family and I love Israel, support it through the national funds and visit from time to time. We rejoice in its achievements.

I myself am most interested in the kibbutz, visit Givath Brener and enjoy the meetings with my old friend - Bath Sheva Shtok (Ayalon). When Bath Sheva visited the United States, as the delegate of the Workers Union, I was very proud of her, and was happy to receive her in my home and help her as much as I could. I have also been involved for many years in the women's movement "Pioneer Women" on behalf of the Workers Union - Na'amat in Israel. Eretz Yisrael is in my blood and I am always excited when I visit Israel and tour its cities and villages. Finally we have realized the Zionist dream and established a Jewish state, after thousands of years in exile, and I regret I was unable to come and live in it.

Time is passing. Together with my contemporaries we are marching towards the unknown, carrying on our shoulders the burden of the sweet and bitter memories. We will never forget the terrible events of the Holocaust - the destruction of our homes and the murder of our dear ones. Yurburg, the cradle of our youth, will remain engraved on our hearts forever. The destruction of Jewish Yurburg will continue to haunt us for as long as we are on this earth. We will remember the beautiful town of Yurburg and its Jewish community - and we will never forget our loved ones, who were murdered in cold blood and not laid to rest in Jewish graves. God bless their memory.

Helen (Feinberg) and David Schrage
[Photo not in original book]
Photo courtesy of Diana Berzaner Tobin

Feinberg Women: Grandmother, Itel, Miriam, and "Mutter" Feinberg

Top: Raizel, Miriam, Bottom in Middle: Diana

[Photo not in original book]

Photo courtesy of Diana Berzaner Tobin

Kizell Family assembled in about 1922 when some family who were already living in Canada came back to Jurburg for a visit. All members of the original family are in the picture.

Left to right top Row: Samuel, David, Chiene, Chiene's husband, Michael, Bella (Michael's wife), Norman, Sarah (Archie's wife), Archie, Esther (Jacob's wife)

Second Row: Nettie (Rachel Leah's sister), Gitel, Moshe Teuvia, Robert, Rachel, Leah, Tilly, Jacob

Front row: Robert (Jacob's son), Helen, Francis (Tilly's daughter)

[Photo not in original Yizkor Book - Courtesy of Herb Beilis, son of Helen Kizell Beiles].

TRANSLATION OF PAGES 149 - 159

ONE FAMILY OF MANY IN YURBURG

THE STORY OF THE SMOLNIK FAMILY

By Zevulun Poran

On an ordinary summer day I happened to arrive, after many years of separation from this area, at the main street of Kiryath-Motzkin. In the afternoon hours there was very little traffic on this road. Children rode their bikes, shouting at the top of their young voices, and the noise of the bells pierced the silence. Summer weariness. The trees bordering the houses cast their shadow over the sidewalks - and the main boulevard, rather shaded, was almost empty of people. Only here and there an old man sat half asleep on the bench, close to cheerful fountains. A girl perused a book while walking along, before returning it to the library. A quiet, pastoral street of a town that was not really a town, growing modestly among the sands. The fountain incessantly sprayed water on its surroundings and the blue water was crowned by foam. A western wind brought along cool, humid air from the nearby sea, blowing life into people.

I remembered that nearby, but a few footsteps away, there was a parallel road, Barak Street. In the past it was a small street with small houses in the sand, square, looking like chocolate boxes. I passed a narrow passageway, almost like a street or a garden, to Barak Street. I looked at the sign on one of the houses to ascertain the name of the street. I was right, it was indeed Barak Street . . . Barak, and Devorah's song immediately came to mind. "Get up, Barak Ben-Avinoam and take your prisoner."

Perhaps, in those days, not far from here, Barak's chariots hurried along, looking for Sisra's hooligans - it might just be true - and therefore we renew signs and names and places.

We are on Barak Street, a narrow, long road. Gardens and thick trees line the street and the houses behind them. And see here: the little houses of the past have grown in size - two-stories and some of them even have three and four stories.

The small houses stand in awe of the huge homes and are afraid that the saying "Remove the old and bring out the new" will come true. I approach house number 52, which is my target. A two-story house covered in green; the building has changed since I knew it as a small, modest house, cast in concrete, with a flat roof, like all the homes of the workers and new immigrants in the small neighborhood. Everything here has changed and is unrecognizable.

I walk along the pavement that leads to the courtyard. In the yard there is a small garden, flowerbeds and greenery. And see here - even a dove-cot, looking like a poultry-pen with doves fluttering around in it, afraid of the guest, and creating a stir, their voices heard all over the courtyard. And there is a small poultry-pen as well, a sort of small cage, with two little ducks in it, still covered in a yellow down. Seeing all this, one feels that those who live in the house have always had a deep love for flora and fauna. The large house is quiet, as if it and all those in it have fallen asleep at twilight time.

- "Shall we knock on the door?"

- "No, no, let's wait a while- we have plenty of time!"

There are chairs and a table on the balcony. You sit down, look around you and see a yard which has everything; nothing is missing - no, no - however, when you think of the yard there, in the old house, which belonged to the people who lived there a long time ago in their little town of Yurburg in Lithuania, "all this" is but a sad memory of what they had there. There is an open area, a large plot, a well-kept vegetable garden, and mountain slopes planted with fruit trees, leading to the Imstra River, which flows along peacefully. It is clear, cold water, and calm and quiet, but then, after a moment of dwelling on the past and dreams that were shelved, you come back to the present, take up courage and turn to the entrance door, glance first at the small sign and realize you were right. In clear letters it says: "Smolnik family." Right, that's it, you have arrived at the address written in the book and with your right sense of direction. However, everything has changed here. How much time has passed since then? How the years pass. I remember that in the past, when I came on aliyah to Israel and joined the kibbutz group of former Lithuanians, I would often visit this charming little house, where Aharon Smolnik and his wife Devorah would warmly welcome me, pleased to open their doors to the next visitor, an old friend from Yurburg, who set up his tent (in the true sense of the word!) nearby, together with his friends on the yellow sand of the beach. As a kibbutznik, worker or porter in the Haifa port, he dried the swamps of the Nieman River, flowing over its borders and spreading malaria flies - worked with the members of his group during the week, but remembered his old friends, the Smolnik family, every Sabbath.

He would come to chat over a cup of tea and take a bite of the fresh cake, "with the old taste of Yurburg," which Devorah would prepare for the Sabbath. Sometimes we would taste the leftovers of the "khamin" - the Lithuanian "cholent," a memory of days gone by.

Thus we used to talk for hours at the family party, in which the two sons, Nathan and Gershon, also took part. Nathan, still a young man, already supported the family while Gershon was still a young boy. The youngsters, as always, left their place in the Diaspora without any qualms and found friends in their new surroundings. They quickly turned the pages of the past, but for the adults, matters were different, they found it harder to get used to their new place of living. The daughter, Hannah, who built her home at kibbutz Mishmar Ha'Emek, also found her place among friends. In those days Hannah would visit her parents from time to time, and help them wherever she could. Only those close to Hannah, know how she helped her parents and how much love and warmth she bestowed on them, to help them get used to their new surroundings, where the difficulties of language and way of life in the neighborhood divided even those living next to each other. It was a mixed neighborhood, immigrants from different countries, speaking in many different tongues, who had brought different customs from their former homes. Father Smolnik had no problem finding work at the "Ata" factory, and though in Yurburg he had never set foot in a textile factory, he quickly got used to the work, and even excelled at it. He liked his job and was popular with his fellow-workers and the owners of this large industrial plant. Matters were different where Devorah was concerned; she sat at home and felt lonely. The sandy garden did not satisfy her love of land and vast spaces. She particularly missed her oldest daughter, Esther. Since Esther had immigrated voluntarily to distant Siberia, near the Chinese border, relations with her had almost been cut off.

However, Aharon Smolnik, once he found the work he liked, put his family into a good mood; he would enthusiastically speak about his work, although he was no longer young when he came to Israel, yet he was still strong. He was broad-shouldered, had a strong body and hands that were good at every job. And above all - he was a resourceful man. He built his modest home almost by himself, and Devorah decorated her new home with flowers - beautiful shrubs and trees, some of them fruit trees, others not bearing fruit. Devorah also cultivated a vegetable garden next to her home, in the small plot available. When Devorah would show me the garden, and we would pass from one flower-bed to another, her face glowed, but then she would heave a deep sigh - "yes, of course, this is not the garden." She meant the large garden the Smolnik family had in Yurburg.

Devorah would take care of the garden in Yurburg all by herself. She never asked for help. However, if the family members "volunteered" to work in the garden it would make her very happy.

Needless to say that that was the greatest joy of her life. And what was not in that garden?- we shall refrain from mentioning all the different kinds of fruit trees and the different kinds of vegetables, there was plenty of everything!

Aharon, her husband, was usually absent. He was busy working as an agent supplying alcoholic beverages of the government factory in Kovno. This factory was well known and famous all over Lithuania. In Yurburg too, of course, these beverages were drunk; the Lithuanians loved to sip them until they got drunk. The Jews also put alcohol on the table, on religious holidays, and particularly at family celebrations. As Yurburg was far away from Kovno, the beverages were transported on steamships, and when the Nieman was frozen, in winter, horse-drawn carriages were used, which transported the beverages over a dirt road, for there was no train to Yurburg. Neither was there a decent road in those days.

The "gentiles" in Yurburg envied the "little Jew" Smolnik, who had received the franchise to supply alcoholic beverages in Yurburg and its surroundings. They complained to the authorities in Kovno, but to no avail. Then they decided to take revenge on Smolnik. What did they do? One night, when Smolnik joined his "gentile" assistant, and they transported a large shipment of alcoholic beverages in the winter carriage - three young gentiles jumped on him and started to attack him and his gentile assistant with sticks. The fight went on for a long time and although he took a severe beating, Smolnik, bleeding and hurt, managed to ward off his assailants, and inflict a deathly blow on them. The assailants fled. Smolnik returned home and required medical assistance. This attack was known all over town and everyone referred to Aharon Smolnik as a hero. Finally, the matter was brought to Court. Smolnik won the case and the assailants received a long prison sentence.

The Smolnik family was well off. Like his wife Deborah, Aharon was also diligent and energetic. The Smolnik family was a happy family, they were hospitable and gracious; their home was always and never boring.

Smolnik's country home in Yurburg was situated in a quiet neighborhood, close to the Jewish Park "Tel Aviv" and its Hebrew Gymnasium. It was a wonderful area for outings. The Smolnik vegetable garden bordered the small Imstra River, which flowed almost all year round, except for the winter days, when it froze and was used for ice-skating.

As the Smolnik home stood in the middle of the road taken by all, everyone, young and old, knew Aharon and Deborah, who would welcome those passing by in their carriages and offer flowers or fruit from the garden to their friends. The young really became "attached" to the Smolnik home and everybody was friendly with them. The students at the gymnasium were particularly fond of the Smolnik home and garden, they would go there from time to time and hide there, and find little corners for a quiet talk. Sometimes students would skip classes, or be expelled from class (yes, that too happened. . .) and where would they then find a "hiding place" if not with the Smolnik family?. . . There, at the Smolnik home, the students found understanding and forgivingness for their "sins" and here too they would receive a "reward" - light refreshment offered by Devorah, who welcomed guests.

In due time the house became a youth movement center. The "Scouts Troop" was formed in town, and Hannah Smolnik was among the first to join. Hannah was an enthusiastic scout. She faithfully observed Baden-Powel'ls scouting rules; wore the uniform, put on the tie and badges, as required, and observed the "Ten Scout Laws" imposed on the individual regarding moral behavior.

Hannah was deeply attracted to the scouts' movement and had a wonderful time there. Excursions, camps in the forest, song and dance, all this was the focus of the charming, slender young girl.

After a while talk started at the movement about the future of the members who were growing up. New ideas were launched . . . new concepts . . . "Zionism," " pioneering," etc. The movement's envoys, who had come to visit the Yurburg group, started to speak in a new style. Being a scout was no longer the movement's ideal, but rather a means to form and educate the personality . . . new words, ideas that caught on.

Hayim Sigar, a teacher at the town's elementary school, also joined the movement. As a teacher, he was older, and more educated than the youngsters who were members of the movement. His joining gave a strong impetus to the movement. Its name took on new meaning; from now on it was called the "Hebrew Scouts - Hashomer Hatsair." Hayim Sigar was attracted to these new, modern ideas and promoted them among his followers in the movement.

One day Hayim Siger lectured to Hannah's group of teen-age scouts at the Smolnik home about the movement's path, and afterwards, as he always did, he burst into song - popular, Zionist and romantic songs. Hayim liked to sing solo as well, Bialik's "Put me under your wing" or Shne'ur's "Delightful hand." These songs were an emotional highlight, the sound of his voice merged with the sound of Hannah's mandolin in wonderful harmony, and the youngsters were enchanted. Hannah received the mandolin as a reward for her outstanding scholastic achievements, when she completed elementary school. The members of the Smolnik family witnessed this vision of the youth movement and they too absorbed its inspiring atmosphere. At the end of the "kibbutz" (as the group's meeting was called) the parents suggested Hayim Sigar stay with them in one of the rooms in their home. Since then, the Smolnik home became the second clubhouse of the movement in Yurburg.

Hannah Smolnik was attracted to new ideas raised at the discussions, such as being pioneers, training, aliyah, kibbutz etc. - concepts that were gradually capturing the minds of the youngsters in the local group. However, it would not be correct to say that all the youngsters were attracted to the Zionist ideas. There were other opinions too that were accepted at the Smolnik home.

Esther, Hannah's older sister, moved in a circle of youngsters who were attracted to revolutionary ideas rampant among the masses. "Palestina," they said, is not a solution for all the Jewish people. It is a deserted land settled by Arabs. The British incite the Jews against the Arabs and blood is spilt there needlessly. . . and what is the solution? Emigration. Indeed, many youngsters from Lithuania emigrated to the U.S.A., the land of gold, or to South Africa. In those days there was a rumor that the Soviet Union was ready to allocate an area of fruitful, unpopulated land and put it at the disposal of the Jews in distant Siberia, on the Chinese border. There, i.e. at Birobijan, as the proposed area was called, an autonomic area would at first be set up and a Jewish state would perhaps be established there.

The leaders of the Soviet Union headed by Kalinin encouraged the Jews at the time to settle the area. Although the idea of settling in distant Birobijan did not seem very attractive to many, there were a number of people, perhaps only very few, who liked the idea and implemented it. Esther and her friend Hayim (Chaim) Frank, her future husband, decided to spend their life in Birobijan.

Hannah came the 1930s to visit her parents in Yurburg to convince them to make aliyah to Israel

From this point on the peaceful and calm home of the Smolniks became the center of discussion about the best path for Jewish youth. The discussions were fierce, accompanied by mutual accusations. The discussion, therefore, went beyond the Smolnik home. The two girls - the oldest and the youngest - were about to realize their dream. Esther left for a distant place, to realize her dream of building a new homeland for herself and the people of Yisrael in Birobijan. And young Hannah, faithful to her beliefs and ideals, started preparations for realizing her dream in Eretz-Yisrael.

Esther left - and immediately disappeared. Letters did not arrive, and rumors that fell from heaven were not encouraging at all the new settlers in Birobijan were deeply disappointed and even desperate.

Hannah started to make plans to go on training [for life in Palestine] together with a group of friends from "Hashomer Hatsair." The parents, although they approved of the Zionist idea and its implementation, wanted to postpone Hannah's departure. They were very proud of her, and wanted her to continue her studies and acquire a profession. The movement inspired her and instilled ideas of a new life in her. Hannah's decision to go on training turned her into an example at the "nest" (as the local branch of the movement was called), for she was the first of Hashomer to go on training. Her girlfriends loved and admired her, and even more so, the boys. At the last Pesakh, prior to her departure for training, a merry Seder was held at the local branch and Hannah was elected "Queen of the Seder."

Hannah was convinced that her departure for training should not be postponed, although she knew this would sadden her parents. One night, in the third night watch, Hannah "disappeared" from home and joined the activist Hashomer group. Although the parents were saddened by what their daughter had done, they finally resigned themselves to the idea, after they received an enthusiastic letter from the training group in the Memel area. There, at the estate of a German landowner in Dompen, Hannah took the first real step towards the realization of her dream.

There were only two girls in this Dompen group, which consisted of 12 people; one of them worked in the kitchen and the other - alternating with her friend- in the field.

Hannah liked the work in the field, especially in the garden, which reminded her of her parents' garden. She quickly adapted to her new surroundings. Although the group was far away from Jewish settlement, without a broader group of youngsters, it took the experience in its stride, as a corridor to future life. Work in the field was hard.

The members got up at sunrise and worked almost until sunset, with an hour's break at mid-day. They were not rewarded for their work, except for food. The work with the "gentiles," who were used to hard work from birth, demanded a great effort on the part of the pioneers, and they tried to comply, to prove that a Jew too knows how to work. . . There were Germans too among the workers, who were influenced by Hitler's propaganda.

When Hannah completed her training, the gates of Eretz Yisrael were closed, and certificates of aliyah were handed out sparingly. Hannah's family in Yurburg was pleased that her aliyah was postponed for a while. Since she left home, their small world had become empty, and only worries had been added.

Esther, who had gone to Birobijan, did not find happiness there. All the dreams about a "Jewish area" disappeared the moment they were faced with reality. Enthusiasm disappeared and deep disappointment filled every corner of her heart. But how does one go back? - And how could the parents help their daughter in her troubles?

The movement's local group was full of joy. Other girls started to follow in Hannah Smolnik's footsteps and prepare for training. Hannah always served as an example to them. She returned from training, more experienced in life and more of an adult. "The daughter's revolt" had succeeded.

Soon the first group of "Hashomer" from Lithuania started the fifth aliyah. It was in January 1929. There were six people in the group: Reuven Blumzon (Shemi) and Batyah Zhuk (Shemi) at kibbutz Beth Zera; Arieh Khalavin at kibbutz Sarid; Sara Weiner, Hannah Kovensky and Hannah Smolnik. This group laid the foundation of the first Hashomer Hatsair kibbutz from Lithuania. It was the social nucleus that would welcome those coming after them, but this took a while. The gates of Eretz Yisrael were not open, and therefore it took years before the Hashomer members from Lithuania formed a true settlement nucleus.

After a number of events in Israel the nucleus obtained its goal, when it joined "Beth Zera" in the Jordan valley. Here, on the shore of the Jordan, they set up an exemplary kibbutz village, together with pioneers of German origin.

Hannah, who was together with her friends at the Shomer nucleus, did not go with them to kibbutz Beth Zera, but to Mishmar Ha'Emek, one of the oldest kibbutzim in the country. Here Hannah found a warm home. She was influenced by the Hashomer movement atmosphere. The first educational institution for Hashomer kibbutz children was opened at Mishmar Ha'emek and here the "Hashomer Hatsair" forest was planted, with donations by the movements' members.

However, Hannah was not very lucky in this place, and in due course she had to leave Mishmar Ha'emek, for family reasons, and move to Tel Aviv, the large, noisy city which she, the country girl, did not like.

When she was at Mishmar Ha'emek, Hannah's parents moved to Eretz Yisrael. Hannah was very happy to have her parents close to her. When her parents set up their home at Kiryath Motzkin, to a large extent with her help, Hannah would often visit them and help them get used to their new surroundings.

A lot of water flowed through the Jordan. Hannah lived in Tel Aviv, her home was always open to her friends (and who was not a friend of hers?), and she and her husband, engineer Yosef Polan, would warmly welcome everybody. Many artists of the theater would come to Yosef, and many kibbutznikim would visit Hannah, who had shared their life for many years. The children grew up in this home - the son Gideon and the daughters - Ruthi and Amira. The Polan home extended education and learning to its children. Indeed, the children learned a lot from their parents. They are married now and active in culture and art.

Hannah has strong ties with her parents' home in Kiryath Motzkin. She is the link between all of them. Nathan set up his home in Kiryath Bialik close to Kiryath Motzkin. Gershon and his family settled in the Smolnik family home and their old father, Aharon Smolnik, lives with them.

Devorah, Aharon Smolnik's wife, died a long time ago. Since she passed away the home got empty. The modest, diligent woman died young and did not have the opportunity to enjoy the success of her children.

Esther lived on the second floor of the home. Yes, the same Esther, from Birobijan, who at long last, after endless efforts, managed to leave the place, after her husband died. She left for the free world with her two sons.

She spent three years with her sons in the U.S.A. Worked and made a good living, but was not happy there. Thus, she arrived at Kiryath Motzkin, at her parents' home and she lives close to her family. Her son, Hayim (Chaim), also set up his home nearby and he also has a family and sons, and Esther has grandchildren. Her second son, David, lives in the U.S.A. Only her son Yosef did not have the good fortune to come to Israel. When he studied in Kovno, war broke out and he perished in the Holocaust, together with his family.

The Aharon Smolnik family expanded in Eretz Yisrael. His sons and daughters are here. Their sons and grandsons will live here. The Smolnik family was fortunate enough to witness the establishment of the State and live a free life in its homeland. Quite an achievement for a Jewish family from Yurburg!

While the memories of days gone by pass though our head - the door of Aharon Smolnik's home opens, he lives in the apartment of his son Gershon and his family. A clean and well cared for home, with a special room for the old father. Aharon Smolnik lies in his bed, half-asleep, a very old man, 98 years of age, at the end of the long road from the little town of Srednik, via Yurburg, to Eretz Yisrael. A path strewn with hard work, joy and sorrow. Bringing up the children, small daily chores and large events, wars and blood-spilling. He was a king in his home and an ordinary man among his neighbors.

Aharon Smolnik, no longer healthy, does not see the end of his life, but he can feel it coming in all of his aching body; furthermore - he longs for rest, and the peaceful end that lies in store for every human being.

In a sudden awakening, Aharon Smolnik tells his visitor who has come from distant Jerusalem - "all is well, my children look after me, I have no complaints, really, no complaints at all. What else can a man of my age ask for? Only Hannah is far away from me and I am waiting for her. She must come, yes, she will come, will come."

Smolnik pauses- it is hard for him to speak- and then goes on: "I am so happy today that a friend from "there," from our Yurburg has come to visit me; it is priceless, such a visit is worth millions, millions. "Old Aharon Smolnik gathers his strength, gropes, finds his stick, and starts to take a few steps. He touches the objects around him, as if he once more, one more time wants to feel the world, as if he no longer belongs to it, the old Aharon Smolnik already belongs to another world, a world of truth and eternity, as he says "die ewige Welt, die ewige Welt."

He is happy to accept his friend's kiss and shakes his hand as if he wants to express that it is farewell forever. Aharon Smolnik is still alive and breathing, but his days are like the page torn each day from the calendar of the year that comes to an end.

TRANSLATION OF PAGES 160 - 162

THE MOST FAMILY

A SAD EVENT IN THE FAMILY

By Yoninah Most-Efraimi

The event about which I want to speak here is the most striking event among my childhood memories, and I cannot forget it. It was one of the most shocking family tragedies that happened to us when I was a little girl.

We lived in Yurburg. I remember my father and my parents' home very well. My father was a learned man and a scholar. He used to get up early in the morning, to study a Gemara page and pray before he went on his way. My father would hitch the horses up to the wagon and in winter to the sledge, travel to villages and buy grain from the farmers, mainly corn, for export to Germany. It was tiring work; he would leave early in the morning and return home two days later. Father loved his home and paid a lot of attention to the children. In spite of his weariness he would play with them as if he was a child like us. Mother, Hayah-Rivkah, took care of our education.

My father was always traveling, and hardly ever at home, until that bitter and sudden day (3 Shevat - 1917) which is deeply engraved on my memory to this very day.

I remember it was a cold day, it had snowed during the night, and the ground was covered in snow. When I got up that morning, my father had already left. He left in the morning vigil, as always after he had said his prayers and studied a Gemara page; he bade good-by to mother and the sleeping children, kissing them on the forehead, sat down in his sledge, covered in fur, and went about his business. That day he was supposed to meet a farmer at his estate. The farmer invited father to conduct business regarding the purchase of a grain wagon. Midway, at Shimkaitz, there was a Jewish inn where the Fainstein family lived. Here one would rest, feed the horses, drink a glass of tea and warm oneself.

The farmer was already waiting for my father at the inn, and the deal was concluded there. It was the custom to change wet clothes at the inn. The farmer followed my father's movements. Once father had taken off his boots in order to change his wet socks, the farmer noticed that father had put the money in the stocking, and apparently at that moment the gentile got it into his head to commit murder and steal the money.

After a short rest, my father left the inn with the gentile and went to the estate owner's storerooms to receive the grain. They had barely left the inn and had gone into the forest, where on both sides of the road there were thick trees, when in the middle of a dust road murderers attacked my father, led by the farmer who held a sharp wood-cutters ax in his hand, and scattered his skull. They threw my father's body into the woods, after they had taken off his clothes and galoshes and removed his boots and taken the money out of his stocking. The murderers fled into the woods with the money and left my father bare-foot and bleeding from his head in a pool on the white snow. . .

A few hours later the horses returned with the sledge to the inn's yard. The innkeeper knew immediately that the horses belonged to Rabbi Yisrael-Yitskhak Most, but their owner was gone.

Fainstein understood immediately that a tragedy had occurred, as there were signs of blood in the sledge. The innkeeper and his assistants immediately went to look for my father with the horses. They followed the sledge until they reached the forest, when they saw a terrible sight: my father was lying on the white snow in a pool of blood. They immediately understood that a brutal murder had taken place here. The innkeeper lifted my father's body onto the sledge and took it to my grandfather, who lived on an estate not far from Yurburg, called Skriblina. A heartbroken scene took place there all night long, crying and fainting.

The next morning my father's body was taken to the synagogue in Yurburg. The Jews were deeply shocked by this tragedy; relatives cried and mourned my father's death. This was the first time I heard "Kadish" (prayer for the dead) at the synagogue, recited by my brother who was in tears.

The terrible event deeply hurt my mother, she was obsessed and murmured all over again "my children are orphans, my children are orphans."

The police interrogated the farmers, but did not find the murderers. On the third day after his death my father was buried. All the shops closed, and a deep mourning enveloped Yurburg. All the residents of the town accompanied my father to the cemetery. Raseiniai Street was full of people. My mother fainted all the time and the doctor stood next to her and injected tranquilizers. The Rabbi and a Jew from the group with whom my father studied Gemara at the synagogue eulogized my father.

All year long a minyan (10 men) was held at our home that was in deep mourning. My mother remained a young, 32-year old widow with 8 little children, the oldest of them being 14 years old, and the youngest, a daughter, a year and a half. After the year of mourning my mother, Hayah-Rivkah brought us up with her small means and taught us Jewish and cultural values. She sent us to study at the Hebrew Gymnasium and took good care of her family.

I remember the first year after my father's death because of an event that is deeply engraved on my memory. When I was five years old, we heard an orchestra far away. Youngsters from all the Jewish schools marched along with blue-white flags, singing Hebrew songs. We wanted to join the merry parade, but my mother said: "although this is an important day for the people of Yisrael, the day of the Balfour Declaration, and we will have a Jewish national home in Eretz-Yisrael, we are still in mourning for the head of our family and therefore we must not take part in this event."

We stood next to the house, waved our hands and cried for joy. We read in Hebrew *"Am Yisrael khai"* (Long live the people of Israel) Even then I understood the meaning of those words.

My mother was a Zionist all those years; she knew the Bible almost by heart; it was her dream to go to Israel. We spoke Hebrew at home; we read a Hebrew newspaper and Hebrew books. We studied at the Hebrew Gymnasium. Until I immigrated to Israel I was a teacher at a little town near Raseiniai; after that I went to Kovno, studied bookkeeping there with the teacher Tovin.

In Kovno I joined the *"HaPoel HaMizrakhi"* pioneer movement. I went for training to Gorzd near Memel, and in the beginning I worked in farming and later on as a teacher. I taught Hebrew and Zionist history to children of Gorzd.

In 1934 I received a pioneer certificate and went on aliyah to Israel. I said good-by to the members of my family, hoping that the day would come when they would all join me in Israel, but that hope did not come true.

War broke out in Europe and Hitler destroyed our towns and villages. My entire family was wiped out in the terrible Holocaust.   Only my sister Lea was saved and the daughter of my brother Mordekhai (Mordechai) Most, from Yurburg. They went through the terrible hell, the concentration camps and atrocities, but they survived.

My relatives established wonderful families, and they are involved in the life of our land and love it.

Tel Aviv

TRANSLATION OF PAGES 163 - 166

THE HOME OF THE FRANK FAMILY

By Sarah Frank-Shapira

I was born in Yurburg to my father, the late Yehudah-Leib Frank (he was active in the "Hamizrakhi" party, and a candidate on its behalf for the community council) and my mother Khavah-Malkah (Chava Malka). My father died when I was a young girl. I had a brother - Mordekhai (Mordechai)-Eli and a sister Libe-Beile, who were younger than I. Unfortunately they all perished in the terrible Holocaust, May God avenge them.

Our family lived on Kovno Street (Kovner Gass), Yurburg's main street. On the other side of the street, opposite our home, was the town's central square, also used as a market. Beyond the square, on the side of the road leading to the Nieman River, the Old Synagogue stood (Di Alte Shul), a wooden building with a very special form. People would come from all over the country; Jews as well as gentiles, to look at the beautiful synagogue built in 1790. The synagogue was famous far beyond the borders of Lithuania and many tourists came to take a look at it.

The stone building of the Beth Hamidrash (prayer house) stood not far from the synagogue, it was used as a prayer house and a yeshiva (college) for scholars. Usually the light was on at the Beth Hamidrash and many people prayed there.

Our neighbors on the east, in the direction of Kovno, were the Efraim Heselowitz family. They were well to do, and lived in a large house. Efraim Heselowitz was a linen and grain trader who employed many workers in the storeroom in his yard. I studied at the Hebrew Gymnasium together with one of the daughters of the Heselowitz family, Etti. Etti survived and lives in Canada. On the other side, to the west, the Yehudah-Leib (Alter) and Malkah Petrikansky family lived (the parents of Zevulun Poran, who now lives in

Jerusalem). It was a large family with boys and girls, with whom we studied together at the gymnasium. Alter Petrikansky was a linen merchant and two workers were employed in his yard that improved the quality of the linen, packed it and sent it abroad. Behind the Petrikansky home lived the Leib Bernstein family. He was a rich merchant, related to the Heselowitz and Petrikansky families. After a while the Bernstein family left Yurburg and the Feinberg family moved into their home with their daughters Batyah and Pipa, who studied at the gymnasium.

Further on, beyond the Petrikansky family, the Reuven Hirsh family lived, the mother and her three daughters. One of the daughters, Tsilah, went to Israel at the same time as me. She lived in Haifa. The Hirsh family had a bakery and patisserie where we used to buy fresh bread and warm rolls. After a while the daughter Pesia also came to Israel.

Our family had a quite large grocery-store. After my father died, my mother took care of the family. When there was pressure at the store my mother took on outside help and we children also helped when we did not have classes.

We lived in our own stone house, the grocery-store was at the front and beyond it the living quarters, the yard with its store-room. Work was usually calm during weekdays, and only on market days, on Mondays and Thursdays, there was a lot of work. On market days many farmers would come from all the villages in the area and bring their wares along. Once they had sold the goods to the Jews, they would disperse among the shops of the Jews and buy all sorts of items they needed. On market days there was a lot of tumult. Some farmers liked to drink; they would crowd into the pubs, drinking till they were drunk and lost their senses. The farmers who drank too much would create uproar in the streets of town until they got sober. However, in general, the Lithuanian farmers were moderate; they would come with their wives - buy and sell with good sense.

The farmers would come to our grocery-store too to buy; many of them were regular customers and good acquaintances. We allowed the regular customers to enter our home and eat and drink the farmer's dishes they had brought along. We had good relations with the farmers. It seemed to us that the farmers were good people, who showed the Jews respect and were friendly to them. They would usually drink Vodka on cold winter days, or beer, but would not get drunk. One should not forget that the Lithuanian winter was very cold, and the alcohol would warm body and soul. On market days the store was full of farmers. When I did not have classes, or after school, I would immediately help my mother, as much as I could. I was happy to assist my mother. My younger brother and sister also joined me and helped my mother.

As a child, I studied at the elementary school and afterwards at the "Herzl" Hebrew Gymnasium. The gymnasium building stood in a beautiful park called "Tel Aviv." There was a time when Jews were not allowed to enter the large park. **"Jews and dogs not allowed"** - said the sign on the entrance gate of the park.

This vile act made the Jews very angry and induced them to establish their own park. An area of land was bought in a beautiful leased area at the rear of town and this became a beautiful park of which the Jews of Yurburg were very proud. A large and beautiful building stood on this site; it was leased to the Hebrew Gymnasium. We loved the park, would stroll in it and have a good time together with the other students. It was nice to study at the gymnasium, We had good and devoted teachers who instilled the love of Eretz Yisrael in us and taught us the Hebrew language. I remember that during the break, when we would play, the teachers would walk among us and see to it that we spoke only Hebrew. The slogan was: "Hebrew speak Hebrew." We loved the gymnasium and our studies. Social life gave us many values and pleasant experiences. We shall never forget the years we studied at the gymnasium. We shall always remember the enchanting village landscape, the Imstra River flowing slowly along and the flights of merry birds; those were happy days, the years when we were young.

When I completed the sixth grade, my mother decided I should learn a profession, towards the future. She therefore sent me to Memel (Klaipeda) to study at the "Handels-Schule" (commercial school) there. When I graduated from this school, I received a certificate and returned to Yurburg, where I got a job at the Komertz Bank, managed by Shmeryahu Bernstein. My mother was very happy that I had found work, was gaining experience and making progress at my job. However, I did not remain at the bank for long.

In those days a revolution was taking place among the youngsters. Matters got worse. The economic situation of the Jews in town deteriorated. The youngsters felt uncertain. The future was shrouded in uncertainty. Some youngsters emigrated to other countries and tried to make a living there, and many looked towards Eretz Yisrael. Yurburg was a Zionist town and our family was Zionist too. The members of my family were therefore also interested in going to Eretz Yisrael. Two sisters of my mother had already gone to Eretz Yisrael a long time ago and they were living in Jerusalem. One of them already went on aliyah in 1905. We always had ties with Eretz Yisrael.

In the early thirties young men and women from Yurburg started to become members of the "Hekhalutz" movement which aimed at training youngsters to go on aliyah to Eretz Yisrael. Like many others, I too decided to do so. As I came from an observant family I decided to join *"Hekhalutz Hamizrakhi"* and after a short while I went on training. Kovno was my place of training, Yanever Street. I worked at a knitwear factory and alsoat a kitchen too for a while. During the training period we learned a lot about Zionism and Eretz Yisrael. I was on training for about two years, and after that I had to wait a long time before I received the *"Sertifikat"* - the permit to go on aliyah issued by the British mandate government.

I was grieved at waiting for the certificate. I was impatient, like many others. Finally, however, one day the good news arrived - "we are going on aliyah." I was informed by the "Hekhalutz Hamizrakhi" center that I could go to Israel, linked to another pioneer, as husband and wife, who also received permission to go on aliyah. This was called a "fiction." It was not very pleasant, but the main thing was to go on aliyah, under any circumstances.

When I arrived in Israel in 1936 my grandmother also joined me, she was "summoned" by her daughter living in Jerusalem. And here the longed -for day of aliyah arrived, and together with my grandmother I arrived in Jerusalem. Here I built my home. My dream had come true and turned into reality. Here too I married Yerukham Shapira and gave birth to three sons (physicians) and a daughter, a university graduate and teacher in Israel.

Since that day I am a Jerusalemite; happy to live in our capital; only the bitter memories of the home that was destroyed in Yurburg, and the brutal murder of my family during the Holocaust makes me sad. It is hard to forget and erase the memory of my beloved ones - I shall never forget them.

Blessed be their memory.

TRANSLATION OF PAGE 167

MY FAMILY IN THE DAYS OF THE FIRE AND THE SHOAH (Holocaust)

By Rachel Hes-Grinstein

I always think of Yurburg, the town where I was born, with mixed feelings of joy and sorrow. I had a very happy childhood and adolescence; however, this changed when the tragedy of the fire occurred. Yes, the great fire . . . I can not forget the fire, it still upsets me when I think of it. Whenever I close my eyes, I see horrible pictures -- flames of fire rising up . . and I also see the house -- our home -- enveloped in heavy smoke, flames of fire bursting forth from it. A truly terrible sight!

Our house went up in flames and nothing was left of it. Not only our house, but also all the homes of our neighbors burnt down as well as many other houses in our area, where Jews were living.

Our house was among the first to burn down in the great fire -- we were unable to save anything whatsoever. The fire spread and burnt down one house after another -- nothing was saved. Some Jews claimed the fire was caused deliberately, that it started at the Feinberg mill and spread from there to the Jewish homes in our town. As we lived close to the Feinbergs, I heard -- and indeed can still hear -- the terrible cries for help "Fainberg's (Feinberg) Mill brent! Fainberg's Mill brent!" But even before it was possible to grasp the extent of the tragedy the fire had already spread to many houses, ours among them.

Everyone in Yurburg knew that the Germans had committed the terrible deed from Smalininken, together with the Lithuanians, in response to the Russian decision, in 1940, to join Lithuania to the Soviet Union. The fire therefore was a warning to the Jews not to cooperate with Soviet authorities. We, the Jews, were the scapegoat, the victims of hate ....

The result was destructive and very sad indeed. Our family, like many other families, remained homeless. We had to lie down outside, on the area of the Zarda next to the Nieman. Afterwards my family received a room at the Neviazhski home, on Kovno Street.

1940 - The great fire in Yurburg. Hes family is standing in the street.

Living conditions were hard; there was a shortage of apartments for the Jews who had been affected by the fire. Finally we had to leave Yurburg after a few days and settle in Kovno. It was hard to leave Yurburg. We could not stop thinking about our burnt-down home, or those of our neighbors. I was very sad, for I loved Yurburg, that lovely and beautiful little town. It seems to me that nothing equals Yurburg, with its luscious rivers -- the Nieman, the Mituva and the Imstra, which lent it freshness and a beautiful view. Yurburg was surrounded by greenery, there were forests and parks everywhere.

As I remember, there was a very active social life in Yurburg, its citizens lived in an atmosphere of friendship and harmony and helped each other.

Yurburg, our town, is engraved on my memory, and I shall never forget it. I shall always remember Yurburg, the beautiful town, as it was before the fire.

From the time the Nazis entered Lithuania till this very day, I can not forget my relatives who were killed in the terrible Holocaust. Whenever I think of them, I feel profound pain -- an entire family was destroyed and is no longer.

Shraga, Rachel and Beines Hes

[Not in original Yizkor Book - courtesy of Rachel Hes Greenstein]

I remember my childhood days in Yurburg -- happy and merry times. I lived amongst a large family in an atmosphere of friendship, everyone helping each other. We had a single story wooden house with a large yard around it. There were buildings in the yard, stables and sheds for cows and horses. My father, Reuven Hes, was a cattle trader; he would send the cattle to be sold in Kovno by gentiles. He made a good living and we lived a calm and quiet life. My mother Pesia skillfully managed the household and was a good and devoted mother to her children. We were five brothers in our family -- Nekhemyah, Yisrael, Shraga, Beinish and Mosheh-Mendel. There were three daughters -- together with me four -- Golda, Gittel and Miriam. The parents watched their children grow up and drew great satisfaction from this.

However, after a while, a terrible tragedy befell my family -- my father, Reuven, contracted coronary disease and died. After my father's death a series of tragedies descended on us, among them the fire, of which I spoke, and the Holocaust. The family was separated. My brother Nekhemyah, who married, moved to Tavrig, before the Nazi Germans entered Yurburg, and he died there. My sister Miriam and my brother Shraga perished in the days of the Holocaust in Yurburg.

I, my mother and brothers -- Yisrael, Beinish and Mosheh-Mendel -- were living in Kovno. When the Nazi hooligans entered Yurburg many people fled from Kovno in the direction of Russia. My mother, brothers and I, who were living in Kovno, also fled in the direction of Yanova. On the way the Nazi pilots attacked the poor people who were trying to escape and many were killed. The Nazis who pursued us caught my family and me. The murderers separated the men from the women. My brothers -- Yisrael, Beinish and Mosheh-Mendel, were sent to Fort VII near Slabodka and, as far as I know, they perished there.

I remained behind with my mother. We were taken to the Kovno ghetto. After a prolonged stay at the ghetto we, my sister and mother, were sent to the labor camp at Palemon. At the camp we were forced to work carrying bricks. Living conditions were poor. Many had no energy left especially the elderly. One day an "Aktion" was announced of old women and children. A S.S. (Nazi) officer came to me and brutally took away my poor mother, the only one of my family left to me. I never saw her again..and I remained all alone.

I tried all the time to overcome the difficulties and used all my energies to escape the claws of the Nazi beast. The end of the war was near, when I was sent together with other women to the Stutthof camp in Germany. While I was in Germany I passed through six camps, where I worked very hard until my liberation in March 1945. I was safe. The war was over -- and I, the only one of my large family, survived. I was free, but I felt no joy. The feeling of deep sorrow never leaves me.

True, I finally attained peace and quiet. I immigrated to Israel, founded a family and I am happy to be in my own country and among my own people.

However, how can I forget my past -- my childhood days and my parents home in our Yurburg -- or forget what the Nazis did to us? It is impossible to forget such a Holocaust, such a terrible tragedy, and we should never forget or forgive those who murdered our people.

Translated from Yiddish -- Paz

TRANSLATION OF PAGES 171 - 172

MY PARENTS HOME

By Yafah Levin-Taitz

My family, the Levin family, was an old and well-known family in Yurburg. My father, Mordekhai (Mordechai) (Motel) Levin, was born in Yurburg, and so was my mother, Golde-Gittel-born Hes. We were four children in the family - Meir, Raphael, Jafah (I myself) and Rivkah.

Unfortunately, all of them, except for myself, perished in the Holocaust, which affected the Jews of Yurburg, like all other Jewish communities in Lithuania. I remember all of them. I fondly remember their lovely personalities.

My mother was a beautiful woman. Those who knew her when she was young say that she was always elected beauty queen at the charity functions in Yurburg, and received many awards. Nevertheless, my mother was a devoted mother - a modest woman, a good and noble soul.

My father was a well-known merchant in town. He had business ties with German merchants. He was always traveling between Yurburg and Memel (Klaipeda) and Koenigsberg, Brikenkap, Smalininken etc. for business purposes. My father was an upright businessman, very popular both among Jews and gentiles, and always ready to help. Many of those who knew him spoke of his love for others.

Our family was a good family - it would be a blessing if there were many like it.

In June 1941 World War II broke out. I myself was not in Yurburg when the Nazi hooligans entered town. I did not witness the terrible atrocities and was not with my family when destruction came. I shall always be sad about this.

About a week before the war broke out I went to visit my grandmother in Kovno. When the Nazis invaded Yurburg there was no way of return anymore. I was worried about my family, but in those days I was in a difficult position. I entered the Jewish ghetto of Slabodka, a little girl alone, and I lived through this hell together with the Jews of Kovno.

I was lucky enough to come out alive and at the end of the war I was transferred to the labor camps in Germany. I was fortunate enough to be liberated on the 10th of March 1945 in Luenburg, close to the Polish border.

"I am free"! Together with the others in the camp we planned our future - "where shall we go?"

Together with many other refugees, I fled to Germany and from there to France. I was still a young girl, so I joined a youth aliyah group and was fortunate enough to go to Eretz Yisrael, my final destination.

In Israel I was sent to school at Magdiel. Before the War of Liberation I joined the "Gadna" led by Arik Sharon, a native of Magdiel, now a famous general in Israel. After a while I joined the *"Palmakh"* and fought in the War of Liberation together with all the other young Israelis.

After the War of Liberation I got married. We have three children, and I presently have seven grandchildren. A new generation grew up in Israel. I am happy to live in my own country, but memories constantly bring me back to Yurburg, my parents' home, my relatives and friends - all the Jews of Yurburg I loved in that beautiful town.

All those people from Yurburg are no longer. I shall never forget them.

TRANSLATION OF PAGES 173 - 175

THE ZE'EV (VELVEL) LEVIN FAMILY

By Rachel Levin-Rozentsveig

Ze'ev (Velvel) Levin was one of Yurburg's long-standing inhabitants and a well-known merchant. He dealt in timber and export. In the early twenties an export company was set up in Yurburg, for the purpose of preventing competition and increasing the exporters' scope of activity.

The company's name was *"Export-Handel,"* i.e. export company. Each export sector had a special committee. Ze'ev Levin was elected to the committee dealing with timber export. Ze'ev played an important role on the committee, for he was an expert in his field. His wife helped him.

When Lithuania's nationalistic government started to limit the rights of the Jewish merchants, Ze'ev's brothers left Lithuania and immigrated to the United States.

Ze'ev and his wife Golde had five sons - Yerakhmiel, Yekutiel, Khanan, David and Hilel. The boys were educated at the local school and afterwards at the Hebrew Gymnasium, where they received a Zionist education.

Thus life went on until the Nazi occupation in the summer of 1941. The Nazi murderers, assisted by their cruel Lithuanian helpers, put an end to the Jewish community in Lithuania. For three months the murderers tortured the defenseless Jews, until they were covered by dust; but a few managed, in one way or another, to escape from the murderers. The Levin family was almost entirely wiped out. The only survivors were the two sons, Khanan and David, who were not from Yurburg in those days.

KHANAN (Chanan) LEVIN

Khanan Levin, born in 1914, fled with his wife Bluma -born Blumenthal- to the Soviet Union. On the way their oldest daughter Nina was born. Khanan was recruited to the Red Army and joined the 16th "Lithuanian" regiment, composed mainly of Jewish soldiers. Khanan served as the division's photographer in the army. Here his gift for photography was discovered. His photographs of the division's fierce battles were published in Moscow and the United States. Khanan became famous for his sharp eye and artistic talent.

In 1944 Khanan arrived in Lithuania with the division and saw the destruction of the Jewish communities, the loss of Yurburg and his family. He had but one moment of solace when he met his brother David who was saved when he hid with a farmer, after he escaped from the Kovno ghetto. Khanan went on with the conquering army to Germany, his camera in hand. The photographs he took in the period of the war are included in the illustrated book **"Along the Battle Path,"** a document of the battles, soldiers and officers up to the decisive victory over the enemy.

When the war was over, Khanan's family closed ranks; his wife and daughter arrived in Vilna and established their home there.

Khanan joins the Lithuanian newspaper TIESA (Truth) as a senior press photographer. In this function he accompanies the heads of state and their actions. His photographs are published in the press and at exhibitions and he receives praise and awards.

In 1983 a book appears in Vilna which is dedicated to his life and activities **as** a press photographer - Chanonas Levinas Gyvenimo Zingsniai - the book is written in three languages, Lithuanian, Russian and English.

Khanan and his wife presently live in Vilna together with their daughter and son Moshe. His children founded families and they all live in Vilna. His daughter Galia immigrated to Israel in 1972 and is an English teacher at present. Khanan has close ties with Israel, but his wishes have not yet been realized.

David Levin   **Khanan Levin**

[Photos Courtesy of Rachel Levin]

DAVID LEVIN

Khanan's brother, David Levin, was born in 1915 in Yurburg. He studied at the local school and then completed his studies at the Hebrew Gymnasium in Yurburg. His complementary studies were in accounting. Like his friends, he too was a member of the Zionist youth movement and absorbed the love of Eretz-Yisrael.

In the days of the Holocaust David was in Kovno and was put into the ghetto, where he passed through hell, but survived. Before the ghetto was destroyed, he escaped and hid with a farmer's family.

When the war was over the "Brikha" (Escape) to Eretz-Yisrael movement was founded in Kovno and Vilna. At the start of 1945 David left Kovno, together with his girlfriend-wife Rachel -born Rosentsveig - and joined the groups of blockade-runners who arrived in Eretz-Yisrael in unconventional ways. After a long, daring and exhausting journey David and Rachel reach the shore of Israel, David's goal has been reached, and his dream has indeed come true.

David settles in Tel Aviv and establishes his home there. He gets a job at the "Hasneh" insurance agency as senior accountant. He serves the company faithfully, is popular and well liked by all.

David was a nice man, and with his quiet way and love of mankind he made many friends and companions. David often meets his old friends from Yurburg, his place of birth, which he never forgets, and together with a number of friends they set up the "Former Residents of Yurburg Association." It is the purpose of the association to gather together all those who have come from Yurburg, in order to commemorate their Jewish community, which was destroyed by the German murderers. David took part in all the association's plans - the conventions, the planting of the forest named after the Yurburg community, the commemoration in the Holocaust basement, etc. He also served as the association's auditor. His home was always open to former residents of Yurburg, city-dwellers as well as kibbutz members. He totally identified with the association and its aim to commemorate the Yurburg community. However, before he could witness the realization of the association's plans he died at an early age, at the age of 56. David's absence is deeply felt by the Former Residents of Yurburg association, whose members are naturally getting sparse. He assisted the association in its activities, and was a friend of many of its members. However, David's home has remained open. Rachel tries to keep up the family tradition, is active in the Lithuanian Jewish archives, which include the Yurburg community. David's only daughter, Khasiah, is a mathematics teacher and established her home in Ramat Aviv; her son is named after David.

The home established by the late David in Tel Aviv still constitutes a warm corner for the entire Levin family, both those in Israel and relatives arriving from abroad; Rachel keeps in touch, and hopes the relationships will continue as long as possible.

November 1989

THE HESS FAMILY

By Tsevi Nekhemyah Hess

The memories of Yurburg, my town of birth, go back to 1929. That was the year when I graduated from the Hebrew Gymnasium in Yurburg and left town. I used to return to my parents' home for a few days once or twice a year. My parents' names were Tuviyah and Menukhah. My grandfather on mother's side was called Hirshel and on father's side Nekhemyah; when I was born in 1920 I was named after them, Hirsh-Nekhemyah.

I spent my childhood years in the little town of Shaudine on the other side of the Nieman. At the start of World War I, when father was recruited to the Russian army, it was hard for my mother to support her three young children, therefore she sent us to Shaudine, where my mother's brothers Meir and Aba and her sister Hava and grandmother Lea lived. When the German army conquered Shaudine, they opened a primary school there in the German language and I studied at that school.

When father returned from the army we also returned to our home in Yurburg. We were seven children in the family - four daughters and three sons. I studied at the "kheder" (religious elementary school) with a "Melamed" (teacher at a kheder) and later on at the Hebrew Gymnasium until my graduation. We lived on Yurburg's main street opposite the Christian church. We were a close-knit family, and observed tradition, like most other families in town. At home Yiddish was spoken. At an early age I went with father to pray at the prayer house, close to the town's market. On the "high holidays" we prayed at the Old Great Synagogue, a beautiful building with woodcarvings on the Holy Ark and Eliyahu's beautiful chair. [Photo of Eliyahu's chair can be found in the section on the synagogue.] Father had fixed seats ("Shtot") at the two great synagogues, which he had inherited. My father was a merchant and traveled to the villages, bought cattle, poultry and sold them to the butchers in town.

Family life took its usual course, without any particular problems. I studied languages at the humanities faculty of the Lithuanian State University in Kovno. I made a living as a private tutor. After a while I was recruited to the Lithuanian army. I was sent to the army officers' school (Karo Mokykla). After my army service I took a complementary course at a physical education institute and served as a gymnastics teacher at the Hebrew Gymnasium in Kovno. At the same time I was a trainer at the *"Hapoel"* sports association.

World War II broke out in those days. The Nazis invaded Lithuania and our town of Yurburg was among the first casualties. The Jewish community was destroyed and our family perished. My parents, two brothers - Yisrael and Leibel- and the two sisters - Devorah and Bilhah - were murdered together with all the other Jews and no trace is left of them.

My sister Golda and her husband Shelomoh Klininsky survived. They went to Israel. Shlomo passed away in Israel in 1977. My sister Hannah, who was saved together with her husband Yitskhak Shleifer, had the good fortune to go to Israel as well, and they passed away - Yitskhak in 1973 and Hannah in 1981. Both Golda and Hannah were in the Kovno ghetto and the Stutthoff camp in Germany.

I managed to flee to Russia with my wife Sonia. After we passed through hell we reached Uzbekistan and there we worked as high school teachers. After World War II we returned to Vilna. I taught at the technical college and the Lithuanian University, as senior lecturer, for almost thirty years.

In 1976, after 20 years of denial of an exit permit, I was finally able to realize my dream and received an exit permit to immigrate to Israel, together with my wife Sonia. In Israel I worked for three years as a clerk at the municipality of Bat Yam and in 1979 I retired. In 1986 I moved from Holon to Jerusalem, where I now live in the Ramoth quarter, close to my family. My son, Eliyahu, immigrated to Israel after 13 years of denial of an exit permit. He is a graduate of the Vilna University, a mathematician.

I often ask myself what the most pleasant memories are that I have of Yurburg. The answer is - they are many and unforgettable. I will never forget the Hebrew Gymnasium on "The Gaon of Vilna" street, as the street was called by many Jews. The Jews called the Gymnasium "Tel Aviv" and the park around it was called "Tel Aviv Park."

I remember the names of the teachers who taught us - Zantkovsky, the bible teacher - to this very day I am able to recite select chapters from Amos and Yeshayahu which I learned from him. I also remember the excellent teacher Kosotsky, who taught literature and history, or Mordekhai (Mordechai) Taikhman who taught mathematics and also was the principal of the gymnasium.

Then there were teachers like Movshovitz and Dembo and the chemistry teacher, engineer Khen and the German language teacher, Mr. Lerman, who was an expert on German language and it was said that he knew Goethe's "Faust" by heart. And while I am writing these lines, I recall the profound sermons of Ha' Gaon Rabbi Avraham Dimant, which were so impressive. I was also deeply impressed by Chief Cantor Alperovitz, a tall and handsome man, who would sing with the choir at the synagogue on holidays and sometimes on the Sabbath as well. He was well-versed in music and composed many beautiful melodies for the holidays.

I recall many Jews in Yurburg, among them the physician Dr. Gershtein, the pharmacist Bergovsky and hundreds of other scholars, as well as "simple people," honest men.

However, my most pleasant memories of Yurburg are from the days when we were young, when I was a member of the "Hebrew Scouts - *Hashomer Hatsair*" movement. I remember the scouts club at the end of town and its lively and cultural atmosphere. I was most impressed by the chief youth leader, Hayim (Chaim) Sigar, whose lectures were full of the love of Israel and Eretz-Yisrael. "Older brother" Hayim Sigar devoted many hours to educating the scouts and the scouts loved him in return and remember him. I can still hear the sentimental songs we sang and the unforgettable patriotic songs.

I also remember the outings in the beautiful landscape surrounding Yurburg, and the scouts' camps in the heart of nature. It is impossible to wipe any of this from my memory.

Yurburg was and is no more. There was a Jewish life there; there were dreams and hopes. All that is gone, never to return. I shall never forget our dear ones in the town where we were born and our community, which was destroyed.

Beautiful Yurburg - along Imstra stream - May 2001

[Not in original book - photo by Dr. Leon Menzer]

TRANSLATION OF PAGES 179 - 183

THE PETRIKANSKY FAMILY

By Zevulun Poran

My family arrived in Yurburg from Russia in 1922 and settled at the home of Uncle Leib Bernstein on Kovno Street, opposite the square of the Great Synagogue.

My grandfather, on father's side, Zevulun (Zavel) Petrikansky, was born in the little town of Kazlu-Ruda (in Yiddish: "Kazlove-Rude) in 1865, the homeland of the Petrikansky families. Kazlu-Ruda is a very special little town; entirely covered by forest trees and in the center of town there is a relatively large railway station, mid-way between Kovno and Germany. The Petrikansky families, and among them my grandfather Zevulun (Zavel) Petrikansky, were timber traders, owners of lumber mills and guesthouses. My grandfather married Toibe (Tovah) Lapidoth and they had a son Yehudah Leib (Alter), an only son after two of his older brothers died of diphtheria. My grandfather was a trader, like all the Petrikansky families, and he was a partner in the family enterprises; he died at an early age and my grandmother died in old age in Novo-Poltavka, a Jewish settlement of farmers in south Russia.

My grandfather, on mother's side, Yosef Bernstein, was born in 1855 in Naishtot -Shirvint, on the German border. He married Hayah and they had two daughters and one son, Leib Bernstein (1875). Yosef's wife Hayah died at an early age. One of Yosef's daughters is Malkah who married Yehudahh Leib (Alter) Petrikansky. Grandfather Yosef Bernstein died in Novo-Poltavka in south Russia.

My father was born in 1885 in Kazlu-Ruda. When he grew up he continued his father's business and settled at an estate near the lovely little town of Visoke-Rude, near Kazlu-Ruda. This was the estate of his father-in- law Yosef Bernstein.

When World War I broke out in 1914, the family was exiled to Kherson in south Russia.

During the years of the revolution in Russia in 1917 and the hunger, our family moved to the Jewish farming settlement of Novo-Poltavka, where we made a living. My father was appointed officer of the Independent Jewish Defense in the days of the pogroms. In Russia we studied at Russian-Soviet schools and in private we studied Hebrew and Jewish studies. From here we moved after a couple of years to Minsk, the capital of White Russia (Belorussia), in order to reach Lithuania where Uncle Leib Bernstein lived, in Yurburg. After about two years in beautiful and hungry Minsk we finally reached our destination, independent Lithuania where we settled, as mentioned before, in Yurburg.

Uncle Leib Bernstein himself moved to Shavli, where he set up a large plant for linen processing called "Semlinas."

My father entered the world of business and joined an exporters company in Yurburg called "Export-Handel." He headed the linen and linen seed section. In 1928 the Lithuanian-nationalist government took over the import-export business, removing it from Jewish hands. The injustice cried to heaven. My father then went to manage the Semlinas factory in Shavli, which was a unique factory in Lithuania. In the early thirties our family went to live in Kovno.We were seven people - my father in Shavli, my mother and three brothers - Yakov, Mosheh, Yitskhak and three sisters- Hayah, Rachel and Shoshanah in Kovno. I no longer lived at home at that time. My brothers, who had not yet graduated from the gymnasium in Yurburg, continued their studies at the gymnasium in Kovno. My sisters studied at the State University. My sister Shoshanah went on training to life on a kibbutz. The years we spent in Yurburg were pleasant and prosperous years. We got attached to the beautiful little town and its charming surroundings. Its beautiful sights were an integral part of us. When we were children and teenagers we saw many beautiful places in Russia, but none of them as charming as Yurburg. Wherever we went, when we left Yurburg, we saw ourselves as Yurburgers in heart and soul. We shall never forget that wonderful Jewish community.

Our family was a traditional family, very close, a Zionist family, aspiring to go on aliyah and realize its ideals. However, from all the family members only two managed to go to Israel - my sister Shoshanah and I. The others, all the members of my family, parents, brothers and sisters, were murdered in the terrible days of the Holocaust at the Kovno ghetto. They suffered terribly at the ghetto. My oldest sister Khayah, a graduate in literature and philosophy of the Lithuanian university married the author and poet Ari Glasman, one of the editors of the *"Yiddishe Shtime"* and they and their five-year old son Giora were put into the ghetto and lived together with our family. (Just before the war Ari Glasman published a first novel in *Yiddish "A Fenster zu der Welt,"* he also belonged to the group of young authors and poets of which Leah Goldberg was a member. Avraham Shlonsky, the writer, sent him a S*ertifikat*, but too late . . . .) When he entered the ghetto, Ari Glasman was immediately taken in the action of the 550 "intellectuals" to a place from where he never returned. My sister Rachel, a surgeon, worked at the illegal hospital at the ghetto, where she was murdered together with the patients and the doctors. My brother Yakov died from physical exhaustion and suffering at the ghetto and he was buried at the Jewish cemetery in Slabodka.

The story goes that my brother Mosheh, who was an engineering officer in the army, introduced arms into the ghetto, and trained those going into the woods.

All my other relatives were murdered in the underground bunker at the end of the bloody war. All of them were the victims of the horrible Nazi-German crime!

Little Giora, the son of Hayah and Ari Glasman, who grew up in hiding, died together with the family, and already at an early age, as told by the survivor Gail, he wrote a diary and songs, part of which she remembers by heart -

The time will come

Indeed, it is not far away -

When we will torture the Germans

With a prickly whip

(Translated by Paz)

He too, Giora, the young child, went together with the others.

My sister Shoshanah, who went to Israel before me, married Aharon Knishinsky. Shoshanah was a teacher in Ramat Gan, where she lived, until she retired. The Knishinsky family had two sons, Avraham and Aviyahu, university graduates, who live in Arizona, U.S.A., with their families.

I went to Israel after a long stay in Lithuania. I studied in Kovno at the teachers college and the university. As a teacher, I was sent to the little towns of Kalvaria and Zhezhmer, and after that I served as the pedagogic director of the children's home in Kovno. I was active in the "Maccabi" youth movement and then in *"Hashomer Hatsair"* as a youth leader and member of the chief management and head of the group in Kovno. For a couple of years I was the movement's representative at the *"Hekhalutz"* center and the *"Dos Wort"* editing committees, a member of the *"Keren Hakayemeth"* center and other institutions. I took part in the 20th Zionist Congress as a representative of the Eretz Yisrael Haovedeth list and in Zionist-pioneer youth conferences in Europe.

In the agricultural training I was a member of the Dompen group in the Memel district and I went to Israel with the pioneering aliyah in 1938. In Israel I changed my name to the Hebrew name *Poran*, a kind of rebirth . . .

When I came to Israel I joined Kibbutz Kefar Masarik, when it was set up, including the "Khomah u'Migdal" (Tower and Stockade) days. I worked as the movement's envoy at the educational institute in Mishmar Ha'Emek. I was a member of the *"Haganah"* and after the War of Independence and military service in the besieged capital I settled in Jerusalem. I worked at the head office of *"Keren Hakayemeth"* as the director of the Zionist-education department, in educational publications and in teachers training. At present I am retired and a member of the Former Residents of Yurburg association, I am the editor of this Memorial (Yizkor) Book of the Community of Yurburg, where I was educated and where my personality and Zionist outlook were formed. I had the good fortune to go to Israel, assist in its building and live in the independent State of Israel. In Jerusalem I coordinate the activities of the Former Residents of Lithuania Association, which aims at facilitating the absorption of emigrants from Lithuania in Israel and especially aims at commemorating the Lithuanian communities which were destroyed in the Holocaust.

In Israel I married Tsiporah Kandel, a Holocaust survivor from Dresden, Germany, who is my all-time companion, and encourages me in my work and public activities. In Jerusalem - at Kiryath Hayovel - Tsiporah and I established our home and here our two daughters were born -Anath, who is a teacher in Jerusalem, married Tsevi Remetz, an artist and printing studio owner. Our first grandson - Shakhar - is presently serving as a paratrooper in the IDF, and the two girls, Shani and Shiran are getting on with their studies, one at high school the other at elementary school. The parents of Tsevi Remetz, Shelomoh and Rivkah, Holocaust survivors, live in Jerusalem. They come from the Vilna area. Osnath, my daughter, is a teacher and educator, married to Nekhemyah (Nemo) Ari; an engineer and they have three sons - Nimrod, Yiftakh and Itamar, pupils at school. The family lives at "Omer" near Beersheva. The parents of Nekhemyah, Gideon and Yokheved, Holocaust survivors, live in Jerusalem. They come from Vilna.

The members of my family in Tel Aviv, on my mother's side are the Tolia Kapulsky family, the daughter of Clara and Ze'ev Dushnitsky, the granddaughter of my uncle Leib and Vitel Bernstein. The daughter Tolia is married to Arieh Kapulsky, the owner of the "Kapulsky Enterprises." Their son, Dr. Raziel Kapulsky, was a physician and their daughter Vitia and her family. Uncle Leib Bernstein died in the first days after his aliyah to Israel and was buried at the municipal cemetery in Haifa. His daughter Clara Dushnitsky died in Tel Aviv and her two sisters - Mihalina Kantor and Dora Haber live in the United States.

Three sons of the Leventhal family, grandsons of my grandfather Yosef Bernstein - Dr. Yedidyah Leventhal, was a volunteer in the War of Independence, helping to rehabilitate those wounded in the war; the brothers Sol and Lou are also doctors and they live in the United States, all of them love Israel. From those of Petrikansky origin - those in Israel coming from Kazlu-Ruda - the late Hannah Petrikansky, Gita Petrikansky-Levinson (Netanya) and Yosef Petrikansky, Holocaust survivors in Tel Aviv. One of the Petrikansky families who were saved lives in Montevideo in Uruguay and another family in Canada.

This is the story of my family, the Petrikansky family, comes to an end, the generation of fathers and sons, who died like martyrs, killed by bestial German-Nazi and Lithuanian murderers.

Those who are left of the family will always remember their dear ones and bequeath their heritage to the next generations.

The Petrikansky family before Zevulun's Aliyah to Eretz-Yisrael in 1938

From left; brother Ya'akov; Zevulun; Mother Malkah; sister Klara (Hayah); father Yehudah (Alter); sister Dr. (Med.) Rachel; writer and poet Ari Glazman-Klara's husband. Missing are the sister Shoshanah (in Eretz-Yisrael); Brother Mosheh (officer in the Lithuanian army); brother Yitshak (studying).

TRANSLATION OF PAGES 184 - 185

FAMILIES IN YURBURG

By Zevulun Poran

In 1982 the Association of Former Residents of Yurburg sent questionnaires to its members in which they were asked to fill in the personal details requested in the form - about them and their families.

Replies were received from over thirty former residents of Yurburg. This is a quite impressive number of replies. After we edited and revised the material we obtained thirty concise surveys which provide an overall picture of the Yurburg community in its days of glory as well as in the days of the terrible tragedy.

From the concise surveys we learned about thirty homes in Yurburg - grandparents, parents, children and relatives. We became acquainted with their activities and way of life. The majority of the families were well off economically and had a very high standard of living according to the norms of Yurburg. All the parents had links with synagogues, some more others less so. The way of life at home was traditional. The parents received a religious or general education.

All the families showed a positive attitude to Zionism and donated to the national funds. In addition, they also donated to charity funds. Almost all the children received a Zionist-Hebrew education at the schools and this was reflected in their Zionist outlook. The family members spoke Yiddish among themselves. The Jews were not assimilated. The children spoke Hebrew at the educational institutions and youth movements. Few also spoke Hebrew at home. The 30 surveys provide a picture of the individual lives as well as that of the whole Jewish community in Yurburg.

The articles in the chapter about "Family Homes in Yurburg" complement the survey and emphasize the picture of the way of life of the families in the Jewish community.

The picture we received of the fate of the families in the days of the terrible tragedy in the period of the Holocaust is very gloomy.

We saw a shimmer of light in the stories of the survivors who came to Israel, built their homes there and were absorbed into the Israeli community, founded families and gave birth to a splendid next generation in Israel.

Unfortunately the handwriting of some of the answers was not clear, and this made it difficult to understand the text. At other times the text was incomplete. Errors may therefore have occurred here and there and there may be some inaccuracies in the surveys, we apologize for this.

Nevertheless, it seems to us that the surveys drawn up in accordance with the replies to the questionnaires, are an important and significant contribution to this memorial book and commemorate the families' dear ones.

With the publication of the recordings we have fulfilled our moral duty to commemorate our beloved martyrs forever.

Blessed be their memory.

Zevulun Poran

We owe it to our fathers, nameless and humble,

To remember them and their actions

To inscribe them in golden and shining letters

In our nation's book of eternal life

Blessed be their memory!

Feinberg Family in late 1930s
Courtesy of Diana Berzaner Tobin
[Not in original Yizkor Book]

TRANSLATION OF PAGE 186

THE ELIEZER ELYASHUV FAMILY

By Aharon Elyashuv

Members of my family:
> Father - Eliezer; Mother - Toibe
> Sisters - Ite, Braine, Sarah and Rivkah
> Brother - Yekutiel

Relatives:
> Uncle - Hayim (Chaim)-Eliyahu and Aunt Hinda-Rachel
> Sons - Leibel, Yekutiel, Hirsch, Mosheh
> Daughters - Beile, Miriam and Hayah

Died in the Holocaust:
> Mother - Toibe
> Brother - Yekutiel
> Sister -Braine
> Sister - Ita and her husband Yekhezkel

Survivors:
> Aharon and the sisters Sarah and Rivkah.

I had the privilege of being among the few survivors of my family. After the bloody war and the Holocaust, Yurburg no longer existed for me. None of my family members or those close to me remained. I decided to leave Yurburg, where I was born (1908), and where I grew up. When I was young I loved Yurburg and its beautiful surroundings. My parents worked at the family store and the children helped out. The family made a living and was able to donate to the poor and the Jewish National Funds.

We lived on 2 Butchers Street. Our home was traditional. My parents prayed at the synagogue. We observed the religious holidays. On the Sabbath and holidays we enjoyed the pleasant atmosphere at home. Our parents spoke Lithuanian and Russian, but at home Yiddish was spoken, just like at other homes in Yurburg.

In 1972 I came to Israel. I lived in Binyaminah and worked at a paper plant and at the Dan Caesarea hotel.

My relatives in Israel: Arieh (Leibel) Elyashuv and his family.

We live in our country, far away from Lithuania, but we remember Yurburg and will never forget it.

TRANSLATION OF PAGE 187

THE HAYIM ELIYAHU ELYASHUV FAMILY

By Arieh Elyashuv

My family - the Elyashuv family - lived in Yurburg, on Yatkever Street. My father, Hayim (Chaim)-Eliyahu and my mother Hinda-Rachel had two daughters - Beile and Miriam and two sons - Yekutiel, and Shelomoh-Mosheh. My sister Beile married Yekhezkel Yafe and they had a son called Yitskhak.

There were aunts and uncles in my family - my uncle David-Leizer Elyashuv, Aunt Taibe Elyashuv, who had six children. Aunt Liuba Kopelovitz had three sons - Yitskhak, Arieh and Yeshayahu.

Survivors in my family: Arieh, Yosef, Tsevi and Hayah. All the others perished in the Holocaust. My parents had a sewing shop. My father prayed at "Tifereth Bakhurim." He was religious. Had a Zionist inclination and supported the Jewish National Fund. The family donated to mutual assistance funds such as for brides, etc. Yiddish was spoken at home. There was a pleasant atmosphere in our home. Relations between children and parents were cordial; the children respected their parents. I will never forget this wonderful family atmosphere.

I was born in 1906. I studied at the local school. I helped my parents in their work at the sewing shop. I was a member of "Maccabi" and was active in sports. When World War II broke out, I was saved and lived in Vilna after the war. My brothers Yosef and Tsevi lived in the Middle East till 1956. After that they were united in Vilna. In 1979 I went to Yisrael. I live in Holon at present. I am a pensioner. My relatives in Israel are - Aharon Elyashuv, Rivkah Midah, Hannah Meltzer, Yakov and Yentel Levin.

March 28, 1982

Yudka Kopinski in Kaliani Forest with his new bicycle.

[Photo not in original Yizkor book. From photo album of Jack Cossid.]

TRANSLATION OF PAGE 188

THE APRIYASKI FAMILY

By Hannah Apriyaski-Abel

My family lived on Kovno Street. The following are the names of my family:

Reuven - Grandfather on my father's side.

Mosheh - Grandfather on my mother's side; Beile- grandmother on my mother's side.

My parents - Father Hayim (Chaim); Mother Khyene

Brothers - Yerakhmiel, Michael, Yakov, Yekhezkel, Reuven.

Sisters - Ethel, Bathsheva, Rachel, Hannah.

My family, like the other families in our community had a bitter fate. Almost all of them were destroyed by the cruel Nazis and their Lithuanian helpers.

The members of my family who were murdered in the Holocaust are:

My parents - Hayim (Chaim) and Khyene

My brothers Yerakhmiel, Yekhezkel, Reuven and their families.

My sister Bathsheva and her family - her husband Eliezer and her son Mosheh.

The few survivors are:

My sister Ethel Aronovsky and her late husband Alter;

My brother Yakov lives in Tel Aviv.

My family is gone, and I live with the pleasant memories of the past. I remember each and everyone. My father, the head of the family, who was all the time occupied with trade, and my mother, who was a housewife. We kept an observant household. Father prayed at the Great Synagogue. He had a Zionist inclination and donated to the national funds, Keren Hayesod and Keren Hakayemeth. My parents naturally donated to the mutual assistance funds and particularly to the poor. The children respected their parents and observed tradition. We spoke Yiddish at home. It was a friendly and pleasant home.

I was born in 1910. I studied at the Hebrew Gymnasium in Yurburg. I was a member of "Hashomer Hatsair." I spent my agricultural training at the Birkenheim estate near Memel. I went to Israel in 1932. I was a kibbutz member and belonged to the working women's organization. At present I am a housewife and I live with my family in Givatayim.

My relatives - those who survived the Holocaust - are my brother Yakov (pharmacist); Rachel - housewife, Ethel at an old-age home.

March 28, 1982

TRANSLATION OF PAGE 189

THE BEIMAN FAMILY

By Yakov Beiman

Our family settled in Yurburg in 1922. We arrived in Yurburg from Kovno. Our home was on Kovno Street.

The members of our family in Yurburg were: -

Grandfather Mosheh Beiman and Grandmother Leah; they owned a bakery; Father Zalman Beiman and mother Gittel, of the Yundler family. My father was a painter.

The daughters: Shoshanah Beiman (1916); Hannah Beiman (1918), the son - I myself - Yakov (1912).

The members of my family who I remember:

Yakov Beiman, uncle (Father's brother), Mottel Beiman, uncle (Father's brother), Yankel Beiman (Father's brother); Mirel Beiman (Father's sister).

The members of my family who were murdered in the days of the Holocaust in Yurburg are:

Zalman Beiman (Father); Mottel Beiman (Father's brother); Yankel Beiman (Father's brother), Mirel Beiman (Father's sister).

That is how my family in Yurburg came to a bitter end.

I, Yakov Beiman, studied in Yurburg at the elementary school and after that I studied electricity. Our home was religious-traditional. Our family members were Zionists. Yiddish was spoken at home. I have very pleasant memories of my life at home. My sister Shoshanah (Sokolovsky), who was a member of "Hashomer Hatsair" went to Israel and joined kibbutz "Amir" in upper Galilee.

I went to Israel in 1976. I worked in Israel as a locksmith at a factory. My wife Ella - a bookkeeper, my daughter Leah (Shuster) is an electronics technician; my son Isaac is a student at "Bezalel." My family lives in "Kiryath Sharet" in Holon.

March 21, 1982

TRANSLATION OF PAGE 190

THE BARSHTANSKI FAMILY

By Miriam Barshtansky - Verpulis

My family lived on Kovno Street opposite the police station, at the Yudel Kushelevitz house.

I remember the following members of my family: -

Grandfather Yosef and **Grandmother** Rachel- Musha Berker.

My parents - Betsalel and Ida Barshtansky.

My **brothers -** Mosheh, Hayim (Chaim), Benjamin.

Uncles - Nathan and Luba Berker, Shalom and Rachel Berker, Berl and Hayah Berker.

The bitter end: - all the members of my family were murdered, some of them in Yurburg, in Tavrig, in Vilna and in Ponivezh. And I, Miriam, am the only one of the Barshtansky family who was saved.

As long as I live on this earth I shall remember all of them.

I was born in 1921 and I went to Israel in 1966, taking my memories along. My parents were good people. My father worked in a shop and my mother was a housewife and also helped him. My father was an orthodox man and a Zionist. I too received an orthodox education at Talmud-Torah. I continue to live in Israel according to the tradition of my forefathers, light the Sabbath candles and attend synagogue.

The few relatives I had - two brothers, Gershon and Yitskhak Barshtansky and my sister Yokheved - passed away.

The children who live in Israel are - Duba and Anath Lifshitz (Arad); Ida Bornstein (Kiryath Hayim (Chaim)); Golda Verpulis (Kiryath Yam Gimel); Yosef Verpulis (Kiryath Yam Gimel).

March 19, 1982

TRANSLATION OF PAGE 191

THE REUVEN HESS FAMILY

By Rachel Hess - Grinstein

My family lived on Yatkever Street and was one of the oldest families in Yurburg.

My grandfather on my father's side, the late Nekhemyah, was born in 1837. He was a businessman; my grandfather on my mother's side - the late Shraga (Feivel), was born in 1853; four uncles on my father's side - the oldest, the late Yakov, was born in 1862. He was a businessman; three aunts on my mother's side. The oldest one was Esther.

My father, Reuven Hes, was born in 1877, and traded in livestock; my mother Pesia, of the Rochzo family, was born in 1883;

The daughters and sons in our family: Golda-Gitel, the oldest (1903); Nekhemyah (1905) a businessman; Miriam (1907); Yisrael (1909) a businessman; Shraga (1912) a businessman; Beinish (1914), I myself, Rachel-Mina (1922); Mosheh-Mendel (1924).

Family members murdered in the days of the Holocaust:

Except for grandfathers and uncles who died a natural death, all of them were murdered, in various places, where they lived. I, Rachel-Mina am the only survivor, together with Yafah Levin (Taitz), my niece Golda-Gitel. I live with the terrible memory of the Holocaust and remember each and everyone.

I remember my happy childhood, my large family, and our home with its large yard, the horses, cattle, sheep and poultry.

I studied at the "Talmud-Torah" school and at the Hebrew Gymnasium. My father was an orthodox Jew. He prayed at the old synagogue. We, the children, respected our parents. During the Jewish holidays our family got together, the married couples and their children and grandchildren, and our home abounded with joy. My father was a Zionist and contributed to the national funds, Keren Kayemeth and Keren Hayesod. They also supported the poor, the Frauen Verband etc. I was a member of the "Hashomer Hatsair" youth movement, my brother Beinish was a member of Beitar. I still remember the excursions in the Yurburg area - the frozen Nieman, the parks, the rivers and the forests.

After World War II I was happy to leave my past in Lithuania behind, and I came to Israel. After a long journey I arrived in Cyprus and from there in Atlith.

I found work in Israel - at "Assis," Kapulsky, the General Health Fund and a shop in Haifa. I am presently living in Kiryath Motzkin and keep in touch with my relatives - Jafah Taitz, my niece, with my cousin Yisrael Rochzo (a pensioner) and with Hannah Barsky.   **March 15, 1982**

Bassia Ess (Hess) and Leah Krelitz

Leizer Peisachson

[Both photos were not in original book - from Leah Krelitz Sherman's photo collection - Bassia and Leizer did not survive the Shoah (Holocaust)]

THE HESELKOVITZ FAMILY

By Yafah Heselkovitz -Lupiansky and Bluma Heselkovitz-Feldman

Our family lived in Yurburg, almost at the town's border. It was impossible to spot the beautiful house from the street, for a large garden full of trees and bushes crowned it with green.

The following were the members of my family:

Grandfather and grandmother on my mother's side - Yisrael and Pesia Lubin;

Father Shakhna Heselkovitz, born in 1880;

Mother Zelda Heselkovitz of the Lubin family, born in 1875;

The sons: Menakhem (Mendel) and Mosheh;

The daughters: Hayah, the oldest daughter and her husband Tuviah Pollak;

Yafah (Sheine), at present Lupiansky and the youngest in the family, Bluma, presently Feldman.

In the days of the Holocaust, the parents and daughter Hayah were murdered along with her husband Tuviyah and their four daughters. The son Menakhem (Mendel) was saved; he was a soldier in the Red Army and died in 1980. The son Mosheh - was murdered by Lithuanian youngsters who attacked him during a soccer game (see separate article and photo); we - the daughters - Sheine (Yafah) and Bluma went to Israel in the thirties. Yafah lives in Pardes-Hannah and works as a nurse at the General Health Fund. Bluma lives in Tel Aviv, worked as a clerk and is now a pensioner. We both have children and grandchildren, and we are the survivors of the family and take care to keep alive the memory of the family we had in the town of our birth.

It is hard to forget our home in Yurburg, our parents and the Jewish family atmosphere. Our parents were traditional. My father prayed at the synagogue and there was a warm atmosphere at home during the religious holidays.

My father was a businessman and my mother was a wonderful housewife, in addition to working hard in our garden that provided fruit and vegetables for our family. Our large garden contributed towards creating the country atmosphere in which we lived.

We both studied at the Hebrew Gymnasium and we were both members of "Hashomer Hatsair" which taught us Zionism, and encouraged us to be pioneers and go to Israel. And indeed we both went to Israel in the thirties and built our home there.

Our parents, who were Zionists too, and supported the Jewish National funds, were happy to see us go to Yisrael and to read the letters we sent them from there.

In the difficult days of the Shoah we thought of them and remembered them.

TRANSLATION OF PAGE 194

THE VAINBERG (WEINBERG) FAMILY

By Rivkah Vainberg (Weinberg)-Ravitzky

I was born in Yurburg (1914). My family lived on 1 Ugniagesiu. My parents were Yakov Shelomoh and Esther Rachel Vainberg (Weinberg).

My brothers were Yekhiel and Avraham and my sisters were Batyah, Nekhamah and Leah.

From among my family members I remember my grandfather and grandmother - Avraham and Tovah Haselovitz, my Uncle Joshua Vainberg (Weinberg) and my uncle and aunt Tsevi and Bertha Vainberg (Weinberg).

On the street where we lived we had our own home, a grain shed, a stall for the family's needs and a small fruit garden. My father was a grain and flax dealer, and he had export connections with German traders. My father was an educated man and a Torah scholar. He was a well-known public figure, active in various charity institutions. He was one of the founders of the Hebrew Gymnasium and contributed considerably to its development. We kept a traditional-orthodox home. My father prayed at the Feinberg Kloiz. During religious holidays there was a pleasant atmosphere at home. We spoke Yiddish at home.

We fulfilled our commitment to Eretz Yisrael by supporting Keren Hayesod and Keren Kayemeth. The fate of our family was bitter. When the war broke out our family was in Shvali and they were all murdered there.

I studied at the Hebrew Gymnasium and after that went for pioneer training in Kovno. I came to Israel in 1938. I joined kibbutz Givath Brener. I married and founded a family. The memories from Yurburg, good and bad, remain with me all these years; it is impossible to forget them and we must never do so, as long as we live.

TRANSLATION OF PAGE 195
THE CHAIMOVITZ FAMILY
By Niunia Chaimovitz-Slovo

I was born in 1920 in Kharkov (Russia) and I arrived in Yurburg with my family in 1923. We lived on Kovno Street, my father, Hayim (Chaim) Chaimovitz, owned a flourmill and a lumber mill near Sudarg.

I studied at the Hebrew Gymnasium in Yurburg. At home we spoke Yiddish, Hebrew and Russian. I was a member of the "Hashomer Hatsair" youth movement. Our home was traditional. Our parents supported charity institutions and as Zionists they contributed to the Jewish Nationalist Funds, Keren Kayemeth and Keren Hayesod. My brother, David Khaimovitz, went for pioneer training in the Memel region and immigrated to Israel in 1932.

I have fond memories of my home and family and I shall never forget them.

The following are the names of my family members:

Grandfather Yisrael-Hayim (Chaim) Khaimovitz;
Grandmother Golda-Feige Goldstein;
Father Hayim (Chaim) and mother Helena Khaimovitz;
Tania, my sister, lived in South Africa, as a physician, and she is presently in Israel;
Misha, my late brother, was a lawyer.
David, my brother, was a sea captain in Israel and has now retired.

Close family members who were murdered in the days of the Holocaust:

My father and mother; the Kretchmer family - father, mother and sister; the Goldberg family was entirely destroyed in the little town of Sudarg, near Yurburg.

Family members who survived:

My sister Tania, presently Dr. Khaimovitz-Ip, my brother Boria, was in the U.S.A. at the time; David Khaimovitz, Avraham Krechmer in Israel - Herzeliyah.

In spite of the terrible tragedy the survivors keep on living with the memories of the Holocaust. I, who survived, married Hayim (Chaim) Slovo and went to Israel in 1966. We worked as self-employed for 8 years.

My husband died and I am presently a pensioner. Our son is an officer in the standing army. The son of my sister Tania - Dr. Eli Ip - is a doctor at the "Hadassah" hospital in Jerusalem. I hope that the young generation will remember its origin.

TRANSLATION OF PAGE 196

THE LEVINBERG FAMILY

By Hinda Levinberg-Beker

My family was one of the oldest families in Yurburg. We lived on 11 Raseiniu Street.

The members of my family are:

My father, Yisrael Levinberg, born in 1880;
My mother Ethel, born in 1882;
My brother: Dov (Berl) born in 1903;
Shelomoh was born in 1909.
My sisters: Golda was born in 1905;
Sheine was born in 1913;
Judith was born in 1914.

All the members of my family perished in the Holocaust.

My brother - Dov (Berl) lived with his family in Canada and in Florida till he died. He was a Zionist activist and paid a number of visits to Eretz Yisrael.

My father was a timber dealer (A Wald Soicher), owned steamships and underwear and cellulose factories.

My father was an observant Jew. He was one of the "Gabbais" at the old synagogue. He assisted the poor and donated to the nationalist funds - Keren Hayesod and Keren Kayemeth.

We spoke Yiddish at home. The atmosphere was pleasant and friendly.

I left Lithuania and went to South Africa with my husband. When my husband died I went to Israel in 1972 together with my son and his family. My relatives in Israel - Hannah Karabelnik - Trainin. Rachel Karabelnik-Niv who lived in kibbutz Beth Zera, passed away.

October 4, 1982

(Parts of Hinda Levinberg's diary appear in this book)

THE LEIPZIGER FAMILY

By Alizah Leipziger-Porath

Our family lived in Yurburg, on Kovno Street. My parents had two houses, a residence and a house for a large sewing shop, where my mother worked and taught trainees. My two sisters also learned to sew. My parents had a vegetable garden and a large fruit tree garden. My father also had a workroom at home, for he painted houses, billboards and also drew. My family lived for many years in this house and I grew up there.

The following are the members of my family:

My grandfather Berl-Feivel and my grandmother Sarah Berlovitz;

My father Yitskhak and my mother Devorah-Leah (1871) Leipziger;

My sister Rachel (1894) and her husband Mosheh Hes;

My sister Hannah (1899), her husband Menakhem Gitelson;

My brother Tsevi Leipziger, born in 1896; went to the U.S.A.

My brother Eliezer Leipziger (1903), a lawyer, his wife Fania of the Krechmer family.

Members of my family:

Members of the Krechmer family, among them Sonia, the sister of Fania Krechmer.

My Aunt Menukhah Goldstein, my cousin Shelomoh Goldstein, born in 1914; my Uncle Hirschel Leipziger.

The members of my family and relatives who were murdered in the Holocaust:

My mother, my sisters Rachel and Hannah, my Aunt Menukhah Goldstein; my Uncle Hirschel Leipziger;

My brother Eliezer Leipziger, his wife Fania and their children the late Tuviah and Ezer (murdered in Ponivezh). Eliezer was the Principal of the Hebrew Gymnasium there.

My parents Fania and her sister Sonia Krechmer.

The members of my family who survived:

Shelomoh Goldstein - my cousin Menukhah Goldstein - presently in Chicago, U.S.A., a manufacturer, Zionist leader, philanthropist and important donor to Jewish Nationalist Funds and particularly Keren Kayemeth.

I must also mention myself among the survivors, for going to Israel saved me.

I was born in Yurburg (1909). I studied at the elementary school and the

Hebrew Gymnasium. I completed my high-school education at Vilkomir, for at that time there were no upper grades at the Hebrew Gymnasium in Yurburg. At the end of my high-school studies I studied at the "Tarbuth" teachers college. I belonged to the Socialist Zionists. Our home was traditional. My family was active Zionist. I used to converse in Hebrew with my brother Eliezer. The family spoke Yiddish among themselves.

I loved my home, which was friendly and cordial. I shall never forget the religious holidays at home and the wonderful atmosphere.

I shall never forget our town Yurburg - the nature walks, the beautiful scenery, sailing along the rivers and bathing in the Nieman. It was a beautiful world - gone forever.

I went to Israel in 1936. In Israel I joined kibbutz Afikim in the Jordan valley. I farmed, looked after children, taught. My late husband, Yitskhak Porath (Poritz), worked in farming, accountancy, training of young kibbutzim and founded the local school. My family consists of a daughter, Razia, member of Kibbutz Yotvatah, a high-school teacher. Twins, David and Jonathan. David is a biology teacher and works in various fields. Jonathan is a physical education teacher. And that is my part in the building of this land.

TRANSLATION OF PAGE 199

THE MAGIDOVITZ FAMILY

By Hannah Magidovitz - Goldman

I was born in Yurburg (1920). My family lived on 21 Yatkever Street.

The members of my family in Yurburg were:

Grandfather Herschel-Yudel and Grandmother Mikhal Heselkovitz, on my mother's side;

Grandfather Velvel and grandmother Magidovitz on my father's side.

Parents - Father Shalom and Mother Feige Magidovitz.

Brothers and sisters: My brother Heshel (1912); my sister Suzka, my brother Velvke; my sister Zeldke and I myself Hannah Magidovitz (1920).

Members of my family who were murdered in the Holocaust:

My parents, my brother Velvke, Zeldke with her husband, Yudiske (Judith)with her husband (Zarkin) and two children; and also Hayah.

The place and details of their burial are not exactly known.

Family members who survived:

My brother Heschel (presently in Vilna) and my sister Hayah (at present Hayah Abramson) who lives in Pardes Hannah.

Our family was traditional. We were a close-knit family. A warm and respectful atmosphere reigned at our home. My father prayed at the great synagogue and we were observant at home. My parents were involved with Zionism and Eretz Yisrael. I don't remember to which funds they contributed. We spoke Yiddish at home. We learned Hebrew at school. I was a member of the Zionist youth movement "Dror" and I wanted to go to Israel.

And indeed, I went to Israel in 1949, from Cyprus to Atlith, after I passed through all the horrors of the Holocaust in Yurburg. I married and I have two daughters - one is a nurse and the other a teacher, married with two children. My husband is a pensioner at present. I am a housewife. I keep in touch with my sister, who is a widow and lives in Pardes Hannah with her daughter. Many years have passed since the horrible murder in Yurburg, but it is impossible to forget all the terrible things that happened and the loss of my family.

March 21, 1982

Sister of Hannah Magidovitz
[Not in original book- from Leah Krelitz Sherman's photo collection]

THE MOST FAMILY

By Leah Most

My name is Leah Most. I was born in Yurburg in 1916. We lived on 26 Raseiniu Street. My great-grandfather Yitskhak Chaimovsky, my grandmother's father, was born in 1825. He was a timber merchant;

Grandfather Shalom Fleischer was born in 1860. He owned an estate;

The son Shelomoh-Hirsch lived in Rasein, died in Mexico;

The son Hillel (died in New York); the son Yisrael-Mosheh (died in New York); the son Meir was murdered in the Holocaust; the son Yehudah - presently lives in Vilna.

The daughters: Sarah Fleischer, Miriam Fleischer and Mosheh Fleischer were murdered in the days of the Holocaust.

My father, Yisrael Most, was murdered in the Yurburg area in 1917;

My mother, Hayah-Rivkah Most Fleischer, was murdered at a labor camp in Estonia.

Families and relatives murdered in the period of the Holocaust:

The Arstein family, at the Kovno ghetto;

The Fidler family in Yurburg;

Mordekhai (Mordechai) Ben- Yisrael Yitskhak with his wife and son in Yurburg;

Shraga, Ben-Yisrael Yitskhak with his wife and son in Yurburg;

Moshe was killed in battle during the war;

Hillel was shot at Fort VII in Kovno.

Yehudah died in the days of the Holocaust at the Kovno ghetto.

The survivors in our family:

The daughter of my brother, Dovele (**Duba - pictured below**) Most-Rosenberg was saved when she was at the Stutthof concentration camp; Yehudah Fleischer was saved when he was a soldier in the Red Army, during the war; I, Leah Most, was saved when I was at the Stutthof concentration camp.

Indeed, only very few of my family remained alive and we live with the bitter memory.

My family was long-standing in Yurburg. My father had a franchise to transport goods on a transport bus in Lithuania itself- Kovno, Klaipeda and Germany.

Our home was orthodox-traditional. My father prayed at the "Tifereth Bakhurim" synagogue.

Our family was active Zionist. We belonged to "Poel Mizrakhi" and its youth movement. My father contributed to Jewish Nationalist Funds - Keren Kayemeth and Keren Hayesod and also to the various charity funds to help the poor.

I cherish the memory of my family. It was a close-knit family and we had excellent relations with each other; we all respected our mother. We spoke Yiddish and also Hebrew at home.

My sister Yoninah and I studied at the Hebrew Gymnasium. My sister Yoninah went to Israel as a pioneer. We corresponded with her and were informed about what went on in Eretz Yisrael. I went to Israel only in 1963, having passed through all the horrors of the Holocaust. In Israel I worked at the "Ort" school in Kefar Saba. I live in Kefar Saba at present as well.

I am close to my sister Yoninah and the Efraimi and Reznik families - who are teachers in Israel. The Reznik family - Miriam and Shraga - live in Herzeliyah.

In Israel we live with the problems of our country and the memories of Yurburg, which is no longer.

March 14, 1982

Duba Most Rosenberg at the site of the mass murders at the Yurburg Jewish Cemetery in May 2001   [Photo not in original Yizkor Book]

TRANSLATION OF PAGE 202

THE MAZOR FAMILY

By Mina Mazor-Simon

I was born in Yurburg (1918). My family lived on 36 German Street. My father, Mordekhai (Mordechai) Mazor, owned a sewing shop. My mother, Feige, was a housewife. I had three sisters - Sarah, Fruma, Rachel and two brothers - Yakov and Gershon. Grandfather and grandmother lived in America. My relatives lived in America, South Africa and France.

In the days of the Holocaust in Yurburg the following were murdered: my sister Fruma with her husband and two children, my brother Gershon and my dear mother Feige. My father died before the Holocaust.

Survivors are my brother Yakov, who lived in South Africa (died 12 years ago) and my sister Rachel Mazor, who lives in Givatayim.

I have happy memories from my home in Yurburg. I particularly remember the religious holidays, celebrated according to tradition, with all the delicacies and prayers. Our home was traditional. My father prayed at the great synagogue. He was a Zionist and belonged to the "Poalei Zion" party. The family contributed to Keren Hayesod and Keren Hakayemeth. Yiddish was spoken at home.

I studied at the Hebrew Gymnasium, and after that at the "Red Cross" nursing school in Kovno. I worked for a while at the "Bikur Kholim" hospital. I was a member of the "Hatsofim -Hashomer Hatsair." I realized my dream and went to Israel in 1935 with "Hamaccabiyah."

I worked as a licensed nurse in Tel Aviv at the "Hadassa" hospital. When I married my husband, Dr. Simon, we moved to Haifa, to the "Moriyah" neighborhood.

When this page was published - Mina was no longer alive.

1982

TRANSLATION OF PAGES 205

THE NAIVIDEL FAMILY

By Mordekhai (Mordechai) (Motel) Naividel

Translation by Regina Naividel, daughter-in-law of Motel

I was born in Yurburg (1904) [1] to my parents Meir and Tovah. We lived on Kovno Street. My father had a store and was a salesman.

I remember about my family - my grandfather Meir [2] Naividel and my grandmother, Rachel. My brother, Hillel Naividel (1905) - a lawyer. My stepmother was Fania and her children were Reuven, Shalom, Hayah, and Fruma[3].

My relatives - aunts: Rivkah Litman[4]and Pola Gurvitch.

All members of my family were murdered during the Holocaust in Yurburg. My wife Cherna (Karabelnik) was murdered in Stutthof and my daughter Elinke was murdered in the Kovno Ghetto.

Mordechai Naividel 's first wife Cherna Karabelnik and their daughter, Elinke. They were murdered in the Shoah [photo was not in original Yizkor Book]

Saved: My brother Hillel (died in 1969), my niece Rachel Naividel-Gershovitz, a doctor, who lives in Kefar Saba.

The way of life in our home was traditional. My parents used to go to services in the Old Synagogue. My father was a member of the "Poalei Zion" (Workers of Zion). We donated to the Keren Kayemeth (Jewish National Fund). At home we spoke Yiddish and Russian. After the death of my mother, I was raised in my grandmother's home[5].

I studied law in the U.S.S.R. I was an attorney. Today I am retired as well as my wife. Our son David[6] is a student. I live in Be'er Sheva.

March 28, 1982 Mordekhai (Mordechai) Naividel

Note added: Mordekhai (Mordechai) Naividel died in Israel in 1993

Notes added by Regina Borenstein Naividel - daughter-in-law: (It is assumed that these mistakes were made in the intrepretation of Motel's handwriting or in the editing of the book.)

1. Motel was born in 1903.

2. Motel's grandfather was Shalom.

3. Fania and Meyerelia had only 3 children: Hayah (Chaia), Reuven and Fruma. *(Possibly Shalom died young and was not remembered by others in the family.)*

4. Gita Abramson Bereznitsky and Bella Abramson Kaplan (cousins) advise that the name of Motel's aunt was Hayah Rivkah Lipman (not Litman).

5. Motel was raised by his Aunt Pola, not his Grandmother.

6. Motel's son's name is Benjamin, not David.

Cherna (Karabelnik) and Mordechai Naividel and a cousin

[Photo was not in original Yizkor Book]

Photos courtesy of Benny Naividel

See additional article on Mordechai Naividel in the Appendix on page 666.

גרקבוצת ניבידל "מכבי" יורבורג 39

The Naividel Macabbi Group (Kvutzat Naividel)

Hillel Naividel in the center [photo was not in original Yizkor Book]

Top from left to right bottom: **, Rodansky, -, Yitzhak Rochzov, Melnik, Lieb Krelitz (son of Meir Krelitz and brother to Moshe Krelitz) .

Bottom from left to right bottom: Feldman, Miki Melnik*, Hershel Eliasov+, **, - Married to a Bass, Hillel (Lushka) Naividel*, - , - Mazar.**

**** Brother and sister**

* Hillel Naividel was in Kovno when the Nazis invaded Lithuania, so had time to flee East with the Russian army and spent the war in Uzbekastan, near the Chinese border. Hillel and his family returned to Lithuania after the war and lived in Vilna. Hillel eventually became the President of the Supreme Court in Vilna, and died in 1969 in that capacity.

*** Miki Melnick died in a heroic way, killing a number of Lithuanians and Nazis. Described in this Yizkor Book, according to Jack Cossid.

+ Lives in Israel

If not otherwise indicated, they did not survive the war.

TRANSLATION OF PAGE 203

THE MELNIK FAMILY

By Geulah (Grunia) Melnik-Rabinovitz

I was born in Riga, Latvia (1916). In 1928 I came to Yurburg from Russia together with my family. We lived on Raseiniu Street. I was part of a large family.

My father's name was Daniel and my mother's name Miriam.

I had two sisters - Mania and Bronia. Bronia was married and had a little daughter called Avivah.

My father was a grain merchant. My sister Mania worked at the Komertz Bank managed by Shmeryahu Bernstein. I finished the Hebrew Gymnasium in Yurburg and the kindergarten seminary in Riga.

We kept a traditional home. My father and mother prayed at the old synagogue. We spoke Yiddish and Russian at home. We were active Zionists. We contributed to Keren Hakayemeth and charity funds in town. I was a member of "Hashomer Hatsair" and my sisters of "Maccabi." There was a pleasant atmosphere at home. We always felt at ease and peaceful at home.

My family came to a bitter end. All the members of my family perished in the Holocaust.

I went to Israel in 1936, after pioneer training in Memel (Klaipeda). In my first year in Israel I worked as a kindergarten teacher in Yokneam and from there I moved to Tel Aviv. I married Yehoshua Rabinovitz, who became the mayor of Tel Aviv. We have three sons, two of them in Israel and one is studying abroad.

The editor (of the Hebrew volume) takes the liberty of adding that the Rabinovitz family was a well-known and popular family in Tel Aviv. The home of Mayor Yehoshua Rabinovitz and his wife Geulah opened its doors to anyone in need as well as to intellectuals and important people. Yehoshua Rabinovitz served as mayor for many years, and he was esteemed and admired by all the town's inhabitants for his many achievements in improving the town.

After his death, institutions and enterprises were named after him: The city' s award for culture and art as well as the well-known and splendid project "Ganey Yehoshua" - one of his many projects for the benefit of the town - are a handsome monument to his name and achievement.

TRANSLATION OF PAGE 204

THE MINTSER (Menzer)FAMILY

By Sheine Mintser-Pulover

I, Sheine, of the Mintser family, was born in 1919. We lived on 4 Kovno Street.

My father was a businessman. We had a pastry shop at home.

The following is the list of members of my family and their fate:

Grandfather and grandmother Mosheh and Rivkah Lubin, died before the Holocaust.

My father Aharon-Yehudah Mintser, died in 1933.

My mother Sarah Mintser-Lubin died in 1979 in Vilna.

My brother Dov (Berl) died in 1947 in Vilna.

My brother Nekhemyah died while he was in the Russian-Soviet army in 1943.

My brother Eliyahu (Luka) died in Vilna in 1982.

I, Sheine Mintser, went to Israel in 1971. After I went through the tortures of the Holocaust I lived in the U.S.A.

My relatives:

Uncle Gavriel and Rachel Lubin died during the Holocaust.

My cousin Hayah Lubin (Meirowitz) was saved and lives with her family in Vilna.

Members of my family who were saved:

Judith, the daughter of my brother Dov, Mintser (Walker), lives with her family in Equador. The son of my brother Eliyahu (Luka) lives with his family in Vilna.

The home of my parents in Yurburg was traditional. My parents were Zionists. We contributed to the Jewish Nationalist Funds - Keren Kayemeth and Keren Hayesod. We also contributed to the needy of the town. We spoke Yiddish at home, like all the families in Yurburg. My husband Mosheh Pulaver wrote books in Yiddish about the Jewish theater, his last book "Ararat" was published by I.L. Peretz, Tel Aviv, 1972.

In Israel we lived in Tel Aviv, 46 Shelom Zion Hamalkah.

March 31, 1982

TRANSLATION OF PAGE 206

THE SMOLNIK FAMILY

By Hannah Smolnik-Pulan

My family lived in the little town of Srednik on the Nieman, mid-way between Yurburg and Kovno. We moved from Srednik to Yurburg in 1915.

In Yurburg we lived on the street of the Hebrew Gymnasium and "Tel Aviv" park. Our family owned a large home with a fruit and vegetable garden. When they strolled in the neighborhood, our friends would pause near our home, enjoy the garden and receive a flower or fruit in season.

The members of our family:

Father Aharon Smolnik; Mother Devorah Smolnik;

Two sons - Nathan and Gershon;

Two daughters - Esther, and I, Hannah. Esther married Hayim (Chaim) Frank - who died abroad.

During the days of the Holocaust my family was already in Israel and no one was hurt, I was the first to go to Israel in 1929. My family followed and they settled in Kiryath Motzkin. Father worked at the "Ata" factory and mother was a housewife. My late parents passed away a long time ago. My brother and sister live in Kiryat Motzkin, and have children and grandchildren. We have heard nothing of our relatives, apparently they did not survive.

My children, Gideon, Ruth and Amirah and I live in Tel Aviv. My husband, engineer Pulan, died, and my children are married and active in culture and art. I have lived in Israel for many years now, but I still remember my past and the past of Yurburg.

Our home in Yurburg was a traditional home. We celebrated our holidays in a happy family atmosphere. We were a close-knit family that took care of its own needs and of the needs of others.

I studied at the elementary school and the Gymnasium and was a member of "Hashomer Hatsair." Our home was Zionist and my parents supported the Jewish National Funds.

in 1927 I went on agricultural training on behalf of "Hekhalutz" to the Dompen group, at an estate near Memel; two years later I went to Israel to the Benyaminah and Petakh Tikvah kibbutz nucleus. After a while I joined kibbutz Mishmar Haemek. In 1933 my family from Yurburg joined me in Israel

As in Yurburg, in Kiryath Motzkin too, my parents' home opened its doors to visitors and friends from Lithuania. We do not have any relatives from Lithuania in Israel, but many friends from Yurburg to whom I am very close.

1982

TRANSLATION OF PAGE 207

THE PULEREVITZ FAMILY

By Shoshanah Pulerevitz

I was born in Yurburg (1914). We lived on 50 Kovno Street. We had our own home, shops and and workshops.

My father was an orthodox Jew. He prayed at the great synagogue and founded the "Tifereth Bakhurim" company. My parents donated to the needy and contributed to charity. In addition, my parents were active Zionists. They donated to the Jewish National Funds, Keren Hayesod and Keren Hakayemeth. At home Yiddish and Hebrew wer spoken. I was sent to the Hebrew Gymnasium in Yurburg; I completed my studies by acquiring a profession - accountancy.

My father Nathan and my mother Batyah Pulerevitz

I was a member of the Beitar youth movement. I passed pioneer training and planned to go to Israel, but due to the restrictions on immigration certificates, I remained in Lithuania - until my family and I were hit by the terrible Holocaust.

The names of the members of my family:

Grandfather Eliezer and Grandmother Zlata Pulerevitz (grandfather was a goldsmith); My father Nathan and my mother Batyah Pulerevitz;

My sisters Hayah and Zahavah; my brother Reuven.

All the members of my family perished in the Holocaust. Only my sister Zahavah and I survived.

I went to Israel in 1973 and I live in Arad. My relatives in Israel are - my only sister , Zahavah, her husband Eliezer and their son - the BenYehudah family.

I live in our country with mixed feelings - the memory of the Holocaust and the joy of life in our country - our state.

March 15, 1982

TRANSLATION OF PAGES 208 - 209

THE FAINBERG (FEINBERG) FAMILY

By Mina Fainberg

Our family - the Fainberg family -was a large family in Yurbug. We lived on 1 Market Square.

The following are the members of my family:

Zalkind Fainberg, grandfather (1854), scholar, studied the Torah;

Hayah-Tovah Fainberg, grandmother (1860), shop owner;

Benjamin Fainberg, father (1879), businessman;

Henya Fainberg, mother (1886), housewife;

Yekhezkel Fainberg (1881), industrialist;

Tamara Fainberg-Blokh (1885), housewife;

Sheine-Reize Fainberg-Gut (1888);

Esther Fainberg-Goldberg (1890); housewife

Leibe Fainberg (1892), farm owner;

Shmaryahu Fainberg (1894), industrialist;

Rafael Fainberg (1896), industrialist;

My brother Shimon Fainberg (1918), clerk in the Ministry of Finance, Israel.

The members of my family in Yurburg:

Heshel Heselzon (1892), agent;

Gittel Shoham (1890), store-owner, wholesaler;

Avraham Yitskhak Kopelov (1896), dentist;

Mordekhai (Mordechai) Shimonov (1890), dentist and shop owner.

Family members who were murdered in the Holocaust:

Benjamin Fainberg in Yurburg (1941); Leibe Fainberg and his family in Kovno;

Tamara Bloch and her family in Vilna; Sheine-Reize Gut and her family in Esthonia;

Esther Goldberg and her family in Kovno.

Family members who survived:

Shimon Fainberg, died in Israel, Bat-Yam, 1977.

Tosia Blokh-Rosentsveig, Israel, Bat-Yam;

Shelomoh Pridham [a.k.a. Seigmund Feinberg, Steven Pridham] Los Angeles, U.S.A.

I was born in Yurburg in 1915, I studied at the Hebrew Gymnasium. My father had various businesses - a farm and a textile and rubber factory. Our home was conservative. My father prayed at the great synagogue. We spoke Yiddish at home. My father contributed to various charity funds and to the maintenance of synagogues. we also donated to Keren Kayemeth and Keren Hayesod. My brother Shimon and I belonged to the "Hashomer Hatsair' youth movement and participated in its educational activity. My fondest memories of Yurburg are the Zionist youth movement.

Due to World War II my brother's and my own aliyah to Eretz Yisrael was held up. Shimon went to Israel in 1948 and I in 1975. I work as an accountancy clerk.

My relatives in Israel are - the Rosentsveig, Dvoretzky, Shimonov, Uliamperl and Bader families.

I live in our free country, but the memories of the past are with me always.

TRANSLATION OF PAGE 210

THE FRANK FAMILY

By Sarah Frank-Shapira

I was born in Yurburg (1914). Our family lived on Kovno Street, opposite the great synagogue. My parents on mother's side lived in Sudarg, a small town on the other side of the Nieman, close to the German border. Their family name was Fein. My late grandfather died in 1928 and my grandmother went with me to Eretz Yisrael in 1936; she died in Jerusalem.

I did not know the family on my late father's side, Yehudah Leib Frank, for his parents died when I was still a small child. My father died at an early age, when I was still a toddler.

I had an uncle, Shimon, in Naishtot-Shaki, and an aunt, Golda. Their family name was Goldberg. They had three children: Mordekhai (Mordechai), Leibe and a son whose name I don't remember.

My entire family was murdered - my mother Malkah, my brother Mordekhai (Mordechai)-Eli and my sister Libe-Beile. I don't know how they were murdered and died. I know nothing about them.

My mother was a widow and worked in her grocery store, which was next to our home. I studied at the elementary school and the Hebrew Gymnasium. Afterwards, I studied at the "Handels-Schule" in Memel. Our home was traditional. We prayed at the great synagogue and observed Jewish tradition at home, especially on Sabbath and the holidays. We respected mother and helped her as much as we could in her work. We spoke Yiddish.

We had strong ties with Eretz Yisrael, for mother's two sisters lived in Jerusalem. We were Zionists and contributed to Keren Kayemeth. I went on agricultural training to a "Mizrakhi" training kibbutz, and I went to Israel. I settled in Jerusalem. I married and had three sons - physicians - and one daughter (Avigdorah), a university graduate.

My relatives in Israel died. So did my husband, Yerukham Shapira. I only have a male and female cousin in Ramat Hasharon, a geologist, works at a bank.

1982

TRANSLATION OF PAGE 211

THE KOPELOV FAMILY

By Emanuel Kopelov

My parents were Avraham-Yitskhak and Miriam-Mosheh Kopelov. My father was a customs clearance clerk and my mother a housewife. We kept a traditional home. My parents were orthodox. My father came from a Hassidic family. He prayed at the Fainbergs-Kloiz in the Yatkever Gas.

From the ideological point of view my parents belonged to the Zionist Federation, and they were General Zionists. My father was very active on behalf of the Jewish Nationalist Funds. He had power of attorney on behalf of Keren Hakayemeth and Keren Hayesod in Yurburg. For many years he worked as a volunteer, and his devotion knew no bounds. We spoke Yiddish at home, Hebrew and Russian as well. The atmosphere at home was very Zionist, it was a warm Zionist home.

When the Nazis entered Yurburg, my parent's lives came to a bitter end. My sister Dasha was imprisoned in Auschwitz for a while and went from there to Paris. She died there at the end of December 1980. My four other sisters were in Russia since World War I, where they had arrived together with my parents, who were exiled there in 1914. Only one of my sisters is still alive and she lives in Moscow.

I, Emanuel (1914), grew up in Yurburg. I studied at the Hebrew Gymnasium. I was a member of "Hekhalutz" and I trained for aliyah to Israel, at a kibbutz-training center and in Ponivezh.

In 1935 I went to Israel and settled in Rehovot. Here I got a job at the Toner Sprinklers Factory Ltd., where I worked till 1938.

When the Ethiopian crisis erupted, the factory was closed down and I was unemployed, like so many others. For two years I worked at all sorts of jobs, among other things, at the Rehovot agricultural research station.

In 1941 I got a job at "Kupath Kholim" (General Health Fund), where I worked till 1950 as assistant bookkeeper. Later on I was appointed as chief bookkeeper at Kupath Kholim, (Heath Maintenance Fund) Rishon le Zion district. In 1951 I became auditor at the district tax office (*of Kupath Kholim*) in Rehovot. I carried out this task till my retirement in 1979.

1982

TRANSLATION OF PAGE 212

THE KARABELNIK FAMILY

By Hannah Karabelnik-Trainin

My family lived in Yurburg on Ugniagesiu (Fire Brigade) street. Before they came to Yurburg my family lived in Rasein, the district town.

The members of my family are:

My grandfather (on my father's side) - Yonah Karabelnik

My grandmother - Rikla of the Rodensky-Karabelnik family

My father - David Karabelnik

My mother - Mina Karabelnik of the Levinberg family.

My parents were born in 1884/5 (approximately); my sister Cherna (1906); Rachel (1908), Rivkah (1911); myself -Hannah (1915); my brother Arieh-Leib (1918).

The members of my family who were murdered in the Holocaust are: my parents (David and Mina); my sister Cherna (wife of Mordechai Naividel) with her little girl; my sister Rivkah with her husband Hayim (Chaim) Siger and their children, my brother Arieh-Leib.

My father was a merchant dealing in forest trade, and a partner in a steamship company. My father prayed at the old synagogue and we observed a traditional religious lifestyle at home. We spoke Yiddish. Our home was a Zionist home. We contributed to the national funds - Keren Hayesod and Keren Hakayemeth. We were brought up at the Zionist-pioneering youth movements and my sister Rachel emigrated to Eretz Yisrael before me and became a member of kibbutz Beit Zera in the Jordan Valley. She is no longer alive. I remember my parents' home as being open and hospitable.

I emigrated to Eretz Yisrael in 1934 after I completed my studies at the Hebrew Gymnasium. At first I worked as a clerk and after my marriage to Dr. David Trainin (Lithuania) we moved to the Yizrael Valley and returned to Tel Aviv again.

March 3, 1982

Note: Photo of the Karabelnik family appears in the Appendix in the additional article on Mordechai Naividel on page 667.

TRANSLATION OF PAGE 213

THE RODENSKY FAMILY
By David-Mordekhai (Mordechai) Rodensky

My parents moved to Yurburg from the small town of Vilon, around the year 1900. We lived on Raseiniu Street at my family's home. My father was a clerk and worked with a timber trader and my mother Mina owned a grocery store. I had two brothers - Dov, a physician, and Hayim (Chaim), a clerk. My sisters - Yafah-Rivkah and Devorah were married and housewives.

I remember my grandfather and grandmother - Yakov and Keile Rodensky. My brothers and sisters were married and they all had sons and daughters. The large family would meet during the religious holidays and there was a truly festive atmosphere at home. We kept an orthodox-traditional home. My father prayed at the old synagogue. He contributed to charity funds and the Jewish National Funds - Keren Hayesod and Keren Hakayemeth. We spoke Yiddish at home.

No one of my large family survived. All of them died. Most of my relatives were murdered in the Pashvente forest, 6-8 kilometers from Yurburg. My brother, Dr. Dov Rodensky, a physician, died at Fort VI in Kovno; his wife Ania and their son Aliz died at the Stutthof concentration camp.

I was born in Yurburg (1911). I graduated from the Hebrew Gymnasium and continued to study at the Kovno and Vilna universities. In Yurburg I was a member of "Maccabi" and then of "Hashomer Hatsair." I was on pioneer training in Memel in 1931-1933. I went to Israel in 1971. I live with my wife (a pharmacist) and with my son Emanuel (an engineer) in Kiryath Ata. I worked as a computer engineer at "Elbit Computers" in Haifa.

When I went to Israel I found my relatives Mosheh Yashkuner, Hanna Karabelnik-Trainin and Rachel Karabelnik -Niv at kibbutz Beth Zera.

My wife and I are retired. When I look back, my life in Yurburg seems beautiful and nice to me, particularly my studies at the Gymnasium and the youth movement. My memories are with me always.

March 24, 1982

TRANSLATION OF PAGE 214

THE RABINOVITZ FAMILY

By Yakov Rabinovitz

My name is Yakov Rabinovitz. I was born in Kovno in 1905. We arrived in Yurburg in 1917. We lived on 1 Kalishu Street. My grandfather Yehudah Rabinovitz had three houses on this street and a large plot with cowsheds and stables.

The following are the members of my family and their occupations:

My grandfather on father's side, Yehudah Rabinovitz, was a very wealthy man, he had a lot of money and many children. He was a timber trader.

My grandfather on mother's side, Yakov Norvitzky, lived in Koenigsberg. He was an accountant;

My grandmother on father's side, Sarah Rabinovitz, and my grandmother on mother's side, Batyah Norvitzky.

My grandfather Yehudah Rabinovitz had eight sons and three daughters, as follows:

The sons: Iliya - a pharmacist; Isaac, a general physician in Yurburg; Tsezar, a physician at Tiflis (Kavkaz) and Leo was a pharmacist; Ossip and Max were timber traders; David was a banker in Kovno. Another son was a dentist in Petersburg (Leningrad at present), I don't remember his name.

The daughters: one daughter, Tsilah, married Magister Smargonsky. Another daughter married pharmacist Rekhes and a third daughter - Hannah, married Rabbi Khaskin, who wrote the religious book - " Kalkalath Shvi'it."

On my mother's side I had a brother, Herman, who was a physician in Kissingen.

My brother Alexander Rabinovitz was a pharmacist, he was born in 1899.

Family members murdered in the Holocaust:

My mother was murdered at the Stutthof concentration camp; my wife Hayah and my daughters Rayah and Geulah.

Survivors: I, Yakov Rabinovitz, am the sole survivor of my whole family.

I live in Holon, and am an engineer by profession. The majority of my family members were academics and in the free professions. We spoke Yiddish and German in our family. We kept a traditional home. My father and grandfather prayed at the great synagogue in Yurburg. Our family had a positive attitude towards Zionism and activities for building Eretz Yisrael. Rabbi Haskin and his son Yitskhak went to Eretz Yisrael and became very involved with the country. We donated to the Jewish Nationalist Funds - Keren Hayesod and Keren Kayemeth, and supported all the charity funds in town.

In Israel I was the manager of the Technical-Pedagogical department of the "ORT" professional schools.

My relatives in Israel are: my wife Hel, a nurse, and my cousin Sarah, a housewife.

Cousins on my mother's side: Hannah Levin, Albert Levinson in Ramat Hasharon and his brother Levinson who lives in Kiryath Bialik.

That is the story of my family, only a few of them survived.

TRANSLATION OF PAGE 216

THE ROCHZO FAMILY

By Yisrael Rochzo

I was born in Yurburg in 1910. The members of my family lived on Yatkever Street. My father was a businessman.

The members of my family:

Beinish; Avraham; Sheine-Golde; Yitskhak; Shemuel-Bentse
My relatives were Pesia Hes; Avraham Rochzo; Aunt Beile Goldstein

The members of my family who were murdered in the Holocaust:

My brother Yitskhak Rochzo - Dachau;
Sarah Barsky - concentration camp;
Miriam Barsky - concentration camp;

Members of my family who survived:

Rachel Hes and Hannah Barsky

The survivors found their way to Eretz Yisrael. Yurburg only exists in our memory. And so does our home; we always sadly remember our parents' home which is no longer. My father was an orthodox man and the atmosphere at home was traditional. My father prayed at the Fainbergs Kloiz. Our home was Zionist. We belonged to Z.S. and we donated to Kupath Poalei Yisrael.

We also donated to the nationalist funds - Keren Kayemeth and Keren Hayesod - and to charity funds. My mother, as far as I remember, contributed to the Frauen Ferein and to the needy. Yiddish was spoken at home.

After my studies at the Gymnasium I joined the "Hekhalutz" movement and went for pioneer training to Kalvaria. In 1935 I went on alyiah. In Israel I worked in farming and industry.

My family lives in Ramat Gan. My daughter is a teacher and my son a technician. We have contact in Israel with our relatives from Yurburg - the Rachel Hes-Grinstein family, the Hannah Barsky family and the Yafah Levin-Taitz family.

March 24, 1982

TRANSLATION OF PAGE 217

THE RAIZMAN (REIZMAN)FAMILY

By Sarah Raizman-Yagolnitzer

I remember the following members of my family:

Grandfather Zalman Hassid and Grandmother Rachel. My grandfather worked in wool processing;

Grandfather Shalom Raizman and grandmother Dinah; they lived in the Girdzi village near Yurburg;

My father Shmaryahu Raizman and my mother Pessia.

My brothers - Yakov, Michael, Mosheh, Shalom.

My sisters - Rivkah and Zeldah.

Members of my family murdered in the Holocaust:

My parents, brother Yakov and his family and Yehudah, David, Daniel and Mordekhai (Mordechai), and my sister Zeldah.

(Michael died in 1979).

My sister Rivkah (Kuperman) and her two sons live in Rishon le Zion.

Shalom with his wife Sarah (Peres), daughter and son live in Be'ersheva.

I would also like to mention the names of my family members who are not in Israel and were murdered in the Holocaust and no one will remember them.

They are: The Eliezer Chosid family, who were murdered together with my family members. Of the Chosid family Doba (Dorothy) was saved and after the war she emigrated to the U.S.A. and lives in Milwaukee. Her brother Yakov (Jack Cossid) lives in Chicago, He left Yurburg in 1937. Their father Eliezer was my mother's brother.

My mother's sister, Doba Hassid (Lurie) and her husband died with everyone in Yurburg. The daughter Rachel was saved and is in Russia.

The names that are very dear to me are my mother's cousins: Hannah Levinson, died close to the outbreak of the war and Leib-Hanan Levinson, who died with everyone else in Yurburg.

My parents owned wood processing machines and that was their occupation. Our home was traditional. My father prayed at the new prayer house. My parents' attitude to Zionism was positive. They donated to the Jewish National Funds - Keren Hayesod, Keren Hakayemeth and to charity funds. Yiddish was spoken at home. My parents saw to it that the atmosphere at home was cordial. The religious holidays and Sabbath were beautiful and pleasant days.

I, Sarah (1912), studied at the elementary school and at high school.

When I was young, I was a member of "Hashomer Hatsair" and "Maccabi." I was on pioneer training at the urban kibbutz in Memel. I went to Israel in 1936. I joined kibbutz "Plugath Hayam" in Kiryath Hayim (Chaim) and in 1939 I moved with my husband to Pardes Hannah, Givatayim and afterwards to Kfar Meishar near Gedera, where we worked as farmers.

My son lives in "Omer" near Be'ersheva, a chemical engineer, works at Oron. My daughter lives in Kiryath Matalon, a secretary.

My relatives in Israel - my brother, Mosheh, was a member of "Hashomer Hatsair" and went to Israel at the end of the twenties. My other brothers survived because they served in the Red Army during the days of the war.

April 29, 1982

Images from a 1938 postcard of the Menzer Family
Not in original Yizkor book - Courtesy of Dr. Leon Menzer

TRANSLATION OF PAGE 219

THE RIKLER FAMILY

By Aharon Rikler

Regina Rikler and Friend in Yurburg - mid 1930s
[Not in original book- from Leah Krelitz Sherman's photo collection]

My family lived in the center of town, 69 Kovno Street. My father, Mosheh Rikler, born in 1880, was a dentist and owned a pharmacy. My mother Rachel was born in 1890. In addition to myself they had three daughters - Fanny, Hannah, Regina and a son - Yakov. I was born in 1912.

The members of my family are members of the Altman family, of them - Nathan, Sarah, Miriam, Tsevi, Avraham, Fanny and Khyene.

My father was a public personality and looked after the needs of the Jewish community. He was one of the founders of the Gymnasium and looked after its budget during all the years of his life. He himself donated considerable sums when he saw that many people were unable to pay tuition fees. He was a devoted and active Zionist, who cared about the problems of Eretz Yisrael. He supported the Jewish Nationalist Funds - Keren Hakayemeth and Keren Hayesod and when the Tel Khay fund was established he donated to this as well.

In addition to donating to the nationalist funds, my father also donated to mutual assistance funds for the needy.

Yiddish was spoken at home. My father prayed at the prayer house and there was a special atmosphere at home during the religious holidays.

In the Holocaust the following were murdered: my father in Yurburg, my mother and sister Regina in Kovno. The survivors from among my family are: Fanny, who lived in Nahariyah (she passed away) and Yakov who presently lives in Klaipeda (Memel) in Lithuania.

I studied at the Gymnasium. I was on pioneer training in Memel and I went to Israel only in 1973. I now live in Tel Aviv. I worked as a civilian in the I.D.F. (Israel Defense Force) in Israel.

I have fond memories - memories of a happy childhood in Lithuania and studies at the Gymnasium, but it is impossible to forget the tragedy of the Holocaust.

February 15, 1982

TRANSLATION OF PAGE 220

THE SHMULOVSKY FAMILY

By Avraham Shmulovsky

My father, Eliyahu Shmulovsky, was born in Rasein (1885); my mother, Mina of the Yozelit family, was born in Yurburg (1885). My parents had two daughters - Alte-Leah and Ita and three sons - Shemuel, Benjamin and I, Avraham.

My family had a tinsmith workshop. My father was a religious man and prayed at the great synagogue and at the Fainberg (Feinsberg) Kloiz, during the winter. There was a cosy Jewish atmosphere at home. We spoke Yiddish amongst ourselves and Lithuanian with the farmers. I still remember the merry feasts and religious holidays at home. We remembered "Zion" which was being built and donated to Keren Hakayemeth.

During the days of the terrible Holocaust my family was annihilated. My parents were murdered as was their daughter Ita and Uncle Yakov-Eliezer Shmulovsky from Rasein. My two brothers, Shemuel and Benjamin, are in Canada and the U.S.A.

I, Avraham (1913), found my way to Eretz Yisrael. I carry with me the memories of my home. I also remember the wonderful community of Yurburg, the youngsters and the surroundings where we would roam. The "Maccabi" sports events and the scouts' camps of "Hashomer Hatsair." I still remember the Jewish Park "Tel Aviv," the rivers and forests.

When I grew up, I joined "Hekhalutz" and went on agricultural training at the estate near Memel (Klaipeda). My parents supported my aspirations and were happy when I went to Israel (1933). In Israel I was a construction supervisor, on behalf of the Government.

1982

TRANSLATION OF PAGE 221

THE SHTERN - FIN FAMILIES

By Erika Katz

My family was one of the oldest and most long-standing families in Yurburg. It was a family of rich businessmen, with broad business interests that reached abroad as well. From the correspondence they conducted in various languages and in Hebrew as well, we may understand that the family members were on a high Torah and educational level.

My great grandfather - Eliezer Mosheh Shtern (1844-1893) traded in grain, wool and linen. In addition he dealt in banking business. My grandfather was wealthy, but he was always ready to help others.

My great-grandfather was an educated man and was fluent in Hebrew, Yiddish, German, and Russian. He was a very religious Jew and a learned man. He married, for the second time, my great-grandmother **Sarah Perlman**, a descendant of Rabbi Shelomoh Zalman, who was a Talmud scholar and observant. He died in Yurburg (1877).

My great-grandfather and great-grandmother had a daughter in 1870, called Basha-Freide. The daughter married **Avraham-Aba Fin** in 1889, who came from Naishtot-Shirvint. he was a wealthy businessman, who traded in grain and linen. The Fin family built its home on German Street in Yurburg.

Basha-Freide and Avraham Aba Fin had four children:

   Naftali-Nathan, born in 1890;

   Sarah, born in 1892;

   Helena, my late mother, born in Yurburg in 1894, died in Israel in 1978;

Lidiya, my aunt, born in Yurburg in 1897, lives in Capetown, South Africa, her family name is Salsing.

The family of Avraham-Aba Fin and his wife Frida of the Shtern family lived in this house in Yurburg in the 19th century.

The Fin family, the parents and their four children, left Yurburg and moved in 1903 to Budapest (Hungary). From 1920-1927 they all emigrated from Budapest to South Africa.

Only I, Erika Katz of the Shtern family, born in Capetown in 1922, went to Israel and was followed by my mother, Helena.

The name of my husband is Michael Katz, born in Rosh Pina.

Our only son, Yakov, serves in the I.D.F. while I am writing this page, with the paratroopers.

I work as a communication disorders clinician.

I must emphasize that I am very happy to live with my family in Israel, yet I don't forget the town of my forefathers, Yurburg, which is no more.

CHAPTER 3
PERSONAGES AND PUBLIC FIGURES

The Author Avraham Mapu   **Israel Stamp Honoring A. Mapu**

TRANSLATION OF PAGES 225-230

AUTHOR AVRAHAM MAPU IN YURBURG

By Zevulun Poran

Each day the Jews of Yurburg saw a tall young man, with a short black beard, innocently walking along the street, towards the open alleys leading to a spectacular green landscape. Such were the ways of the man. Since he arrived in Yurburg, he walked slowly each day through the town, disappearing among the hills beyond the horizon. The Jews of Yurburg watch the man walking along in this strange fashion and wonder who he is.

Days go by and the unknown figure becomes part of the human landscape, part of the town's daily life. Sometimes he would walk along the shores of the town's many rivers, looking into the clear, slowly flowing water. At other time he would look at the broad river where ships were heading towards distant places, and barges and towing boats were flowing along the strong current to the ocean, his eyes shining, immersed in thought.

The young man would wander about for hours, return to his place of residence, to be warmly and respectfully welcomed by his hosts. Slowly he would recover, pursue his daily chores, till nightfall, when in roaming dreams he would weave a wondrous tale created by his burning imagination. Who is this man? - The answer is as follows.

Avraham Mapu, who would one day attain fame as one of the bright "Haskalah" (Enlightenment) authors, was born in Slabodka (1807), a suburb of Kovno, in a miserable, poor house, more like a wooden shed. His father, Rabbi Yekutiel was a teacher ("Melamed"),scholar and a man of dreams. While still a young boy, the son already excelled in Gemara (Talmud) and other Jewish studies. As was the custom in those days, he married at the age of eighteen.

His natural inclination for broadening his outlook induced Mapu to study foreign languages and get acquainted with the world beyond Judaism. Thus he adopted the ideas of "Haskalah" which broke through the Jewish ghetto's boundaries. His father, an observant Jew, found it difficult to see his son "become an infidel." He also found his son's walking alone in fields and forest strange. However, the young Mapu, the dreamer, continued to walk alone in the Aleksot Mountains, far from the town and the society of man, he sat in a hut, seeing yet not being seen. He absorbed nature and lived in a world of mystery. In his imagination he saw a link between the landscape around him and the distant landscape of the Bible.

His eyes beheld noblemen and prophets, simple people, vine growers and yeomen. The imagination flows, and the hand writes, writes and erases, writes and erases; all beginnings are hard. Nevertheless, the list of words becomes longer and but a few men of word and mind look at them and praise and laud the future writer.

One day Mapu moves from Slabodka to a village not far from Kovno. The house has become very crowded and poor. He has to support his family - a wife and two children. At the village, Mapu gets a job as family teacher, as was the custom in those days. He is enchanted by the village atmosphere, but feels lonely.

After a short while, Mapu is invited to serve as teacher in the home of a wealthy man in the town of Yurburg. This is an immense change. According to the biographers, Mapu found peace and quiet in Yurburg. At the home of his wealthy, friendly host, he led a comfortable life, in a quiet, pleasant and cultured atmosphere. As Yurburg was close to the German-Prussian border, its inhabitants were more accustomed to the western-European style. There were no zealots here as in Slabodka, who interfered in the individual's life. Here everyone lived as he pleased. In Yurburg Mapu finds "Haskalah" books in Hebrew and other languages, and they broaden his outlook. Mapu arrived in Yurburg in 1832, a young man, barely 24 years old. The few people who read his early attempts at writing complimented him and encouraged him to write. There is no doubt that Yurburg was the proper place for him to make progress in his literary endeavors.

Yurburg is not a metropolis, but here he found a small window to the world at large. The contacts the Jews of Yurburg had with Germany in general, and Jewish Germany in particular, indirectly affected the socio-cultural atmosphere of the town. There was a fresh spirit in Yurburg. The "Berlin Haskalah," which stood for progress, had not yet been accepted in the Jewish community in Eastern Europe. Yurburg, therefore, was the bridge to the New World. Here Mapu breathed top-of-the mountain air. He read and studied. The beautiful landscape around Yurburg served as the background for his literary creations."IALAG" (I..L.Gordon) said that in Kovno he secretly learned the language of the past and wrote in secret, but here, in Yurburg, he was free to do as he pleased. During his stay here, without his family - his wife and children remained all the time in the town where he was born - Mapu could devote himself to furthering his autodidactic studies without disturbance, and also note down his thoughts.

The biographer H.A. Medalye and his close friends, the authors Kaplan and Friedberg, testify that already in Kovno in 1830, i.e. two years before he arrived in Yurburg, he started to write the book "Shulamith," which would later be called "The Love of Zion." Indeed, here in Yurburg, thanks to the comfortable circumstances, and the beautiful surroundings, the mountains and forests, the fields and the water flowing through the town's three rivers - the Nieman, Mituva and Imstra, Mapu was able to concentrate on the writing of his book. The strong impressions of the quiet village life, near the town, gave Mapu a feeling of peace, and induced him to write. **The landscape of the Aleksot Mountains near Kovno was also impressive, but the landscape of Yurburg left a stronger mark on him and he identified more with the inhabitants of the town and the village.**

The magic of the spectacular Yurburg landscape caused his pen to bring to life the world of the Bible, with a clearness that is unparalleled in our literature. Nevertheless, it appears that, as he himself testifies, Mapu had many doubts, as he wrote to his friends -"I built and destroyed, built and destroyed." . . both in Kovno and in Yurburg. The wish to produce a perfect oeuvre drove him to be very strict with himself and to be his own harshest critic.

Mapu's years in Yurburg were very fruitful. We have no tangible proof, but it seems likely that here in Yurburg Mapu completed his writing and polished his book "Love of Zion" and perhaps here he started to weave the tale of his next creation - "The Guilt of Shomron (Samaria)" which is in fact a continuation in style, character and spirit.

Yurburg, therefore, was an important interim stage in Mapu's life and literary creation. How many years did he spend in Yurburg? Some say seven years, others claim more. The biographers differ in opinion. There are no documents.

It is important to mention that Mapu felt comfortable at the home of his master in Yurburg. Mapu's relations with his host were excellent and they shared a sincere friendship. All the members of the family, both young and old, liked and respected Mapu the teacher, and so did the residents of Yurburg. He made friends, people of intellect, interested in writing and knowledge. Here he was able to discuss any subject with his friends, in the spirit of the time. Mapu liked the liberal atmosphere. When he left Yurburg, he did so with fondness in his heart. He also liked his work as a teacher at the Russian-Jewish school.

However, we cannot end Mapu's Yurburg story without mentioning the composition which bibliographers consider his Yurburg adventure. In his teachings, Mapu realized that he did not have a reading book to give to his pupils, as was the custom in enlightened countries. Mapu wanted to spare his pupils abstract dialectics. He therefore decided to draw up a text for students called "Pedagogic training," a sort of student handbook to study Hebrew and grammar and acquire general knowledge. In this book Mapu included his own original story called "Beth Khanan." The story is based on what he experienced in Yurburg. The two heroes of the story are Khanan and Nekhbi. Khanan is an entirely positive person, symbol of kindness and purity, while Nekhbi is the complete opposite, entirely negative, an evil person. According to the critics, Khanan in fact personifies the man at whose home Mapu stayed in Yurburg, he knew him well and was acquainted with his lifestyle. The didactic-educational trend is clearly reflected in the "Beth Khanan" story by presenting a good example to the children.

The following is the opening chapter of the "Beth Khanan" story, in order to give the reader an idea of what it is all about. Thus Mapu describes in the "Beth Khanan" story his master and benefactor in that town of Zefron - the pseudonym for Yurburg:

> **"There are two rich men in Zefron. One is called Khanan, the other Nekhbi. Khanan is a generous person who grants every wish to those close to him: old clothes to some, money and bread to others.**

Nekhbi is a miser, unable of giving, who tells his parents: I did not see them, ignores his brothers and relatives - - -

In his (Khanan's) house there is pity for the poor, and sympathy for those close to him. The hungry knock on Khanan's door and leave it satisfied - - - Khanan is successful in all his undertakings, for the Lord has mercy on him - and the inhabitants of Zefron praise Khanan, for he is a cherished person, without any envy or hatred in his heart. Nekhbi hates him, yet Khanan does not hate Nekhbi. Nekhbi chases the poor away; Khanan is kind to the poor.

---Zefron is a small town, but there are many poor people there. They are not worried about the Passover holiday, for they are certain of Khanan's charity, he buys flour and his assistants bake matsoth (unleavened bread) for the poor. Once the (khametz) leaven is removed from the homes, food is sent to the poor: matsoth, meat, wine, oil and sweets for the holidays, and those who receive assistance, eat and drink merrily and bless the home of the righteous man. --"

The more we read about Khanan's home and his activities, the more curious we get as to who this "righteous" person is, this man from Yurburg; we will probably never be able to discover the secret, but suffice it to say that there were such righteous people as Khanan in Zefron - Yurburg, they were the fathers of this small town of which we are proud.

Mapu left Yurburg and took the "Pedagogic training" book with him-the cherished pedagogic- didactic asset so hard to find in those days. However, Mapu did not consider "Pedagogic training" an important creation. He thought it was a useful handbook merely made for teaching. Thus the book was forgotten, until Yosef Klauzner, the historian and critic, found the "Pedagogic training" book at the end of his life; he took the "Beth Khanan" story and published it. The story became very popular with the young, and was an innovation at the end of the 19th century. When the book was published, Mapu was no longer alive.

After Mapu left Yurburg, he remained in Rasein for a while. In this town too, he found educated friends who had great esteem for the author with whose writings they had already become familiar. From Rasein, Mapu returned to Kovno. In those days he also visited Vilna, met the "Haskalah" authors - Adam Hacohen, Michal (Mihah Yosef Levenson), Shemuel Yosef Fin, Shulman and the young "Yalag" (Yehuda Leib Gordon). They had all read his work "Love of Zion" and recommended it be published. Indeed, in early 1850 Mapu submitted the "Love of Zion" book first to the Russian censor and then had it published. However, publication was held up, and the book was only published in 1853. The book left a deep impression on the readers. Authors and intellectuals demanded he also publish his other books. Mapu was very happy. The publication of "Love of Zion" lifted Mapu's spirits. All the wise men of Israel took pleasure in praising the book.

**The author Peretz Smolenskin compared Mapu to the prophets of Israel.
No other Hebrew author had received such honor before him.**

The young were charmed by him, but there were also those who envied him,
harassed him and spoiled the little happiness fate had reserved for him.

Those who read Avraham Mapu's "Love of Zion" - and indeed who did not
read this wonderful book? - were deeply impressed by the host of wonderful
descriptions of ancient, beautiful and spectacular landscapes.

The author of this creation which artfully describes these attractive landscapes
in Judea and the Jerusalem mountains - had never set eyes on them, for though
he saw them in his mind's eyes, Mapu never became acquainted with the land
of his fathers, and had no idea of its beauty.

However, apparently there is no good without evil. In the meantime his wife
had died, and he himself was weakened by a malignant illness. He was no
longer able to provide for himself, and had to accept a position as teacher in
Vilna, this time at the home of a rich but difficult man, who insulted him. His
friends then commented sadly and carelessly -"Mapu is forced to swallow
insults so that he will know that in addition to the home of Khanan in Yurburg,
there is also the home of Nekhbi in Vilna." Without the encouragement and
material help of his brother Matityahu, who lived in Paris, Mapu's situation
would have been very bad.

We, the students at the Hebrew Gymnasium in Yurburg, merely heard the
stories remembered by our fathers' fathers about Avraham Mapu in Yurburg,
but at the Gymnasium we read his books - "Love of Zion" and "Samaria's
guilt"- and were taught to understand them by our excellent teacher, Avraham
Kosotzky

We enjoyed the biblical-ornate style of the books, their fascinating contents
and exciting adventures.

We were very fond of the heroes of the book "Amnon and Tamar" -the fruit of
Mapu's imagination. We were particularly impressed by the descriptions of the
enchanting landscape. But we, the students of the Gymnasium, were not
surprised at the descriptions, for Mapu who spent quite a few years in Yurburg
(more than seven!) walked in it surroundings, and formed a strong attachment
with its landscape. We, the students, did not doubt that the Yurburg landscape
formed the background of Mapu's descriptions in his books. Therefore, we
students were very proud. Avraham Mapu was not a Zionist, according to
Herzl's definition, but he was a subconscious Zionist, the man with the vision
of the Return to Zion, such as Rabbi Yehudah Halevy, Moshe Hess, Rabbi
Leivi-Yitskhak from Berditshev and Heinrich Heine in their time.

When we, the sons of Yurburg, read his books "Love of Zion" and "Samaria's
guilt" we too experienced the vision of Return to Zion. We got up and went to
our land, the land of the Bible, in order to assist in the resurrection of its ruins,
build its towns and make the land bloom, for us and our sons after us.

TRANSLATION OF PAGES 231-234

ZELIG SHAKHNOVITZ - AUTHOR AND INTELLECTUAL

By Pinkhas Volman

The author Zelig Shakhnovitz was the brother of Pinkhas Shakhnovitz, and the uncle of Frida Shakhnovitz. He was born in Yurburg and emigrated to Germany, where he studied at institutions of higher education and became a famous and prolific author.

The following is the history of the life of Zelig Shakhnovitz-author and intellectual.

Zelig Shakhnovitz studied at a "Kheder" and at the famous Lithuanian yeshivoth. He subsequently complemented his studies at institutions of higher education in Germany. Here he also worked as a teacher and took his first steps in the field of literature.

His adventures, crises and moves from one spiritual sphere to another, as well as the confrontation with his bitter fate in which he had the upper hand, left their mark on his character and perception which is rooted in historical Judaism, and awakened and developed his creative power and poetical gift. In 1908 he was invited to Frankfurt as the editor in chief of "The Israeli," the central organ of conservative Judaism in Germany, replacing the late Dr. Lehman, the man who had founded this weekly in 1860 in Maintz. Indeed, Shakhnovitz brought a new spirit to the paper. With his personal attributes, his fair combination of East and West - having been born in Eastern Europe and educated in the west, he knew how to bridge these two worlds. His stories about the life of the Jews in the east managed to bring this world closer to that of the Jews in the west, to whom this had been totally foreign. He created understanding for the suffering of the Jews in eastern Europe under the reign of the Czar, and the translation of his articles in the Jewish press showed the Jews in the east the beauty and cultural lifestyle characterizing the Jews in western Europe. His personal attributes were very helpful, his erudition, intimate knowledge of Jewish literature and history. Not in vain, he was considered one of the most prolific journalists of his time. However, Shakhnovitz became mainly known as an author in the Jewish world because of his series of historical novels. His language is cultural, exquisite, diversified and full of linguistic subtleties. He builds his characters in an artful manner and takes a deeply personal part in their considerations. The specific Jewish psychology and the warm and delicate Jewish feelings leave their mark on his characters and their actions, their conversations, and they abound with intimate, friendly Jewish charm.

However, Shakhnovitz does not use his faith as a goal in itself ,but as an ultimate, lofty way to educate the young to love Israel and their people's history. That is why Shakhnovitz chose historical subjects for his books.

In this respect Shakhnovitz fulfills a national-educational task. This trend is not emphasized or felt in his books, and it is only in the way that he describes fascinating adventures in previous generations, in various historical periods, and thus the rich past of our people penetrates and leaves its mark on the young reader's brain. The lives of the great men of Israel, the wise old men, the ancient morals of Israel, the manner of response, the way of thinking and the Jewish feeling, the modesty, humility and true heroism - the mental heroism of the eternal Jew.

Only few religious authors wrote in German, especially authors of religious-historical novels, and after Dr. Lehman and Rabbi Dr.Herman ("Judeos"), Shakhnovitz was the only Jewish author, writer of important historical novels, of religious Jewry.

A list of 16 books is proof of his literary work and broad output over a quarter of a century:

Notes from Lithuania, among them characters from Lithuanian villages;

The Rabbi from Suvalk;

Marlika, a novel about the life of the Jews in Galitzia.

People in the air (Air People), a novel about the present;

Over the border, a Jewish tragedy in the land of the Czars;

In the shadow of the World War (I);

In the Jewish Kuzarian kingdom, a historical novel, translated into the Hebrew by S.L. Tsitron, published by "Omanuth" in the year 1924. One of the best historical books ever published;

Maikimeir's way to the Kremlin;

Shelomoh the Falasha, about the life of the Falasha Jews in Ethiopia, discovered by Dr. Faitelovitz;

Mashiakh's bride; a historical novel about the Shabtai Tsevi movement in the 17th century;

Torches, a historical novel about the great fire at the Frankfurt Ghetto in 1711;

Avraham Ben Avraham, a historical novel about the conversion of Polish Count Pototski. A heroic tale of suffering, wanderings and persecutions at the time of "Hagara" (Hagaon reb Eliyahu) and the proselyte's tragic end;

From ruins to the building of Eretz Yisrael, (impressions from a journey to Eretz Yisrael) a song of praise, full of enthusiasm, about the country being built. The book called up longings, mainly among the religious Jews, for Eretz Yisrael and the idea of the Return to Zion.

Light from the West, a historical novel about Khatam Sofer, his deliberations and actions from his youth to the day of his death. Translated into the Hebrew - the first time by Ovadyah Hacohen, the second time by Mosheh Shenfeld, published by "Netsakh" publications, Tel Aviv (1942);

Escape to the Homeland (document of the time), the author's last novel in which he describes the conservative circles and the Frankfurt characters, the atmosphere in the "Adath Yeshurun" community founded by the late S.R.Hirsch, the bourgeois and the cultural life, and mainly the scholarly life at the houses of prayer. In this background, he describes the life of a rich "Yekish" family in Frankfurt, who go to Eretz Yisrael as tourists, to visit their sons who live on a kibbutz ("Khafetz Chaim"), their impressions, and what happens to them when they see this new world and are confronted by it wherever they go, until finally they too remain in Eretz Yisrael;

Rabbi Mosheh Ben Maimon (monograph).

It is a pity that to date the two books "**In the Jewish Kuzarian kingdom**" and "**Light from the West**" have not been translated (into Hebrew). It would be worthwhile to redeem this spiritual- Jewish property and translate it into Hebrew for our youth who lack this material [An English translation of the Love of Zion bears the title <u>Amnon, Prince and Peasant</u>, by F. Jafie (1887). Mapu's stories have been often translated into other languages. n.b. JA]

In addition to these novels, Shakhnovitz wrote many short stories, feuilletons and articles, and they too are outstanding in their genuine Jewish gaiety, optimistic, positive Jewish spirit and love of creation. There are the stories about his various journeys to the east or west, to spas in the mountains and near the sea. A light and subtle humor runs through his tales. When he looks at the wonders of nature he experiences a profoundly religious feeling, which is expressed in his writing. His work is deeply Jewish, full of the love of Israel, simple, natural and with profound feeling. When at first, he brought Eastern European Judaism closer to the hearts of the Jews of western Europe, and managed to introduce them to the best ideas of the East, he also prepared the ground and the hearts of the religious Jews in the West for the idea of building Eretz Yisrael, and returning to it in heart and soul. In this too, he succeeded and he convinced many to adopt the idea of Return to Zion. Here we must mention another merit: he was the first to found Hebrew study circles in Frankfurt, and was among the most fervent supporters of spreading the Hebrew language there.

He did much to strengthen religious and cultural life, mainly among the people, each day he taught at the "Makor Hayim (Chaim)" hall, and each Sabbath he would lecture about the week's Torah portion. Young and old hurried to listen to his lectures, which were very well presented, and full of personal charm.

He was also a teacher of Talmud at the small yeshiva for working youth and pupils of the "Hirsch" secondary school.

Many appreciated his optimism and belief that the eternal glory of Israel will not fail, his modesty and humbleness, his pleasant nature and love of Israel from east and west. All these good qualities made him very popular and granted him special charm.

He maintained his journalistic and cultural standards in Frankfurt till the end. Until Hitler's henchmen attacked him in the street in 1938, threw him to the ground and beat him till he bled. By a miracle he was saved by the Swiss Ambassador (Shakhnovitz was a Swiss citizen) who was summoned by telephone, and on that very day he left for Switzerland under the patronage of the Ambassador. In Zurich Shakhnovitz continued his literary work till he died.

Old Wooden Shul
[Not in original book] Courtesy of the Vilna Jewish Museum

Kuschelevitz homes - June 2003
Not in original Yizkor Book - Courtesy of Dr. Leon Menzer

TRANSLATION OF PAGES 235-247

SHELOMOH (SOL) GOLDSTEIN

A Jewish Leader and Humanist

By Zevulun Poran

Shelomoh (Sol) Goldstein is known as a prominent leader among Jews and non-Jews alike in the United States. He is known as a proud Jew, popular and admired by the national and philanthropic institutions. He is an example to many in his devotion to the needs of the Jewish public, is a benefactor and fund-raiser.

After World War II Shelomoh Goldstein, the Holocaust survivor, arrived in the United States, destitute, hurt and wounded by the nails of the Nazi beast Eastern Europe, where he fought a fierce battle to remain alive, and succeeded; he managed to make a living and secure his existence.

Shelomoh Goldstein, a Zionist and pioneer since his youth, very much wanted to go on aliyah to Israel, but destiny caused him to deviate from this road and led him to the United States. Here, as a chemical engineer, graduate of the universities in Kovno and Rome and by virtue of his intellect and good business sense, he succeeded and climbed the ladder of the materialistic society. He strengthened his status as a successful industrialist.

However Shelomoh Goldstein is famous not only for his success in business, but mainly because of his activities in public life. Shelomoh Goldstein never remained aloof; he always considered himself part of the general community. As a public figure, with a well-defined social outlook, he found himself morally obliged to help the Jewish community. The public circles that knew him appreciated his contribution and humanitarian activities.

Government circles in the U.S. opened their doors to him - Congressmen, Senators and even the President himself. He was well known, both in government circles, as mentioned above, and among the American people.

However, with all his obligations to the country where he lived, Shelomoh Goldstein never forgot he was Jewish. His Jewishness was part of him; he had deep Jewish nationalist roots and was a Zionist in body and soul. The man who was miles away from the country of his dreams, breathed its air from far away. The concerns of the state of Israel were his concerns, and its joys were his joys. Indeed, Shelomoh Goldstein played an important part in the development of our country, its villages as well as its towns. At Keren Hakayemeth, Keren Hayesod and the Israel Bonds they appreciate his contribution. His name is registered in the "golden book" of Keren Hakayemet as one of the most important liberators of land, who contribute to the blossoming of the land and aspire to develop it. With good reason Shelomoh Goldstein received the "good name crown" on behalf of Keren Hakayemeth in the United States, only very few people have received this reward.

As one of the main activists in the Zionist movement Shelomoh Goldstein was chosen to serve as the representative on the Zionist executive committee, at the Jewish Agency and the Israel Bonds. From time to time he leaves his personal business in the United States and comes to Israel in order to take part in the discussions and decisions of the Zionist Federation and Jewish Agency. His words at the Zionist executive committee make good sense and are practical and constructive. His proposals are appreciated. The echo of his speeches in fluent English and Hebrew carries far away to his listeners at Zionist conferences and meetings.

Left: Shelomoh (Sol Goldstein Tamara
Right: Goldstein with President of the United States Jimmy Carter

As an intellectual Shelomoh Goldstein found it his duty to strengthen not only the materialistic but also the intellectual layers, such as the educational and cultural institutions of the State of Israel. Halls at the Hebrew University and Technion carry his name, and so do other institutions that he generously supports. When he visits Israel Shelomoh Goldstein has the opportunity to see the country that is being built and the progress being made in all wakes of life. He always returns home enchanted by what he has seen. Each visit to Israel increases his love for the country and his longing to be there.

Those close to him say that when he returns home, he feels guilty about not being part of those living in Israel, building it and moulding its image.,

Many people will probably ask who this man - Shelomoh Goldstein -is, where he comes from and how he came hither from Yurburg in Lithuania, a small town on the German border. There is no doubt that the landscape of the town where he was born with its wonderful Jewish community influenced him and formed the character of the little Jewish boy "Shloimele." Yurburg is a town through which three rivers pass, one large river - the Nieman and two smaller ones. This beautiful area, surrounded by forests and parks with its warm Jewish community, a Zionist community with Torah and educational institutions, among them the splendid synagogue, admired by famous artists all over the world.

The Herzl Hebrew Gymnasium, situated in the Jewish park called "Tel Aviv" was perhaps the greatest wonder of all. . . . Yurburg was a Jewish Diaspora with sparks of light, which the Jews of the little town lit with their meager means, in order to bring some light into the darkness of exile.

The Jewish children in Yurburg spoke Hebrew from an early age and grew up in a Jewish atmosphere without any fear of assimilation. The pioneer movements sprang up in these schools, they taught Zionism and encouraged aliyah to Eretz Yisrael.

Shelomoh Goldstein was a pupil at these schools. His kind mother, Menukhah, took care of him and gave him love, after his father, the late Hayim (Chaim) Meir, a soldier in the army of the Russian Czar, fell in World War I against the German soldiers. Indeed, when Shloimele was a baby in the crib, merely four months old, he lost his father and never knew him.

In spite of all the worries and problems of daily life the child grew up happily, to the joy of his widowed mother, excelled at school and at whatever he did. He was a sharp-witted kid, diligent, persevering and an outstanding student. The home of Shloimele's mother was not a wealthy home, but it was full of the warmth of a mother who loves with all her heart.

His widowed mother worked very hard to make a living for herself and for her only son, to bring him up and educate him to be a good person and send him to Rabbis to learn Torah and to the local schools to learn science and acquire an education.

As all the other homes in Yurburg, the home of widow Menukhah was full of love for Eretz Yisrael, with the "Blue Box" and the hope to emigrate to Zion one day, our Holy Land. It is said that one day an envoy from Eretz Yisrael arrived at the home of widow Menukhah. After addressing the Jews in synagogue and speaking about the pioneers' work in developing Eretz Yisrael, he visited homes to raise funds for Keren Hayesod, the fund that was building Israel. Menukhah, the poor widow, did not have any money at home, but she did not send the envoy away empty-handed. She went to the cupboard, removed some silver objects and said: "here, take these as a donation for the building of the Holy Land."

Another time, when an envoy from Eretz Yisrael came, and she had nothing to donate, as she wanted to, she told the envoy with tears in her eyes - "here, take my only son, he is barely nine years old - take him and he will be a pioneer in Eretz Yisrael." that is how Menukhah, the Jewish mother, brought up her son to love the country that was being built, after two thousand years of exile.

Sixth Graduating Class of the Gymnasia in Yurburg

When Shloimele arrived at the Hebrew Gymnasium he drew the attention of the teachers and educators. By the way, in the 1930s Eliezer Leipziger, Shelomoh Goldstein's relative, an academic, was the principal of the Hebrew Gymnasium called Herzl in Yurburg.

With his graduation from the gymnasium the chapter of Shelomoh Goldstein's life in Yurburg comes to an end. He left the town of his birth and was accepted at the Lithuanian State University in Kovno, studied chemistry and prepared himself for a future linked to Eretz Yisrael. In the lively and Zionist town of Kovno the young student Shelomoh Goldstein was a leader in the *"Hekhalutz Hatsair"* youth movement, and later on he was the secretary of the *"Hekhalutz"* center, aiming to go on aliyah to Eretz Jsrael. In those days he also helped the illegal immigration organization (aliyah beth) and prepared himself to go on aliyah as soon as possible. He showed leadership potential in these Zionist activities and was admired for his achievements.

A man may have many intentions, but reality sometimes plays a different game. That is how one day all Shelomoh Goldstein's plans changed. All of a sudden World War II broke out, the German Nazis invaded Kovno and its Jews were put into the ghetto under a strict and cruel regime. Like all the other Jews, Shelomoh Goldstein fought for his life and tried to survive. He showed initiative in the ghetto, even under the strict conditions of the regime, organized underground activities to save Jews, as much as this was possible. The main purpose at the time was to get the youngsters out of the ghetto to places of hiding. Some organized youth to join the partisans in the woods. The aim was to save Jews as quickly as possible, for the mechanism of destruction was working ruthlessly. Almost every day large groups of Jews were sent to Fort IX from where there was no return, and thus the murderers went on until the very last days of the war (1945) . When Shelomoh Goldstein understood that all hope of rescue was gone, he too left the ghetto. In a daring action he escaped with his girlfriend Tamara and a group of youngsters and hid in a Lithuanian village, until the Red Army entered Lithuania and the Germans fled.

When Shelomoh Goldstein returned to Kovno he found it empty of Jews and only graves all around, of a town that had almost a quarter of a million Jews in Lithuania, only about four thousand remained after the Holocaust, dejected and shocked by the terrible tragedy that had befallen Jewish Kovno and Lithuania as a whole. There is no hope left for the Jews in Lithuania Shelomoh Goldstein told himself - the few remaining Jews concentrated mainly in Vilna should be taken out of there and sent to Eretz Yisrael.

Shelomoh Goldstein and his friends got ready to act. They organized the "Berikha" (escape) to Western Europe in spite of the Soviet authorities' opposition to letting them go. After an eventful journey Shelomoh and Tamara arrive in Italy and join the refugee camps waiting to go on aliyah. The gates of Israel are closed and those waiting - Holocaust survivors - had to wait in Italy. Wait and wait. They had already been waiting for three years. . . . from time to time refugee ships leave, but they are caught by the soldiers of the British Mandate government and sent back.

In Italy Shelomoh Goldstein and Tamara's oldest daughter is born. Under the difficult and hard conditions of living the baby falls gravely ill. The local doctors propose they transfer her to the United States to be treated by specialists.

After lengthy deliberations and realizing there is no hope to go to Israel soon, they leave for the United States, contrary to their plans and deepest wishes.

When Shelomoh Goldstein and Tamara arrived in the United States they first settled in Philadelphia and then in Chicago, Illinois, and from there they moved to Skokie. Here they got along very well with the Jewish community and in general. Goldstein showed enterprise; he went into business, developed an industrial plant in his professional field as a chemical engineer, and his efforts bore fruit.

Sol and Tamara Goldstein established an exemplary home in Skokie and took part in the local Jewish community life. Sol's talent and dynamic personality helped him achieve impressive results in the industrial-business field. His success did not turn his head. Even at the top of success he never forgot his Zionist obligations. The memory of the Holocaust cast a shadow over him; his conscience drove him to help the Holocaust survivors in Skokie, Chicago and in general.

He was elected to head the Holocaust organization in Skokie and was its patron. After that Goldstein was elected to head a number of other national Jewish organizations.

The highest echelons of the American authorities knew Sol Goldstein's public activities. Congressmen and Senators consulted him. Even the President of the Unites States invited him to take part in various events. When President Reagan decided to set up a memorial to commemorate the Holocaust, Sol Goldstein was invited to take part in the advisory board at the President' s home.

In addition to his donations to Jewish institutions, SolGoldstein also donated to gentile humanitarian institutions. Indeed, Goldstein lived in two worlds - in the United States, where he lived and worked, and in the other world, the world of Israel. This reminds us of the song of Rabbi Yehudah Halevi - *"My heart is in the east yet I am at the far end of the west. . . ."*

That is why Goldstein was attracted to activities in the framework of the Zionist movement. The American press published at the time that 1400 guests and VIPs from in and out of town took part in the reception held in Chicago when Sol Goldstein received the "good name award" for his activities and contribution on behalf of the Keren Kayemeth leYisrael.

At the end of the festive occasion the national director of Keren Kayemeth in the United States, Mr. Avraham Salomon, announced that a sum of money had been donated during the ceremony for planting a forest of 100,000 trees in the Yehudah Mountains, near Jerusalem in the name of Sol Goldstein and his wife Tamara, in recognition of their activities.

In his words of thanks to those who congratulated him, among them Rabbi Dr. Arthur Herzberg, the President of the Jewish Congress in America, Sol Goldstein said that he did not deserve any praise for what he had done, for he merely did what his heart dictated him to do, and that he acted out of recognition that his destiny was linked to the destiny of the State of Israel and that therefore all that was his also belonged to Israel.

His Jewish-traditional education and knowledge of Hebrew, familiarity with Zionist ideas and Hebrew literature granted him an advantage over many others who were his friends in the Zionist Federation's institutions. When he visited Israel, Sol Goldstein felt at home and felt part of the Israeli people.

Sol Goldstein, the Holocaust survivor, does not speak much about the Holocaust, but sub-consciously the Holocaust is part of his soul. It is hard to separate oneself from the Holocaust. In their daily lives Holocaust survivors try to forget the horrible pictures and live the life of the present, but from time to time the Holocaust comes to mind and re-emerges on the surface. Every little reminder of the Holocaust may turn into a storm in the minds of Holocaust survivors. And that is what happened to Sol Goldstein in Skokie, on the face of it, a quiet town with thousands of Jews. Among them are Holocaust survivors who live a quiet and prosperous life.

Sol Goldstein with the President Reagan and his wife Nancy

There are industrial plants in Skokie belonging to Jews, beautiful homes, schools, synagogues, charity institutions, and Sol Goldstein established his home here; he also had the honor, as mentioned above, to be the head of its Holocaust Survivors organization.

One day a warning light went on in Skokie. The rumor spread that an organization of neo-Nazis in Chicago and other places planned to hold a protest march against the Jews in Skokie. Some Jews were terrified when they heard this, but others were inclined to ignore the neo-Nazis and remain quiet. Not so Sol Goldstein. He was decisive and determined : " No Nazis will march here!" . . . he said and left no room for doubt. In his mind he saw the writing on the wall of the Kovno ghetto: **"Jews, remember - revenge!"**

One day Sol Goldstein told an Israeli journalist about the "March in Skokie" affair and its results. "When I heard about the march, I convened a group of Rabbis and public figures and told them we must not sit at home and must not remain quiet. These Neo-Nazis did not aim at proving that there was freedom of speech in the United States, but rather they wanted to prove to the Jews in Skokie and the whole world that Hitler's job had not yet been done and that too many Jews remained alive - - - Therefore, said Goldstein - I turned to the courts. I knew that the courts would not decide in our favor, as the laws of freedom of speech were legislated in the United States before the Holocaust and the emergence of the Nazis. So then I had the choice to declare that 50,000 inhabitants of Skokie, Chicago and many others in the U.S.A and all the countries of the world would come to demonstrate with us against the neo-Nazis, a demonstration without violence, a peaceful demonstration."

"When the Ku Klux Klan, the neo-Nazi leader saw the preparations of the Jews, he quickly announced that he no longer intended to demonstrate. One day the telephone at my home rang and someone on behalf of Klans told me that the Nazis would not demonstrate in the center of Skokie, but next to my home . . . I answered him that I welcomed their decision to come to Skokie, but that I could not promise they would leave it live. Since then I have never heard from them again."

This sad episode was photographed and appeared in the film "Skokie," with Danny Kaye. In reality the hero of the film, Max Feldman, is Sol Goldstein. 25 million people saw the film in the U.S.A. and in other countries of the world, Germany among them. The film left a deep impression on all those who saw it. At the end the film indicates "To be continued," i.e. the people of Israel is alive, continues and will continue to exist.

Sol Goldstein's determined stand against the evil plans of the neo-Nazis became known through the film "Skokie" and incited the public against them. The initiator of the film, Sol Goldstein and his assistants were appreciated and admired.

Sol and Tamara Goldstein's home was a unique home, totally immersed in a Zionist-nationalist atmosphere; it was a Hebrew home. Jewish and Hebrew songs were heard around the family home, were absorbed by the girls too.

One of his friends from Lithuania tells the story that one day he received an invitation to the daughter's wedding from the Goldstein family. When he opened the invitation and read what was written there he was greatly moved. The invitation was different from any other wedding invitation he had ever received from his friends; half the invitation was written in Hebrew in brilliant letters.

Shelomoh the father Tamara the mother

Hayim (Chaim)-Leib the bridegroom Menukhah-Miriam the bride

In addition to the Hebrew date inside the invitation there was another date

In the 33rd year of the State of Israel

Such an invitation, writes the friend, Yakov Rabinowitz from Lithuania, a writer and journalist, shows a warm Jewish heart and respect for traditional values.

Indeed, Sol Goldstein personifies the Lithuanian Jewish "Talmid-Khakham" (scholar) whose roots are in Judaism and tradition as well as in Zionism and its nationalist values. This is the source of the great love for the people of Israel and Eretz Yisrael.

This phenomenon was also expressed in the very traditional wedding the family held for their daughter. The four posts were covered by a light-blue prayer shawl. The popular Jewish music was mixed with Hassidic and Israeli melodies. In short - a Jewish wedding recalling the tradition of our forefathers. Indeed, all the "Who's and Who's of America" as well as many guests from abroad took part in this wedding. Among the wedding guests were Jewish leaders and national leaders - Rabbis, Consuls and Senators, industrialists, bankers and the many family friends.

In his speech to the young couple, Sol Goldstein expressed the wish that they would bring up their children in the traditional manner, continue the existence of our people and instill the love of Eretz Yisrael in them, the land of hope of the Jewish people. Indeed, the daughter and her bridegroom promised they would observe the Torah and respect their parents, would follow in their footsteps and that generation after generation would spread the word.

All the family friends and the large and varied group of participants who had come to take part in the joy and congratulate the young couple and wish them luck would remember this wonderful wedding for a long time.

Tamar (Tamara) - born Taitz - Sol Goldstein's faithful companion, was born in the little town of Shkud, near Memel in Lithuania, and grew up in the traditional Jewish family atmosphere. In this little town Tamara received a Hebrew education at the local school and Zionist youth movement. She was known in town as a charming and gifted girl. When the three children of the family grew up, Tamara among them, they joined "Hekhalutz" with the aim of going on aliyah to Eretz Yisrael.

The Nazis put an end to the plans and hopes. The moment the German Nazis conquered Lithuania, the Jews of Shkud were brutally murdered. Tamara, who was staying in Kovno in those days, was also put into the ghetto of Slabodka. There she met Sol Goldstein, her future husband. As his faithful friend, she helped him in his underground activities in the ghetto.

Sol and Tamara, together with their friends, had the courage to try and save souls as far as this was possible under the difficult conditions. Tamara took part, together with Shelomoh, in all the daring actions, such as leaving the ghetto for a Lithuanian village and later on the "Berikha" (escape) to Italy, up to the departure for the United States. Tamara was always at Shelomoh (Sol)'s side, encouraged him and supported him. Until they reached a safe haven in Skokie. In Skokie and Chicago Sol Goldstein showed initiative in his business ventures and Tamara, an exemplary housewife, took care of their two daughters - Judith and Miriam-Mili. The home of the gracious Tamara was a Zionist home and Eretz Yisrael was the love of her life. She brought up her daughters in this spirit of love of Eretz Yisrael. All her hours of respite were devoted to work for Israel and charity for the poor. Tamara's beautiful and well-kept home was the center of Zionist activity for many years, a kind of "embassy" of the State of Israel. The smart-looking and friendly Tamara gave a warm welcome to every guest from Israel. There was hardly a Zionist leader or representative of the government of Israel who was not a guest in this home and absorbed its Zionist atmosphere.

It is said that when Tamara was ill, between one operation and the next, as long as she was in her senses, she was concerned about the situation in Israel. "What is going on in Israel?" she would ask. Nowadays too, after the death of Tamara, Sol Goldstein never ceases his extensive public activity for a moment. This was no doubt the wish of Tamara, who loved Israel so much.

In all we have told in the story of Sol Goldstein, we wanted to speak a little about the activities of the man and his eventful life. Sol Goldstein traversed a long road from his home in Yurburg in Lithuania until he arrived in the United States, his present home. The imprints Sol Goldstein left on the path of his life show his power to face physical hardship and mental anguish and overcome them. Sol Goldstein is not an introvert individualist by nature; he loves man and society. His uprightness always drove him to volunteer as often and as much as possible.

This brought him the appreciation and esteem of others. These were probably the characteristics of all the philanthropists in the world.

When we recall the names of the great philanthropists among our people, like Moshe Montefiori and Edmond Rothschild, who wrote golden pages in our history and the history of the rebuilding of Eretz Yisrael for generations to come, with their generosity. We also think of Sol Goldstein, who with his donations to the nationalist funds and humanitarian funds occupies a place of honor in the row of well-known philanthropists.

According to Goldstein's conception, Israel needs the help of Jews in the world, but the Jews in the world just as much need Israel, for the State of Israel may serve as a refuge for any Jewish community that -God forbid- finds itself in trouble.

The more the Jews in the world do for Israel, the more they do for themselves, ensuring a secure place for their sons and the sons of their sons at times of trouble. That is the motto of Sol Goldstein, the man of the world, who has a universal and far-reaching vision.

Israel needs great leaders, with political understanding, wisdom and vision, able to contribute with their experience and knowledge of life.

We wish Sol Goldstein a long and prosperous life, and hope to receive his blessings for many more years, to enjoy his wisdom and warm affection for the State of Israel.

BORIS BERNSTEIN

The man, his vision, his achievements

By Zevulun Poran

Yurburg, Boris Bernstein's place of birth, was a small town at the beginning of this century, and there were limited possibilities for the young people of the town to get on in life, acquire an education and a profession. It was hard under those difficult circumstances to lift one's head and rise above the common level, yet there were a few youngsters who did achieve a high cultural and social status. Boris Bernstein was one of them. Although as the saying goes "a prophet is without honor in his own country" - his broad outlook and intellectual capacities made him stand out in his little town. When Boris was seventeen years old, his parents sent him to Koenigsberg in Germany to acquire a profession. Here he started to work as an apprentice at one of the banks. He made fast progress in banking and at the same time also studied at the university.

At the outbreak of World War I, Boris Bernstein, as a Russian citizen, was exiled from Koenigsberg, which was close to the Russian-Lithuanian border, to the large city of Berlin. Here Boris got a job at one of the large banks, and in no time he was appointed Department Manager.

After a while, when the managers of the Komertz Bank in Kovno heard about the Jewish boy called Boris Bernstein, who was so successful in the banking profession in Berlin, they invited him to come in 1922 and appointed him Manager of the Bank. The Komertz Bank was the largest Lithuanian bank, and ranked second after the government bank.

The Jews of Yurburg were very proud of their townsman who occupied such a senior position as the manager of the largest bank in Kovno, at that time the central town of Lithuania and its capital between the two World Wars. Much was said at the time about Boris Bernstein's modesty and generosity and about how he supported many people through the bank and his personal contribution.

From personal experience I may say that the generous bank manager helped the Zionist-Pioneer youth movement, which had financial problems at the time, both by his personal contribution and through loans, although he was aware of the fact that they were unable to return their debts.

Furthering the Zionist undertaking took priority with him over narrow party considerations, and therefore he warmly supported any kind of Zionist enterprise. To us, the youth leaders of the time, Boris Bernstein was a great Zionist, warm-hearted and concerned about the fate of the Jews and the building of Eretz Yisrael. For many years he was an active member of the Zionist Center in Lithuania and contributed considerably to furthering the cause of building Eretz Yisrael.

In the thirties I also came to know another aspect of Boris Bernstein, the public figure's character - the humane and moral aspect - Bernstein the man who loved children. At the large bank he worked hard to make progress and manage its business, but at the children's home the "Yiddisher Kinder Haus" in Kovno he found food for his soul. He gave all his love to this "Kinder Haus" on the green mountain, 4 Giedraiciu Street, where poor children, struck by fate, lived. He, Boris Bernstein, was like a father to them, a godfather. His heart went out to these unfortunate orphans and he was overwhelmed with joy when he was able to save a child from misery and distress.

Boris Bernstein's love affair with the "Kinder Haus" started in the early years of its establishment, in the early twenties. At that time, after World War I, children, refugees and starving orphans were adopted by a public council set up to look after these unfortunate beings. Boris Bernstein joined the founding committee of this humanitarian institution for children called "Yiddisher Kinder Haus." At the time the institution was housed at an old building in the old city of Kovno, close to the Jewish hospital. Dr. Siegfried Lehman, a well-known pedagogue from Germany, was appointed Director of the institution. Here the children were fed and clothed and received an education.

When the children grew up and the question of their future came up, the public council was divided in its opinion. Some were in favor of "Do'ikeit," i.e. absorbing the youngsters in the existing community, including learning the spoken Yiddish language and professional training in industry, services and office work. However, the Zionists on the public council, headed by Boris Bernstein, were of a different opinion; they said the youngsters should be trained to go to Eretz Yisrael, be taught Hebrew so as to make it easier for them to be accepted there at an educational institution. When the Zionists' stand was accepted, the public council contacted the Zionist leadership in Jerusalem, and a positive answer was soon received.

At the time there was a deserted educational institution for children near Lod; there were a number of dilapidated buildings there and vacant areas of land of the Jewish National Fund, on part of which the "Herzl Forest" was planted. The Zionist leadership's proposal was accepted by the public council, and in 1927 most of the "Kinder Haus" graduates emigrated to Eretz Yisrael, headed by Dr. S. Lehman, and set up a new educational institution at the deserted spot, namely the Ben Shemen youth village, which still exists today. Boris Bernstein was very pleased with the fact that the youngsters of the "Kinder Haus" went to Eretz Yisrael and with the establishment of the youth village for agricultural education, and he was happy to be among the founders of the Ben Shemen youth village.

Since the Ben Shemen period and until the thirties, the "Kinder Haus" underwent many changes. In the thirties the "Kinder Haus" blossomed once again. At Boris Bernstein's initiative and with his efforts important changes occurred at the institution. The luxurious building was erected on the green mountain, living conditions were improved and the children received better care at the two sections of the home - one for toddlers and the other for kindergarten and school children. The undersigned was invited at the time to serve as the institution's pedagogic director. Boris Bernstein, Chairman of the public council, wanted a Zionist Israeli educator to take care of education. Nearly the entire staff of educators at the kindergarten and school was replaced, educators who had been trained at the "Tarbuth" seminar were accepted for the educational task. Children of school age were sent to study at the "Tarbuth" school on the green mountain. The "Kinder Hois" children learned Hebrew and Hebrew songs. The atmosphere at the institution changed, and it took on a Zionist outlook. When guest envoys arrived from Eretz Yisrael they taught Hebrew songs and told the children about life in Eretz Yisrael , about the towns, villages and kibbutzim.

On the eve of each Sabbath and on religious holidays, Boris Bernstein would visit the institution, together with his wife Ella and his children, and they loved seeing the children shining clean and happy. It was the custom then at the "Kinder Haus" to hold a "Kabalath Sabbath" party before dinner, with merry Hebrew songs and literature readings. Boris Bernstein drew great satisfaction from seeing the children so happy.

Much is to be said about the poetic pedagogic experience, which took place among the children at the "Kinder Haus." Although Boris Bernstein was not involved in the daily educational events, his friendly fatherly attitude towards the children encouraged the educators in their task. Only a great and sensitive soul, such as Boris Bernstein's, is preoccupied with the fate of underprivileged children.

At the end of 1938 the pedagogic director of the "Kinder Haus" emigrated to Eretz Yisrael. Upon his arrival he immediately went to the Ben Shemen youth village. He spent a few days there and talked to the old director of the village, Dr. Z. Lehman, and to the senior educators, Yirmiyahu Shapira and Rachel Katrovsky, about bringing groups of children from the "Kinder Haus" to Ben Shemen. They were enchanted with the idea. However, unfortunately, it did not come about. The sky of Europe darkened in those days and the political situation of Eretz Yisrael became uncertain. The World War already appeared on the horizon. Boris Bernstein was very sorry.

In the terrible Holocaust that befell the Jews of Europe, the Jewish children in Kovno were cruelly murdered, and among them the children from the "Kinder Haus" and their educators. Their place of burial is not known and nothing is left of them, but Boris Bernstein's wonderful deeds will not be forgotten and will never be erased from the Book of Life of the Jews of Lithuania.

Boris Bernstein himself and his family were exiled to Siberia before the Holocaust, when the regime changed in Lithuania. In 1940 Lithuania was attached to the Soviet Union. The new rulers, Stalin's protegees, considered Zionism a reactionist anti-Soviet movement. Therefore most Zionist activists in Lithuania, among them Boris Bernstein, who was a member of the Zionist Center, were accused of undermining the Soviet regime. Boris Bernstein was exiled and imprisoned for 8 years in one of the most terrible camps in the Soviet Union. This camp was described in detail by the well-known Russian author Solzhenytsin in his book "Archipelag Gulag."

Boris Bernstein spent 25 terrible years in distant, freezing Siberia, until he and his family were fortunate enough to immigrate to Israel. When he arrived, he was officially recognized as a "Prisoner of Zion" by the Zionist leadership and government institutions.

Boris Bernstein, the young boy, passed a long and winding road, filled with suffering, from the time he left his town of birth Yurburg until he arrived in the country of his dreams, for which his soul had yearned all those years. Boris Bernstein spent his last years surrounded by family and friends at his home in Natanyah, spent and tired, but as always full of confidence in the People of Israel and the well-being of the State - until he died.

May he rest in peace and may his soul be bound in the bond of life

Dr. Ze'ev Bernstein, Boris Bernstein's son, was exiled, together with his parents, to Siberia at the start of World War II in 1941. In his last years in Siberia he taught German philology at a Soviet university.

In 1972 Dr. Ze'ev Bernstein immigrated to Israel and joined the staff of the foreign language studies faculty at Tel Aviv University. For his many research works and books, published in Israel and abroad, Dr. Ze'ev Bernstein received the title Associate Professor in 1988, [and full professorship in the field of German linguistics (Germanistics) in 1993 and Professor Emeritus in 1997, Z.Bernstein.] the first such professorship in this field at Tel Aviv University [and the first one in Israel; Z. Bernstein]. Indeed, the son followed in the footsteps of the father . . .

See article by Dr. Ze'ev Bernstein in Appendix at the end of this book.

Feinberg Family in 1927 - Most were murdered in Yurburg
Standing from Left: Hannah Feinberg, Grandmother, Cousin, Itel and Max Berzaner, Sitting: Feinberg Cousins
[Not in Original Book - Photo courtesy of Diana Berzaner Tobin]

The Yurburg Yizkor Book

TRANSLATION OF PAGES 253-255

PINKHAS SHAKHNOVITZ

ZIONIST AND MAN OF THE BOOK

Born in Yurburg, Lithuania, Died in the Shoah (Holocaust)

**(Pinkhas Shakhnovitz was the husband of Hayah Feiga Naividel,
daughter of Shemuel Naividel)**

Left: Pinkhas Shakhnovitz and his daughter Frida

Right: Pinkhas Shakhnovitz - Not in original book

Courtesy of Gita Abramsohn Bereznitzky

Pinkhas Shakhnovitz's home was situated in the center of Yurburg, in a big stone building. He and his family lived on the top floor of the building, and on the first floor was his stationery and bookstore (see photo of Kovno St. in Chapter 1). This store was the center for Hebrew and Yiddish book lovers. It was at that place a committee of the prominent Jewish citizens of Yurburg, met to discuss worldly subjects, especially news from Eretz-Yisrael (the Land of Israel) - and eventually of course discussions about the new book.

Pinkhas Shakhnovitz, an intelligent man and impressive looking, was in the center of the discussions; he talked slowly and in are laxed way, as if divinely inspired. And at that "shrine of the book" one could also look at a Zionist Yiddish newspaper as well as books written by Hebrew writers, and natives of Lithuania. Pinkhas Shakhnovitz, who came from a family of writers (see page 228 for an article on Pinkhas's brother Zelig Shakhnovitz), was also interested in the Hebrew revived literature which was different in its style and contents from the Enlightenment literature, which he felt close to in his youth.

At that time, during the 1920s, when we met Pinkhas Shakhnovitz, he was already well known as a writer. And as we found out in "Hamelitz" (the first Hebrew periodical of the Enlightenment and the "Khovevei Zion [Lovers of Zion] " in Odessa Russia 1860-1904), he was a fast correspondent who sent his writings for publishing on Lithuanian Jews, including Yurburg. His Hebrew was a bit flowery and his style was that of the period. During the editing of the Memorial Book we read a few of the articles sent by Pinkhas Shakhnovitz to "Hamelitz," which were mostly up-to-date. From the articles it seems that in his youth he was a trustworthy correspondent involved in the life and happening of the Jewish community in Yurburg and Lithuanian general.

During our studies in high school we knew Pinkhas Shakhnovitz to be a modest man, one of the prominent Jewish citizens of Yurburg, a public person sensitive to people's pains, always ready to assist and help to solve problems. As a Zionist, according to his views, his main interest was Eretz-Yisrael, its development, problems and needs. He was involved in every Zionist enterprise, which could contribute to the development and construction of Israel.

Pinkhas Shakhnovitz did his utmost for the Hebrew High School, which needed encouragement and financial assistance, as it was difficult to keep up such an institution in a relatively small town like Yurburg. Nevertheless the Jewish Zionist community took upon themselves this heavy burden, with the understanding of the importance and value of this national-cultural institution for the Jews of Yurburg. The high school was kind of a mini-university, which contributed to the entire Jewish population, and was the pride of the Jews of Yurburg. Pinkhas Shakhnovitz was also interested in the activities of the Zionist youth. While his daughter, Frida, as a member and a counselor in the Jewish Scouting movement - Hashomer Hatsair (literally: Young Watchmen), he learned to know this movement and identified with its pioneering goals. Frida went through all the stages of the pioneer training leading to her immigration to Eretz-Yisrael, to which her father gave his consent, encouragement and praise. And indeed, one day Frida immigrates to Eretz Yisrael and joins the nucleus of Hashomer Hatsair movement of Lithuania, which is the nucleus of the kibbutz (group) founding Mishmar Zevulun, later becoming Kefar Masarik. Frida adjusted very well to the kibbutz, marrying her friend David and adopting a very symbolic last name - Zevuluni. When their son was born he was named Ilan, Ilan Zevuluni, grandson of Pinkhas Shakhnovitz of Yurburg. Pinkhas Shakhnovitz who followed his daughter's life in the kibbutz was extremely happy. He was very pleased to receive letters from his daughter and had great satisfaction on hearing any news and developments of the kibbutz. But the happiness did not last for along time. One morning the skies of Yurburg were covered with the darkest clouds. Hitler invaded Yurburg, which was located 9 km (5miles) from the German border. And within three months, in the summer of 1941, the entire Jewish community was completely destroyed. People who read the article "The Old Synagogue Tells" by Pinkhas Shakhnovitz may learn that as soon as Hitler came to power,

Pinkhas Shakhnovitz had the feeling that this would be the end of the Yurburg Jewish community, even before it happened...and with this feeling he joined the departed.

May his memory be blessed.

Zevulun Poran

Standing Shmuel Leib Abramson Judith Levenberg Natan Abramson Sitting: Chana Karabelnik, Bella Abramson, Gita Abramson, (2 friends) (friend) Pinchas Shachnovitz, Frida Shachnovitz, Pesha Rochel Abramson

Not in original Yizkor Book - Courtesy of Gita Abramson Bereznitzky

Added Note: The following is based upon a telephone conversation between Charles (Hayim) Tabakin and Joel Alpert and was not part of the original book:

Charles Tabakin (husband of Pinkhas's granddaughter Feiga) related on May 6, 1995, that he and Feiga were married in the Kovno Ghetto during the war. She was also called Fanny. During an action in the ghetto she was taken and sent by train to the Stutthof concentration camp near Danzig. Charles found out from her mother, who survived the war, that Feiga did survive until the liberation of the camp but died a few days later. Charles was in Dachau for ten months, and was very sick at liberation; he was taken to a hospital by a doctor from Kovno. Charles also related that he was an officer in the Lithuanian army and saved Pinkhas Shakhnovitz (Feiga's grandfather) from an action by the Nazis and he later died a "normal death" in the ghetto (understood by Joel Alpert to mean that a "normal death" means that he was not murdered out right).

TRANSLATION OF PAGES 256-257

ELIEZER LAIPTSIGER (LEIPZIGER)

TEACHER, EDUCATOR AND PRINCIPAL

By Emanuel Kopelov

The late Eliezer Leipziger (blessed be his memory) was an outstanding teacher at our Hebrew Gymnasium. He was born in Yurburg. Studied at the Real Gymnasium in Kovno, which in its first years was managed by a principal with orthodox, anti-Zionist opinions. According to his friend, Dr. Shelomoh Kodesh, Eliezer was a diligent and studious pupil at the gymnasium. He had a Zionist outlook. He became a Zionist leader there and led the students' revolt against the orthodox, anti-Zionist ploys of the school's management, which forbade the singing of "Hatikvah" inside the school. The revolt succeeded under his leadership. The students were allowed to speak Hebrew at school and to sing "Hatikvah" under the proper circumstances.

Eliezer Leipziger -Teacher and Principal of the Hebrew Gymnasia

Eliezer completed his studies at the gymnasium. He read law at the University of Kovno and obtained the title of Advocate (law degree). At that time the rights of Jewish lawyers were restricted at the order of the Lithuanian authorities. Eliezer decided to leave the law practice and came to the Yurburg gymnasium where gifted teachers were in great demand, to serve as its principal. He served as a teacher and then as the principal. Later on he had the honor to serve as the principal of the important Hebrew Gymnasium in Ponivezh.

Eliezer considered going on aliyah to Israel but this hope was not realized and he, like many others, perished in the Holocaust.

Eliezer was an enthusiastic Zionist and communal worker in heart and soul. He stood out among the other teachers at our gymnasium in Yurburg with his educational talent, showed a great deal of knowledge in the professions he taught and leadership qualities. The students appreciated and respected him. He was one of those teachers students remember even today, when memories of the gymnasium are brought up. During classes Eliezer was as strict as was necessary and made sure discipline was observed at school. But when one met him in the afternoon, he knew how to be a friend. He would invite us to sail a boat on the Mituva along the park. That was an unforgettable experience. Here he and we had the extraordinary opportunity to talk quietly about various subjects as friends.

Eliezer was involved in every Zionist activity in town. His special, praiseworthy contribution was the establishment of the "Brener" library, which took care of the lack of Hebrew books in town. Eliezer spent all his energy on this task and was tireless, and together with other activists, among them my late mother, who also devoted endless efforts to this enterprise, they set up the splendid library.

Although he was older than I was, I had the good fortune to be his pupil, friend and partner in all the Zionist activities in town. I learned a lot from him and remember him with great admiration.

Blessed be his memory!

TRANSLATION OF PAGES 258-261

Eliezer Leipziger - Friend and Soul-mate

by Dr. Shelomoh Kodesh

I met Eliezer, or as we used to call him "Leizke," when I was a youngster at the Jewish Real Gymnasium in Kovno, in the early twenties. We both arrived at the Jewish orthodox prayer house of Dr. Karlebach (the uncle of Azriel Karlebach, who later on became the editor of "Ma'ariv"), which remained at the Kovno community in Lithuania from the days of the German occupation in World War I. The conquerors wanted to use this educational institution to "Germanize" the Jews of Lithuania, and prepare them for the German cultural occupation of the Lithuanian district. A number of Jewish officers in the German army, headed by Dr. Karlebach, were recruited to carry out this cultural patriotic mission, and were appointed teachers at the Jewish educational institution called *Ober Realschule fur Judische Kinder* (Real School for Jewish Children). It was a German school with a number of hours for teaching Orthodox Judaism based on the model of the orthodox, anti-Zionist community of Frankfurt on Main.

When the Germans were thrown out of Lithuania, and Lithuania became independent, this school remained, and the merger of an expanded general education with ultra-orthodox Judaism was a kind of innovation.

Dr. Karlebach and a couple of German Jewish teachers, some of them outstanding, others less so, remained at the school. Eliezer and I arrived at this school from little towns that were at a distance from each other, Yurburg in the south of Lithuania, Eliezer's town of birth, and I from Kupishok, in the north. We both started in the sixth grade, and soon found each other. We were very much alike. Small, "touched" by the Zionist idea, inclined to public activity. The competition between two boys in the same class did not affect our friendship. Eliezer was more diligent than I was. He showed artistic talent, mainly in drawing, and was very sharp-witted in mathematics. Those were stormy days in the life of the Jewish community in Lithuania. After the Balfour Declaration the Lithuanian Jews as it were received cultural autonomy, and the youngsters had sparks of hope of realizing their dream to go to Zion via pioneer training, towards aliyah in an uncertain future. In those days ideological differences of opinion started to appear which divided the Zionist movement into different streams; the war of languages in Jewish education, Hebrew or Yiddish, and social unrest which also penetrated the Zionist camp, mainly because of the influence of pioneering, status-conscious Israel. A host of ideas and beliefs, hopes and illusions, endless discussions in a new version, unknown till then by east European Jews, penetrated our school, and our class, although it was not the highest grade, turned into the center of unrest, and Leizerke Leipziger spearheaded this agitation.

With *"Yekkish"* (German Jewish) innocence the authorities who had just discarded the epaulettes of the German officer's coat, and their friends, believed that it would be possible to continue the orthodox-anti-Zionist educational line in Lithuania in the German language. They soon found out how wrong they were. A number of Zionist teachers, who returned to Lithuania from Russia after the war, introduced a new spirit at school. On the face of it, nothing had changed. The chief language taught was German, the program was in the spirit of the German high school, strict discipline, including physical punishment for "rebelling" students, and a strict ban on Zionist activity within the school which in reality meant a ban on the Zionist hymn "Hatikvah." It was our class that turned into the black sheep, and became the source of "all evil." Our group started to look for opportunities to break through the wall of opposition to all Zionist activities.

Eliezer stood out as a sharp-tongued speaker, and he had a strong influence on his friends at the boys' gymnasium and its equivalent, the girls' gymnasium.

I remember two episodes from this period, which deserve, no doubt, to be inscribed in the history of the Lithuanian Jews who are no longer. A very ordinary event, such as a slap in the face received by one of my classmates from the Latin teacher incited the miracle of the revolt. Eliezer headed the rebels. We managed to convince our classmates not to enter the classroom. We gathered in a room of a Jewish soup kitchen on Mapu Street (the Kovno municipality named a street after the Hebrew author Avraham Mapu, who had written "Love of Zion" and "Samaria's Guilt," the first Hebrew Zionist novels, he was a native of Kovno), where I lived with the manager of this Jewish soup kitchen. After enthusiastic speeches of encouragement Eliezer wrote a memorandum to the school's management in his beautiful handwriting, specifying the conditions of our return to class. One of the conditions was the right to speak Hebrew at school and sing Zionist songs, in particular "Hatikvah." On Eliezer's advise, we signed in a large circle, in order to confuse management so it would not know who headed the revolt.

We did not go to school for about ten days, without informing the parents of the local pupils. Each morning we would gather at the appointed time at a place we had fixed in advance (usually the abandoned women's sections at one of Kovno's many synagogues), where we received lessons from students who excelled in their study subjects. I, who was not very good at mathematics, learned a lot from my friend Eliezer's teachings, he restored my self-confidence regarding this complicated subject, in the days of the revolt. Whether by co-incidence or not, a few weeks after the revolt, Dr. Karlebach left Kovno, and after his departure another atmosphere reigned at the gymnasium. Those were the glorious days of Eliezer as a recognized, influential and energetic leader, *primus inter pares*. I would also like to mention him in connection with the young leadership unrest in the wonderful event of the conference of students' representatives of the Hebrew Gymnasia in Mariampol. This was when the blossoming Hebrew education in Lithuania with its 16-17 Hebrew Gymnasium recognized by the Lithuanian government and hundreds of Hebrew state elementary schools was at its peak. The illustrious Zionist leadership of which but a few managed to go to Israel, originated from these Gymnasium. In 1922 the best students at these schools decided to convene a students' conference at Mariampol. As main speaker we invited Dr. Yakov Rabinson, the principal of the Hebrew Gymnasium in Virblan, an outstanding educator, clever and well-versed in international law, who became one of the greatest legal authorities in the U.S.A.; he also researched the international Holocaust. In those days, as mentioned before, there was another young educator who was very interested in the Zionist youth initiative and had an impact on the conference.   At our school it was Eliezer who encouraged us to take part in this conference, and he was very active in all the days of the conference during Hanukah 1922.

In countless hours of discussion with close friends we planned our future - law studies seemed the right way to serve the Jewish people, for the Lithuanian authorities started to oppress it and take away its rights. During the years at the university our friendship continued. Eliezer was a very successful student and was popular among friends and the Hebrew Zionist circle. As was the custom in Lithuania in those days, we did not reside at the place of Torah -the University in Kovno, but went to teach at the Jewish gymnasium which were looking for young and enthusiastic teachers. Thus our ways parted. Eliezer married Fanya Kretchmer, my former pupil, and the granddaughter of Rabbi Katzenellenboigen, the Rabbi of the Jewish community in Petrograd.

Eliezer continued to teach and manage, while I ceased my teaching for a couple of years and worked as an attorney for a while.

In those days Eliezer was asked to manage the Hebrew Gymnasium, first in Yurburg, and then in Ponivezh, and did a wonderful job there with his talent, energy, enthusiasm and persistency to fulfill the task imposed on him. However, the glory of Hebrew education in Lithuania was dimmed when the government started to oppress the Jewish minority and restrict its civil rights.

In the meantime, I went to Israel. In the first years of my aliyah Eliezer inquired about the possibility to come on aliyah and settle in Israel. I immediately answered him in an optimistic letter, almost imaginative, and I hoped to see him and his family comes to Israel. He was unlucky. His feeling of obligation towards the circle of Jews he so faithfully and successfully served, made him postpone his aliyah for a number of years, for he wanted to look after the educational project he was managing, see to it that it was not harmed. In the days of the Holocaust the life of one of the most outstanding young leaders of the Jews in Lithuanian exile was lost.

Eliezer was handsome and had a handsome soul, had done numerous good deeds and promised to do many more. . his life was cut off in the middle!

Formerly Jewish homes in Yurburg - May 2001
[Not in original Yizkor Book - Photos courtesy Dr. Leon Menzer]

TRANSLATION OF PAGES 262 - 264

ALTER-MORDEKHAI (MORDECHAI) SHIMONOV - A PORTRAIT

By Shimon (Beba) Shimonov

Our home, where our family lived happily, stood on a raised area, opposite the new synagogue. The family included my parents, Alter-Mordekhai (Mordechai) Shimonov and Malkah-Annah Shimonov and their four children - Shimon -Baba, Yisrael and the twins, Tsevi and Shaul. My father - a well-known man, respected by the community- was one of its representatives on the town council; from time to time he was also asked to carry out official duties and other tasks.

Alter-Mordekhai (Mordechai) and Anna Malkah Shimonov, parents of Shimon Shimonov

My father was a member of the national council of the Folksbank (People's Bank) in Lithuania and also served as a council member of the bank in Yurburg.

I remember very well how father and other notables in town discussed the purchase of the area of the "Tel Aviv" park, which also included the building of the gymnasium. They consulted for a longtime and tried to find the best possible way to represent the town's inhabitants vis-a-vis the authorities.

The Nieman River in Yurburg would cause a flood every few years, inundate the adjacent streets, the very streets where the poor Jews lived. The Lithuanian government would allocate funds to help these residents. My father headed the committee and did his best to see to it that the money was distributed in a just manner.

When the synagogue incurred losses, my late father was asked to serve as its Gabai (treasurer). I remember the days before Rosh Hashanah (New Year) and Yom Kippur (Day of Atonement), when my father would sit down with the big book of liabilities and the members of the congregation were asked to pay their dues. Quite often I saw my father taking money out of his own pocket to help those, who had debts, pay their dues to the synagogue. My father did this with utmost discretion, taking care not to insult anyone and without giving the impression that the person in question was poor and could not pay his dues.

Once a group of wealthy Jews from the United States paid us a visit. The Jews saw the old synagogue and were most impressed by the Holy Ark with its woodcarvings and the beautiful chair of Eliyahu; they expressed the wish to buy the woodcarvings for $150,000. However, my father and the other members of the council were strongly opposed to this.

When envoys of Keren Hayesod came to Yurburg my father was among the first to make a donation. Once it was proposed that the benefactors buy plots of land at "Mishor haCarmel" (Carmel plane) near Haifa; father accepted the proposal to buy a plot of land in Eretz Yisrael and other Jews followed suit. Indeed, the plots of land were bought and the purchasers paid the required sum in full, however the transfer to the rightful owners was complicated and never came about.

At the Hebrew Gymnasium my father was a member of the public council, which fought against the closing down of the gymnasium because of financial difficulties. My father was a dentist by profession, but he did not close down the store he had inherited from his father; when he was unable to manage it, he asked Mordekhai (Mordechai) Levyush to take care of it.

When the Russians entered Lithuania, they immediately drew up lists of Jews whom the authorities decided to exile to Russia. My father was on this list. However, good Jews in Yurburg submitted a letter of opposition to the authorities and asked my father not be exiled, claiming they needed a gifted man of finance, capable of handling the cartel issues in town. The authorities consented, and father remained in Yurburg. However, it so happened [ironically] that the very Jews who were accused animosity towards the Soviet authorities, and exiled to northern Russia and the Ural (Mountains) remained alive, together with their families.

On June 22, 1941, in the early hours of the morning, the Nazi armies invaded

Yurburg. A couple of hours later a steamship left for Kovno, at the initiative of Jews from Yurburg, however, the trick did not work. When the steamship left and was not far from shore, German planes went into the air and dropped a bomb on the ship, which was forced to return from where it had come. The result was one casualty- Shaul Shimonov, my late brother, one of the twins. The second twin was put into hiding with gentiles. However, evil people gave him away and when he was found they crushed his skull and hanged him on an electricity pole.

A couple of days after the Nazi invasion of Yurburg, they and their Shaulist-Lithuanian helpers took my father out of our home and forced him to uproot stones with his bare hands from the paved street. After that they strung him to a horse and dragged him to the shore of the Nieman. Here the torturers and murderers threw him into the river and when they removed him from the water, they put him on a purification board and carried him through town while hooligans threw all sorts of items at him.

This was a degrading and barbaric act. My father died a tragic death in the first "action" of the group of 350 town's people, a week after the Nazi occupation.

My late mother and brother were put into a kind of mini-ghetto setup at Rikler's home. My brother worked with the other men - he was 17 years old - at the German camp set up at the Nieman-Mituva junction.

In September 1941 those Jews of Yurburg who were still alive, were put to death - among them my brother. They were buried in a mass grave on the road to Smalininken.

Blessed be their memory.

TRANSLATION OF PAGES 265 - 267

MORDEKHAI (MORDECHAI) ZILBER

THE MAN AND HIS PEN

By Zevulun Poran

My father, Mosheh-Mordechai Zilber, was born in Yurburg on 13 January 1907, to his parents, Leah-born Eliyahu-Anshl Rodoner- and Aba Pinkhas Zilber, brother to Hinda and Yosef. Mordekhai (Mordechai) studied at the "kheder" at the large prayer house and the Hebrew Gymnasium. He served in the Lithuanian army. He married Rachel - born Erf (Kovno) and went to Israel in 1933.

My father settled in Petakh Tikvah, where his daughter Sarah and son Aba-Pinkhas were born. The latter died in 1967. Most of the time he worked as a farmer. For many years he was active in the "Haganah." During the War of Independence he participated in the defense of the town. My father was a writer and wrote articles and songs which were published in various publications. In his last years he started to paint and received a great deal of praise.

He passed away on August 2, 1976.

(His daughter Sarah Alkoni-Zilber)

Everyone in Yurburg knew Mordekhai (Mordechai) Zilber. He was tall, broad shouldered, had blond hair, blue and straight forward eyes. His face always wore a friendly smile.

That is how his friends at the gymnasium knew him - a tall thin-haired young man, sitting in class, sometimes paying attention, sometimes not. He always seemed deeply immersed in a world of his own thoughts.

The subject being discussed in class did not always interest him, but the next day he showed awareness of the subject's problems and knew how to make the most of it.

Mordekhai was the oldest among his friends in the class that consisted of students from Yurburg and from surrounding towns. When Mordekhai came to the Gymnasium he was already a kind of "walking library."

He read a lot, to satisfy his quest for knowledge. Mordekhai (Mordechai) already then knew how to express his thoughts in writing and verbally in a clear and profound manner. Mordekhai devoted a lot of time to excursions in the area and to spending some time alone in the woods and training himself. He was more self-taught than a regular pupil. In his essays Mordekhai proved to be a gifted young man with an excellent ability to express himself in writing. He loved to write more than anything else.

Mordekhai (Mordechai) Zilber

One day he decided to publish a newspaper on the subject of Yurburg, to print it in shapirograph and distribute it in town. This did not work out. Mordekhai apparently was not very good at business.

Mordekhai was disappointed by the unsuccessful experiment and started to look for other ways to express himself - he found them at the theater, he fell in love with drama, and found relief for his doubts. He already took his first steps on the stage at the gymnasium. Thus, one day, he joined the drama circle in Yurburg, which from time to time staged plays in Yiddish. Mordekhai (Mordechai) stood out among the local actors in the group. In those days he read many drama books and never tired of doing so; while reading he also learned chapters by heart.

Mordechai Zilber in the Lithuanian army uniform in 1928 - Photo not in original Yizkor Book. Courtesy of Lior Alkoni and Sara Alkoni - Silver, grandson and daughter of Mordechai Zilber.

Mordekhai was not always interested in spending time with the students at the gymnasium. He stood out in class. He was critical of the teachers, but not cynical. Mordekhai did not accept all they said; he did not need them. He drew his knowledge from sources outside the gymnasium -from the library, theater, newspaper and conversations with intellectuals and writers.

Mordekhai was enchanted by the beautiful landscape of Yurburg. His absences from the gymnasium grew longer until one day he totally disappeared. His classmates missed their brilliant classmate, whose advice and friendship they valued.

No one knew of his plans, although many felt that the gymnasium's horizon was too narrow for him. He was attracted by the great wide world outside. One day he broke out of the "boundaries of domicile" that was suffocating him and left for far-away places, to gather knowledge and wisdom.

Mordechai Zilber shortly before leaving Yurburg 1925 to study in Nancy University in France. On the back of the picture he wrote his feelings:

"Various changes in life, even those to which we look forward, fill our hearts with sadness. So it is when we leave the *shtetl* to face its end - without us. Even, when having lived one round of life, our time comes to depart from this life, we do so, to start another.

Yurburg 1.6.1925   Mordechai Zilber"

Mordechai Zilber on the right - [Photos not in original Yizkor Book. Courtesy of Lior Alkoni and Sara Alkoni - Silver, grandson and daughter of Mordechai Zilber.]

Thus the days and years passed. Finally Mordekhai found inner peace and came to terms with reality. His education at the Hebrew Gymnasium and the Zionist-nationalist values he absorbed there guided his path. Thus his friends and acquaintances found out one day that Mordekhai (Mordechai) was in Eretz Yisrael and had built his home in Petakh Tikvah. He was a farmer, carrying out his family- and national obligations. It appears that Mordekhai became very humble in Israel. He was satisfied with little and content with what he had. Of his spiritual riches his gifted pen spread but a few crumbs; there was an article here or there. Quality did not turn into quantity. His friends who were aware of his literary talents had expected more of him.

However, it is hard to get to know a man - everyone does what he likes. We heard only recently that he replaced his pen with an etcher and paintbrush. With these he also found a way to express his spirit and he received much praise.

Mordekhai's recordings dedicated to Yurburg, where he was born, were submitted to the editors of the memorial book of the Yurburg community. The recordings are moving and full of love, they are charming and humorous. They are an important contribution to the book. With his clear eye he described with a writer's pen as with a painter's-brush the little town where he was born that was and is no more. Thus he commemorated the Jewish community from which he sprang and where he gathered his inspiration, richness of tongue and power of expression.

How sad that our dear Mordekhai is no longer with us now that we are publishing the memorial book, in memory of his and our unforgettable community.

Blessed be his memory.

**Hind Zilber (Mordechai's sister) in 1939. She was murdered in the Shoah.
[Photos not in original Yizkor Book.]**

Mordechai Zilber's family

From left to right: Aba Pinchas (father), Sheine Leah (mother), Taube (Tova - Josef's wife), Josef (brother). All were murdered in the Shoah.

[Photos on this page were not in original Yizkor Book.]

Mordechai and Rachel Zilber in 1939, shortly before they left their "safe" home to an unknown future. In their new home in the land of Israel they raised two children Sara Alkoni-Silver and Aba Pinchas Zilber - who died at the age of 21. With this trip, they made the continuation and memory of the Zilber family possible - by the book and in life – by their offspring.

TRANSLATION OF PAGES 268-269

CLARA BERNSTEIN-DUSHNITZKI

(WORDS SPOKEN AT HER GRAVE)

By Zevulun Poran

Clara and Vulya, the loving couple who never separated in life or death .

Vulya passed away too early, he never had the privilege of seeing his children and grandchildren. Nor did he witness the development of the city of Tel Aviv, one of whose builders he was. Vulya - Ze'ev Dushnitzki - was a man with a profound public conscience. He had a liberal - Jewish outlook, combined with Zionism without compromise. He was a Hebrew intellectual in the true sense of the word, modest, and pleasant, with a noble and sensitive mind. Woe to the departed - we shall always remember them

Those who knew Clara well, appreciated her noble qualities. She loved books, and had exquisite taste. She was kind to everyone. Only few people knew how much pain she felt in the face of poverty and need, and how she hurried along shelters and synagogues in order to assist the needy. She was always surrounded by friends and received them at her home.

Clara loved her close relations and they returned her love and gave her strength. How happy she was when they paid her a visit - her grandchildren, Dr. Raziel Dushnitzki, with her great-grandchildren and the granddaughter Vitya with her great-grandchildren. Her eyes shone and her joy knew no bounds.

Each encounter with Clara was like a party. We wanted to say -"Clara, how wonderful you are." but we did not dare to do so for we did not want to exchange pure gold for simple old coins.

Now that she is gone, we will no longer see her smiling face and enjoy her wonderful personality. In recent years Clara felt that her days were numbered. She would say: "Soon, very soon, Kinderlech, you will come to me and won't find me. Come now, while I am still alive. Let's talk a little," and she meant talk about days gone by, her parent's home and the town of Yurburg on the shores of the Nieman River; about its wonderful people, the popular nature and elevated spirit of the people whose soul was pure. Now all had perished in the terrible Holocaust. She wanted to commemorate her hometown, Yurburg, and perpetuate the memory of her dear ones in the Book of Remembrance. And indeed, in this book we implement her will and commemorate the Jews of Yurburg as well as our beloved Clara who did not live to see the book published.

Two years ago we still managed to see her on a cold, rainy evening at the meeting of Former Residents of Yurburg meeting. She listened attentively to each word that was spoken there. Clara also took part in meetings of former residents of Lithuania and Kovno, the town where she studied and where her personality was formed. In Kovno, the Jewish and Zionist town, she founded her family, together with Vulya, and dreamt of Zion, a dream she realized when she immigrated to Israel.

She never forgot the warm home of her parents. Her mother, Vitel, was a good mother and outstanding housewife. It was an exemplary home, and her mother's influence was felt everywhere.

Her late father, Leon Bernstein, the well-known businessman, was nicknamed "The Linen King" for he dealt in linen and linen processing. The Lithuanian government, which was interested in his good advice, asked him - the only Jew - to join the country's national trade council. He was a man of the world, spoke a number of languages and was a well-known businessman even beyond the borders of Lithuania. He was fortunate enough to escape the claws of the Nazi beast, and when he arrived at the gates of Israel, after a few stops on the way, in Haifa, he died and was buried at the Haifa cemetery.

Clara treasured the dear memory of her parents. In her last days Tulya Kapulsky, her only daughter, was at Clara's bedside and took care of her as best she could.

Today we stand here at Clara's tomb and we think of her, here in the old cemetery, in Nakhlath Yitskhak, founded by the Jews of Lithuania, close to the memorial of the Lithuanian martyrs - there is a certain symbolism to be found here. Every life comes to an end. Clara passed away in old age. Nevertheless, we have a deep sense of loss for the family, her friends and all those who were close to her.

With her death we have lost a dear person with a rare treasure of moral values. It creates a gap between the generations.

The light that shone out of the shadows of her unique home on the shore of Tel Aviv shines no longer- and we are the poorer for it.

We are orphaned. And we grieve.

Blessed be her memory!

ZALMAN LEVYUSH ACTOR AND DIRECTOR

By Zevulun Poran

About twenty families lived in the little town, or rather village, of Shaudine. There was no school and the children would each day cross the Nieman River on the ferry in order to study at the schools and the Hebrew Gymnasium of Yurburg. Almost all the Shaudine students were educated in Yurburg and took part in its social and cultural life.

Among them was Zalman Ben Mordekhai (Mordechai)-Meir Levyush (1908) who belonged to the Levyush "clan" and studied in Yurburg. The 15-year old son of one of the Levyushes, a relative of Zalman Levyush, he was sent by his parents already in 1913 to study at the "Herzliyah" Gymnasium in Tel Aviv. This Levyush boy was a "paper bridge" between Tel Aviv and Shaudine. Indeed, many youngsters in the town were attracted to Eretz Yisrael and were fervent Zionists.

Zalman Levyush, a faithful representative of the Levyush "clan" in Shaudine grew up in Yurburg. He was popular among the youngsters and a serious and outstanding student. At an early age he liked to read plays and was attracted to theater and cinema performances. He often discussed the theater with his friends who had dreams like his own. When the Hebrew Theater studio was established in Kovno and Zalman joined, he found he was not alone. There were other "drama fanatics" at the studio from Yurburg. Here he found Hayah (Clara) Petrikansky, who shared his dream.

After he graduated from high school, Zalman studied at the Lithuanian University. His evenings were devoted to visits to the Lithuanian Theater and the opera. He also attended Yiddish performances of the local amateur drama groups that came from elsewhere (Zigmund and Yonas Turkov with their ensembles).

Once every few years theater groups from Eretz Yisrael would visit Kovno - "Habimah" and "Ohel." Zalman attended all the performances over and over again. These were glorious days for him. There is no doubt that the drama groups from Eretz Yisrael gave the youngsters the idea to set up the theater group in Hebrew and Zionist Kovno.

Indeed, in Kovno there was a broad public background for setting up a Hebrew theater. There were Hebrew elementary and high schools there, Hebrew libraries, teachers colleges, a Hebrew department at the Lithuanian University headed by lecturer H.N. Shapira, the son of the town's Rabbi. There was the younger generation here that spoke Hebrew, a youth movement and Zionist parties. It was only natural therefore, that in addition to all these, a Hebrew theater would be established too. The idea took on more substance when the "Tarbuth (Culture)" center promised to support a Hebrew Theater studio.

Indeed, the Hebrew Theater studio was set up in 1928, and it aroused great interest among the younger generation. Soon a group of Hebrew students was formed, teachers, writers and others, who expressed the wish to set up a Hebrew theater studio in Kovno. The "theater fanatics" group was a group of serious and visionary theater lovers. Zalman Levyush was the living spirit of this studio. However, a theater studio needs an experienced drama expert. The "Tarbuth" center took care of the matter and invited one of the popular actors of the Eretz Yisraeli Theater - Michael Gur -to be the teacher and guide, and he taught them the basics of drama. Miriam Bernstein-Cohen, the famous actress from Eretz Yisrael, also became a teacher at the studio.

After serious learning and an in-depth study of the various theatrical styles, an attempt was made to perform the **"Peretz Stories,"** four stories adapted to the theater by author and actor Ari Glasman. The "Peretz Stories" evening made a tremendous impression on the Hebrew public. Zalman Levyush stood out as an actor. It was a treat for the young actors and the Jews of Kovno as well. "What a novelty," many said, for they were surprised at the success of the studio. The Jewish press considered the performance an impressive theatrical achievement. The government newspaper -"Lietuvos-Aidas" - also gave an enthusiastic review of the performance and advised the Lithuanian Theater to take a lesson from the studio's actors. . . The Lithuanian Theater was not popular in Lithuania, on the other hand, they liked the opera with Grigaitiene and Kipras Petrauskas, who were famous in the countries of Western Europe.

The studio's second performance was the "Tower of Oz" by M.H.Lutzato (Ramkhal).

In this play two actors from Yurburg also participated; they performed the main parts - Zalman Levyush and Clara Petrikansky (she changed her name to Hayah Sal'it). Hayah Sal'it played the part of the rebellious Ayah who agonized in the flames of her wild love.

The public loved the play, written in the eighteenth century, in near- biblical style; the directors taught the studio members' diction, history of the theater and modern acting styles. The Russian director Gromov and others were quite familiar with the styles of Stanislavsky, Vakhtangov (Russian) and Reinhardt (German). After that they performed a few other classical plays by Moliere and others, with increasing success.

The next play was "The Golden Chain" by Peretz, directed by "Ohel" actor Rafael Tsevi.

However, as it is said, "all good things come to an end." The actors from Eretz Yisrael who discovered theatrical talent at the studio encouraged them to go to Israel. Zalman immigrates to Israel and joins the theater groups there. Indeed, Zalman Levyush's talent as a character actor is a treasure for every theater. He was a gifted actor and fit in very well with the theatrical collective in Israel.

Zalman Levyush's first step in Israel was to join the "Komedia Eretz Yisraelith," where he stood out with his natural humour. From here he went on to "Matatey" where he was also very successful. In1943 Zalman Levyush joined the "Ohel" theater and became famous.

In 1947 Levyush goes to the U.S.A. and serves as a Hebrew phonetics teacher at the Jewish Theological Seminary. At the same time he takes a postgraduate course for directors at Yale University. However, Zalman Levyush longs for his Hebrew public and returns to Israel (1950). This time he joins the "Kameri" theater, plays the main part, and receives much acclaim.

Among his main parts: Tartuffe in "Tartuffe"; Efraim Cabotin "Desire in the Shadow of the Trees," Caesar in "Marius"; George in" Of Mice and Men"; Galileo in "Galileo"; Malvolio in "Twelfth Night"; Shimon Ben Shetach in "The War of the Righteous."

Levyush also directed a number of plays in Israel and abroad, and appeared in solo performances on various occasions - at conferences and national and Zionist congresses.

In the last years of his acting activity in Israel Zalman Levyush fell ill. His wife passed away and he decided to go for medical treatment to the U.S.A., where his sister lived. When he took leave of his friends and acquaintances he told them that he was seriously ill. If I get well, he said, I shall perhaps direct a few plays in the U.S. and then go home. However, his dream disappeared very soon. His state of health deteriorated and he died abroad (1987) and was brought to Israel to be buried.

Blessed be his memory.

Kovno Street

TRANSLATION OF PAGE 273

THE ARTIST WILLIAM ZORACH

By Zevulun Poran

William Zorach was born in Yurburg on February 28, 1887. At an early stage, when he was still a child, his rare gifts in the field of plastic arts were already discovered. Zorach studied in Yurburg. However, after a while he emigrated with his parents to the U.S.A. and settled in Ohio. He made his living working as a lithographer. Later on he moved to Cleveland where he studied at the arts school, and went onto the painting academy in New York.

In 1908 his works were shown at a Paris exhibition and he received much acclaim. However, he became famous because of his wood, stone and marble sculpture. His painting was influenced by cubism, but his achievements as a sculptor were original and innovative.

In the art of sculpture he learned from all generations. With the rhythm, simplicity and charm of his creations he became famous as one of the greatest sculptors of our time. William's artistic creations were exhibited at various museums. He received many awards.

Among his creations: *Mother and Child, Childhood, The Spirit of the Dance, Child Riding a Pony,* and his sculpture of Benjamin Franklin.

William also wrote books in the field of art. William Zorach explains the art of sculpture (New York 1947) [n.b. *Zorach Explains Sculpture: What It Means and How It Is Made* – Cynthia Spikell] and *Introduction to the Art of Contemporary American Sculpture* (New York 1948).

He died on November 16, 1966 in Bath, Maine, U.S.A. His name will be remembered as one of the great sculptors of our time.

In the time of independent Lithuania only few people from Yurburg remembered the name **William Zorach.** However, art lovers in the town read the papers and followed their fellow townsman's achievements in the art of sculpture with great interest. He became very well known in the United States and other countries.

> [n.b. -- William Zorach's birth name was Zorach Gorfinkle. His family took the name Finkelstein after settling in Ohio, U.S.A., before 1895, and he was known as Willie Finkelstein as a child. He studied at the school of art in Cleveland, Ohio. In 1909 he went to Paris and had four paintings shown there. Several of his later works were considered controversial, among them *was "The Spirit of the Dance."* His autobiography, *Art Is My Life: The Autobiography of William Zorach* (Cleveland: The World Publishing Co., 1967), which includes information on his early memories of Yurburg, was published shortly after his death. – Cynthia Spikell, great-niece of William Zorach.]

TRANSLATION OF PAGES 274

AVRAHAM KASIF

EDUCATOR AND MAN OF THE BOOK

By Zevulun Poran

We know Avraham Kasif (Kosotski), as a teacher, for we were his pupils. He started his activity in Yurburg and continued in Israel. Kasif was not one of those teachers who view their profession as a way to make a living, but as a task that has a mission . He considered teaching an important foundation for the teacher's work, but he merely considered it a tool - a medium - to educate the child towards the fulfillment of his future personal and national goals. Indeed, Avraham Kasif was a teacher and educator per excellence. He was deeply rooted in the Jewish experience and history of Israel. As a former yeshivah student he had the gift for in-depth analysis and clear thinking. He had his own Hebrew style and was soft-spoken and charming. He therefore had a direct influence on his pupils.

For a number of years he was a Hebrew language and literature teacher at the Hebrew Gymnasium in Yurburg. He educated a young generation towards Zionism and aliyah; he encouraged a desire not only to get to know our country, but beyond that - to work on its behalf. This meant national funds, pioneering and aliyah. He himself belonged to "Tzeirey Zion," the followers of A. D. Gordon.

By the very fact that he went on aliyah to Israel he served as the living example for teachers and for his pupils in Yurburg that Zionism is realization. Even under the new circumstances of Eretz Yisrael he was able to find his way to the hearts of his pupils, the "Sabras" (native Israelis). He left his mark on them and many of them honored and respected him. He arrived in Jerusalem a few years ago, when he retired. He took part in activities of former residents of Lithuania in Jerusalem, and was pleased to attend every conference that was a pleasant experience for him.

May the memory of his blessed educational activity be a light onto many teachers, and to all of us, his pupils in Yurburg.

TRANSLATION OF PAGES 275-276

HAYIM (CHAIM) SIGAR

TEACHER AND EDUCATOR

By Zevulun Poran

Hayim (Chaim) Siger was born in the little town of Kamai. He was the son of a Rabbi, graduated from a yeshivah and pedagogical courses. He was a teacher at the "Tarbuth (Culture)" school in Yurburg. Hayim became involved in the Hashomer Hatsair movement due to the influence of Nakhum Finkel, who was the principal of the school at Kelm. A wonderful person, a yeshivah graduate in the spritit of the Musar movement founded by Rabbi Yisrael Salanter. From the Musar "Shtibl" he found his way to socialism and "Hashomer Hatsair." Finkel attracted the young by his simple manners and slow and convincing way of speaking. When he addressed the young, the focus of his speech was "the morals of mankind, the new society, the society of the future."

Finkel would visit Yurburg to see his relatives and he would also drop in at the

Hashomer Hatsair nest (clubhouse) for conversation. The youngsters liked and admired him. The teachers of the school in Yurburg were his friends too. That is how he met teacher Hayim Siger. Nahum Finkel influenced Hayim Siger to join the scouts troop -"Hashomer Hatsair" - and he soon became its head. In his position as head of the troop, Hayim would appear as a man of virtue, almost a monk, who observes the ten scouts' laws as if they were religious duties. When a scout would leave the movement they would sit "shivah," try to find points of blame with the leaders and their educational attitude. The members of the troop would rise when Hayim walked up and down the long room and would, as it were, eulogize the departed. He would say "do not cry for the dead, cry for the one who is leaving," his words were uttered in a hoarse and pressed voice and their echoes could be heard in all the corners of the large room.

Hayim was persistent in his moral claims on the scouts and especially the adolescent girl scouts. One day, a social evening was held in town and the program among other things, included a beauty contest. One of the girl scouts of the adolescents group at the troop went to the event out of curiosity, modestly dressed. She arrived at the event without any expectations and she won the "Most Beautiful Girl of Yurburg" award. Indeed she well deserved this honor however, Hayim found this to be aesthetically wrong and against moral standards expected of scouts. Hayim summoned the Girl Scout for clarification and condemned her behavior.

At Hayim's inspiration the troop's meetings became Musarnik conferences. This also marked the parties. Hayim would sing Hassidic songs in candlelight, accompanied on the guitar and sad songs, heart yearning, such as Shneur's "Delicate Hand," Tchernikhovsky's "Play- play along" and Bialik's "Take me under your wing" etc. When he spoke in his soft Hebrew style and attractive voice, everyone listened to him attentively and with truly holy respect.

Hayim exerted a very strong influence on each and every scout. He was unique and unforgettable. Both at the troop and at school.

When the Nazi hooligans entered Lithuania, during World War II, disaster struck Hayim Siger and his girlfriend Rivkale Karabelnik.

Rachel, Rivka's older sister, went on aliyah to Eretz Yisrael (see the article "Rachel Niv from Yurburg to Beth Zera"). Rivka's younger sister, Hannah (Trainin) also went to Eretz Yisrael and established her home there.

Hayim and Rivkah whose eyes were always directed towards Zion, got caught up in the terrible Holocaust and were cruelly killed by the Nazi murderers and their Lithuanian helpers.

The friends of Hayim Siger, outstanding man and educator, will never forget him as long as they live, or the sweet and kind hearted Rivkale. They loved and were loved during their lives and did not part in death - blessed be their memory.

TRANSLATION OF PAGES 277

YISRAEL DIMANTMAN

AUTHOR AND EDUCATOR

By Zevulun Poran

Yisrael Dimantman was a Hebrew educator and author. When he was young he studied at Lithuanian yeshivoth and afterwards at the humanities department of the Lithuanian University at Kovno. When he completed his studies, in the early twenties, he served as teacher and principal of the elementary school in Yurburg. In his time the educational level of studies at the school rose considerably. Dimantman created a Zionist-Hebrew atmosphere at the school and was much appreciated by the parents.

Yisrael Dimantman was a dynamic person and he was well known in the Hebrew public circles in Lithuania. He was a member of the "Tarbuth (Culture)" center and "Hamoreh (Teacher)" union and took part in the publication of the pedagogic paper "On the path of education" in Kovno. Dimantman published many articles on pedagogical and educational subjects. He also wrote a pacifist novel in Russian called "Nakanone" (Not yet).

Yisrael Dimantman was a staunch Zionist and devoted to the idea of building Eretz Yisrael. In 1936 he visited Israel and was very much impressed by its development and progress in all wakes of life. On his return he wrote articles about the Zionist venture taking place in Israel, and mainly about Hebrew as the daily language of students and their parents. He postponed his aliyah to Israel for a couple of years.

In the meantime great events took place in our lives - true upheavals. In 1939 Vilna was attached to the Vilna and Lithuania region. Dimantman was appointed principal of the Epstein Hebrew Gymnasium in Vilna. More than a year later he found himself in the Vilna ghetto. Dimantman, a dynamic person, accomplished a lot even under these circumstances and contributed as much as he could to the cultural and educational life in the ghetto, at first as a teacher and then as principal of schools and the person in charge of cultural work in the ghetto. In those days a Hebrew literature contest was held at the ghetto; Dimantman took part in this competition and won two awards for his story "Up to the gate" and for a play in Yiddish about life in the ghetto.

When the ghetto was dismantled Yisrael Dimantman was sent to the forced labor camp in Kaluga (Esthonia) and near the end of the war he was sent to the labor camp at Schtutthof (Germany) where he died.

It should be mentioned that wherever he was, and under all circumstances Dimantman proved to be a reliable public person, full of initiative and energy to work for others, very devoted until his death. Blessed be his memory.

TRANSLATION OF PAGES 278-280

BERL LEVINBERG

THE MAN AND THE PUBLIC FIGURE

By Zevulun Poran

The Israel and Ethel Levinberg family was well known in Yurburg. The oldest daughter of the family was Golda, the second son Berl (Dov) and then Hinda, Shelomoh, Sheine and Yehudith. The four younger children studied at the Hebrew Gymnasium. Yisrael Levinberg was a wealthy businessman, who traded in timber, stone and celluloid. He was also a member of "Export-Handel" for the export of farming produce and a partner in the business of steamships transporting passengers and merchandise along the Nieman River.

The son, Berl Levinberg, who is the subject of this article, studied accounting. When "Export Handel" was set up in the early1920s, Berl was appointed manager of the company.

Berl excelled at his work at the commercial company, and stood out with his initiative and organizational talent. "Export Handel" was a large company that included 20 export traders, and the scope of its business attained many millions. In the course of his work Berl gained commercial- managerial expertise and made progress in his work.

However, it should be mentioned that Berl was not the kind of person who was satisfied merely with commercial and business matters. Berl found spritual satisfaction in the "Maccabi" federation in Yurburg, the sports club, of which most youngsters were members. Berl was elected Chairman of the branch and managed it in a sensible and strong manner. He was a gifted man and knew ho to express himself. His Yiddish was fluent and a little pathetic.

Berl himself was not a sportsman, perhaps due to a fragile disposition - he looked thin and pale - and perhaps because he was busy with his many occupations. Berl looked after the organization of the "Maccabi" branch and its sports equipment, as well as the cultural activity in a Zionist spirit. He asked teachers and public figures to join the cultural activity. And indeed, everything was very well organized. Berl considered his volunteer task at "Maccabi" a Zionist duty.

One day when a group of friends asked him to establish a "pioneer youth" circle in the framework of "Maccabi," he immediately agreed. The pioneer idea was consistent with his outlook on life and he liked it. Berl offered his home for the meetings of the circle, and even took part in them himself. However, when the circle was established and called the "Trumpeldor Regiment," Berl did not join it, because the circle obliged its members to implement pioneering, i.e. go on training and aliyah to Israel.

After a while the circle members joined the "Hashomer Hatsair" youth movement, headed by Zevulun Poran, committee member. Berl regretted the circle's departure from "Maccabi," but was very happy that friends who had been educated at "Maccabi" would implement pioneering, for aliyah to Israel and building the land were the essence of Zionism.

Berl continued to be active at "Maccabi" with all his heart and soul. Many positive things were done to encourage physical education and also in the cultural field. Everything seemed beautiful, almost perfect. Berl believed that this situation would go on forever. However, reality was different. Fateful events led to serious political and social upheaval in Lithuania. "Export Handel," which was active in Yurburg from the early 1920s, was eventually dismantled, due to the decrees of the nationalist- anti-semitic government, headed by Voldemaras. The government took all the export/import business away from the Jews by government decree. All the different kinds of businessmen in Yurburg and Lithuania became destitute. This decree came as a shock to the Jewish population in Lithuania. Berl Levinberg too found himself cut off from his source of living. He, like his contemporaries, looked for ways to make a living, and when they failed to find them - not in Yurburg and not in Lithuania - they decided to emigrate. Berl wanted to go to Eretz Yisrael, but a certificate was hard to get,therefore Berl immigrated to Canada, where the gates were open to immigration.

Berl immigrated to Canada, and thus exchanged one Diaspora for another, against his wish. In Montreal Berl found a job, and did not change his taste. Wherever he was he always remained the same warm "Litvak" and was a faithful Zionist in his outlook. Berl did not achieve much for himself in Canada, however he achieved much - as a volunteer - for Eretz Yisrael. Berl was elected member of the Zionist center of Canada's Jews and also Deputy Chairman of Keren Hakayemeth. There were many Jewish immigrants in Canada from Lithuania who donated large sums of money to the nationalist funds. The Canadian Jews were particularly generous in their contributions to Eretz Yisrael, and Berl's share in this activity was significant. This was well known in Israel as well, and when Berl came to Israel on a visit, he received a warm welcome. Berl was happy to see the country, breathe its air and spirit, enjoy the act of Jewish creation, and particularly what was achieved with the donations of the Jews from Canada. One day, when Berl climbed to the top of a mountain, to the west of Jerusalem, and saw a large area, entirely covered by forests, named after Canada, his eyes filled with tears of joy.

The dream of the forests, which he had dreamt in Yurburg, had come true in the mountains of Israel!

When Berl visited Israel he looked everywhere for people from Yurburg, in towns and villages. When he found pioneers from Yurburg at a kibbutz, he was very happy. He was proud of them. Praised them, and only regretted he himself had not physically contributed to the building of the country.

In the last years of his life Berl fell ill. He had no energy left. He moved from the cold climate of Canada to the warmth of Florida in the U.S.A. From Florida too he wrote nostalgic letters to his friends in Israel. He wanted to know what was going on. Our concerns were his concerns. Nevertheless, he never forgot Yurburg, the cradle of his birth, the home of his parents. The Yurburg that no longer exists.

When he learned that the Jewish community of Yurburg would become commemorated in a book of remembrance, he was enchanted. He himself sent the first article for the book, in which he nostalgically described Yurburg and its Jewish community, which was totally destroyed. We, his childhood friends, have hereby fulfilled his and our wish by publishing the book of remembrance of the Yurburg community, as we knew it in its days of glory and disaster, a book which will bequeath the values of our fathers in Yurburg to many generations to come. What a pity that Berl did not live to see the book of remembrance published.

Blessed be his memory.

Dora Arshtein was a cashier of the Komertz Bank in Yurburg (owned by Shmerl Bernshtein). Given to Jack Cossid on July 30, 1937 with the message " Remembrance to Jack, I give you this present before you go to America." Dora was murdered in the Shoah.

[Photo not in original Yizkor book. From photo album of Jack Cossid.]

TRANSLATION OF PAGES 281-283

HINDA LEVINBERG-BECKER AND HER DIARY

By Zevulun Poran

Hinda Levinberg, as we knew her when she was young, was a slender and beautiful girl. As a girl she was an introvert and apparently shared her experiences with her personal diary. From an early age -hard to believe - she started to write her diary. The diary shows a keen eye and a serious, adult attitude to what took place around her.

The diary is written in Yiddish - a popular and juicy Yiddish -with a treasure of folklore characteristic of the little Jewish town. The diary speaks of family occasions and various personalities who walked along the streets of Yurburg and we never saw them, and social events which we did not witness.

It was Hinda's ambition to see the diary printed in a special book, but she did not have the good fortune to see this happen. She would certainly have been happy to at least see the two parts out of her diary that were translated into Hebrew for the book of remembrance of the Yurburg community, but even this did not happen, what a pity. It was not easy to translate the parts we present in the book of remembrance. The conversations and dialogues of the simple people in their popular language required the translator to adapt himself to the original language and to adhere - as far as possible -to its special style. Reading the diary, one could feel her great love of Yiddish - the "Mameloshen" - and the atmosphere of the little Jewish town. Hinda remembered everyone by his name, and even by his nickname.

In her diary Hinda takes an interest in every detail of the town's Jews - their occupations, jobs, profession, even the idle Jews, who sat around and gossiped. Hinda's diary reflects the entire atmosphere of the little town as through a looking glass. There are a few romantic stories in the diary as well, but more romanticism and love for the past. When we read the diary we grasp the reality of the man in the street in his daily life in town. In short: Hinda's diary is a fascinating diary about the little Jewish town, an expression of different and strange people, a world in its own .. marvelous!

Perhaps we should have presented the diary as it was written in Yiddish, the Yiddish of our fathers - the "Litvakian Yiddish"! We thought about it and asked ourselves: "for whom is the book of remembrance? For us, the "disappearing generation" who knew Yurburg, or for our sons and their children who did not know Yurburg and the Yiddish language!" The answer was straight and unhesitating-to translate the parts of the diary into Hebrew - and that is what we did.

Hinda Levinberg- Beker (Becker)

We are confident that we "did the right thing" for the next generations, who will wish to read and get to know their forefathers and their history.

Hinda studied at the Hebrew Gymnasium in Yurburg and even graduated from it. She was a good student, but not outstanding in anyway. At that time Hinda did not show any particular love for the Hebrew language or Zionism. She did not join any youth movement -either in sports or the scouts or an ideological circle. She was not interested in any of these, and thought they were childish. Hind lived in a world of her own. She loved to take part in conversations, to go on outings and to dance. She also liked to dress smartly, in order to look special and impress people. And indeed, she received attention. Many curried her favor. Some said she was a "dreamer," a snob - but they were wrong. Hinda was by nature a simple person, friendly, without any snobbery or conceit.

When Hinda went to Kovno to study she did not have any "grand" plans. Her world became richer in the big city, her horizons broadened and her outlook became more keen. Here she acquired intellectual values, met people, and attended the theater and the opera. She had time to herself, did not have to worry about making a living, as many others. Her well-to-do parents took care of all her needs. She did not have to pay dearly for what is acquired at the university. Perhaps she was less interested in dry science than in the school of life. In Kovno too she made many friends. The Kovno period is not registered in Hinda's diary and we do not know if she adhered to her studies or chose another way of life.

One day we found out that Hinda was in South Africa. Married and already a mother. Since then we lost track of her for a long time. In the meantime life took its swift course, worlds were shattered and new worlds sprang up and again we hear that when Hinda got tired of the "wonders" of the South African diaspora - she, her son and his family, decided to go to Israel. Here we realized that the Zionist sparkle which was kindled at the Hebrew Gymnasium in Yurburg lit up again abroad and turned into a flame that lit up her way to the State of Israel.

Hinda was not many years in Israel and she was no longer as agile as in the past. She turned old and her physical strength dwindled. She still had her lust for life and hoped for another day, as before, but the years gone by and her weak body let her down. Nevertheless, Hinda did not disappear from the public eye. She traveled from one place to another to meet relatives and friends, establish contacts and take part in Israeli society. She also spent quite some time in Jerusalem with her friends. Everywhere she looked for people from Yurburg. The voices of the past were deeply imbedded in her personality and never left her. She talked often of the past, spoke Yiddish, told about what happened in Yurburg. She knew a lot about Yurburg, even the smallest details, which none of us remembered. She hardly mentioned South Africa in her conversation. It is perhaps unnecessary to say that even when she was in Israel she lived in the world of Yurburg. Hinda very much wanted to see her diary in print, consulted friends and regretted that her life's dream would not come true.

In the last years Hinda had no strength left. Her body became weaker and she was often ill. How happy she was when we came to visit her at the home of her son and his lovely family, living near Tel Aviv. During the entire visit she told the guests, her friends, in a hoarse voice, about her grandchildren, her eyes shining as in the past - they turned on and out -on and out.

One day we heard that Hinda has passed away. Her heart, so full of the love of life, had ceased to pound. Hind was just like anyone else - and each life comes to an end. There is no such thing as eternity!

Zevulun Poran

Note: If the Yiddish Diary of Hinda Levinberg-Becker can be located, we would like to add its translation to a future English version of the Yurburg Yizkor Book. Please contact: Joel Alpert jalp@comcast.net

TRANSLATION OF PAGES 284-287

RACHEL NIV

FROM YURBURG TO BEITH ZERA

By Yakov Niv (Vin)

Rachel Karabelnik-Niv was born in Yurburg to a wealthy family. Her father was a timber exporter and a partner in the business of the steamships that sailed on the Nieman River. He was also a partner in the "Export-Handel" company, which included all the businessmen of Yurburg who dealt in export.

 The father, David Karabelnik, was a tall man, nice, and respected in Yurburg. The mother, Mina, was a sensitive woman, a devoted mother to her family, concerned about her children's education. The Karabelnik's were well off and this enabled her to keep a beautiful, spacious home and ensure that her children- Cherna, Rachel, Rivkah, Hannah and Arieh - developed and grew up under comfortable circumstances. Rachel passed all the stages of education in Yurburg -studied at the "Tarbuth" elementary school and the Hebrew Gymnasium, as did her sisters and brother. (See photo of family in article on Moti Naividel in the Appendix.

At an early age Rachel joined the "Hebrew Scouts - Hashomer Hatsair" movement and she was among the first in Yurburg to do so. Rachel embraced with the movement's principles with all her heart and soul and observed the "Ten Scouts' Laws" in her way of life. When she became an adolescent, she was appointed youth leader of the young groups in the troop. Rachel loved her trainees and they loved her in return. Rachel took care to wear the movement's uniform and shaped the character of her trainees. She contributed much to the troop, decorated it in good taste and kept it clean.

The "Hashomer Hatsair" movement was, of course, a movement that educated its trainees to active Zionism. When the trainee turned 17or 18, he or she had to implement Zionism, according to the movement's principles, and go for pioneer training, aliyah and live in Israel on a kibbutz. When it was Rachel's turn to go for pioneer training, she decided, without any hesitation, to observe the duty of implementation. Rachel identified with the movement's principles and it's pioneering way.

Rachel's parents were not surprised by her decision; they were well aware of her adherence to the movement's ideals, yet they proposed she postpone her departure for training for reasons of health. However, Rachel did not agree, under any circumstances, to make any concessions whatsoever. Thus, one day she got up and went for training to Memel. Her parents accepted Rachel's decision because they also had a Zionist outlook - and the atmosphere in Yurburg was Zionist and most of the youngsters were affected by this.

Rachel arrives in Memel, a large port city with the "Pioneer House," a handsome two-story building set up by the town's Jews as their contribution to the pioneer movement. In this home there was representative of "Hekhalutz" who sent the khalutzim (pioneers) on training in places set aside for them. The pioneers worked at estates that needed workers in summer. Every such estate owner would invite a group of pioneers to work in the field. It was hard work for youngsters who had not worked on the land before. Some of those who were sent to Memel, a German industrial town in the past, worked in Memel itself. The pioneers who worked at the factories stayed at the "Hekhalutz Home."

It so happened that Rachel had to work in the domestic service of "Beith Hekhalutz" itself. Here, at the "Beith Hekhalutz," a large group of pioneers had settled, and the upkeep of the house required a large team of workers. Rachel was found suitable for work at the "Beith Hekhalutz" and joined the team. Rachel's diligence and her pleasant disposition helped her to adapt to her work and be accepted in society. After one or two years of training - Rachel was found fit to go on aliyah. However, there was a queue to go on aliyah; one had to wait until "His Majesty's" government would kindly agree to send certificates for the pioneers. And till then they waited and waited until they finally went on aliyah after all.

Rachel finally arrives at her much-wanted destination, Israel. She joins the Lithuanian Hashomer nucleus, which started to be absorbed at the Benyaminah settlement. The boys worked in the orange groves and the girls mainly at the farmers' homes. Rachel was sent to work with one of the farmers, to carry out domestic duties and was looked up on as inferior. After a while the nucleus moves to Petakh Tikvah. Others, who had in the meantime come on aliyah from Lithuania, joined the nucleus. In Petakh Tikvah, as in Benyaminah, they worked with farmers. Wages were low, conditions bad, housing primitive - they lived in tents and huts. They passed the time hoping for change. The change they desired was to go to a settlement and set up a farming community. Here the Lithuanian Shomer nucleus was offered a special opportunity. It was proposed that they merge with Beth Zera, a kibbutz settlement that already existed in the Jordan valley, near the Deganiyah Kibbutzim. The Lithuanian Shomer nucleus accepted the offer to merge with Beith Zera; the two parts complemented each other and a large kibbutz was formed. The old timers brought along the culture of the west and the new members the culture of their Lithuanian Jewish roots.

Rachel adjusts to the new surroundings. Conditions here are more comfortable. Although the climate is warmer in summer, one gets used to it. There is a home, a garden and lawn, a pastoral atmosphere. Rachel carries out all sorts of jobs. She is given a task and faithfully carries it out. Although her physical condition does not allow her to work hard in the field, there are branches of farming where she fits in, and the kibbutz appreciates her contribution to work and social activity.

A couple of years later, when she is about to establish her family home, Rachel feels the need to share her experiences with her parents. She longs to see her family and goes to Yurburg for a visit. The many years of separation from Yurburg, the beloved little town of her youth, have created a feeling of distance. Although Rachel loved her parents, the home she had built at Beith Zera drew her back there, and she returned. When Rachel said good bye to her parents she did not know - who could have known? - that this was the last time she would see them and Yurburg, the town of her birth. A short while later the Jews of Yurburg were cruelly murdered by the Nazis and their Lithuanian helpers.

At the kibbutz life goes on as usual. Rachel works; Her family life is harmonious. She has a lovely home. Only the shadow of the terrible Holocaust pursues her. She knows - one has to live with the tragedy. Go on. Bring up the children. Rachel tries to be strong. The years go by and in our country too there is rising concern. Survivors arrive from various countries, they have passed through the gates of hell and they want to find shelter and a safe haven in their national home, but the British mandate government causes problems. The battle for aliyah and - in fact - an independent state in Israel - continues.

The War of Liberation breaks out. The Beth Zera children go to study at an educational institution at Mishmar Haemek. Rachel joins the group that takes care of the children and helps them get adjusted. However, the War of Independence arrives here too. Mishmar Haemek is besieged and attacked by the Arab army with tanks and guns. Mishmar Haemek defends itself heroically and does not yield. The defeated Arab army retreats. Mishmar Haemek returns to life. Rachel passes the war at Mishmar Haemek. While she worries about her children at Mishmar Haemek, the war knocks at her door too ... the battle of the Deganiyas. The war is at Rachel's doorstep.

The children, the boys, wage a heroic battle until the fighting is over and the State of Israel is established.

All these events leave a scar on Rachel's heart and weaken her physical condition, but not her spirit. Rachel continues as usual and is happy with her family and the kibbutz. Thus the years go by. Rachel feels weak, but does not give in. She still makes an effort to work. She wants to carry out her tasks accurately and diligently, as in the past. However, Rachel's efforts are in vain - one day her heart falls silent.

Her relatives and friends at the kibbutz, who have accompanied Rachel for many years and shared her sorrow and joy - will never forget her.

May she rest in peace.

TRANSLATION OF PAGES 288

MEIR LEVYUSH

MAN AND FRIEND   By Zevulun Poran

Meir Levyush was born on March 6, 1912 in Shaudine, a little town on the other side of the Nieman River, opposite Yurburg. Not more than twenty families lived there. The Jews of Shaudine were linked to Yurburg's economic and cultural institutions. Their children studied at the elementary school and the gymnasium there. Every day they had to cross the Nieman River on ferries to get to school in Yurburg. Only on winter days, when the Nieman River was frozen, the two settlements merged into one. In spite of the difficulties of the road and waste of time, the Shaudine students were good students. Among them was Meir Levyush, who graduated from the Hebrew Gymnasium.

From here Meir went on to study at Kovno University, where he studied pharmacology. In the meantime World War II broke out. Meir was sent to the Shavli ghetto and then to the Dachau concentration camp until the liberation in 1945.

After all this, Meir went to Israel with his family in 1950, and settled in Ramat Gan, where he worked in his profession as pharmacist at the General Health Fund. All those who required his services at the pharmacy appreciated his professional standard and humane attitude.

In Israel he was a member of the Former Residents of Yurburg Association and never missed a social occasion to meet former acquaintances. In the article for the book of remembrance Meir commemorated Shaudine, his home and the people he loved.

Meir passed away on September 18, 1989 after a long illness. He left a wife and two sons. He was a fine, well-liked person, Meir, popular among his many relatives and friends.

Blessed be his memory.

TRANSLATION OF PAGES 289

SHIMON FAINBERG

PIONEER AND PUBLIC FIGURE

By Zevulun Poran

On Friday October 21, 1977, we laid Shimon to rest. We, his friends from Yurburg, stood in the crowd of mourners near his grave, sad and grieving. The burial was over and here it said: Shimon Ben-Benjamin Fainberg - blessed be his memory.

The life of a man who had accomplished much had come to an end. We had known Shimon for many years. We sprung from the same land of Yurburg, our town, where together we absorbed the Jewish atmosphere, in its "Litvak" character. Unlike many of his friends, Shimon was spared from the terrible Holocaust. We watched him in the days of his youth and while he grew up. He was a modest person, a pleasant man who enjoyed company. He had a quest for learning and lofty human qualities. He had a warm personality, and was kind- hearted and a true friend.

Shimon was charming, moderate and calm, spoke little but had a heart that was sensitive to the suffering of others. He strove for a just and moral life style. Till the end he sincerely believed in the values he was taught when he was a youngster at "Hekhalutz," when he adhered to the socialist ideal with its humane values and love of man, trust in the simple working man with all his greatness and weaknesses.

Shimon loved the beauty and splendor of the country, but loathed arid and wasteland. He therefore followed the furrows, on foot and by tractor, in order to plough the land and till the soil of the homeland, to be happy when it flourished and rejoices when it bloomed. When the task was accomplished, his heart filled with joy and the love of creation he derived from working in the fields of his beloved homeland, for which he had yearned all his life, especially in the years of war and suffering, as a soldier in the Russian snow and as a fighter in the heavy battle against the Nazi hooligans.

When he came to Israel, after the War of Independence, the gray reality did not cloud his happiness, for the dream of his life had come true. Shimon quickly adapts to life in the country that is being built. He works and establishes his home in Holon, a beautiful dwelling-place that matches his spirit. He makes new friends and broadens his horizons, and in his spare time he does community work where he lives, works for the creation of a working, just and moral society in our country. Shimon loves his friends and they love and respect him in return.

Alas, life takes many turns and fate is blind and cruel! - His active life was cut short by a malignant disease, which he contracted some time ago. He bore his pain patiently and quietly. He did not burden those around him and did not cause depression, until the candle of his life blew out. He took all his dreams, aspirations and expectations with him to the grave.

The Great Wooden Synagogue of Yurburg
Not in original Yizkor Book - Courtesy of the Vilna Jewish Museum

Chapter 4
RELIGION, CULTURE AND COMMUNITY LIFE

TRANSLATED FROM PAGE 293

YURBURG: A JEWISH COMMUNITY DISTINGUISHED BY ITS INTELLECTUAL LIFE

By M. Simon, Tilsit

(Israelitisches Familienblatt, October 22, 1931)

Not far from the border between the Memel district and Lithuania, about 30 kilometers from the German city of Tilsit the former small Russian town of Yurburg (Georgenburg) is situated in a picturesque location on the banks of the Memel (Nieman) river. The Jewish community of about 2,000 souls is distinguished by its lively intellectual life. Besides an elementary school, the community maintains a well-equipped high school run according to modern educational principles. It is subject to supervision by the Lithuanian ministry of education from which it receives substantial support.

It is almost the sole remnant of the rights solemnly promised to the Jews of Lithuania ten years ago: an autonomous network of schools subsidized by the state. All the other rights and privileges were aimed at improving the economic and spiritual conditions of the Lithuanian Jews. The Jewish community councils that were to operate autonomously were appointed according to the old Russian pattern; the Rabbis were again appointed to administer the population registration, and once again, there is no nationwide Jewish council and no minister of Jewish affairs.

What remains is what already existed before: reminders of past good times, memorials to folk art and community life. In Yurburg, the Old Synagogue, a wooden structure, remains the main point of attraction for the Jewish traveler. No reliable data exist on the "age" of this house of prayer. Based on its architectural style and its location, it probably was built towards the end of the 18th century. The unique cupola above the dais in the center of the sanctuary and the Holy Ark deserve special mention.

The aged Rabbi Dimant serves as head of the community. He is famous far beyond the borders of Lithuania.

(Translated into Hebrew by Joseph Valk, son of the late Matityahu Valk, a native of Yurburg)

TRANSLATED FROM PAGE 294

YURBURG IN "QUESTIONS AND ANSWERS" OF RABBINICAL LITERATURE

Edited By Zevulun Poran

Chapter 7 in the Rabbi of Lublin's "Questions and Answers" deals with the problem of an 'agunah' [a deserted wife] whose husband has disappeared and there is no proof that he died or was killed. Such a woman is forbidden by Jewish law to remarry.

When evidence was taken in Vilna in the year 5353 (1593), the book "Questions and Answers" reports, it was told that her husband was killed in the customs house of Jurberg - Yurburg - a town southeast of Memel and northwest of Kovno.

Following is the story on "hearing the evidence," which was written in the Yiddish language which then was in its infancy....

This shows that a Jewish community existed in Yurburg as early as in 1593.

... The third session of taking evidence, in the Rabbi of Lublin's Q&A; (Chapter 7), also refers to an "agunah" [deserted wife], "the wife of Yehuda son of Kathriel, brother of Nathan, Kerpel," and mentions the evidence taken in Vilna in the year 5353, which is 1593 (."... as stated in said evidence taken in the Holy Community of Vilna on Tuesday, the 20th of Tamuz, 5393"). The agunah did not receive the "get" [divorce] very quickly, because four years later, in 5397 (1597) we learn more details about this case from evidence given by one Reuven son of Shemuel, who tells that he had heard about the deceased "at the customs house in Yurburg, which is none other than the Lithuanian town of Yurburg, southeast of Memel and northwest of Kovno: "And so, the evidence given on Monday, the 15th of Shvat, 5357 [1597], by the witness Reuven son of the late Shemuel [in his language, German] was: It is now three years when at the customs house at Yurburg that it had been heard from several non-Jews who blurted out that Feivel (Pavel) was killed (may God revenge his spilled blood); his own son-in-law told me several times that Feivel was killed at Yurburg and that is the place where he was killed."

TRANSLATION OF PAGES 295 - 296

Not in original book - Courtesy of the Vilna Jewish Museum

THE OLD SYNAGOGUE TELLS ITS STORY

by Pinkhas Shakhnovitz

There it stands, humbly, the old synagogue, shrouded in the glory of age - yet still standing upright, its head reaching to the sky.

Inside the empty space of the synagogue one can often hear the moaning of grief and a lamenting voice whispers "Where are they, my sons?" Not one of my sons, those I raised in dignity turns to me. Only mourners and orphans come to me each morning, saying a hasty prayer, they say "Kadish" and close the door behind them. All that remains of me is a locked garden. Rather die than live such a boring life.

I remember days gone by, when I was a crown of splendor and a magnificent mound to God, everyone turning to Him; my gates were wide open from morning to night. Talitoth were worn and folded, tsitsiyoth were dragged, bands wrapped around hairy and smooth arms, half bare, moving in space, each mouth mumbling and each tongue praying, each back swaying and all eyes lifted to heaven. The air filled with many voices, merging in wondrous harmony. I would have taken the echoes of these voices and the words in heart and mouth and sent them straight to the world above, the "household of heaven."

Whenever someone fell seriously ill in town, his family would immediately run to me, to my gates of mercy. Their weeping shook my walls, and I cried with them.

When one of the Jews in town died, the inhabitants would cry bitterly and I would shed a tear with them. On Simhath Torah I would be tipsy together will all the others; they danced in me and I in them; the echo of my beautiful ceiling answered them. The sorrow and joy of my sons were absorbed into my walls every day and every hour, for about two hundred years.

And now, after many years of being abandoned, my gates are wide open again. Many Jews come to me, young and old alike. The young ones are courageous, without a beard yet, but their eyes burn like torches. Many of them speak in the language of prayer. Once one of them took courage and climbed onto the pulpit from where the most honorable Rabbis addressed the people, and he spoke in a loud and courageous voice full of belief.

These were his words: "The best of our sons in the country of our fathers, who freed our homeland and realized the hope of all of us, will never again offer their necks for slaughter. To those who hate us and persecute us we answer with courage, aliyah, defense and building of our country. Salvation lies not only in prayer. Gather every cent for the liberation of the country and it defense." That is what he said and the "Blue Box" was passed along, becoming heavier, filling up.

I stood there, wondering and murmuring; who brought those under my wings and gathered them here? These youngsters seemed different to me from past visitors. I looked at them and saw fire burning in their eyes. Not a strange fire, but a holy fire. They yearn for human sacrifice, build a homeland and wait with open arms for other youngsters to join them. They make the desert bloom, gather in exiles, build a homeland. I am proud of these sons. I too would love to see one of these pioneers with my own eyes, conquer the land and defend it.

One clear morning the sun opened my doors and one of the pioneers who had come on a mission from "over there" entered. I looked at him and was thrilled; I received him as a grandfather receives his beloved grandson, who has come from a distant- near land. Only then did I understand the reason for my boredom: my space was too narrow to hold the flame of thousands of such eyes.

My son is my victory. At my advanced age I shall be satisfied with the old people who come to tell me of their sorrows, and the young ones I will accompany with my blessing and prayer from afar, so that they will build their homes in splendor, as they see fit. I was built as "a little temple" and they are building a "world temple" for centuries to come.

The old synagogue, from 1790, straightens its back and proudly lifts its head, facing the light coming from the East.

After many years a terrible tremor shocked the building, from bottom to ceiling, as if the synagogue cried and lamented silently, weeping about its destruction and the destruction of its community.

Yurburg, April 29, 1938

TRANSLATED FROM PAGES 297-305

THE SYNAGOGUE AND THE COMMUNITY'S RELIGIOUS LIFE

by Zevulun Poran

The synagogues constituted an important center in the Jewish communities of the Diaspora at all times. The synagogue was not only a place of worship and Torah study, but also the center of the community's religious and social life. It was the home of the wise Bible scholars and harbored the organizational and social institutions of the community, such as the various charity institutions, soup kitchens etc.

Jewish history teaches us that once a Jewish community was founded and settled somewhere, a synagogue was immediately erected. At first, it was a small building, enough for a minyan (quorum of ten adult male Jews), and as the community grew, so did the synagogue.

We do not have the exact dates as to when synagogues were erected in Lithuania or Yurburg, our town. No community was formed according to plan, or at a specific date. From the events of general history we know that the Jews of Germany were driven to the land of Lithuania in the twelfth and thirteenth century, following the Catholic-Christian persecutions at the time of the Crusaders. Lithuania's residents, still divided into tribes at the time, were pagans and did not oppose the German Jewish settlers' taking hold of the land, realizing that the cultural level, craftsmanship and commercial talents of the Jews would be helpful to the Lithuanian groups in their villages.

From the direction of Eastern Europe too - from Russia - waves of Jews arrived in Lithuania, due to hardship and sometimes also at the invitation of the rulers (Vytautas -1399). Thus over the centuries Jews from west and east gathered in the land of Lithuania, looking different, speaking a different language, and with different customs. It is presumed that the Russian Jews arrived in Lithuania first; they spoke in Slavic dialects, Russian in particular. The Russian Jews brought along special Jewish customs and tradition. The persecuted German Jews who arrived in Lithuania also had a rich cultural-Jewish background, their own customs and tradition. The German Jews spoke Yiddish, a German dialect interspersed with Hebrew words.

Hundreds of years passed until the two divisions - the eastern (Russia) and western (Germany) found a common language and merged. In the past hundreds of years nothing is left of the Lithuanian Jews' roots and only the family names are a sign of their origin.

Names such as Grinberg (Greenberg), Goldman, Vainstein (Weinstein), Ziman etc. indicate the German origin, whereas names such as Ansky, Kobelsky, Lutzky, Ritov, Rizhov etc. are evidence of their Russian roots. The merging process that affected all the Jews of Lithuania of course also affected the fathers of our town of Yurburg. Therefore, the process of composing the Jewish communities in Lithuania was very lengthy.

When the Lithuanians became Catholic Christians, hatred of Jews increased in Lithuania. The Catholic Christians considered the Jews as their competitors in trade and crafts. Nevertheless, the Lithuanian Jews did not suffer from persecution or expulsions, except for one short expulsion, in 1495. After eight years of expulsion the Jews returned to their places of residence and their belongings were returned to them. The Jews in Lithuania also had privileges, among them the privilege to erect synagogues, on condition they were built of wood, at the same height as the buildings around them, and did not stand out. It is quite probable that as early as the fifteenth and sixteenth centuries synagogues were already erected in the Jewish communities of Lithuania and in Yurburg too. Accurate numbers regarding Yurburg's population only exists from 1766. In that year Yurburg had 7391 inhabitants, 2833 of them Jews. At that time synagogues already existed in Yurburg, although we do not yet have any details as to the life of the Jewish community here.

Exterior of the Old Synagogue of Yurburg (not in original Yizkor Book)

Photographs by Balys Buracas - requests for higher resolution images should be made to Professor Antanas Buracas: anbura@lrs.lt

From the eighteenth century there were already famous Jewish craftsmen in Poland and Lithuania, builders, such as Simkhha-Hayim (Chaim) Ben Habanai, Shelomoh from Lutsk, David Friedlander from Ludmir and Benjamin from Lask. These builders specialized in wood building and they also built a number of famous synagogues in Lithuania. The price of building wood in Lithuania was cheap, for there were plenty of forests near by.

The great synagogue in Yurburg was built in 1790. It was a large and magnificent building. In 1870 the synagogue was expanded and renovated. On its upper level the women's section was installed and downstairs the prayer room. In the attic a room was set aside for welcoming distinguished guests. From the research carried out by engineer David Kotliar, published in the Lithuanian Jewry's Book of Remembrance, we learn that the builders, mentioned above, were those who built the great synagogue in Yurburg.

The Yurburg synagogue was one of the most beautiful buildings from the architectural point of view, and all those who saw it were impressed. It was erected at the end of a broad square and looked very special. Its roof was composed of three slopes, slanting onto each other, creating an interesting architectural combination. Upon entering the synagogue, one could see the traditional petitioning dome over the pulpit which brings to mind the "east" and the land of our fathers. The Holy Ark was particularly impressive - its magnificent woodcarvings were carved in a splendid ornamental style and considered popular art creations. The prayer pillar and Eliyahu's chair were also tastefully installed.

Eliyah's Chair in the Old Wooden Synagogue - 1927
[Not in Original Yizkor Book]   Courtesy of Ben Craine

The Bimah in the Old Synagogue of Yurburg

Photograph by Balys Buracas - requests for higher resolution images should be made to Professor Antanas Buracas: anbura@lrs.lt

The Bimah in the Old Synagogue of Yurburg

[Not in original Yizkor Book]

Photograph by Balys Buracas - requests for higher resolution images should be made to Professor Antanas Buracas: anbura@lrs.lt

Model of the Wooden Synagogue of Yurburg by Mosheh Verbin

The model created by artist Mosheh Verbin, member of Kibbutz Yakum, is a reconstruction of the synagogue in Yurburg. This model, made of straw, was made on the basis of two sketches, one of Andreoli dated 1872, the other of Chekarsky, dated 1903.

The picturesque building of the synagogue drew the attention of artists and painters from Lithuania as well as from abroad. In 1850 the famous painter Andreoli came from Italy and painted the Yurburg synagogue. He was enchanted by its special architectural structure and the composition of the woodcarvings inside. The picturesque motives and the colors of the plants interwoven with animals - deer and lions - and the figures and symbols that have been holy to our people for generations, such as the Tables of the Testimony, the Candelabrum, Star of David etc. were also most impressive. Anyone entering the synagogue stood in awe of the splendor and magnificence he beheld. The Jews of Yurburg were very proud of their synagogue.

Zusiya Efron, the researcher of Jewish art, writes the following in the album "Wooden Synagogues in Poland and Lithuania": "Until World War I there were 350 wooden synagogues, and in the period between the two world wars about 100 wooden synagogues were still standing, some of them outstanding architectural creations. Among these synagogues the synagogue of Yurburg, Volpe and Narobala were particularly splendid. In the Holocaust the Nazis and their helpers destroyed the last remaining synagogues and nothing is left of them at present."

Bimah - 1927   [Not in Original Yizkor Book]
Courtesy of Ben Craine

In the spring, summer and fall, the synagogue abounded with worshippers who loved the building and its special atmosphere. Only in the cold winter days, when there was ice and snow, the synagogue was totally empty. When it was very cold, the worshippers huddled together in the warm house of prayer and the three small synagogues, the "kloisim" of craftsmen and small traders. The "kloisim" also served as "khadarim" (religious elementary school) of the schoolchildren. About twenty children studied in our time in these "khadarim" with Rabbis, according to the old tradition.

Holy Ark - 1927 [Not in Original Yizkor Book]
Courtesy of Ben Craine

Close ups of top, middle and bottom of the Holy Ark. Note the ornate woodwork. [Not in Original Yizkor Book] Courtesy of Ben Craine

"Talmud Torah" students with their Rabbis, 1913 (Students only)

About two hundred children studied at the "Tarbuth" school, which was a Zionist school in spirit. At this school general subjects were taught in Hebrew.

"Tarbuth" elementary school 1920.

Its founder and principal Bekin sits on the right, the teachers next to him.

The former name of the elementary school was "Talmud Torah," here mainly Jewish subjects were taught. This was a sort of "upgraded kheder." Between the two world wars "Talmud Torah" became a modern elementary school, according to the State Laws, and at the wish of the parents, and it was called "Tarbuth." Two Rabbis, Bible scholars, taught the Jewish subjects, they are fondly remembered - Aryeh Leib (Leibchik) Gut and Rabbi Hayim (Chaim)-Nathan Yoziper. The other teachers and principals were graduates of Teachers' Colleges, in accordance with the Law, and they taught all the study subjects in a Zionist spirit. We remember Yisrael Bekin (the first Principal), Hillel Zaks, David Gorshein, Yisrael Dimantman, Hayim (Chaim) Siger, Yisrael Chekhanovsky and others.

In addition to the Hebrew school, there was another small elementary school, where all the subjects were taught in Yiddish. The Yiddish school did not stress the Zionist idea as an ideological principle.

The highest grade of the Gymnasium in the first year of its existence (without external students), the teachers - from right; Kaplan (gymnastics), Lifshitz (Natural Science), Mrs. Efrath-Rosenboim (Languages), Tsentkovsky (Tanakh), Dr. Efrath (Principal, Mathematics) Kosotzky (Literature); (X - x)

The students - from right: Dartwin, Kobelkovsky, Zevulun P., Hannah Fainberg (Feinberg) (x - ?), Shlomovitz; below to the right - Hinda Levinberg, Klara (Clara) Petrikansky

Eighth grade of the Hebrew Gymnasium, students and teachers

It must be mentioned that the Jewish children of Yurburg did not study at the "gentile" schools where studies were in Lithuanian, the official language. Lithuanian was only taught at elementary school as a compulsory official subject. The Jews usually spoke Yiddish among themselves. Many of the older generation knew Hebrew, corresponded and even calculated in Hebrew as early as the eighteenth and nineteenth century.

The pupils of the Gymnasium spoke Hebrew in the framework of the Gymnasium. The slogan was: "Jew: Speak Hebrew!" At the pioneer youth movements activities -mainly talks- were held in Hebrew.

The Jewish community in Yurburg was composed of various groups. There were religious people who observed the religious duties and there were Liberals. The non-religious also respected religion and tradition. The character of the Jewish community in Yurburg may be defined as traditional in its lifestyle, customs and Jewish atmosphere. There were no mixed marriages in Yurburg and no assimilation.

The members of the Yurburg community respected the religious leaders and especially the Rabbi, Rabbi Avraham Dimant, who was the Chief Rabbi between the two world wars and almost up to the bitter end of the Jews of Yurburg.

Rabbi Dimant was a handsome man, a man of learning, who knew how to mix the biblical with Derekh Eretz (respect). He was realistic and sensitive to the spirit of the time. He had a charming, pleasant personality, and was very much liked. Rabbi Dimant was respected in Yurburg, and although he was not in the habit of going to the people, they came to him to consult him. When the Rabbi of the town spoke his inspiring words of substance, the Jews of Yurburg listened and admired him. The Rabbinical Chair in Yurburg was held in great esteem in Lithuania.

Of the Rabbis of Yurburg the best known are Rabbi Yacov-Yosef Kharif, Rabbi Yekhezkel Lifshitz and last but not least - Rabbi Avraham Dimant.

Rabbi Hayim (Chaim)-Reuven Rubinstein, a wise and scholarly man, served as the Dayan (Judge) of the community in the last years. However, Rabbi Dayan Rubinstein was not as striking a personality as his colleague Rabbi Dimant. On matters of Bible Law Rabbi Rubinstein would be consulted. He had a large biblical library in his home which also contained holy books in German. Rabbi Rubinstein devoted days and nights to research on Jewish subjects and he published a number of books at his own expense. He used to give most of his books away in order to spread the word of the Torah among the people. One of his books is called " The Words of Reuven." About a year before the Holocaust he served as the community Rabbi instead of Rabbi Dimant.

Cantor Alperovitz was very popular both among the religious and in general. He was a scholar and also served as the chief "Shokhet" (religious slaughterer) of the community. The cantor will also be fondly remembered for the choir he cultivated and of which he was the conductor. He composed melodies to prayer chapters. In the last year his voice grew weaker, but he made an effort in spite of his hoarseness to fulfill his task. The Yurburg choir made his job easier and pleased the worshippers.

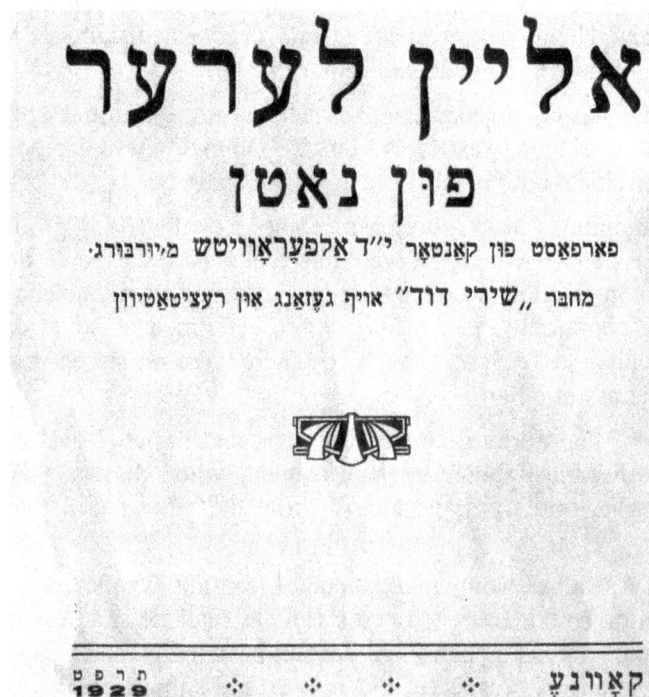

אליין לערער
פון נאטן
פארפאסט פון קאנטאר י״ד אַלפעראָוויטש מיורבורג.
מחבר ״שירי דוד״ אויף געזאנג און רעציטאַטיוון

ת ר פ ט
1929   ✦   ✦   ✦   ✦   קאָוונע

Title Page of Music Theory Book Written by Cantor Alperovitz

נעים זמירות ישראל יצחק דוד אלפעראוויץ.

This is the picture from the book of music written by Yitzhak David Alperovitz, the town Cantor. He gave Jack Cossid this book as a gift as Jack was leaving Yurburg for America. Below is the cover of the book. It was published in 1927 in Kovno.

Not only was he the Chazan (cantor) but also taught music and was the moyel. When Jack left in 1937 he was 84 years old and had the body of a young man and would swim in the Nieman with all the young men.

When the Nazis occupied Yurburg, the Lithuanian hoodlims tied a brick to Chazan Alperovitz's long white beard and forced him to parade down the street. They tortured him to death.

This page and title page of book by Cantor Alperovitz on previous page were not in original Yizkor book. Jack Cossid supplied these items.

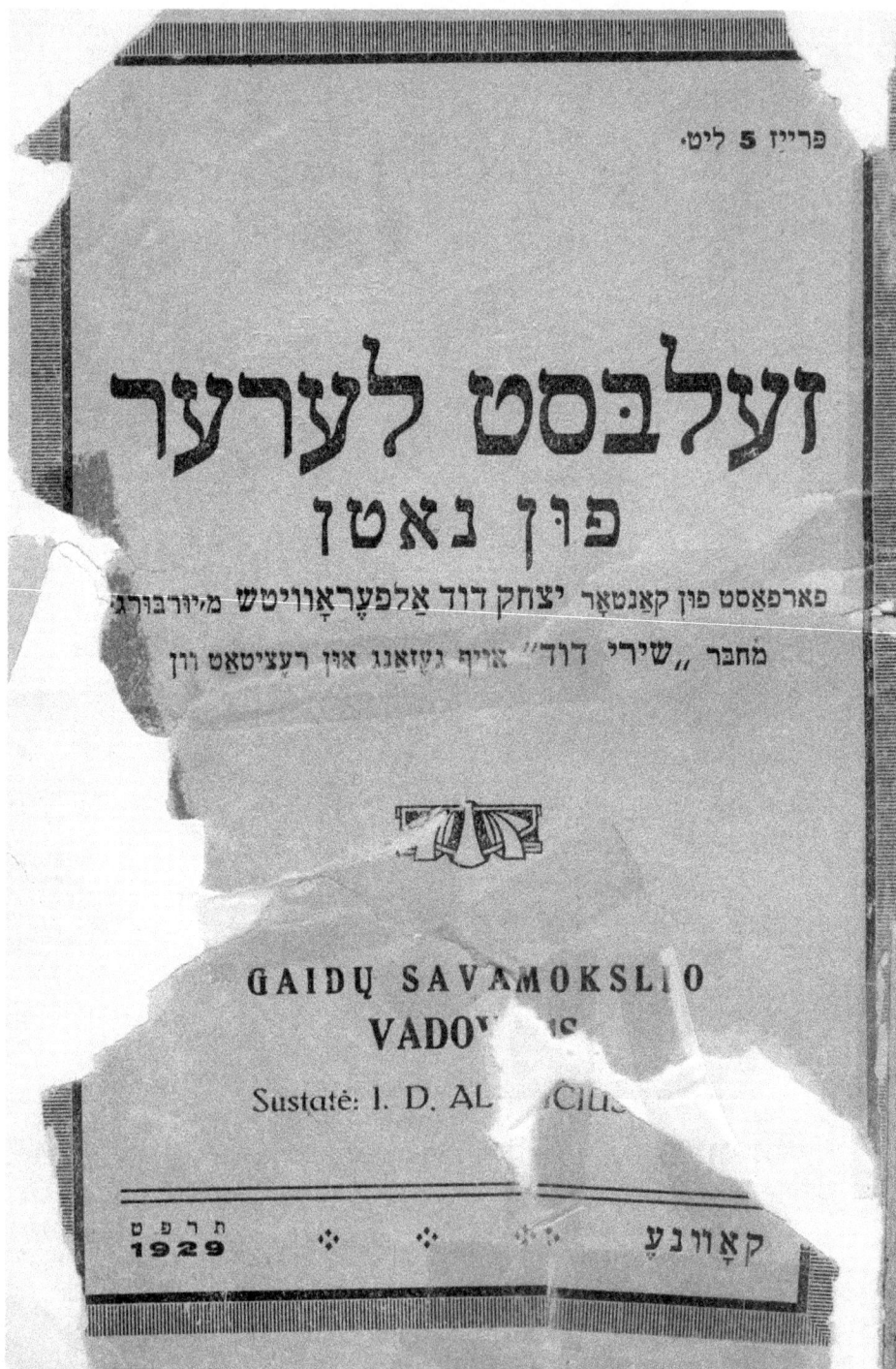

Cover of Music Theory Book Written by Cantor Alperovitz
[Not in original Yizkor book. Provided by Jack Cossid.]

The "Shokhet" (religious slaughterer) Rabbi Aharon Shlomovitz was a Bible scholar and popular. His daughter studied at the Hebrew Gymnasium and was in the first class that graduated.

Rabbi Bishko was an interesting and colorful person among the religious circles. He did not belong to the "holy vessels" of the community, for he was a small- scale industrialist. He had a candy factory at his home, and earned his bread this way. However, Rabbi Bishko, who was a "Talmid-Khakham" (learned man) was not satisfied with his physical work, but also spent a lot of time spreading Judaism among the younger generation.

He was one of the founders of the "Tifereth Bakhurim" (Splendid Boys) company and a small yeshivah where he taught the Torah to youngsters, at nightfall. Although somewhat peculiar, Rabbi Bishko was a simple, pleasant man, and with all his devotion to spreading the Torah among the masses, he was quite close to this world. He sent his children to the Hebrew Gymnasium. It is said that his eldest son, Aharon Bishko, was saved from the Holocaust and is living somewhere in Europe. Aharon also visited Israel.

The Jewish community in Yurburg was composed of many different social groups - Jews with different outlooks lived together in a calm and peaceful atmosphere - each to his own belief. Most of the youngsters lived according to the new life style and wanted to be educated. The graduates of the Hebrew Gymnasium in the town went to study at the State University in Kovno or the Hebrew Teachers College. Some of them also learned technological professions. Many of them made preparations to go to Eretz Yisrael.

As Yurburg was close to the German border, humanistic ideas and ideals were introduced. However, the Jews also went to the House of Prayer and studied the Torah, as was the custom in those days. There was a large biblical library at the House of Prayer and the scholars perused its holy books. No one made light of the other's belief.

Yurburg's Jewish character was carefully maintained, for it was a town with national and traditional nationalistic-religious values.

Notwithstanding the difficulties of the Diaspora, and the economic woes of the community of Israel in Lithuania, Yurburg among them, there was hope for a better future. As always, Jews believed with all their heart that "the eternal glory of Israel shall not fail."

TRANSLATED FROM PAGES 305 -308

ON THE HISTORY OF THE JEWISH COMMUNITY IN YURBURG

DURING THE DAYS OF NATIONAL AUTONOMY

Translated (into Hebrew), rewritten and edited by Zevulun Poran

The Jewish minority in Lithuania was granted national autonomy after World War I. A national council was organized and Jewish community councils were set up in all the large and smaller towns to run the cultural, religious and social affairs. The community councils were elected in all Jewish communities beginning in 1919. In Yurburg, the community was organized with a delay of five years, namely in 1924. The reasons for the delay in setting up the community are not known.

With the help of Prof. Dov Levin, who is currently editing "The Encyclopedia of Jewish Communities in Lithuania" at "Yad Vashem, we obtained important records for documentating the functioning of the Yurburg community. These documentary materials have been brought to Israel from Jewish historical archives in the United States.

Now available to us are copies of the minutes of meetings the Yurburg Community Council held during its early days of activity. After reviewing these minutes we deemed it appropriate to publish summaries from them dealing with the elections to the Yurburg Community Council and with the functioning of the council.

Following are the deliberations of the Council members, their considerations and resolutions. The deliberations were conducted in Yiddish. We are quoting the essential items in Yiddish and the explanations in Hebrew.

Eight lists of candidates were submitted to the Community Council, namely:

1. Non-party list: Jacov (Jacob) Beilis; Hayim (Chaim) Khatskelevitz; Joseph Rabinowitz; Aba Zilber.

2. Orthodox: Rabbi Avraham Dimant; Mordekhai (Mordechai) Kamel; Aba Kaplan; Yisrael Pulovin; Reuven Hirsh; David Dimant.

3. Butchers: Dov-Ber Mer; Shimon-Nakhman Kaplan; Efraim Telzak; Leib Shtok.

4. Bikur Kholim Society [Society to Aid the Sick]: Nathan Revel; Jacob Tumim; David Verblovski; Zalman Neviazhski; Shelomoh Shnaider (Shneider); Mosheh Kretchmer.

5. "Mizrakhi:" Yitskhak-David Alperovitz; Leib Gut; Benjamin Fainberg; Ber-Leib Shtok; Eliezer-Barukh Frank.

6. "Tze'irei Zion" [Young Zion]: Khanan Lintupski; Ida Friedland; Shmaryahu Bernstein; Shakhnovitz.

7. "Khevrah Bakhurim" [Men's Group]: Yitskhak Beiman; Tuviyah Berkover.

8. Workers: Leib Portnoy; Motl Gut; Daniel Kukhter; Avraham Rekhtza; Joseph Levitan; Tsadok Jofe; Bunim Portnoy; Mosheh Shmulovitz; Leizer Khosid (Jack Cossid's father); Yudl Frakt; Yerakhmiel Shmulovitz.

From the minutes No. 1 of the Community Council we have learned that the first meeting was held at the Talmud-Torah [Religious School] building on July 16, 1924, at 9 p.m. Eight elected council members attended the meeting. Three were absent: Rabbi Dimant, Grinberg (Greenberg) and Lintupski. Only one "item" was on the council's agenda - The structure of the Community Council, in other words, the council's organization-

1. Election of the Officers of the Council - Chairman, deputy chairman and general secretary.

2. Election of the chairman - the nominated for election is Shimonov, who is not a member of the Community Council, but was elected by Jews to the Yurburg Municipal Council; Shimonov is known as a man active on behalf of the town's population.

Resolution: Alter-Mordekhai (Mordechai) Shimonov is elected unanimously to serve as chairman of the council. Election of the deputy chairman - those nominated for election are Alperovitz and Motl Gut (Workers), the latter is elected deputy chairman by majority vote.

Election of the general secretary. The candidates are Pinkhas Shakhnovitz and Joseph Levitan. When a misunderstanding arose among council members - probably after a tie vote - no resolution was adopted. The council will again take up the election of the general secretary at the next meeting. The meeting was then adjourned. The minutes are signed by Shimonov, chairman of the council.

The Third Meeting of the Council - a stormy meeting

Minutes No. 3

The meeting was held on August 9, 1924 with 13 members of the community council in attendance. Absent: Rabbi Dimant, Lintupski.

On the agenda - the elementary school. Chairman: Shimonov.

1. The members of the council discussed the claims of the elementary school's teachers that their salaries had not been paid in full last year.

Resolution: After discussion, it was resolved that in principle the council does not have to assume the debts of third parties, but from a moral point of view the council believes it has a duty to solve the problem, so that the teachers would not be treated unfairly. The council's arbitration committee will study the problem and will endeavor to satisfy the teachers, since the debt is not large.

2. Report on the instructional and educational activity of the school. Mr. Shlomovitz, member of the school board, was asked to give a review on the school's problems. This was done.

3. The language of instruction at the school. A sharp and lengthy debate ensued on this important subject. In the end, the following resolution was adopted, which we have copied verbatim from the minutes because of its importance. "The language of instruction shall be Yiddish. In addition, Hebrew shall be taught extensively, as well as religious studies. The teachers shall be impartial in the school."

The meaning of the resolution is that most subjects will be taught in the Yiddish language, but Hebrew and religious studies will also be taught extensively. The teachers in the school must be impartial.

It was resolved to elect a school committee, which will deal with its problems. However, since time is short, it was decided that in the meantime the council's executive committee will deal with matters affecting the school and will confirm the hiring of teachers who will commit themselves to teach in the spirit of the Community Council's resolution.

With this the meeting was adjourned. The minutes are signed by Shimonov.

Actually, no resolution was passed on the language of instruction, either because there were no impartial teachers or because of the desire of the majority of parents to provide the school's students with a Hebrew and Zionist education as a preparatory stage for admission to the Herzl Hebrew High School in Yurburg. The elementary school indeed did join the network of "Tarbuth" schools in Lithuania, which teach the subjects in Hebrew in a nationalist and Zionist spirit.

An additional document we received contained a notice sent to the council members of August 17, 1924, calling the councilmen to a meeting which was held in the Talmud Torah building at 8 p.m.

Agenda of the meeting:
1. Election of the general secretary
2. The elections to the Municipal Council
3. Election of the education committee
4. Election of the budget committee
5. Registry (of births, marriages, divorces, deaths etc.)
6. Current matters

All members of the Community Council are requested to be punctual.

Following is a list of members of community council, from which we get an idea of the names of its elected members

With courteous greetings - M. Shimonov, Chairman
1. Rabbi Dimant
2. Mordekhai (Mordechai) Kamel
3. Dov-Ber Mer

4. Yitskhak-David Alperovitz
5. Khanokh Lintupski
6. Leib Portnoy
7. Mordekhai (Mordechai) (Motl) Gut
8. Daniel Kukhman
9. Abraham Rechtsa
10. Tsadok Jofe
11. Zusman Levitan
12. Pinkhas Shakhnovitz
13. J. Grinberg (Greenberg)
14. Perlman
15. Shimonov

We are missing the minutes of the third meeting of the community council, just as the minutes of the following meetings are also regrettably missing. Still, we believe that even what little material has reached us allowed us to get an idea of the events involving the community in Yurburg and its problems during the period of Jewish-national autonomy in the state of Lithuania.

Jewish autonomy in Lithuania and the activities of National Council were terminated at the end of the 1920s, when the Tautininkai Party, an extreme nationalist party, came to power, suspended the rights of the national minorities and obstructed their economic, cultural and social progress.

TRANSLATED FROM PAGES 309 -310

THE YURBURGER COMMUNITY

Translation from Yiddish

A report on the activities of the Yurburg Community Council, from "Yiddishe Shtime" [Jewish Voice], Kovno, No. 1559 of November 11, 1924.

Our Community Council, finally established after a lot of debate, consists of the following members: five workers, three Zionist-businessmen, two orthodox, two Democrats, one Tze'irei-Zion, one Mizrakhi, one butcher.

Since it was established, the Yurburg Community [Council] has held five meetings, all of which ended up in quarrels. Here, because of a seat on the executive committee, there, because of something else. But with the last two meetings the end has come to the "short term" Yurburg Community Council.

The entire actual work of the council consists in that it has taken control of the Yurburg elementary school (Talmud Torah), in order to support it, alongside the government subsidy, because 70% of the children attend free of charge. Yet no budget has been set up. There is not even an office and the civil registry books and the official stamp are kept by the chairman. It is because of the budget that the council has broken up.

The budget amounted to Lit 1900 a month. And the high school has also asked the community for a monthly subsidy. But since the high school is a private institution (?), the subsidy was deleted. Outside persons were invited to one of the meetings at which the tax and the allocation of funds were to be discussed. A large number of councilmen, who felt insulted that the allocation to the high school had been deleted and with aid of the outsiders, caused a commotion, saying that the total budget is too much of a burden on the town and every item in it should be deleted. They claimed that the elementary school should not get such a large amount, because in reality it is not an elementary school, but a "Talmud Torah" and a Talmud Torah could raise money from synagogue attendance. Moreover, there is no need to have a school doctor. And the same applies to money for the library and "Maccabi" [sports club]. Wouldn't the children of the well-to-do be ashamed to take money from the community?..

Money for the community council office? A 'melamed' [religious studies teacher] could be hired who would do the work for a song. Social assistance? There is a "Bikur Kholim Society" (where you can get a pinch of tobacco as a remedy...) and with these and similar clever inventions they attempted to tear the entire budget apart, except for pocket money. The workers faction therefore found it was necessary to leave the community council.

A Taxpayer

This excerpted article supplements the preceding article on the "Yurburg Community," which was based on the minutes we had received just before we finished editing this Memorial Book. The articles supplement each other and give us some idea about the short-lived days of the Yurburg Community Council. As is well known, an extreme nationalistic party came to power in Lithuania at end of the 1920s, which put an end to the autonomy and also to the Jewish community councils all over Lithuania.

The Great Wooden Synagogue of Yurburg
Not in original Yizkor Book - Courtesy of the Vilna Jewish Museum

TRANSLATED FROM PAGE 311

THE TALMUD-TORAH IN YURBURG

The following is a copy of "Hamelitz," dated June 30, 1889 which describes the Talmud-Torah in Yurburg (Kovno district), methods of learning, achievements and economic problems

Yurburg (Kovno D.) - The Talmud Torah school which has been operating in our town for a number of years, is steadily improving, and even more so since the honorable Rabbi Harav Hagadol Rabbi Yehezkel Liekhshimetz decided to devote himself to improve the school; the boys are scoring success in their studies; many of them have become well versed in Bible studies and grammar in Russian too and in mathematics, and whenever the Rabbi tests his pupils, he is satisfied. Recently the Rabbi decided to renew a special department for studying Talmud, and his efforts bore fruit and ten boys will be taught Talmud by a Talmud teacher. Last Passover they passed the test and were able to answer all of the Rabbi's questions correctly. When the Rabbi and the directors realized there was not enough income to finance the Talmud-Torah, they appealed to the people from our town who live in America, in New York, St.Louis and Rochester to support this noble cause; and the people from our town who are in New York immediately sent their contribution, one hundred Rubels. And though for the time being there are not many former Yurburg citizens who live there, the others who did not make a contribution yet, will undoubtedly also make a donation in the future and participate in this noble cause. We hereby express our deepest gratitude to all those benefactors who sent their contribution and their name will be engraved forever in the pages of "Hamelitz." The following is the list of the generous benefactors, which we received from Rabbi Avraham Yosef Romanisky who resides in New York:

Rabbi Yehudah Ben Yitskhak Mendel Vilensky $7.50; Mr. Eliyahu Fainberg $5; Mr. Zalman son of Yoel Fainberg $5; Rabbi Yitskhak Mendel Vilensky $5, the Rosinsky brothers $5; Rabbi Shemuel Zalkind Fainberg $3; Rabbi Yerakhmiel Vilensky $2.50; the Azriel Yozefer girls $1.50; the Gavronsky partners $2; Mr. Gaishenfeld $2; Mr. Eliyahu Vilensky $1; Rabbi Rafael Markir $1 dollr; Rabbi Avraham Levinson $1; Rabbi Avraham son of Shelomoh Mordekhai Levin $1; Rabbi Yitskhak Leib Mazor $1; Rabbi Hayim (Chaim) Ben Hirsch Bakovsky $1; Ben Elhanan Schilisker 50 cents; in total $45; and the generous brothers Messrs. Shemuel and Eliezer and Aharon the sons of Yacov Kastel sent 15 Rubles.

The Talmud Torah - Hebrew School in Yurburg (from a 1926 postcard)
Names of Students Provided by Jack Cossid in July 1996

Enlarged image of above appears on page 43

Bottom Row from left: 1. -, 2. - , 3. Yankele Goldstein, 4. Schmulovsky, 5. Ben Tzeler, 6. - , 7. Moishe Ess, 8. Noah Stern, 9. Chertock, 10. Smolnik, 11. Mendel Kaplan (USA), 12. Shoemaker's son, 13. Shakhnovitz, 14. Yudel Krupinsky (Jack Cossid's cousin), 16. (girl) Goldstein.

Second Row from Bottom from left: 17. Berl Heselkovitz, 18. Yudel Tsukernik, 19. Avrom Vainberg (Weinberg), 20. Simon Fainberg (Feinberg), 21. - , 22. Mordehai - Shoemaker's son, 23. Shmerl - (baker's son), 24. Yankel Khosid (Jack Cossid - USA), 25. Hanele Berkover, 26. - , 27. Orke Hess (Jack Cossid's first cousin) 28. Sandra Glazer, 29. Judith Lebovsky, 30. - Levin, 31.Miriam Ess, 32. Sarah Elyashev, 33. Miriam Elyashev, 34. Alter Stern, 35. Feivel the Blinder.

Third Row from Bottom from left: 36. Baker's daughter, 37. Yente Berkover, 38. - Alexander, 39. Baske - , 40., Rivkah Feldman (Israel), 41. - Szertock, 42. Rachal Hess Grinstein (Greenstein) (Israel), 43. Leizer (George Feinberg's cousin)

Fourth Row from Bottom from left: 44. - , 45. Avraham - , 46. Sholom Raizman (Jack Cossid's first cousin), 47. (girl) Abramovitz, 48. - , 49. (girl) Krelitz (Joel Alpert's cousin), 50. Yudel Raizman (Jack Cossid's first cousin), 51. (girl) - , 52. - Bershtansky, 53. Hayah (Chaya) Khosid (Jack Cossid's sister), 54. (not visible), 55. (not visible), 56. (not visible), 57. (not visible), 58. Esther Elyashevitz (Eliashevitz) (Joel Alpert's cousin), 59. Hana Beiman, 60. Lieba Kopelov, 61. Yankel Ess, 62. - , 63. - , 64. - , 65. -

Fifth Row from Bottom from left: 66. Hayim Sigar - Teacher (His picture is in the Yizkor book), 67. Teacher -, 68. Motel Komel (Head of the School), 69. Archik Solomovitz (Shochet - Ritual Butcher), 70. Hayim (Chaim) Nosen (Rabbi - taught the Bible), 71. Chekhanovsky - Teacher, 72. Beinish Ess, 73. Gershon Kobelkovsky, 74. Shimon - . Standing by the Drain Pipe: 75. Itsik Kopelov.

Sixth Row from Bottom from left: 76. (girl) Berkover (Israel), 77. Rivka Rizman (Jack Cossid's first cousin - Israel), 78. Mordechai Berkover, 79. Baske Hess (Jack Cossid's first cousin), 80. Baske Berkover.

Seventh Row from Bottom from left: 81. - , 82. Shlame Elyashevitz (Eliashevitz) (Joel Alpert's Cousin), 83. Miriam Ess, 84. Hanna Magidovitz (Israel - her article appears in the book - witness to the destruction of Yurburg's Jews), 85. - Alexander, 86. - Elyashevitz (Joel Alpert's cousin), 87. Mendel Abramovitz, 88. Moishe Elyashevitz (Joel Alpert's cousin ??).

Top Row (Hard to see) from left: 89. Mendel Shapiro, 90. - Frank, 91. Avraham Shmulovsky (Israel).

May they be blessed. And may the name of the directors and supervisors also be fondly remembered from the time the house was founded til today, Mr. Leon Valk, Mr. Matityahu Hirsch Kostin and Mr. Leon Baner, who implement their tasks faithfully and carry out the sacred work with devotion.

We would appreciate it if the American publishers would reprint this article in their publication and bestow honor and esteem on those who deserve it.

By the Registrar of the Talmud Torah

Insert from photograph on page 340

From Left: Mordechai Komel (Head of the School), Archik Solomovitz (Shochet - Ritual Butcher), Rabbi Hayim Nosen (taught Bible)

The Yurburg Yizkor Book

TRANSLATED FROM PAGE 312

THE ELEMENTARY SCHOOL IN YURBURG

By Zevulun Poran

In 1918 Lithuania became independent and the Jews gained nationalistic-cultural autonomy. The Jews were allowed to set up their own schools, in Hebrew or Yiddish, at their discretion. The study program was general and studying the Lithuanian language, its literature and history were compulsory. Bible classes (Old Testament) were included in the study program. The teachers' salary was paid by the Government. The elementary school in Yurburg was a Zionist school in spirit, and therefore it was ideologically close to the "Tarbuth" schools in Lithuania.

The school's first principal was Yisrael Bekin, an upright man and gifted teacher. The other teachers were graduates of Hebrew-pedagogic courses, among them we would like to recall Yisrael Dimantman, Gorschein, Hillel Zaks, Chekhanovsky, Hayim (Chaim) Siger and Rabbi Leibchik Gut, who taught bible classes and Jewish concepts. The school was housed in a handsome, large building, donated by Yehudah Rabinowitz, an important businessman from Yurburg. The classrooms were full of light; there was a beautiful hall, which was also used for weddings.

Unfortunately the schoolyard and its building were the place where the Jews of Yurburg were gathered in the war and sent to their death in the forests surrounding the town.

Student Identity Card of Gymnasium Student: Toibe Most

TRANSLATED FROM PAGES 313-317

THE HEBREW GYMNASIUM IN YURBURG

By Rivkah Vainberg (Weinberg) Ravitzky

When I received the invitation of the founders of the Society of Yurburg to attend a meeting of former residents and graduates of the Hebrew Gymnasium, in honor of the jubilee of the organization's foundation, my heart missed a beat. Memories and events of those distant days, of childhood and adolescence, the best times of one's life, which leave their mark on an entire lifetime, came to mind.

When I was asked to say a few words at the meeting, recall a few memories pertaining to the period of the Gymnasium and the days of its foundation, I was reluctant at first, when I looked at the people participating in the meeting, by far outnumbering those at previous such meetings, for I am not very good at "making a speech," and in general, should we let our nostalgia flow freely along the stream of beautiful memories, yearning and cherishing them, without any restraint. However, I was led by a certain inner need to share the memories of those days, to give in to my feelings - and see here - I have the courage and the words are coming.

This meeting of ours has an additional and different dimension than those similar experiences of people at meetings such as these, where common memories are being recalled and cherished, when in everyone's life there are those moments of "once upon a time" for in our case there is the heavy burden of the tragic events of the Holocaust which was part of each of us. While we are meeting here, other members of our families, beloved ones - parents, brothers and sisters - who were murdered and destroyed by the terrible Nazis and the Lithuanian beasts -may they rot in hell - cry out in anguish and fury. It is hard to come to terms with the cruel reality, for our town Yurburg is the Jewish Yurburg, full of Jewish life, initiative and resourcefulness, which set up social, cultural and economic projects, in spite of the hostile environment. This Jewish community was entirely wiped out by human Satans and nothing is left of it, except for us - we who continue, in our country, to weave the thread of Jewish tradition and pride.   *The poet writes:*

> **Youth is fatherland! And no matter where,**
> **Here - or there;**
> **It is the nucleus of the distance**
> **And the navel of the world**
> **Therefore - no wonder - let's be honest**
> **All of us - and why deny?**
> **Carry in our heart, in a hidden corner**
> **The town of our youth, forever and ever.**

{Shimshon Meltzer: Meir the Kleizmer (popular singer) becomes Komisar.}

All of us can identify with the words of this song. And the accompanying feelings?

We are the second generation, we left our parents' homes and were uprooted from the haven of our childhood and youth - we are happy that we settled and built a new life in Israel and have a new family. Nevertheless, we carry with us the memory of the town of our childhood, and we are sensitive to this and aware of it.

Among the memories of my childhood and my parents' home are the days when the Gymnasium was established in the town. I recall vague moments, from the days when I was a girl listening and absorbing the conversation of adults discussing the need to set up an educational institution for their children who were growing up. My late father, Yacov Shelomoh Vainberg, agreed with Mr. Perlman and the late Mr. Rikler and others about the establishment of the Gynmasium in our town. My father's frequent trips to Kovno, the capital, to the Ministry of Education in order to lobby for the establishment of the Gymnasium which was about to be established, the reports and consultations at our home on his return. I was too young to understand the details of what my late father and his friends were discussing.

I particularly remember my first day at the Gymnasium. We wore festive attire, my brother, the late Yekhiel and I. Thus we went to the Gymnasium. Father held us by the hand, leading us along. I can see the imposing image of Mr. Efros (Efrath), the principal, who welcomed us while we followed father into his room. I still remember the entrance exam, when the principal gave us a test and our hearts beat and throbbed.

I will never forget the excitement we felt at that moment. And thus the years passed - childhood, adolescence, and adulthood. Years of growing up and taking part in life. These were the days in which our minds were formed, days of the joy of youth, but there were also days of disappointment and sadness, as is usual in our world.

The Hebrew Gymnasium Building named Herzl in the "Tel Aviv Park"

Same building as photographed in May 2001 by Dr. Leon Menzer
[Not in original Yizkor Book]

The Herzl Gymnasium Teachers in Yurburg at end of the 1920s

Who will enlighten educators and teachers? Learning the Hebrew language, the Old Testament and the relation to them.

I owe a lot to teacher Tsentkovsky who, with his intimate knowledge of the Old Testament and his great love for Hebrew language and literature, stimulated and swept us along and guided us, even if he sometimes tended to exaggerate in his eloquence and made us, students, sneer - as teenagers are wont to do. And the singing lessons with teacher Movshovitz, and the students' choir set up with great effort, which appeared at the school parties - even after all those years they bring a smile to the face. The gymnastics classes with the teacher Gans, the former officer, who later on became famous at the Vilna Ghetto, and whose personality remains controversial even to this very day. The history lessons with teacher Kosotzky - with his quiet nature and balanced approach he knew how to create an atmosphere of attention and interest in the subject.

A long list of teachers and educators without whose devotion (they did not earn much and their salary was not always paid on time and strikes were not yet known) and their view of education as being a mission, this important project which went on for so many years could not have existed.

Then there was the building and yard of the Gymnasium; I can see the large building and the garden in which it stood, called "Tel Aviv" after the name of the new town Tel Aviv, which symbolized the building of Eretz Israel in those days.

I find it hard to understand now how these Jews - our parents - were able to set up and maintain this institution, which demanded a lot of money; the maintenance of a high school without government or local funding, in a town without a large Jewish population - in total 2,500 people. There were no large industrial plants there, or rich landowners. We must admit that the personal financial effort of the parents must have been quite important, probably they often saved and economized at the expense of their own needs. This was the traditional Jewish devotion to give their children's education. Another point must be made, with pride, even though it may sound haughty and chauvinist.

It may be said that Jewish Lithuania, between the two world wars, maintained a wide network of Hebrew educational institutions, which were unparalleled in the rest of the Diaspora. There were 14-15 high schools in the towns of Lithuania and pre-high schools as well. Towns and villages that had a far larger Jewish population than Yurburg were unable to keep high schools. However, the parents in Yurburg made a great effort and gave their children the opportunity to study at a Hebrew, national and Zionist school.

I have many memories of this concern and struggle for the material existence of the Gymnasium, the constant worry about the teachers' salary, housing expenses etc. Indeed, during all my years of study, our home was the focus of all these concerns. The meetings of the Gymnasium's public council were usually held at our home. Many hours were spent in discussion and deliberation about the material existence and educational direction of the institution. I have many memories of these "heroic sounds" which I absorbed deep into my soul.

This educational project of the Hebrew Gymnasium with its professional aims and ideological atmosphere left its mark on the entire Jewish population in town, and particularly on the younger generation. The challenges and targets of the Hebrew Gymnasium were never restricted to obtaining educational aims only, but mainly focused on teaching the nationalist, cultural and traditional values.

Without the ideological and moral values the students acquired at the Gymnasium, and the demand for personal fulfillment, the pioneer movements would not have been so important. We were educated according to the Hebrew book, the tradition of Jewish history and the love for Eretz Israel and denial of the Diaspora. Even if it was unconsciously and not on purpose- all this was absorbed and penetrated deep into our minds, as the saying goes "with our mother's milk" The ideology of the Zionist youth movement found the fertile ground here, together with the pressures brought on by the distress of the Jewish environment. Moreover, these values, of Torah (Bible) and religious duties formed us, accompanied us in our fulfillment, Aliyah and settling down in Israel.

We may perhaps add, that the proof of these values that are deeply rooted in us, is our very presence and creation here in Israel, in the village and the city. In spite of all we went through till we arrived here, we still carry the memory of the past, of Yurburg our town, our cradle, it is nor forgotten, and will never be forgotten, as long as we live.

Givath Brener

First Graduating Class of the Hebrew Gymnasium (High School) of Yurburg, 1927 - students and staff of teachers

Third Graduating Class of the Hebrew Gymnasium (High School) of Yurburg, 1929

[The above photo was not included in the original Yizkor book, but is included here because it is fitting - Provided courtesy of Ashley Levinsohn]

Bottom row, left to right: Meir Levyush, Golomovitz, Kaplan, S. Heselkovitz, Picture of School, L. Shtok, N. Ess, Rachel Levyush, Leviteh.

Second row from bottom, left to right: G. Kovalkovskit, R. Petrikanskit, H. Baron, J. Tsikovski, A Altman, T. Khaimovitz, Moskovitz.

Third row, left to right: B. Fainberg, H. Levinsohn, Navossitis, Dr. Rotshtein, Y. Lerman, D. Pinkus, Mendelovitz, Bluma Heskelovitz.

Top row, left to right: Vainberg, Colombus, A. Leiptziger, Headmaster Engineer D. Khen, Deputy Headmaster Y. Tukhman, H. Lintupski, H. Shakhnovitz, Y.

**Seventh class of the Hebrew Gymnasium - students and their educators
I. Grinberg (Greenberg), teacher of literature.**

**Students of the Hebrew Gymnasium - sixth grade - with their teacher
Eliezer Leipziger. Second row to the right (in the middle) the writer of the
article about the Gymnasium. Next to her (above) Shelomoh Goldstein.**

Students of the "Herzl" Hebrew Gymnasium in Yurburg and their teachers in the study year 1925/26. Partial picture.

See page 44 for an enlarged version of this photograph.

Hebrew Gynasium (High School) of Yurburg - 1927/1928

[The above photo was not included in the original Yizkor book. Provided courtesy of Ashley Levinsohn]

See page 45 for an enlarged version of this photograph.

גמנסיון עברי יורבורג מחלקה ז׳ דזמותכת

Gymnasium Yurburg 7th Class (Mahlaka) with Form Master (main teacher). Written on the back: "Winter 1928"

[The above and below photos was not included in the original Yizkor book, but is included here because it is fitting - Provided courtesy of Ashley Levinsohn]

7th Class (Mahlaka) 28th November 1927. Written on back "Hadassah Levinsohn 7th Class in memory of the day we did not attend Gymnasium because of the famous 'Solidaritet' 6 Jan 28.

TRANSLATED FROM PAGES 319-328

ZIONISM AND ZIONIST ACTIVITY IN YURBURG

By Zevulun Poran

For hundreds of years Jews in the Diaspora were active on behalf of public funds. The public funds in every Jewish community reflected Jewish solidarity, mutual assistance and the general public's concern for the needy individual. However, in past generations, in the period of national awakening, new funds were added, result of the times.

In the last quarter of the previous century, Jews "Khovevey Zion" (those who cherish Zion) arose and started to go to Eretz-Yisrael, as individuals or in small groups. They bought land and set up agricultural settlements with the few means at their disposal, and with the assistance of benefactors. It was mainly a central-European immigration, and the Jews from Lithuania were prominent among them.

In Jerusalem too, people started to move out of the "old city" walls, among them Jews originating from Lithuania, one even from Yurburg, who set up house at the Nakhlath Shiva neighborhood (founded in 1869). The idea of settlement in Eretz Israel gained momentum in the countries of the Diaspora, but a joint national effort was required to achieve this lofty goal which a single individual could not achieve.

In these days Dr. Theodore (Benjamin Ze'ev) Herzl formulated his idea of the foundation of a Zionist Federation. And indeed, in 1897 Dr. Herzl convened the Congress of the Jewish representatives in the world, mainly "Khovevey Zion," in Basel (Switzerland), and the Jewish Federation was founded. This was an important historical event. Among those invited to the Congress was also Prof. Herman Shapira from Heidelberg (Germany), who proposed the establishment of a national fund, whereby land would be bought and prepared for settlement. Every Jew had the right to lease land for agricultural settlement for 49 years. Those who settled on the land were not allowed to sell it, for the land belonged to the Jewish National Fund forever. The proposal was enthusiastically accepted at the Zionist Congress; and indeed the Jewish National Fund was founded in 1901 and called "Keren Kayemeth Le'Yisrael" (The Jewish National Fund). We, who come from Yurburg, should be interested to know who this Prof. Herman Shapira, who proposed the establishment of the Jewish National Fund, was - so let us provide some information about the history of his life.

Tsevi (Herman) Shapira was born in the small town of Erzhvilky, near Yurburg, and he was a very gifted child. When he was three years old he could already read, at the age of four he studied Mikrah and Gemarah and at the age of eight he was already well versed in Talmud. While he was still a young boy he became a licensed Rabbi. After a while, the boy was appointed Rabbi at the small town and he became famous. However, the young Rabbi was not satisfied with his life, and one day, perhaps on one of his visits to Yurburg, where he was at home, he happened to find a book on mathematics and discovered the magical world of science. From that moment he found no peace. On his wanderings through Russia he did not find what he was looking for, until he came to Germany to drink from its source of knowledge and learning. Shapira went without food and slept on a bench in Berlin and later on in Heidelberg, where he studied and made progress at astonishing speed and obtained the rank of Professor of Mathematics. Nevertheless, he did not forget his origin; he took an interest in the "Khovevey Zion" movement and published articles about Judaism and Jewish nationalism. That is how Dr. Herzl, who was impressed by his personality, discovered him and invited him to the first Zionist Congress (1897). Thus the young Shapira, who was at home in Yurburg, put forth his proposal at the Congress to establish the Jewish National Fund, the national fund for the purchase of land in Eretz Yisrael (1901).

When the Jewish National Fund was established, Jewish consciousness underwent an upheaval. The fund gave them hope and they felt that by donating to the Jewish National Fund they became partners in the Grand National project. It was not hard to understand for a Jew that the land - the Promised Land - was in the hands of strangers and that without the land there simply would not be any building or settlement. Therefore the first priority was to redeem the land which would be the foundation for the national home.

The Jews of Lithuania, those from Yurburg among them, lent a faithful hand to the project of the Jewish National Fund. It is not known when the Jews of Yurburg started their activity on behalf of the Jewish National Fund, but we may presume that it was immediately after the establishment of the Fund, and from the time of the Balfour Declaration (1917) organized activity increased. An action committee composed of the representatives of all the parties and organizations in Yurburg was set up. There were volunteers too - "crazy about the idea" - who joined the activity and made it the center of their life. The main attraction of the fund was its popular appeal and the modest demand of all layers of the population, sort of "everyone gives according to his heart."

Especially the children were enchanted by the Jewish National Fund, for to them it was not an abstract idea, but a real one, and we all know that children love action. Indeed, this activity on behalf of the Jewish National Fund was a sort of competition, a positive "match of brains" - the more the better. The Jewish National Fund's manners of operation suited everyone - old and young - and we will name a few here.

The Stamps. The Jewish National Fund stamp was already printed in the first year of the fund's establishment. It was a small stamp, light blue with a Star of David and it had the name "Zion" on it. This small stamp, printed in millions of copies, had tremendous propaganda value and was very popular. "We too have a stamp" -said the children. The stamp also turned out to be an important source of income for the Jewish National Fund. We still remember our stamp collections, which we collected as children in albums or copybooks, and which served as important study material for becoming acquainted with places and people in Israel. And this is what we sang:

כִּי יִדְבִּיקוּ בּוּל אֶל מוּל

נַעֲרָה וָנַעַר —

יִגְאֲלוּ שָׂדֶה, יְבוּל,

וְיַצְמִיחוּ יַעַר.

Let's stick on stamp after stamp

Boys and girls -

Redeem the field, the crop,

And let the forest grow

The song was written by Dr. Yehoshua Fridman, the Principal of the Real Gymnasium for Girls in Kovno.

The teachers recommended collecting the Jewish National Fund's stamps, stressing their educational value. At present, the small Zion stamp, first issue, is a rare and important item for collectors of Judaica, and is worth a lot of money.

The "Blue Box." One of the most efficient educational and financial tools, of interest to young and old, was the Jewish National Fund box, called according to its color - the "Blue Box". The box was born in 1904. The man responsible for the box and, as a matter of fact, for the Zion stamp as well, was the first President of the Jewish National Fund, Yonah Kremenetzky, Dr. Herzl's faithful assistant, an industrialist from Lithuania. Interestingly enough, the "inventor" of the box was a Jew called Hayim (Chaim) Kleinman. When Kleinman heard of the establishment of the Jewish National Fund, he made a small box and put it on his desk at the bank where he worked as a clerk. The result was astonishing. All those who came to Kleinman's office put coins into the box, fully aware that they were helping to redeem the land of Israel.

When Kleinman told the Jewish National Fund heads about his box and his successful experience in collecting donations for the Fund, they liked the idea.

Since then, the "Blue Box" became an asset and the national symbol of all the Jewish communities. And thus sang the pupils:

על הקיר תלויה קופסה
היא קופסת התכלת —
כל פרוטה שנכנסה,
אדמה גואלת.

יהושע פרידמן, כנ"ל

קרן קימת לישראל

צבי (הרמן) שפירא

A box is hanging on the wall

The "Blue Box"

Each penny put inside

Redeems the land

The song was written by Dr. Yehoshua Fridman, the Principal of the Real Gymnasium for Girls in Kovno.

Those who come from Yurburg remember the box very well. We may safely say that the Jewish National Fund box could be found in almost every Jewish home. Some Jews took care to put a few pennies in it every day, others added coins when the volunteer pupils came to empty the box. The pupils of the Yurburg Gymnasium, as well as members of the youth movement, carried out the task of emptying the boxes. Sometimes women too would volunteer for this task. Upon emptying the boxes a receipt with a drawing would be given. The boxes would usually be emptied once a month or once every two months. A few people were needed each time to empty the boxes.

The Jewish National Fund boxes were placed in offices, shops and schoolrooms. When the boxes were emptied, written information was handed out as well as pictures explaining the Jewish National Fund's activity and its achievements in Israel, in the purchase of land and settlement. From this publicity material everyone understood why they were donating and what was being done with the money; this information created a feeling of joy and trust in the Jewish National Fund.

Activities at the synagogue. The Jewish National Fund used various opportunities for obtaining donations on behalf of its activities. All circles in the community took part in the synagogue actions - both secular and religious. We would like to mention two actions on behalf of the Jewish National Fund, which was the custom at our community and revived a new tradition.

Alyiah to the Torah. During the calls to the Torah it was customary to donate a sum of money "to he who blesses" to the worshippers, such as, for example, the man who married off his son or daughter, or the man who had recovered from an illness etc. It is interesting to note that it was Dr. Herzl himself who started this custom, when he was called to the Torah, on the Sabbath after the establishment of the Jewish National Fund.

Herzl blessed the Jewish National Fund and promised to donate a sum of money to it. After him, David Wolfson was called to the Torah, and he too blessed and made a donation to the Jewish National Fund. Of note, Wolfson was elected second President of the Zionist Federation after Herzl's death. He comes from a small town in Lithuania.

Another custom of the Jewish National Fund was " The action of the bowls," which were placed at the synagogue before the "Kol Nidrei" prayer. Members of the Jewish National Fund Board or volunteers sat next to the bowls, at the synagogues. It was a new tradition - and the Jews donated. The religious Jews were happy that with their donations the land was also being freed for the erection of synagogues and Torah institutions in Israel.

The books of honor. Already in the second year of the Jewish National Fund's establishment the first edition of the "golden book" was prepared, in which people are registered who are active on behalf of Zionism and the Jewish communities. Those who register their friends in the "golden book" donate to the Jewish National Fund. It is said that when Dr. Herzl's friends wanted to register him as the first person in the "golden book" he rejected this outright and wanted to register Prof. Tsevi Shapira, the man who invented the idea of the Jewish National Fund, as the first person in the book. At the time of registration, Prof. Shapira was no longer alive. A few months after the First Zionist Congress, he volunteered to go on a publicity campaign in Europe to explain the essence of Zionism and the Jewish National Fund - he caught pneumonia on the way and died.

Those who visit the main office of the Jewish National Fund in Jerusalem may see the many editions of the "golden book" with lists of names, among them from Lithuania and Yurburg as well.

Two special books of honor were dedicated to children, the Bar-mitzvah and Bat-mitzvah book, in which children who reach the bar- and bat-mitzvah age are registered. Children's photos may be added to the registration.

Children were registered on their birthday in the "Children's book" -the book for children from birth to the age of bar-mitzvah.

All those registered in the books of honor receive an illustrated certificate as a handsome souvenir. The school pupils too were in the habit of registering their teachers and principals in the book of honor, at the end of the study year or other events.

Donations at special events. Immediately after the establishment of the Jewish National Fund, Menakhem Usishkin, one of the leaders of Russian Jewry - Lithuania too at the time - writes as follows: "I call on you, my brothers, to carry out a difficult and tiring task, however of grand and noble purpose - the redemption of the Land of Israel for the People of Israel, no opportunity should be missed, no social meeting, no party, at each and every joyful occasion, money should be collected to win hearts for the Jewish National Fund." The Jews of Russia and Lithuania responded to Usishkin's call and donated many "kopeikot"(a kopeika = a cent, 1/100 of the Ruble). Donations by Russian and Lithuanian Jews in the days prior to World War I amounted to 62.5% of the total donations of Jews all over the world on behalf of the Jewish National Fund. Usishkin asked for "Kupeikot," i.e. cents, so that everyone, poor and rich, could take part in the national target of redeeming the land of Israel. The cent too, said our wise men, is very important, for one cent and another together make a large sum."

Dr. Herzl, who was very enthusiastic about the idea of the Jewish National Fund, set a personal example on how to use every opportunity to raise funds. Once he was at a party with friends. At a certain moment he got up, took his hat and passed it along, asking for a donation to the Jewish National Fund - and the participants donated very generously.

This custom of donating at every festive occasion existed at each Jewish community and in Yurburg too. At every festive occasion - wedding or bar-mitzvah - the member of the Jewish National Fund board appeared and organized a donation. Sometimes he brought along a few blessings from people who blessed the person celebrating the event. The blessings were printed on special forms of the Jewish National Fund. Sometimes such forms were sent by mail, and, by the way, there were even forms of condolences. . .

The Jewish National Fund board in Yurburg did not only collect donations at existing events, but also initiated and organized special cultural-social events, whose income was dedicated to the Jewish National Fund.

The board also asked to donate a certain percent of various events organized by organizations in Yurburg to the Jewish National Fund. The organizations did not always agree, and often there were "quarrels" on the subject.

The board's actions were usually respected - it consisted of distinguished organizers, but some considered them "a nuisance."

The Keren Hayesod (Jewish Foundation Fund) - We must mention that there also was a committee in Yurburg active on behalf of "Keren Hayesod" ("The Jewish Foundation Fund"), the national fund of the Zionist movement, established in 1920. "The Jewish Foundation Fund"'s purpose primarily was to finance the needs of the "emerging state," such as immigration, absorption, building, settlement, security, health, education etc. Wealthy people usually donated to this fund, which was a sort of official fund, according to their means. The "Jewish Foundation Fund" committee in Yurburg raised considerable sums, for the Jews of Yurburg lived up to their reputation.

Yurburg had the privilege of counting among its residents a number of faithful Zionists who did an excellent job on behalf of the national funds. We should mention the name here of one of the activists, Avraham-Yitskhak Kopelov, the father of Emanuel Kopelov, who lives in Rehovoth and is a member of the executive committee of the Society of Yurburg. A.I. Kopelov was active on behalf of the national funds for many years and he was the official representative of the Jewish National Fund and the Foundation Fund; he was dedicated and devoted to the Zionist ideal, launched campaigns and urged for action: he represented the Jewish National Fund and the Foundation Fund at meetings and national conferences and was greatly respected and admired for his devoted and tireless effort. Kopelov's activity contributed a great deal to the national funds and was a great honor to Zionist Yurburg.

We must also mention that the Zionists in Yurburg were responsible for setting up the "Herzl" Jewish Gymnasium, in a small town such as Yurburg. In its first year the gymnasium was Yiddish, but the Zionists turned it into a Hebrew nationalist -Zionist gymnasium. We recall the names of some people who should be praised, such as: Vainberg, Rikler, Shakhnovitz, Shimonov, Perlman and others, who undertook a heavy burden and maintained the cultural institution which granted cultural values to Yurburg, and educated its youth to be Zionists and fulfill the Zionist dream. Blessed be their memory!

Youngsters active on behalf of the Jewish National Fund. - The youngsters in Yurburg showed a sense of duty and obligation towards the Jewish National Fund. They were attracted by the goals and activities of the Jewish National Fund and were happy to assist on its behalf. Indeed, the youth movements fought for their place in the activities, to show their devotion. Members of Maccabi, Hekhalutz, Hashomer Hatzair, Hanoar Hamizrakhi and Beitar all worked together for the Jewish National Fund - until the latter split from the Zionist Federation and established its own fund, the "Tel Khai" fund (1929), whose aims were different from those of the Jewish National Fund. In Yurburg they did not take part in the activities on behalf of the Jewish National Fund. The members of the sports club I.A.K in Yurburg did not take part in the Jewish National Fund's activities, nor did the Yiddish circles who were active in the "Mendele" library and read the "Folksblat." They did not identify with the Zionist aims and did not donate to the national funds. The Yiddishists - Folksists laughed at the naive Zionists who believed they could set up "a Yiddishe Melukhe in Palestina." They also claimed that the funds' sums did not reach their targets and scorned Menakhem Usishkin, the Jewish National Fund head, under whose leadership the valleys in Israel and other areas in its mountains were redeemed. However, the majority of the people rejected the Folksists' lies and enthusiastically embraced the activities on behalf of the Jewish National Fund. The arguments with the anti-Zionists merely unified the youngsters, sharpened their feelings and strengthened their desire to increase their actions in order to realize the Zionist dream.

Holidays and festivities at the youth clubs. In the wake of the activity on behalf of the Jewish National Fund some holidays and festivals were created and renewed and the youngsters observed them with gusto at their clubs. One of these festivals was "the 19th of Teveth Day" - the day of the Jewish National Fund's establishment - which became a happy festival day at the clubs. Towards this day the clubhouse would be decorated with pictures and slogans such as:

Redeem the land
For the land will not be sold forever
Come to the land and plant
Those who donate redeem the land - those who till the land bring it to life

(Usishkin)

"19th of Teveth" day would be mentioned in all the daily papers, together with the Jewish National Fund's achievements. Above all, this was a good reason for the youngsters to hold a party at the club and sing the songs of the pioneers and the Jewish National Fund, such as the popular song about the Jewish National Fund's activity:

A dunam here, a dunam there
Clod after clod -
Thus we will redeem our people's land
From the north to the Negev

(From Dr. Yehoshua Fridman's song mentioned above)

As they sang along, they became ever more enthusiastic - and they started to dance the Horah - till they had no energy left.

Tu be Shevat (15th of Shevat) - The festival of nature in Israel - was mainly celebrated by children and youth. On that day they would place a pin depicting a blossoming tree to their clothes - in return for a donation for the planting of trees. Outside, as always in Yurburg, the winter is cold, the streets and houses are covered in snow, and here come the youngsters, merrily carrying their pins, to remind us that today the almond tree is blossoming in Israel and hundreds of children and youth are going out to plant trees in the mountains, singing -

**Tu be Shvat has come - to celebrate the fruit trees
Tu be Shvat has come - to plant and build ----**

Two opposites - the cold and icy Diaspora, and the warm and blossoming Land of Israel. Due to this difference in climate, Tu be Shevat was almost forgotten, however, something was kept in our tradition - to arrange a meal and bless the fruits of the Land of Israel. It was impossible to obtain fresh fruit from Israel in Yurburg, therefore one was satisfied with dry carobs, at least to get a taste of Israel. The carobs were bought in the stores and thus the carob became the symbol of Tu be Shevat in the Diaspora.

The children were very interested in the trees and forest, finding them truly refreshing. Every child was acquainted with the pictures of the Ben-Shemen forest, planted in the name of Herzl (1908), after his death. Herzl himself managed in his lifetime to serve as a good example of a man who attaches importance to planting in the Land of Israel. When Herzl visited Israel (1889) he planted a cedar in the yard of the farmer Broza at Upper Motza. After a while the cedar was maliciously uprooted and a pine-tree was planted in its place. It may be seen at the "Arzah" park. Youth movements planted groves and forests, such as the "Hashomer Hatzair" forest in Mishmar Ha'emek, "Gordonia" at Ginossar etc.

Lag B'omer (33 in the Omer count) was another historical festival, the day on which students had a good time in the fields and forests. The trip to nature brought forth longings to return to life on the land and forest in our country.

Yurburg's activity on behalf of the Jewish National Fund was very much respected at the Jewish National Fund's central board in Kovno. The author of this article had the honor of representing the youth movements at the Jewish National Fund's central board in the last years before he went on Aliyah to Israel (end 1938). As member of the central board he had the opportunity to watch Yurburg's activity on behalf of the Jewish National Fund, compared to other cities and small towns. When I perused the monthly reports, I was happy to note Yurburg's achievements, which were praiseworthy. When I drew the attention of the central board members to Yurburg's achievements, they would say - "but of course, Yurburg has many good Zionists."

The central board members were right. The majority of the Jews in Yurburg were Zionists and did an excellent job for the Jewish National Fund and the National Foundation Fund; Yurburg brought up pioneers who looked towards Zion - however, regretfully, due to fate, only a few managed to go to Israel - the others were lost there, they and their hopes.

The National Association of Lithuanian Jews planted a forest at the "Martyrs' Forest" site in the mountains of Jerusalem - a memorial forest to commemorate former Lithuanians, who were murdered in the terrible Holocaust.

Our organization, The Society of Yurburg In Israel also planted a special grove, in the Modi'in area, to commemorate the Yurburg martyrs, a kind of living memorial to the community that no longer exists.

Home and store of the grain merchant Moshe Tuvia Kizell on Haupt Street in about 1922. The family lived above the store. Photo not in the original Yizkor Book. Courtesy of Herb Beiles.

TRANSLATED FROM PAGES 328-331

YIDDISHISM AND FOLKISM IN YURBURG

By Zevulun Poran

The Yiddishists circles in Yurburg were not homogenous - the majority were Folkists and the minority Jewish Communists. The Folkists operated legally in Lithuania, as a true political party. The party's leadership published a daily newspaper in Kovno called Folksblat, i.e. the newspaper of the people.*

> *A number of daily newspapers appeared in Yiddish in Lithuania, s.a. "Yiddishe Shtime" (Jewish Voice), a General Zionist newspaper; "Dos Vort" (Davar) a Zionist newspaper supporting the working class in Eretz Yisrael; "Letzte Naies" (Latest News), a general evening paper; and there was a paper for the orthodox as well, in Yiddish.

The Folksblat preached Folkism ideas, ideas of a popular, liberal, Yiddishist and anti-Zionist Jewish party. The Folksblat was distributed in Yurburg as well, among the I.A.K. members of the communist Jewish circles, there was no legal newspaper in Lithuania, but rather bulletins which were published and distributed underground.

According to the Folkist outlook the Diaspora countries, Lithuania among them, are not a temporary place but rather a permanent residence; our forefathers lived in Lithuania for hundreds of years and **here** ("do" in Yiddish) Jews would live forever. The way of life of the Jews in the Diaspora should therefore be strengthened, the Yiddish language and culture should be encouraged, and thus neither Zionism nor Hebrew, "idle dreams" according to their outlook, would ever be realized. The main struggle should be directed towards achieving national autonomy for the Jews in Lithuania, as it existed at the start of Lithuanian independence and was taken away a few years later. In fact, the Zionists also fought for achieving national autonomy in Lithuania, as essential to the proper physical and spiritual existence of the Jewish minority. National autonomy was not seen as opposed to Zionism, which meant concentrating the Jewish people in its historical homeland and reviving its culture and Hebrew language.

In fact, in the years when the Jews enjoyed national autonomy in Lithuania, this was mainly due to the pressure of the Zionists and they, the Zionists, were its leaders. As long as Zionism was not realized and the people dwelt in the Diaspora they had to fight for a proper Jewish life from the economic, cultural and social point of view. However, the Folkists and the Jewish communists as well saw everything with "Do'ikait" (here and now) i.e. in the daily life of the Jews in the Diaspora. From this point of view the Folkists angrily fought Zionism which squandered the people's energy and money.

Thus writes Ozer Finkelstein, one of the leaders of Folkism and among the editors of Folksblat: - "Each penny Jews spend for the [Jewish] national funds (Keren Hayesod, Keren Kayemeth, Kapai) goes down the drain. The pennies that are spent do not even achieve constructive goals for Eretz Yisrael, but find their way to the pockets of the Zionist officials ..." (Folksblat 169)

Shanah Tovah Greeting

Association of the Yurburg Library Named "Mendele"

Wishing to all members, teachers, a "Good Signature"

(To be written in the "Book of Life").

Translated by Rosi Sherman-Gordon, Mexico City

Others wrote in the same spirit as Finkelstein: Yudel Mark, Dr. Mendel Sudarski, Esther Elyashev, Helena Khatskeles and others, they were totally opposed to Zionism and its achievements in Eretz Yisrael. Many Jews in Lithuania and in Yurburg, who read the Folksblat, adopted the Folkism ideas.

There was constant dispute between the Folkists and the Zionists, but it became much more marked in the days prior to the municipal elections and community council in Yurburg. The two blocs - Zionists and Folkists- wanted to be on the town council, together with the Lithuanians and exert their influence on municipal matters so as to see to it that the Jews would not be discriminated against in the budget for development of the residential areas and that a heavy municipal tax would not be imposed on the poor population. And indeed, the Jews who were elected to the municipality made every possible effort on behalf of the Jewish minority in Yurburg. That is how we know that Shimonov, the Zionist, was put in charge by the municipality of providing assistance and relief to the victims of the terrible floods which plagued Yurburg.

At the Jewish council in Yurburg there were always loud discussions about the distribution of the budget. The discussion was usually about matters of principle. For example, when members of the community council demanded that money be given to the Hebrew Gymnasium, the Folkists -Yiddishists were strongly opposed, claiming that the Hebrew Gymnasium educated towards Zionism and aliyah, and that Hebrew was being taught there, an unnecessary evil. The discussions often broke up and the meetings were halted. After a while a compromise would be reached when the Yiddish school in town received a grant from the community council.

Thus the discussions and debates continued every year until the bitter end. None of them realized that the ground was burning under their feet and that the rope was being tightened around their necks - and that the murderous enemy was lurking at a distance of merely 9 kilometers from Yurburg.

Before we end the story of the ongoing debate of the Zionists with the Yiddishists in our Yurburg - we remember the last chapter of the life of Yudel Mark, the ideologist of Yiddishism and partner to the idea of Folkists at the time.

It so happened that Yudel Mark was saved from the bloody events in Lithuania and emigrated to the U.S.A., where he tried to promote Yiddish and Yiddishism. However, to his and our regret there was no demand for Yiddish in the U.S.A. Yiddish papers were closed down for lack of readers and Jewish - Yiddish schools that existed before were closed down for lack of pupils. All his efforts were in vain. Mark accepted the Jewish historical verdict. When the State of Israel was born a sparkle of affection for our country and hope for our people lit up in his Jewish heart.

One day Yudel Mark got up and went to Israel where he received a warm welcome, befitting a most important linguist of the Yiddish language. Here in Jerusalem, our capital, he built his home and joined a team researching the Yiddish language at the Hebrew University and also worked as the editor of the Yiddish encyclopedia. Talking to former Lithuanians in Jerusalem he speaks Hebrew and his face glows with happiness, he is glad that many people in Israel still speak Yiddish on a daily basis and that Yiddish is being taught at a number of schools to understand the history of our forefathers. How astonishing - in Israel, the new, Zionist country, books appear in Yiddish and there are Yiddish newspapers and a Yiddish theater etc., Yudel Mark had never dreamt this. The circle comes to a close and the dispute of the past is left behind. In the national Pantheon Yiddish will be kept as an important national cultural asset which the people of Israel created in the Diaspora.

When Yudel Mark was asked to participate in the memorial service for the Lithuanian martyrs at "Yad Vashem" he spoke in moving words in his rich Yiddish about the destruction of Jewish Lithuania.

However, Mark did not have the good fortune of a long life and he was unable to finish his creative work in Israel. He died in Jerusalem and was buried in the Land of Israel. At a meeting commemorating the Jews of Lithuania in Jerusalem, the writer of this article eulogized Yudel Mark, the great humanist who loved the people of Israel. In the history of Lithuanian Jews Yudel Mark occupies a place of honor.

The bitter dispute between the two outlooks on life -Zionist and Folkist - ended in tragedy. The "war of languages" ended and there was reconciliation with the new historical reality created in Israel. It is a great pity that all this happened after millions of Yiddish speakers in Europe were lost, including in our Lithuania and Yurburg, our hometown.

TRANSLATED FROM PAGES 332-333

YURBURG

A Song to the Ttune of a Lithuanian Folk Song

By Emanuel Kopelov

Kur Bega Sesupe

There among the shores of the Sesupe
And along the Nieman River
There was a homeland once -
The beautiful Lithuania.
There farmers spoke Lithuanian
There pioneers spoke Hebrew
There was Yurburg on the shores of the rivers:
The Nieman River, the Mituva,
And the Imstra in the middle
There dreams were dreamt
Much hope was there.
Only some of them managed to realize their hope
To come to Eretz Yisrael and settle there
Others were not so fortunate

And remained behind:
Some fought and survived
Others were destroyed.
Only some of them finally joined us
After they went through the sufferings of the Shoah
And were able to build a new life.
May the memory of Yurburg
Remain in our hearts forever
Its inhabitants, its public personalities
Its prominent citizens and institutions;
The "Tarbuth" Gymnasium
Its books in the name of Brener
"Mendele" Library
The "Talmud Torah"
"Hekhalutz" in the little town
And the training kibbutz
The steamships that set sail
Along the Nieman River
To the capital and back.
The beautiful girls in town
Remembered by all
To this very day.
Jewish porters
Along the shores of the Nieman River
And coach owners
Strange types in the streets:
Berele Malchik
Yudel Dratse
The "Turks" ("Di Terkn")
And other crazy people.
Dondolis, the postman
Who could be relied upon in days of distress.
There were many honorable Jews there
Who are no longer!
All of them enhanced the glory
Of the little town
Where we were born
And which we left to go to Israel
But we shall never forget it!

About sixty years ago we left our town
To go on our way
Some to Eretz Yisrael, some elsewhere
Our ways parted
And many of our friends

Are no longer!
Nowadays we meet those who are left
Of the little group of good and kind Jews
Who lived peacefully in their little town
With all their worries to make a living
And bring up their children
They wanted to realize
The dream of better days
But these did not come
Times only got worse
We here in Israel
Had a better life
Although we too had our problems:
World War II
And our little wars with our neighbors.
A lot of blood was spilt here too
And sorrow and loss
We saw - heroism and victory.

Now we are in a country
That belongs to us and us alone
And it does not matter if someone thinks
He can question this right.
We have the power
To face each enemy
Thanks to our sons who hold the gun
Of whom we are very proud!
Thanks to this power
We had the privilege of welcoming the new immigrants
Who joined us
From behind the iron curtain that was opened
From East and West.
We look
And can't believe
Is it true that all of them came
And are with us here?
We wish that all those from our town
Who arrived from nearby
Settle down and become citizens
And absorb new immigrants in their turn
As many others did
Who arrived before us

TRANSLATED FROM PAGES 334-336

Yurburg Loved the Theater

By Motl (Mordekhai) Zilber

Yurburg was not a town of fanatics, but everybody loved the theater sinfully.

At an evening play the theater would fill with Yurburgers of both genders.

Yurburgers simply adored the theater.

Apparently, wind of the ardent Yurburg fans reached the professional actors, and they would come to Yurburg often.

Shows were presented by such groups as "Kadish and Khash," Sokolov, actor Rotblum and often by our local ensemble. We can remind you the names of our local actors: Beinish Levinzon, Rokhele Portnoi (she would play "mother" roles), Hilel Flier, Hinde Levinberg, the script writer, Yisrael'ke Ziser (the agent), Avraham Altman, Fanichke Altman, Hanah Meirovitz, Yehudah Arshtein and others.

Yehuda Arshtein would present a special monologue from "The Madman in the Hospital" where he would climb the table and announce: "Today I will become the King of Spain-I will split the sun and the moon," and then with great enjoyment he would engage in an hour-long monologue.

We played the "The Empty Bar Room" by Hirshbein, "The Spanish Inquisition" by Shomer, we organized rehearsals of "Moshke the Swine" by Berkovitz (but never played this play on stage). In the hall of the Hebrew high school we played "Two Deaf People " and at the front terrace we staged a "Parody on the Jewish Theater" by Tunkeler. The play would begin like this:

(Here several rhymes from the play in Yiddish follow, not translated)

For whom we played? (for whom we donated the income?)

"For the Fire Brigade and the Bikur Kholim."

One person, Mr. Fainberg (Feinberg) was in charge of the theater finances. We were happy we had an audience to play to. And there was nothing missing as far as we were concerned.

We had our own directors who attempted to direct the plays. The directors were Mr. Khanokh Lintupsky, a teacher at the Hebrew high school, Mr. Kopelov-the dentist, Mr. Zundelovitz, the manager of the Folksbank and others.

Different props needed for the show could be found in our own town, and people lent us their things willingly.

I once borrowed a crinoline and a lorgnette, and at a fancy ball I impersonated an old woman from a century before and won the first prize.

The arrival of a theater group would quickly become news in Yurburg, and we, the theater fans, would gather outside the widows of the Bilman Hotel to listen to the singing at the rehearsals. From the other side of the windows sweet tunes of operettas would fill the air around us.

Actress Nekhamah Khash from the "Kadish and Khash" ensemble was a beautiful brunette, with a slender body and black eyes, a perfect gypsy type - She would appear dressed in a hussar uniform with a small cane in her arm and would sing the part of Malkah'le from the play "Malkah'le the soldier." (Three rhymes of the play are not translated).

Believe me, it was impossible to remain untouched by this, and nobody could really remain indifferent to Nekhamah Khash!

Professional actors played "God, Man and Devil" from Y. Gordin and other Gordin's plays. "The Golem" by Leivik was staged as well. I envied the role of Golem- such a rewarding part. I dreamed to play this role.

The play had a wonderful plot: the Golem (made of clay) created by the Maharal [famous Rabbi from Prague] rises against its creator. At the end he is defeated and when Maharal takes away the note with the inscription "Shadai" (God) from him, he becomes again a lump of clay.

To my regret my dream to play the role of the Golem never materialized.

Yurburg Youth Theater Ensemble 1938 -1939

TRANSLATED FROM PAGES 337-341

MEMORIES OF PEOPLE AND EVENT

Astonishing actions in Yurburg

By Avraham Shmulovsky

A Powerful Coachman

Yurburg had a coachman. Manly and unusually strong. When a wagon full of merchandise ran into mud, he would volunteer, load the wagon onto his shoulders and extricate it from the mud. I was told that in winter, when the Nieman River was frozen and the tradesmen would travel to Kovno for business in sleighs this coachman would take them on his sleigh. Once tradesmen went to Kovno with him in the afternoon and spent the night at Vilon (Veliuona), a small town almost midway between Yurburg and Kovno.

Early in the morning the tradesmen were about to leave. They ordered an abundant meal, for themselves and the coachman. The moment the innkeeper left the kitchen the coachman jumped inside, threw a handful of salt into the pot and ran away. When the tradesmen wanted to eat their breakfast they were unable to do so, for the food was very salty. However, the coachman went to the pot of food and finished it all.

Father Saves his son from Drowning

One day a young boy, still a student at the Hebrew Gymnasium, went for a walk on the ice of the river near the beach. It was before the Passover holiday, when the Nieman River started to melt. All of a sudden the block of ice detached itself and started to flow away from the coast. People ran to the father and told him what had happened to his son. What did the valiant father do? He jumped onto a horse and rode while the horse was swimming in the Nieman among the blocks of ice; he overtook his son and saved him from drowning. The name of the father was Aharon Smolnik.

Crazy Etka

Who does not remember crazy Etka, whose father used to live near the Tiflah (Church) (their plot was adjacent to the Talmud -Torah). He would pass along Raseiniu street and the German street every day and close the gates.

The Rabbi's daughter The Rabbi's daughter, blessed be her memory, fell in love with Doctor Gershtein, a tall and handsome man. However, the Rabbi's daughter was not on the doctor's mind. She would wander around the windows of his house for hours, hoping to catch a glance of him.

Shloimele Meirovitz

His family had a building material shop on Kovno Street. Shloimele liked to play the guitar and he played very well. The residents would ask him: " Shloimele, play us a happy tune" and Shloimele played a happy tune. In winter he would volunteer to play a funeral tune" "He that dwelleth in the secret place of the most High shall abide under the shadow of the Almighty" *(Palms 91)*

Shelomoh the Mute

Shelomoh the mute lived in the synagogue yard of the tailors, Die Schneidersche Shul. And what happened? - He fell in love with the daughter of Mota Kimel, who lived in the corner, opposite the building of Shakhnovitz, a wealthy Jew. However, she did not want him and he decided - to keep silent.

The Shames (Caretaker) Who Sees with his Senses

The shames and his family lived near the inn, the "hostel for the poor," at the end of the market, not far from the Nieman and the magnificent synagogue "Die groise Shul."

His family name was Markir. The shames had a blind son called Meir, who had a special sense of knowing people by touching their body. Apparently he remembered people even after he had met them only once.

Early in the morning Meir the shames would go to the synagogue to light the oven, only using his senses, for after all he was blind.

The War of the Ritual Slaughtering

I remember Rabbi Shelomoh Shakhnovitz who was the children's tutor. He used to read the Torah scroll at the synagogue. He was also a cantor. He lived in poverty and distress and wanted to be slaughterer, apparently he knew the job. However, the ritual slaughterers in Yurburg did not agree.

He then took the initiative to announce to the public that he was willing to receive poultry for slaughtering. The Rabbinate in Yurburg forbade his slaughtering. Instantly the "war of the ritual slaughtering" broke out in Yurburg. . .

Our Rabbis

Nekhemyah Yozefer an expert on Torah and Talmud. He taught at the "Talmud Torah," and later on at the "Tarbuth" school.

Leibchik Gut. A nice and good man, he also taught Jewish subjects at the "Tarbuth" school. His son was a Maskil (enlightened). He liked Yiddish and its literature.

Rabbi Nekhemyah. He taught children at the "Fainberg (Feinberg)" school at Yatkever Gas. Went to America. I remember one of his sayings: "And the boys moved around in her womb" - referring to Rivkah our Mother.

Who Remembers the Revolution?

I moved to another school. From the Yiddish school to the Hebrew school. The main person active on behalf of the Hebrew school was the "Tsukernik," Rabbi Bishko, owner of the candy factory. He used to live near Dayan Rabbi Rubinstein, in the yard of the Pulovin family. Rabbi Bishko was active in two matters - Torah and "Tsukerkes" (sweets). . .

Tel Aviv Park

There was great joy in Yurburg when a park was bought and called "Tel Aviv Park." Here the Hebrew Gymnasium was founded. There were beautiful paths in the park and the Jewish youngsters played here at the recesses and after classes in the romantic corners.

Youth Movements

The Jewish youth was composed of "Hashomer Hatzair" members. The main leader of "Hashomer Hatzair" was Hayim (Chaim) Siger, a teacher at the "Tarbuth" school; the "Maccabi" sports federation with the devoted and active Yitskhak Rakhtsa; and the "Beitar Camp."

There was also a semi-leftist youth organization called I.A.K. which fought against Zionism, and issued a newspaper "Folks- Shtime." All this was like "a storm in a teacup."

Rabbi Dimant - the Rabbi of "Beth Hillel"

Rabbi Dimant, *may he rest in peace,* was a wonderful and clever Rabbi. Most of his sermons were given before Passover and the New Year (Rosh Hashanah). I remember how glorious he looked. Once he was asked: "What should we do with an egg that has a drop of blood in it?" And he answered: "If it is possible to separate the drop of blood from the egg - it is kosher, but if the owner of the egg is a wealthy man - he should throw it away." He was the kind of Rabbi who decided in the way of "Beth Hillel," whereas it was said about Dayan Rubinstein that he was stricter and that his decisions were of the "Beth Shamai" school.

I remember one of Rabbi Dimant's sermons on the Lithuanian Day of Independence, in Yiddish. I hope, he said in a festive manner about the Nazis, that the day will come

"When the red cocks will save the world."

Dayan Rubinstein speaks to the ***"Yinglekh and Meidlekh"***

He once urged the youngsters to donate money to charity. He said in Yiddish:

"Yinglekh and Meidlekh - boys and girls - get together and make children"

He meant: arrange a party to collect money for the poor.

Pogrom in Yurburg

In the early years of the rule of the anti-semitic Voldemaras an annual mobilization was carried out. The mobilization took place on the Sabbath at the "Talmud Torah" building.

Many people, from the villages, presented themselves. All of a sudden the villagers started to riot in the streets, broke windows, beat and hit the Jews. The police went away. All the Jews, myself among them, went out onto the street to defend ourselves; we gathered heaps of stones. The commander of the action on Yatkever Gas was Alter Petrikansky, the father of Zevulun Petrikansky (Poran), who had experience in the organization of self-defense in southern Russia. When the gentile hooligans saw the courage of the Jews they dispersed in all directions and ran away terrified.

Black Friday

I remember that one warm summer day, on Sabbath eve, a few youngsters went to bathe in the Nieman River. When they were already in the water, they saw a steamship (Damfer) returning from Kovno. The swimmers wanted to show how they could swim against the waves created by the steamship, but were unable to do so. They started to drown. Three youngsters drowned: Itzik Zarnitzky, Fainberg (Feinberg), his neighbor from across the road, who lived near the water pump (Pluma), and the name of the third boy I don't remember. I will never forget that tragedy. All the residents of the town wept, but continued to bathe in the Nieman. *(Noted added: The third boy was Nathan Bernstein. Information supplied by Bella Abramson Kaplan in Dec. 1997)*

Acts of Heroism

Young couples used to walk in the large park on summer nights, near the large "mushroom" near the Pravoslavic church in the large park.

At 22.00 hours three "ghosts" covered in white sheets approached the couples, and threatened to strangle them. This happened every evening. The youngsters consulted each other as to what they should do, and they decided to come to the park dressed up as couples.

The dressed up couples were only men who stood on a few dark corners of the park and waited, the "ghosts" appeared, of course, and were beaten up by the guys. Since then quiet returned.

Deserves Praise

Everyone knew about the devotion of Frida Shakhnovitz - *may she rest in peace*- to the "HaShomer Hatzair" group. The parties she would organize each Friday were fantastic. With her knowledge and sensitivity, she was an outstanding person.

The Magnificent Synagogue

We cannot forget the magnificent synagogue, with its high Torah scroll adorned with many animals from Noah's Ark. On the New Year (Rosh Hashanah) and the Day of Atonement (Yom Kippur) the cantor and his choir would pray next to the beautiful Holy Ark. Sometimes the slaughterer (shokhet) the pleasant ba'al koreh (lector) would replace him.

Shaye der Terk

The old Shaye would distribute the "Yiddishe Shtime" newspaper. His sons were tailors and they were a very peculiar family. Why was Shaye called "der Terk"? - Really why? One of his sons was Ore -Shmer der Terk, a peculiar person. Terk the son of Terk.

Left: Newspaper seller with "Di Yiddishe Shtime" - likely old Shaye

Right: Ore Shmer, der Terk - a peculiar character in Yurburg's streets

Ore Shmer, der Terk Above were not in the original Yizkor Book.
Provided courtesy of Jack Cossid. Photo taken in Yurburg Feb. 14, 1934.

Elke da Hotz (Elka the horse - he loved horses)
Another Yurburg Character
Above were not in the original Yizkor Book. Provided courtesy of Jack Cossid.

Yes, those were the days . . . .

TRANSLATED FROM PAGES 342-343

THE RABBIS OF THE YURBURG COMMUNITY DURING THE LAST GENERATIONS

By Nakhum Eliezer Duskes

Editied by Zevulun Poran

Over the generations, the Yurburg community had many rabbis. We do not have a complete list of all the rabbis who occupied the seat of the Yurburg Rabbinate, except for just the last few generations.

From the history of these rabbis we learn that some of them, who left Yurburg, were appointed rabbis of large and esteemed communities. Among the Yurburg rabbis were heads of yeshivas and gifted writers who left behind valuable books in field of Jewish learning. The chief rabbi of Yurburg was always a luminary, steeped in the halakhah [the part of the Talmud dealing with religious laws], esteemed and honored by the public. One must not overlook that a good number of learned Jews lived in Yurburg, who were Torah scholars and not just any rabbi could be the first among them. In addition to the rabbi, the Yurburg community had a "Dayan" [judge under Jewish law], who also performed administrative duties, such as keeping the community register, etc. He, too, was expected to be well versed in Jewish learning.

We have compiled the list of Yurburg rabbis from a variety of sources, including from the Book of Lithuanian Jewry. We hope that the following compilation of short articles on the Yurburg rabbis of last generations will give us some insight into their personalities, their esteem and the work they did for their community.

Among Yurburg's rabbis:

Rabbi Aizik son of Rabbi Eliezer;

Rabbi Aryeh- Yehudah-Leib;

Rabbi Mosheh son of Rabbi Shemuel Levinson (5621-5645 [1861-1885]);

Assistant Rabbi Ze'ev-Wolf Shteinfeld (5639-5640 [1879-1880]);

Rabbi Yekhezkel Lifshitz (5649 [1889]);

Rabbi Avraham Dimant; Rabbi Hayim-Reuven Rubinshtein (the author of "Divrei Reuven" [Sayings of Reuven].

May God Avenge his Blood!

RABBI MOSHEH
SON OF RABBI SHEMUEL LEVINSON

Yurburg (through Kovno) - On the Holy Sabbath, of the "Ekev" weekly Portion of Law (August 8), the bad news reached our town by telegram that the Chief Rabbi of our town, Rabbi Mosheh, son of the Rabbi Shemuel, Levinson expired and departed from life on that day in the city of Koenigsberg in Prussia. It was only last Passover holiday that the Rabbi fell ill (with a stomach disease) and traveled to Konigsberg to consult physicians, and from there he was sent to take the healing waters of the sources in Krantz; two days before his death he returned from Krantz to Konigsberg, and on the Sabbath eve he went to pray in the synagogue; at night, he lay down to sleep, never to wake up, for in the morning he was found dead. When the bad news reached our town, all its inhabitants were in mourning, and on Monday, when the deceased was buried in Konigsberg, all the people in our town sat in mourning, and the acting rabbi from Kovno, who was called to come here, eulogized the deceased in the synagogue. All the shops were closed by lock and key and the workers and craftsmen laid down their work on that day. - The late rabbi was seventy-one years old when he died and he had occupied the Rabbinate seat in our town for thirty years. He will be held in blessed memory.

In the name of this community I address myself to the rabbi sages, who may wish to come here to occupy the Rabbinate seat, that they should not hurry here, to our town, to prevent any disputes in this town; in particular since our community will not wish to make the appointment to the Rabbinate as if it were a piece of property. The rabbi who will be selected after careful consultation and is found to be worthy and the right choice to be the Rabbi, he will be given the honor and called to come here, and in this manner both the rabbi's and the community's honor will be enhanced.

From the "Hamelitz" Newspaper, No. 92, of August 18, 1886

RABBI YAKOV - YOSEF KHARIF

(1848-1902)

Yacov-Yosef Kharif was born in Kruz. His father was a poor workman. At an early age he went to look for places of Torah. When he arrived in Kovno he became the pupil of Rabbi Yisrael Salanter, who advocated the Musar movement in Lithuania in the nineteenth century. Rabbi Israel Salanter shaped his character and guided his way in life. At an early age he was already accepted as a rabbi in the small town of Vilon and he opened a proper yeshiva there, with special hours for studying Musar. The yeshiva was successful and attracted students from all over Lithuania.

After five years of service in Vilon he was accepted as rabbi in Yurburg where he became popular among the town's Jews. He exerted a very strong influence on the community.

In 1883 he was invited to serve as Moreh Tsedek and Town Magid in Vilna. Here too the masses were fascinated by his sermons.

A few years later he was invited to be the rabbi of a Kolel in New York, where he organized the community and also had to take care of public and educational activities.

Rabbi Yakov-Yosef Kharif passed away in 1902. About 50,000 people took part in his funeral. A yeshiva was established in his name in New York - the **"Rabbi Yakov -Yosef Kharif Yeshiva."** Before he died the rabbi published a compilation of sermons and Torah called "For the House of Yakov" which was also translated into English.

RABBI YEKHEZKEL SON OF RABBI HILLEL-ARYEH LIFSHITZ

(1862-1932)

Rabbi Yekhezkel Lifshitz was born in Rasein. He had a vast knowledge of Judaism and a broad general education.

For a number of years he was the Rabbi of Yurburg, where he was greatly respected by the community.

From Yurburg he was invited to serve as rabbi in Kalish until he died.

His publications: When he was young he published songs in the "Ha'asif" compilations. He translated stories about the life of Jews from Germany. He signed under the name: "Fast Writer." His main book "The Midrash and the deed" - sermons in three parts.

After a while he was chosen to head the rabbis in Poland. In 1929 he took part in the founding conference of the expanded Jewish Agency in Zurich (Switzerland) and was also elected to the Administrative Council of the Jewish Agency.

TRANSLATED FROM PAGES 344 - 345

RABBI AVRAHAM DIMANT

YURBURG'S LAST RABBI

By Zevulun Poran

Rabbi Avraham Dimant - son of Rabbi Asher-Dimant.

Rabbi Avraham Dimant was one of Lithuania's most important Rabbis. The Jews of Yurburg were very fortunate to have such an illustrious personality as Rabbi Dimant as their teacher and rabbi. He became the rabbi of Yurburg at the beginning of the century and served till his last day. He passed away on Monday, 24 Adar 1940.

Rabbi Avraham Dimant was a learned man and a great bible scholar. He was sharp-witted and intelligent. He studied day and night, learning and exploring. He was a learned man and a gifted teacher. Jews in Yurburg avidly absorbed his words, and respected and admired him. The Rabbi, with his pleasant personality, was very popular and everyone treated him with respect. He was always smartly dressed and looked very respectful. We remember his words on the eve of Yom Kippur when he would address a large crowd at the Great Synagogue, taking moral stock of the individual and the community in general. The public would tremble when he stressed " For here we are as clay in the hands of the Creator," his words sounded philosophical. The Rabbi knew there were highly educated people among his flock but also "common" people, and he knew how to make himself understood by all. The Rabbi was clever enough to know that he could not ignore the cultural and spiritual revolution of his generation and therefore he always looked for the best ways to explain and convince his listeners. Rabbi Dimant never reprimanded his followers, did not moralize or intimidate but explained the importance of belief and the happiness of man living in accordance with the religious laws and tradition. He always knew how to emphasize the positive and the beautiful, for he loved man and believed he was good.

However, his innocent belief was disappointed. Inhuman people came to power in the neighboring country of Germany and they cruelly trampled on human morals and the humanistic ideals of the enlightened community of man. A year after his death these wicked people destroyed the community of Yurburg. Rabbi Dimant did not witness the terrible scenes, but deep in his heart he felt them coming and they hastened his death.

TRANSLATED FROM PAGE 346

RABBI HAYIM (CHAIM)-REUVEN RUBINSTEIN

THE RABBI IN THE DAYS OF THE HOLOCAUST

By Zevulun Poran

In addition to Rabbi Dimant, there was also a Dayan (Religious Judge) in Yurburg, who was mainly in charge of managing the community records, personal law etc.

The Dayan would assist the Rabbi in guiding the community in his way. He would also address a mixed public at the synagogue. He had a pleasant personality and was an educated man. He knew how to explain the Halakhah and wrote a number of books on the subject, which he published at his own expense. His books were translated into German for the benefit of the Jews in Germany. The Rabbi-Dayan was a social person and loved to talk to old and young, without any arrogance.

As a child, the undersigned knew Rabbi Rubinstein, who lived nearby, had the privilege of perusing his publications and listening to his explanations about their profound meaning.

When Rabbi Dimant died, Rabbi Rubinstein took his place as the Rabbi of the community, for only one year. His name was thus registered as the last Rabbi in the history of the Yurburg community.

When the Nazis entered Yurburg - his fate was as bitter as that of all his followers. The murderers tortured him and forced him to bring his rich library to the large pile of Holy Books, which were put on fire, while the Jews, men and women, were ordered to sing and dance. The wicked barbarians humiliated him and tortured him to his death.

He was murdered by the German-Nazi beasts in the summer of 1941, together with his community at the cemetery, when he bitterly protested against the evil actions of the Nazis and their Lithuanian helpers.

RELIGIOUS SCHOLARS WHOSE NAMES ARE LINKED TO YURBURG

By Zevulun Poran

RABBI SHELOMOH SON OF RABBI ARYEH-LEIB

(Born in 1821)

Rabbi Shelomoh was born and grew up in Yurburg. When he was grown up he taught Torah, first in Yurburg and then in Vilna. He left a handwritten essay called **Be'er-Sheva** on the subject of **Tractates of Sabbath, Eiruvin and Beitsa.** At the end of his life he wrote a booklet of new conceptions about the Rambam called "Stones of Shoham."

Rabbi Shelomoh's pupils thought he was a very charming and highly moral person, of sensitive mind and noble spirit. He had a broad European and Jewish education.

RABBI YITSKHAK-ELIYAHU SON OF RABBI SHEMUEL LANDA

Rabbi Yitskhak Eliyahu learned Torah from Rabbi Shelomoh the son of Rabbi Aryeh-Leib from Yurburg, who was a great and learned Torah scholar. After he married he settled in Dubno. There he became a businessman. He would hold sermons to the public and his listeners were greatly impressed with his words.

Rabbi Yitskhak Eliyahu was a Jewish delegate at the Rabbi's Conference in Petersburg in 1868. Later on he was asked to serve in Vilna.

He wrote and published many books on religious and Jewish subjects.

SHELOMOH LEVY BEN YISRAEL FAINBERG (FEINBERG)

He was born in Yurburg in 1821. He received a traditional education and was well versed in the Talmud and its commentators. He inherited a large business from his father in Yurburg and eventually became one of the biggest bankers in Lithuania and Russia.

In 1857 he settled in Kovno and married Baroness Rosa Von Hartenstein from Vilna. He became a well-known philanthropist. He lent a helping hand to all the needy inhabitants of Lithuania. He was also noted for his deeds of charity. He particularly assisted those who studied the Torah and observed religious duties. He had a wide range of business enterprises all over Russia. In 1887 the Czarist government granted him the title "Commercial Counselor."

After a while he moved to Koenigsberg (Prussia) and there too he became famous for his charity. He took an active part in public life and participated in various councils and committees in Vilna and Berlin. He also took part in the Rabbinical Conference in Petersburg in 1881. Famous for many deeds of charity, he passed away in 1893.

The Fainberg (Feinberg) dynasty in Yurburg continued until the last tragic days of Yurburg.   **Blessed be his memory.**

Great rabbis, famous and distinguished men
faithfully and devotedly served
the Jewish public in Yurburg.
Each one in his time did all he could
to strengthen the religious- spiritual
moral-social life of the community.
This they did for many generations, one after another,
the spiritual leaders and their special moral contribution
to shaping of Jewish personality and deepening of the Jewish faith.

Blessed be their memory.

The building of the Old Synagogue which was destroyed by the murderers.

Chapter 5
YOUTH ACTIVITIES IN YURBURG

The Maccabi Soccer Team in 1924. Mosheh Heselkovitz - Second from the right in the first row. Top from left: Kizel, Yosel Miasnik, Arnstein, Mosheh Heselkovitz, and Moskovitz. Middle from left: Z. Poran, Gedallah (George) Zarnitsky (? was in Lithuanian Army), unknown
Bottom from left: Moskovitz (went to US), Hilka Flier, Unknown
Identification by Jack Cossid

TRANSLATED FROM PAGES 351 -357

THE "MACCABI" ORGANIZATION IN YURBURG

The name "Maccabi" brings up an association with the Maccabians, who valiantly fought against the Greek and won. According to our Fathers, the source of the name "Maccabi" is the combination of the first words of the verse - **M C B I** ("Who is like You among the Gods").

Nevertheless, some - among them the historian Shimon Dubnov - claim that the correct spelling of the name is not "Maccabi" but "Makabi" which derives from the word Makeveth (hammer). Over the centuries we did not find another use for the word "Maccabi" other than its reminder each year at Hanukkah.

Only in 1894 the name of a sports organization called "Maccabi," founded in Kushta (Constantinopol, Turkey) was registered.

However, at the first Zionist Congress -in Basel in 1897 - Dr. Max Nordau for the first time raised the issue of strengthening our people's body and said: "We need muscular Jews and not only people of mind and spirit." Dr. M. Bodenheimer, Dr. Herzl's friend and adviser, also demanded at this Congress that Jewish sports associations be establish in order to train the youngsters and make them vigorous. Only after World War I "Maccabi" sports clubs sprung up all over Europe and in the U.S.A. The first "Maccabi" association in Israel was established in Jaffo in 1906.

At the "Maccabi" council in Karlsbad (1921) the world organization of "Maccabi" was founded.

In 1932 the first sports Olympics took place - the "Maccabiyah" in Tel Aviv. The " Maccabiyah " takes place once every four years.

After World War I branches of "Maccabi" were established in Lithuania, while the largest of them was the Kovno branch. In 1932 "Maccabi Hatzair" (Young Maccabi) was founded as a Zionist-Pioneer movement.

"Maccabi" - the Pride of the Jews of Yurburg

The "Maccabi" branch in Yurburg was established in the early twenties and included almost all the local Jewish youngsters. The "Maccabi" club operated at the town center, in a large stone building. The large, paved yard also belonged exclusively to "Maccabi" and served as a meeting place and a large part of the sports activities were held here in summer.

The "Maccabi" club was the essence and the center of Jewish power in Yurburg. As "Maccabi" was a national organization, without any political affiliations, all those who loved sports found a home there, without any connection to their personal outlook on life. The majority of the Yurburg Jews were "Maccabi" supporters, except for a small anti - Zionist group which set up its own sports club - Y.A.K. - Yiddischer Athletik Klub.

The Jews of Yurburg loved to watch the rows of young Maccabi members dressed in white, march in the street with their national flag, blue and white. The onlookers who stood on the sidewalk and watched the march were filled with pride and applauded. The mothers may have shed tears of pride when they watched their sons, "the Army of Israel," marching proudly along and singing the Zionist folksong:

> **Carry the flag and banner to Zion**
> **The flag of the camp of Yehudah**
> **On wheels or foot**
> **Join the association!**
> **Together we shall go, nay return**
> **To the land of our Fathers,**
> **To our beloved land**
> **The cradle of our youth!**

(Rosenboim/ Folksong)

The proud march encouraged the Jews who dwelt in the Diaspora among strangers. Each "Maccabi" march was a true feast in Yurburg - but how many national feasts do the Jews have? - And then there were the marches of the "Hebrew Scouts" - those in white and the others in green. The Jews created a sort of illusion and hope that this kind of life would go on forever and ever.

Anyhow, sports created a new experience in town. Parents would come to the "Maccabi" hall to watch the gymnastics exercises and the use of the sports equipment, such as parallel bars, horizontal bars, springboards, reins, weights etc.

The "Maccabi" sports instructor was a Christian German, a true professional and an excellent coach at the sports equipment. He was past fifty, but those who saw him demonstrate at the equipment, his elasticity and agility had the impression that a young man was carrying out these complicated exercises.

The instructor studied the subject of sports in Germany, shaped the muscles of his body with continuous exercise and attained full control over his body and the equipment.

The "Maccabi" sportsmen also made steady progress. But the instructor demanded more; when the "Maccabi" sportsmen had problems with one exercise or another, he would cynically say: "You Jews eat Weissbrot (white bread), you should eat "Schwartzbrot (black bread), for if you don't do so, you will not be real sportsmen."

Perhaps the instructor did not like Jews, but his devotion and efforts to make his pupils strong and sporty were praiseworthy. True, the quality of food of some of the Jewish sportsmen was inferior, and that made it difficult to attain a high level of performance. And, said the instructor; exercise must be started at an early age, for it is hard to attain real achievement in sports at a riper age.

Nevertheless, after a period of sports exercise and intensive preparations - the "Maccabi" sportsmen would succeed. Then they would put up a show for the public at large at the "Tel Aviv" park. If the show was a success and the public was satisfied with the sports achievements, the instructor too would praise his pupils. The event would begin and end with blessings and expressions of gratitude to the sportsmen and the instructor by the Chairman of "Maccabi," Berl (Dov) Levinberg, who contributed much to the sportsmen's success.

THE SOCCER SECTION AT "MACCABI"

"Maccabi" had a special section - "the soccer section." There were a number of soccer teams at "Maccabi" who usually played among themselves, and sometimes also against the soccer teams of the Lithuanians. The "Maccabi" soccer players were not always successful, but there were victories. The "Maccabi" players also played against the soccer teams in the area, but their performance was mediocre. The "Maccabi" team was the best in its area.

"Maccabi" did not have a special soccer coach in Yurburg. Only in the summer months it was possible to obtain a "Maccabi" soccer player in Kovno (Epstein), who would be able to make some progress with the "Maccabi" soccer players in Yurburg. Soccer games were not yet as popular as they are today, nevertheless, many people would come to watch the games, Lithuanians as well as Jews.

There were some excellent players in the "Maccabi" team (A) in Yurburg, who were good at the level of Yurburg, but not yet good enough for the level of the Kovno or German teams.

We recall that one day a soccer game took place between "Maccabi" (A) and the German team of Smaleninken, a small border town in the Memel region, 9 kms. from Yurburg. Although Yurburg's "Maccabi" team was confident in its ability to win, when they arrived at the field in Smaleninken and saw the tall, strong German youngsters, their spirits fell. The Yurburg players tried hard to win the game, but were unable to do so. The Germans soon took over the field and scored a few goals. The "Maccabi" players gathered all their forces and tried their best, but they lost. When the "Maccabi" players went home tired and exhausted by the game they lost against the German team, they had to do some stocktaking. It was clear to "Maccabi" that the team (A) needed a good coach and good conditions for regular training. Now they understood the meaning of the word "muscular Jews," mentioned by Dr. Nordau at the Zionist Congress. Actually the ancient Greek and Romans already understood this when they coined the phrase "*Mens sana in corpore sano*" - *a sane spirit in a healthy body.*

Since the defeat in Smaleninken the "Maccabi" soccer players increased their training, in order to be able to face future challenges, and particularly the battle against the Lithuanian soccer team (A) in Yurburg. The Lithuanians envied the "Maccabi" team for its success and always played against it in a very brutal manner, disregarding proper conduct and civilized sports manners.

A SAD EVENT AT THE SOCCER GAME

One day the Lithuanian mayor announced a reward would be given to the outstanding soccer team in Yurburg. Two teams were supposed to contend - the "Maccabi" team (A) and the Lithuanian team. The Lithuanians and the Jews were most interested in the game and many came to watch. Tensions rose high. The Lithuanians started the game with physical violence; they did not observe the rules, kicking and pushing all the time.

The Jews - on their part - tried to play a correct game. "Maccabi"s two outstanding players were Mosheh Heselkovitz and Meirke Hess, both fast and very fit runners. Mosheh Heselkovitz, a sturdy young man, very resourceful, proved to be full of tricks; he outwitted the Lithuanians each time and already in the first half of the game he "determined" the game at the Lithuanian goal.

The Lithuanian players became enraged and decided to attack Mosheh physically in order to remove him from the game. And this is how they went about it: two Lithuanian players attacked Mosheh, pushed him and threw him onto the ground and one of them - a hooligan - used the occasion to lay on top of Mosheh and strangle him with his knee. All the efforts to revive Moshe were fruitless and he died there on the spot.

The Jews in Yurburg were shocked by this tragic event, and so were all the Jews of Lithuania. The incident was widely covered in the Jewish press but hardly mentioned in the Lithuanian papers. A special public committee was set up in Kovno, which demanded a national investigation committee be set up-, but the government circles closed their ears and did nothing. The heads of the government sports bodies merely asked for an apology.

After a while the public committee set up a **memorial monument** (see below) on Moshe Heskelovitz's grave at the Yurburg cemetery. The members of the public committee attended the funeral and tried to comfort the family and the Jews of Yurburg who were deeply shocked by the tragic event. It was a terrible blow to "Maccabi" in Yurburg, the family and the town's Jews. The funeral was over, but the Jewish community was deeply shocked and the tragic event left a deep scar in their hearts.

The "Maccabi" sports committee decided to go on playing soccer, in spite of the pain, and to improve the training of the team members, and prove to the "Goyim" (Non-Jews) that they were strong and had it in their power to implement the "Maccabi" slogan "Be strong and brave"!

SOCIAL-CULTURAL ACTIVITY AT "MACCABI"

After the tragedy the "Maccabi" committee decided to increase the socio-cultural activity and cheer up the youngsters. The "Maccabi" cultural committee drew up a socio-cultural activity program. In the framework of this program "Maccabi" decided to hold "excursions" - i.e. sailing on the steamboats from Yurburg to Kovno. The "Maccabi" members in Yurburg met their friends in Kovno and hosted each other, usually on the Sabbath, in a friendly atmosphere. "Maccabi" in Kovno paid a return visit. When the guests - 500 to 600 in number - filled the streets of Yurburg, the whole town would take on a festive atmosphere full of youthful joy.

The guests and the hosts would walk in the parks of Yurburg, enjoying the beautiful scenery and the social encounter. These were good days for the Jews of Yurburg, and for a moment they forgot their problems and their worries.

In addition to the sports activity to "stretch the muscles," the "Maccabi" committee also took care to enhance the cultural and spiritual life of the sportsmen. Berl (Dov) Levinberg, the Chairman of the "Maccabi" committee, a diligent and resourceful man, did much to increase the socio-cultural activity among the branch members.

For this purpose he enlisted the help of teachers and public figures, active Zionists, who spent time and money in order to further Jewish culture, Zionism and Eretz Yisrael among the "Maccabi" members. Eretz Yisrael was always the priority of "Maccabi" in Yurburg. Its members volunteered for Zionist activity, such as " distributing "Shekalim" to Congress, activity on behalf of the funds etc. Often literature and cultural trials were held on cultural and moral issues. In the years of the Zionist Congresses propaganda meetings were held on Zionist subjects in the background of global politics, in order to update the **"Maccabians"** about what was going on in Eretz Yisrael and the possibilities of aliyah, etc.

The "Maccabi" club was home to all of Yurburg, a sort of cultural and social center that united Zionists of all political streams.

"Maccabi" in Yurburg counted 300 active members in various branches of sports. There were many expenses and little income (membership due and support of the assistance committee). Berl (Dov) Levinberg, Chairman of the Committee, was not an active sportsman, but he fully understood the importance of sports for the Yurburg youngsters and did all he could to obtain the necessary means to encourage sports and strengthen the Zionist-nationalist awareness among the "Maccabi" members.

Members of the "Maccabi" Organization in Yurburg, 1925

Gravestone of Moshe Heselkovitz, (the brother of Bluma and Sheine). "Maccabi" soccer player. From left: Moshe Krelitz, Yoske Miasnik, Headstone, Rochzo, Rozansky, Frank, Feivel Chossid, and Hannah Magidovitz (Identification by Jack Cossid). Photo most likely by Moshe Krelitz.

"MACCABI" IN THE LAST DAYS

In the thirties the situation of the Jews in Yurburg and in all of Lithuania worsened. The nationalistic policy of the Lithuanian government restricted the commercial activity of the Jews. Import and export business was totally banned. "Export Handel," of which Berl (Dov) Levinberg was the treasurer and executive manager, was liquidated and all the businessmen, big and small, were left without anything. Hitler came to power (1933) and instilled fear in all the Jews, especially his neighbors in Lithuania. Economic development in the town came to a halt. Cultural institutions were closed down, the Hebrew Gymnasium among them. The youngsters felt an "earthquake" was approaching; the gates of Eretz Yisrael were closed.

Only few people managed to get out with a "Sertifikat." Many left for distant countries. Berl Levinberg immigrated to Canada, where he remained faithful to Zionism.

"Maccabi" remained active in Yurburg, under the guidance of Kizel and others. Activity slowed down in all the youth movements and also in the Zionist parties - till the bitter and violent day arrived. In the summer of 1941 the Yurburg community was destroyed.

The survivors, wherever they are, will always remember the wonderful achievement of "Maccabi."

Committee members of the Macabi Organization of Yurburg. Sitting from the right: Rafael Kizel, Berl Levinger, and Avraham Altman. Standing from the right: Yitskhak Rakhtsa, Zevulun Petrikansky (Poran); Elyashev, Miasnik, Yosef Gutman *(emigrated to El Paso, Texas).*

TRANSLATED FROM PAGE 358

Jewish Scouting Movement - HaShomer HaTzair

In 1908 Lord Robert Baden-Powell, officer of the British Army, published a book "Scouting for Boys." The book attained a lot of publicity and was used as guide for the organization of the scouts' movements in many countries, according to the system of "scouting."

In Lithuania, right after the founding of the country, scouting groups were founded under governmental patronage. The goal of the scouts was to equip the youth with virtues, strong character, love of the nature and to educate them to good citizenship. At this time, also Jewish youngsters joined the Lithuanian scouts' movement; in the beginning they were in mixed troops, however, later on in separate troops.

The scouts movement "HaShomer HaTzair" was founded in Virbalen by the director of the Jewish Gymnasium, Dr. Yakov Rabinson, who was one of the leaders of Jewish settlements in Lithuania. At about the same time, at the beginning of the twenties, additional scouts troops were founded in Kovno and in Ponivezh, and later on in nearly every town and settlement in Lithuania. The Hebrew translation of the "Scouting" book by Baden-Powell was used as the educational guide of the Hebrew troops.

A scouts organization was founded in Yurburg at the beginning of the twenties. During these days, one could see two youngster, dressed in the khaki-green scouting uniform, a cord with a flute around their neck and the long "scouting stick" in their hands, walking through the streets of Yurburg. These two youngsters with their unusual uniform caused amazement wherever they were seen. These two youngsters were Menakhem Pukhert and Dov Mintser. Menakhem Pukhert, the elder one, was a tall, slim, serious, self-thought young man. Dov Mintser was a very charming boy, a student of the Hebrew Gymnasium in Yurburg. The two were accompanied by younger children, who were also dressed in scouting uniforms. Their appearance seemed to be strange, because of its novelty, but it marked the beginning of a change for the young generation in Yurburg.

TRANSLATED FROM PAGE 359-367

THE HOSTEL AND THE EDUCATIONAL ACTIVITY

By Zevulun Poran

In the course of time an apartment was rented - a hostel in the terms of the scouts - in the northern part of town, a quiet, sparsely populated street. The hostel was situated in a one-story building; it contained two rooms.

The atmosphere at the hostel was pleasant and pastoral. The voices of singing would always be heard there. The hostel's rooms were decorated and in the center were pictures of Baden-Powell, Herzl, and Trumpeldor. The hostel was usually quiet, clean and orderly.

The scouts in the troop were divided into three groups: the group of the "Lions," scouts and the adolescent scouts.

The **"Lions" group** included children aged 9-12. The name "Lions" referred to the saying "Yehudah is a lion cub" - a name with a nationalist meaning. The non-Jews called this group the "Little Wolves."

In the "Lions" group boys were not separated from girls, they operated as one group and went on outings together; they learned to recognize plants, birds and the animals of the forest. When the "Lions" were at the camps they acquired a variety of scouts techniques - walking, tree- climbing and lighting bonfires. They also learned how to use a compass, look at the stars and the moon in order to find their way.

The "Lions" leaders taught them to dress properly, be clean, polite and obedient. To broaden their knowledge the "Lions" were told about Eretz Yisrael in the days of the Bible, about historic heroes and heroes in the new country, such as the heroism of the watchmen, pioneers etc. After a while the "Lions" group was called "Khabirim" like the members of the Hebrew desert clan who wandered in the desert and conquered Eretz Yisrael.

THE SCOUTS GROUP IN THE TROOP (KEN)

The basic-educational cell at the troop - the group - included 8 to 10 scouts. The group was divided separately into boys and girls. The scouts would meet twice a week, at the hostel or outside for meetings ("kibbutz") with the head of the group (the "Kevutsaii"). The scout was required to appear in uniform, obey the Kevutsaii's orders to be accurate, orderly and obedient.

The "kibbutz" started with the order "Be prepared! Stand still! And the blessing "Be ready!" while the reply would be "Ready always!" Activities would start with a short march, singing, sitting down and talking and finally dancing "Be merry Galileans, heroes and soldiers," the hora dance of those days. The group's main goal was to create a close social structure, good friendship and openheartedness. In the "character" talks they would talk openheartedly about the character of the group's members and find a way to amend distortions. Each group had a triangular flag made of cloth on which the name and symbol of the group was sewn - the picture of an animal, fowl or flower.

On Saturdays the scouts would hold a meeting of the troop which included four groups, the kevutsaim and the head of the troop. It would start with a festive roll call; similar to the group's meeting. If there were a festive occasion they would bring the troop's flag along - made of dark green silk with the symbol - three fig leaves under which was written, "Be prepared." Down at the flag's helm was written: "Scouts troop - Yurburg troop." When the troop's flag was brought in they would have to stand at attention. The troop's head would order "Honor the flag- salute!" - silence all around and everyone saluted the flag. (The salute was by lifting the hand while the thumb would press the pink and the three middle fingers were raised). Each troop meeting was a feast to the scouts; the atmosphere and the elevated mood left a strong impression on the participants and provided them with an unforgettable experience.

SCOUTING IN THE FIELD AND FOREST

**Advance brother, to the top of the mountain
In the forest among the trees;
On the river bed,
On the wide meadow
Where Hebrew scouts pause.
Not among the walls and not in the city -
Laughter in their eyes, a song on their lips
And joy - so much joy in their hearts**

Yitskhak Katsenelson (Katznelson)

One of the scouts' rules says: "A scout loves nature." The scout generally observes all the scouts' rules out of understanding and recognition of their importance, however, the rule regarding nature he accepts with enthusiasm. Indeed, the scouts in Yurburg observed this rule in its true sense. Yurburg was surrounded by forests; thus the scouts did not remain inside the hostel but went on outings, to the camp or settlement. There were many trips and camps held by the Yurburg troop in the beautiful landscape around the town. These trips left a deep impression on the scouts' hearts. There were many preparations before departure and much sports training had to be acquired before leaving for the camp.

- Measuring the distance at eye level - height of a tree, width of a river, how fast the stream flows;

- Determining the world's winds according to compass, sundial, movements of the moon and stars;

- Signs: Morse code; semaphore;

- Walking a kilometer at scout's pace in seven minutes, walking seven km. at scout's pace, notice and remember striking things in landscape;

- Set up a tent, know 20 uses of the scouts stick and 10 knots in the rope;

- Know how to light a bonfire with two to three matches and cook a three-course dinner;

- Know at least eight sports exercises to strengthen the body;

- Know first aid in case of injury and daily hygiene at the camp.

When the camp ended in an exalted spirit - the scouts would say: "One day at camp is better than a whole month in town."

We would not be telling the truth if we did not mention the sport of sailing on the rivers. Yurburg had three rivers and that was an advantage not enjoyed by every troop. Indeed, the Yurburg troop used the sailing advantage; who does not remember the hours of sailing on the Mituva, the songs and laughter that filled the eyes with tears.

THE SCOUTS RULES

The rules were an indication for each scout from the day they joined the troop. Violation of the scouts' rules was considered very serious. Each scout had to know the rules by heart and explain their essence. However, merely knowing the rules was not enough; the scout had to live according to these rules and implement them in daily life. These were the rules:

A. A scout observes the truth

B. A scout is devoted and faithful to his country

C. A scout helps others

D. A scout is a friend and brother to all other scouts

E. A scout is polite and ready to serve

F. A scout is frugal and takes care of his own and other people's belongings

G. A scout is diligent and defends his views

H. A scout is merry, alert and in high spirits

I. A scout is modest

J. A scout is pure of thought, words and deeds

(Observes sexual purity, does not smoke and does not drink alcohol).

The above rules, as defined here, are based on Baden-Powell's "Scouting Book," and they applied to the first years of the movement. However, when the movement adopted the Zionist-pioneer outlook - the rules were changed accordingly. However, the scouts' principle remained valid as an educational guideline in the movement.

THE STEPS

The steps served as an educational work system for the scouts groups. All the steps' subjects were divided into three parts. The scout studied them in his group and passed a test on them. These were the parts of the steps:

Scouting with everything it included the rules and educational principles.

Information about the world and homeland. After the movement passed through ideological changes the new program was formulated for "the steps" in the Zionist-pioneer spirit.

The "steps" program included:

Judaism - A selection of Bible chapters, parts of Ethics of the Fathers, traditional holidays and nature holidays, periods in the history of Israel, personalities, heroism in Israel etc.

Eretz Yisrael - General information about the country, various generations of aliyah, settling the country in the last generations, "Khibath Zion," the first settlements, the Bilu'im, town and village in Israel, Jewish workers in Eretz Yisrael, "Hashomer," moshav and kibbutz. Hashomer Hatzair in Eretz Yisrael. As background study material the following books were used: Self-emancipation by Dr. I.L. Pinsker, The Jewish State by Dr. T.Z. Herzl and the books "Dreamers and Fighters" by Ya'ari Poleskin, the "Yizkor" (Remembrance) book, the study book "The Railway Track" the book about the life of Yosef Trumpeldor (written by Pesakh Lipovetsky) - the man of labor and Hagana and the founder of "Hekhalutz." (His last words "It is good to die for our country" became holy words to the scouts. On the 11th day of the month Adar a memorial day would be held at the troop to honor his memory. Selected parts were also read of the authors - Akhad Ha'am; Brener, A.D. Gordon, H.N. Bialik, S. Chernikhovsky, A. Shlonsky, Yitskhak Lamdan ("Masada") and others of their generation. The scouts hymn - "Be prepared" -

was exchanged for the song by Hayim Nakhman Bialik "Blessing of a people" (first verse) which encourages the pioneer workers who build the country.

Hold the hands of all our gifted brothers

Young harts where they are

Let them be cheerful - be merry and glad

Lend a shoulder to help the people!

And of course they also sang Imber's "Hatikvah" at the time- the hymn of the Zionist Federation. The scouts' greeting "Be prepared" "Always prepared!" was also replaced by "Khazak Ve'ematz" (Cheer up - cheer up and be strong)

Later on in the "process of change" parts of the social theory were also introduced into the "steps" and in the ideology of the Zionist- pioneer labor movement.

THE PUBLIC OATH

It was the custom at the adolescent scouts group that the adolescent scout would deliver a public oath reflecting his commitment to the movement, its aims and values. A scout who received a favorable opinion from the members of his group regarding his good behavior would be fit to deliver the public oath at a festive occasion. The troop's head, the older brother, would speak about the responsibility of the scout who took the oath.

When the troop head finished his speech, the troop's flag would be brought forth and they would all salute the blue flag.

The scout, who delivered his oath, would stand upright in front of the flag and the troop's leader, who would ask as follows:

Head of the troop: "Are you aware of the value of man's honor and his word of honor?"

The scout: "Yes, I am aware of it and I and my word of honor are to be trusted."

Head of the troop: "Can I trust you and your word of honor that you will do your duty to your people, help others and observe the rules of the scouts?"

The scout: "Yes, I am aware of this and I and my word of honor are to be trusted."

Head of the troop: "Take your oath." (The scout salutes the flag and delivers his oath).

The scout: "I hereby take a public oath, confirmed by my word of honor, that I shall do my duty to my people and my country, help others and observe the rules of the scouts."

Head of the troop: "I trust you and your word of honor that you will do as you say, from now on you are our brother, a brother in the large family of scouts."

Head of the troop: "I wish you success!" He attaches the pin to the scout's uniform and gives him the blue tie.

THE SCOUTS SING THE HYMN

That is the end of the ceremony. There are no words to describe the scouts' excitement. The members of the group embrace the scout who delivered the oath and he returns their embrace. Everyone is happy and glad and they start to sing and dance the hora.

That is, in fact, the Baden-Powell version of the public oath, which existed as long as the movement existed.

THE NEW FACE OF THE MOVEMENT

There was an increasing trend at the movement to change its nature and objectives, but there were others who wanted to adhere to Baden-Powell scouting and were opposed to adding Zionist-pioneer aspects. However, the majority of the adolescent group agreed, without hesitation, to give the movement a Zionist-pioneer outlook. The troop continued its activity; scouting remained the same as far as organization and the movement's system of education were concerned, but became richer in substance. From now on the troop was called "The troop of the Hebrew scouts Hashomer Hatzair." The movement considered itself the successor of "Hashomer," i.e. kibbutz -work, settling the country, protecting and defending it.

"HaShomer-HaTsair" youth before leaving for"Hakhsharah" (Training Kibbutz)

A group of friends got organized in those days at the "Maccabi" branch in Yurburg, among them Zevulun, member of the committee that identified with the ideas of pioneering Zionism. The members of the group considered Yosef Trumpeldor their teacher and mentor - and they were called "The Trumpeldor Troop." The "troop" members joined "Hashomer Hatzair" and strengthened the Shomer troop. Zevulun occupied key positions in the troop, together with Hayim (Chaim) Siger. Since then the troop became more important and its rising power was felt in all fields of Zionist activity in town. Chaim Siger met the expectations of the "Trumpeldor Troop" members with his strong personality and Zionist outlook.

THE SHOMRIM GROUP - TOWARDS IMPLEMENTATION

When a scout at the troop turns seventeen, he joins the Shomrim group, which obliges its members to implement the Zionist ideal. The first stage of implementation is to go on training.

The Shomer now faces a crucial decision about his personal life in the near future. Some Shomrim decide without hesitation, others have a problem with the decision, for personal reasons. They usually consult their parents, and the answer is not always positive. Then the Shomer faces a difficult decision. Particularly the parents of girls would make it difficult for them. We remember a case when one of the girls at the troop, Hannah Smolnik (Polan), decided to go on training and faced strong opposition by her parents. Hannah did not give in to her parents and one night she got up and left her home to go on training. In this case she joined a farming group in Dumpen, an estate owned by a German in the Memel (Klaipeda) district. Hannah was the first person in the troop to go on training and the first to go on aliyah to Israel (1929).

Mosheh Raizman also went on training to Dumpen. Zevulun joined the same group, three days after he graduated from high school, in his case also against the wish of his parents.

The move from scouting romanticism and the boisterous life of the young to life on a distant farm was not easy. The hard work started early in the morning *and ended late at night*. Living and economic conditions were poor. Nevertheless, they got used to it. "Once a scout - always a scout." This saying becomes reality when confronted with difficulties. The good scout-Shomer passes the test. Training in town was not easy either; but the hope to go to Israel boosts the spirit.

When the training period was over, the problems of aliyah started. No certificate. "His Majesty's Government" caused disappointment. They wait and wait and the waiting causes frustration and disappointment. There is a long queue for aliyah. That is why the aliyah flows slowly, although there is great demand and the fight for the Certificate is difficult.

A group of "HaShomer-HaTsair" at "Hakhsharah" in the Dumpen farm in Memel (Klaipeda) region, summer 1927, first group from Yurburg at "Hakhshrah." Standing from right; Mosheh Raizman, Hannah Smolnik (Polan), between them is Zevulun Petrikansky (Poran)

When the Shomer goes to Israel he joins the nucleus of the Shomrim from Lithuania, who are of the same age, in order to set up a new kibbutz. In the meantime they are in tents near one or other settlement, and they work, some in the orange groves and others paving roads or building. When the Keren Kayemeth announces to the kibbutz nucleus that land has been allocated to it somewhere for settlement, their happiness knows no bounds. Usually two or three kibbutz nuclea merge for joint settlement on the land.

However, we did not intend to speak about settlement, but about the fact that the Shomrim, the immigrants from Yurburg, joined the settlement nuclea and together set up kibbutzim. The Hashomer Hatzair movement from Lithuania set up six kibbutzim:

Beith Zera in the Jordan valley, Kefar Masaryk in the Zevulun valley, Amir in Upper Galilee, Ramat Hashofet in the Menashe mountains, Ma'anit in Samaria (Shomron) and Lehavoth Habashan in Upper Galilee. Among those who settled in these kibbutzim you will find branches from Yurburg who realized their life's dream at the kibbutz. There are Shomrim from Yurburg too who joined other kibbutzim for personal reasons, such as Givath Brener, Afikim and others. Quite a few Shomrim from Yurburg are to be found in Israel's towns and villages.

Unfortunately, the number of Shomrim from Yurburg at the kibbutzim and in general is getting smaller and smaller. There is no eternity.

People pass away and presently their relatives represent Yurburg. Many people from Yurburg, who left the town even before the Holocaust, are dispersed over all the corners of the world.

Is this the end of the Yurburg story? Will the name of our community still be remembered? The name of the Shomer-scouts troop in Yurburg?

It is hard to imagine that these youngsters we knew - the trainees of the Hebrew scouts troop - who were so much loved and liked in their lives, who filled the streets of Yurburg with laughter and joy - are no longer alive . . .they, who at the time were a source of pride to their parents and the Jews of Yurburg, were cut by a cruel and criminal hand from the land of life.

And now, the Shomer hostel is empty. There is the silence of a cemetery around it. The paths breathed. The crowds and joy of youth have gone. The song of their lives has fallen silent. Hayim (Chaim) Sigar, their leader and mentor, Rivkah Karabelnik, his girlfriend, are no longer. They are gone forever. Only their sacred memory will remain forever in the hearts of those who knew them and were close to them.

This in short is the dramatic story of what happened to a group of young boys and girls, members of an illustrious youth movement, called Hashomer Hatzair. The scouts and Shomrim were active at their modest troop for about twenty years, an exemplary troop in the town of Yurburg, a charming corner where one could widen the horizon and enrich the soul with the exciting experiences of youth.

This troop, as many other troops of Hashomer Hatsair in Lithuania, constituted a glorious page in the history of the Zionist-pioneer youth movements. These youngsters who dreamt of Zion, were cruelly murdered, and did not manage to fulfill their dream to go to Israel and take part in its building and development on behalf of themselves and for the people of Israel.

Scouts from HaShomer HaTsair in 1925

Scouts in Yurburg

The leadership of the Scout troop in Yurburg 1927.

Sitting from left: Leah Shtok (sister of Bath-Sheva Shtok-Ayalon), Rachel Karabelnik, Zevulun Petrikansky, Hayim Siger, Meirovitz, Hannah Braun, Eliezer Shapira.

Youth Camp of the Betar Organization in Yurburg

(Zahavah Pulerevitz is in the middle row from the bottom)

Top row, third and fourth from the left: Yakov Chosid (Jack Cossid) and Mosheh Krelitz

TRANSLATED FROM PAGES 368

The Betar Movement in Yurburg

By Zahavah Pulerevitz Ben Yehudah

A strong movement named Betar developed and grew in the streets of Lithuania before World War II. The young movement had the philosophy the famous Zionist leader Ze'ev Zabotinsky. And of course the Betar group also started and was built in Yurburg, our birthplace. In almost all Jewish communities in Europe there was a Betar group.

The movement Betar was quite active and spread throughout Yurburg. It was a strong movement here. Whoever passed through the Betar camp, felt like if he entered the drawing room, from there we would became strong leaders to defend our homeland Israel.

The Zionist education that we received in the courses and in the Betar camp was based upon a special program: an education with national basis. We became fluent in the Hebrew language and learned to love our homeland Israel.

The goal to emigrate was instilled in everybody, and it was not executed in parts. We would first have to get a strong preparation in the courses and in the camp in order to emigrate. We would all learn the background of Zionist education under the special leadership of Yehudah Most and Mosheh Krelitz.

This preparation would find the interest in many activities, in the courses we would get a strong leadership and we became close friends like a family. Our leaders were always there for us.

In those days when we all dreamed that a Jewish state would be founded. We did not know about the coming of the Holocaust. And thus occurred this horrible tragedy to the Jewish people of Europe. We did not know that the dream of many would not materialize and many of us would be murdered.

Some members of the movement from our city escaped the Holocaust, and made their way to the land of Israel.

We cannot forget those days that passed of the magnificent group of the Betar movement in Yurburg.

Maccabi Band in 1925

TRANSLATED FROM PAGES 369

The "Hekhalutz" (Pioneer) as the Head of the Camp

By Zevulun Poran

The "Hekhalutz" movement was very popular in Yurburg, in spite of the difficulties of the pioneer training and the unceasing anticipation for the emigration (Aliyah) certificate, there were a lot of people who joined the "Hekhalutz" movement. In the last years before the Holocaust, a Kibbutz for pioneer training was founded in Yurburg. "Hekhalutz" was in need of support from the public, and hereunder is one of their financial operations:

Each one takes part in the unification of the "Hekhalutz"

Each one who takes part in the unification gives the "Hekhalutz" a chance to establish it's economic situation.

Mr. **Hayim (Chaim) Siger** and Mr. Elimelekh Park (who in Israel became a professor and head of the agricultural faculty in Rekhovoth) asks you to help with 10 lit. and to contact:

Miss Ida Fridlender, Yurburg

Miss Hanah Fainberg (Helen Feinberg), Yurburg-Tavrig

Mrs. Sheine Rabinovitz, Marijampole

Mr. David Gorshain, Yurburg, teacher

Mr. Yisrael Chekhanovski, Yurburg, teacher

Mr. Mordehai Taikhman, Yurburg, head of the Jewish Gymnasium

Mr. Khanokh Lintupski, teacher

Mr. Eliezer Leipziger, Yurburg, teacher

Mr. Yekhiel Blizovski, Posvol, teacher

In the very comprehensive book of Sarah Nishmith - "There Were Pioneers in Lithuania" (published by "Beit Lokhamei HaGhetaoth," Kibbutz of the Ghetto Fighters, 1983) some numbers about the "Hekhalutz" movement in Lithuania were published. According to this source, the "Hekhalutz" movement in Lithuania was, in relation to the population, the largest of these movements in the world. In 1933 there were 5,000 members in 110 branches of the "Hekhalutz" in Lithuania, thereof about 1,500 in more than 50 Kibbutzim for pioneer training and about the same number in divisions of the pioneer training program.

The request for emigration was very large and the number of certificates did not fulfill the demand. In 1935, for example, the "Hekhalutz" center in Lithuania received certificates only for 33 male members and 28 female members.

It was like a drop in the sea. The "Hekhalutz" center had to find alternative ways out of the Diaspora.

Yurburg "pioneers" at "Hachshara" (agricultural training camp for Betar movement) across the river from Yurburg, in Saudine. They worked with Lithuanian farmers to become familiar with life on a kibbutz.

[Not in original Yizkor Book. Photo courtesy of Jack Cossid.]

Betar group was taken in honor of a fellow member Bayneski Hess, second seated from the left. He left the Lithuanian Army. The rest are old friends and members of the Betar in Yurburg. Sitting in the middle from left to right, Weinstein, Bayneski Hess, Pulerovitz, Moshe Krelitz and Simka Rochzo. Jack Cossid standing just above Simka Rochzo. Photo taken in the Tel Aviv Park by Foto K. Levino on Oct 11, 1935.

Betar group. Moshe Krelitz is third from the left. Jack Cossid is in middle just to the right of the five women. March 19, 1935.

Photos not in original Yizkor Book. Photos courtesy of Jack Cossid.

The "Vad" (board) of Betar From left to right: Simka Rockzo, Ark Rickler, Moshe Krelitz, Pinki Kopinski and Jack Cossid as the secretary of the organization. December 1, 1937.

Betar Group with the Moment, the Betar Newspaper. Moshe Krelitz on left sitting in front. Jack Cossid in back on right top.

Photos not in original Yizkor Book. Photos courtesy of Jack Cossid. Both photos by Moshe Krelitz.

Moshe Krelitz in his Betar Uniform
[Photos not in original Yizkor Book. Photo courtesy of Jack Cossid.]

Jack Cossid and Moshe Krelitz pictured on right side just to the left of the fellow in light coat with hand pointing up. Photo taken in 1933.

Betar members in Lithuanian Park. From left to right a gentleman from the Betar organization, from Kovno, Moshe Krelitz, Chana Rickler, Benski Hess, Dora Gittleman (Krelitz) and a fellow from Czechoslovakia. Photos not in original Yizkor Book. Photos courtesy of Jack Cossid. Photo by Moshe Krelitz.

TRANSLATED FROM PAGES 370

J.A.C. - the Jewish Athletics Club

By Zevulun Poran

In addition to the Maccabi Sports Club, there was another sports club, named J.A.C. in Yurburg. Their activities were rather narrow. Their main activity was a club that trained gymnastics groups for men and for women separately.

J.A.C. also had a soccer group of rather low performance level. They also had an active volleyball group. J.A.C did not organize sports festivals for the public, nor parades in the streets. During the summer, the members of J.A.C. organized excursions, meetings and sports activities in the nature. Since they did not have many members, they would meet in the woods or in the parks of the town.

The only language spoken at J.A.C. was Yiddish. Also the orders - "Stand in line," "Stand at ease" "Quick-march" were given in Yiddish. Also at Maccabi, Yiddish was spoken, but the orders were given in Hebrew and the whole atmosphere was Zionist.

J.A.C. also organized a broad cultural and social program. In these activities, not only the athletes of J.A.C took part, but also other Yiddish-oriented people, for example members of the Folkist movement and also Jewish communist who had to remain undercover, since the law forbade meetings of leftist movements.

The J.A.C. was sponsored by few "Yiddishists," well known persons, who would lecture about cultural issues, as for example the publication of a new book in Yiddish, the Yiddish literature and culture etc. One of the well-known people was Mordechai Gut, son of Rabbi Aryeh-Leib (Leibchik) Gut, who also was a teacher at the elementary school (Talmud Torah). Gut was a serious and educated person, who had a broad knowledge of, and a love of Yiddish. He had no interest in Hebrew literature, although he spoke the language well.

Also the head of the Yiddishists of Lithuania, Yudel Mark, was among the lecturers at J.A.C. Mark was, together with Helena Khatskeles, was the founder of the Yiddish school of Yurburg. This was a small school, but the pride of Yiddishists in town. There was also a Yiddish library, named "Mendele library, in Yurburg. Also many Zionists who did not speak Hebrew, made use of the "Mendele" library.

Chapter 6
THE DESTRUCTION OF JEWISH YURBURG

THE DESTRUCTION OF JEWISH YURBURG

The Sun Shined, the Acacia Blossomed and the Slaughterer slaughtered.

Hayim (Chaim) Nakhman Bialik

סֵפֶר הַדְּמָעוֹת

הַדְּבָרִים יָצְאוּ מִן הַלֵּב

הַמִּלִּים נִכְתְּבוּ מִתּוֹךְ כְּאֵב –

כָּל מִלָּה

בְּדָם טְבוּלָה

דַּם־אָדָם

דָּם שֶׁל עָם.

סֵפֶר דְּמָעוֹת

מַזְכֶּרֶת לְדוֹרוֹת.

דִּמְעָה – לְהוֹרִים שַׁכּוּלִים

דִּמְעָה – לְאָחוֹת וּלְאַחִים יְתוֹמִים

דִּמְעָה – לְסָב יָשִׁישׁ וּלְסַבְתָּא קְשִׁישָׁה

דִּמְעָה – לִקְהֵלָה קְדִישָׁא.

דִּמְעָה – לְרֶצַח תִּינוֹק קָטָן

קָרְבַּן רִשְׁעוּת בְּנֵי הַשָּׂטָן,

נֶפֶשׁ קְטַנָּה, שְׁסוּעָה

בְּפַרְפּוּרֵי גְּסִיסָה.

מָוֶת בַּחוּצוֹת –

נֹאד מָלֵא דְּמָעוֹת.

קוֹלוֹת זָעֲקוּ – "הַצִּילָהוּ"

פִּיּוֹת הִתְפַּלְלוּ – "הוֹשִׁיעָה!"

אַךְ אֵין שׁוֹמֵעַ וּמַאֲזִין

וְאֵין קוֹרֵעַ גְּזַר הַדִּין,

אֵין מֵנִיד עַפְעָף

וְאֵין פּוֹרֵשׂ כָּנָף...

וְהַשָּׁמַיִם אֲטוּמִים

וְאֵין שׁוֹמְעִים זַעֲקַת שְׂרִידִים –

הָעוֹלָם שָׁחוֹר־מִשְׁחוֹר

וְאֵין לִרְאוֹת שְׁבִיב־אוֹר.

וְהַהֶרֶג רַב

לֹא שָׂרַד בֵּית־אָב

כָּל הָעִיר שׁוֹאָה

קְהִלַּת יוּרְבּוּרְג חָרְבָה.

★

הַשֶּׁמֶשׁ שָׁקְעָה,

חֲתוּלָה יִלְּלָה –

אֵין כֹּל

רַק שְׁכוֹל.

וּבַלַּיְלָה –

בְּחֶשְׁכַת לַיְלָה, רַק נֵר זִכָּרוֹן יָאִיר

אֶת קְדוֹשֵׁי הָעִיר.

זְבוּלוּן פּוֹרָן

TRANSLATION OF PAGES 373

THE BOOK OF TEARS

The words come straight from the heart
They were written in great pain
Each word
Is drenched in blood
The blood of man
The blood of a people.
A book of tears
To be remembered for generations to come.
A tear - for the bereaved parents
A tear - for the sister and brothers that were orphaned
A tear - for the old grandfather and grandmother
A tear for a sacred community.
A tear - for the murder of a little baby
Who fell victim to the evil of the devil's sons
A small heart that was torn
And whispers its last breath.

Death outside
A vessel full of tears.
Voices cried to heaven - "Help us!"
Lips murmured prayers - "Save us!"
But no one heard, no one listened
No one removes the decree;
No one raises an eyebrow,
No one stretches out a hand. . .
The heavens are closed
They do not hear the cries of those who remain
The world is blacker than black
Not a ray of light is to be seen.
There is much killing
Not a family is spared
The whole town is a Holocaust
The community of Yurburg is destroyed.

The sun went down
A cat howled -
Nothing is left
Only bereavement.
And at night -
In the darkness of night, only a memorial candle will shed its light
On the martyrs of the town.

Zevulun Poran

TRANSLATION OF PAGE 374

THE SHOAH IN WORLD WAR II

THE STRUGGLE AND DESTRUCTION OF THE YURBURG COMMUNITY

By Zevulun Poran

The word Holocaust, which means destruction, liquidation, annihilation refers to the destruction of the Jews of Europe in World War II (1939-1945). The Jewish people numbered 16 million when the War broke out and over 6 million of them were killed by the Nazis and their collaborators. Jewish communities in Europe were destroyed in twenty-one countries that were conquered by the Nazis.

Adolf Hitler came to power in Germany in 1933; he was a brutal, bloodthirsty man who hated Jews. In 1939 Hitler started war with the aim of conquering the countries of Europe. The war went on for about six years, and it drowned the world in a sea of blood. The Nazi army conquered almost all the countries of Europe. Millions of people were killed. Many towns were ruined. Millions were uprooted from their homes. However, the greatest tragedy of all befell the Jews. The Nazis decided to destroy the Jewish people. Every Jew was destined to be killed.

On 20 January 1942 Hitler convened the heads of the Nazi regime in the Berlin quarter Wannessee am Grossen in order to discuss the subject of the **final solution of the Jewish question**. At this "historical" conference the head of the security police and S.D., Ober Gruppenfuehrer Heidrich, submitted a detailed plan to liquidate 11 million Jews in Europe. For 90 minutes the participants discussed in cold blood the preferred method of murder, the organization, transport problems etc. The plan was approved in all its details in order to be executed in stages. Indeed, the major part of the plan was carried out.

The following is a list of the countries in which the destruction of the Jews was carried out in Europe (in %):

Poland (85.7);   **Soviet Union (42);**   **Romania (50);**
Hungary (50.4);   **France (33.3);**   **Czechoslovakia (84.6);**
Germany (81);   **Austria (66.6);**   **Luxembourg (83.4);**
Latvia (89.5);   **Holland (73.3);**   **Belgium (50);**
Lithuania (90);

> **[Figures for Lithiania is cited by Rabbi Efrayim Zuroff, Simon Wiesenthal Center in 2002 yields over 95%, n.b. J. Alpert]**

Yugoslavia (75);   **Greece (80);**   **Italy (26.3);**
Bulgaria (14);   **Denmark (7.1);**   **Norway (50),**
Estonia (90).

Now, let's describe the route of suffering the Jews of Europe passed during the course of the War:

The Jews of Germany were the first to be destroyed, then came the Jews of Poland, the largest Jewish settlement in Europe, which numbered 3.5 million Jews prior to World War II. To facilitate the destruction the Nazis gathered together all the Jews in the large cities into ghettoes of Warsaw, Lodz, Bialystok, Riga, Vilna and Kovno and Shavli (a relatively small ghetto) etc.

At the ghettoes the Jews were employed in forced labor, such as: industrial enterprises, paving of roads, building of bridges etc. The conditions of living and nourishment were poor.

In addition to torture at the ghetto, the Nazis set up **the death camps** at Auschwitz, Maidanek, Buchenwald, Treblinka, Chelmno, Belsen etc. At these camps gas chambers were installed and furnaces that accelerated the destruction process of millions.

Immediately after the Nazi occupation of the Baltic States: Lithuania, Latvia, Estonia and Soviet Russia as well, the Nazis and their local collaborators carried out brutal killings. Entire communities were destroyed.

In Lithuania the majority of the Jews were already killed in the first days of the Nazi invasion (1941). The Jews of the little villages in Lithuania were the first to be killed. The Jews of Yurburg shared the fate of those in the other villages of Lithuania. Only in the large cities ghettoes were set up, where the Jews were kept, like in Vilna (60.000), Kovno (20,000 to 30,000) and Shavli, a relatively small ghetto, about 3000 people. The destruction at the ghettoes was in stages. Those who were not fit were executed. From Vilna they were sent to Ponar and from Kovno to Fort IX and Fort VII near Kovno and there they died. Those who remained were employed in forced labor until they were liquidated. Near the end of the War the Nazis took those Jews who were still able to work to Germany, where they were employed in forced labor. Many of them were saved when the Germans were defeated in the war, among them were some survivors from Yurburg who were at the Kovno ghetto.

In Yurburg all the Jews were destroyed, as mentioned above, in the first months of the Nazi invasion. In these months (June through September) Yurburg was a kind of ghetto, where no one could enter or leave. Here too everything happened in stages. Groups of Jews were taken to the woods, one after the other, on the way to Smalininken, at the cemetery and other places where the elderly, women and children were brutally murdered. In Yurburg it was impossible to set up a resistance movement. The foreign surroundings alienated the Jews. And the Lithuanian "friends" -- if there were any -- were afraid to help.

However, in spite of everything, a few -- oh so few -- managed to organize into a group of Partisans and they went to the woods around Yurburg. They were joined by people from the Kovno ghetto and together they numbered 70. (See the article "People from Yurburg in the Forest" in the Book of Remembrance). Some of those from Yurburg in the forest were extremely brave and courageous; one of them even turned out to be a leader and daring warrior. This group carried out a number of daring actions, fighting as Partisans against German military units. The group of "people from Yurburg" in the forest became known as a brave group, which intimidated the Lithuanian villages in the area. The villages had to supply to the Yurburg Partisans everything they required and even shelter to women and children in their homes. Unfortunately, at the end of the war the "Yurburg" group was defeated. However, with their daring fighting, they survived for a long time and saved Jewish honor. Some youngsters from Yurburg at the Kovno ghetto joined the Kovno Partisans in the woods (see the article, "Daring Fscape of the Partisans in the Forest" on page 474).

A few of the youngsters, who were outside Yurburg when the War broke out, enlisted in the Lithuanian division, in the framework of the Red Army in Russia. The majority of the Lithuanian division was in fact composed of Jewish young men. Those from Yurburg played their part in the war as best they could and had the good fortune to return with the division to Lithuania and liberate it. In Jewish Yurburg the Jews did not live to see the day of liberation. They were no longer there. Only dust and ashes remained of the Jews of Yurburg.

THE HOLOCAUST REMEMBRANCE LAW
YAD VASHEM

"A memorial authority is hereby established -- YAD VASHEM -- to commemorate the six million Jews who were murdered by the Nazis and their collaborators; the families of the House of Jacob who were killed and destroyed by the oppressor, the communities, synagogues, movements and organizations, military, cultural, educational, religious and charity institutions that were destroyed by evil action, to protest and cry out to heaven on behalf of the People of Israel and its culture, the courage of sacred Jews who gave their life for their people; the courage of Jewish soldiers in the armies and underground fighters in settlements and forests, who found their death in the battles against the Nazi oppressor; the courageous deeds of the survivors of the ghettoes and their fighters; who rose up and started the revolt to save their people's honor; the glorious and persistent fight when countless Jewish homes were about to be lost with their humane outlook and Jewish culture; the daring efforts of the Christians, that never ceased, and the devotion and heroism of brothers who strove to save those who survived and liberated them, and the righteous gentiles, who gave their lives to save Jews."

TRANSLATION OF PAGES 377 - 387

YURBURG DESTROYED

The Story of Hannah Magidovitz as Recorded by Zevulun Poran

We are sitting in the home of Hannah Magidovitz, in the center of Rekhovoth. The apartment is spacious, furnished with taste and spotlessly clean. Around the table are also her husband, Shelomoh Goldman, Manager of the town's Post Office branch and her two charming daughters, one a teacher at the Ashkelon state school, the other, a nurse at the "Kaplan" hospital. The family extends a warm welcome to the guests. There is a festive atmosphere in the house. It is not every day that two such welcome guests appear. One has come from Tel Aviv and the other from Jerusalem; both are true Yurburgers, Shimon Shimonov and Zevulun Poran.

There are refreshments on the table and a pleasant conversation is taking place in a friendly and warm atmosphere of old friends. However, the clock does not stop ticking, and we hint at the purpose of our visit, the hosts are fully aware of it. It is getting late and everyone understands time has come to bring back the memories of those terrible days, in which the tragic history of Jewish Yurburg ends.

The husband and daughters leave the room, and we, the three Yurburgers, remain alone with our sorrow about the bitter fate of our Yurburg.

A moment of silence passes, and another one of heavy thoughts. Hannah's face is getting pale and red in turn. There are tears in her eyes and she finds it hard to swallow.

"To speak about Yurburg, the tragedy, it is impossible. Impossible! Those who were not there will not believe what I am saying."

Hannah is struggling with herself, overcomes her reluctance and starts to tell her story. Words in Hebrew and Yiddish, a medley of tongues, sounding like lamentation, sad.

The wailing of Hannah, the Jewish mother, daughter of the town of Yurburg, who calls to heaven: "Why, Oh God, why?" She speaks out against the cruel and indifferent world that brought destruction on Yurburg. For a moment we remember Hannah as a young girl, full of joy, and it is hard to imagine that this is the same Hannah, speaking in anger, avenging the women and children, young and old. An entire Jewish community was wiped out and is no longer - and only she, Hannah, the only witness, remains in order to tell the terrible story.

. . . It started one summer morning. The dawn disperses the misty watches of the night, a slight breeze, drops of dew; the pleasant odors of field and garden are in the air. The birds twitter, singing happily towards the start of a new day. Yes, a new day, Sunday, June 22, 1941. Yurburg is slumbering at this hour, sleeping as usual. Everything is restful and pleasant -until suddenly a terrible sound rips through silence,

"Jews, war, w-a-r. . . "

The sound ripped through the house, startled the whole family and made them get up from their beds. When we went outside we already saw many others; windows were opened nearby and far away, Jews looked out in surprise and awe. "What is going on?" Here and there those standing outside noticed airplanes raging through the sky, approaching Yurburg with a terrible noise, dropping bombs and destroying the surroundings of the town. Luckily most bombs fell into the Nieman and did not damage houses or people.

We spent hours waiting anxiously, tensely whispering "Hoi, what will happen?" Thus, without knowing what would happen to them, the helpless Jews stood around in small groups, whispering, their faces full of gloom.

Eight o'clock in the morning. The first rows of motor vehicles appeared in the streets and behind them the German "Wehrmacht" and behind the "Wehrmacht" rows of marching soldiers, facing West, on the road to Kovno. The Jews shivered and watched in terror as the German army took over the town, without any resistance from the Lithuanian army units which formed part of the Russian army.

After the "commandos" passed, the "Wehrmacht" infantry spread out onto all the roads, took over the government institutions and started to look for Russian and communist soldiers. Tumult broke out in town. Lithuanians and Jews, who were connected with the government institutions started to hide, and those who could flee, fled. Only a few managed to escape on the first steamship which left in the morning along the Nieman to Kovno. There was a situation of uncertainty in town. Jewish families started to gather together in order to ease the fear. Children cried and wailed and it is hard to describe what went on among the Jewish population on the morning of that cursed day. Many burst out and vented their feelings of frustration. When one of the neighbors shouted: "Jews, let's protect ourselves, let's hide in the public bath" they all got up and without a thought ran to the public bath, a large, strong building.

It seemed to many that its strong and thick walls would protect those inside. Fear is the Devil's Advocate. They thought that together they might be able to protect themselves. The public bath was full to the brim, a multitude of people pressed into this dubious shelter. And as the popular saying goes, a drowning man grasps at a straw, when he wants to save himself. Food was brought to the public bath for the little children and later also for the grownups, to strengthen their bodies and souls, enabling them to face the enemy when the time would come. These were difficult hours for those who had deliberately imprisoned themselves in this gray and depressing building on this first day, there are no words to describe their gloomy spirit.

Building that was reported to be the bathhouse - photo taken by Dr Leon Menzer in May 2001. [Not in original Yizkor Book]

At 4 p.m. the German soldiers discovered the hiding place. Four soldiers broke open the door and one of them entered and shouted the order: "Come out immediately!" In order to convince the people not to huddle there, he added: "it is more dangerous here, if the air force sees a large building standing out in the area - it may decide to bomb it!" However, no one agreed to leave the building, a discussion started with the soldiers, women and men implored and begged to be allowed to stay, but the soldiers had no mercy. At this stage the "Wehrmacht" soldiers did not yet show their true face. They started to calm the desperate Jews and assured them nothing bad would happen to them. The soldiers also told the agitated crowd that the Russians had attacked their country and that they had no choice but to defend Germany, their fatherland. One German soldier even boasted: " Never mind, in two weeks we will be in Moscow." He said this in an arrogant, self-assured manner as if this was wonderful news to the Jews as well. However, there was one soldier who stood aside and secretly whispered to the Jew standing next to him - "Yes, in two weeks we will be in Moscow, and in two years the Russians will be in Berlin." This was apparently an unusual German soldier; in fact, they all received orders and carried them out ruthlessly.

We must admit that the German soldiers, who were very aggressive, were courteous in their first meeting with the Jews, and even tried from time to time to calm the frustrated crowd. Having no choice, the Jews started to leave the public bath. Sad and perplexed they returned, stumbling, to the homes they had abandoned. We, unfortunate Jews, had no inkling yet of the German policy of misleading us.

The Jews of Yurburg passed the first night in great fear. No one removed his clothes or took off his shoes. No eye was closed. They had no appetite, were depressed and confused by so much fear of what lay ahead.

The next day, Monday, no one left his home. Jewish Yurburg was paralyzed. Business came to a complete standstill. There was no hunger yet. Jews sold part of their belongings to Lithuanians and bought food. All the neighbors and relatives gathered together in one house, it was very crowded, but the situation was still bearable. Jews said *"Zol nor nisht sein erger"* ("things should not be worse"). Nevertheless, we felt that the Lithuanians, the former Shaulists (now they called themselves partisans or activists) started to make themselves available to the Germans, enthusiastically assisting them, taking over the street. The attitude of these Shaulists towards the Jews was hostile and brutal. Their influence on the other Lithuanians grew by the day. Already on the second day the Lithuanians carried out severe beatings. The new rulers ordered all the Jewish boys, without exception, to assemble on Raisen street (Raseiniu Gatve) on Mordekhai (Mordechai) (Motl) Levyush's plot, a place later known as "Arbeits-Lager" (i.e. labor camp). From here Jews were sent for service in town such as: cleaning the streets, working in vegetable gardens and any assistance required by the Lithuanians. A Jew was appointed manager of the "Arbeits-Lager" and he was asked to carry out the authorities' orders.

Everyday another bad thing happened to us. The Lithuanians started to show their rudeness and tyranny. On the third day of the war an order was issued that the Jews had to wear a yellow patch on their clothes. Where to find yellow cloth? Here we got the idea to use the cloth of the Lithuanian flag, one of whose colors is of course yellow. We therefore tore up the Lithuanian flag, without any pangs of conscience, and sewed the patches for our clothes. Thus "adorned" with the yellow patches we were ordered to march along the pavement of the street. These and others were the orders we received every morning. The more the Lithuanians' atrocities increased, the more depressed we became, yet we tried to stand firm, as far as we could.

One day the Jews were ordered to destroy the Old Great Synagogue, break up its walls and everything inside, and distribute it all to the Lithuanians. It is impossible to describe how this order affected the town's Jews. This old synagogue was the pride of the Yurburg Jews. It was not only a house of prayer, but also a valuable cultural attribute of art. It was said that its construction was completed in the seventeenth century by the best Jewish artists of the time. The sacred ark was made of wood, carved by hand, with beautiful engravings of animals, plants, leafs, turtles, lions and birds. Then there was the beautiful chair of Eliyahu, used for brith-milah (bris). The old building was gray, but full of splendor and inspiration. The synagogue was "a little temple" not only for the Jews of Yurburg, but also for all the Jews of Lithuania, who came from far to see the Temple.

The building was famous beyond the borders of Lithuania as well. Then here comes the oppressor and orders: "get up and destroy your synagogue," the

"Holy of Holies" of Yurburg's Jews! But the order was given and the Jews had to implement it and those who did not observe it were beaten and forced to carry it out. The knees failed and the hands were shaking, but who could oppose these beasts? With tears in their eyes and broken hearts the Jews had to carry out this shameful job. Many Lithuanians came to watch the terrible deed, but only a few dared to take the loot.

Not far from the synagogue stood the "shekhite shtibel," a small building used for poultry slaughtering. This building too had to be destroyed. There were many feathers there, which were dispersed over the area; these feathers stuck to the Jews and they were so dirty it was hard to recognize them. Therefore the Shaulists, Lithuanians who were overseeing the crime, ordered them to go down to the Nieman River and wash in its water. During the destruction and also at the river the Shaulists tortured them, kicked them and pushed them into the water, an offensive and degrading sight.

The German soldiers stood next to the Lithuanians all the time and took pictures of the "action" carried out faithfully by their Lithuanian helpers. The Germans, for whom and at whose behest the Lithuanians gladly carried out these actions, cynically asked the Jews "why do the Lithuanians hate the Jews so much?"

Another thing that degraded and angered the Jews took place the next day. One of the religious ministrants in town was Cantor Alperowitz. An old man, tall and distinguished looking. On religious holidays he would appear with his chorus at the synagogue or the great seminar and pray and sing the melodies he himself composed. He was a learned man, very popular and venerated by the worshippers. The sons of the devil turned to him as well. They took him to the center of town, many Lithuanians thronging about; they attached a brick to his white beard and ordered him to march through the streets of the town. The Jews were called upon to watch the painful sight; some Jews pleaded for mercy and volunteered to take the old cantor's place on the shameful march, but they were refused. Thus the cantor had to go on his shameful walk, accompanied by the enemies' shouts of joy and the wailing of the Jews of Yurburg who were forced to watch this terrible ceremony, the likes of which had not been created by the devil yet.

Time passed, and there was no end to the malicious acts. One day the Jews were assembled and ordered to carry Stalin's statue in a parade through the streets of the town, to sing and dance, while the Lithuanians, the German soldiers at their side, marched along and tormented them, beat them and kicked them from one side to the other. Finally the parade reached Zarda, a broad square near the Nieman River. A high heap was made of Jewish books and writings and Stalin's statue was set in the middle. When the paper burned the Lithuanian's joy knew no end and they tortured the Jews. Children, women and men were ordered to sing and dance.

The Jews were forced to sing until the flame went out; they sang psalms and the well-known folk song "Arum dem fai'er mir singen lieder" (around the fire we sing songs), a Jewish revolt song, in front of their oppressors.

The acts of the Germans and the Lithuanians undermined our morale and we slowly became ever more indifferent to our fate. Nevertheless, when disaster struck our home and hit our family- says Hannah Magidovitz - we completely broke down. One day the Lithuanians, at the orders of their German masters, came to the Jewish homes looking for workers, they said. They took my father and younger brother somewhere. In this action 350 Jews were taken away. They were all ordered to bring along a shovel for digging. Thus our dear ones left on a silent road from which they never returned. A long, dreadful night fell over our home and over many homes in town, from where the men were taken forcefully, never to return. Only the next day did we learn of the terrible disaster. A Lithuanian, a farmer, was witness to the horror. After they were led into the forest they were at first ordered to dig pits, according to the witness, as deep as possible, and then to kill each other with the shovels in their hands.

Thus the earth swallowed them forever, without a sign or a mark on the large common grave. One day short letters were received from the "enlisted men" sent, as it were, to work. In their letters they wrote us that they were working on the floating of tree barges (traptim) and that there was no cause for concern. . After the horrors we had gone through, we had no illusions that our beloved ones were still alive.

A few days later another calamity took place. One evening, another count took place, this time under the pretense of concern for the sick and elderly. They promised to take the sick and weak to hospital where they would receive proper treatment. This was another deception which no one believed. We knew they were led to their death; women cried and pleaded for mercy, but there was no mercy.

Thus the sick and elderly were led on the road to Raseiniai at a distance of 18 kilometers. from Yurburg. The Lithuanians did not bother the sick and elderly with digging pits. The graves were already waiting to receive the dead. From this "action" no one returned either and no one was left alive. Again, according to the testimony of Lithuanian villagers, they were all brutally killed. Most of them were buried alive. The next day, when we were called to the "Arbeits - Lager" ("labor camp"), we found remnants of clothes and jewelry, removed from the dead.

Hundreds of Jewish men were led to the cemetery where they were brutally killed. 520 people, among them the leaders of the community, including Rabbi Rubinstein, revolted, shouted, shook their fists and fought to the bitter end. There were no illusions left. We knew our days were counted. Only women and children remained in the Jewish homes. However, the cruel fate did not spare them either. German planning and deception were constantly active. One day the women were called to headquarters, while the children had to remain at home. When we heard this, says Hannah, we hid mother on the attic, and we presented ourselves in her place. The women were told to stand together in the yard of "Talmud Torah," the large elementary school of the town. Hundreds of women were brutally taken to the headquarters, babies crying in their arms. We remained at the "Talmud Torah" from morning to night, says Hannah, without any food or drink. The Lithuanians behaved like cruel animals.

Early in the evening, Shaulists-Lithuanians arrived with automatic weapons and ordered us to line up, two in a row; they kicked and beat us to make us hurry. The wailing of the mothers and the cries of the babies went up to heaven, but the hearts of the murderers remained cold as stone. The Germans, masters of the land, stood at a distance with their cameras, as usual, watching their Lithuanian servants-helpers' actions with much interest and satisfaction.

There was much confusion, as the crowd of Shaulists-Lithuanians surrounded the poor women, hitting them brutally with the butts of their rifles. They particularly hit those who walked too slowly, children and they threw them onto the ground, to induce them to carry on. Late at night we reached the end of the road. We were in the thick Shventshani forest, frightened to death by the shadows of the trees. In the darkness we saw a deep pit, dug that day. Tumult broke out, and a terrible panic took hold of the women. The murderers fired into the air and shouted in frightening voices "Throw the children into the pits," they ordered the women to take off their clothes and leave them behind. It is hard to bring back to memory those awful moments at the place of murder. Mothers jumped with their children into the pits, some of them were shot, and others still breathed. At those crucial moments in a person's life -as strange as this may seem - the life instinct is extremely strong. My entire being started to throb with the instinct to live and a voice from deep down in my soul cried out "Live, live" says Hannah Magidovitz.

Among the Lithuanians I met near here was a young man, a shopkeeper from the Kalyani village, and he whispered to me - "Escape Hannah, escape!" The plan to escape had already come into my mind along the way. I told myself - I must return to save mother and my little sisters, who still remained hidden at home. Therefore I quickly took the decision to escape at all costs! - And thus at a certain moment, when confusion took over and the women started to cry and flee to the forest, and the Shaulists -Lithuanians ran after them and fired at them, bewildered and without thinking what I was doing, as if a spirit of madness had taken hold of me, I jumped behind a bush, a jump and another one and here I am behind a tree, and another tree and a third one, my legs carrying me in a mad race, further and further away into the darkness of the thick forest towards an unknown place. Shots? -They no longer frighten me: the quest for life throbs in me, hope, revenge! Thus I finally fell down on the cold earth, exhausted. The Lithuanians did not manage to harm me. They were drunk from alcohol as well as from victory. The lust to murder and the smell of blood prodded them to carry out these bestial acts.

When I recovered and my energy returned, I started to walk towards Yurburg, but I lost my way, and almost ran into a German (patrol) guard who called to me from afar "Wer ist hier?" (Who is there?). I went back from where I had come and at dawn I arrived at my home in Yurburg. At first I said nothing to my mother and sisters Zelda and Judith, who were still alive. Yet I was bothered by the idea - **"I must tell."** Those who remained had to know what the Lithuanians, the helpers of the Nazi Germans, had done to us and then I told them the bitter truth and I said:"we must escape immediately, find a place with the Lithuanians, otherwise we will be destroyed. Don't be deceived!"

We tried to look for a hiding place with Lithuanian gentiles, but we soon found out that all the gentiles had betrayed us. They regretted the murder and were afraid for their own lives. Perhaps they were afraid of being denounced [and being accused of helping the Jews]. That is how we were stuck between hammer and anvil, all we could do was to pray for mercy.

Only three days passed and the sword hit us again. In the morning all those who were left, without exception, had to gather in the notorious yard of Mordehai (Motl) Levyush, where the "Arbeits-Lager" (labor camp) was.

All day long Lithuanian soldiers, accompanied by the Germans, searched through all the Jewish homes to check whether anyone was left there. Indeed, no one was left. The few who were still alive knew their fate - death! However, a day of brutality and torture still lay ahead of us: intimidations, blows and humiliations. Towards evening we were ordered to leave the "labor camp" and go on a journey, the last journey of the last survivors of Yurburg.

When the last one left, Yurburg remained empty of its Jews, who had lived there for hundreds of years, built and cultivated it, borne children and raised generations faithful to their nation and the land of Lithuania, reliable partners for obtaining its independence. Now - the end had come! There is no Jewish Yurburg any longer! But no, there are still some survivors, and they are marching on their tragic march of death, straight towards the Shventshani forest, to the deep pits, which are opening their mouths to swallow up the murder victims. This time the survivors knew very well where the road was leading. No, they did not accept the judgment: they revolted, shouted, pleaded with the murderers, "what did we do wrong?" - Why kill human beings born in the image of God, but in response there were only impudent answers and severe beatings. Mothers told their older children to run away, not to surrender, to beat the murderers, save their lives. But what power do weak women and small children have in the face of the sophisticated Nazi machine? In a terrible battle of unequal forces they arrived at the end of the journey. Everything was prepared in advance, the murderers well trained, and the victims offered for slaughtering are pathetic and have no energy, they are pure and just in their soft existence and desperate struggle. No, this time they do not give up easily. Women attack the murderers, bite, hit, and shout. But the murderers close in on their victims. Shots are fired, the automatic rifles do not stop, shooting from every corner at anyone trying to escape, and they are many. The murderers run after them. There is panic and chaos and a struggle for life and death accompanied by shouts that tear apart the walls of the earth.

I, the young girl, already experienced in this fateful test, am standing among the girls of my family, my mother crying bitterly, my little sisters holding on to me with all their might. I feel the throb of life in them and at the same time a shot is fired, mother is shocked - she throws me her scarf (patshele) - and shouts **"Run away my daughter - Hannale, flee! Remember - Revenge mein Tochter (my daughter), revenge! "**

And I, I don't know how I dared throw myself into the turmoil this time, into the thick bushes. I jump behind the Germans and Lithuanians and flee, flee, while the murderers are running after me, steadily firing at me, but the bullets don't hit me. The murderers hit trees and bushes, and I manage to escape from their murderous hands. I have no energy left in me, but I continue to crawl and go away as far as possible from the valley of death. I did not look back, I knew that behind me was death, destruction, and I have to go on living. **My mother had placed an important responsibility on my shoulders: To avenge my family and the Jews of Yurburg.** This time I knew I was not going to Yurburg, there was no longer any Yurburg for me. When the last group of Yurburg Jews died, my Yurburg died too.

At that time I did not know whether I was the only one who had been saved or if other women too had managed to stay alive. I went into the direction of the town of Erzhvilki, where I had Jewish acquaintances. I hoped to find a few survivors there. I walked through fields and forests, slept awhile under the open sky, was hungry, and towards morning I arrived, exhausted, on the second day of my wandering, at the entrance of Erzhvilki. I was very thirsty. I went up to a farmer and asked for water, but he chased me away. I drank water from a puddle I found, and continued to knock on farmers' doors. Finally, one farm woman agreed to let me stay in the cowshed, near the pigsty, although she knew I was Jewish. She told me that only yesterday an "action" had taken place of the Erzhvilki Jews, and that they had all been brutally murdered, and buried in a mass grave, close to the town.

I met but a few "good" Lithuanians, but even the most humane among them were not inclined to take in a Jew. Finally I found shelter for a while in the home of an intelligent man, broadminded. He told me that two Jewish boys, who had been saved from the "actions," were hiding in the town and that they came from Yurburg.

With the assistance of my landlord a meeting took place with them and to my joy I knew them well, they were Tsevi (Hirshke Abramovitz) and Klein (I forgot his first name). They looked sad and thin. They smoked a lot and told me they had managed to escape, after their families were murdered. Now they intended to return to Yurburg, not in order to live there, but to set it on fire. They talked of their plan with burning eyes. I said good-by to them and did not see them again. Later I was told that Yurburg was set on fire and burnt. I don't

426

The Yurburg Yizkor Book

know if the two really managed to take revenge on the murderers of the Yurburg Jews, but it is true that a large part of the town center burned and went up in flames. Revenge? Maybe, but even if they did take revenge, it is small compared to the terrible, horrendous crime perpetrated against the Jews of Yurburg by beasts. This awful shame, the mean and planned murder to destroy the Jewish communities will not be wiped from our memories, it will cry out forever, and as long as we are alive we will not forget or forgive!

After a long wandering, dangers lurking everywhere, I reached the Kovno Ghetto, in order to tell the Jews there the bitter truth about the destruction of the Jews of Yurburg. In those days the Jews in the Kovno Ghetto did not yet know what lay ahead of them. Jews still had false hopes, inside the ghetto, and I felt sorry to disappoint them and disperse their illusions.

When the survivors of Yurburg left the graves of their families and relatives behind, they embarked on a difficult journey to Eretz Israel, it was their yearning and the yearning of the martyrs of Lithuania who did not have the good fortune to arrive hither.

Among the immigrants, the survivors of Yurburg, was also Hannah Magidovitz.

The few survivors of the holocaust, will continue to spin the thread of continuation forever, here in the independent State of Israel, they, their sons and the sons of their sons after them, as revenge on the murderous gentiles, and for the establishment of a secure shelter for the people of Israel in centuries to come.

ADDITIONAL DETAILS ABOUT THE ANNHILATION OF THE JEWS OF YURBURG

The Testimony of Hannah Magidovitz

At the end of World War II, when Hannah Magidovitz was in Germany, she was asked to testify in person about the destruction of the Jewish community of Yurburg. Her testimony was written down by L. Koniukhovsky, at the municipal hospital of Munich, the MUNCHEN KRANKENHAUS, in Germany, on April 30, 1947, and signed by Hannah Magidovitz and Dr. Peisakhovitz, the Chief Physician (Chef Artz) of the hospital.

This testimony is kept at the Yad Vashem Archives in Jerusalem.

On June 22, 1941, German soldiers were already marching through the streets of Yurburg at 6 o'clock in the morning. Only very few people managed to escape and save their lives. Hannah, her father Shalom and her three sisters hid in the farmer Grinberg's cellar, behind the Jewish cemetery. The German soldiers burst into the cellar and checked whether there were any Russian soldiers there. They sent the Jews back to their home in Yurburg. The German army units continued for a number of days to march on to the town of Kovno and pursued the retreating Russian army from there.

Jews belonging to the communist party, among them Hannah's brother Heshel, went to Russia. The moment the German army entered, the Lithuanians gathered their courage and organized into active gangs - active Shaulists - put a green ribbon on their arms and became the town's rulers. The commander (Kommandant) of the town belonged to the German army and the student Mikas was the Chief of Police, his assistant was a policeman from the period of presidency of Smetona, Kilikevicius. Shukaitis was the leader of the Lithuanian gangs. A German, a citizen of the town, was appointed mayor. During the time of the communists he was the manager of the public kitchen and he supported the communists. His surname was Gefner. Hannah still remembers a few active Lithuanian gang members, among them: two brothers, from the Gymnasium, Vakseliai, the kiosk owner Tselkis and the nationalist from Smetona times, Blatvinskis and others.

One of the murderers' first evil "actions" was to gather many Jews next to the synagogue, take a purification board, put the barber (Parikmakher) Yitskhak Kopilovitz and Bibles on the board, and take them to the Nieman River. Here the Jews were ordered to "drown" the barber Kopilovitz and also drown each other. The barber saved himself by swimming. The Germans ordered Hannah's younger brother, the 13-year old Velfke, to drown the manly Jew Tetke Levinzon. Levinzon too saved himself, and Velvele returned home, started to cry and told his family the terrible story.

One day the Jews were ordered to destroy the Great Synagogue and house of learning. They removed the Torah Scrolls from the house of worship; the hooligans unrolled them and danced on them. The Jews were also ordered to bring their prayer shawls, prayer books and mezuzoth from their homes, putting them all into one big pile. The Jews of Yurburg were very upset by this demeaning and cruel act and even the non-believers among them cried bitterly. The Lithuanian mob shouted "Bravo" and was full of joy and merriment. The next day the Jews were ordered to destroy the old synagogue and the coachmen were ordered to gather the boards and panels and bring them to the yards of the Lithuanians. Only the bare walls remained of the house of worship that was built of stone. The Jews were forced to transfer all the holy books to Zarda (an empty lot near the Nieman River) and put them in one big pile. The women were ordered to clean the destroyed places of prayer on the Sabbath. The hooligans put Mrs. Berzaner on a wheelbarrow (a Tatschka) and a 12-year old boy was ordered to take her to the Nieman River. On the way Mrs. Berzaner saw a German officer. She jumped from the wheelbarrow, ran to the officer and begged him to shoot her. The officer replied he could not do so, as the Lithuanians now were the rulers. The hooligans continued to torture her and hit her. Everybody was ordered to enter the Nieman and "bathe" with their clothes on, Hannah Magidovitz was among them. The men were ordered to "bathe" fully clothed every day after work.

Each day, at 6 o'clock in the morning, men and women were ordered to present themselves at Levyush's yard, in order to go to work. The women were under the command of the Jew Friedman, the former owner of the "Versailles" hotel. He was close to the Lithuanians, for he had belonged to the "Shaulists" In the end, he too was led to his death in the last "action," just like the others. He was tortured and it is said he was even hung from a tree.

On July 10, the men were ordered to bring digging tools (shovels, spades etc.) and go to work. The order was particularly tough this time. The Lithuanian overseers carried rifles and there were a few Germans among them as well. It was a secret "action."

In the evening, when the women returned from work, they did not find their husbands. Hannah, too returned from work, and did not find her father, Shalom or her brother Velvele. The next day it was rumored the men had been shot at the cemetery.

The woman Dobe Lam went to the cemetery to find signs of graves, but found nothing, the large grave was well hidden. Most women could not imagine that their husbands had been shot, although the Lithuanians living next to the cemetery knew, and told the story about the sadistic acts that had taken place there.

It was said, for example, that the men were ordered to dig the graves and kill each other with the spades they held. Fathers were ordered to kill their sons and sons their fathers, a truly terrible sight, 550 Jews were shot. Among the dead were the physicians Dr. Karlinsky, Dr. Gershovitz (from Ponivez), Dr.

Reikhman, the pharmacist Bergovsky, the dentist Dr. Shimonov and the dentist Dr. Kopelov, the lawyer Segal, the cantor Alperovitz, the ritual slaughterer Aharon (Archik) Shlomovitz, Rabbi Rubinstein, businessman Levyush, Shalom Magidovitz, Hannah's father, and her brother Velvele; textile merchant Hirsch Purveh and his brother in law Mendel Furman and his 16-year old son Mosheh, Reuven Naividel - a businessman and owner of an iron shop; Hayim Rodensky and his father in-law Levinberg, the owner of the steamships and Karabelnik, his partner in the boats and barges business, etc. One Lithuanian brought Mrs. Vilonsky her picture that he found in the pocket of K. Levin's clothes. Torture and problems were a daily occurrence, but the tragedy of the cemetery was never forgotten.

Immediately after the "men's action," Hannah Magidovitz's mother, Feige-Mirel, arrived in Yurburg from Kovno, as well as Hannah's sister Judith, with her husband Hirshel Zelik and their two children, the 2-year old Gershon, Yudele and the one and one-half year old Tsadikel. Those were the days of the humiliation of men and women. On Sunday morning women and children were ordered to organize in rows in the streets and walk to the Zarda, the area near the Nieman River. They had to sing and dance on the way. However, this was merely a "rehearsal." The "performance" only started at 12 o'clock, when the worshippers at the Catholic house of worship went out into the street and saw the humiliating parade of the Jews. Four men, Alter Stern, Notl Mendelovitz, Velvel Portnoi and another person (?) "had the honor" of carrying a few boards tied together (a Trage-nasilke) with pictures on them of the Soviet leaders - Stalin, Lenin, Molotov and others. In the middle, among the pictures, was Stalin's statue. The entire parade arrived at the Zarda, close to the Nieman River, and here the women were ordered to form a circle around the pictures, the men behind them.

They all had to sing Soviet and Jewish songs, and dance around the fire in which the pictures of the Soviet leaders were burnt. In the course of the "procession" the men were ordered to throw stones at Stalin's statue and in the end, to kneel and kiss the Lithuanian earth. Hannah and her sisters Zelda and Zisa also "took part" in the humiliating performance.

One Tuesday, before Rosh Hashanah (the Jewish New Year), all the childless women were ordered to present themselves at Levyush' yard. The Lithuanian policeman Mikas Levitskas addressed the women and advised them not to sell their belongings, as the husbands would soon return and receive wages for their work. They believed him. The next day they were again ordered to present themselves at 6 o'clock in the evening, this time they numbered 200. Again they were advised not to sell anything and to hope "*Az man wet noch darfen leben*," i.e. "all the belongings will be needed in the future." And again there was an "invitation" to meet on Thursday.

This time there were already 300 women, among them sick women too, who had been taken from their beds by the murderers. Armed Lithuanian guards took up position at Levyush's yard. A curfew was imposed on those remaining at home, including the men. The men were told that work would start at 8 o'clock Friday morning. When the men came to work at Levyush' yard, the women were no longer there, and only a few remnants of clothes were left behind. Others also found hidden jewelry and money. One young girl, Yokhke Kushelevitz, found her mother's handkerchief in the toilet. Everyone understood the 300 women had been murdered. Lithuanians said the women had been taken to the Kalnienai village during the night, 5 kilometers from Yurburg, in the direction of Smalininken, and there they had all been shot. Policeman-murderer Butvinskis told the women who came to work that the women had been given clothes and they had been taken to do farm work in villages. The murderers continued to spread the rumor that all the women were well and that they were working on farms. It was also said that 70-year old Mrs. Pulovin wrote a letter that she was working and all was well with her, but no one saw the letter.

Immediately after the "action" of the women, the policemen passed among all the houses of the town and collected the sick and weak. One Jew, Hirschel Kobelkovsky had to bring his 65-year old neighbor, Mosheh Kaplan, to the labor camp and the man died on the way. When the women arrived at the labor camp the next day, they no longer found the sick and weak. Lithuanians said they had been sent to Rasein on carriages and had been killed on the way. There were no accurate details in those days.

On September 6, 1941 the hooligan policemen again burst into the Jewish homes and took away all the children and women who no longer had husbands and led them to "Talmud Torah." Here they were told that a sort of Jewish ghetto would be set up, where mothers and children would be taken care of. Only very few women obeyed and went to the gathering point. Many women fled and hid. On September 8, 1941, the hooligan policemen searched the homes and gathered all the women who had no husbands to support them. On this day many women who did have providers were also added. Mrs. Polak, for example, who had three daughters working at the labor camp. One of the daughters, Miriam, quickly ran to the leader of the hooligans, Sukaitis, and asked him to release her mother. Shukaitis demanded 25,000 Rubles as a redemption fee. Miriam and her sisters claimed they only had 15,000 Rubels. Shukaitis refused to release their mother who was imprisoned at "Talmud Torah." Miriam then turned to the German Kommandant of the town, and he replied that her efforts were useless. They are all going to work. Having no choice, the three girls went back to labor camp, crying.

On Monday afternoon Hannah was at home with her sister Judith and her two children. Suddenly policeman Kilikevicius burst into their home with his friend Motskus and urgently demanded to see their mother. Hannah replied that mother was not at home and that she was ready to come instead. They agreed and asked her to put on a coat. Hannah refused to put on the coat and said "you'll be able to shoot me without a coat too." The hooligans hit Judith on the nose, and she started to cry. At that time her husband Hirshel-Zelig was still working at the labor camp and therefore he was not taken to "Talmud Torah."

This time Hannah was spared too.

The next day, September 8, Friedman called Hannah to the labor camp. Friedman promised her no harm would come to her. On the same day the chief of the region (Rasein) arrived with the awful Sukaitis, and they ordered all the women without husbands to go to work. They all burst out in tears. Hannah too bade farewell to her sister Zelda, whose husband was still working at the labor camp. It is believed the order was a reaction to the Polak sisters' denunciation of Shukaitis and his demands for money. The women were led to "Talmud Torah" and from here they were all taken in the direction of Smalininken. Farmers with tools joined the hooligans accompanying the women, volunteering to help the policemen. Hannah knew a few farmers from Yurburg and the little town of Skirstamun, from where the Jewish women were also taken.

One of the hooligans from Skirstamun, who knew Hannah, advised her to escape, as the women were led to hard labor. Hannah decided not to separate from the women at this stage. After a tiring march of 7 kilometers on the road, the women were directed towards the town of Tavrig. After another 1/2 kilometer they arrived at the forest, where they saw large pits that had been dug. It is hard to describe what took place at the forest. The murderers ordered the women to climb on the heaps of earth forthwith. The women panicked. They embraced their children, cried, lamented and swore. The murderers, on their part, started to beat the women with their tools and ordered them to throw the children into the pits. Under the pressure, some women threw their children into the pits and jumped in after them. One woman, Mrs. Perl Beder-Stern, from Yurburg, refused to throw her child into the pit. She went crazy and started to smash the child's head against the tree next to her. All the women screamed and fought the murderers. Then the murderers used their weapons and the battle between the poor women and the inhuman, armed hooligans went on till the bitter end.

During the tumult, a Lithuanian from among the group of murderers, who knew Hannah, went up to her and said: "Run away, you'll catch up with death later." Hannah, who had already considered escaping on the way, immediately decided to run away from the pits of death. It was dark outside already, and it rained now and then. Hannah jumped and disappeared among the trees. They shot at her, but missed their target. Hannah ran away from the place of tragedy and for a long time she heard shots and women's shouts and children's cries. When she grew tired, Hannah sat down on a sawn-off tree trunk to rest. When it grew quiet, and hundreds of women and children had been swallowed up by death. Hannah heard the voices of the hooligans, quarreling about the loot: watches, rings, jewelry etc. Finally they got drunk and went away. Hannah is convinced that on the part of the Germans, only the Kommandant of the town and one of his assistants, a Wachtmeister, took part in this terrible "action." She does not know who gave the order to fire.

Hannah remained in the forest till early morning, and when she started to walk, she lost her way. When she saw a farm, she went in to ask for a drink of water, but the farmer chased her away. Here the hooligans found and caught her. They decided to kill her, but luckily her Lithuanian acquaintance was among them. He took it upon himself to carry out the murder. The others went away and her Lithuanian acquaintance demanded compensation for saving her life.

He led her to Yurburg as a "prisoner" and took her to her home. In the afternoon the Lithuanian came to fetch his compensation, and Hannah gave him her late father's gold watch.

Hannah returned home, her feet wounded. She needed rest and recovery, but she was unable to find peace. She could not put the terrible sights she had witnessed out of her mind. She told the truth of what had happened to the group of women in the forest to everyone. Not everybody believed her, thinking such barbaric behavior, killing women and children in cold blood, could not be possible.

On Thursday September 11,1941 the Lithuanian policemen and their hooligan helpers again demanded that all the Jews, women and men, present themselves at the labor camp at Levyush's yard.

On Friday, September 12, 1941, the Lithuanian policemen and their hooligan helpers searched all the homes and took away all those who were still alive, including the children. The Jews had become numb and indifferent and took the "mobilization" into their stride. The hooligans came to Hannah's home too, and found her mother, Feige-Mikhal and her sisters. The policeman Valechkus was among the hooligans, he knew Hannah from the previous "action" near the pits in the forest. He wanted to separate Hannah from the others. She refused to go with the policeman, but her family told her to go and, should she remain alive, take revenge on the hooligans. "You must go," her mother told her, even if it means destruction. Thus her mother and sisters said good-bye to Hannah, with tears in their eyes, following in the path of many others. The policeman took Hannah to Levyush' house and locked her up in a tiny room, on the upper floor of the house. The room contained the clothes of the women who had been taken to the death pits.

Through a small peephole Hannah saw how cruelly the hooligans treated the Jews, the men, women and children, the remnants of the Jewish community in Yurburg. The hooligans demanded the Jews hand over money and valuables, such as gold, silver, jewelry etc. The hooligans tortured the poor unfortunate people, the last Jews in Yurburg. The mob stood outside, close to the place of detention, waiting for the loot.

On Friday September 12, 1941 at 4 o'clock in the afternoon, things came to an end. All of the unfortunate Jews were led on their last journey to the forest, closely guarded by the hooligans. The sobbing children were put on a carriage. Preceded by the carriage, men and women marched in the direction of Smalininken. Hannah saw the dreadful scene from the peephole in the little room where she was imprisoned. She was heartbroken, and on the spot she decided "to escape to safe her life!" That same night she forced open the door leading to the roof and climbed down to her freedom. The hooligans were drunk, rejoicing in their victory, and did not pay attention to her.

Hannah roamed through the villages for a number of weeks. Alone, dressed up in farmers' clothes, she decided to go to the Kovno Ghetto. And indeed, on the night of October 27,1941 she reached her goal. In the ghetto she met her sister Hayah Abramson, whose husband was no longer with her.

The next day, October 28, 1941, the major "action" took place at the Kovno Ghetto. Hannah was saved and shared the fate of the other Jews of the ghetto. She worked in labor camps and at the time of the evacuation she was sent to Germany, spending time at the Stutthof and other labor camps. When she was at a camp near Danzig, Hannah contracted typhus. Many women fell sick there and died. Hannah was lucky, and on March 10, 1945 the Red Army liberated the camp and took the sick women to the hospital. Hannah recovered and remained in Germany until she went to Israel together with all the other refugees.

Hannah goes to Israel. She leaves the Diaspora. Yurburg is no longer. Hannah left behind many graves in Yurburg of her family, and bitter memories of the last days of the unforgettable Yurburg community.

Testified: Hannah Magidovitz

Translated into Hebrew from Yiddish by Zevulun Poran

Photo reported to have been taken in Yurburg
[Photo not in original Yizkor book.Courtesy of the Vilna Jewish Museum.]

TRANSLATION OF PAGES 395-397

A FAMILY IN DIRE STRAITS

By Bela Bernstein - Mering

Bella Berstein - Mering, born in Yurburg, testified at the Landsberg camp in Germany to L. Koniukhovsky, on 16 January 1947, describing her fate and the fate of her family during the holocaust.

(From the collection of "Yad Vashem"documents, Jerusalem)

Bella, the daughter of Wolf Bernstein, was born in Yurburg. Her father was a wealthy Jew and her family was well known in Yurburg. Bella married Leo Mering and lived in Memel (Klaipeda) until after the evacuation of the town's Jews by the German Nazis. Bella, her husband and daughter Yetti, moved to Kovno.

When war broke out they were sent, like all the Kovno Jews, to the ghetto on August 7, 1941. On that day Bella and her daughter was already in the ghetto, but her husband remained behind for a day, busy transferring their belongings to the ghetto. He was caught by the Nazis and together with 550 other men they were taken to the Fort VII near Kovno. Later it was said they had all been shot......A short while later Bella's brother, Shmerl Bernstein, arrived at the Kovno Ghetto, together with his wife Khavah, born in Kybartai, their daughter Yetta and their son Ze'ev-Wolf (See article in Appendix). They had been saved, as will be described hereunder, from the terrible "actions" in Yurburg and arrived at the Kovno Ghetto. Shmerl Bernstein was born and lived in Yurburg until the outbreak of World War II. In Yurburg Shmerl Bernstein was the Manager of the Kommertz Bank. He lived in his private, two-story home, on the German Street (Daitsche Gass). There was a large fruit garden around the house. The moment the Germans entered, the Jews of Yurburg could not to escape. Yurburg was only 9 kilometers away from the German border. On Sunday, June 22, 1941, the Nazi soldiers arrived in the Kovno streets too. The town was captured without a battle.

When Shmerl Bernstein arrived at the Kovno Ghetto, he told Bella what had happened to him and to the Jews of Yurburg. The Germans had already entered Yurburg in the early morning hours, said Shmerl and they immediately took over the town. The Germans also came to Shmerl's beautiful home. The German officers thought the house was an elegant place of residence so they confiscated the house and turned it into their home.

The Germans found a visiting card (Visit-Karte - Visa) in Shmerl's home on which was written: Shmaryahu (Shmerl) Bernstein, Manager of the Komertz Bank in Yurburg. One of the officers read what was written on the card and commented cynically: "Jezt wirst du nicht mehr Bankdirektor sein, du wirst bei uns ein Stiefelputzer sein " - i.e. Shmerl would no longer serve as Director, but as a shoe-shiner. Indeed that is what happened. They turned him into the shoe-shiner of the officers in his own home, where they resided.

From left to right, Dora Arshtein, Fievel Chosid (Jack Cossid 's brother) and Miki Melnick. This was taken in front of the Komertz in Yurburg before Fievel Chossid entered the Lithuanian Army on Dec. 30, 1931.

[Photos not in original Yizkor book. From photo album of Jack Cossid.]

Komertz Bank Employees

From left to right: Jack Cossid, Miki Melnik, the sister of Schmerl Bernshtein (the bank director), Schmerl Bernshtein (brother of Boris), Fievel Chosid, (Jack's brother) and Dora Arshtein. Jack replaced his brother at the bank when Fievel went into the Lithuanian Army.

[Photos not in original Yizkor book. From photo album of Jack Cossid.]

In the first week when they took over Yurburg, the Nazis, assisted by the Lithuanian hooligans, arrested the well-known physicians: Dr. Karlinsky, Dr. Gershovitz, the dentist Shimonov, the dentist Kopelov, and the owner of the pharmacy Bergovsky, as well as other prominent people of the town. The cruel Lithuanians, who worked in the service of the Nazis, tortured and humiliated them, and took them to the Jewish cemetery, where they were all shot. The pharmacy owner's wife, Genya Bergovsky, arrived at the Kovno Ghetto a few days after Shmerl Bernstein. Genya said her husband had been forced to leave the pharmacy, dressed in his white coat, preparing drugs for the sick. Genya's pleas and supplications were to no avail. The murderers merely reassured her that her husband would return.

In the course of polishing the German officers' shoes, Shmerl Bernstein became friendly with them. When the Lithuanian murderers arrested the prominent townspeople, they also wanted to arrest Shmerl. But the German officers protected their efficient shoe-shiner, and did not arrest him. Shmerl told all this, as well as other stories, to Bella when he arrived at the Kovno Ghetto. One day the murderers took the women, children and elderly out of their homes and gathered them together at the "Talmud Torah" yard. Here the murderers kept them for several days and nights, hungry and exhausted. Later, they led them a few kilometers along to the Kalnienai village, where they were all cruelly shot. The men were shot one or two months later. No one was left in Yurburg. Bella no longer remembers all the terrible things that happened in those days, but she remembers one detail connected with her brother. During the days when the women, children and elderly were detained at the "Talmud Torah" yard, Shmerl managed, after many efforts, to remove the dentist's wife Mrs. Kopelov, (nee Goldheim in Mariampol), together with her two daughters. Mrs. Kopelov left Yurburg with her two daughters, heading for Kovno. However, they disappeared, and it is not known what happened to them.

When the last Jews in the Kovno Ghetto were sent to camps in Germany, at the end of the war, Shmerl Bernstein, his wife and children hid in a "malinah," a kind of cellar in the ghetto. The "malinah" was blown up by the Lithuanian murderers and everyone inside was killed.

Thus quite a few Jewish families and persons who tried to save themselves were killed, betrayed by destiny. They failed to escape from the claws of the Nazi beast and found their death and burial under the ruins of the "malines" at Slabodka.

In those days there were no Jews left at the ghetto -and Jews no longer walked on the earth of Kovno.

May their souls be bound in the bond of life.

Bela Bernstein - Mering

Translation into Hebrew by Zevulun Poran

Ghetto Kovno (Slabodka) - *Valley of Tears of the Jews of Kovno and other places including the escapees from Yurburg - Esther Luria*

TRANSLATION OF PAGES 398 - 403

YURBURG IN THE FIRST DAYS OF THE SHOAH

From the Yiddish book *"LITE"*

Published in New York in 1951, pages 1849-1854

By Tsevi Levit

Yurburg lies in the western part of Lithuania, 10 kilometers from the German border, at the time of the holocaust about 2,000 Jews were living there. The Germans conquered the town without any resistance, and on June 22,1941 at 8 o'clock in the morning the German warriors were already walking through the streets of the town. The Yurburg residents, Jews and non-Jews alike, were stunned, and many of them, especially those who had connections with Soviet authorities, tried to escape. Some of them managed to flee by boarding the steamship that left that morning.

The regular German army was the first to take over the town. They did not single out the Jews, or treat them badly. The Jews sensed something might happen to them, and huddled together. It is not known where it originated, but a call was heard to go to the bathhouse. It was a large, strong building, with thick walls and the Jews thought they would be safer there. They all went to the bathhouse and crowded there. At first, food was brought only for the babies, but later for the adults too.

The moment they arrived in town, the Germans started to look for possible pockets of resistance, and that is how they noticed the crowd that had gathered at the bathhouse.

Four soldiers broke open the doors of the bathhouse and ordered the Jews to leave. They tried to convince the crowd that it was a very dangerous place, explaining that the building drew attention, due to its size, and a plane might bomb it, causing far more casualties to those inside than outside. They also told the Jews they had nothing to fear, for no harm would come to them. The Jews were impressed by the German soldiers' courtesy and insistence, and they left the bathhouse.

In the first days the Lithuanian "activists" were already starting to get organized. They put themselves at the disposal of the Germans, and started to take part in the government. Their influence grew by the day, and the Germans gradually transferred handling of the local population to them. A Lithuanian Police was immediately set up, headed by the teacher of the Gymnasium Levitskas. Hoffner was appointed mayor.

On the second day of the war an order was issued obliging all the young Jews, without exception, to gather at Motl Levyush's yard, on Rasein Street. This place became the labor camp. Each day the young men were sent on different kinds of jobs in town. They cleaned the streets, worked in the parks and carried out all sorts of public work.

Each day a new decree was issued: it was forbidden to walk on the sidewalks, a yellow patch had to be worn, etc.

One day the Lithuanian soldiers' wrath fell on the Great Synagogue. It was a very special building, dating from the seventeenth century. Its Holy Ark, the pulpit and Eliyahu's beautiful chair were decorated in splendid woodcuts. This synagogue was the pride of the Yurburg people. Now the Jews were ordered to destroy the synagogue, tear down its walls and distribute everything inside to the local Lithuanians. The Jews carried out the order with tears in their eyes, their knees trembling. The Lithuanian throngs stood around them and looked on, but only a few agreed to take the spoils.

Next to the synagogue stood a small building, used as a poultry slaughterhouse "a Shekhita Shtibel." The Lithuanians ordered its destruction as well. The building was full of feathers, and when the Jews started to destroy the building, the feathers stuck to them and they got very dirty. The Lithuanian "activists," who were overseeing the destruction, ordered the Jews to go down to the Nieman River and wash themselves. During the destruction and near the river they tortured the Jews, beat them, kicked them and chased them into the water.

The Germans stood around and took photographs. Some asked: "Why do the Lithuanians hate the Jews so much?"

The next day, the torture continued. This time Cantor Alperovitz was the town's victim, an old Jew, tall and distinguished looking. They took the cantor to the center of town, tied a stone to his gray beard and dragged him through the streets of the town.

On June 28, 1941, on the Sabbath morning, all the Jews were ordered to go to work and pull out weeds in the streets. They were also ordered to bring all their books, at 4 o'clock in the afternoon, to the synagogue yard, and the old rabbi, Dayan (religious judge), Rabbi Hayim Reuven Rubinstein was forced to bring his books and manuscripts there on a wheelbarrow.

At 5 o'clock the Lithuanians ordered the Jews to remove the Torah scrolls from the synagogues. They were put on the pile of books, and everything was set on fire. The next day all the Jews were ordered to gather next to the town's bookstore, and it was threatened that anyone who refused would be shot. The Jews lined up in rows of three.

Four of the strongest Jews were ordered to remove a statue of Stalin from the store. Pictures of the most important Soviets were placed next to the women. They had to parade through the streets of the town. The teacher Levitskas and the policemen Butvinskis and Kilikevitshus were in charge of the parade. They arrived at the sports grounds near the Nieman. The Lithuanians were already there, "the intelligentsia" up front. They were very happy to welcome the parade. Stalin's statue was placed on a table prepared for the purpose, and all the Jews were ordered to stand around it. One of the homeowners was ordered to read a speech from paper handed to him, containing degrading and nasty words about the Jewish people. After the speech, the statue and pictures were thrown into the fire, and the Jews were forced to dance around the fire and sing. They sang psalms, from the bottom of their heart. The Germans took photographs of the scene.

The Jews used to buy food at the food stores. They were the last in line. Only after the non-Jews bought everything they needed, could the Jews buy something.

Yurburg, or as the Germans called it, Georgenburg, is 10 kilometers from the German border, and it is included in a 25 kilometers strip for which the Gestapo in Tilsit received an order to exterminate the Jews.

The head of the Gestapo at Tilsit, Boehme, immediately started to plan the extermination. Thursday July 3, 1941 was to be the day. After consultations with mayor Hoffner, the Jewish cemetery was chosen as the place of murder.

Details about the process of preparations and events on the day of the mass murder were heard at the German Court in Ulm, where the members of the Gestapo in Tilsit stood on trial. The record shows the following:

On the morning of July 3, 1941 Boehme and his helpers arrived in town together with 30 to 40 Germans from Smalininken (the border town on the German side). Small groups were formed of the Gestapo, together with Lithuanian assistants, policemen, who were ordered to take the Jewish men from their homes. When the number was insufficient, the teams went back once more to look for Jews and they returned with another 60 men. Three women with their children, who did not want to separate from their husbands, joined the group of men. During the arrest, a Lithuanian doctor asked one of the Gestapo leaders called Karsten, to release the Jewish doctor who was among the detainees. He said the Jewish doctor was a surgeon, and the population needed him badly. When the Lithuanian doctor repeated his request to Boehme, the latter hit him severely. The arrested Jews numbered over 300.

The detainees were led on foot through the town to the Jewish cemetery. Here they had to hand over all their valuables and take off their clothes. The Jews were ordered to dig more pits, as the existing ones did not suffice for all the detainees. During the digging of the pits, the Germans ordered the Jews to hit each other with the spades, and promised that those who won would live.

The victims were led along by the Germans and the Lithuanians with threats, shouts and blows, their cries went up to heaven. They had to stand next to the pits, facing their graves. Some of them were forced to kneel down. The murderers went up to each of them, shot them in the neck, and kicked them into the pit. As the victims were brought in at great speed, those who arrived witnessed what happened to the others. The Lithuanians, who resided at the two neighborhoods close to the cemetery, looked on.

Among the victims was a Jewish customs clearance agent, who during World War I had served in the German army, and received the most distinguished service award, the "Iron Cross" Grade 1. He attacked Boehme, but was immediately silenced by a murderer's bullet.

Many ran away from the pits. The murderers and guards pursued those who tried to escape. A few Germans and Lithuanians were hurt during the chase.

In this "action" 322 Jews were murdered, among them five women and children. Once the murderers had finished their job, a meal was prepared and there was plenty of vodka.

That same day another 80 men, who had been hiding, were caught and arrested. At 10 o'clock in the evening, policeman Butvinskis told them they would be shot at 3 o'clock. According to the report, the Jews were not particularly impressed, no one cried and there even was someone who had an annual Remembrance Day (Yahrzeit). All the detainees ardently prayed "Ma'ariv" (afternoon prayer) in a group of ten (minyan). The order was not carried out, and they were not shot. Those aged 15-50 who were still alive, were taken to work, and the old men were forced to present themselves at the police twice a day.

On July 21, 1941, 45 old men were arrested when they presented themselves, and were transferred on three carriages of Jewish coachmen to Rasein for a medical check-up, it was claimed. On the way to Rasein, at kilometer 15, they were murdered, together with the Jewish coachmen and the Jews of the small towns in the area. Before they were killed, the old men were forced to write to their families that they were working and did not need anything, and many in the town believed this was true.

On August 1, 1941, all the old women were forced to present themselves for a roll call. They were all put together in the "Talmud Torah" yard. Hundreds of women were cruelly dragged to the roll call, babies crying in their arms. They were held from morning till evening without any food or water.

Towards the evening Lithuanian "activists" arrived and ordered the women to line up in rows, two by two in each row. They were cruelly beaten, in order to urge them to hurry up. The dreadful event started when the women were surrounded by armed Lithuanians who hit them with their rifle butts. They especially tortured those who walked slowly. Children were hit, thrown down and trampled to death. The march went on until they arrived at the dense Shventshani forest. Through the light of the murderers' torches it was possible to glimpse a deep pit dug that same day. The women panicked. The murderers fired in the air and shouted in frightening voices: "Throw the children into the pits!" They ordered the women to undress and leave their clothes behind. Mothers jumped with their children into the pits, the Lithuanians firing all around. Many were buried alive and some managed to escape amidst all the chaos.

On September 4, 1941 the last women and children of the Yurburg community were taken to the Jewish elementary school. On September 7th, they all had to come to Motl Levyush's yard, which had been turned into a "labor camp."

All day long groups of Germans and Lithuanians passed along the Jewish homes in order to check no one was left behind. And indeed, not one Jew remained.

When they started to take the last of the flock, everyone understood where they were going, and what awaited them there. The poor women did not remain silent.

They shouted and pleaded with the hangmen, asking why human beings were being put to death. The Lithuanians merely answered by more beatings. The women started to shout to their older children, admonishing them to run, and they themselves attacked the Lithuanian guards with their fists. They bit, hit, shouted and swore. The murderers tightened the circle; shots were fired from all kinds of guns. It was a struggle for life or death between the poor women and the cruel murderers.

In the chaos a few young women managed to escape, and thanks to their testimony we know what happened to the Jewish community of Yurburg in its last moments.

Only 50 men and their families, who worked for the Germans remained in Yurburg for a week and then they too were all killed.

At the entrance of the town a sign was then put up, reading: "This place is free of Jews."

In the list of mass graves, published in the book "Mass murders in Lithuania," Part 2, mass graves in Yurburg, the following is written:

1. 322 people are buried in the eastern part of the Jewish cemetery. Date of murder - July 3, 1941.

2. Near the Kalnienai village, 7 kilometers from Yurburg on the left side of the road to Memel, 300 meters from the road - 200 people. Time - August 1941.

3. Barantsinas forest, 5 kilometers from Yurburg, 2 kilometers from the road - 500 people. Time - September 1941.

4. Shilinas forest - 1 kilometer to the west of Yurburg - 200 people. Time - September 1941.

Sources:
Zevulun Poran, according to the story of Hannah Magidovitz .
Tsevi Levit, "The Destruction of Yurburg."
World Trial Report, Mass Murder in Lithuania, Part 2.
From the Book of Lithuania - LITE 1951, New York

PAGES 404 - 407 APPEARS TO BE THE ORIGINAL YIDDISH OF THE PREVIOUS ARTICLE ENTITLED:

YURBURG IN THE FIRST DAYS OF THE HOLOCAUST - by Tsevi Levit

FROM THE BOOK *"LITE"* (Published in New York in 1951)

TRANSLATION OF PAGES 408 - 410

Yurburg in the Days of Its Destruction

By Rabbi Ephraim Oshry

Translated from Yiddish by Maurice Tsoref

The town of Yurburg was situated in the region of Raseiniai, ten kilometers from the border to Germany near Smalininken, resting along the shores of the Nieman River. The Nieman River runs from Grodna, passes Kovno and Yurburg, until it finally spills into the Kurish Bay (Kurisches Haff) a part of the Baltic Sea. Two thousand Jews lived in Yurburg.

There were two parks in Yurburg. One was called "Tel Aviv," the other was Lithuanian park.

The Jews of Yurburg derived their livelihood from the river. Families like the Levinbergs and the Aizenstatts owned their own steamships or Parakhods, as they were called, and maintained a passenger line from Kovno to Smalininken. There were also freight ships delivering goods from Memel to Kovno, as well as rafts that would go to Kovno or Memel. The river supplied the main income for the inhabitants of the village; others were merchants, shop owners and craftsmen.

Yurburg was world famous for its old Shul (synagogue), which had been built in 1790. But it wasn't so much the wooden structure that was famous, as was its Holy Ark (Aron Kodesh), with its woodcarving. It was hard to believe how such wonderful birds, animals and flowers could be carved out of wood, climbing from the floor all the way up to the ceiling. Anybody, who laid his eyes on that Holy Ark, was enchanted by its beauty and the artwork of its woodcarvings, its meticulous finish. The Holy Ark has been photographed hundreds of times, the images sent and sold throughout the entire world. Tourists visiting Lithuania would come to Yurburg especially, in order to see the great, wonderful antique piece, **the Holy Ark of the Shul of Yurburg**.

The men of the town were taught and educated people, such as Hirshl Fin, Aba Kaplan, Kalman Fridlender, Pinkhas Shakhnovitz, Yisrael Levinberg, Shmaryahu Fainberg (Feinberg), who was vice mayor of the town, Alter Shimonov, Meir Zuse Levitan, Rikler (Apteiker), Reuven Olshvanger, Dr. Karlinski, Cantor Alperovitz and the "Shokhet" Shmulovitz.

The Rabbis were: Rabbi Yakov Joseph Kharif, of blessed memory (later the Rabbi of the Collel of New York), Rabbi Yekhezkel Lifshitz, of blessed memory (later Rabbi in Kalish), Rabbi Avraham Dimant of blessed memory, a great scholar in religious as well as in worldly studies, and the (Dayan) Judge Rabbi Reuven Rubinstein.

Jewish institutions in the village were the Hebrew Gymnasium and a Public School. There were also a Folksbank (Popular Bank), institutions for the Hakhnasath Orkhim (Hosting Guests), Bikur Kholim (Visiting the Sick), two libraries and other institutions.

A curious figure in the village was Leibele Yisrael-Borukh's, a Jew who would sit in the study house, the Beth Midrash, all day long and study. His was the breadwinner of the family. He would be the first to enter the Beth Midrash in the morning and the last one to leave at night. He would wait until all the poor people received some food from some housewife someplace, especially Friday nights, when there would be many visitors in the village, so that God forbid, they would not remain hungry. He would see to it that the visitors were sent to the patrons. And when a visitor, sent by Leibele Yisrael-Borukh's, would come to a patron, he was happily welcomed. It was not a small thing, when Leibele Yisrael-Borukh's sent somebody.

His brother Velfke, too, had made it his job to take care of poor people on Shabat. Velfke, who was an old single man, would collect Khaloth (challes), fish, and meat on Friday and bring them to the homes of the poor for Shabath.

One of the distinguished anonymous donors was Israel Levinberg. Levinberg would help out patrons, who failed in their businesses, but it all took place away from the eye of the public.

On June 22, 1941, when the Germans attacked Russia, the Jews of Yurburg were immediately involved, as their village was situated right on the German border. The Lithuanian murderers soon engaged in killings and robberies. The first victim was Reuven Olshvanger.

On June 28, 1941, the Germans issued a decree, ordering all Jews to assemble in front of the municipal bookstore. Anybody disobeying that order and staying home, it said will be shot. When all the Jews had assembled, the men were forced to carry a bust of Stalin, and the women had to carry pictures and images of other members of the Soviet leadership. It was in this fashion that they were marched to the town square. There they were photographed, and Friedman was ordered to read out loud derogatory statements about Jews. Stalin's bust and the pictures were burned, and the Jews were forced to dance around the fire.

It didn't take long. Only a few days later all-important patrons of the village, 320 men, together with Rabbi Reuven Rubinstein, were called together. They were taken to the Jewish cemetery and ordered to dig out graves. Everybody was devastated and cried, but Rabbi Rubinstein comforted them: "Jews, let us be proud and brave. After all, we will be buried amongst our brethren, in Kever Yisrael." When the graves were ready, they were ordered to undress completely, and then were shoved into the graves.

They tortured Shimon badly. He was forced to tear down the stones from the bridge, and suffered other tortures. As he was already losing his strength, they laid him down on the Purification (Tahara) board (which the Jews used to purify their dead) and threw him into the Nieman River.

Around September 1941 the women and children were driven into the Jewish public school. For three days they left them there, hungry and suffering. Then they drove them to prepared graves in the forests of Smalininken.

The annihilation lasted a mere two days. The Christians from the village of Pashvente said that the earth around the graves moved for three days, because the Jews had been buried alive.

The murderers also burnt down the old Shul with its Aron Kodesh, the Holy Ark.

Thus Jewish life of many centuries was erased, and a piece of past Jewish continuity was torn out by its roots.

New York - Montreal (1951)

[Rabbi Ephraim Oshry died in New York on Sept. 28, 2003]

TRANSLATION OF PAGES 411 - 414

CASES OF THE SHOOTING OF WOMEN AND CHILDREN

(Ulm Trial, Tilsit)

1. Georgenburg [Yurburg in German]

(See decision to bring the suspect to trial dated 29.1.1958, page 14, item 19, and Page 24, pages 4148 and 4158).

(1) **Findings:**

One day in July or August 1941, again it is impossible to determine the exact day, at least 100 (among them a few old men, one rabbi and the others merely women and children) were shot to death in an exposed place in the forest, at a distance from the Schmalleningken - Georgenburg road about 30-80 kilometers from the German border and about 9 kilometers from the Lithuanian town Georgenburg. The execution was carried out at the general order of the accused Boehme, issued to those under his command in the framework of the Stahlecker order.

The accused Carsten, commander of the border patrol at the border town of Schmalleningken (at a scope of 4:1) had already arrested the Jews earlier by means of the Lithuanian Ordnungspolizei, by virtue of a general power of attorney on behalf of the accused Boehme in the guise of a "cleansing order."

While the Jewish men were already shot on July 3, 1941, the Jewish women and children were held under arrest together with some old people by Lithuanian assistant policemen, among them the Lithuanian assistant policeman, Urbanas.

The prisoners were led along on a 9-kilometers march at night, at the command of the accused, Carsten, by his Gestapo officers and Lithuanian assistant policemen, to the site of the killing. There were women with little babies among them. Before the start of the march the women were told they were about to join their husbands and that they should take all their valuables along with them. At the site of the killing there was a 5m by 6m (16 ft by 20 ft.) hole. The victims were forced to hand over the valuables and undress, i.e. the men to keep on their underpants only and the women their skirts and underpants.

After that the rabbi prayed with his flock and then they were shot, in the early morning hours, by the Lithuanian assistant policemen, who were drunk, at the command of the accused, Carsten.

There are no further details as to how the killing was carried out. The accused Carsten reported the killing and the number of people killed to the Gestapo in Tilsit and from there to the main Department of Defense of the Reich (RSHA) and Dr. Stahlecker.

There was no particular mention of this incident of killing in the report of the head of security police and security service (SD) submitted in the Russian region.

Next day the accused Carsten traveled together with his close friend, the customs officer Oselies, who appears as witness, from Schmalleningken to Georgenburg. On the way he stopped near this forest clearing and went on foot with witness Oselies to the mass grave. Here he gave him a description of the killing of the day before.

Later on the accused Carsten brought chlorine plaster [lime], which was thrown over the mass grave, as the odor of decay started to be evident.

2) **Evaluation of the testimonies:**

The accused Carsten denied he had taken part in this killing. In any case, he admitted there was a possibility that he had received the order to kill Jewish women and children, but he claimed he had not carried out this order. He even received information from Lithuanians about two instances of killing Jewish women and children, and reported this to the police department at Tilsit. Furthermore, he claimed, he did not know the place of the killing, although he hid behind the mass graves when he went hunting. It was true he had brought chlorine plaster [lime], but this was only for the graves in the Jewish cemetery.

The jury did not believe Carsten's claim that he had not taken part in the killing. Throughout all these court sessions the accused Carsten did not create a trusting impression.

Carsten was mainly proven guilty by witness Oselies. He delivered a believeable testimony to the effect that some time before the trip in question with the accused Carsten, the Lithuanian assistant policeman Urbanas, who was in charge of guarding the Jewish women and children, together with other assistant policemen, had told him that he earned a lot of money for this, as the Jewish women always offered him money to prolong their lives. A short while later, in July or August 1941, one morning he traveled with the accused Carsten beyond the border. About 3 kilometers from the border the accused Carsten stopped in the forest and went on foot with him to a clearing in the woods, about 80 meters from the road.

Here he showed him a mass grave, and said that the day before Jewish women and children as well as a few Jewish old men and a rabbi had been shot here by the Lithuanians. The Lithuanians had been drunk. The women had been ordered to undress, leaving on their bras and panties and the men their underpants. The rabbi had still managed to speak to the people and pray.

The witness Oselies gave an accurate and clear description of all this and he added that he was so shocked by the accused Carsten's story that he was speechless and merely looked at him in silence. According to the accused Carsten's overall behavior and on the basis of his detailed description of the killing delivered in a matter of fact way and without any signs of emotion, he was convinced that the accused Carsten had taken part in the killing of the Jewish women and children by the Lithuanians. The jury considers this fact to be proven.

Witness Oselies added that shortly after this trip policeman Urbanas also told him about this incident of killing. According to his story the victims were forced to walk to the site of the killing, about 9 kms. Among them were women who had just given birth. Witness Stanat also testified against the accused Carsten. He served as Evangelian priest in Georgenburg from 1934 to July 3, 1941. He rendered trustworthy testimony according to which during his visit to Georgenburg between the end of 1941 and early 1942. The Mayor, Hoffner, and the Evangelian priest who served in Georgenburg at the time told him that the accused Carsten had played a decisive role in the killing of the Jewish men, women and children. He had ordered the Lithuanians be given rifles and bullets. Before they were brought to the site of the killing the Jewish women were advised to bring along all their valuables, as they would be joining their husbands.

Witness Obremski, a former adjutant in the Tilsit police battalion, rendered trustworthy testimony which he had heard from the men in his police unit, that Jewish women and children from Georgenburg were shot by the Lithuanian police at the order of the Gestapo. In his opinion the Gestapo were present at the killing by the Lithuanians, also because the Lithuanian police at that time did not have any weapons of its own. Obremski also testified about an incident that which happened to him. He said he was traveling to Georgenburg with his commander when he saw a confused Jewish woman with a little child run out of the woods and flee along the road.

They stopped the police car to ask the woman what she was doing. However, the Jewish woman continued to run. In addition, a Gestapo man was seen coming out of the forest, and that is why they let the matter rest.

A short while later a drunken Lithuanian policeman came out of the woods. They asked him what was going on and he answered Jewish women and children had just been shot. Later on they heard in Georgenburg that the Lithuanian police had received alcohol from the Gestapo and had then shot Jewish women and children; many of the Jewish women were pregnant.

In spite of the accused Carsten's denial, the jury is convinced that he gave the order, by virtue of the general order of the accused Boehme, to let the Lithuanians - who had earlier gotten drunk, shoot the Jewish women and children, and that the murder had taken place under his command.

According to the testimony of witness Oselies that little children and even babies had been killed and that the mass grave took up an area of 5m by 6m [16 ft by 20 ft] the jury determined that at least 100 people had been shot.

The accused Boehme denied he had taken part in this killing of Jewish women and children. He claimed he could not remember this incident. True, he had repeatedly been told that Jewish women and children had been shot by Lithuanians, but his share in this affair was limited to receiving the information and passing the facts about the number of casualties on to the main Defense Department of the Reich (RSHA) and Dr. Stahlecker.

However, the jury did not believe the accused Boehme's claim that this had been carried out without his participation and knowledge. The jury was convinced that this killing too, was only carried out at the general order he had issued to his Gestapo troops. Here we must rely on previous statements and findings submitted in the verdict.

It is impossible to prove that the accused Hersmann took part in the killing. In the decision to put the accused on trial he had been accused of the same number of crimes as the accused Boehme.

Yosef Ben Matityahu Valk
Born in Yurburg
Blessed be his Memory

Remembering the Victims at the Mass Murder Site of the Yurburg Jewish Women and Children off the road to Smalininken, in May 2001 - Fania Hilelson Jivotovsky, Nancy Lefkowitz and Lottye Brodsky approaching to light Memorial Candles

[Photo not in original Yizkor Book - Courtesy of Dr. Leon Menzer]

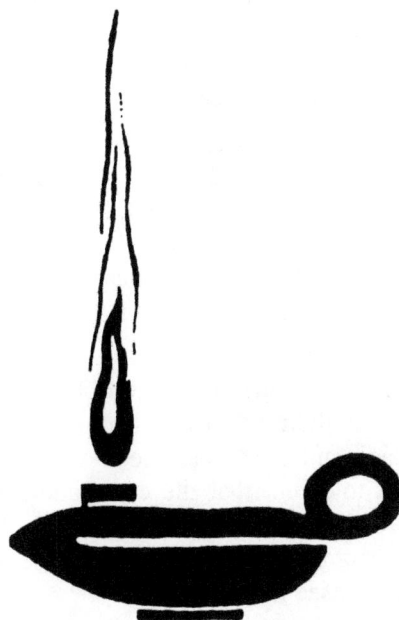

This next section was not in the Original Hebrew Yizkor Book, but is included because it is a translation of the testimony of the transcript of the Ulm Trial directly from German into English and it also contains the sentences.

Ulm Trial Testimony Transcript: 3 July 1941

Translated by Dr. Ulrich Baumann

On the third of July in the morning, Boehme, Hersmann and their Gestapo and SD assistants, numbering 30 to 40, came to Yurburg; there, the accused Carsten, and the Gestapo members from Smaleninken subordinated to him, were already there, among them Kriminalassistent Schlegel and Hof. From the Tilsit Gestapo there were, among others, Kommmisar Gerke (witness) and Krumbach (witness) and from the SD the motorist Ju. (witness) and Pap. (witness). ["SD" means "Sicherheitsdienst der SS" which was a special branch under the leadership of Reinhard Heydrich. n.b., U.Baumann]

In the courtyard of the building of the Lithuanian "order service," the accused Carsten reported to the accused Boehme about his preparations. He also reported the number of arrested and about the reasons for the arrests, based on the list of names written in German language. Beside a few communists, the prisoners were [primarily] male Jews. Among the arrested communists were two women, among them a telephone operator.

Now, between the accused Boehme and Carten a severe dispute began, because the accused Boehme complained that the preparations were not sufficient (...copy is not readable, U. Baumann)....

As a result, small groups of Gestapo and SD members, among them witnesses Krumbach and Gerke, were formed and ordered, together with Lithuanian police assistants, to remove the Jewish men from their homes where they had been held in detention. Through this action, at least 60 additional Jewish men were arrested. Three women with their children followed them.

During the arrest, the Lithuanian doctor turned to the accused Carsten, and asked that the Jewish doctor be freed. He explained that the Jewish doctor was a surgeon and the citizens urgently needed him. The accused Carsten told him he should address himself to the accused Boehme. After very urgently conveying his request to Boehme, the Lithuanian doctor was beaten by Boehme. His request was not listened to, and he had to leave without any result.

The accused Hersmann in the meantime was looking for the execution commando of the police battalion, because it had not been at place in spite of the agreement with the adjutant of the battalion. After finally having reached the adjutant, the adjutant told him that the commander had not allowed the execution of those arrested by members of his battalion. The accused Boehme and Hersmann were very angry about that because of the additional arrests, the number of arrested had increased to 300.

The prisoners were marched by foot through the town to the Jewish cemetery. There, they were forced to turn over all of their valuable things and also to remove their top clothing.

The accused Boehme had been driving, together with the accused Carsten, to the execution site on the Jewish cemetery and had meanwhile ordered the digging of an additional mass grave by the Jewish prisoners, because the excavated grave was not sufficient due to the additional people arrested. With the help of the accused Carten, he ordered the necessary additional equipment.

After the prisoners arrived at the cemetery, the accused Carsten tried successfully to convince Boehme to release his two former agents who were arrested in the additional action as well.

The arrested Jews were then forced to dig the second mass grave. During that time two Jews were beating each other with spades in the presence of the Gestapo member Wiechert, probably as a result of his order.

Then, the victims were led by the Gestapo and SD members from the nearby assembly site to the execution site, partially urged on by loud shouting and beatings with sticks. The outcries of the victims filled the air. They had to stand in front of the holes, facing their own graves. Some were ordered to kneel. They were shot in the neck. At the same time, they received a push, so that they fell into their graves. Since the victims were constantly led to the execution site, the next ones had to witness the murder of their fellow sufferers. Inhabitants from two neighboring farmhouses watched the killings, which was observed by Carsten. He directed the attention of the accused Boehme to this and ordered the accused Carsten to prohibit the inhabitants from watching. The accused Carsten followed the order.

During the execution, several incidents occurred, which were also observed by officers of the police battalion, who had come to this place after finishing their exercise, driven by curiosity. A Jewish custom's agent, who had fought in World War I and had been awarded the Iron Cross, Class A, for excellent fighting, attacked Boehme and hit him. A deadly shot stopped him.

One or two prisoners attacked Kriminalkommissar Krumbach and were shot. When several Jews tried to escape, the accused Boehme and Hersmann each shot one escapee. At these turbulent episodes a SD man was inadvertent shot in his leg. In his place, the SD motorist Pap. (witness) came to replace him, and he killed three prisoners by shots into their necks. The police battalion reported about these incidents and the bad organization to higher authorities. This had the consequence that the accused Boehme and Hersmann had to accept the responsibility for these actions to the RSHA. However this brought no disgrace to them.

In this action, 322 Jews were killed, among them were five women and some children who did not want to be separated from their parents.

The accused Boehme and Hersmann reported, as they did in every instance, the number of those executed and the place of the execution to the leader of the Einsatzgruppe A, Dr. Stahlecker, and to the RSHA, which reported itself in the Incidents Report SSSR Nr. 19 of 11 July 1941 (Source 9i, page 1): "Together with SD-district Tilsit, the Gestapo Tilsit carried out another "Grossaktionen" (larger actions). In Georgenburg (Yurburg), 322 persons, among them five women, were shot on July 3rd."

After finishing the execution, a joint meal was held, a so-called "Sakuska," which had been ordered by the accused Carsten by order of the accused Boehme. This meal was paid by the witness Gerke by order of the accused Boehme, with the money that was taken from the Jews before their execution.

Directly after he came back to Georgenburg, the accused Carsten told his good friend Os. (witness) on the same evening, without any emotions about that execution. He introduced the discussion with the words: **"This morning we have bumped off the Jews of Georgenburg."**

After the killings of all the Jewish women and children, a sign was posted at the entrance of Georgenburg with the inscription: **"This Place is without Jews. (Judenrein)."**

ULM TRIAL SENTENCES

[Not in Original Yizkor Book]

Translated by Dr. Ulrich Baumann

Sentences from Schwurgericht (Jury) Ulm August 29, 1958:

Boehme: Crime of a joint of offense of accessory to the **murder of 3,907 cases: penitentiary 15 years, loss of citizen's honor rights 10 years.**

Hersmann: crime of a joint of offense of accesory to the **murder in 1,656 cases**, in account of the sentence of jury court of Traunstein (Bavaria) of 21. Sept. 1950 which was eight years penitentiary and five years loss of citizen's honor rights, which are subtracted, to a **total punishment of 15 years penitentiary, loss of citizen's honor rights 10 years.**

Carsten: crime of a joint of offense of accessory to the **murder in 423 cases: penitentiary four years, loss of citizen's honor rights three years.**

TRANSLATION OF PAGE 415

THE OPPRESSORS - LEVITSKAS AND KAMINSKAS

By Shimon Shimonov

Justice has a long arm, and even if many years have passed since our community was destroyed, we did not give up nor will we ever give up the wish to see the murderers punished, wherever they may be.

At the end of 1974, I was asked to come to the American Consulate in East Jerusalem to identify, according to pictures, the criminals Levitskas and Kaminskas.

In coordination with the Nazi crimes investigation division of the Israeli police, I appeared at the Consulate, however the pictures of old gentiles that were presented to me made it difficult for me to identify the criminals.

At the end of 1974, I received a request from the Israeli police to submit the names and addresses of former residents of Yurburg who would be able to identify the criminals, and so I did. A number of people were called for interviews and the matter was forgotten again.

In October of this year [probably 1990 - before publication of the Hebrew Yizkor Book] I once again turned to the Nazi crimes investigation division of the Israeli police and asked for a report about the matter.

I was told the file had not been closed. As far as they knew, Kaminskas had been traced, brought to trial and a verdict had been issued to deport him from the United States. However, the execution of the verdict was postponed from year to year due to his poor health.

As far as Lawitzkas [Kevitskas] is concerned, the investigation department has no information yet. **[If anyone has any further information about these criminals, please communicate with the editor Joel Alpert so that we can add the information to later editions of this book.]**

Romualdas Levickas, Lithuanian War Criminal
Born on February 7, 1908. He took part in the murder of Jews in Jurbarkas. After the war he escaped to the USA, where this photo was taken in 1958. From Ghetto Fighters' House Archive Department Collection. Catalog Number 26597. Provided Courtesy of the Ghetto Fighters' House.

THE JEWS OF SHAUDINE WERE THE FIRST TO BE EXECUTED

By Avraham Levyush

To the martyrs of Shaudine - a faithful tear

True, one might say: thousands of towns and villages in the Diaspora were destroyed by the Nazi oppressors, so what difference does another tiny town with 16-18 Jewish families make! The answer is: it does, oh yes it does! Both because of its particularly bitter fate and because of some of its Jews, this small town deserves special mention.

Shaudine was one of the first little towns to be slaughtered, even before the ghettoes, before the gas chambers, before Maidanek and Auschwitz.

The Jews of the little town of Shaudine had a "special privilege:" they were the first to be executed. Perhaps this fate was shared by other small towns in Lithuania that were close to Germany (such as Sudarg and others), but the writer of this article received accurate information only about Shaudine. A week after the Nazi invasion, which took place at the end of June 1941, the Nazis rounded up all the adult Jewish men at the little town in order to, as it were, "send them to Shaki." On the way there they were all murdered. Two weeks later all the Jewish women in the town and their little children drank [from] "the cup of poison."*

> * According to the version of the Igdalski brothers from Shaki (I met them in Munchen, Germany) and also according to the version of Rachel Bendelin, the men were killed near the town of Shaki on the eleventh of Tamuz 5701(July 6, 1941). The women were killed by the Germans and their faithful Lithuanian helpers, who outdid them in cruelty, on 21 Elul 5701 (September 13, 1941).

Thus they lie there, till today, in two mass graves, close to each other. Who can describe the terror in the eyes of the poor women when they realized the bitter fate of the men! Thus they were murdered and thus they were thrown into mass graves, the Jews of Shaudine, without a tear of pity, without a funeral, without a eulogy, without the prayer for the dead. They died like impure animals and were buried like donkeys.

Among the women who were killed we should mention the devoted mother who at the time had become a legend because of what she did: her only son contracted diptheria. He would soon suffocate if he did not receive an injection by a physician, but there was no doctor in Shaudine, only on the other side of the Nieman River in Yurburg. It was in the cold days of winter. The Nieman

River had just frozen, but was still covered by a thin layer of ice, and no one dared to walk on this thin ice. What did this mother do? She put her sick son on a small winter carriage, and with the rope in her hands she drew the sled over the thin ice, until it reached the safe shore.

And among the murdered men was the great father who planted the love of Israel in the heart of his son. This father gave everything to his son, saved every penny, to send him to Zion, to be educated there. This was before World War I when merely a handful of lucky people went to Eretz Yisrael. There was no greater joy to this father than the letters he received from his son in Eretz Yisrael, he would read them six days of the week, and on the seventh day he would read them together with the week's Bible portion.

A steamship, that had left Kovno to go to Yurburg, was sailing along the Nieman River. A young, enthusiastic passenger stood on deck, his bright eyes looking in the distance. Here, here, the two towers of the new church of Yurburg appeared on the right side of the river. Here come the parks and houses of Yurburg. Opposite these houses, to the left of the river, there is a broad range of forest. There are large stone houses there with many trees. Those are the buildings of the Kidul estate, Shaudine's neighbor on this side. Closer to the viewer on the boat, large wooden houses become visible - the Kimmel estate, Shaudine's neighbor on the other side. Between these two estates, parallel to the river - broad green pastures in between, the little houses with the thatched roofs of Shaudine continue.

About twenty Jewish families lived in Shaudine at this time (before World War I). The Jews here were no intellectuals, but they were not ignorant either, neither rich nor poor and made a living here and there on trade and here and there on farming. There was a synagogue (Kloiz), but the town was too small to be able to keep all the "religious ministrants." It did have its own ritual slaughterer, while it shared the rabbi with Sudarg. And - God forbid - a Jew who died was brought to Sudarg for burial, 8 kilometers away from Shaudine.

Only the Nieman River, which is not very wide at this spot, separates Shaudine from Yurburg, but the mental distance with the "Poilishe," as the people in Yurburg would call the Jews of Shaudine, was very great indeed. These were two different worlds. The Jews of Yurburg considered their town (only 5,000 inhabitants in all) a metropolis, while the Jews of Shaudine were provincial villagers to them. In addition there were geographical and ethnographical differences. Here the Suwalk Region (Gubernia), formerly Poland, there, the Kovno Region, Russia. Here they say Mauer Sauer, there: Moier Soier. Here they are plain, stubborn Jews who don't mind eating mutton, especially when it is smoked, there they are spoiled towns people, where there is a law and they would never dare serve **warm Beigels** for breakfast. When Lithuania gained independence and the Hebrew Gymnasium was established in Yurburg, used also by the children of Shaudine, many differences were set aside.

Only one of the hundred Jews of Shaudine survived. The houses were not
burned or destroyed, but "our homes became the homes of strangers" -
Lithuanian gentiles occupied them. I don't know what happened to the "Kloiz"
(synagogue), but whether it was occupied and used for another purpose or not,
"save me from the insult of the one that remains silent, without anyone coming
to celebrate."

Hitler may be credited for not distinguishing between one Jew and another. He
directed his poisonous rage at all of them. Only very few Jews from Yurburg
and Sudarg survived.

On their last journey...

TRANSLATION OF PAGES 419-428

LAST DAYS IN YURBURG AND THE SURROUNDING AREA

The Story of Aba Vales

By Zevulun Poran

The story of my life in the Nazi hell covers a long period, however, it is well-known that it is the nature of man to forget many things and this applies even more so to someone like myself who has reached a very old age. There are, however, chapters of life that leave such a deep impression on the heart that it is impossible to erase them. I shall never forget what happened to me in the evil years of the Nazi occupation in Lithuania. Those who were not there and did not feel the physical and mental anguish will not believe our story, for it is beyond comprehension.

When I remember those terrible days, dreadful scenes come to mind, torture and killing. I witnessed the death of our relatives and brothers, the Jews of Yurburg; I witnessed the loss of my family.

In the last years before the Holocaust I lived in Yurburg. Jews had lived in Yurburg for many generations; they are there no longer. Jewish Yurburg was destroyed and erased from under the sky of Lithuania.

I was born in the little town of Shaudine. The Nieman River, as is known, separated Shaudine from Yurburg. Although Shaudine belonged to the Shaki region, as the entire area beyond the river, we from Shaudine considered ourselves as belonging to Yurburg. We were all attached in heart and soul to Yurburg, where we studied and spent the years of our youth.

After World War I, Shaudine became quite large, but the number of Jewish inhabitants diminished. Many left, especially the young, who did not see a future there for themselves. Of the hundreds of families that had lived there in the past only about twenty were left when World War II broke out.

The majority of the Shaudine residents were farmers and some dealt in the trades. The tradesmen bought fodder from the farmers, cattle, linen, poultry, eggs etc., and they would sell their goods to the Jewish tradesmen in Yurburg, who dealt in the export of goods to Germany and Western Europe.

I remember a number of families in town, among them my brother Meir Vales and his family, and my uncles, Nathan and Leizer Vales, my father's brothers, and also Hirshel and Itzik Goldin. I also remember Orchik and his wife Ilana, Leibe Meigel, Yankel Bendelin, who was a wholesale tradesman and Meir Pesakhson. I remember Meir Feldman, whose daughter Hannah joined the "Hekhalutz" movement, went on training and on aliyah to Eretz Yisrael and to the kibbutz. There was the Levyush family: Mosheh Levyush, whose son Meir is presently in Israel and works as a pharmacist at "Kupath Kholim" (Health

Fund). The Mosheh Levyush family was also well-known, their son Zalman, a gifted young man, studied at the Yurburg Gymnasium and Kovno University; he joined the "Habimah" studio while he was still a student and emigrated to Israel. Zalman Levyush became very well known in Israel as an outstanding actor and famous director in Israel and America.

There were many Zionists in the little town of Shaudine and there was a great love for Eretz Yisrael there. The youngsters studied at Hebrew schools and belonged to pioneer youth movements. The town did not have a rabbi. The Shaudine residents used the rabbi of Sudarg, a little town 8 to 9 kms. (6 miles) away on the German border. The two towns shared a cemetery. We had a religious slaughterer, called "Rabbi Alter mit die sieben Techter," i.e. Rabbi Alter with the seven daughters. We also had a prayer house in our little town, but there was hardly a real school. Most children studied at the schools and gymnasium of Yurburg. Indeed, what separated us from Yurburg, only the Nieman River on the ferry. Except for the days when the snow melted, the trade, cultural and social link was never cut off between Shaudine and Yurburg. Many Shaudine residents even settled in Yurburg itself, in fact that is what I did; when the Nazis came I had been a Yurburg resident for quite a while.

My forefathers were Shaudine residents. They were peasants. They had fields, cattle, and horses. The land did not disappoint them. I inherited the love of land and animals from my parents. We were very close to nature, rooted in simple farm life, just like all the gentile peasants around us; however, in the last generation people left the town, as mentioned above. The young men wanted to acquire an education, they went to study and did not return to the little town; I also left, after I got married, and I settled in Yurburg, although I still continued the farming business. Three children were born to me in Yurburg, Hayim (Chaim) Shelomoh, Nathan and Zelda. I was happy with my life; I earned enough and was able to take good care of my family. There was no room for any particular concern. In those days I could not imagine that heavy clouds were already hovering over our sky. Soon our entire way of life changed completely. Disaster hit us like a thunderstorm.

On the evening of June 22, 1941, Hitler's hooligans entered Lithuania. Already in the early hours of the morning, airplanes appeared in the sky of Yurburg, immediately followed by the army. There was shock and tumult. People tried to escape to all possible directions. I had a horse and carriage and thought they would save us. As I lived at the outskirts of town I said to myself" I'll run, I'll run." . . . The moment the idea occurred to me I urged my wife, Henya, to put all the things that could be taken along on the carriage. We did everything in a great hurry, put our little children on the carriage, and in the early hours of the morning I left with my wife and children. We went to the east, to Rasein. The road was difficult and full of vehicles; it was a tiring and exhausting trip, while the terrible enemy was behind us, a narrow path of hope in front of us. However, after a short while, when we reached Shimkaitsh, our hope dissipated.

The Nazi soldiers had arrived there before us; they confronted us, rifles drawn, searched us and our belongings, took a photograph of all of us and sent us back to Yurburg. When we returned tired and depressed to Yurburg we found our house had been taken over by the Germans. After we begged and pleaded, they vacated a space in one of the houses for us and thus we passed the first days, under the patronage of "our German neighbors." We lived in fear and were terrified, yet we had no idea of what would happen to us in the coming days.

A couple of days after the Germans invaded Yurburg; the German hooligans passed along the homes of the Jews, together with their Lithuanian helpers, and took some of the Jews away, according to a list. Later on it transpired that this was aimed at the Jews who were educated and influential among the Jewish population of the town. I also joined this respectable group, which consisted of 520 people. There were 20 in the group who were not Jewish, communist leaders, who had ruled Lithuania for over a year. This group of people was led to the Jewish cemetery by the German soldiers and their Lithuanian guides. Here we were told to form groups and dig deep holes. The work was hard and we were very depressed. It is impossible to describe what went on there. I immediately understood what to expect in this place. I don't know how, but I suddenly got the idea and decided to rebel, "to be saved, to hang on to life." I saw a piece of large plot of land in front of me with a deep decline behind it and a steep slope. I quickly threw myself onto the ground and rolled myself into the deep abyss, which went down to the Nieman River. After a few seconds I saw myself hurt and beaten, but all alone, and far from the place of evil. I gathered my last strength and got up. "Where should I go?" In front of me was the slowly flowing Nieman River, cows in the meadows and fields in the distance. I decided to hide in the cornfields. The moment I started on my way I found a horseshoe. I took the horseshoe into my hand and put it next to my heart, perhaps, I said to myself, this is a sign that I shall be able to survive. Our forefathers were superstitious and believed the horseshoe is a sign of luck and success, who knows? At that moment the horseshoe lifted my spirits and gave me hope that I would be able to reach my home and see my wife and children. Thus, I continued on my way. I climbed mountains and went down valleys until I reached the area where I lived. On the way shepherds and peasants told me what had happened to the group of Jews at the cemetery. Their story was no surprise to me. I knew their fate would be bitter. I was told that Dr. Karlinksy delivered a speech at the cemetery, before he died, he spoke out against the murderous Nazis, who condemned them to death. As far as I know I am the only survivor of this group.

When I approached the garden of my home I saw my wife from afar; I was sure that I had reached my goal. This was not the case. All of a sudden two Lithuanian Shaulists blocked my way, grabbed me and ordered me to follow them to the police station. I begged them to let me spend the night at home and promised I would present myself at the police station the next morning. "Anyhow," one of them said, "you are about to die, so what difference does it make to sleep one more night at home." However, one Shaulist almost granted me my request; I saw that my pleading had aroused his pity, but the other one was as hard as stone. He had murder in his eyes. In short, I was taken to the police. My wife and children remained at home and were certainly waiting for me. We all passed a sleepless night.

Thus, after all the hurdles I had overcome that day I walked and crawled with the last force left in me, while the Shaulists urged me along, swearing and hitting me all the way. The police commander sent me to prison. At the prison I found 46 Jews. I was number forty-seven. They say that it is possible to find solace in sharing one's troubles with others. It was no solace to me to find so many Jews at the prison, yet I cheered up somewhat, perhaps I would be lucky this time too. After a while the order was received to take us to the Levyush courtyard on Rasein Street. We were unaware of the reason for this and did not know what to expect. In the evening a German officer came, accompanied by a Lithuanian policeman, and told us to line up in the courtyard. We were divided into two groups: old men on one side and healthy young men on the other side. The old men were allowed to go to sleep at home. They were told unequivocally that if they failed to return next morning all the young men, who remained at the Levyush courtyard, would be shot. Thus, I too remained at the Levyush home to spend the night there with the young men. We found a place for ourselves somehow in the home and courtyard, where we were guarded. Shmerl Bernstein, who was the manager of the bank in our little town, was put in charge of our group, which included about forty people. We passed a terrible night. Everyone tried to guess what would happen to us. We each crouched in our little corner and took stock of our life; the night passed without much sleep until the sun rose at daybreak. The old men returned from their homes, one after another. They looked sad, as if they knew the end was near. After a while the Germans and Lithuanian Shaulists came, counted the old men, making sure none of them was missing. Immediately the order was issued to take the group of old men out of the courtyard and beyond.

We still saw them dragging their feet. We could still hear their sighs and saw them taking a last look at those left behind and at the streets of Yurburg where they had grown up, lived, raised children, grown old. Now the bitter end had come, they went on their way, and, as we heard from Lithuanian acquaintances, they were taken to the Shimkaitz forest where they were shot. To this very day their graves are nowhere to be found.

The group of young men that remained in the courtyard was divided into two units. I too was placed with one of these units. We were taken to the Nieman River, where we were ordered to load stones on to steamships, while the policemen and the oppressors stood over us and urged us coarsely and cruelly along. The loading went on for three days. It was hard labor. We received prison fare - but we accepted our verdict. We said to ourselves: "as long as it doesn't get worse." All those days when I was loading the stones I was thinking how to escape and run far away beyond the hills of darkness, in order to disappear from the eyes of the murderers; however, I knew this was an idle dream. One day, as we finished loading the stone, I went up to the German officer who was guarding us. I told him that I was a peasant, a farmer, and that if I did not reap the harvest everyone would go hungry, and that was more important than the slave labor I was carrying out here. The officer asked a gentile Lithuanian to corroborate my words that I really had a farm. To my joy, the Lithuanian testified in my favor. That is how I received a certificate from the police, at the orders of the German officer that released me for a month. My joy, of course, knew no bounds. I went home with the passport to salvation in my pocket, free for a month.

The next day, early in the morning, I went to the Nieman River in order to cross the river on the ferry to Shaudine. Near the Nieman River I found a Jew who had been ordered to set up a guard booth. He had been given wooden boards, but he did not have a saw or tools. I helped him a little, as far as I could, and I went to my parents' home in Shaudine. And here, imagine how pleasantly surprised I was, I found my mother at home, my sister and all the other members of my family, healthy and well. I can't tell you how happy we were; here I am, sitting at home, my childhood home, among my family, while outside the evil wind of Hitlerism is blowing and the sword is poised. Many Jews of Shaudine had been taken out of their homes and taken in the direction of Shaki. No one knows what happened to them. There was a great deal of fear. Everyone was counting his last days and hours.

Nevertheless, let's cross that bridge when we come to it. In the meantime I was enjoying my long "holiday." During the day I did not work at all. "Who cared about the fields?" - a sword was hanging over our heads. I went into the fields, looked for a place to hide from the Germans and Shaulists and in the evening I crossed the Nieman River on the ferry and went to my home and family in Yurburg. Each time I heard terrible news there, which depressed me. After a month I received an extension of another month; "was I an important and useful man?" I deceived them as far as I could, that was my only weapon.

In those days I received the terrible news that the women and children of Yurburg had already been taken out of their homes and led to the forest. From the Lithuanians I heard about their bitter end and about the tragic fate of my wife and children. I find it hard to believe the terrible testimony about the crimes committed by the Lithuanians, the Nazis' helpers, how could they . . ? How could they murder women and children in cold blood, weeping babies ?.. and throw them all into a hole . . .I can hear their voices deafening my ears . . . how? . . . how?

I remained alone, the only one of my small family to survive. There was nothing left for me in Yurburg. Yurburg without Jews did not exist for me. My world had fallen apart. However, the urge to live is apparently stronger than man is. I recovered from the blows of destiny and the suffering of Job. Now I only felt the instinct of wrath.

One day I was summoned to the police. I understood the end had come. I had to think of a way to save myself this time too. Up until now I had managed to outwit them, but what would happen now. Perhaps someone had denounced me? Could that be true? Until now I had been lucky, had my luck run out now?

And then, at the very time when I was deliberating, an idea struck me. I shall not go to the police of Yurburg. What do I have to do with Yurburg, what is it to me? Those who hate me are there, those who murdered my family, I shall run away, I shall not surrender, I want to live. Perhaps I would do well to run to my mother and my relatives who are still in Shaudine. When the Germans find out that I don't have any fields or gardens and that I lied to them all along, they will kill me, for they are murderers. I can still hear the cries of the old men, women and children they murdered and whose skulls they crushed and now they want to do the same to me. No, I said to myself, they won't be so lucky.

I shall not be a slave to you, or fall victim to these wild bloodthirsty animals. I must escape, immediately, but where to? Where shall I go? Certainly not to Yurburg, that is clear. Nor will I go to Shaudine. I remembered that not far away, in this area, I knew a gentile, who was a frequent guest at our house. I knew him and trusted him. I somehow got to him. Yes, he knew me. He did not ignore me, although I saw he was full of fear. At the home of this farmer I hid for seven days. I ate of his bread and drank of his water. I might have remained with my Lithuanian acquaintance longer, but something happened. Close by, almost next door, the Jew called Moshke Yoks was caught. He too had hidden with a Lithuanian farmer. The Germans and Lithuanians arrested him and shot him on the spot, and after that they also shot the gentile who had helped him. This news spread to the entire village and to other villages as well. From now on no one dared harbor a Jew under his roof, it was too risky, and the local population was not too fond of Jews anyhow. Many now found an opportunity, under the German occupation, to take revenge on the Jews whom they had hated for a long time.

When it became known that the Lithuanian farmer had been killed for hiding the Jew, my benefactor said to me "I am very sorry, you must leave, for if they find out they will kill me." Outside it was winter. It had snowed and it was ice cold. "Where shall I go?" - tears welled up in my eyes - "where can I go?" The farmer saw how I felt and understood my tragic position that I was homeless and was being thrown out of the house like a dog. He took pity, got up and said: "go to my father in-law, he is a Lithuanian farmer of German origin, no one will suspect him, go to him, tell him I sent you, and you'll be able to stay with him for a couple of days." That is what I did. It did not take long before I saw that he disapproved of me and I was afraid he might hurt me. One day he said to me: " why fall victim to those who want to kill you, why don't you just go through the gate of the yard and take your own life there, that is your only choice." I told him: "if I really have to die I shall not die here, and be devoured by the wild animals of the forest, I prefer to go to the Jewish cemetery, dig a hole for myself and be buried on the land of my fathers." As it was night, I asked for permission to sleep in the attic for one more night before I would leave. The gentile showed signs of nervousness and I felt he was planning to kill me. I climbed to the attic, but I could not close my eyes, I was afraid of my hosts' evil schemes. I was already experienced in those days. I knew how to distinguish between one person and another.

After I had tossed about for an hour, unable to fall asleep, I made a small hole in the straw that covered the roof, and went outside, leaving the farmer's house far behind. All night long I trampled in the snow, while my legs froze and my head was spinning. I reached Papushok, a scarcely populated village, on the way to Shaki, about ten kilometers (6 miles) away from Shaudine. I knew the angel of death was waiting for me. Until today I don't know how I managed to get through those difficult days and arrive here. Till I die I won't know. However, I knew one thing, that I was determined to overcome the difficulties and stay alive and witness the downfall of our people's enemy and my family's murderers. This hope kept my spirit up, and helped me overcome the hardship and sufferings.

It was morning. At a farmer's home I saw that the door of the stable was open. I went in. The farmer saw me and was startled. I knew him and he knew me too. His wife also came to take a look at me. He told me the Jews here were in great danger. And he also told me that Levyush from Shaudine had been caught and had been killed here in this area. I started to cry. I had no energy left and I did not have the strength to go any further. If I had to die in this stable then let this be my grave.

When the farmer saw how miserable I was, he took pity. He ordered his wife to bring me some bread and butter to cheer me up. Once I had eaten I no longer had the strength to get up, but the farmer said: "go into the home, never mind what happens. I am not afraid of those who live in my home, they won't tell anyone, for another Jew is hiding in my home." This was a simple, poor peasant, who barely made a living from the plot of land and the animals he had. In winter he would be a shoemaker, would stitch one patch to another, for anyone who asked. That was how he barely made a living, particularly in those difficult days, when everyone was hungry. The German conquerors starved and humiliated the population, for they took the Lithuanian harvest to the front. "My" farmer was unable to understand how so many Lithuanians cooperated with the Germans and helped them.

In short: the farmer, with whom I found my home, was my true benefactor. He arranged a place for me in the attic where I spent, who would believe it? - Three and a half years! The farmer shared his food with me. Often the members of his family would go hungry and I was one of them. He had one condition. "If you hear my dogs barking, be aware they may search my house. If so, run away, my friend, don't bring disaster on me."

Luckily, there were Germans who needed shoe repairs and used the farmer who was a shoemaker; however, they had no idea that in the attic, in bundles of straw, a Jew was hiding, poor fellow.

My life at the farmer's home was boring; each day resembled the next. The days and nights were very long, endless. It is impossible to convey the thoughts that tortured me and weakened my strength to face the hardship and suffering.

One day I found a crystal radio that was equipped with earphones. I barely managed to hear the news from a distance. Each day the Germans would enthrall the Lithuanian population with stories about the German army's heroic victories on all fronts. And here, on that same day, I heard that the German divisions had been beaten in battle and fallen into Russian custody. This was encouraging news, from that moment I felt that Hitler's days were numbered and that the murderer would die on the gallows. From that moment I felt some relief in my sorrow.

One day, it is hard to believe we were free. The enemy had been beaten and dealt a mortal blow. Now I was free to go, could breathe fresh air, enjoy the warmth of the sun - yes, yes, I - the survivor - who had lived through the terrible Holocaust- could leave my place of hiding and . . .go, go, go...

"Where to go, where shall I go?"

And then, without a minute's hesitation, I made the decision:

"I shall not return to Yurburg or to Shaudine! Those places - without the Jews- mean nothing to me."

I got up and went to look for other survivors. I wanted to find my fellow Jews, and I found them - very few in Kovno and many more in Vilna. I decided to settle in Vilna, which was now the capital of Lithuania, under the Soviet regime. I also found work, which came as a great blessing. From the physical point of view my life was not particularly difficult. It was difficult, though, to forget what our enemies and prosecutors had done to us. The shadow of the terrible Holocaust haunted me and my soul found no rest. That went on for a long time. Then I understood my place was not here among the whispering ashes of my dear ones. I was the only one left of my family and the Jewish community, what was I doing here?

In those days my dreams were taking me to our country, the country of the Jews, Eretz Yisrael, which had come alive again, after two thousand years of exile. I asked the Soviet Lithuanian authorities to allow me to leave Lithuania, in order to immigrate to Israel, but they refused. I asked them again a number of times. I did not give up. Only in 1967 I received permission to leave Lithuania. I went on aliyah and Israel has been my home since.

I am very happy to live among my people with the family I was lucky enough to establish after the years of the terrible Holocaust.

All we need is health, the health to go on living in our beautiful country, the land of our dreams, in revenge on the beastly murderers of our people.

TRANSLATIOTRANSLATION OF PAGES 429-437

THE GROUP OF "YURBURGERS" IN THE FOREST

Eye-witness account by Yehudah Tarshish, a Partisan Survivor

Edited by Zevulun Poran

At the end of World War II, one of the most cruel wars ever to take place, what was to be expected indeed happened to Nazi Germany. Hitler's army was defeated. Fascism proved to be a total failure. The people of Europe felt relieved, after their desperate battle against German vandalism aiming to destroy them. A period of recuperation and renewal started - the time had come to rebuild and create a world free of fear of persecution and force. Such was the world and thus were all the people of Europe who had known much suffering. However matters were different for the people of Israel, dispersed and exiled all over Europe. They had come out of the horrible battle bruised and wounded. A few were left here and there, one in a village, two in a family. They were unable to rebuild their ruined communities on the soil that was drenched with the blood of their dear ones. As soon as the war was over, therefore, the Holocaust survivors started to move towards Eretz Yisrael, the shelter of those who longed for national salvation and human dignity.

One of those survivors on Lithuanian soil arrived at a safe haven at the end of the war, after he had gone through many difficult experiences in the Kovno ghetto and forests near Yurburg. His name was Yehudah (Yudel) Tarshish, who presently lives in Tel Aviv, and he is a survivor of the group that lived in the forests and was called "The Yurburgers." Some of them were a nucleus of Jews from Yurburg (11 men and women under the leadership of Antanas {Mosheh}), others were Jews who had come to the forest from various places, among them the Slabodka ghetto, to join small units that fought against the enemy.

Professor Dov Levin, the famous Holocaust researcher at the Hebrew University of Jerusalem, talked to Yehuda Tarshish. We found important testimony in his words regarding the fate of the survivors from Yurburg and its surroundings, who went to the forests to fight for their physical safety and take revenge on the enemy who had destroyed their families and community. Furthermore: the Jewish nucleus from Yurburg maintained a connection with the Kovno ghetto, by special envoy, and took tens of imprisoned Jews who were in distress out of the ghetto.

We thought it important to present Yehudah Tarshish's words as an eye-witness account of the courageous survivors from Yurburg and others in the forests surrounding the town. In the end most of them were defeated and fell in the battle in the Yurburg area and their place of burial is unknown. It is a terrible story with a bitter, tragic end.

. . .At the Kovno ghetto (Slabodka) - says Yehudah Tarshish - I was known as a brave guy, who would come and go through the fence that surrounded the ghetto, without a yellow patch and without a Star of David, i.e. without "Lates." A Hoz (rabbit), they were called. Armed with a gun I would cross the ghetto fence in order to smuggle in food and arms from the outside.

In March 1944, after the children's "Aktia" (Action) acquaintances from the ghetto approached me and asked me to help them get to "Inkaras," a rubber factory 5 or 6 kilometers from the Slabodka ghetto. They wanted me to lead them there in order to reach the Yurburg forests from there. I agreed at once.

In those days I also transferred small children from the ghetto to the Lithuanian orphanage called "Lopshialis" (Lopselis). An old woman worked at this orphanage and she would receive the children from me. She was particularly interested in little girls. Once a baby who I was about to transfer to the orphanage was given an injection to make him fall asleep before I would take him out of the ghetto so that he would not cry when I crossed through the fence. I put the baby in a bag at an agreed upon spot near the back door of the orphanage, and when I came next day and brought another bag of sleeping children, the old women told me the child had died. Apparently he had received an overdose.

Those who approached me regarding their transfer to "Inkaras" were in contact with someone called Fainstein. He was a "Brigadir" at the ghetto, i.e. in charge of those leaving on forced labor outside the ghetto. This Fainstein had two brothers in the forests near Yurburg. The Fainstein brothers were quite familiar with the area for they had been born there. Before the war they owned a sawing workshop [sawmill] (*Segewerk*). They spent three years in the forest, armed with Russian submachine guns and other weapons; they inspired fear in the Lithuanians who inhabited the villages and received them at their homes.

When they heard that the Russian army was approaching Lithuania and that the war would soon be over, they asked Jews be removed from the Kovno ghetto and be concentrated in the forests until the war was over. In one of the villages a woman lived who was a convert and wanted to reconvert. This woman risked her life to bring a big ship to the Viliya riverfront near "Inkaras." But, how does one leave the ghetto? I of course had almost free passage to get out of the ghetto, for I knew the militia (Lithuanian police) whose guard post was near the Christian cemetery. Here a few policemen stood guard and in return for money they would turn a blind eye, so that one evening I could take about thirty people out of the ghetto. I often bought arms from these policemen, mainly rifles. I would dismantle the rifle butts and smuggle them into the ghetto for self-defense and for those who were about to join the "Partizanka" in the forests.

I knew the way to "Inkaras" very well, so that I was able to lead those who went to the forest without a problem. We left in the early evening hours and arrived at the boat at midnight. Here the converted woman was waiting for us and she agreed to let me be one of the sailors, although I was not on the list of those going to the forest.

My mother and two sisters remained at the ghetto; they did not know the secret of my going to the forest. My father was killed in 1941, the moment the Germans entered Lithuania.

All those who went to the forest had money to buy food, and light arms mainly. As far as I remember the Bek brothers were with us (Hirshke and Shlomke), Moshke Levin, Fain, the butcher, and other men who possessed arms. The group consisted of 15 men and 12 women, two young women among them.

The members of the group crowded on the bottom of the ship. It was a foggy night. We flowed along the stream of the Viliya, which joins the Nieman River near the "Schloss," the old fortress of Kovno. We were headed for the Yurburg area. We went down stream at a speed of 10 kilometers per hour. I rowed. It was a quiet night, but all of a sudden, an unpleasant surprise: we ran into a steamship. We heard Lithuanian songs and German voices as well. Apparently they were policemen and soldiers. They were heading towards Kovno and we were heading towards Yurburg. We immediately covered all the passengers with canvas, and we tried to get as far away as possible from the boat. The converted woman beckoned to me to go on rowing quickly, and if questions would be asked, only she would answer, for she spoke Lithuanian fluently, like a true gentile. I wore a light peasant coat, so that it was impossible to recognize me as a Jew. It was a fishing boat that had space for forty people. We advanced slowly to our destiny. It was clear to all of us that many surprises lay in stock for us. We had therefore taken along arms to defend ourselves. All those who went to the forest knew they would live the life of "Partizanka" in the forest, under the command of the Fainstein brothers, who were experienced in the life of the forest. We were prepared for this.

The plan was to accommodate the women and children at peasants' homes, while the men and young women would be organized into guard groups. It was explained to us that the Fainstein brothers planned to concentrate 200 to 250 men of army age, armed, in the forest to form a fighting force. They also planned to "absorb" people who had been trained by Hayim (Chaim) Yelin's organizations and the Zionist movements. Till now there had been no contact between the Fainstein brothers and these organizations, except for the connection the converted woman maintained with the ghetto every couple of months.

After hours of energetic and exhausting rowing all night, we arrived at the Shakai shore in the morning, not far from Yurburg. A few terrifying encounters awaited us on the way, but the important thing is that we arrived at our destination, although here another unpleasant experience was waiting for us.

This is what happened. We went down to the beach and hid among bushes growing on the sand dunes, not far from the Nieman River. It had been agreed that a Lithuanian would wait for us on the beach; however, apparently we were mistaken. The converted woman went to look for the Lithuanian, and it took two hours before she finally returned with him. The Lithuanian's name was Kazis. The Fainstein brothers had promised him payment for his efforts and had assured him that once the war was over he would receive a lot of money, as all those who were coming were wealthy people from Kovno who had homes and a lot of property.

Kazis led us to the nearby forest and he himself went to look for food. The promise was kept. A couple of hours later he came, bringing along bread, butter and all sorts of porridge on his wagon. We rested and waited for nightfall, getting organized under field conditions. The Fainstein brothers came and issued orders, which we obeyed. The women and children were accommodated at peasants' homes and the men were divided into two groups that would operate in the forest. I was put in charge of one group. In addition to the Fainstein brothers we knew another Jewish commander in the forest, nicknamed Antanas. Antanas' family was killed by the Lithuanians and Germans.

He himself had escaped and roamed the forests, armed from head to toe. I was given the nickname Vladas, for everyone here had a nickname. I was given a F.N. gun, made in Belgium with a Lithuanian emblem. The gun came with thirty 9-mm. bullets.

A couple of days later we were introduced to an officer, a Russian pilot, via Antanas. At a special roll call we were told that the pilot's plane had been downed over Yurburg, and Antanas had found him in the forest. He was a senior lieutenant who had been decorated. We were sure we would hear details from him about what was going on at the front and we very disappointed when we heard nothing new. About 30-40 armed men were at this meeting, but the Lithuanians in the area who observed us were convinced that we were a military force of hundreds of men. They were afraid of us and even the Lithuanian policemen in the villages avoided entering the forest area.

That evening, people were appointed to special functions, such as food supply, guarding the camp and sabotage. In those days we went onto the roads and attacked German vehicles.

Others went on procurement missions, i.e. to obtain food in the Lithuanian villages, particularly from those about whom we knew cooperated with the enemy. Once we even had to shoot a Lithuanian, who cooperated with the Germans, for refusing to hand over a few cows.

Most actions were planned by Antanas (Mosheh), he was a serious, poised man, a well-known war hero and all the Lithuanians were afraid of him. He was familiar with the Yurburg area and spoke Lithuanian like a gentile, although his dark face revealed his origins.

In the Lithuanian War of Independence (1918) he was a "Savanoris" - a volunteer in the Lithuanian army. The Fainsteins also followed his orders without question, and so did the officer, the Russian pilot.

In the summer of 1944 another 15 men arrived from the Kovno ghetto. The ghetto was about to be completely liquidated. When they learned about our group in the forest around Yurburg a few managed to escape from the ghetto and came to us on foot, a 70-80 kilometers (about 50 miles) walk, in spite of the hurdles and risks on the way. In those days the plan was to take hundreds of people out of the ghetto, in spite of our limited ability to accommodate them under forest conditions. Unfortunately, the ghetto was liquidated within a week. The soldiers on the Russian-Lithuanian front advanced and arrived at Rasein. The Lithuanian division that took part in the conquest of Zemaitija was already at the front. Most of the soldiers in this division were Jewish and the Russians and Lithuanians formed a minority here. Among them was Wolf Vilensky, the well-known general who earned the title "Hero of the Soviet Union."

The horror stories of the Kovno ghetto survivors enticed us to take a course of action aimed at preventing the enemy from carrying out his plans and beat him. We were 75 men in total. Half had some kind of weapon, rifles, sub-machines, pistols and grenades. We were an independent unit. We came into contact with a Partisan battalion (Otriad) only once. They had come from the Rudniki forest and were advancing towards Yurburg, there were Jews among them. They wanted to strike at the enemy's back. They were armed with heavy Soviet machine guns.

We wanted to join them but they refused, thus we were forced to continue to operate against the German troops on our own, in the area where we were, to hinder their movement and avenge the Jewish people. It is superfluous to point out that the fire of wrath burned in all of us and we were always ready to volunteer for the most dangerous actions.

The security situation in the forest grew worse by the day. Therefore all the people from Yurburg were divided into two groups; one counted 30 people and the other 40. The Fainstein brothers and I were appointed to head one group, while Antanas and the officer, the Russian pilot, led the other group.

Bunkers were dug in the forest for both groups, although this was done without an adequate engineering plan. Each bunker had one entrance and exit and this proved to be a serious pitfall. We equipped the bunkers with water, which we filtered through bed sheets.

One night we encountered two soldiers. We were sure they were Germans, but they spoke Russian and told us they were Latvians who had deserted from the German army. They said that in Latvia they had been forced to enlist and they were now ready to join the Partisans against the German army. We wondered whether to believe them. Tt was well known that there were many murderers among the Latvians who cooperated with the Germans. We had a difference of opinion, but in the end we took pity on them. Jews are known for their compassion and therefore the warm Jewish heart is incapable of killing, in spite of the doubts we felt. Some, among them the officer, the Russian pilot, thought that we might learn details about the front from them and about the German movements in the areas near us. In short: after we put them to some sort of test we accepted them amongst us. One of them was called Volodia and the other Mishka. Antanas ordered they be transferred to my bunker, and that is what I did. After they were interrogated we found out that they had indeed been Latvian "Partisans" in the past and had taken part in the liquidation of Jews in the Riga ghetto, at the order of the Germans. They also spoke about the coming German strategy on the front, about the communication trenches, lighting devices, barbed wire fences, minefields etc. Some of us offered the idea of breaking through the German front and joining the Soviet army, others rejected this idea. When we saw that the Germans reinforced their troops and brought a lot of ammunition and stoves for the winter to the forest, we decided to try to break through the front together with the Latvians and cross over to the Soviet fighters.

Both the Russian officer pilot and the Fainsteins volunteered to be among those who would break through the front. Thus we left, ten of us, to a post opposite the enemy's positions. We saw the change of guard in the German communication trenches. We left the Latvians and the Russian officer behind, for good reason. We heard the exchange of fire between the Germans and the Russians. Someone from the communication trench switched on a torch.

All of a sudden the two Latvians jumped up and started to run, shouting, towards the communication trenches, presuming we would all follow. The Germans started to shoot and to shout "Halt!" (Stop). "Halt!" …but we did not run. One of the Latvians (Mishka) was wounded in the foot and we turned back and ran away.

The Germans ran after us, shooting all the while, but they were unable to catch up with us in the dark of night. When we sat down to rest, exhausted, we saw the two Latvians come close, one of them limping and leaning on his friend's shoulder. We tied up the injured man's leg and informed Antanas about what had happened.

We passed a quiet night. In the morning, at about ten o'clock, a group of military policemen of the German field police suddenly appeared. The armed policemen took up position close to us and aimed their rifles at us. The moment I saw them I shouted at the top of my voice to Fainstein, "Yurgis Pazurek!" i.e. "Look Yurgis, look!" We immediately understood that we were lost. We opened fire, but they outnumbered us and surrounded us on all sides. We saw them face to face from a 15 meters (50 feet) distance. A doctor or medic stood out among them. They did not enter into battle with us, but allowed us to escape, although they ran after us with their trained dogs. We shot at them and they returned fire. Thus, running and exchanging fire; we ran about 5 kilometers from the bunker. We managed to pass from one part of the forest to another. When the shooting died down and there was no sign left of the Germans, we sat down to rest among the bushes, when suddenly we heard the noise of shots and explosions. We knew that our force inside the bunker had grenades, and they probably used them against the Germans. In truth, we were just guessing. Our heart was beating strongly but our force was too weak to help. Only later did we learn the bitter fate of the bunker from young woman called Frida (Frieda). Without Frieda, those who were in the bunker would have taken their secret with them to the grave. Genia Angel was saved from the second bunker and she too is a witness who survived.

The following is Frida's story. First of all, it immediately became clear that the two Latvians were part of the German field force. As they managed to fool us and became well acquainted with our bunkers and everything concerning them, they passed this information on to the Germans. The Germans approached the opening, assisted by the Latvians, and one of them issued the order "Ihr geht mahl raus. Wenn nicht, schmeisse Ich meine Grenaten herein!" (If you don't come out I'll throw the grenades inside) Those inside the bunker did not surrender. They opened fire from within. The exchange of fire went on for a while.

Those inside the bunker were at a disadvantage. The Germans came slowly closer to the opening of the bunker and threw the grenades inside. Some were killed instantly, others were mortally wounded, and their legs were torn off, hands and other parts of their body. It is impossible to describe the horrendous scene inside the bunker. Finally all those who were still alive surrendered.

Outside, the Germans lined them up in rows and searched them for money and other valuables. Some Germans even went down into the bunker in order to find loot there.

Frida (Frieda) too was standing in the row, she asked the German medic to allow her to step aside "for personal needs" due to her illness. The medic consented. When Frida went a short distance away from the row and started to carry out "her personal needs" the medic turned his face away for a moment, probably out of embarrassment. When Frida noticed this, she drew forth her courage and quickly started to run away. The medic drew his gun and shot at her. The bullet hit the top of her finger, covering her hand in blood, but Frida overcame the pain and continued to run as fast as she could in a muddy swamp, until she found a place of hiding in the woods. That is how Frida was saved, the only one of those who was in the bunker. The others were led, heavily guarded, to Yurburg, where according to testimony by the Lithuanians, they were all cruelly murdered. They took the bitter truth with them to their graves.

At night our group of guards decided to return to the bunker to see what had happened to those who were inside. We walked silently along, in the darkness of night, and approached the bunker. The horror scene became immediately clear, even the devil had not yet thought of this, heads, legs, hands and body parts that were impossible to identify, covered in blood and mire. We were only able to identify the leg of our doctor Mordehai (Mottel) Aharonson by the color of his pants. Tt was terrible . . . awful and terrible. . . .

Shocked we climbed out of the bunker into the open air, depressed and in despair. "What shall we do now?" How can we go on?" One of us got up and said that if everyone was dead there was no sense to our lives any longer: "Let's commit suicide!" Some were inclined to accept this idea. But I, the youngest of the commanders, said: "If they killed everybody, we have nothing to lose, we will get up and avenge their blood." After a long moment of silence and much deliberation, my proposal was accepted.

However, if at that moment someone would have drawn a gun and shot, everyone would have committed suicide and nothing would have been left of any of us. The fate of the second bunker would have been the same as the fate of our bunker. Those who remained alive there were led to Yurburg where, as mentioned above, they were shot.

When we had drunk the cup of poison down to its last drop, we decided to accept the Fainstein's advice and go to Yurburg. Here the Fainstein brothers knew a Lithuanian, an old acquaintance, who lived near Yurburg. We hoped we would find shelter there and would perhaps even manage to pay back the murderers in kind. We gathered food and arms, someone still had a few gold rubles left and we went ahead. We walked the whole night and towards morning we arrived, tired and exhausted at the home of the gentile who lived at the entrance to Yurburg. The Fainsteins knew him well. At first the gentile was alarmed, but when he saw his old friends, the Fainsteins, he started to kiss them. It was a rather forced scene, but that was unavoidable under the circumstances. In short: he received a few golden rubles and became very friendly.

We found temporary refuge in the gentile's barn under the bundles of fodder. Once Germans came to the gentile's home and looked into the barn, but this time we were lucky and they did not find us. As time passed, we witnessed exchanges of fire between German soldiers and the Soviets in Yurburg and its surroundings.

One day our patience came to an end. We decided to break out of our quarantine and go to the Russian front. That is what we did. After many risks and hurdles we encountered a Soviet reconnaissance platoon. The Russians asked us: "Who are you?" - and we answered "Partizans." They immediately disarmed us, took off our watches and boots; we had nothing left. When we complained they said "Vi Yevrei Pomogli Niemzem"- i.e. "You, Jews, helped the Germans." They intended to blame the Jews for having worked at the forced labor camps of the Germans, thereby strengthening the enemy.

Our attempts to explain that the Jews who had been imprisoned in the ghettoes had been forced to work under threat, failed. The Russian soldiers were stubborn and did not listen.

The unexpected disappointment came soon enough. Only when we met a Jewish officer did we get back our boots, thanks to his swift intervention. The watches were no longer to be found and the weapons were no longer needed.

In the end we received certificates (a piece of paper) that we were Partisans and entitled to go to liberated Kovno. The Fainstein brothers decided to remain to receive back their property, while we three, Fein, Koniukhovsky and I, went to Kovno.

In Kovno we found total chaos. We had trouble finding a Jew who took us into his sorry home. We saw the destruction and ruined life of the few Jews who had survived and been absorbed by the town, most of them had already packed their suitcase in order to leave the valley of death as soon as possible. They all wanted to leave and not remain in the valley of tears. They were looking towards Eretz Yisrael, of course, but how to escape from here? Though I longed to leave Lithuania, I had a strong urge to settle accounts with the murderers of my family and relatives. On my way "there" I joined those who fought against our people's enemy inside Germany, and as a former investigating judge of Nazis I took a great deal of revenge, our revenge on the Germans.

From the murderous land of Germany I arrived after many events in my own country, to build and be built by it.

Monument to Remember the Murdered Heroes: " In this place on August 12, 1941 were murdered 28 children, 19 of their mothers and one man by the German fascists and the Lithuanians ....." ------- Standing alongside the monument is Aba Vals and his wife Miriam, who were responsible for building this monument. [Note: no mention of Jews, JA]

The mass grave is located at Kokhovskina near Kidul.

DARING ESCAPE OF THE PARTISANS IN THE FOREST

THE PERSONAL STORY OF MORDEKHAI BEN TUVIYAH AND RACHEL BERKOVER

By Mordehai (Mordechai) Ben Tuviyah and Rachel Berkover

I left Yurburg a long time ago. I have no idea of what is going on there. The news coming out of there is terrifying. Destiny has taken me to Kovno and from there to the Slabodka ghetto. I am not the only one from Yurburg in the ghetto. There are other Jews from Yurburg here who had arrived one way or another.

We all share a cruel fate. We live here under crowded conditions, a degenerated life. However, the fear of becoming fewer and fewer is even more terrible. The actions, ah yes, the actions! From time to time Jews are being abducted; old men, women and little children are being taken to Fort XI, near Slabodka, from where there is no return. Those who are able to work are sent to forced-labor camps. Those who can still contribute to the German war machine, stay alive. To stay alive, that is the aim of every Jew in the ghetto, but chances are slim.

Each day there are fewer people left in the ghetto. What to do? Young people get organized into underground resistance groups and go into the woods. I too liked the idea and became obsessed with it, until one day I implemented it.

This is what happened.

On 11 June 1944 a Gestapo order was issued whereby all the men in the Kovno ghetto had to gather the next morning on the plot between the big blocks, to move to a labor camp. It was clear to us what "leaving the ghetto" meant. Where we were going, this was not explained to us. An order is an order and must be obeyed.

I did not sleep a wink all night; neither did many of my friends. There was a tense quiet at the ghetto. In every corner people huddled together and asked each other how to escape the evil. I had decided to run away. But how? Where to? The ghetto was closed off by a tight ring of Gestapo and the German army. I lay there, thinking of a solution but, unfortunately, did not find one.

I got up at dawn, took my rucksack which contained all my belongings and went out to join all those who were going to the plot. People were coming from all corners of the ghetto, those who were still alive after all the selections and deportations. Those who had a family gathered together. I had no one I could join; I was all alone. My brother Yosef had run away when the war broke out with my mother to someplace beyond the borders of Lithuania, hoping to be saved. My brother Eliezer with his wife and my sister Hayah with her husband remained in Yurburg, my sister Devorah was at the Keidani camp during the children's action with her little son. She refused to hand over her son to be killed and decided to die with him. Indeed they were both killed together with the other babies. The other 18 babies were killed too and thrown into transport vans, like slaughtered poultry.

My sister Tsiporah was at the Vilna ghetto with her husband; my two sisters Hannah and Scheinale, who were at the Keidani camp, were sent to the Ponivezh camp. The whole family dispersed in the days of the Holocaust as chaff before the wind. I have no idea what happened to my dear ones, I guess I shall never know. Thus I was left alone, the only one of my family who remained. I was tormented and did not know what to do. Even today I face the same problem. Then I remembered the bible passage, Book of Psalms, "Look to your right and see here, I know no one, there is no escape, no one cares about me. I called out to you, Almighty God, I said you were my shelter, my part in the land of life. Hear my lamentation, for I am very miserable, save me from those who persecute me, for they are stronger than me."

Here I stood among many others, like a man who had been found guilty and was waiting for his bitter destiny. We waited for an order to be issued. It soon came - "Go!" We left with the heavy feeling that perhaps we would never see our town and our family again. We walked in the direction of the suburb of Kovno, Aleksotas, on the other side of the Nieman River. We saw a look of malicious joy on the faces of the gentiles who lined both sides of the road. Their look was humiliating and repulsive. And then I remembered the lofty words of the prayer: "Almighty God, I am a member of the bond you created Look down from heaven and see how humiliated we are and mocked by the gentiles, they are leading us like sheep to be slaughtered, to be killed, to be beaten and disgraced." They stood on the sidewalk and we had to walk on the borders of the road. I was deeply grieved. Thus we passed over the bridge and approached the railroad tracks. From far away we saw a series of wagons, and tens of armed S.S. soldiers were waiting for us. Before we even came near the wagons we heard wild shouting, "Get on to the wagons!" They were cattle wagons. There was uproar. All the people from the ghetto quickly climbed onto the wagons and tried to find a space. I also climbed onto the wagon with my rucksack and sat down. Some of my acquaintances joined me. The wagon was overcrowded. Everyone was waiting for the journey into the unknown. There was a mood of depression in the wagon. We were closed in like animals. A 60-year old German soldier was positioned next to the door and he had to guard us and make sure we did not escape, God forbid.

After lengthy preparations the train left. The soldier guard stood up and said to us: "You'd better know that I shall not hesitate to shoot anyone who tries to escape, so watch out!" It was 11:30 o'clock. The wagon rattled and the soldier guard fell asleep. Not so the people who were led to slaughter like cattle.

Everyone stood lost in thought, tired and depressed. One of my friends wanted to tell me something but he suddenly fell silent. He was unable to utter a sound. I was very sad, but after an hour or so I pulled myself together. It was 12 o'clock. One of my friends peeped through a crack in the window, recognized the place and whispered in my ear: "We are in the Kazlu-Ruda area." This struck me like a bolt of lighting. I knew that the place was in the area where the Jewish Partisans operated who had escaped from the ghetto. I immediately got the idea to escape, to flee to the forest. In the meantime I saw that the soldier guard was drowsy and had perhaps even fallen asleep. I told myself this was the best time to escape. But how to go about it?

All of a sudden I thought of the psalm, "I shall raise my eyes unto the mountains, my help will come from there. Help from God, who created heaven and earth. God will guard you against all evil and will guard your soul. God will look after you wherever you come and go, now and forever." I got up my courage and told my friend that I had decided to jump through the window and escape. Those who wanted to were welcome to join me. They hesitated. One of them started to grumble, if you run away, then they will kill us. At that moment the soldier-guard fell asleep and he fell into deep slumber. Yes, I said to myself, this is the right time. I asked one of the woman passengers called Feige Vislitzky from Kovno to hide me from the sleeping guard's eyes. She kissed me and wished me good luck. I immediately climbed on the boxes standing next to the small window, opened the window carefully, moved my head and part of my body out and when my friends pushed me from behind. I found myself outside the window. I fell onto the small ramp at the front of the wagon and was about to jump into the passageway when I saw a train approaching on the other track, in the opposite direction. I doubled up for a moment, allowed the train to pass and then jumped down into the bushes lining the road. I got scratched by the bushes and was slightly wounded. It is not too bad, I told myself; I shall overcome. Better be injured and free than prey to the Nazi beast.

When I recovered from the daring act, I crawled away from the railway track and lay down to rest in a hidden corner. When I raised my head I saw that three people were coming towards me. They spoke Lithuanian and this encouraged me. They had apparently seen me jump off the train and offered help. I did not want to go with them, for I did not know who they were. However, they suggested I turn to the railway guard who lived in a little house behind the tall tree, they told me he was a good man and he would help me if he could.

They also told me to be very careful, for the area was full of German soldiers. I thanked them for their advice, got up and went straight to the house of the railway guard.

I slowly and hesitantly approached the guard's house. I saw a little girl in the yard, about seven years old, who started to call her mother who was in the garden. When the guard's wife approached I said hello to her in Lithuanian. The woman answered me very politely and invited me into her home.

Inside, I told her that I was the son of a mixed marriage between a Jewish woman and a gentile, and that I had been put into the Kovno ghetto. I went on to say that I had been put into a train wagon, together with many Jews, and that I had jumped off the train, for I was about to be exterminated. That was how all the Jews were treated. I have come to you to ask for help. I have heard that there are Jewish Partisans near here and I want to join them. "You will have to ask my husband," she said. In the meantime, until my husband comes, wash yourself and eat something. I did as I was told. I washed myself and she gave me a bowl of soup. In the meantime her husband, the railway guard, arrived. He heard my story from his wife. He nodded his head and told me my life was in danger if I was seen at their home. Nevertheless, he suggested I go to the estate, 4 kilometers away and there I would be told how to achieve my goal. I thanked the guard and his wife and was about to leave. The good people were very kind to me and gave me some food to take along.

Encouraged, I went on my way and turned towards the estate. I stopped at the forest for afternoon prayer and was about to go on when I suddenly remembered the psalm: "Please, God, guard me against evil, save me from the evil man, from those who want to divert my steps." I said to God; "You are my God, please, oh Lord, hear my call for mercy." I continued on my way, hoping God would lead me on the right road to my goal. After about an hour I arrived at a large estate. When I entered the yard a dog started to bark. I was immediately welcomed by the estate owner and his two sons. They asked me to come in and sit at their table. I told them my story, who I was, and what I wanted to know. The estate owner told me that German soldiers came to his estate each day to buy food and that if they saw me there it would be harmful to him and my life would be in danger. After he had told me this, he suggested I sleep on straw in the barn and at dawn I would have to leave the estate. This I did. I slept soundly on the straw, which to me was better than a king's canopy. When I went to the estate owner's home to bid him farewell, I found a wonderful breakfast on the table, two eggs with bread and butter, tasty cheese and a can of milk. I did not want to bother him, but he insisted. I ate and satisfied my appetite.

When I left his house, the estate owner accompanied me, and pointed out the way to me along the forest paths to an estate owner who, he said, would be able to offer more help than he. Thus, I took leave of my benefactor, but he did not forget to give me a parcel of food and put 100 Chervontses, Russian money, into my pocket. I left this estate with a wonderful feeling and with the hope that God would continue to lead me on a successful road.

I went to the second estate owner with a feeling of certainty. When I entered his house, I immediately saw a carpentry workshop, where he, his wife and sons were working. I said hello and they answered me in a friendly manner. They also asked me if I had eaten breakfast and if I was no longer hungry. I told them I had eaten at the home of estate owner Stankevitz and that he had filled my rucksack with a lot of food. After this initial encounter, I repeated my story and added, of course, that I wanted to know where the Jewish Partisans were. The house owner, a carpenter listened attentively to what I said, took paper and pencil and started to draft the lines of a map. When he was finished he explained the details of the map to me. This road, he said, leads to the narrow railway tracks that go on for about 25 kilometers in the forest area. When you reach the end of the forest you will see an overturned locomotive there. Turn to your right onto an empty lot, here you must be very careful for there are many German soldiers there. From there, turn to the nearby woods, on the right, and continue on the straight road which leads to the village marked on the map. He attached a note to the map for his cousin in that village. I thanked him from the bottom of my heart. I would have kissed him. Thus I went on my way. I knew the road was difficult and full of mines, but there was no way of return. I burned all of my bridges behind me and had to go forward.

With the map and the note I walked along with confidence, although from time to time I had my doubts. I sat down to rest along the road. I took out my phylacteries which I had received before the selection from my neighbor Rabbi Mans. He was was later executed, together with his family by the Nazis. I look after the phylacteries as if they were the most precious objects of my life. This time too I put on the phylacteries and prayed. It was a prayer of thanks to God who till now had helped me along. After the prayer I ate and went on. It was 12 o'clock, and all of a sudden I looked up. I saw the locomotive at the side of the road, marked on the sketch of the map. From here I walked with a lot of hope in my heart. In the distance I saw a man in the forest. I was a little frightened, but when he saw me he ran away. I laughed. Did I look so frightening?

In short, I walked on. It was 7 pm. Finally I saw a house. I approached the house, knocked on the door and went in. I saw a young man sitting in front of a sewing machine, sewing in the light of an oil lamp. I said hello and he answered me. He was not afraid of the stranger who had come to his house. He immediately asked where I had come from and where I was going. I told him what I had told the others.

He saw that I was tired. Soon, he said, my wife will return and she will bring food for dinner. I saw that he was not a rich man. I immediately told him that I had enough food for him and his wife too. I only needed a place to sleep and some guidance as to how to reach the Jewish Partisans in the forest. My host told me that he had seen two young men in the morning, apparently the forest people, who had asked about the road to Kovno. I was happy to hear there were signs of the Partisans in the area. In the meantime, the woman had returned with a basket full of food. I was asked to dinner. When I told her I had enough food, she urged me to at least have a cup of fresh milk. After my meeting with my hosts, I went up to the barn and fell asleep. I slept soundly, as if in my mother's bed when I was born.

Early in the morning my host woke me up. Breakfast was already on the table. I ate and shook his hand. Before I left I asked him about the village which the carpenter had sketched on the note intended for his cousin. He told me the village was nearby. He indicated the direction, and as far as the man was concerned to whom the note was sent - he told me - he was a cowardly man, not to be relied upon. Although he knew much, he would not tell me anything worthwhile. We separated and I shook his hand once more.

After about an hour's walk, I saw a house in the distance that looked like the one I was looking for. Indeed, someone I met on the way referred me to the man to whom I was supposed to give the note. As I approached the house, I saw that the door was open and a few people were sitting inside around a radio. I said hello to them and asked about the man to whom I was supposed to give regards from his cousin. The man got up and beckoned me to step outside. He was apparently afraid that someone would hear about his connection with me. I came straight to the point and asked him where the Jewish Partisans were. I saw that he turned pale and started to stammer. I did not understand whether he was afraid or if he did not want to reveal his secret to me. In any case, from what he said I understood that I had to follow the path in the forest for about 8 km, and from there get to a village called Shtura. Partisans came to this village about every two days.

I left, believing he had told me the truth. However, a gentile I met on the way told me I should go in the opposite direction. I understood the tailor had been right.

What to do? I turned around and walked a long and tiring way until I reached my destination. I saw a large estate in the village, where I was told to go. I entered a house where I saw a woman speaking to a man in Russian. I stood there for a moment, waiting for the woman to be available. When the man left, I turned to the woman and told her my story and why I had come. She immediately answered that she knew nothing about the people I was looking for. True, various people passed through the village, but she did not know them. She added it would not be a good idea to stay here. If the authorities found me, it would be very bad for her and me.

Disappointed, I left her house and asked myself "where will I find help" for I had met so much contempt, but I gathered my strength, " for those who believe in God will "find mercy." All sorts of thoughts crossed my mind. While I was deliberating, I saw wagons with wooden boards enter the yard and a young man was sitting on it. I did not know whether he was Jewish or not. But the young man saw me and jumped off the wagon, came up to me and looked at me as if we had agreed to meet here. He asked me whether I spoke Lithuanian and I replied I did, he grabbed me with both his hands and held on to me as if he was drowning in the sea, God forbid. We were both very moved and just looked at each other. Once we calmed down he told me he and another group of Jews had worked at the labor camp under the command of Nazi Germans. One day the German camp commander told the Jews they were leaving the place.

He told me his story:

"We knew this meant our life was in danger. We got organized immediately and we planned to leave, as we were told, but we bribed the Ukrainian guards we paid them a lot of money to allow us to disperse in the forest while we were walking. That is indeed what happened. In the evening we presented ourselves to the camp commander, and after an accurate count, we were led through the forest in the direction of the railway tracks. Those guarding us were the Ukrainians. When we were walking to an unknown destination at midnight we heard a sharp whistle and shots, this was the sign that had been agreed upon with the guards to disperse in the woods. That is what we did. We dispersed in the forest. The Ukrainian guards disappeared and we were left to ourselves. There were about 30 people in the group, families among them. Now we were living together. We set up a temporary camp and wanted to join the permanent camp of the Partisans. Nearly all of us are from Vilna."

He said, "We do not know Lithuanian. You will be able to help us with the Lithuanian population in the area." The armed young men who were with the young man, who owned the wagon, also spoke Lithuanian. I recognized one of them as someone from the Kovno ghetto. Then I knew that "God had heard my lamentations and prayers."

The young man from the Kovno ghetto knew me. He had fled from Fort IX. I asked him about my brother-in-law Yehudah Meister, who came from Yurburg and I received the positive answer that he was in the Partisan camp. My joy knew no bounds. I said to myself, " God be blessed each day and God shall bestow salvation on us, Sela."

With the help of God I have come to this point. The young men suggested I join their unit. I full heartedly agreed, for this is what I had wanted all along. I helped the young man to buy food for the group and to make contact with the Lithuanians, for I spoke the language fluently. We loaded all the purchases on the wagon. I sat next to the young man who owned the wagon, and the two armed young men who accompanied him sat crowded in the back.

When towards evening we arrived at the place where those who had fled with the assistance of the Lithuanians were, there was a lot of joy. They were happy, and so was I. We had found each other. However, I had no one there with whom I could share my experiences of the recent days. However, I adjusted to my situation. We ate the food we had brought with us on the wagon. We were in high spirits. At 11 pm at night we left. We went to join the Partisans' camp. We were ordered not to utter a word on the way. We walked through the forest all night long. We were tired and exhausted.

Towards morning we saw smoke in the distance. The leaders told us we had arrived at our destination. We arrived at the Partisans camp in the morning. The leaders were allowed to enter by the Partisans who carefully guarded the camp. We entered one after another. We presented ourselves to the camp commander. When I entered the commander's tent my heart pounded, I was so excited. The commander asked me all sorts of questions about my family and myself. In the end he told me that a relative of mine, Yehudah Meister from Yurburg, was at the camp, that he was now on guard duty and that I would be able to speak to him the moment he came off duty. I was so moved that I started to cry. I cried for joy that I had reached my destination and in sorrow that none of my brothers and sisters had had my good fortune to be saved.

Once I had made myself at home at the Partisans camp, I sat down on the mattress and waited for my brother-in-law. Soon my brother-in-law came to me. We fell into each other's arms and started to cry like babies. The first question my brother-in-law Yehudah (Yudel) Meister asked me was what had happened to his wife and little two-year-old son.

I wanted to postpone the subject, but he would not let go of me and I was forced to tell him the bitter truth: how they had been cruelly murdered. I am not sure my brother-in-law heard all I told him about them, for he was sitting there, crying and tearing out his hair. When my brother-in-law said good-bye to them, his son was a year old baby. He had not yet had time to get to know him and enjoy his company. After a year he had been abducted by the German murderers in the children's action at the Kovno ghetto, and taken to Fort IX, a place of no return. Thus we sat and talked for a long time, until we were called to lunch. After the meal we continued to talk. I preferred not to speak about the disasters that had befallen the family, for I knew I would make him sad. I learned from my brother-in-law that Mosheh Magidovitz from Yurburg was also at the camp. I was very excited and went to see him. We were overjoyed. Three people from Yurburg at the Partisans camp, three Partisans, three out of many from Yurburg, who did not have this good fortune. We were the few who had been lucky.

Towards evening I was given a rifle with bullets. Within an hour I passed accelerated training in the use of arms. Here I am holding a gun and I am able to defend myself against the enemy. I also received an explanation about the arrangements at the camp and rules imposed on the Partisans. Thus I passed the first day at the Partisans camp.

Towards evening we received the order to carry out a raid on one of the villages in order to equip the camp with food. The farmers knew it was no use to argue with us.

We received what we needed and also a wagon to carry the food. We returned tired and exhausted from this action. After a while we went to the villages to look for gentile infiltrators, who cooperated with the Germans and provided them with information about the Jewish Partisans' whereabouts. When we found them, we liquidated them. Everything was done at the commander's decision and at his orders.

One evening we were told that at midnight a plane would deliver equipment to us. The plane would drop the equipment at our airport with a parachute. Our airport was situated near the camp. It was 2 kilometers long and was on muddy land. We had to light six bonfires as a signal to the plane. Indeed, at the prescribed time we heard the noise of the approaching plane. There was a great deal of tension. We were afraid the German soldiers would spot the plane and then we would be lost. We were trained before the action. We stood in silence and saw the plane flying overhead when suddenly; a huge parcel was thrown out of the plane.

We all hurried to extract the heavy parcel from the mud. We carried it on our shoulders to the wagon that was waiting for us. We loaded the parcel on the wagon together with the parachute. We aimed our rifles and accompanied the wagon until it safely reached the camp. We unloaded the parcel and folded the parachute. There were Russian arms and ammunition in the parcel, cigarettes and even chocolate. The action was successful and we all enjoyed it. In the morning we heard the buzzing sound of a German plane which had apparently spotted us at night, but it did not dare come near us. The Germans were afraid of us and we of them. We were always tense. We would listen to the radio broadcasts about the situation at the front. The news was better recently. We, from Yurburg, would from time to time meet and exchange memories of our dear town Yurburg and our loved ones who had been killed in the first months of the war. We were lonely and we all waited for the day when we would be able to avenge the blood that had been spilled.

The days passed by and almost every day there were actions of some kind or other.

One day we went to look for food, as usual. I was in charge of the action. My brother-in-law, Yehudah Maister, was with me as well as two Russian soldiers who had escaped from a prisoner camp, and others. On our way we arrived at the house of a rich estate owner. We knocked on the door and entered. Two women and a man stood in front of us. I politely bid them good evening and they replied in kind. Before we had even explained our request to the estate owner, he said he knew why we had come. "Come," he said, "I will give you what you want." While we were still talking, one of the women asked a question in Yiddish. I was taken by surprise. It turned out that she was a Jewish girl from Kovno who had been here for two years, and that here she had found protection against all bad. We were very moved by her story. In the end I got up, told my friends the story and said, "here we will not take anything." A gentile, who risks his life in order to rescue a Jewish soul, is a friend of ours. The estate owner was surprised by my decision, but thanked me and all the people in the group. From here we went to the next estate owner and took all the food we needed from him. We loaded everything onto the wagon and returned to the flourmill, the meeting point of the other groups in the village.

Here something unexpected happened. All of a sudden automatic fire opened at us from all sides. We had no choice but to leave the place in a hurry. When we counted, it appeared that two were missing. The commander was furious. In many cases [like this] we went back to a village after a while to repay them in kind. This happened this time too.

Immediately after dinner we received the order to go on an important and dangerous mission. Where to, we did not know. When we were gathered together we were given tin boxes with a lace. We took the boxes with us as well as our personal arms. At the roll call we were told what the purpose of our nightly mission was. We were led to the flourmill in the village from where the mortal fire had been opened at us. Here we were told to disperse and place the boxes near the wall of the mill after all the laces had been tied together. We were immediately ordered to run the distance of at least a kilometer from the mill and here we waited for the results of our action. All of a sudden we heard a tremendous explosion and saw a sea of fire rise up to the sky. This was the retaliation against the German fascists. We returned to camp where a pleasant surprise was waiting for us. The two young men who had been missing from yesterday's action had returned healthy and well.

Sometimes life at the camp was very meaningful and sometimes it was boring. We were merely interested in one thing, what was going on there in the terrible war? What about the Kovno ghetto, who had survived and who had not? The news we received was very sad. We talked about Yurburg, the cradle of our youth, with love and longing, as if it still existed, as in the past. Thus many days passed by. One day the person in charge of reconnaissance, the only gentile at the camp dressed in the uniform of a Gestapo officer asked me to join him on a tour. I joined him and we went to a village not far from our camp. It was on July 30, 1944. We entered a house known to the gentile. We found girls at the house who were sewing clothes and listening to radio broadcasts. And see here, what did we hear, an important and pleasant bit of information. The Russian army battalions had liberated Vilna, Lithuania's capital. Our joy knew no bounds. It was as if we were drunk. We hurried back to the Partisans camp through the cornfields, to tell them the good news. When we approached the camp, the gentile said, "let's shoot a round of fire in honor of the liberation of our capital." We both enthusiastically fired a few shots. Suddenly we heard shooting at us from the other side of the cornfield. The gentile ordered me to run and inform the camp that a group of fascist soldiers from the Lithuanian army was in the area and was shooting. I did as he told me. While I was running I saw a Lithuanian soldier not far away who was operating in the framework of the German army. I shot at him and when he fell to the ground I went up to him and did not check whether he was alive or dead. I took his rifle and ran to our camp, to tell them that Lithuanian soldiers serving in the German army were near us. The commander of our camp immediately ordered the shock troops to go. We went with 25 men, while I was their guide.

We had barely left the forest when we already heard the sound of the attackers' shooting. We were in the line of fire. Our commander issued the order, "Advance!" "Hit them!" The battle was fierce. We pursued the fascist Lithuanian soldiers and killed some of them. Two of our men, the Russian Partisans were killed. We were very grieved. We did not find consolation in the fact that many enemy soldiers had fallen. Each Partisan was dear to us. When the battle was over we went back with the Lithuanian gentile to one of the estates to drink some water. Suddenly the dog that was tied up there started to bark. The gentile was annoyed at his barking; he was furious at the dog, went up to him and hit him with his rifle butt. Unfortunately a bullet came loose, which struck the Lithuanian gentile who fell and was dead. We all stood around him in silence, very sad. We had lost a good reconnaissance soldier and a kind hearted man. We collected the three casualties and took them to the camp on a wagon. We dug holes and buried three good and dear Partisans, who did not have the good fortune to be with us when we celebrated the victory over the Nazi Germans.

On our return to camp we were immediately informed that the retreating German army would pass near us. In the headquarters' instructions it was stated that we had to hit them till they were destroyed. That is what we did. We waited for them somewhere and when they approached, we opened fire at them from all the weapons we had. Our blow was so heavy that they did not even know where it was coming from. They panicked. We pursued them and hit them. Then they started an unorganized escape and left a lot of booty behind - expensive equipment, food and mainly, many casualties in the field. However, we pursued them and hit them till morning came. We were happy to see the Nazi enemy beaten, but it was too little for the murderers of our people. Our joy was mixed with sorrow that they had managed to destroy the communities of Israel in Lithuania.

When the battle was over, we collected our Partisan fighters and returned to camp. Fortunately we had no injured or damage. A lot of booty had fallen into our hands. On the way we captured three wounded German soldiers and the camp commander brought them to justice, a just verdict. When we returned to the camp I met my brother-in-law, Yehudah (Yudel) Meister, and the third man from Yurburg, Mosheh Magidovitz. We shook hands and were happy that we would very soon return to Kovno. Although we knew there was no one left for us to meet there, we nevertheless would be happy to live among free Jews, in spite of the gentiles. Deep in my heart I still believed, perhaps? Perhaps I would find a sister or someone from my family, and I would not be the only survivor of my large family.

A day passed, it was night now and in the morning we were ordered to get organized towards leaving the camp. A month ago I had not yet believed that I would live to see this day. Four difficult years had passed. The danger of extermination had hung over our head each and every day. Now the great day had come, August 3, 1944, the day of the great victory.

We leave the Partisans camp, bid farewell to close friends we had known and go with a heavy heart to Kovno, which we had not dreamt of seeing again. We traveled by car and on foot until we reached Kovno. Now we were in Kovno. There were but a few survivors in Kovno, the [most] important Jewish town. Kovno, the Jewish community, the town that had been full of Jews and Jewish life, and that now merely contained Holocaust survivors, few, oh so few survivors. Partisans who found relatives joined them. I and many like me, who had no family, were sent to the police departments in town. My brother-in-law Yehudah (Yudel) Meister, who was a tailor by profession, was sent to work at the prison, to work there as a tailor. I was sent to the police department at

Daukshos Street number 1. As I had no choice, I agreed to this appointment. I received a large room to live in for my brother-in-law and myself and together we started our gray life all over again. Although I was living in a large city, I felt like a stray lamb in the forest. Yet I started to breathe fresh air in Kovno, like free people, equal to the gentiles who had always ruled over us. We lived under the communist Lithuanian regime. Then I felt like praising and blessing and saying: "God be blessed for helping us to survive and arrive to this time."

"We shall sing your praise and God will not be silent and I shall thank him forever."

A few in Kovno were able to tell me about the fate of Yurburg, my town of birth. The story was sad, very sad. There were no Jews at all left in Yurburg. All of them had been exterminated and were no longer. There was nothing left for us to do in this Yurburg, the Yurburg without Jews. It no longer existed for us; however, the Jewish community of Yurburg will go on living in our memory forever.

After a while the story of the exile and its sufferings ended and the story of a new life was born in the State of Israel, our independent State of Israel.

Mordehai (Mordechai) Berkover

Left picture: Mordehai Berkover a free man-full of sad memories from the time of the Nazi occupation and the struggle of the partisans in the woods against the wicked conqueror, unforgettable emotional memories.

Right picture: Mordehai Berkover in the Nazi labor camp in Keidan

TRANSLATION OF PAGE 451

A LETTER FROM THE JAIL IN YURBURG

This letter was originally written in Lithuanian by Mika Liubin when she was at the Yurburg prison, to a Lithuanian friend called Genia.

Mika Liubin managed to escape from the murderers (8.9.41) and found shelter at the homes of Lithuanians for a year and a half, until she was caught. Apparently she was denounced and put into the Yurburg prison, where her friend Genia visited her. After the visit at the prison, Mika Liubin managed to send a letter in Lithuanian to Genia and no trace was found of Mika ever since. . .

At the end of the war Genia found Haike, the only survivor of the Liubin family and gave her Mika's letter, translated here by Shimon Shimonov and ZevulunPoran, which tells the story of her bitter personal fate and that of her family who were lost in the war.

March 14, 1943

Dear Genia!

Thank you so much for your visit to the prison. I longed to see you. All the time I was thinking what we would talk about, but when I saw you I was so confused that I couldn't utter a word . . .

Did you ever imagine, Genia, that I would return as a dangerous criminal to the place where I was born and grew up, where I spent the wonderful years of my youth and lived a happy life? Oh, dear Genia, how hard it is to wait for death and count the last hours in torment and tears. If the thick stone walls of the prison could talk they would tell you about me and my bitter tears and how I tear out my hair and torment myself. Many times I have tried to commit suicide; I am fed up with this life, but I don't have the courage to put an end to it. Therefore, darling, I have to wait for death patiently until my persecutors come and take me away, still so young, to the holes of death in the green Oshanti forest, from where there is no return.

Genia, dear, I am not afraid of death, for you know the saying: " all troubles come to an end in the silence of the grave." And indeed, I had so many troubles; life was not at all kind or interesting to me. I have only seen suffering and sorrow in my life. Try to imagine, Genia, what I felt when I saw with my own eyes how they shot and killed my sister Esther'l and many many others.

All night long I heard the sighs coming out of the fresh graves, the groans of children before death, for almost all of them were thrown into the holes while they were still alive. Oh, what a terrible and awful night that was! Yes, that night I also heard the trees around the holes weeping, it was the night of the eighth of August 1941.

After the tragedy, when I managed to survive, from 11 August the "outlaw" part of my life started with all the troubles inherent in such a miserable life. True, the people where I found shelter helped me were fond of me, but from the mental point of view I found no rest. Imagine, Genia, it is spring outside, flowers are blooming, and I have to remain locked up inside, hide and close my eyes. All day long I had the feeling I was being pursued and shot at. I am no longer thinking about the past, for it is impossible to turn back the clock, and I can't dream about the uncertain future; I don't want to fool myself, for I know very well what to expect. I would like to be the last victim of the tragedy that has befallen our people. You should know, Genia, that those who think they can obtain victory by trampling on corpses and washing their hands in the blood of innocent people are wrong. The evil people who are capable of carrying out such vile acts should be hung from posts of shame, denounced in front of everyone.

Genia, I can't stand the way people around me look at me. They all think that I am afraid to die and that is why they tell me they will take me to Kovno. I know it is hard for you too to tell me the truth and I don't need any pity. I am helpless. I shall die with a clear conscience, for I have never wronged anyone, never hurt or caused pain to anyone on this earth. Yes, I shall die with a clear conscience.

I am confident, Genia, that you will not forget me soon. On days when the sun shines again, the fields are green, the forest whispers its mysterious secrets, the birds twitter and sing the hymn of freedom, you will remember me. Genia, very often, think of me and of the days we spent together. I hope your life will be full of sun and light, that you will know no suffering, torment and humiliation, pain and tears.

Thank you so much, Genia, for the clothes. I no longer need them in prison. From the faces of the horrible, almost beastly people around me, I know my days are numbered. Thank your mother for the food. All the prisoners here are fond of me and help me as much as possible. They give me cigarettes to lighten my pain. Therefore I smoke a lot.

I had no idea how hard the hours of waiting would be. Finally my life will come to an end. It may be tomorrow or the day after, and then my "eternal salvation" will come and everything will fall silent forever and ever.

Genia, if you find my sister Haike who may still be alive when the terrible war is over, tell her about my family's terrible tragedy, and about me. My father and brother are buried in a mass grave, my mother and Esther'l in the forest 6 - 7 kilometers from Yurburg. Perhaps there is some sign of a grave there?!...

I am going to die without fear...

Please give my regards to your family, be healthy and happy.

Embracing you,   *your Mika*

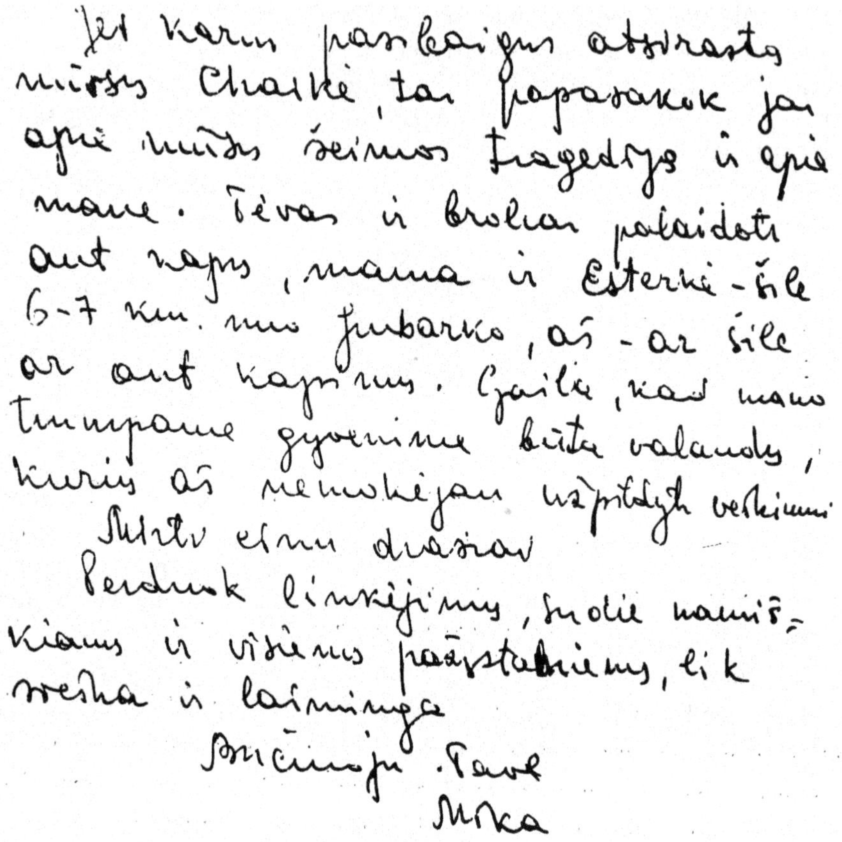

Jei karui pasibaigus atsirastų
mūsų Chaikė, tai papasakok jai
apie mūsų šeimos tragediją ir apie
mane. Tėvas ir broliai palaidoti
ant kapų, mama ir Esterkė - šile
6-7 km. nuo Jurbarko, aš - ar šile
ar ant kapų. Gaila, kad mano
trumpame gyvenime būta valandų,
kurių aš nemokėjau išpildyti verkimu.
Sudiev esmu drąsiai
Perduok linkėjimus, svočiai namiš-
kiams ir visiems pažįstamiems, tik
sveika ir laiminga
Bučiuoju Tave
Mika

The last part of the original letter

TRANSLATION OF PAGE 454-455

At the Seventh Kilometer on the Road from Yurburg to Smalininken

By Leib (Aryeh) Elyashev

After the storm of the terrible Hitler period and the horrors of hundreds of European mass murder sites, it was found that the seventh kilometer from Yurburg to Smalininken was the fatal place of murder of Yurburg Jews.

Here, at the seventh kilometer from Yurburg to Smalininken, was the site of the mass grave of the murdered Yurburg women and children, killed by Lithuanian Hitlerist Nationalists only because they were Jewish.

The mass grave in the forest was hidden from the surrounding world for seventeen years, with not one single sign or monument to commemorate the victims. Only eyewitnesses, who hid in the villages, knew about this sad place, and the memories were engraved deep in their minds.

This is how it was all these years from 1941 until 1958.

In 1958, after significant efforts and demands were exerted, the government finally gave its consent to transfer the bones of murdered Yurburg Jews to the Jewish cemetery of Yurburg.

It was Mikhalovsky and his wife, Meigel and his wife, Zelde Frank, Shalom Raizman, Yehudah Fleisher, Yankl Levin, Leibl Elyashev and other Yurburgers who took part in the sacred work of commemorating the dead, after the bones were exhumed and transferred to the Jewish Cemetery.

During the painful process of exhumation, everybody could see the scene how "in life and in death we did not part." In the upper rows of heaps of dead bodies only bones were left. In the lower rows entangled human arms were lying covered with lime. Trying to exhume them hands and feet disintegrated.

This terrible sight remains before my eyes as I am writing these lines and they will never be erased from my mind.

Miriam Mikhalovsky standing by the bones of the martyrs that were
exhumed from the mass grave near Smalininken before they were brought
for burying at the cemetery in Yurburg.

Same place of Mass Murder of the Yurburg Jews off the road to
Smalininken, as seen in May 2001.

[Photo not in original Yizkor Book - Courtesy of Dr. Leon Menzer]

The bones of the murdered at the seventh kilometer between Yurburg and Smalininken, were exhumed by the survivors from the death pits and brought to a mass grave at the Jewish cemetery in Yurburg.

1960, Yurburg survivors, living in Lithuania, came to the Memorial of the Martyrs, who were murdered by the Nazis. The monument was established by the Yurburg municipality.

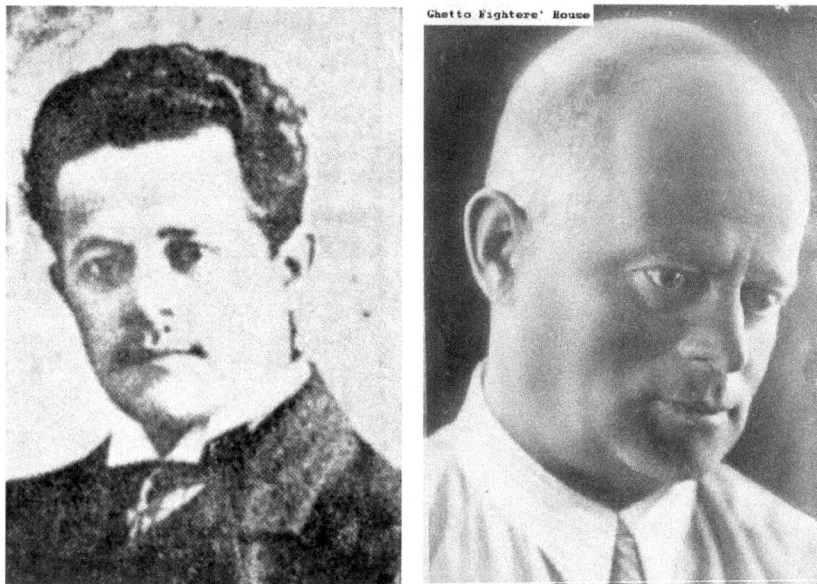

Yitzkhak Katznelson (July 1886 - April 1944)

Born in Lithuania (see the song "My Lithuania" in the Book of Remembrance page 91). He went from Lithuania to Poland when he was young. He was a well-known educator, author and poet. Many of his poems became folk songs. He took part in the uprising against the Nazis at the Warsaw ghetto. At the Vittel concentration camp in France he wrote the incredible song of lamentation - "Songs of the Murdered Jewish people," one of the most important songs about the Holocaust. He died in Auschwitz.

Right hand image was not in original Yizkor Book. Courtesy of the Ghetto Fighters House, Israel.

TRANSLATION OF PAGE 457

I Dreamt a Dream

I dreamt a dream,
Most terrible:
I have no people, my people
Are no longer.

I woke up with a cry-
Alas, alas!
My dream
Has come true!

"God in heaven!"
I tremble and implore:
Why and what for
Did my people die?

Why and what for
Died in vain?
Not in war,
Not in battle . . .

Young boys, old men,
Women and children too -
They are no longer, no longer
Lament !

I am shrouded by sorrow
Day and night
Why, my Master?
Why, oh Lord?

Y. Katzenelson

TRANSLATION OF PAGE 458

FLOWERS OF THE HOMELAND GROW ON THE MASS GRAVE IN THE FOREIGN COUNTRY

By Zahavah (Zlata) Pulerevitz - Ben Yehudah

Former Lithuanians in our country remember the visit to Israel of the Lithuanian Christian woman Mrs. Binkiene, wife of the author Binkus. Mrs. Binkiene is a noble lady with a warm heart, one of the righteous gentiles. This noble woman supported the Jews in Kovno in the terrible days of the Holocaust.

Holocaust survivors in Lithuania invited her to visit them in Israel and she accepted. She came to Israel to see her friends in Israel and express the ongoing spiritual relationship that had been created with them.

It was an emotional visit for her and for those she saved.

Before she returned to Lithuania I asked her to take along some soil that I had collected near my home in Givatayim and flower seeds and give these to the few Jews, Holocaust survivors, in Yurburg.

Mrs. Binkiene graciously accepted my request, and when she returned the people in Yurburg received the bag of soil and flower seeds of the homeland. On Memorial Day they scattered the soil over the mass graves of the victims of destruction. They also scattered the flower seeds there so those flowers from the Hebrew homeland would grow on their graves in the foreign country.

From now on, the flowers of our homeland will grow on the graves of the martyrs who were killed by evil men and the flowers will glorify the names of our loved ones like memorial candles. They did not have the good fortune to come to the land of the Jews and realize their life's dream, to live here and rebuild the country.

TRANSLATION OF PAGE 459

THE BITTER END OF THE COMMUNITY OF YURBURG

Oh, that my head were waters

My eyes a fount of tears!

Then that I weep day and night

For the slain of my poor people. (Jeremiah 8: 23)

The bitter fate was a terrible disappointment for the Yurburg Jewish community, indeed for all the communities of Israel in Lithuania and Europe.

When the enemy soldiers raised the hatches of destruction, they did not distinguish between man and woman, young and old. All, yes all of them, were sent like sheep to slaughter to the pits of death in the Shventshani forest, the cemetery, on the road to Raseiniai and other places.

HO, HEADSMAN, BARED THE NECK - COME CLEAVE IT THROUGH!

NAPE ME THIS CUR'S NAPE! YOURS IS THE AXE UNBAFFLED!

THE WHOLE WIDE WORLD - MY SCAFFOLD!

AND REST YOU EASY; WE ARE WEAK AND FEW.

MY BLOOD IS OUTLAW. STRIKE, THEN; THE SKULL DISSEVER!

LET BLOOD OF BABE AND GRAYBEARD STAIN YOUR GARB

STAIN TO ENDURE FOREVER!

H. N. Bialik (In the City of Slaughter)

After World War II, the few Yurburg survivors in Kovno, Vilna and other places, organized an annual trip to the mass graves of the Yurburg martyrs in the Shventshani forest. Thanks to the efforts of the Yurburg survivors it was finally possible to transfer the bones of the dead from the mass graves in Shventshani to the old cemetery in town.

We remember the innocent beings of our loved ones

Who were murdered in cold blood

We will remember them always, for

The pain is great and there is no solace.

By Zevulun Poran

Chapter 7
SURVIVORS OF YURBURG PERPETUATE THE MEMORY OF THEIR COMMUNITY

TRANSLATION OF PAGE 463

THE ASSOCIATION OF FORMER RESIDENTS OF YURBURG AND ITS ACTIVITIES TO COMMEMORATE THE COMMUNITY

By Zevulun Poran

At the initiative of the organizing committee, of which **Mordekhai (Mordechai) Berkover** (Ramat Gan), **David Levin** (Tel Aviv), **Zevulun Poran** (Jerusalem), and **Shimon Shimonov** (Tel Aviv) were members, we convened at the Association of Former Lithuanian's building in Tel Aviv, on Tuesday, 23 Shevat 5725 (January 26, 1965), about 60 men and women, former residents of Yurburg, situated on both sides of the Nieman River, Yurburg and Shaudine.

It is hard to describe how excited they were, the people from Yurburg, who were unaware of the existence of the others and/or had not seen them for many years. Suddenly they felt how the common past bound them together into one family, and how important it was to them not to extinguish the hidden connection in their hearts.

At that first meeting Leah Most and Yosef Grinberg reported about what was going on among the few survivors from Lithuania, only one woman had returned to Yurburg, Zelda Frank.

A committee was chosen at this meeting, composed as mentioned above, and to this were added Bathsheva Ayalon (Givath Brener) and Alizah Porath (Afikim). Shimon Shimonov was elected Chairman and committee coordinator. It was decided to hold regular meetings and take action to commemorate the Yurburg community. One of the first actions of commemoration was the planting of the forest in memory of the Yurburg martyrs.

It was agreed upon with the Israel National Fund to plant a memorial forest of 1,000 trees, donated by former Yurburg residents. The forest was planted in the Modi'in region, not far from the tombs of the Maccabeans. At the entrance to the forest a statue was erected in memory of the community's martyrs and the following words are inscribed on the marble plaque:

THIS FOREST IS IN MEMORY OF THE MARTYRS OF THE COMMUNITY OF YURBURG IN LITHUANIA

IT WAS PLANTED BY FORMER RESIDENTS OF YURBURG IN ISRAEL AND THE DIASPORA

JEWISH NATIONAL FUND

The planting ceremony took place on Wednesday, 28 Iyar 5726 (May 18, 1966) with the participation of over 60 people. Nathanel Ben Yosef, of the Israel National Fund, started with Mordekhai (Mordechai) Gebirtig's song "The Town is Burning." Shimon Shimonov started his speech by pointing out the importance of planting the forest, which would be used as a memorial site for the Yurburg martyrs and be a living memorial for generations to come. Alizah Porath added emotional words about the destruction of Yurburg. Her words are published in this compilation (see page 473 in the original Hebrew Book).

Rachel Karabelnik-Niv and Yosef Grinberg had the honor of unveiling the plaque. "Yizkor" was said by Zevulun Poran, "Kadish" by Aharon Smolnik and the "Eil Maley Rakhamim" prayer by N. Ben Yosef. The ceremony ended with the public singing "Ani Ma'amin."

Before the first saplings of the forest were planted Zevulun Poran read the scroll of planting (see page 472 in the original Hebrew Book). The following were honored with the symbolic planting of 10 trees: Yosef Grinberg, Yakov Shapira, M. Zarnitsky, Gutshein, Yosef Berkover, Rachel Karabelnik-Niv, Ulya Yasvonski, Zahavah Pulerevitz, Malkah Levin and her husband, guests from South Africa.

On Sunday 28 Adar Beth 5726 (April 9, 1967) a memorial plaque commemorating the Yurburg martyrs was placed in the Holocaust basement on Har Zion (Mt. Zion) in Jerusalem. The memorial plaque carries the following inscription:

In eternal memory of the martyrs of the community of
Yurburg and its vicinity - May the Lord avenge their blood -
Who were murdered by the German Nazis and their helpers
- cursed be they -
in the years of the Holocaust 5701-5705
We shall never forget them
Association of Former Residents of Yurburg and its vicinity in Israel and
the Diaspora

After this memorial plaque was installed, former residents of Yurburg, who had arrived on a special bus, paid a visit to the Memorial Mountain at "Yad Vashem." The ceremony of lighting the torch was held at the "Ohel Yizkor" and the martyrs of the Yurburg community and its vicinity were remembered. It was a very moving and painful moment, and all those who took part will never forget it. Zevulun Poran placed a bunch of flowers on the unknown person's tomb.

I VOWED TO REMEMBER IT ALL

TO REMEMBER - AND NEVER TO FORGET!

Avraham Shlonski

The General Zionist Organization in Yurburg - 1934

Zevulun Poran reads the scroll of planting in memory of the martyrs of Yurburg. Nathanel Ben-Yosef said the memorial prayer: *EIL MALEI RAKHAMIM* (God of Mercy).

Aharon Smolnik recites Kadish, former residents of Yurburg

Rachel Niv (Karabelnik) and Josef Grinberg uncover the Memorial to remember the Community of Yurburg that was erected at the grove

The Plaque in the Picture above Reads:

This Forest is in Memory of the Martyrs of the Community of Yurburg Lithuania.

Planted by the Emigrants of Yurburg in Israel and the Diaspora

The Jewish National Fund - "Keren Kayemeth LeYisrael"

On Sunday, 21 Tishrey 5732 (September 7, 1971) a special meeting was held to commemorate the 50th anniversary of the Hebrew Gymnasium named after Dr. Theodore (Benjamin Ze'ev) Herzl in Yurburg. Memories of the days of study at the Gymnasium recalled through the works of - Rivkah Vainberg (Weinberg)-Ravitzky (her words are published in the book on page 313 in the original Hebrew Book). Emanuel Kopelov recounted interesting episodes of life at the Gymnasium, which caused laughter as well as tears.

Since the start of the activity of the Former Residents of Yurburg Association in Israel until 1988, 16 meetings were held in Tel Aviv, Jerusalem, Givath Brener and the forest in the Modi'in region. The majority of the meetings were held at the building of the Former Lithuanians Association in Tel Aviv, on 70 Ibn Gevirol Street. The meetings were always well attended and very interesting and there were many requests to hold the meetings.

Indeed, the association's committee made countless efforts to satisfy the members' requests to hold the meetings so that the connection among the members would continue. Indeed, almost every year meetings were held to recall common memories and say "Yizkor" together in memory of the dear ones who had been murdered by beastly murderers.

Recently the committee has been trying to approach the second generation of former residents of Yurburg, hoping that when the time comes they will continue the tradition of the meetings and consider it their sacred duty to continue the tradition of their parents.

Today another important item joins the memorial plaque in the Holocaust basement in Jerusalem and the memorial forest at the Modi'in region, namely the **Book of Remembrance Commemorating the Yurburg Community**.

We hope that this memorial book will serve as an important historical document to commemorate our lost community. We hope that the book of remembrance will be found in every family of former residents of Yurburg and its vicinity, to be perused by our sons and the sons of our sons so that they will become acquainted with the heritage of their fathers and pass it on to coming generations.

Joel Alpert (Editor of English edition) Lighting Memorial Candle at Mass Murder Site at the Jewish Cemetery in Yurburg - May 2001

[Photo by Leon Menzer - Not in original Yizkor Book]

The Yurburg Yizkor Book

TRANSLATION OF PAGE 466

MEETING OF FORMER RESIDENTS OF YURBURG IN JERUSALEM

By Frida Shakhnovitz-Zevuloni

Blessed be my few remaning friends who are full of love for their place of origin and the little town where they were born, and each year we, the few survivors left, collect and organize a social meeting of former residents of Yurburg. The meeting of the lucky few who managed, some earlier some later, to find their place in our country. Childhood memories apparently have an endless nostalgic power; a power capable of bringing together people from all corners of the country; a power whereby countless years of life and creation in our country have not diminished the fondness and link with those who share the same town of birth. Life takes its course; everyone has acquired a new circle of friends with whom he has passed the long road of his personal life; most have spent more years in Israel than they ever lived in Yurburg.

In spite of this, after a day of work, almost all of them respond to the call: "Yurburgers, come and meet!" This time too we met, on a spring day, again in the same corner of Tel Aviv. We had come from all over the country, and we have a common goal: **placing a memorial plaque** commemorating our loved ones, a memorial plaque for the cradle of our youth, at the **Holocaust Cellar on Har (Mt.) Zion**, in the eternal city of Jerusalem! Will such a small, silent marble plaque be able to commemorate the memory of our peaceful, honest life in Yurburg? May this plaque serve as a meeting place and a place of commemoration. In addition to all the painful memories, the informal meeting of various immigrations and different age groups is always warm and welcoming. The atmosphere is, as always, very emotional, the spiritual bond of the few who survived, few of many fine people, as we once were. This year's meeting, held at the initiative of our executive committee, and hosted by our dear friend Zevulun Poran from Jerusalem, was very impressive. The ceremony of the unveiling of the plaque commemorating the Yurburg martyrs on Mount Zion was full of bitter memories, immense sorrow for all that was dear to us and had been lost for no reason.

How can one forget and be free of this pain, this deep sorrow? Indeed, when I stood among the others, next to the plaque illuminated by memorial candles, I suddenly saw my loved ones coming towards me from every corner, those I had loved so much, with their noble souls, personalities from our unforgettable little town, and my mind wandered to the narrow streets of Yurburg, that no longer exist. Each corner, every tree, river, each path, each house had its memories. Yes, it was a little town like many others in Lithuania, yet it had something different, something near, full of the love of youth, childhood memories and the echo of first steps on the path of life. And then destruction came, inflicted on us by murderous men, and wiped away all the beauty without leaving a trace.

The visit to "Yad Vashem" was very impressive and emotional. An atmosphere of a generation that had been lost filled the hall. Here I felt that a tombstone had been placed that most suited the commemoration of our martyrs, those who lived in our town of Yurburg.

When we left "Yad Vashem," full of memories and sad feelings. We all found a certain consolation in the beautiful landscape of Jerusalem and in all that symbolized the creation and building of the state, in the willpower to live and be a people, in spite of all that had happened and in spite of the "final solution" of the Nazi devil.

The feeling of being a family, being close, spiritual closeness, are so beautiful and enrich us all so much that every effort both by individuals and by the organizers to continue the meetings and encourage this cherished tradition is worthwhile.

Kefar Masarik, (April 9, 1982)

TRANSLATION OF PAGE 468

WHAT THE NAME "YURBURG" MEANS

TO US

WORDS SPOKEN AT A MEMORIAL MEETING OF FORMER RESIDENTS OF YURBURG

By Zevulun Poran

One Saturday in the winter of 5725 (1965), I visited Kibbutz Kefar Masarik with my family. We were the guests of my friend Frida Shakhnovitz, sitting here with us. We enjoyed being entertained at the kibbutz among whose founding members we had been, and particularly Frida's warm welcome. We talked a lot about Yurburg and the meetings of former residents of Yurburg.

When we returned from Kefar Masarik, my daughters, 9 year old Anath and 7 year old Osnath, asked me why Frida had been so emotional when she spoke about the meeting of former residents of Yurburg and about Yurburg itself. Of course I answered them as best as I could. I found it difficult to give them a full answer to their questions without much thought. Anyhow, they would not have understood the thread binding those from Yurburg to each other. To my daughters Yurburg is a strange name; it has a strange sound, which means nothing to them. This is true for my daughters as well as for your children.

We are the last people to whom the name Yurburg and its sound bring up associations, memories and moving experiences. The name Yurburg is dear to us, for it is linked to our past, to memories of our youth, which are the most pleasant memories in a person's life. We are linked to Yurburg by the love of our dear ones, our fathers, brothers and sisters, relatives and friends and the entire Jewish community of Yurburg.

Let's also ask ourselves the question: "what does Yurburg mean to us?" Will we be able to express it in words, we who come from Yurburg? After all, to us Yurburg is all and everything, a world full of feelings and experiences. We all have memories that never leave us.

It seems to me that when we think of Yurburg, we immediately see the enchanting landscape, which charms the eye and heart. All the views around Yurburg are beautiful, but I think the view of the Nieman flowing slowly towards the town is the most beautiful of all. Yurburg's two smaller rivers are beautiful too, the Mituva and the Imstra, crossing Yurburg, a joy to everyone. Who can't forget the town's streets full of life and its busy center, Kovno Street, its paths and alleys, gardens and luscious parks? All these colorful scenes always charmed us and left their mark on us, it has already been said, "man is merely a reflection of his childhood landscape." Man merges with nature and turns into an integral part of it. I don't know, perhaps we are not objective when we say: "Yurburg is different from other towns!" Although we can't deny the truth that Yurburg is very special and different from the other towns. Yurburg is also different in the special nature of its population, soft spoken and pleasant in its mutual relations and peace of mind.

We remember the members of the youth movements, who walked through the streets of town, upright and strong with their national and human pride, singing the song of Zion. The youth movements where we grew up, like "Maccabi," "Hekhalutz," "Hekhalutz Hatsair," "Hashomer Hatsair" and "Beitar," which gave us moral values and shaped our personality. We shall remember the schools too, where we acquired an education and knowledge, the primary school ("Talmud Torah"), the Hebrew Gymnasium called Herzl and the small Yeshivah at the Kloiz.

The old synagogue is also unforgettable; Splendid, everyone who saw it was impressed by it -it inspired the love of art in us, with its woodcarvings, the love of beauty. Indeed, this Yurburg of ours inspired us with wonderful values, human values, love of man, love of life and joy of life.

This Yurburg, the cradle of our youth, Hebrew Jewish, no longer exists. Everyone is gone; no one remains. They were murdered in cold blood and slaughtered by the Nazi murderers. No trace is left of our loved ones, no sound to be heard. But the name Yurburg still rings in our head, the survivors' head, and won't leave us alone.

We shall never forget our sacred duty, to remember, to remind and commemorate their memory, the memory of the members of the Yurburg community.

TRANSLATION OF PAGE 470

YURBURGERS HELPING YURBURGERS

Mordekhai (Mordechai) Zilber

Petakh Tikvah   August 26, 1956

Dear Zevulun,

I was very happy to receive your reply, which helped me solve the mystery of your silence. Indeed, I was most impressed by your readiness to help our joint friends, to get them out of the Soviet "paradise."

Once I have written this letter, I shall write a letter to Menakhem Kravet.** with whom I want to make an appointment, whenever it suits him, I shall come to him, or he to me. Due to the strike, the "Dan" company's bus schedule was disrupted, as a matter of fact; it is non-existent for the time being. So it is better to decide at present that I shall faithfully carry out the part of which I am in charge.

> ** This refers to Tuviyah Kravetz, the Holocaust survivor from Kovno, who wants to go to Israel, but emigration certificates are only handed out to people who have relatives in Israel. I therefore looked for a man called Kravetz, an Israeli citizen, who could be turned into a "relative, a brother."

I read your Israeli *curriculum vitae*. Indeed, a lot has happened since we left the Hebrew Gymnasium in Yurburg, the wooden building in the "Tel Aviv" park, looking out over the little hill on the Imstra river, the willow trees bending over its quiet waters, the little wooden bridge and the road leading to the park of Prince Vasilshchikov.

Were it not for the national, family and personal tragedy that befell us when all our dear ones there were murdered, Lithuania and Yurburg would have remained enveloped in the glory of romanticism, the romanticism of youth. However now, a screen of blood separates us now, and I have torn any feelings for that country out of my heart.

The search for the "relative" via the telephone directory led me to ask Mordekhai (Mordechai) Zilber for help. He lives in Petakh Tikvah and knows Menakhem Kravetz, the "so-called brother" of Tuviyah Kravetz.

I have had some news from Yurburg from which I understand that it is a ghost town now; it hardly exists, it was destroyed and burnt down and has but a few Jewish inhabitants. "He" too, the writer of the letter, begged me to help him, but I am heartbroken that I am unable to do so.

I had the opportunity to meet people from Yurburg in Canada, where I visited three years ago (I spent a year and a half there, not as an emissary). I meet very few people from Yurburg in Israel, for I hardly ever leave Petakh Tikvah. About 8 months ago I met Bathsheva Ayalon from Givath Brener and her husband Yankele Vilensky. She made a wonderful career for herself at the Working Women's Federation (today called Na'amat). She was sent on missions to England, U.S.A., Canada. I also met Tsivyah (Tsevika) Levitan (graduate of the first class at the Gymnasium). She has a brother, Yoske, who presently lives in California (he is also a graduate of the first class). Tsevika came from Toronto, Canada, on a visit to Israel.

Indeed, time passes, it seems to me we are now at the point of "Minkhah," almost "Ma'ariv," soon we will have to say "Kryath Shema."

I was really very happy with your letter. I am corresponding with a certain Yitskhak Levinson from South Africa, formerly from Yurburg. I wrote to him about your letter and he will surely be very pleased too. He wants to help Tuviyah Kravetz and Bathyah (Fainberg), his wife.

I hope to hear more about you and to see you too.

Best wishes to you and your family and Happy New Year,

Affectionately yours,

Mordekhai (Mordechai) Zilber

A youth choir participating in the assembly to commemorate the Balfour proclamation to establish the Jewish State on November 2, 1919.

TRANSLATION OF PAGE 472

WE SHALL REMEMBER - THE SCROLL OF PLANTING THE YURBURG GROVE

By Zevulun Poran

WE SHALL REMEMBER.

With sorrow and indignation we shall remember our parents, our brothers and sisters, our relatives and friends who were deprived of their innocent life by cruel and beastly murderers.

We shall remember our beloved children, mere babies, torn away from their parents by the Nazi oppressors and their Lithuanian helpers and led like sheep to slaughter in the Shventshani forest, the cemetery, on the way to Rasein, and other places, where they were murdered in cold blood and thrown, still alive, into the pits of death, their lives cruelly cut off. We shall remember all the members of our community in Yurburg, men and women, young and old, exterminated, their honor wounded, their blood spilt by beastly people, in sanctification of the Holy Name. We shall remember and never forget.

SCROLL OF PLANTING THE MEMORIAL FOREST FOR THE YURBURG COMMUNITY

On behalf of former residents of Yurburg in Israel, old time settlers and new immigrants, and on behalf of former residents of Yurburg in the Diaspora, we have today, Tuesday 16 Iyar 5725 (May 18, 1965) planted the first saplings in the forest commemorating the martyrs of the Yurburg community.

By planting this forest we are erecting an eternal memorial in the Modi'in region, the cradle of the Maccabeans, for the people of our town. The trees we planted today are trees of remembrance for the entire community of Yurburg, destroyed by beastly people. We shall bind the memory of the Yurburg martyrs into the eternal life of the trees in the forest, always fresh on the land of Israel, a symbol of the eternal bond of our loved ones with the homeland to which they did not have the good fortune to arrive during their lives.

In the shadow of the trees turning green, in the memorial forest of the Yurburg community, we shall meet from time to time, to proudly and painfully remember our town, the cradle of our youth, fondly remember its glorious past and mourn its bitter fate.

We shall remember and never forget the crimes of the Nazi Germans and their Lithuanian helpers, those who destroyed and exterminated our community until the last generation.

TRANSLATION OF PAGES 473 - 474

ADDRESS ON PLANTING OF THE GROVE

By Alizah Leipziger-Porath

Here I stand, trembling and in awe on this piece of land, where the grove commemorating our dear ones is to be planted. What shall I say, what can I say that has not been said already? The heart grieves bursts and flows over, and the words must come out. However, it is hard to find the right words to express what we all feel. You and I, we are one of a kind, united in our pain and sorrow. We share a bitter fate. We have gathered here as people who share the same past, people who are bound by many open and hidden threads; we were all born and raised in the same town called Yurburg, where we absorbed the tradition of our fathers and where our spiritual nature was formed. We all dreamt our youthful dreams there, and it is only natural that the period of childhood and youth enhance the happiest memories in a person's life. The not-so-good memories sink into an abyss and only the happy ones remain with us. Indeed, we had happy memories and we had a wonderful past. Our Yurburg, I pronounce its name with pride, and refer to its wonderful people with great esteem. Warmth flowed out of every Jewish home, for in each Jewish home a warm Jewish heart was to be found. Not only official charity and organized aid institutions were to be found there, but also daily individual deeds of charity, anonymous gifts, acts of mercy not expecting to be rewarded. I remember the Fridays, when my late mother would send me on missions of charity, to bring the "khales" (challas - Sabbath bread) and fish to the needy. And I know very well that my late mother was but one of many in our town who helped the poor, not only our own people, but the gentiles as well; all this kindness derived from the love of man and the belief that it was deserved. There are many more beautiful humane acts of which I could speak. Perhaps one day a book will be written in their memory, describing their good deeds and their aspirations for education. How hard they worked, and what tremendous efforts they made to provide an education for their children; how the first ones learned Hebrew and were drawn to Zion. Many dreamt of national redemption. The Zionist activity, cultural as well as public, was carried out with endless devotion, enthusiasm and perseverance.

Our Yurburg brought forth the best of youth, glorious youngsters, splendid idealists determined to implement their ideals, but when the terrible enemy arrived, all was destroyed. Our home, together with the cradle of our youth, went up in fire. It is no longer. Turned into ashes.

We were told many tales, but many other things remained obscure, for the voices have fallen silent and there is no one left to tell. However, we are sure that in that last hour of their lives they thought of us, and their only consolation was that we were not with them, and that luckily some one was left to remember them, and perhaps take revenge. And indeed we shall remember them forever!

We have gathered here to plant this grove to honor their last wish. We plant in order to commemorate uprooting, the terrible uprooting! It is particularly symbolic to us, Jews, the people of peace. Against the destruction, ruin and devastation, building and planting. It is also a symbolic response: the enemy wanted to uproot, and we plant. There is something else we should know: our dear ones did not die in vain. The shattered, sooted stone remains from the destroyed town has turned into the cornerstone, the foundation stone of our life. The song that suffocated there in the flames sprang up again in the voices of the divisions of our fighters, here in Israel. Thanks to them we received our State, thanks to them we love it even more, and thanks to them we shall look after it even more. They therefore play an important part in the building of the State and its defense, even though they were not here, did not have the good fortune to be here. They probably also ordered us, in their most difficult moments, to go on, continue the story of their life in Israel. I remember the Sutskover song, the words expressed in the camp by the father to his son in Tel Aviv:

"Dig into the ashes and if nothing is left there, silently take out a fragment of destruction and take it with you and bury it with your own hands in the garden where your children will sing"

Friends, in the spirit of this legacy, we should come here often with our children to this grove, and tell them who and what their grandfathers and grandmothers were. Our fathers used to say: "may their souls be bound into the bond of life." Indeed, the souls of our martyrs will hover over this place which has come to life, they will live in the bond of our life, the bond of our people and its homeland. The trees will grow, take root and send up a branch above; this grove will be their tombstone and carry the message of eternal new life in the homeland in memory of our beloved. We shall meet here from time to time in their shadow and remember those who we shall never forget, will remember forever and ever.

Kibbutz Afikim

TRANSLATION OF PAGE 475

A MEMORY FOR OUR GRANDCHILDREN AND GREAT-GRANDCHILDREN

That they should make them known to their children
That the generation to come might know them
(Psalms 78 -6)

Dark nights in the forest
In the dark nights in the Shventshani forest
Children stood in front of open pits -
Crying and wailing .. .
The cruel people hit and kill
And spill their blood . . .
One after another they throw them into the pits -
Jewish children . . .
A boy, another boy, and a little girl too
They die there, screaming -
MOTHER! . . MOTHER!. . .
And the mad murderers trample on their bodies
And pile them into a heap
Growing higher and higher
And the night is dark, a cold wind is blowing
A wind of terror . . .

IN THE SHVENTSHANI FOREST   **By Zevulun Poran**

Oh, the Shventshani forest,
The victims' burial place
You swallowed them all
For always and ever

There, over the pits of death
An evil spirit roams
Over the bones of our loved ones
Lying in your earth

Over the top of the trees
The terror hovers
And the sounds of a mother embrace
The wounds of its victim

WHY, MOTHER, WHY

Why, mother dear,
I ask - why
Did little Rivkah'le
Became silent forever?

Why, why, why,
Are my brothers and sisters no
       longer -
What crime did they commit
That evil men devoured them?

Mother, Mother, why
Don't you answer me?
Shall we ever see
The sun shine again?

Statue by Ze'ev Ben Tsevi

The Valley of the Destroyed Communities

The Memorial to the Five Thousand Jewish Communities Destroyed During the Holocaust

THE VALLEY OF DESTROYED COMMUNITIES AT THE YAD VASHEM MEMORIAL SITE.

THE VALLEY OF DESTROYED COMMUNITIES located in Jerusalem at Yad Vashem. There are names 5,000 communities, whose names are written in the Jerusalem stone.

THE VALLEY OF DESTROYED COMMUNITIES. It was created for the purpose of commemorating our parents, brothers and sisters, commemorate the Jewish communities and that includes the names of our loved ones. From the Jewish people in Israel and in the Diaspora.

THE HOUSE OF YURBURG IN JERUSALEM

By Zevulun Poran

In the second half of the nineteenth century the Jewish population in the old city of Jerusalem grew. It was estimated that 13,340 inhabitants lived in the old city in 1859, 6,000 of them Jews, 4,000 Muslims and 3,340 Christians. The Jewish quarter was terribly crowded. In the Bible verses there is a shocking description of the living conditions of the Jews in the old city. This is what is written:

"Those who see the places of living that look like dusty holes will be most astonished. If kind-hearted souls want to help these poor people, then the first thing they need is a clean and healthy place of living."

Their economic conditions were also poor. The majority lived on "distribution" funds, collected by emissaries in the Jewish communities in Europe. Few were small tradesmen, had a grocery store or workshop. There was endless poverty and suffering. The majority of the Jewish population were Sephardic Jews, who had lived here for many generations, and a few were Ashkenaz Jews. All of them lived in terrible circumstances and unbearable poverty. Nevertheless, aliyah to Israel did not cease, from Kurdistan, North Africa, Eastern Europe. The holiness of Jerusalem attracted them in spite of the economic difficulties and living problems. In those years the philanthropist and public personality **Sir Moses Montefiori** (1784-1885), helped the Jews in Eretz Israel. He visited Israel seven times, together with his wife Judith. Montefiori was well aware of the Jews' difficult living conditions and decided to do something about it. Montefiori thought of a daring idea, to move the Jews out of the suffocating quarter to beyond the walls of Jerusalem. The financial means to realize this idea were also found. At that time, 5614 (1854), a rich and generous Sephardic Jew called **Turo** died in the town of Orleans in the U.S.A. In his will Turo left a sum of money, about $60,000 to the poor people of Jerusalem. This donation was handed over to Montefiori by the administrator of Turo's estate, and he decided to use it to realize his plan, i.e. to purchase a piece of land and set up a neighborhood for the Jews outside the walls of the old city.

That is what happened. In 5620 (1860) the first building for the Jews was completed outside the walls of Jerusalem, on a rocky hill, opposite Mt. Zion. The quarter was called **Mishkenot Sha'ananim.** Half of the settlers were Sephardic and the other half Ashkenaz.

In 5628 (1868) a new neighborhood was established, the second one, of Jews of Moroccan origin, (presently: to the west of the "King David" hotel), and this quarter was called **Makhaneh Yisrael** or in the popular tongue: the neighborhood of the western people.

A year later Ashkenaz Jews bought an area of land to the west of Makhaneh Yisrael and here on the second of Ayar 5629 (1869) the third quarter was established, called **Nakhlath Shiv'ah**, named after its seven founders.

Further on I plan to speak about the Nakhlath Shiv'ah quarter and the interest it holds for us, former residents of Yurburg.

Rabbi Yoel-Mosheh Salomon, one of the quarter's founders and one of the editors of the *"Torah miZion"* ("Torah from Zion") newspaper says the following in his memoirs:

On Lag ba Omer 5626 (1866) Mosheh-Yoel Salomon went for a walk on the road leading to Yaffo. On the same road (opposite the Russian compound and the police, at present) he came upon a field where lentils and beans were growing and peasants were working. Salomon struck up a conversation with them regarding the purchase of the land for building there. The peasants agreed to sell the land and asked for half a cent per cubit. Yoel Salomon informed his friend Rabbi Yosef Rivlin, the man whose dream it was to further Jewish settlement, about his offer to buy the area, and he encouraged him to do so.

Next day Mosheh Yoel Salomon found another five partners for this idea and they were:

Yehoshua Yelin, the founder of the well-known Yelin family in Jerusalem;

Mikhael Hacohen, a partner in the newspaper business;

Benjamin (Beinish) Salant, the son of Rabbi Shemuel Salant, the chief Ashkenaz Rabbi in Jerusalem;

Hayim (Chaim) Halevy (Kovner), the first emissary who went abroad to collect donations for building the "Hakhurvah" synagogue;

Arieh Leib Hurwitz in whose wife's name, she was a Turkish national, the quarter's land was registered and to whom the property certificate was registered. That is why at the time the jesters of the "Nakhlath Shiv'ah" founder's generation would say: " seven people held on to one woman."

After a while, Yosef Rivlin, called "Yoshe der Shtetl Makher (Yoshe the town maker)" laid the foundation for a number of neighborhoods in Jerusalem and was the first man to build his home at Nakhlath Shiv'ah and also the first to settle there. When all the houses of the quarter had been built, all seven families settled there.

Soon Nakhlath Shiv'ah became a very lively neighborhood. Apartments were rented there, shops and even coffee shops; slowly it became the nucleus of the new town outside the walls of Jerusalem. Two streets in the neighborhood are named after the two founders today, Yoel Mosheh Salomon Street and Yosef Rivlin Street, both of them old timers of Lithuanian origin, the grandsons of the pupils of the Gaon from Vilna.

This is where it becomes interesting to us, from Yurburg, to tell the story of the Nakhlath Shiv'ah quarter:

One day, one hundred years after Nakhlath Shiv'ah was founded, the writer of this article went for a walk along the alleys of the aging neighborhood in the center of Jerusalem, which, by the way, is being renovated these days. All of a sudden I saw an old marble plaque attached to the front of a two story stone house, at the corner of 18 Salomon Street. When I looked closely at the letters inscribed on the marble I noticed the word **"Yurburg,"** yes, Yurburg, who would believe it, Yurburg at Nakhlath Shiv'ah. Here I stood wondering in front of the plaque on which Yurburg was clearly inscribed. It was hard to read the entire text of the plaque, for the letters had become unclear. The text was a rabbinical text.

What to do? I decided to contact a few of my friends from Lithuania and Yurburg. I also shared the secret with the Chairman of the Former Residents of Yurburg Association, Shimon Shimonov. A photograph was taken of the plaque, and once the text was deciphered we indeed found a connection between this house and its owners, formerly of Yurburg. We were curious to know who owned the house now and who was living there, and we approached the entrance floor of the house and knocked on the door. An old woman opened the door. We saw a few rooms in the apartment, most of them in disarray. We asked her what she knew about the house of Yurburg. The woman was surprised and alarmed. "Yurburg, Yurburg, she whispered. I have never heard that name," she said. She had lived in this house for many years, and didn't care what was written on the plaque. She said the house belonged to the municipality and she was merely a tenant, paying rent. She now planned to leave town with her family. If we were interested in the apartment she was ready to let it to us for "key money", as was the custom. When we heard this we immediately got an idea into our head. If we would get this house we could turn it into a "Yurburg house." Former residents of Yurburg would come to it from all over the country and remember the past, relax etc. etc. all sorts of ideas and thoughts ran through our head. We asked the house owner what the sum of "key money" would be and she mentioned an astronomical amount. We were disappointed. The association would never be able to raise such a sum. We no longer wished to climb to the second floor. We turned to the Jerusalem municipality to check her connection with this house to which she had rights. The clerks at the municipality only knew that the house had been registered as municipal property for years, perhaps even from as far back as the Turkish period and perhaps from the British mandate period. They collected rent and that was all.

We told them of our connection to this house and how important it was to us as historical property. They replied: "try to reach a compromise with the tenants. "

We left the house very sad. We had to let go of a dream, but we were very disturbed about the history of the house and its initial owners, as written on the plaque. We contacted our old geographer friends, researchers of Jerusalem, and they were the late **Ze'ev Vilnai** and **David Benvenishti**. We showed them photographs of the plaque testifying to the connection with former residents of Yurburg and the house, those who had built it, its owners and first inhabitants. Unfortunately the researchers found nothing. The house remained a mystery even when we deciphered the handwritten text of the historical marble plaque. Here we would like to take the opportunity to show you the photograph of the marble plaque and its text:

In this home and these walls I have given them a worthy memorial for sons and daughters, an eternal name that shall never be erased, God shall remember them on the Holy Mountain in Jerusalem, may it be built soon in our days. Amen.

For these premises were dedicated by the honorable, illustrious and gracious Rabbi, our Rabbi Yehudah Leib, the son of Rabbi Mordekhai (Mordechai). Blessed be his memory - from Yurburg - May God look after them.

He donated it for the glorification of his soul.

It shall forever be to the benefit of the poor from the Kolel-Vilna and Zhamut.

This philanthropist passed away on 28 Sivan 1894

May his soul live on forever, his gracious deeds shall be remembered

And God will keep him until the dead rise again on the Mountain of Zion

Soon, in our days, Amen.

To this very day our heart pounds when we pass this house on 18 Salomon Street. Salomon Street flourishes at present. It was totally renovated and has turned into a promenade linked to the Ben Yehudah street promenade. The entire neighborhood of Nakhlath Shiv'ah has turned into a kind of historical museum, in the center of Jerusalem. We hope that those who develop the quarter will also discover the historical plaque and give it the prominence it deserves.

As former residents of Yurburg we are proud of this Jew, Torah scholar, who left Yurburg and immigrated to Israel a century ago, guided by his love for Eretz Yisrael. The text of the marble plaque shows that when the owner died the house became public property, for Lithuanians who would come to live in Jerusalem. Former residents of Yurburg who come to Jerusalem should go to this corner house and look at the plaque of the old stone house.

The Yurburg House in Jerusalem

Plaque that is on the Entrance of the House

The word "m' Yurburg" appears at the beginning of the eighth line from the bottom.

Once upon a time there was a town called Yurburg, a glorious Jewish settlement in the land of Lithuania, now it exists no longer. Any memory of Yurburg is dear to those who come from this town and the house in Nakhlath Shiv'ah is one of the dearest memories for those who have come from Yurburg to the State of Israel.

Mrs. Alizah Porath (Leipziger), is lamenting the Jewish victims from Yurburg who were murdered by the German Nazis and their helpers

On the left: Shimon Shimonov In the middle: N. Ben Joseph On the right: Zevulun Poran

People attending the ceremony: Former Residents of Yurburg in Israel and representatives from abroad, listen to the speakers of the ceremony of the planting trees to remember the martyrs of Yurburg.

Former Residents of Yurburg Gathering in the Memorial Forest at Modi'in to Remember the Holy Martyrs of Yurburg Succot 1969

Former Residents of Yurburg Plant a Forest in Memory of Their Beloved

Hereafter List of Those Who Planted

Name of the Planter   **In Memory of:**

Hannah Abel (Apriyaski)

> Hayim (Chaim) and Khyene Apriyaski
> Yerakhmiel and Etel Apriyaski
> Yekhezkel and Merl Apriyaski
> Reuven, Bath-Sheva Apriyaski
> Hannah Meirovitz and her son Eliezer Apriyaski
> Leizer, Mosheh, Rachel-Leah Landsman

Tsevi Ahuvi (Lubovski)

> Hayim (Chaim), Dov, Etel and Rivkah Lubovski

Adah Obfeier

> Shimon, Yehudah, Aba Berkover
> Ita, Rivkah Berkover
> Risha and Zisse, daughters of Aba Berkover
> Eliyahu, Hannah, Bath-Sheva, children of Yehudah Berkover
> Sarah and Zalman Berkover-Dartvin
> Yitskhak Rochzo

Esther Atlas (Atlas-Pukhert)

> Yakov and Hayah Pukhert
> Henia Gruzin and family
> Sonia Lubin and family
> Yonah Pukhert and family
> Esther Beker and family
> Malkah Salomon and family
> Tsiporah Grinblat

Esther Atlas and Frida Pukhert

> Menakhem Pukhert

Herbert Idelson

> In memory of his family

Bath-Sheva Ayalon

> In memory of her family

Aharon Eliyashev

> Tovah, Yekutiel, Ite and Braine

Pesia Eliyashev (Nevyaski)

> Eliyashev Tsevi, Beile, Mosheh, David and Yekutiel Eliyashev

Yoninah Efraimi (Most) and Leah Joselevitz (Most)

Yisrael-Yitskhak Most
Hilel and Yehudah Most
Khayah-Rivkah Most
Mordekhai (Mordechai) Most and family
Shraga Most and family
Mosheh Most and family

Zahavah Bar-Yehudah (Pulerevitz)

Nathan, Yitskhak, and Sarahh-Batyah Pulerevitz
Hayah, Reuven Pulerevitz

Helen and Isaac Beiles

Khyene Beiles and family
Gitel and Isaac Tsukerman and family

Yakov Beiman

The Beiman family

Shoshanah Birger (Tarshish)

In memory of the Tarshish family

Shoshanah Birger, Portnoi

Mordekhai (Mordechai) Mendelovitz
M. and Ch. Pak, Iva, Rabai, I. Sigel,
E. Efron, P. Epstein, A. Atlas

Rivkahh Blokh-Levanoni (Feldman)

Mosheh, Yakov Feldman
Leah, Sarah, Jafah (Sheinele) Feldman
Dobe Feldman and her children

Rachel Ben-Artsi

Mosheh, Sheine and Aizik Levyush
Bluma, Mosheh, Devorah, Benjamin and Jafah Volovitski

Howard Bendelin

In memory of the Bendelin family

Rachel Bek (Apriyaski)

Hayim (Chaim), Yerakhmiel, Yekhezkel, Reuven Apriyaski, Zini
Apriyaski, Bath-Sheva Apriyaski (Landman)

Rivkah Baron

Pesia Baron-Shakhnovitz

Boris Bernstein

Menakhem-Mendel, Shmaryahu-Yonah, Yisrael Bernstein,
Hannah-Devorah Levinson
Khayah Weinstok
Ida-Rachel Tsherniak
Sarah Fridland

Hannah Barski (Meltser)

Tsevi, Golda, Sarah-Rivkah, Miriam Barski

Mordekhai (Mordechai) and Yosef Berkover

Tovah, Rachel, Hayah, Devorah, Tsiporah Berkover

Eliezer, Elkhanan-Reuven, Asher Berkover

Hannah, Sheine, Hannah-Miriam Berkover

Miriam Barshtanski (Verpul)

Hayim (Chaim) Barshtanski

Gershon Barshtanski

Benjamin Barshtanski

Michael and Jekl Gotshtein

Eliyahu, Golda, Tsilah, Aharon Gotshtein

Mosheh, Bluma, Pesia, Pesakh Gotshtein

Hayim (Chaim)-David, Miriam, Sarah-Pesia Rozenberg

Mosheh Gotshtein

Eliyahu, Golda, Aharon, Pesakh, and Pesia Gotshtein

Miriam Gold

Motel, Itel, Reizel Brezaner

Hannah Goldman (Magidovitz)

The Magidovitz Family

Miriam Gurvitz

Mosheh, Shemuel Hess

Khayah-Gitel, Mina, Khyene, Sarah Hess

Golda (Eliashevitz), Leizer Chosid

Malkah Ginzberg

For her family

Yosef Grinberg

Yitskhak, Etel, Yosef, and Beti Markus

Heshel, Berl Grinberg

Leon, Henrieta Mering

Rachel Grinstein

Reuven, Khanan-Nakhman, Pesia, Golda-Gitel Hess

Miriam, Nekhemyah, Yisrael, Feivel, Beinish, Mosheh-Mendel Hess

Hayim (Chaim)-Nathan, Leah Yozefer

Yosef Grinberg and Grunia Melnik (Rabinovitz)

Zalman, Heshel, Avraham-Mordekhai (Mordechai), Meir Grinberg

Mikhal, Grunia, Zhenia, and mother Grinberg

Pola, Wili, Grunia, Ezra Aizikovitz

Grunia, Dinah, Rachel, Grisha Margolis

Yosef, Dinah, Grunia Shabashevitz

Mosheh, Etel, Mendel Kaplan

Olga, Yehudah, Sherl, Grunia Arsh

Daniel, Merl, Mania, Braina, Avivah Melnik
Sarah, Gitel, Aba Lubovski
Beile Cahan
Yakov Shapira
Artur, Yokheved Ziman

Mina Dimant-Julius Salanski

David Dimant and his family

Yosef Vilenski

Iser, Batyah, Ita, Hayim (Chaim) Vilenski and their daughter
Yitzchak, Shimon, Mirel, Rachel, Perl children of Iser Vilenski
Nathan Shvartz and Meilakh Kaplan
Khayah Sarah, Meir-Reuven, Sonia Meltser

Leah Vitko - Rozenberg

Yakov-David, Malkah, Belka Vitko
Malkah-Belka Rozenberg

Frida Zevuloni (Shakhnovitz)

Yakov, Tsipa Shakhnovitz
Shelomoh Shakhnovitz and family
Pesia-Rachel and Nathan Abramson

George Zerry (Zarnitzky) and Max Zarnitzky

Leib and Elka Zarnitzky
Yisrael-Mosheh Zarnitzky, his wife and two children

David Khaimovitz

The entire Yurburg communiy
Lena, Hayim (Chaim), Mosheh Khaimovitz

Dinah Tobin (Berzaner)

Motel, Itel, Reizel Berzaner
Henia, Sarah Fainberg
The Peisakhson family

Jafah Taitz

Mordekhai, Golda-Gitel, Meir, Rafael, Rivkah Levin

Sarah Tamshe (Yozelit)

Miriam, Tsadok Yozelit
Betty, Liova, Genia Aizenshtat (Eizenshtat)

Hannah Trainin (Karabelnik)

In memory of her family

Sarah Yagolnitser (Raizman) and Mosheh Anaki

Shmerl, Pesakh, Yakov, Golda, Yehudah Raizman
David, Daniel, Zelda, Mordekhai (Mordechai) Raizman
Leib-Hanan Levinson
Eliezer and Golda (Eliashevitz) Chosid

Ulia Jasvonski

>Ilusha, Feiga, David Jasvonski
>
>Pinkhas, Hayah-Feiga Shakhnovitz

Mosheh Jarovski

>Arie and Mosheh Jarovski

Meir Cohen

>Tsevi Hess and his family

Meir Cohen

>His family

A. Kasif

>The Yurburg community

Meir Levyush

>Mosheh, Sheine, Yisrael-Aizik Levyush

David Levin

>Ze'ev, Zahavah, Yekutiel, Arieh, Hilel Levin

Rachel Levin

>David Levin

Dov Levinberg

>The Levinberg family

Hinda Levinberg and Berl Levinberg

>Yisrael, Yeta, Shelomoh Levinberg
>
>Yakov, Avraham Ela Ivanski
>
>Jafah Levinberg (Gedalski) and her family
>
>Yehudith Levinberg (Rodensky) and family

Jafah Lupianski and Bluma Feldman

>Shakhne and Zelda Heselkovitz, Mendel, Hayah, Tuviyah, Miriam, Leah, Sarah and Mosheh

Ida Levinson

>Feivel Levinson

Lapinsky-Rabinotvitz

>David, Bruriyah, Tsilah Lapinsky
>
>Yosef and Yehudah Rabinovitz

Reuven Magidovitz

>In memory of his family

Tsilah Maizel and Pesia Hirsh

>Rachel Hirsh

Sheinele Mintser

>Dov, Luka and Nekhemyah Mintzer (Mintzer)

Meir Mendelovitz

> Nathan, Rachel-Leah, Hinda, Golda Mendelovitz
> Ben-Tsion, Sarah, Hayah, Miriam, Nekhamah Mendelovitz

The Margalith Family

> Yehudah-Arieh, Hayah, Shmaryahu, Esther Margalith
> Meir, Rosa, David, Zelig, Miriam, Mordekhai Margalith
> Lipshe and Theodor Lipetz
> Leah, Shalom, Hayahle Ingerman

Shoshanah Martin (Pulerevitz)

> Nathan, Batyah, Hayah, Reuven Pulerevitz

Khasyah Markuze and Meir Derori

> Khayah-Rivkah, Shemuel, Dinah, Hannah-Leah Akhpasander

Hannah Niv (Zakher)

> Aharon Yehudah Mintzer
> Elka Shapira Zakher
> Tsevi and Yosef Zakher
> Henia Berman

Shoshanah Sokolovski (Beiman)

> Zelig, Sherl, Merl Beiman

Mania Simon and Rachel Zigelman

> Tsipora-Feiga, Fruma, Gershon Mazur
> Dov and Daniel Katz

Niunia Slovo Khaimovitz

> Helena, Hayim and Mosheh Khaimovitz

The Smolnik family

> In memory of our family and the Community of Yurburg

Hannah Sandler (Beiman)

> Gitel, Zelig Beiman

Leo Portnoi

> Sheine-Rachel and Hayim (Chaim)-Dov, Bunim-Dov and all the members of the Portnoi family
> Eliezer and his family, Ze'ev-Wolf and family, Gita-Malkah and family Portnoi
> Menakhem-Mendel, Ephraim-Mordekhai (Mordechai), Eliyahu Mosheh Abramovitz
> Toibe-Zelda, Mordekhai (Mordechai), Elimelekh, Eliyahu Kaplan and family
> Aharon and his family, Reine Kaplan
> Simkhah, Heniale Sefbranski
> Sheine Sefbranski and family

Gabi Pukhert (USA)

> Yakov and Hayah Pukhert
> Henia Gruzin and family
> Sonia Lubin and family
> Yonah Pukhert and family
> Esther Beker and family
> Malkah Salomon and family
> Tsiporah Grinblat and family

Meir Polovin

> David, Khyene, Mordekhai (Mordechai) and Leah Polovin
> Lina Polovin-Chekhanovski and family
> Hannah Polovin-Soloveichik and family
> Mosheh Polovin, Golda and family

Hannah Polan

> In memory of the family and the Yurburg community

Mosheh Forbin

> Yisrael Rudnitski

Leah Furman

> In memory of the Hess family

Zevulun Poran

> In memory of the Petrikansky Family and Yurburg community
> In memory of Ari Glazman, his wife Klara (Petrikansky) and their son
> Giora

Alizah Porath-Leipziger

> Devorah-Leah, Eliezer, Fania, Matityahu-Tuviyah Leipziger
> Ezra, Hirshel Leipziger
> Rachel and Mosheh Hess
> Hannah and Nekhemyah Nakhumzon

Shimon Fainberg

> Benjamin, Henia, Rafael Fainberg, David Gut

Fainberg

> Shimon Fainberg

Shoshanah Petrikansky-Knishinski

> Yehudah-Leib (Alter) - (the father), Malkah (the mother), Klara,
> Rachel (the sisters), Yakov, Mosheh, Yitskhak (the brothers) of
> the Petrikansky family

Hannah Feldman

> Meir, Reizel-Tovah, Dov, Eliezer, Tsevi, Rivkah Feldman

Tsevi Feldman

> Mosheh, Leah, Sarah, Yakov, Sheina'le (Yafah) Feldman

Shulamith Feldman

> Dobe Feldman and her children

Lili Fridmans

    Leibel and Yakov Shoham

Sarah Priskel (Jozefovitz)

    Hayim (Chaim)-Tsevi, Hannah, Yosef, Shulamith Jozefovitz

Leibel Frank

    Yitzchak, Hannah-Leah, Berl, Itzel, Henek Frank

Avraham Chertok

    Tsevi, Hannah-Miriam, Zalman, Sarah, David Chertok

    Aizik, Pinkhas, Shimon, Dov Chertok

Rivkah Kadmon

    Yisrael Rudnitski

Emanuel Kopelov

    Avraham-Yitzchak, Masha Kopelov

Rosa Kanter

    Avraham, Daniel, Mosheh Berman

    Tankhum Berman, his wife and children

Batyah Kravitz and Akiva Flier

    Fania, Mendel, Nadya Fainberg

    Yehudith Fainberg and her son Benjamin

    Hilel, Khasya Flier

Yakov Rabinovitz

    Eliyahu, Marta, Hayah, Raya, Geula Rabinovitz

Rivkah Vainberg (Weinberg)-Ravitzki

    Yakov-Shelomoh, Esther-Rachel, Yekhiel Vainberg

    Avraham, Batyah, Nekhamah, Leah Vainberg

David Rodenski

    The Rodenski family

Yisrael Rochzo

    Yitskhak, Bernard, Avraham Rochzo

    Sarah and Rivkah Bresky

Yeta Reznik

    Mordekhai, Rachel, Tsilah, Malkah, Zlata Perlman

Aharon Rikler

    Mosheh, Regina, Hannah Rikler

Frida Straus

    Yosef-Dov Bekin

Shimon Shimonov

    Mordekhai, Malkah, Yisrael, Tsevi, Shaul Shimonov

    Yakov-Yosef Shimonov

Bela Shekhter (Bernstein)

> Leon, Henri Mering
>
> Hannah Luzin and her family
>
> Khayah Vainstein (Weinstein), Ida, Shertok, Sarah Fridland, Mendel Bernstein, Shmerl Bernstein, Yisrael Bernstein and their families

Avraham Shmulovski

> His family

Dora and Yakov Shapira

> David, Sarah, Hayim (Chaim) Verbelovski

Sarah Shapira (Frank)

> Malkah, Mordekhai (Mordechai)-Eli, Khavivah Frank

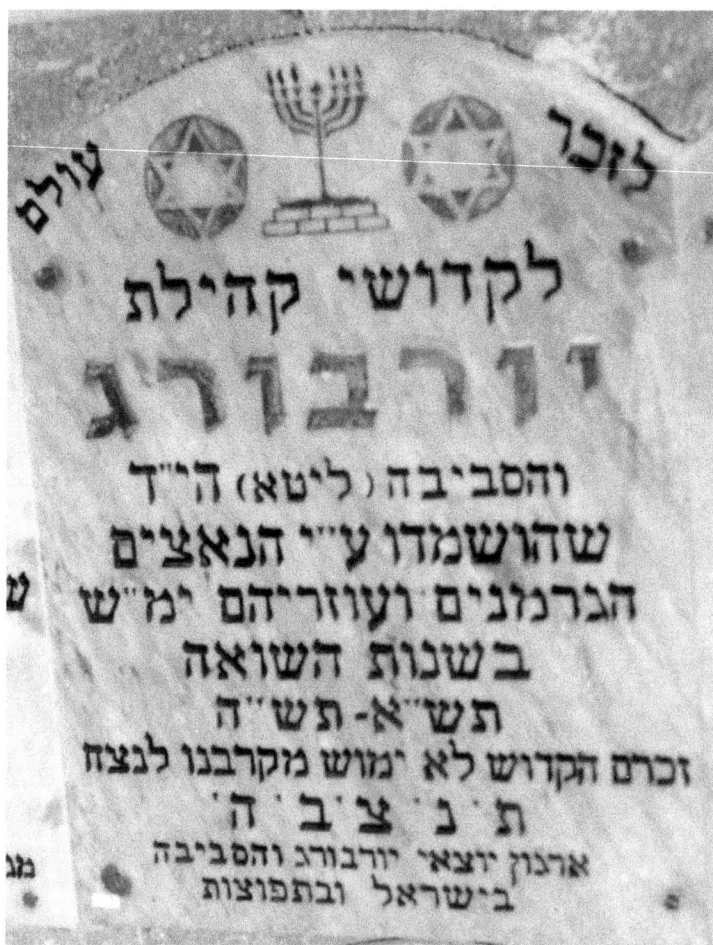

The Memorial Plaque in the Holocaust Cellar in Jerusalem

TRANSLATION OF PAGE 492

I SHALL ALWAYS REMEMBER THEM

I shall always remember the members of my family, my relatives and friends, members of the Jewish community of Yurburg, who were cruelly murdered although they were quite innocent.

I shall always see them in my mind, innocent sons, proud Jews, true to their people, Zionists who loved Eretz Yisrael, striving to go there to build and be built there.

Their hope did not come true.

Bloodthirsty murderers, mad Hitlerists and their Lithuanian helpers, criminals and murderers, put an end to the glorious Jewish community that had existed in Yurburg for hundreds of years.

Blessed be their memory.

Lovingly remembering all of them

Hannah (Feinberg)-Shraga   (Helen Feinberg Shrage)   Miami

TRANSLATION OF PAGE 493

A MEMORIAL CANDLE FOR MY FAMILY

With deep sorrow I cry for the members of my family who were killed in the years of the terrible Shoah in Yurburg by the Nazi-German murderers and their Lithuanian helpers, shameless, inhuman criminals.

These are the names of my relatives who were killed:

My father: **Mordekhai (Mordechai) Berzaner**

My mother: **Ethel Berzaner**

My sister: **Raizel (Raizale),** the lovely little girl

We shall always remember what the Nazi criminals did to our families and community; we shall never forgive them for the murder of innocent human beings.

The memory of our loved ones will be with us forever.

Always, always we will remember them with a sacred tremor.

God will avenge them!

Sadly remembering them,

Diana (Dinale) Tobin (Berzaner)

The photo below did not appear in the Yizkor book but is included here because it is relevant to the material above.

For our sister -
Raizale Berzaner 1924 - 1941
And for her two dear friends -
You will forever be in our hearts -
With love Dina'le [Dina] and Mute [Miriam]

At the Site of the Mass Graves in Yurburg Cemetery in June 1998
Photo by Gerrard W. Rudmin

Refer to page 177 for photos of Raezal, Danale (Diana) and Muta (Miriam).

TRANSLATION OF PAGE 494

IN ETERNAL MEMORY

SHULAMIT MILLER (FELDMAN)

To my dear family - My parents, my brothers and my sisters, who were killed in cold blood by the Nazi-Killers and their helpers the Lithuanians. They were innocent people.

And those are the members of my dear family and they are unforgettable.
My father: **Mosheh Feldman.**
My mother: **Leah Feldman.**
My brother: **Tsevi (Hershel) Feldman,** his wife **Devorah,** and their children **David and Aba.**
My brother: **Yakov Feldman.**
My sisters: **Sarah and Sheine (Sheinale).**
Their names will be remembered in eternal memory with great love.
They will always remain in my heart.
Forever their memory. The sacred memory.
I will never forget my family and the dear ones from the Yurburg Community.

May their souls be bound up in the bond of everlasting life.

Shulamith Miller (Feldman)   **Los Angeles**

TRANSLATION OF PAGE 494

IN MEMORY

FRIDA EPSHTEIN-PUKHERT

My sister Esther Pukhert and I weep and mourn the deaths of the dear children of the Yurburg community, who were murdered in the Shoah by the murderers, the German-Nazis and Lithuanians helpers.

Their inhuman acts shall never be forgotten.

The Jews will not ever forgive the perpetrators of these horrible crimes toward us and the Jewish community.

We will remember forever, our relatives, our friends, our city, our homeland - Yurburg.

Frida Epshtein Pukhert

TRANSLATION OF PAGE 495

In Memory of the Victims

With great sorrow and pain, I mourn the deaths of the children of my dear family, who were killed by the Nazis and their Lithuanians helpers.

And here are the names of my dear family who were the victims:

My father: **Meir**

My mother: **Henia**

My sisters: **Golda and Mendel Furman** and their children **Mosheh, Yakov, and Leib; Sheine** and **Hirshel Purve** and their children **Yonah and Berele; Rivkah** and **Aharon Kliachko** and their children **Avraham, Fruma, Yonah** and **Toibe**

My brothers: **Michael, Tsilah** and **Leah'le**

Hirshel Tarshish, the first victim to be shot by the murderers in front of my eyes at the Kovno prison on June 27, 1941.

I shall always remember my parents, my brothers, my sisters and relatives who were murdered while they were still young by the Hitlerist criminals, in the years 1941 -1944.

I shall remember the members of my dear family fondly and with respect.

May their souls be bound up in the bond of everlasting life.

Roza Shoshanah Birger Tarshish.

The youngest daughter from a big and special family.

Chicago, Illinois

TRANSLATION OF PAGE 496

In Eternal Memory

With a heavy heart, I mourn the members of my family, my parents, brothers, sisters and relatives, who were murdered by the evil German Nazis and their Lithuanian henchman - with terrible cruelty.

We shall never forget the barbaric acts of horror and we shall not forgive the murderers. These are the members of my family; may they rest in peace:

My Father: Eliezer Chosid

My Mother: Golda (my stepmother)

My Sister: Miriam-Rivkah, her husband Eliyahu Miasnik and their children

My Sister: Hayah-Beile and her husband Pinkhas Fields

My Sister: Batyah (Basa) -Rachel

My Brothers: The twins - Zalman-Yitskhak and Mosheh-Ze'ev

My Aunt: Dobe Luria, her husband Yerakhmiel and their son, Zalman-Shne'ur

My Aunt: Tirtsa Krupinski and her children - Pinkhas and his wife, Yehudith

My Aunt: Sarah Pesia, Yehudah and her little daughter Miriam'l

My Uncle: Daniel Hess and his wife Mina, daughter Batyah Eikhman and their child Lusy

My Uncle: Aryeh Meler, and his son Mosheh-Aharon Hess

My Uncle: Tsevi Hess, his sons David-Leib, Mosheh-Yitskhak, Chayim (Chaim)-Avraham and their children Nekhamah Eikhman, Aharon Segal and their children

My only daughter: Pesia-Tsipa (Tzipora'le), who was killed at age three and a half.

Blessed be the memory of my large family.

I shall always remember each and every one of them.

Dorothy Chosid-Bodnoff (Milwaukee, Wisconsin)

Dorothy passed away in April 2003

Sister of Jack Cossid

TRANSLATION OF PAGES 497 - 502

JEWS OF YURBURG - LIST OF NAMES
List from Memory - Mordehai (Mordechai) Berkover
Italic Notations is information added by Jack Cossid

TRANSLATION OF PAGE 497 [See page 736 for a map showing streets]

KOVNO STREET
Rabbi Arieh Leibchik Gut
Freyman Eliezer
Mintser Avraham
Khamenski, non-Jewish
Jasunski
Hayim (Chaim) Nathan Yozifer
Hasneh Shapira
Heselkovitz Shakhne
Pollak's tavern
Yisrael Mazur
Menukhah Goldshtein
Gutshtein family
Heishel der Teper (potmaker)
Rabbi Artsik Yozifer
Heselovitz Ephraim
Frank Malkah
Petrikanski Yehudah-Leib (Alter)
Bernstein Leib (Leon)
Lapinski
Hirsh pastry store
Tilla Weitsman
Fidler Mordekhai (Mordechai), barber's shop
Goldin
Rubinstein-Dayan
Bishko, candy factory
Pulovin
Soloveichik
Eliashevitz Meir - (Grocery)
Grinberg Mordekhai (Mordechai)
Grinberg Yosef
Komertz (Commerce) Bank (Bernstein)
Perlman Mordekhai (Mordechai) (store)
Lapinski (store for drinks)
Fin Hershel
Fin Pharmacy
Frank Yoel

Vainberg (Weinberg)
Krelitz Mosheh *(Bagel Bakery & lived upstairs)*
Mordehai Kimel's house
Hotel Aharonson
Shakhnovitz Pinkhas - Book store *(Pictured on page 33 of original book)*
Jasvonski *(store) (Pictured on bottom of page 33 of original Yizkor Book)*
Zarnitsky *(hat & cap shop, lived upstairs-see bottom page 33 of original book)*
Hannah - Itse Mayer's
Sausage shop Shmulovitz *(butcher shop)*
Yudel Kushelevski (leather shop)
Per David
Reizel Levin
Beker brothers
Yisrael Mazur (leather shop)
Meir Krelitz
Beile Bernstein *(Shmerl Bernstein's sister)*
Yekhiel Bernstein
Yente Bernstein *(Shmerl Bernstein's sister)*
Blumental

TRANSLATION OF PAGE 498

Berman (soda factory)
Leshts Yakov-Mosheh
Zalman Neviazhski
Yakov Pulerevitz
Nathan Pulerevitz
Leizer Pulerevitz
Nathan Vladislavovski
Zeider Mosheh
Berkover Eliezer
Abramovitz Zuse
Bader Mordekhai (Mordechai)
Pine der Staller (carpenter)
Berchik Malchik
Pukhert Yakov
Margolis Mersh (?)
Beile Kagan
Yekel Meirovitz
Khina Beilis
Rassel Gamler
Zelig Beiman
HaParush Rabbi Akiva
Khina Telzak
Nathan Verbelovski
Beiman family

Temke Heselzon Shelomoh
Pulerevitz grocery
Aizenstat (Eizenstat) Liba
Kantor
Glazer Hirshel
Eliyahu Naividel
Leah Revel
Christian house of prayer
Chertok (the tailor)
Beker
Tsevi Kobelkovski
Yekutiel Kobelkovski
Pazrinski Zalman
Pazrinski David and Barukh
Tana Levinson
Rabinovitz Yudel
Shmulovitz Yerakhmiel
Pollak Tuviyah
Meras
Telzak (sausage shop)
Vainstein
Mendelovitz Mordekhai (Mordechai)
Kobelkovski Gershon
Kobelkovski Ze'ev
Portnoy Yehudah Aharon
Mintser Aharon Yehudah
Hotel Hirshel Fin
The Great Synagogue
Beth HaMidrash
Mosheh Eliezer Beker (the attendant-Shamash)
Hostel for the poor
Yitskhak Kobelkovski
Yehudah Berkover
Zundelevitz Shmaryahu
Heselzon family
Benjamin Fainberg
Lipski's store (Gut)
Shimonov Alter, dentist
Kopelov - Shugam
Kopelov, dentist
Rikler, pharmacy
Tarshish *(Rosa Birger's brother)*
Purve (textile store) - *Tarshish's brother-in-law*
Nieviski Tsevi

TRANSLATION OF PAGE 499

Bernstein (hardware store)
Levitan Meir-Zusha (textile store)
Rochzo Shimon (grocery store)
Pulerevitz *(bicycle & jewelry stores)*
Simna (stationary store)
Kopelovitz (barber)
Vitko Yakov Dov (store)
Reuven Olshvanger *(hardware store)*
The Folksbank
Hayim (Chaim) Yosef Kobelkovski
Goldstein Mosheh Hayim (Chaim)
Putnoisheitel
Henia Fainberg
Leizer dem Dayan's (store)
Naividel Reuven *(bicycle shop)*
Naividel Rivkah (Puckale)
Fainberg (Feinberg) Meir *(George Feinberg's father)*
Yozefovitz Hayim (Chaim) Tsevi
Berzaner Mordehai (Mordechai)
Sarah Verbelovski
Grayevski (leather store)
Meierovitz Shemuel
Lubin Dov (barber)
Elyashuv (grocery)
Yozelit Tsadok
Leibe Popkaimer
Flier Akiva
Berkover Shimon
Rozin Hillel
Appelboim (leather store)
Rabbi Shelomoh Gershon the Tsadik
Berman the tinsmith
Zuikis store
Arpakhsander Sheftel
Krechmer Mosheh
Mekhel the ironer
Polak Avraham
Gery's tavern - non-Jewish
Fainberg Gavriel
Fainberg family
Heselkovitz Yitskhak Hessel (cinema)
Leibe Heselkovitz
Beiman David Yitskhak
Tuviyah Ess
Salmon (tailor)

Apriyaski Hayim (Chaim)
Mintser family
Leipziger Yitskhak
Ess
Meirovitz house (Hirshele Klein)
Levin Mordekhai (Mordechai) - on the other side of the bridge

UGNIAGESIU (Fire Brigade) STREET

Mikhlovski Hayim (Chaim)
Peisakhzon Devorah
Karabelnik David *(Cheka's father)*
Mikhelson Mordekhai
Hayim (Chaim) Sigar (the teacher)
Raizman Shmaryahu
Zalman (der Volkratzer-cleans wool)
Yozefovitz (the policeman)
Fire brigade
Hillel Skirstmunski

KALISHU STREET

Rabinovitz Ossip
Doctor Gershtein
Nathan Abramson (photographer)
Bilman's tavern
Post Office

TRANSLATION OF PAGE 500

Kalman Fridland
Mosheh Levin
Ze'ev Levin
Milkreit (non-Jew)
Meirovitz Eliezer
Aba Silver
Peres Mosheh
Minevitz Hayim (Chaim)
Zusman Levitan
Aba Verblovski
Shvedis tavern
Sarah Prusak
Yarovski Mosheh family
Leizer Meirovitz (Dem Dayan's)
Leibe Elkhanan Levinzon *(the watchmaker - Jack Cossid's great-uncle)*
Kopelov Zalman
Zakher family
Kizel family

UZH IMSTRA (Beyond the River) STREET

Berkover Shelomoh
Berkover Jonah Yakov
The Lithuanian Gymnasium
Hillel Danilevitz
Mikhelson
Grayevski
Altman
Berkover Yudel

HAMEKHES (Customs) STREET

Nathan Kaplan
Zilberman Hayim (Chaim)
Levinson Shraga
Tsofnath
Kushnir Aba

YATKEVER (Butcher's) STREET

Reuven Ess
Mosheh Yosef Ess
Shtok Arieh-Leib (bakery)
Aba Kaplan
Apelboim (Appelboim)
Reuven Hirsh, bakery
The Shokhet Arieh Shlomovitz
Vilonski Shimon
Shimshon
Avraham Kobelkovski, bakery
Die Bulvalakh (potatoes)
Synagogue on the name of Fainberg
Yakov Mintser
Hayim (Chaim) Eliyahu Elyashuv
Rochzo Shimon
Rochzo Yisrael
Kaplan Ita
Dov Bresky (bathing house)
Eliezer Chosid *(Jack Cossid's father & family)*
Mosheh Krupinski
Synagogue
Eliyahu Shmulovski
Tsivyah die Tsukhne (the clean one)
Mosheh Ess
Tsevi Kobelkovski
Mosheh Kaplan

Ess Nakhman
Heselzon family
Berski family
Abramovitz David
Kobelkovski Yitskhak
Avraham Pollak
Fruchter Daniel
Magidovitz Zelig

TRANSLATION OF PAGE 501

Tovah die Hutsikhe (Happy-Go-Lucky)
Shtern Wolf
Avraham Ber Abramson
Eliashevitz Meir
Megidovitz Hannah
Fruma Kraid (bakery) - Ben Craine's gradmother
Yudel Frank
Tovah Tirtsah Michelson
Tsevi Michelson
Barukh Mikhlovski
Rachel Kaplan (butcher shop)
Shimon Nakhe Kaplan
Aharon Arieh Kaplan
Mordekhai (Mordechai) Kaplan
Sheine-Leah di Zorgerke (the caring)
Yakov Hess (butcher shop)
Dov Mer (butcher shop)
Zelig Kobelkovski
Shie der terk (the Turk)
Miasnik family
Mosheh Shmulovitz
Yosef Ess
Dov Ess
The Khazan Alperovitz (cantor)
Mordekhai (Mordechai) Ess
Mosheh Beer (the Tehilim sayer)
Aba (the coachman)
Yakov Stern
Arieh (Leibe) Shtok
Peer family
Eliezer Eliashuv
Jonathan (the Melamed)
Yekhezkel Vilonski
Vasilov tavern
Hayim (Chaim) Reuven Danilevitz

Dr. Krolinski
Daniel Ess
Fridlender (bakery)
Shelomoh Levin
Tsevi (Hersh) Ess
Shulamith (Shlame) Moskovitz
Hertz (grocery)
Shmerl Polak (Pollak)
Shelomoh Polak (Pollak)

RASEINIU STREET
Goldstein Yosi Khemia
Eliyahu Miasnik
Talmud Torah (school)
Mendelevitch Nathan
Mikhel Leshtz
Yisrael Markovitz
Zuse Danilevitz
Tovah Polak (Pollak)
Dratvin Shemuel
Dratvin Zalman
Ita Zaks
Yudel Kushelevski
Barshtanski Betsalel
Berkover Shimon
Berkover Tuviyah
Asher Zaider
Yerakhmiel Shmulovski (tailor)
Meilakh Kaplan
Sarah Hene Kushelevski
Shemuel Faive Veitsman (Weizman)
Leibe Portnoy

TRANSLATION OF PAGE 502
Aba Zilber
Yosef Burker
Mina Glazer
Mosheh Odel Gavronski
Yudkovski
Yisrael Levinberg
Yisrael Kovalkovski
Yakov-Shelomoh Vainberg (Weinberg)
Eliezer Mikhlovski
Mosheh Feldman

Leah Kovalkovski
Yekhezkel Yafe
Elkhanan Vladislavovski
Niskale
Photographer Zidov (not Jewish)
House of Archik Nakhmis (?)
Aharon Verbelovski
Gavriel Lubin
Beit HamitbaHayim (Zamski Nachalnik)-Abattoir
Jewish Cemetery
Hayim (Chaim) Dovid Rosenberg
Hillel Fidler
Mordekhai (Mordechai) Most
Rabbi Avraham Dimant
Ita Feigin
Leibe Pres
Hayim (Chaim) Katsav
Nathan Aronovski
Dov Lubovski
Eliyahu Yokovitser
Yisrael Zilber
Rivkah Most
Yosef Melnik
Gitelson
Simna Family
Antsel Family
Verbelovski
Yakir Lubin
Hirshel Vainberg (Weinberg)
Sudak
Shelomoh Armian
Yakov Arnshtein
Zlatah Di Kekhin (Magid)
Eta Faikin

SODU GATVE (GARDEN STREET)
Mosheh Kaplan
Emanuel Kopelov
House of Yekhiel Bernstein
Aharon Smolnik
Hannah Frank
Herzl Gymnasium (Hebrew High School)
Alexandrovitz

GERMAN STREET

Bergovski Drugstore

Shimon Zundelovitz

Mordekhai (Mordechai)-Aryeh Mazur

Meigel

Kruger

Mordekhai (Mordechai) Perlman

Tsevi Shtok

Kopel Gutman

Shmaryahu Bernstein, Head of Komertz (Commerce) Bank

Alleyway in Yurburg in the 1930s
[Not in original Yizkor Book]

Members of The Organization of Former Citizens of Yurburg and the Vicinity in Israel

Compiled by Shimon Shimonov

Hannah Abel (Apriyaski) - Bereshith 11, Givatayim
Mosheh Abramovitz - Harkavi 5, Tel Aviv
Ada Oberfeier (Berkover) - Yarkonah 38, Ramat Gan
Tsevi Ahuvi (Liubovski) - Kibutz Yagur, M.P. Yagur
Bath-Sheva Ayalon (Shtok) - Givath Brener
Peninah Oren (Rikler) - passed away
Tania Ip, Dr., (Haimovitz) - Mendeli 5/8, Jerusalem
Arieh Eliashuv - Tsefath 9/9, Kiryath Shareth, Holon
Aharon Eliashuv - Shikun Khadash, Blok 10/8, Binyaminah
Yakov Apriyaski - Hapalmakh 16, Yad Eliyahu, Tel Aviv
Yoninah Efraimi - Kiryath Shalom, Mesilath Yeshurun, Maimon 10, Tel Aviv
Yakov Beiman - Mosheh Shareth 52/13, Kiryath Shareth, Holon
Hannah Beiman (Sandler) - passed away
Rivkah Levanoni-Blokh (Feldman) - Yavneh 28/5, Holon
Zahavah Ben Yehudah (Pulerevitz) - Hagalil 13, Netanyah
Rachel Ben Artsi - passed away
Rivkah Baron - Kibutz Yagur, M.P. Yagur
Mordekhai (Mordechai) Berkover - Tsuriel 6, Ramat Gan
Yakov Berkover - passed away
Yosef Berkoer - passed away
Boris Bernstein - passed away
Prof. Ze'ev Bernstein - Netanyah
Leib Bernstein - passed away
Klara Barnstein-Dushnitzky - passed away
Hinde Beker (Levinberg) - passed away
Menakhem Beker
Prof. Tsevi Barak
Baron Leah
Gershon Barshtanski - passed away
Yitskhak Barshtanski - passed away
Betsalel Barshtanski
Mosheh Gutstein - Simtath Mezadah 20/6, Ramat Hanasi, Bath Yam
Michael Gutstein - passed away
Yakov Gutstein - passed away
Hannah Goldman (Magidovitz) - Herzl 161, Rekhovoth
Yakov Goldstein - passed away
Fania Gamzu - Kefar Daniel, M.P. Merkaz
Miriam Gurevitz (Hess) - Nazereth Ilith 90/14
Yosef Grinberg - passed away

Rachel Grinstein (Hess) - Bar Ilan, Kiryath Motzkin, Haifa
Meir Drori (Akhpersander) - Akhad Ha'am 57, Tel Aviv
Pesia Hirsch - Michael 47, Haifa
Yafah Hirshheimer-Shitz 11, Tel-Aviv
Tsevi Hes-Ramoth, Jerusalem, Tsondek 21
Yosef Vitko - Talpiyoth, Shikun Amami, Jerusalem
Aba Vales
Mrs. Vladislavovski - Kiryath Shareth, Hashiloakh 10, Holon
Mark Verbelovski - Balfour 213 A, Appt. 9.10
Miriam Verpol (Barshtanski) - Kiryath Yam G, Joseftal 36/9, Haifa
Frida Zevuloni (Shakhnoviz) - passed away
Frida Zurinas (Mintser)
Rachel Zigelman (Mazur) - passed away
Shemuel Zakher - Ibn Gevirol 183, Tel Aviv
Kalman Zakher - Kefar Pines, M.P. Karkur
Mordekhai (Mordechai) Zilber - passed away
Max Zarnitzky - passed away
David Hayim (Chaim)ovitz - Nekhemyah 21, Naveh Sha'anan, Haifa
Jafah Titz (Levin) - Katzenelson 8, Bath Yam
Devorah Titz (Peiskhovitz) - Hashiloakh 14/3
Sarah Tamshe (Yozelit) - Helsinki 6, Tel Aviv
Hannah Trainin (Karabelnik) - David Yelin 19, Givatayim
Sarah Yagolnizer (Raizman / Reizman) - passed away
Leah Joselevitch - (Most) - Rupin 5, Kefar Saba
Mosheh Yanovski - passed away
Ulia Yasvonski - passed away
Eliyahu Kagan - Hadasah 9, Tel Aviv
Frida Kagan (Reznik) - Dakar 25, Neve Shareth, Tel Aviv
Meir Cohen (Hess) - passed away
Erika Katz - Hazamir 8, Ramat Gan
Zalman Levyush - passed away
Meir-Eliyahu Levyush - passed away
Rachel Levin - Yekhezkel 13, Tel Aviv
David Levin - passed away
Rinah Levit (Berkover) - Hadekalim 4, Ramat Gan
Michael Lazovski - Harav Kook 13, Tel Aviv
Mosheh Levite, Dr. - Pinkas 4, Tel Aviv
Jafah Lupianski (Heselkovitz) - Neve Asher, Pardes Khanah
Sarah Lupianski (Rabinovitz) - Chlenov 17, Petakh Tikvah
Berl Lapinski - passed away
Reuven Magidovitz - Poalei Tzion 151, Neve Amal, Herzliya
Mosheh Magidovitz - Sireni 32/5, Rekhovoth
Rivkah Moshkovitz - Levi Eshkol 101/12, Kiron
Hannah Moshkovitz
Rivkah Mida (Eliashuv) - Eilath 18, Holon
Hannah Meltser (Hess) - Struma (?) 18, Netanyah

Frida Mintser - passed away

Tsilah Maizel (Hirsch) - Michael 47, Haifa

Miriam Mikhlovski - Tsahal 13/10, Kiryath Yam

Meir Mendelovitz - passed away

Ronith Margalith (Gut) - Yeshayahu 32, Tel Aviv

Shoshanah Martin (Pulerevitz) - Ben Yair 37/31, Arad

Khasiah Markuze (Achpesander) - passed away

Hannah Niv (Zakher) - Kefar Pines, M.P. Karkur

Rachel Niv (Karabelnik) - passed away

Pesia Neviaski (Eliashuv) - passed away

Mordekhai (Mordechai) Naividel - Shiloh 15/12, Be'er Sheva (passed away)

Niunia Slovo Hayimovitz - Shderoth Deganiah 15/6, Kiryath Hayim

Shoshanah Sokolovski (Beiman) - Kibutz Amir, Hagalil Ha'elyon

Aharon and Devorah Smolnik - passed away

Nathan, Gershon and Esther Smolnik - Barak 52, Kiryath Motzkin

Mina Simon (Mazur) - passed away

Mosheh Anaki (Raizman / Reizman) passed away

Meir Polovin - passed away

Sheinele Polover (Mintser) - passed away

Barukh Portnoy

Menakhem Pukhert - passed away

Hannah Polan (Smolnik) - Motzkin 25, Tel Aviv

Alizah Porath (Leipziger) - Kibutz Afikim, Emek HaYarden

Zevulun Poran (Petrikanski) - Hantke 1, Jerusalem

Leah Furman - passed away

Beile Pulerevitz - Joseftal 32/12, Kiryath Hayim (Chaim) 3

Yehoshua and Mosheh Purvin (Rudnitski) - Ben Nun 54, Tel Aviv

Shimon Fainberg - passed away

Mina Fainberg - passed away

Devorah Peisakhson (at S. Shatz) - Nakar 12, Armon haNasi, Jerusalem

Hannah Feldman - Kibutz Yagur, M.P. Yagur

Bluma Feldman (Heselkovitz), Gezer 7, Tel-Aviv

Ida Per (Mostovitz) - Misgav Dov, M.P. Emek Sorek

Sarah Priskal (Josefovitz) - passed away

Leibel Frank - passed away

Rachel Tsevi (Blumental) - La Guardia 65, Yad Eliyahu, Tel Aviv

Zanun Chertok - passed away

Emanuel Kopelov - Herzl 208, Rekhovoth

Rivkah Kuperman (Rozman) - Tiomkin 7/2, Rishon LeZion

Golda Kaliski (Hess) - Basok 10/1, Neveh Shalem, Yad Eliyahu

Hayah Kurtzman (Elyashuv) - Ben Yehudah 74/17, Herzliyah

Shoshanah Knishinski (Petrikanski)-Shderoth Ha'am Hatzarfati 62, Ramat Gan

Ita Kalinski - Simtath Hasharon 4/28, Ramat Hanasi

Geulah Rabinovitz (Melnik) - Bareli 10/8, Tel Aviv

Rivkah Ravitzki (Weinberg) - Kibutz Givath Brener

Yakov Rabinovitz - passed away

Elkhanan Rudnitski - Kibutz Yagur, M.P.
David Mordekhai (Mordechai)) Rodenski - Olifant 3/3, Tel Aviv
Jetta Reznik - passed away
Leah Rosenberg (Vitko)
Yisrael Rochzo - passed away
Michael Raizman (Reizman) - passed away
Shalom Raizman (Reizman) - passed away
Aharon Rikler - passed away
Fruma Shokhat (Vladislavovski)
Bela Shekhter - passed away
Miriam Shlivak (Josefovitz) - Beith Yosef 20, Tel Aviv
Hannah Shleifer (Hess) - Kiryath Giora 161/1, Or Yehudah
Avraham Shmulovski - Pinkas 4, Tel Aviv
Shimon Shimonov - Harav Herzog 20, Tel Aviv (passed away)
Sarah Shapira (Frank) - Rambam 44, Jerusalem
Dora Shapira (Verbelovski) - passed away

PAGE 508   Originally in English

People of Yurburg Abroad

Alphabetized and spelling corrected

(Parenthesis material added here by Joel Alpert)

Submitted by S. Shimonov

L. Abrams	Skokie, (Illinois)
Esther Atlas	Brookline, (Massachusetts)
Lena Berman	Detroit, (Michigan)
J. H. Beiles*	Montreal, (Canada)
(Helen Kizell Beiles*	Montreal, Canada)
Ben-Berk	Chicago, (Illinois)
L. Bernstein	Chicago, (Illinois)
Haward Bendalin	Phuenie
Rosa Birger	Chicago (Skokie, Illinois)
Dorothy Budnoff*	Milwaukee, (Wisconsin)
R. Cable	Brookline, (Massachusetts)
Jack Cossid	Chicago, (Illinois)
Sol Ellis*	Detriot, (Michigan)
Max Ellis*	Oak Park, (Michigan)
Bob Ellis*	Southfield, (Michigan)
Joe Ellis*	(Delray Beach, Florida)
Freda Epstein	Brookline, (Massachusetts)
Quen Faktor	S. Africa
Pauline Freeman Feldman*	Milwaukee, (Wisconsin)
Isidore Fainberg*	Detroit, (Michigan)
George Fainberg	Detroit, (Michigan)
(Yehuda Fleisher	Lakewood, New Jersey)
Ellis Gans*	Detroit, (Michigan)
Olga Zapolsky Gans*	Detroit, (Michigan)
Molly Ginsberg	Montreal, (Canada)
Miriam (Berzaner) Gold	Southfield, Michigan
M. Goldstein	Skokie, (Illinois)
Sol Goldstein*	Skokie, (Illinois)
Ethel Goldstein	Chicago
(Joe Goodman - Guttman)	El Paso, Texas
Greenman	Chicago, (Illinois)
Dora Haber	New York
Hebert Idelson	S. Africa
Michalina Kantor	New York
Max Kissel*	Canada
Joe Levin	Chicago, (Illinois)
Toni Levinsohn	Transwal

Rose Levin	Chicago, (Illinois)
Ruby Levin	S. Africa
Lazar Levin	S. Africa
Herbert Lyon	Canada
R. Mazur	Brookline, (Massachusetts)
S Meller	Los Angeles
Harry Michelson	Brookline, (Massachusetts)
Sarah Mendelowits	Mattapan, (Massachusetts)
Betty Much	Detroit, (Michigan)
P. Rosenfield	Lincolnwood, (Illinois)
Lena Rubinowich	Canada
Hannah (Helen) Shrage*	Michigan
S. Smolin	Skokie, (Illinois)
H. Schaffer	Chicago, (Illinois)
Diana (Berzaner) Tobin	(Boca Raton, Florida)
Lazar M. Wallace	Charlotte, North Carolina?)
Iritt Wenokur	Detroit, (Michigan)
Rina Wenokur	Detroit, (Michigan)
I. Vilonski	Los Angeles
George Zerry (Zarnitsky)*	Detroit, (Michigan)

* Known to be deceased

TRANSLATION OF BOTTOM OF PAGE 510

SURVIVORS OF YURBURG, SHOAH SURVIVORS (HOLOCAUST) IN LITHUANIA

Yurburg: Zelda Frank (deceased-2000)

Kovna: Hayim (Chaim)-Wolf Joffe (deceased-1996); Shalom Rosenberg, (Duba Most Rosenberg)

Vilna: Hanan Levin; Haike Lubin; Asher Meirovitz; Berl Minevitz, Hayah Kobelkovsky, Zalman Kaplan; Hannah Shimna-Konisky; Eliezer Shapira.

Immigrated to Israel: Beilinke (Bela) and Gitale (Gita) Abramson [Gita Abramson Bereznitzky passed away in August 2000 in Tel Aviv]; Shimon Beiman.

Visited Israel: Hannah Shimna; Zalman Kaplan.

Died - blessed be their memory -: Heskeh Magidovitz, Yisrael Moshkovitz.

TRANSLATION OF PAGES 507 AND 509

WE SHALL REMEMBER

We shall remember our friends from Yurburg, who managed to arrive in Israel, many of them after many difficulties and the sufferings of the Holocaust, but did not live to see the Book of Remembrance of our town's martyrs published. They walked a long way with us, took part in our meetings and excursions, participated in the activities to commemorate our loved ones - contributed towards the placing of the memorial plaque in the Holocaust basement, planted trees in the Yurburg forest in the Modi'in region and initiated the publication of the Book of Remembrance, but did not see it published. Among them: David Levin, member of the Association's council, a man of vision, active and among those who took the initiative to publish the Book of Remembrance.

The pages of the Book of Remembrance include the names of those who are absent - they were not forgotten.

Blessed be their memory!

Shimon Shimonov and Zevulun Poran

"In Memory"

GREETINGS FROM FORMER RESIDENTS OF YURBURG IN LITHUANIA

Upon completion of the Book of Remembrance of the Yurburg community, in the fall of 1990, an unexpected guest arrived from "over there," from our Yurburg, the Yurburg which is engraved on our memory, for better or worse. This important guest, Holocaust survivor **Zalman Kaplan**, came to tour the country. Here he was traveling along, looking at its towns and villages, inhaling the country's fresh air and absorbing its pleasant odors.

The guest sees our country as a summer dream - a thriving and developing Jewish country, absorbing new immigrants even in days when there are plenty of political, economic and cultural problems. Indeed, in spite of the problems in Israel, life is exhilirating and creative. He, the guest, returns - as he says - to his friends, the survivors, excited about the wonderful things he has seen and experienced in Israel in general and the intimate and moving meeting he had with former residents of Yurburg in particular.

We here in Israel, formerly of Yurburg, send cordial greetings to our friends and acquaintances, survivors, who are over there - and say to them: we shall be very happy to see you as guests and as residents - our country is your country!

Shimon Shimonov and Zevulun Poran

Zalman Kaplan in May 2001

The Story of the Life of Zalman Kaplan and His Family in the Terrible Days of the Holocaust

By Zalman Kaplan (see previous page for his picture)

I was born in Yurburg on 28 May 1921. My father's name - Aba and my mother's name - Ethel. My grandfather on father's side was Mordekhai (Mordechai) (Motl) Grinberg. We lived on Naujos street, next door to Emanuel Kopelov.

I studied at the "Talmud Torah" elementary school and at the Lithuanian high school. When I graduated from high school in 1939 I went on to study at the universities of Kovno and Vilna.

When World War II broke out, I was sent to the Tambov area in Russia. From October 1941 till February 1946 I served in the Red Army. In 1943 I graduated from officers' school and took part in battles against the Nazi enemy.

The fate of my family was like the bitter fate of all the families in Yurburg. My brother Mendel, 15 years old, was murdered on July 3, 1941 in the cruel "Action" of the Jewish group at the Yurburg cemetery.

My father was murdered in Kalniya on the way to Rasein. My mother was murdered in the big *Aktia* at the Slabodka (Kovno) ghetto. She was sent to Fort IX and died there on October 28, 1941. The members of my father's family, among them his brothers Yakov-Ber, David, Meir, his sister Merel and his uncles and aunts and cousins were all killed.

The father of my mother Mordekhai (Motl) Grinberg and her brother Yosef (Yosel) .and their families were exiled to Siberia. Of them Yosef (Yosel) Grinberg (Greenberg) and his son survived. My mother's sisters - Dinah and Polia and their families were exiled to Riga and from there to the Aushwitz gas chambers.

Each year we visit the graves of our dear ones in Yurburg. It is sad in Yurburg. The streets of the Jews are gone. The synagogues were destroyed. There is no sign left of the hundreds of years old flourishing community. Only graves, graves all around. Yurburg's Jewish cemetery has been abandoned. Weeds, bushes and thorns cover the graves. The survivors have renovated the cemetery, as far as possible, but the graves and fence require further thorough repair. Former residents of Yurburg have approached the local authorities on the matter, but nothing has been done to date. The Former Residents of Yurburg Association in Israel has participated in donations for these requirements.

Once upon a time there was a Jewish town called Yurburg, now it is a town that exists merely in the memory of those who used to live there once.

Update 2014: The above wishes of Zalman Kaplan were carried out by The Friends of the Yurburg Cemetery and Project Preservation of Dartmouth College who built a new fence around the cemetery and carried out extensive restoration in summer of 2007. For more detail see   *http://kehilalinks.jewishgen.org/yurburg/yurburg.html,* and in the Appendix

TRANSLATION OF PAGE 511

EPILOGUE

WORDS SPOKEN AT THE CEREMONY OF PLACING THE ASHES OF THE JEWISH MARTYRS FROM LITHUANIA AT "YAD VASHEM"

Not long ago we buried the few ashes brought from the graves of Lithuanian Jewish martyrs.

A tiny remnant, merely a symbol of the many heaps of ashes dispersed in each town and village; heaps of ashes that remained there as angry witnesses to the terrible Holocaust that befell our dear ones, the Jews of Lithuania. **The martyrs' ashes cry out to us: Remember, do not forget!**

And each generation will tell the next, father will tell his son about the terrible Jewish tragedy of one tribe, out of all the Jewish tribes in Europe, that was cruelly destroyed and exterminated although it was quite innocent.

Let us lament and mourn the blood that was spilt and the Lithuanian Jewish tribe that was destroyed and is no more.

IN SOLEMN REMEMBRANCE

While we light the eternal candle, at this shrine of mourning, near the sacred ashes, we remember them:

The six million of our people who were destroyed as martyrs

Slaughtered and exterminated by the Nazis and their helpers;

Of the communities and families of Beith Yakov who were murdered and destroyed

Out of the evil intent to erase the name of Israel and its culture from the earth.

Let us tell our sons and grandsons how six hundred years ago we, Jewish refugees, terror-stricken and persecuted in pogroms, settled on the marsh land under the gray sky of Lithuania Here the Jews set up their tents as unwelcome guests; they suffered and were persecuted, but they had no choice but to hold on to this land and consider it their permanent shelter.

In this miserable valley the Lithuanian Jews sacrificed their existence and their blood; they left nothing behind, only hard work and contributed much to the country that absorbed them and to its material and spiritual culture. Many generations developed Jewish culture, created a spiritual tradition.

Alas, they built in vain.

When the bloodthirsty Nazis came to the land of Lithuania, the Jews found no cover there, and their Lithuanian neighbors did not stretch out a helping hand and did not stand by them in their hour of need.

The land of Lithuania became one big grave to its Jews.

Its Nazi gravediggers and their Lithuanian helpers ended the hopes, the dreams and the wish to find a secure home for Jews in the land of Lithuania, as in all the countries of the world.

95% of the Jews of Lithuania were destroyed in the terrible Holocaust.

The last survivors return to the borders in the land of birth of the Jewish people.

This is the bitter Jewish fate and that is the cruel conclusion!

No statues were erected for the Jewish fighters against the Nazis.

We here in the free land of Israel, in our independent state, set up the statues and tombstones.

The fate of the Yurburg community is like that of the communities of Lithuania - it was lost and is no longer.

Our dear ones, who climbed the gallows there, gave us our life, the continuing existence and creation in the country of the Jews, together with the tribes of Israel forever.

We shall carry out our fathers' and father's fathers' last will in Israel.

Zevulun Poran

TRANSLATION OF PAGE 513

WE SHALL REMEMBER

WE SHALL REMEMBER

With pain and sorrow our fathers, our brothers and sisters, killed by beastly murderers;

WE SHALL REMEMBER

The loss of the treasures of our Torah, wisdom and knowledge, the rabbis of the community and the people of noble mind, the glory of mankind;

WE SHALL REMEMBER

The great synagogue, the house of prayer and kloizes, the libraries and studios, Talmud Torah and the Gymnasium, the charity institutions, the love of others, the love of Israel and Eretz Israel;

WE SHALL REMEMBER

Our loved ones, all of them, who were murdered in cold blood by evil men who destroyed our community - the Yurburg community - forever. The martyrs' blood that was spilt cries to heaven and there will be no atonement.

Amen

Zevulun Poran

TRANSLATION OF PAGE 513

Memorial for the Murdered Jews and Anti Fascists - Erected by the town of Yurburg. Along side the memorial are the surviving sons of Yurburg who came to commemorate the Jewish martyrs of Yurburg.

Memorial at the Mass Murder Site and Cemetery in Yurburg

[Photo not in original book - Courtesy of Gita Abramson Bereznitsky]

TRANSLATION OF PAGE 512

The Only Tombstone

Befitting the memory of the Jewish community of Europe that was destroyed by the Nazi murderers is THE STATE OF ISRAEL, the country where the hope of the Jewish people has come true, for all generations to come, and it is a free and reliable shelter for all the Jews in the world who want to live a free and independent life.

DAVID BEN GURION

Overlooking the Nieman River in Yurburg in June 2003 (to the South).
Top photois to right, middle is in center, bottom is on left.
Photos not in Original Yizkor Book - Courtesy of Dr. Leon Menzer

APPENDIX

New Materials Collected After Publication of the Original Book

Appendix Was Not Part of the Original Yizkor Book

Preface for this Appendix

We hereby take advantage of the opportunity to add new material that has come to light since the publishing of the original Hebrew book in 1991 and hence it is included here. Since the tone of this material is different from the material in the original Yizkor Book, the editor hopes that the reader understands the intent of including this material is to enrich the content of the book, enhance the history of the town and its descendents and make it more appealing to a wider readership, who can read the history of our community of Yurburg.

This chapter contains new material from the autobiography of Professor Ze'ev Bernstein about his father, Boris, a newly written history of Yurburg written by Professor Dov Levin and Josef Rosin, editor and assistant editor respectively of the Hebrew volume ***Pinkas Kehilat Lita, Encyclopedia of Jewish Communities of Lithuania***, descriptions of the lives of Yurburgers who settled in Israel, Canada and the United States, and a description of a trip to Yurburg and Sudarg taken by descendants of Yurburgers in 2001.

Yurburg

By Professor Dov Levin and Yosef Rosin

English edited by Sarah and Mordehai Kopfstein

*Note: This article was written by Professor Dov Levin and Josef Rosin, Editor and Assistant Editor, respectively, of **Pinkas HaKehilat Lita**, **Encyclopedia of Jewish Communities of Lithuania** (Yad VaShem, 1996). This article is based upon and expanded from their article on Yurburg in that book. This article was written especially for this book and was requested by Joel Alpert, compiler of this book.*

Yurburg is situated on the right hand shore of the Nieman (Nemunas) river where the tributaries Mituva and Imstra converge. The town used to be about 12 km (7.5 miles) to the east of the Prussian border, surrounded by woods. It began as a stronghold of the Knights Order of the Cross in the thirteenth century named Georgenburg or Jurgenburg, but after the border between Lithuania and Germany was defined in 1422, Yurburg became a border town and a customs point. During the thirteenth century the importance of Yurburg increased due to the harvesting of trees in the surrounding woods for commercial purposes, when the logs were floated on the Nieman River to Prussia. Thanks to the ethnic diversity of its inhabitants, its location on a main sailing route - the Nieman - and its proximity to Prussia, Yurburg became a communication and commercial center between east and west. During Russian rule (1795-1915) the town was included in the Kovno Gubernia (province).

As a result of railway construction and road improvement in the region during the nineteenth century, sailing on the Nieman subsided and the growth of Yurburg slowed down. The town was taken over by rebels for a short time during the Polish mutiny in 1831, but after the mutiny was repressed by the Tzar, Yurburg returned to its former life.

German culture from across the border influenced the social life greatly and affected the mode of living in town, which also continued to be the case during the period of Lithuania's independence (1918-1940).

Because of its topographic situation and location between the two rivers and the Nieman, the town frequently suffered from floods. In 1862 eighty houses were inundated and their residents rescued themselves by climbing onto the roofs. Yurburg also suffered from fires, the greatest fires being in 1906 when 120 of its houses burnt down.

Jewish Settlement till after World War I

Yurburg was first mentioned in the book of Rabbi Meir ben Gedalyah (1558-1616) from Lublin "Sheloth uTeshuvoth" (Questions and Answers) concerning the case of an "Agunah" (deserted wife) whose husband had been killed in Yurburg. The testimonies of this case were reported in 1593 and 1597. During the period of the autonomous organization of Jewish communities in Lithuania "Va'ad Medinath Lita" (1623-1764), Yurburg was included in the Keidan district, and by 1650 there were already seven Jewish houses in town.

In the middle of the 17th century, some Yurburg's Jews earned their living by renting the right to collect taxes for the government in Yurburg, Birzh and other towns, and this was done under the cover of Christians.

At the beginning of the 18th century the community wanted to replace the officiating Rabbi, but he complained to the authorities and received a " letter of protection " from the king. On the 17th of November 1714 Rabbi Aizik. Leizerovitz was mentioned in an official document, but detailed information of Jewish settlement of Yurburg exists only from 1766. At this time there were 2,333 Jews in the town who owned a few prayer houses, among them the magnificent wooden Synagogue built in 1790, one of the oldest in Lithuania. There was also a Jewish cemetery, as well as welfare and religious education institutions. In 1862 there were 2,550 Jews in Yurburg.

Yurburg Jews suffered during the Polish mutiny in 1831. A local resident, Reuven Rozenfeld, was hanged by rebels, who blamed him for aiding the Russian rulers. After the mutiny was quelled, a trial of those involved in the hanging took place for many months, among the accused was a Jew named Tuviyah ben Meir Danilevitz. After being imprisoned in Rasein for 13 months, he was acquitted due to lack of evidence.

In 1843 the Czar issued an order stipulating that Jews living in an area within 50 km of the western border of Russia should be transferred to some of the Gubernias (provinces) inside Russia. Yurburg's community was one of 19 communities that refused to obey this order.

Most of Yurburg Jews made their living from the timber trade, floating timber to Germany, commerce, customs commission, transport and shopkeeping. In 1865 a branch of one of the greatest commercial firms in Germany "Hausman et Lunz" opened in town.

The local garrison was also situated there, providing a living for Jewish merchants. In 1861 Jewish soldiers of the garrison donated money for writing a new "Torah Scroll," which was later brought into the synagogue by the Jewish soldiers, with due festivity. The celebration was attended by respected local people, headed by the commander of the garrison.

At the end of the 1880s a cooperative credit company was established, for which it took three years to receive permission from the authorities.

As a result of the general atmosphere in Yurburg, the "Haskalah" (Enlightenment) movement flourished there among the Jews more than in Zhamut's (Zemaityja region) other communities. This was demonstrated by the cooperation of the community heads in the establishment of a quite modern Talmud-Torah in 1884, where 100 poor children studied, and in addition to religious subjects, Hebrew and grammar, mathematics and Russian were also taught. Members of the management of this institution were: L.Valk, M.H. Kostin and L.Boger, one of the teachers being the famous Hebrew writer Avraham Mapu. Although the school was under the supervision of the government, its financial maintenance was mainly the responsibility of the community. Due to the fact that the 900 Rubles received from the "Meat tax" was not sufficient, the community heads appealed to former Yurburgers in New York, Saint Louis and Rochester in the United States for help. A partial list of donors (who donated from $0.50 to $750) was published in the Hebrew newspaper "HaMeilitz" in July 1889.

The Yurburg Jewish institutions also served smaller Jewish communities in the vicinity, such as Shaudine, Pakelnishok, Gaure. (After World War there were no more Jews in Pakelnishok).

In the Hebrew newspaper "HaMagid" from 1872 there is a list of 39 Utyan donors of assistance for starving Persian Jews. (See Jewishgen-Database-HaMagid-by Jeffrey Maynard).

During the years of famine (1869-1872) which affected many parts of Lithuania, Yurburg suffered less and its Jewish residents donated money to needy communities. The fundraisers were Yitshak-Aizik Volberg and Shelomoh Bresloi.

In a list of donors for the Settlement of Eretz-Yisrael dated 1896, names of 20 Yurburg Jews appear (see **Appendix 3**). The fundraisers were Tsevi Fain and Avraham-Yitshak Kopelov.

In the old Jewish cemetery in Jerusalem there is a headstone of Rivkah Gitel bat Mordehai Margalioth from Yurburg. During World War I many of Yurburg's Jews left the town, some returning later.

During Independent Lithuania (1918-1940)

After the establishment of independent Lithuania, Yurburg was included in the Raseiniai district. The number of Jewish residents in Yurburg was smaller than before as some of those who had left did not return and also due to immigration abroad. However, their proportion amongst the whole population increased, as can be seen from the first census performed by the government in 1923. There were 4,409 residents including 1,887 Jews (43%), while in 1897 there were 7,391 residents, of them 2,350 Jews (32%).

In 1922 the elections for the first Lithuanian Seimas (Parliament) took place, with 774 Utyan Jews participating. 477 voted for the Zionist list, 199 for the

Democrats and 98 for the religious list "Akhduth."

According to the autonomy law for minorities issued by the new Lithuanian government, the minister for Jewish affairs, Dr. Max Soloveitshik, ordered elections to be held in the summer of 1919 for community committees in all towns of the state. In Yurburg a committee was only elected five years later, in 1924, after much pressure from the National institutions of Lithuanian Jewry (Va'ad HaAretz). The committee (Va'ad) comprised five members of the Workers list, three Zionist-Merchants, two Religious, two Democrats, one "Tseirei-Zion", one Mizrahi and a representative of the butchers. The committee, which collected taxes as required by law and was in charge of all aspects of community life, was active till the end of 1925 when the autonomy was annulled.

Among the 14 members at the local council (later the municipality) elected in 1924, six were Jews, one of them serving as deputy chairman and another as a member of the management. The elections of 1931 resulted in three Lithuanians, one German andone Russian being elected, as well as five Jews: Z. Levitan, M. Shimonov, Y. Grinberg, Sh. Zundelevitz, Adv. H. Naividel, one of them as deputy chairman. In the elections of 1934, when two Jewish lists were presented, four Jews, four Lithuanians and one German were elected.

At right: stamp of the office of the Minister for Jewish Affairs
At left: stamp of the Jewish National Council in Lithuania

During this period, as previously, Yurburg's Jews made their living from trade with timber, fish, poultry, fruits and eggs that were exported to Germany. Others dealt in crafts, fishing and shipping, a large part of economic activity taking place on weekly market days (Monday and Thursday) and during the 24 annual fairs.

According to the government survey of 1931 there were 75 businesses in Yurburg, 69 being owned by Jews (92%).

The list of traders according to the type of business is given in the table below:

Type of the business	Total	Owned by Jews
Groceries	3	3
Grain and Flax	4	4
Butcher's shops and Cattle Trade	13	9
Restaurants and Taverns	4	2
Food Products	9	9
Beverages	2	2
Textile Products and Furs	13	13
Leather and Shoes	4	4
Haberdashery and Utensils	6	6
Medicine and Cosmetics	3	3
Radio, Bicycles, Sewing Machines	1	1
Tools and Steel Products	5	5
Heating Materials	3	3
Books and Stationary	1	1
Others	4	4

According to the same survey there were 19 light industries in Yurburg, including 18 owned by Jews (95%), as can be seen in the following table:

Type of the Factory	Total	Jewish owned
Power Plants	1	1
Sawmills and Furniture	2	2
Paper Industry: Printing Press	1	1
Food Industry	8	7
Dresses, Footwear	3	3
Others	4	4

In 1937 there were 93 Jewish artisans: 19 tailors, 12 butchers, 12 bakers, 8 shoemakers, 6 barbers, 5 stitchers, 4 painters, 3 hatters, 3 glaziers, 2 oven builders, 2 locksmiths 2 electricians, 2 watchmakers, 2 jewelers, 2 photographers, 1 tinsmith and 8 others. In 1925 there was also one Jewish doctor and 2 dentists.

The Jewish popular bank (Folksbank), established in 1922, which later had up to 400 members, played an important role in the economic life of Yurburg's Jews. Among the great businesses in town the private bank of the Bernshtein family, the "Export-Handel" company and the shipping companies in the Nieman River, should be mentioned.

One of the steamships wharfing in Yurburg

By 1939 there were 116 phone owners, 41 of them belonging to Jews.

Throughout the ages mutual tolerance existed between the different ethnic groups in Yurburg, and this also continued during Lithuanian rule. However, there were exceptions from time to time, as in 1919, when Yurburg Jews complained to the minister for Jewish affairs in Kovno about a decision by the local authorities that all signs should be in the Lithuanian language only. Previously there had been some signs on Jewish shops in Yiddish or in Hebrew. One of the factors that fostered strong mutual relations was the local branch of the Organization of Jewish Combatants for the Independence of Lithuania, but during the thirties a significant decline took place in the relations between local Lithuanians, Germans and their Jewish neighbors. It expressed itself by the suppression of Jewish commerce, such as the closing of the "Export-Handel" company, in assaults and in the burning of Jewish property, i.e. the flourmill of the Fainberg family.

To the deterioration of the economic situation of Yurburg's Jews, the lower and middle classes in particular, added the many fires and floods caused by the rising water level in the Nieman during the melting of the ice.

Yurburg was famous in Lithuania for its nationalistic atmosphere and Hebrew culture that dominated it. One of the two public parks was almost officially called "Tel-Aviv," and the Hebrew high school was called "Herzl" after the founder of the Zionist organization. In addition to the old Talmud Torah, which was turned into a modern elementary school, a new Hebrew school of the "Tarbuth" chain was also established. There was a public Yiddish library called after "Mendele Mokher Sefarim" and a Hebrew library called after Y. H. Brener.

The "Maccabi" sports organization with about 100 members, an urban Kibbutz of HeHalutz named "Patish" and branches of all Zionist parties, were established. There was also much activity by Zionist youth organizations, such as "HaShomer-HaTsair," "Beitar " and "Benei-Akiva"

The Leftist-Yiddishist movement, the "Jewish Knowledge Society" and the sports organization the "Jewish Workers Club" were also active among Yurburg's Jews. Communist youth too had their supporters.

The table below shows how Yurburg Zionists voted for the different parties at five Zionist Congresses: (See the key below the table)

Congr Nr.	Year	Total Shkalim	Total Voter	Labor Party		Rn	GZ		Gm	Mz
				Z"S	Z"Z		A	B		
15	1927	64	40	29	6	---	5	--	--	---
16	1929	118	44	28	2	11	3	--	--	---
17	1931	53	40	20	10	4	6	--	--	---
18	1933	---	143	101		19	9	--	10	4
19	1935	---	359	257		---	14	40	19	29

GZ = General Zionists Gm =Grosmanists
Rn = Revisionists   Mz= Mizrachi

During Nazi rule a member of the illegal Communist youth organization named Yekutiel Elyashuv, who had managed to escape to Russia at the beginning of the war, was parachuted in Lithuania. He fell in battle.

For the list of Rabbis who served in Yurburg during the years, see **Appendix 1**. For a partial list of personalities of Yurburg, see **Appendix 2.**

During World War II and Afterwards

World War II broke out on the first of September 1939, when the German army attacked Poland. A German-Soviet agreement of August 23rd 1939 had stipulated that Lithuania would be under German influence, but that same year, in September 1939, Germany and the Soviet Union decided that Lithuania would be under Soviet influence. Accordingly the agreement of October 10th 1939 stipulated that the Soviet Union return Vilna to Lithuania, this ending its occupation by Poland. This included an area of 9000 square kilometers around the town, and Soviet troops were allowed to establish bases all over Lithuania.

On June 15, 1940, Lithuania was forced to establish a regime friendly towards the Soviet Union, and after the new government headed by Justas Paleckis was installed, the Red Army took over Lithuania. President Smetona fled, Lithuanian leaders were exiled to Siberia, and political parties were dissolved. A popular Seimas was elected, 99% of its members being communists, and decided unanimously that Lithuania join the Soviet Union.

Newspaper seller with "Di Yiddishe Shtime" in his hand

Following new rules, the majority of factories and shops belonging to Jews of Yurburg were nationalized and commissars were appointed to manage them. Most of the artisans were organized into cooperatives (Artels). Some flats and buildings were confiscated. Some enterprises were turned into government institutions, others into public and communal companies.

After these events the supply of goods decreased and, as a result, prices soared. The middle class, mostly Jewish, bore most of the brunt, and the standard of living dropped gradually.

All Zionist parties and youth organizations were disbanded, the Hebrew "Tarbuth" school was closed, and the Yiddish school which was broadened, became an official Soviet institution. At this time Yurburg numbered about 600 Jewish families.

On the 22nd of June 1941 the war between Germany and the USSR began, the German army entering Yurburg on the same day. Many people connected to the Soviet regime tried to escape, but only a small number managed to board a steamer, which sailed to Kovno. Very few managed to escape to the USSR. **(See also the BA Thesis of Ruta Puisyte from the University of Vilnius "Holocaust in Jurbarkas " in the next article on page 570.)**

Those Jews who remained in town hid in the bathhouse, but German soldiers discovered them and forced them to return to their homes. Although the Gestapo should have processed Jews from Tilzit, during the first weeks of the occupation the fate of the Jews was in the hands of the local Lithuanian police and its newly appointed head, a teacher in the local high school. The Lithuanians forced Jewish youths to work in various jobs, including cleaning the streets. The Lithuanians also forced Jews to destroy the old and magnificent wooden synagogue (built in 1790) with their own hands, including the "Bimah" and "Eliyahu's Chair" with their splendid ornamental wooden carvings.

During this work, Jews were beaten and mistreated, one example being when a brick was fixed to the town cantor's beard (Alperovitz) and he was thus led through the streets. On Saturday, June 28, 1941, Lithuanian police forced the old Rabbi Hayim-Reuven Rubinshtein as well as Jewish family heads to bring all Torah scrolls and other holy books to the synagogue yard to burn them. The next day policemen made Jews run through the streets in a so-called procession, while a sculpture of Stalin was carried ahead. In front of a curious crowd, Jews were forced to dance and humiliate themselves by declaiming speeches that were dictated to them and similar actions. Several Jewish doctors and learned people were murdered, after having been humiliated and tortured by local Lithuanians.

On the 3rd of July 1941 (7th of Tamuz 5701) German and Lithuanian police detained 322 Jews, whom they led to the Jewish cemetery cruelly beating them on the way, and then shot them one by one near the pits which had previously been dug. One of the victims was the exporter Emil Max, who as a German soldier during World War I, was decorated with an Iron Cross, first degree. He attacked a Gestapo officer, and was shot dead immediately. After the carnage a party for the murderers was arranged in town.

On the 27th of July, 45 elderly Jews were put on carts to be taken to Rasein for a supposedly medical inspection. After a journey of 15 km they were murdered together with the coachmen who transported them and with Jews from neighboring villages. On the first of August, 105 elderly Jewish women were murdered in the same manner. On the 4th of September, 520 women, children and relatives of the 322 men, victims of the carnage of the 3rd of July, were imprisoned for 3 days in the yard of the Jewish school, after which they were transferred to the yard of Motl Levyush which served as a labor camp. At midnight, the 7th of September, these women and their children, who resisted and hit the Lithuanian murderers with their fists and shouted with anger, were led to the Smalininkai grove (seven kilometers from Yurburg), where they were shot with rifles and machine guns, with only a few girls managing to escape. One week later the last 50 Jews, who had been left temporarily in Yurburg for work, were murdered too. Only a few were hidden by peasants.

During the three years of Nazi occupation, several Jews who managed to sneak away from the hands of the rulers and also from local residents who were liable to betray them to the police, roamed around in the surroundings of Yurburg and Staki. The Fainshtein brothers, armed with automatic weapons, met a Soviet pilot whose plane had been shot down, and together they acted as a partisan group.

Later on several tens of Jews from the Kovno ghetto and from other places joined this group and in the spring of 1944 they numbered 35-40 armed fighters. From time to time they attacked German vehicles on the roads and punished Lithuanian collaborators. When the frontline approached their base, they were suddenly surrounded by German gendarmerie and after a short fight all fell in battle. From this group only two wounded women and five men (among them the Fainshtein brothers who were absent from the base during the fight) survived. Among Yurburg's Jews those who survived were those who had managed to escape to Russia, those who arrived in the Kovno ghetto and several others who fought with the partisans.

After the war a monument was erected on the mass graves.

In 1991 **"The Book of Remembrance" of Yurburg Jewish Community"** was published in Hebrew and Yiddish, edited by Zevulun Poran (Petrikansky).

The number of Jewish survivors who returned to live in Yurburg decreased, in 1970 there were nine Jews, in 1977 there were four, in 1998 only five, and in 2001 there were none!

In 1991-92 the government cleaned and restored the old Jewish cemetery.

Sources:

Yad Vashem Archives: M-/Q-1314/133; M-9/15(6); TR-10/40,275 Koniukhovsky Collection 0-71, files 49,50.

Central Zionist Archives-Jerusalem, Z-4/2548; 13/15/131; 55/1788; 55/1701; JIVO, Collection of Lithuanian Communities, New-York, Files 507-509, 1388, 1523.

The Oral History Division of the Institute of Contemporary Jewry, the Hebrew University in Jerusalem, evidence 65/12 of J.Tarshish.

Gotlib, Ohalei Shem, -page 93 (Hebrew).

Kamzon J.D., Yahaduth Lita (Lithuanian Jewry), pages 147-154 (Hebrew), Rabbi Kook Publishing House, Jerusalem 1959.

Levin Sh.- "Lithuanian Jews in the 1831 Uprising"- YIVO Pages.

Poran Zevulun-Sefer haZikaron leKehilath Yurburg-Lita, (Hebrew and Yiddish) Jerusalem 1991.

Dos Vort -daily newspaper in Yiddish of the Z"S party, Kovno-30.10.1934; 11.11.1934; 12.2.1939.

Di Yiddishe Shtime-daily newspaper in Yiddish of the General Zionists-Kovno, 24.8.1919; 3.9.1919; 4.4.1922; 25.4.1923; 19.10.1924; 23.11.1924; 19.6.1931; 28.8.1931; 5.10.1937.

HaMeilitz, St.Petersburg, (Hebrew), 18.8.1886; 3.1.1889; 19.4.1889; 19.2.1899; 2.7.1893; 6.3.1901.

Folksblat - daily newspaper of the Folkists, Kovno (Yiddish), 7.3.1933; 10.4.1935; 16.7.1935; 21.3.1937; 29.3.1937; 5.10.1937; 20.11.1940.

Funken, Kovno (Yiddish), 8.5.1931.

Di Zeit (Time), Shavl (Yiddish)-5.6.1924; 6.5.1924.

Hamashkif - daily newspaper of the Revisionist party, Tel-Aviv (Hebrew) 22.4.1945.

Forverts -New York (Yiddish)-4.4.1946.

The Small Lithuanian Encyclopedia, Vilnius 1966-1971 (Lithuanian).

The Lithuanians Encyclopedia, Boston 1953-1965 (Lithuanian).

Lite, New-York 1951, volume 1 & 2 (Yiddish).

Yahaduth Lita, (Hebrew) Tel-Aviv, volumes 1-4.

Masines Zudynes Lietuvoje 1941-1944 (Mass Murder in Lithuania 1941-1944) vol. 1-2, Vilnius (Lithuanian).

Pinkas haKehilot Lita (Encyclopedia of the Jewish Settlements in Lithuania) (Hebrew). Yad Vashem. Jerusalem 1996, Editor Dov Levin, Assistant editor Yosef Rosin.

The Book of Sorrow, Vilnius 1997 (Yiddish, Hebrew, Lithuanian, English).

Cohen Berl,. Shtet, Shtetlach un Dorfishe Yishuvim in Lite biz 1918 (Towns, small Towns and Rural Settlements in Lithuania till 1918) (Yiddish) New-York 1992.

Gimtasis Krastas - (Country of birth) (Lithuanian) 8.9.1988.

Naujienos ,Chicago-(News) (Lithuanian) 8.9.1949.

Sviesa, Jurbarkas, (Light) (Lithuanian) 12.7.1990; 8.8.1990; 11.8.1990.

Valstieciu Laikrastis-(Farmers Newspaper) (Lithuanian) 26.4.1990.

Appendix 1

A list of Rabbis who served in Yurburg

Aizik Leizerovitz - mentioned in an official document in 1714.

Aryeh-Yehudah-Leib - during the18th century.

Yehushua-Zelig Ashkenazi (about 1785-1831), refused to accept a salary because he had a rich father-in-law.

Mosheh haLevi Levinson, from1861 in Yurburg.

Ya'akov-Yosef ben Dov-Ber (1841-1902), from 1888 a Rabbi in New York where he died.

Yehezkel Livshitz (1862-1932), in Yurburg 1887-1891.

Avraham Dimant (1863-1940), in Yurburg for several tens of years until his death.

Hayim-Reuven Rubinshtein (1888-1941), the last Rabbi of Yurburg, murdered by the Lithuanians.

Most of the above mentioned Rabbis published books on religious matter.

Appendix 2

A partial list of personalities in Yurburg.

Shelomoh Fainberg (1821-1893), philantropist, moved to Kovno in 1857, married Baroness Rosa von Lichtenstein from Vienna, in Koenigsberg from 1866. He received the title of " Councellor of Commerce " from the Czar, and died in Koenigsberg.

Shelomoh Shakhnovitz - author of the book "The Skill of Reading the Torah" (Keidan 1924).

Mendel Shlosberg (1843-??), moved to Lodz, where he participated in the development of the Polish textile industry.

Shelomoh Goldstein (1914-1995), a graduate of the Hebrew high school in Yurburg and a graduate of Rome university in chemical engineering, one of the leaders of "HeHalutz" in Lithuania, was imprisoned in the Kovno ghetto. Lived in Skokie, USA, from 1948, a philanthropist who supported many Jewish and Zionist institutions in America and in Israel, among them the Hebrew University in Jerusalem. For many years a member of the Zionist executive.

Zalman and Tuviyah Samet, born in Yurburg in 1857 and 1858, founders and directors of the big firm "Brothers Samet" in Lodz.

William Zorach (1887-1966), sculptor and painter, also painted many pictures on Yurburg. He died in Bath, Maine, U.S.A

Shelomoh ben Yisrael Bresloi, a learned man and philanthropist, donated 500 Rubels for establishing a "Gemiluth Hesed" in town.

Hirsh Noteles, sent a Hebrew poem to the Czar and received a letter of thanks and a golden ring as a memorial gift.

Appendix 3

List of donors for Settlement of Eretz-Yisrael, published in 1896

Gut Leib	Segal Ya'akov
Garzon Mordehai	Fainberg Gavriel
Homler Avraham-Leib	Pustapedsky A.H.
Helberg Shemuel	Kopelov Avraham-Yitshak
Hershelevitz Avraham	Kaplitz Hertz
Yablonsky David-Shelomoh	Rubinovitz Max
Yozefer Hayim-Nathan	Dr.Tsezar Rabinovitz
Yozelit Hayim	Rochelson Shimon
Leibovitz Aba	Rivkin Dov
Mendelson Leib	
Myakinin Avraham	

The fundraisers were Tsevi Fain and Avraham-Yitshak Kopelov.

Holocaust in Jurbarkas

The Mass Extermination of Jews of Jurbarkas in the Provinces of Lithuania during the German Nazi Occupation

B.A. Thesis of Ruta Puisyte

Tutor: Prof. M. Subas (Shub), Head of the Center of Judaic Studies

University of Vilnius, The History Faculty

The Department of Contemporary History

Vilnius 1997

Translated into English by Joseph Rosin (Haifa, 1998)

Contents

Preface by Professor Mejeris Subas (Meyer Shub)

In 1941-1943 the Lithuanian Jewish Community, which had existed in Lithuania for centuries, was struck by a catastrophe never experienced before in world history: the community was cruelly massacred by the Nazis and their local collaborators. Only the graves, a handful of the living and a never-fading memory remained. Though more than half a century has passed since this horrible catastrophe, historians in Lithuania still have not conducted research into how and when such a regional community was destroyed. From this prospective, Ruta Puisyte's bachelor's thesis on the massacres of the community of Jurbarkas is the first attempt to fill this void. The author was not driven merely by scientific interest. She is a young and talented Lithuanian historian, whose conscience demanded that she reveal one of the bitterest truths in Lithuania's mid-century history.

One outstanding feature of this thesis is that the author details not only the dates and the places of massacres, but she also names the victims, their executioners, and those righteous Lithuanians who saved Jews.

I hope that the English translation of the paper will be useful to those people all around the world who carry out investigations of the Holocaust.

Professor Mejeris Subas, Head of the Center for Judaic Studies
The University of Vilnius

Preface by Professor Dov Levin

As a person who has learned from his own personal experience about the massacre of the Lithuanian Jewry, fortunate to arrive to Eretz-Israel in 1945, and actually take part in the establishment of the State of Israel and for tens of years has been engaged in researching Lithuanian Jewry and its annihilation, I have a particular interest in presenting to the "Litvaks" (Lithuanian Jews and their descendants) and the general public the important work of Miss Ruta Puisyte. Her thesis was completed to fulfill the requirements of her Baccalurate degree under the guidance of my longtime colleague Professor Mejeris Subas (Meyer Shub), Head of The Center of Judaic Studies of the Vilnius University. Miss Puisyte systematically reviewed the history of the Jewish Community of Jurbarkas (Jurburg, Lithuania) and in particular its terrible fate during the Holocaust. She also precisely documented the names of the murderers. Her findings not only reveal her patience and the arduous work needed to collect data from a variety of sources, but the work also displays her objectivity in documenting the horrific details describing the cruelty and murders perpetrated on the Jews. In the social reality of present-day Lithuania she also exhibited a great deal of personal courage, integrity and bravery to reveal, by name, those who were the murderers. Therefore this work has a greater significance than it's scientific merit because it can serve as a model to others to also seek and report the truth intelligently and with integrity. As a consequence of this thesis it is clear that it would not be an exageration to say that such work merits respect and dignity to the Vilnius University which is striving to earn its place among the other research institutions in the western world.

It is my honour and pleasure to thank my good friend Joseph Rosin who volunteered to translate this book from Lithuanian into English so as to enable the English-speaking population all over the world access to its contents. Mr. Rosin was also my assistant in editing the Encyclopedia of the Lithuanian Jewish Communities (Pinkas haKehilloth. Lita, Yad Vashem, Jerusalem 1996) which also served as a primary source to Miss Puisyte in preparing her thesis.

Jerusalem, June 1998-Sivan 5658

Professor Dov Levin, Head of the Oral History of the Institute of Contemporary Jewry, The Hebrew University of Jerusalem

A few comments on the English translation:

1. All the books and articles mentioned in this thesis were written in Lithuanian except The Encyclopedia of the Jewish Communities in Lithuania *(Pinkas haKehiloth Lita)* which was written in Hebrew.

2. All the Jewish names mentioned in this thesis were written without the Lithuanian endings in the English translation and spelled as they were pronounced in Yiddish.

3. I thank my friends Sarah and Mordechai Kopfstein for helping to translate this thesis.

J. Rosin

Text added by Joel Alpert in further editing for clarification is contained in {brackets}.

J. Alpert

Introduction

During the years of the German Nazi occupation of Lithuania several hundred thousand people were murdered, among them about 170,000 to 180,000 Jews, i.e. about 94% of the Jews living in Lithuania before World War II. After three years of war, out of the 200,000 Jews who had lived there before the war, only 8,000 to 9,000 Jews remained alive in Lithuania.

After Lithuania regained its independence, the subject of the Holocaust (*Katastrofa* in Lithuanian) was opened up for investigation. The murder of the Jews in Lithuania during the years of World War II was not only a great numerical loss of the country's citizens, but also an historic problem strongly related to justice being done for a crime actually committed and to the punishment of actual persons. It is a pity that this historic tragedy is essentially only being investigated half a century after it happened.

The mass extermination of the Jews in the chronological margin of the 1941-to-1944 period is part of the now popular research in Lithuania being carried out by historians and non-historians with regard to the 1940-to-1956 period. During this period, people experienced Soviet occupation and reoccupation, the uprising of June 23, 1941, resistance after the war, and exile. When conducting research into all the aspects of this period or of particular problems in it, the theme of the Jewish Holocaust became just one part of the whole process.

The search for the accused in the mass murders is a painful question for the Jews as well as for the Lithuanians. Is the nation guilty (moral responsibility)? Is the government guilty? Or maybe only individual people are guilty? Historic research could help to investigate the many aspects of this problem and answer these questions, also for people from the extreme fringes of society, amongst whom "all Lithuanians were Jew killers", and "all Jews were communists."

This work deals with events in Jurbarkas during the period of the three months (June to September 1941), starting from June 22, 1941 till the middle of September 1941. If we divide the extermination of Lithuania's Jews into three periods - a) June 1941 - December 1941; b) January 1942 - June 1943; c) July 1943 - July 1944 -, then the above three months take up less than a half of the first period and in this short time the town of Jurbarkas lost half of its inhabitants. 2,000 Jurbarkas Jews among the 170,000 murdered are but a drop in the ocean when referring to numbers, but we are dealing with human beings and therefore 2,000 people is a very significant number.

In 1941, the town of Jurbarkas was 10 kilometers (6 miles) distant from the Lithuanian SSR-German border. At 8 o'clock on the morning of June 22, 1941, the German Army marched into the town. The town was situated within the 25 kilometers border strip controlled by the Tilzit operative group. The future of the Jews was determined by German politics, but the fate of individual Jews depended on the friendship or hate of individual Lithuanians. During the first months of the war the Nazis did not as yet have an official plan for solving the Jewish Problem. "The Final Solution" was only drawn up in January 1942, during the Wannsee Conference.

One of the particular characteristics of Jurbarkas was that it was a border town, and the other, that it was situated in the Lithuanian provinces. Here the mass murders of the Jews were performed abruptly and quite "silently, with the same cruelty as in the big cities, and the perpetrators did not expect any massive resistance from the victims or other disturbances.

During the years of Soviet rule the Jews' mass extermination by German fascists and local collaborators was not investigated. Many books were published about the crimes of the Hitlerites and the "bourgeois nationalists." There were many documents[3,4,5] and books dealing with particular regions of Lithuania and particular locations, such as Panevezys[6], Kretinga[7], Dzukija[8] and others.

Some data about Jurbarkas can be found in the collection of documents "Mass Murders in Lithuania." In the second part of this book, where the crimes of the Tilzit operative group are detailed, mention is made that "on July 3, 1941, 322 persons were shot in Jurbarkas." Furthermore, mentioning the fate of the survivors, (the murderers knew that the number of the victims was greater), it said: "In some indefinite place on some indefinite day an indefinite number of people...."[9] This intensifies the motivation and importance, from a Jurbarkas point of view, to search the archives for documents and supplementary collections of memoirs.

In the collection of memoirs of Mrs. S. Binkiene[11], there is a story about the fate of Jurbarkas's Jews, by S. Rozental "Macijauskas." During World War II this man hid a few Jews and among them a native of Jurbarkas, David Levin.

Among the recent literature it is worthwhile mentioning a specially published book[12] about Jurbarkas in which, in separate articles, particular themes are discussed, i.e. schools, the vocations of its inhabitants, healthcare and more. The information in this book was very important when writing the first part of this thesis - i.e. the economic, social and cultural life of the Jews in Jurbarkas between the two world wars.

This thesis also used a particular article from the Encyclopedia of Jewish Communities in Lithuania[13] published in Israel, about the history of Jurbarkas Jews. I am very grateful to the Vilnius resident Mrs. Riva Bogomolnaja for her translation of the Hebrew text into Lithuanian.

This work was supported by documents from two archives: **The Central Lithuanian State Archives (LCVA)** and the **Special Archives (LYA)**. From the central archives file Number 1753 was used, the documents of the municipality of Jurbarkas, paragraph Number 3, in which there were orders from the Siauliai (Shiauliai) Gebietskomissar, head of the Raseiniai region, from the mayor of Jurbarkas and others. Also statements and correspondence on the execution of orders by the town's occupation power, personal, economic and financial questions. Many files were reviewed, but there were only a few documents relating to the subject of this work.

In the special archives many files were found regarding the murderers of the Jews. But the murder of Jews was of minor importance, because the accused mentioned in these files very often took part in other "punishment deserving" activities - he would be a partisan (against the Soviets), or belonged to some "nationalist" organization and the like, which interested the Soviet courts a lot more. In these courts the questions to the accused were designed in such a way as to take into account that the answers had been arranged beforehand, always weighted against the accused. This does not mean that the files in the aforementioned archives are not a credible historic source. After these archives became accessible to researchers, the possibility opened up investigation into the Holocaust in Lithuania by relying not only on memoirs or the press of those days, or archives material of high German and Lithuanian institutions, but also took into account the evidence given after the war by murderers and witnesses in Soviet hearing and court institutions. A critical approach to these sources helps the historian to remain objective.

The second part of this thesis describing the Holocaust of the Jews in Jurbarkas, tries to record the events of this four-month period chronologically. It was impossible to order all the events chronologically by relying only on documents from government archives, and it was essential to obtain additional historical sources.

The bases of this work are the collected and recorded memoirs of Chayim Jofe. Chayim Jofe (1916-1995), a Jurbarkas Jew, who dedicated the last ten years of his life to collecting material about his murdered fellow-citizens. I am very thankful to his widow, Mrs. Brone Jofe, who willingly allowed me to use her husband's archives. I used them for the part they tell about the Holocaust, for parts 1 and 3 of this work, and the Appendices were taken from copies of Chayim Jofe's archives existing in the Lithuanian State Jewish Museum (LVZM).

Some of the events of June-September 1941, mentioned in short articles, were taken not from Chayim Jofe's personal archives, but from those published in the newspapers.

Speaking about the investigations of some Lithuanian authors into the Holocaust after the re-establishment of independence, it is worth mentioning that there were no wider studies and it was difficult to get a many-faceted view of the subject. Apart from this, almost everything which was written about Lithuanian - Jewish relations, was neither scientific nor journalistic, but rather emotional, with many prejudices and stereotypes being involved.

The goal of this B.A. thesis was to use the scientific research methodology to analyze the Holocaust in Lithuania.

The topics of this work include:

1. The economic, social and cultural life of Jurbarkas's Jews before the Holocaust (during the years of independent Lithuania and the Soviet occupation).

2. The description of the mass murder of the Jews in Jurbarkas, in the Nazi occupied Lithuanian provinces, referring to:

- the course of events
- the places of the mass shootings
- the Ghetto in Jurbarkas
- the number of victims,
- persons who took part in the torturing and shooting of the Jews
- Lithuanians - saviors of Jews
- Jewish survivors after World War II

Jurbarkas was not chosen as the object of inquiry on the assumption that there would be source material available. On the contrary, this thesis' theme was chosen before having any knowledge of where to obtain any material. Therefore I am very thankful to the people who helped me collect material and delivered it to me. They were: Mr. Gediminas Grybas[14]; Mrs. Rachele Kastanjan[15]; Mr. Iliya Lampert; Mr. Josef Levinson[16]; Mr. Asher Meirovitz[17]; Mr. Zalman Kaplan.

1. The economic, social and cultural life of Jurbarkas Jews in Lithuania (1918 - June 1941)

Jurbarkas (in Yiddish - Jurburg/Jurburk) is situated in the valley of the river Nemunas (Nieman), on its right bank. It is difficult to state the exact period when the first Jews settled there, but it is known that in 1650 there were seven Jewish houses, i.e. about eight families[18] in Jurbarkas. During the follwing years this number increased significantly.

During the years of the Lithuanian Republic, Jurbarkas was the regional center in the Raseiniai district. According to the first population census of Lithuania in 1923, Jurbarkas then had a population of 4,409 people, among them 2,031 (46%) Lithuanians and 1,887 (43.2%) Jews (880 men, 1,007 women)[19].

There now follows a description of the economic, social and cultural life of Jurbarkas's Jews during the period of the Lithuanian Republic, with emphasis on the end of the fourth decade - the eve of the Holocaust.

Due to the geographic situation of Jurbarkas throughout its history the main occupations of the town's citizens were concentrated in commerce. Most of Jurbarkas's merchants, i.e. 70 to 80 %, were Jews[20], in other words, about 92% of Jurbarkas's Jews were engaged in commerce[21].

In 1931 there were 73 shops in the town, of which 66 belonged to Jews[22].

Type of business	Total	Jewish Ownership
Various shops	3	3
Grain and flax trade	4	4
Butcher shops	13	9
Restaurants and taverns	4	2
Food trade	9	9

Alcohol trade	2	2
Textile products	13	13
Leather products	4	4
Domestic utensils	6	6
Cosmetics	3	3
Bicycles, sewing machines, radio	1	1
Agricultural tools and machinery	5	5
Heating materials (wood, peat)	1	1
Miscellaneous	5	4

The Jewish merchants were different: there were small shops (selling so called 'colonial' merchandise) and they were owners of big shops and warehouses, such as: Yakov Golde who owned a shoe warehouse; Bela Nevjark - cotton knitwear; Max Simonov traded in iron products and agricultural machines; Moshe Krelitz - silver and other metal products; Sarah Israel dealt with office equipment.

It should be mentioned that although it was a small town, at that time commerce was already quite specialized.

According to 1931 data, 19 light industries were actively producing in Jurbarkas, of which Jews owned 18:

Type of Industry	Total	Owned by Jews
Flour mill	1	1
Wood processing (sawmill and furniture production)	2	2
Paper mill	1	1
Food processing	8	7
Dresses and shoe production	3	3
Miscellaneous	4	4

Most of these industries were small, employing one to three workers. But they also had shop outlets, i.e. the owner of a meat products factory also had a meat shop, a bakery owner also had a bread shop, etc.

There were also bigger factories or workshops. The brothers Fainberg owned a flourmill, a power station and a sawmill; Itzik Geselowitz had a lemonade factory (he also owned the cinema "Triumf"); Girsh Margolis, O. Sefler, K. Krom - each had a furniture workshop.[24]

Many of Jurbarkas's Jews were the owners of various means of transportation, such as, in those times were very expensive, buses, trucks, floating barges and steamships on the river Nemunas. For example, Yakov Golde was the owner of four buses and three trucks. In 1940, 14 steamships, 15 motor ships and 39 barges were sailing on Lithuanian rivers, a third of them belonging to Jews from Jurbarkas as follows: Israel Levinberg, L. Aizenshtat, J. Fainberg, Moris Arshtein, J. Lubin, Arel Aremjan and David Karabelnik[25]

There were two Jewish banks in Jurbarkas, one of which was established in 1922 and called the "Volksbank" with about 400 members, whereas the other was a private bank and belonged to Bernshtein[26].

In 1939 Jurbarkas had 116 telephones, 41 belonging to Jews.[27]

In 1940 there were five hotels and lodging houses in Jurbarkas, of which four belonged to Jews. The hotels were owned by Yitzchak Fridman, Roza Berkover and Shmuel Limas and the lodging house belonged to Chashe Finberg. Chaya Polak, Motl Kaplan and Moshe Kaplan each had a restaurant. Mrs. Kabilkovsky[28] was the owner of a teahouse.

The most popular crafts among the many Jewish craftsmen in Jurbarkas were shoemakers, tailors, blacksmiths and stove builders. There were also unskilled and part-time workers, such as porters, coachmen, raftsmen etc. being representatives of the less prestigious professions[29].

There were also workers in the liberal professions, in health and in education. N. G. Naividel was a lawyer.

In 1925 a government lung hospital was established in Jurbarkas, but there were also people engaged in private medicine. In a journal called "Medicine" (1920, Number 5) two practicing doctors are mentioned in Jurbarkas: Elias Levin with fully certified papers because he was a graduate of Dorpat University and passed the examinations in Russia, and Leib Gershtein, who did not pass those examinations.

In this "Medicine" journal (1920, Number 7) there is a list of dentists, mentioning two Jurbarkas citizens, Mordechai Simonov and Moshe Rikler.

Later on the Health Department started to publish, in the "Medicine" journal's supplement, lists of the practicing doctors, veterinarians, pharmacists and health institutions in Lithuania. In its list of 1922 there were three doctors who had temporary permission to practice medicine, being: Leib Gershtein, born 1891, completed medicine in 1923 in Kaunas; Tuviah Goldberg, born 1887, graduated in 1914 in Petrograd; Elias Levin, born 1890, graduated in 1916. Of them only L. Gershtein, who received his rights to practice in Kaunas in 1923, was mentioned in the list of 1928 to 1929[30].

Sources dating back to 1888 already mention the Jewish pharmacist Markus Bregovsky. His pharmacy continued to exist, managed by his heirs, till 1940, when it was nationalized. In 1923, two pharmacies were in business in Jurbarkas, belonging to Fania Bregovsky and Shmerl Fin. Josl Shabashevitz worked as assistant pharmacist, having concluded his studies in 1914 in Dorpat. Elias Rabinovitz - graduated in 1888 in Moskow - was a qualified pharmacist. Later Goldberg, M. Bregovsky, J. Fin, G. Zundelovitz were added to the list. In the list of 1923, a new doctor appeared, named Josef Karlinsky, born 1880, having received his rights to practice in Kaunas in 1923. In the list of 1936 another two new doctors are shown: Josef-Ber Girshovitz, born 1901, graduated in 1933 and Basia Naividel-Maizler, graduated in 1928 in Kaunas. In 1936 four dentists practiced in Jurbarkas, two of them Jews: Miriam

Kopelov-Goldengeim, born 1902, graduated in 1926 in Kaunas and the already mentioned M. Simonov. During the fourth decade the number of pharmacies in Jurbarkas stabilized. There were two, one belonging to Bregovsky (director Miss Libe Katz, born 1906, graduated 1933 in Kaunas), and the other, the so-called " Central Pharmacy" (Owners Sh. Fin and L. Flier). In the list of 1938 we found the assistant pharmacist Elena Flier-Surasky, born 1895, who graduated in 1918 in Petrograd. Doctor Boris Reichman[31], not mentioned so far, worked in Jurbarkas's hospital in 1940.

The Jewish children of Jurbarkas were able to study in three schools[32]

On September 1, 1921 the Jurbarkas Jewish High School was inaugurated, with Hebrew as the language of instruction. The initiator of the project for the establishment of this school and its organizer was J. Fainberg. At the end of 1921 the school had enrolled 104 pupils in four classes and during this year seven teachers worked there: the director A. Efros, Itzik Tzintovsky, D. Verblovsky, Miss E. Rabinovitz. In 1922 a fifth class was established and by the end of that year the school consisted of 140 pupils and nine teachers. According to 1924 data, 140 pupils studied in the school at that time. The tuition fee was then 30 to 60 lit ($1=10 lit) per month, but about 20% of the pupils were exempted from payment of tuition.

Being a private school, it did not receive any financial support from the Ministry of Education. By 1925 this school grew to include seven classes, 139 pupils and nine teachers. In 1926 there were eight classes and 144 pupils. On April 24, 1934, the director of the high school D. Kagansky, not being able to solve the financial problems of the school, announced that as from the first of July the Jewish High School in Jurbarkas would be closed down. In 1934 there were only 46 pupils studying in this high school, whose scholastic achievements were quite low.[33]

Two of the town's elementary schools were Jewish. One of them was school Number 3, called "Talmud-Torah", in which the teaching language was Hebrew. In 1944 the withdrawing Germans set fire to it. During the years 1924-1939 five teachers worked in this school: the director D. Gershon, Tchechanovsky, Chayim Sigel, Chayim V. Jozefer, Miss M. Joselzon.

Another Jewish elementary school was school Number 5, called the "Volksschule." In this school, situated in the poor Jewish neighborhood, the teaching language was Yiddish and there was no tuition fee. It had been established in 1921 and was kept going with the help of the Jewish Community. Its first director was Miss Dora Fainberg, and during the years 1931 to 1940 the director was Basia Gut. Forty to fifty pupils attended this school in four classes.

Jurbarkas Jews also participated in the town's administration. The town council of 1918 had 23 members, consisting of 16 Lithuanians, three Jews, three Germans and one Russian. On April 30, 1919 the town's social care department was established and on its board there also served a Jew, I.Rabinovitz. In 1931 three Lithuanians, one German, one Russian and five Jews (Levitan, Simonov,

Grinberg, Zundelovitz, and Naividel) were elected to the town council. In the elections of 1934, four Jews won election to the town council, and one Jew, Sh. Fainberg, became the alternate mayor[35].

Honorable and intelligent people were elected as leaders of the Jewish community[36], so that at different times there were such leading figures as Hirsh Fin, Pinchas Shachnovitz, Israel Levinberg, Shmaya Fainberg, Alter Simonov, Meir-Zuse Levitan, Reuven Olshvanger, Josef Karlinsky. The members of the social committee in 1923-1924 consisted of five laborers, five merchants (two of them wholesalers), and two delegates of the intelligentsia and three of the synagogues.

The Rabbis of Jurbarkas: Jakov Josef Charif (emigrated to USA and became a Rabbi in New York); Jechezkel Lifshitz (later Rabbi in Kalish); Avraham Dimand (1863-1940, famous as a Gaon) and the last Rabbi Chayim Reuven Rubinstein (1888-1941, famous as a writer, who published his own book)[37].

At the end of the eighteenth century the Jurbarkas's Jews had been able to build a big wooden synagogue, an interesting and valuable architectural structure, its interior being a carved work of art, the most beautiful wooden synagogue in Lithuania. During the nineteenth century and not far away, the Jews also erected a synagogue built of brick. Both were the center of the spiritual and public life of Jurbarkas's Jews.

Jurbarkas Jews had an extensive, varied cultural and public life, and following herewith is a description of some of the Jewish organizations.

The Jewish national- democratic educational association, which directed the athletic club "JAK", a library, a reading room, art circles. "Hapoel" (The Worker) - a leftist sports organization.

The Zionist organizations: Hashomer Hatsair" (Young Watchman) connected to the "Scouts." Their uniform was green blouses and blue neckties. "Hechalutz" (The Pioneer) prepared Jewish youth for agricultural work in Palestine. On the extreme right there was "Betar" (named after Joseph Trumpeldor) with its militant wing "Beit Hahashmal. There was also "Maccabi", the Zionist youth sports organization.

The Jewish volunteers who took part in Lithuania's battle for independence had their own association[38].

Quite a few charity associations were active in Jurbarkas: "Hachnasat Orchim" (Shelter for Passersby) and cared for beggars; "Hachnasat Kala" collected money for poor brides' doweries; "Bikur Cholim cared for the sick; "Somech Noflim" aided the impoverished; "Gmilath Chesed" provided loans to poor people on easy terms; "Tzdaka Tatzil Mimaveth" (Charity Saves from Death) collected money for funerals.

A Jewish drama group also existed in Jurbarkas, whose members were: J.Arshtein, I. E. Pelbaum (or Perlbaum), D. Tchertok, M. Fidler, D. B. Portnoy, I. Purvas, Miss B. Jozefer, B. Shmulovitz, G. Kravetzky, H. Sh. Michelson, M. Beder, H. Zarkin, M. Shmulovitz, Katriel Levin and others (mostly youths)[39].

The Jewish community of Jurbarkas, having a valuable cultural and a wealthy economic life had to face two foreign occupations of the Lithuanian Republic, one following the other.

On July 21, 1940, Soviet rule was proclaimed in Lithuania. This thesis does not deal with the Jews' reaction to this situation in detail, but it is interesting to note how many communists and commsomols (members of communists youth organization) were among Jurbarkas's Jews. In Chayim Jofe's list of Jurbarkas's Jews who were killed, there were four[40]: Miss Sheine Geselkovitz, Miss Mika Lubin, Leib Polak (these three were comsomols), Boris Reichman (a communist)[41].

During this year of Soviet rule, the organizations were closed down, private and public property was nationalized, and this disaster included both Jews and Lithuanians. The banishment into exile of June 14 and 15, 1941 badly effected several Jurbarkas Jewish families. In the list of those "deported to Soviet Russia"[42], drawn up during the years of the German occupation, these Jews can be found:

Efraim Geselovitz, son of Avraham, born 1878,

Chayim Polovin, son of David, born 1896,

The family of Moshe Polovin, son of David, born 1896; his wife Tzile Polovin-Golberg, daughter of Shlomo, born 1917; his daughter Tzile (?) Polovin, born 1939,

Asher Meirovitz, son of Levi, born 1909,

The family of Yakov Leshzh, son of Yankel (?), born 1895; his wife Lika Leshzh-Finkelshtein, daughter of Motel, born1904; her mother Dveire-Chane

Finkelshtein-Maltovsky, daughter of Yudel, born 1861,

The family of David Lapinsky, son of Yankel, born 1874; his son Berl Lapinsky, born 1904; daughters Feige, born 1900 and Yese, born 1908;

Referring to additional sources investigating their banishment[43] [44], a few more of Jurbarkas's Jews should be added to this list:

The family of E. Geselovitz: his wife Tzipa, daughter of Avraham, born 1890; his daughter Bete, born 1915,

The daughter of J. Leshzh, Hanna, born 1927,

The children of M. Polovin: son Faivel, born 1937; his daughter Gita, born 1935,

Rachel Shugam, daughter of Leon, born 1904 with her children Yankel, born 1920; Kushel, born 1924; Sheitele born 1927; Lina, born 1940. Although he was the head of this family, Mr. Shugam was not mentioned in these sources, he was also oppressed.

Zalman Kaplan, a Jurbarkas Jew living in Vilnius, pointed out the exiled Grinberg family members: Motel Grinberg, son of Zalman, born 1864; his second wife Ema, his daughter in law Zhene and his son Robert, born 1928[45].

Speaking about all Jurbarkas's citizens, we may suppose that in the wagons taking them to exile on June 14, 1941 there were no less then 60 people[46] and among them 29 Jews.

In this part of this thesis many Jewish names and family names have been mentioned, but almost none of their special vocations, such as merchants, teachers, coachmen etc. This is important, because {*note added in editing by Joel Alpert:* it was due to that fact that} all of them or their offspring were shot during those few months in 1941.

Every name and family name belonged to an individual human being. It is a fact that in history a person often becomes a mere number. For this reason it is important to know who the Jews were who lived in Jurbarkas on the eve of the German occupation.

The Encyclopedia of Lithuania indicates that in 1940 the town's population numbered 5,400 inhabitants, of them 42%, about 2,300, Jews[47]. The data of the Central Lithuanian State Archive (LCVA) show different numbers: ."..according to the registration of the citizens on December 26, 1940, there were within the boundaries of Jurbarkas 4,439 people, of them 1319 Jews, i.e. 29.7%[48]." C. Jofe refers to the number of 2,500 Jews. From the Encyclopedia of Jewish Communities in Lithuania published in Israel one learns that in 1941 2,000 Jews (600 Families)[49] lived in Jurbarkas.

2. The Mass Extermination of the Jews in Jurbarkas (June 1941 - September 1941)

2.1 Events in June 1941

In 1941 Jurbarkas was about 10 kilometers distance from the German border. On June 22, 1941 the war between Germany and the Soviet Union began and on that same day the German army entered the town at 8 o'clock in the morning. Jurbarkas's Jews quickly felt the changes of the new order.

After the German occupation of Lithuania, local government authorities were established in the provinces. All the former functionaries from the time of the Lithuanian Republic returned to their previous jobs, this being done in accordance with orders of the Temporary Government of Lithuania, but local initiative was important in establishing institutions of self-government, committees, police. These institutions, established *de facto*, were later legalized *de jure*, mostly without any changes[50].

Jurgis Gepneris, an elderly Jurbarkas citizen acquainted with every resident of the town and fluent in Lithuanian, Russian, German, Polish and Yiddish, again became Mayor of Jurbarkas. On the order of Tchaponsas, the commander of the town, Mykolas Levickas was appointed head of Police on June 24, 1941 and thereafter. He organized a group of policemen, composed mainly of former policemen and soldiers; an auxiliary police company was also established in sufficient numbers for defense purposes, from which members from the civilian security units were recruited [51]. During the years 1941 to 1943

Romualdas Levickas served in the Jurbarkas Gestapo and wore an SS uniform.

Jurbarkas was inside the 25-kilometer zone operated by the Gestapo of Tilzit. Among the Germans arriving from Tilzit as SD agents were the officials in charge Grigalavicius, Voldemaras Kriauza, Richardas Sperbergas, Oskaras Sefleris and Karstenis[52]. The Germans played the managerial role, but the responsibility of the local executors for the fate of the Jews is indisputable.

The first Jewish victims in Jurbarkas apparently were the Es brothers. In a letter written by J. Gepneris on January 6, 1941 to the principal of the Raseiniai District it was said that "at this time there was no registration of those killed, but according to unofficial reports two Jews (the Es brothers) were killed during the shooting in the town"[53]. I wrote "apparently", because in another document J. Gepneris wrote to the Commissioner of the department about the victims in Raseiniai, that in Jurbarkas " no people became invalids or were killed by German weapons"[54]. On the first days of the occupation the Germans conducted themselves in a "calm" manner, in order to convince the Jews to obey the orders of the government and not to frighten them. One day a German took Chatzkel Jofe[55], Leib Meigel and Leib Karabelnik to a nearby abandoned beer factory, ordered them to dig a hole, to undress and kneel by the side of the hole. Stepping back about ten steps, he used an automatic weapon to shoot over their heads. After that he approached them laughing, offered them cigarettes and released them, saying, that Germans do not shoot people. On their return they told their families and neighbors everything. This had a soothing effect, but nevertheless the Jews instinctively felt great anxiety and fear[56]. These events happened during the very first days, but soon the murder of the Jews started, although not yet the mass murders. Mykolas Levickas, during investigation, admitted "the first shooting of Jews took place on the fourth day of the German occupation. The perpetrators were Germans SS members, the place - the Jewish cemetery. How many were shot - I don't know"[57]. Witness J. Keturauskas testified to these facts: "One night at the end of June 1941, policemen V. Ausiukaitis and V. Muleikas went to carry out a special task, from which they returned with many valuables." Later, in the summer of 1941, J. Keturauskas had an opportunity to speak with V. Muleikas. He told him that during that night, together with V. Ausiukaitis, they took part in the shooting of Jews and Soviet activists, and for this they got 3,000 Mark[58]. Witness P. Mikutaitis related: "I saw (policeman) Kairaitis rushing up the street to a Jew whom I knew, whose first name was Yoshke, I have forgotten his second name, arrested him and took him to the Ghetto. Yoshke was about 60 years old, did not work anywhere and lived with relatives. He was kept in the Ghetto for three days and then shot in the Jewish cemetery"[59].

Those events had occurred by the end of June. J. Bogdanskis also reported that the chief of police ordered him and P. Greiciunas to arrest the Jewish doctor B. Raichman and about a week later, on July 3rd, the doctor was shot to death[60].

2.2 Events in July 1941

On July 3, 1941, a Thursday afternoon, in the office of J. Gepneris the Mayor of the town, the first Jewish mass extermination was decided upon, to be carried out in the Jewish cemetery[61]. A group of 40 Gestapo men[62] arrived in the town, and together with the local policemen began to round up Jewish men, pulling them out of their houses or their places of work. N. Bregovsky the pharmacist was arrested in his pharmacy in similar manner by policemen K. Almonaitis, P. Kairaitis and M. Urbonas, who also performed "a personal search" on him. N. Bregovsky was led through the town[63]wearing his white gown. (By the way, the policemen exploited these situations - when arresting a Jew they would steal some of his valuables. For example, A. Dravenikas, who worked in the Jurbarkas police as an interpreter, was arrested by the Germans and imprisoned for two months in Siauliai prison because of "stealing a lot of Jewish property, with which he afterwards speculated" [64]). The policemen gathered up groups of about 30 Jews and led them to the police station. Policeman P. Krescinas, the leader of one of these groups which included the Most family, snatched a little child from Most's hands and banged him down onto the road, while at the same time Most himself was pushed forward. Jewish women picked up the child, but they were also shot later. The above mentioned policeman arrested many Jews: Karabelnik, Michelson, the brothers Most and others[65]. A large empty shed was filled with people, who had been evicted from their homes to the market place. By one o'clock about 300 Jews were gathered there as well as several tens of Soviet activists[66]. Lacking the required number, 60 more Jews and three women with children, who did not want to be separated from their husbands (the fathers of their children), were brought along. Upon the command: "One step to the left - we shoot! One step to the right - we shoot! One word - we shoot! March!" the column moved in the direction of the cemetery. During the first "actions" a column of about 350 was assembled, three in line, who were then driven to their death. At the end of these columns there would be a few motor cars. The first car held the machine guns, Germans sat in the others, and a car with shovels[67] brought up the rear. On that day policemen K. Almonaitis and A. Dravenikas found Most and his son hiding in the kitchen garden. They were torn away from their family and pushed into the death column[68]. The town's doctor J. Karlinsky was shot as an enemy of the (German) Reich. A Lithuanian doctor, A. Antanaitis, tried to save him, asking the German in charge of the execution to free the doctor from the column since he was needed as a specialist, but the SS man struck A. Antanaitis several times with his stick and threatened to push him too into the column of the condemned. Doctor J. Karlinsky even turned to the chief of the Auxiliary Police Mykolas Levickas whom he had treated and cured. But Mykolas Levickas made a helpless gesture with his hands and, turning away, shouted "Forward!"[69]. Those Jews who had been driven to the cemetery earlier, had already dug a long trench, and were to dig three more later on. The people arriving now (who were not made to dig, because there were not enough shovels for all) were ordered to break branches from the trees in order to camouflage this place from the road and the town. After finishing this task, the condemned were ordered to beat one another "as much as possible, and whoever refused to do so, would be whipped to death." Nobody moved; nobody raised a hand. Then Jankel Rizman was ordered to climb onto a nearby pear tree and chirp like a lark. He climbed to the top of the tree, shots rang out and Yankel's body fell through the branches[70]. Emil Max, who had served in the German Army during the First World War and had been decorated with the" Iron Cross", was among the Jews. Standing at the side of the trench, he took hold of a German policeman and tried to throw him into the trench, but a shot "silenced" Max [71]. The story of witness Narjauskaite[72] confirmed of Chayim Jofe's reports: " At the cemetery the condemned were ordered to break branches from the trees, to dig trenches and to beat each other. The actual shooting was carried out by Germans from the "Dead Head" battalion, the Lithuanians guarded the site. The shooting took place at 4 o'clock in the afternoon, before which the condemned were tortured, and the moaning and crying was even heard in Jurbarkas"[73]. Several tens of Lithuanians were among those murdered there - communists, comsomols, trade union activists and the Jurbarkas sculptor Vincas Grybas. Some people found themselves alive in the trench, managed to scramble out and escape, among them Antanas Leonavicius[74], Povilas Striaukas[75] and Abel Vales[76]. Also Leizer Michailovsky survived this "action", but by different means. When in the death column march, he walked last in line and managed to escape, at the beginning to "some ditch where he hid", later Lithuanian peasants harbored him[77].

After the "action" of the men on July 3, 1941, the Jurbarkas occupation authority ordered all elderly Jews to register every morning and evening with the police department. On July 21, 1941, 45 aged men were detained during registration. They were put on carts and each was given a shovel. The official version was that they were going to Raseiniai for a health check up, after which those not fit for physical work would be brought back, whereas the others would be left in Kalnujai to repair a gravel road. "The carts started to move. Rotuliai, Antkaniskiai, Molyne, the small towns of Skirsnemune (already "cleansed" of the few local Jews), Zvyriai, Siline ...passed out of sight. On arrival in Kalnujai, the policemen ordered the Jews to write letters to their families. Leading them farther away from the road and the individual farms, they were ordered to dig a "gravel pit." The men dug slowly, knowing what awaited them, and for that the policemen beat and kicked them. The carrier David Portnoy (whose 12 year old daughter was raped) came to blows with a Lithuanian, called on the other Jews to take the shovels and attack"[78]. But the end was predetermined and final - all 45 Jews were shot.

From a document dated July 23, 1941 written by the town's mayor J. Gepneris to the Raseiniai district office in connection with the population survey, we learn how many Jews still remained in alive Jurbarkas at this date:" They numbered 1,055 Jews, including 25 children of up to two years old, 39 children aged two to four and 46 children from four to six years old"[79].

On of July 25, 1941 the occupation authorities ordered the Jews to tear down the wooden synagogue and with trembling hands they obeyed the order. A group of spectators {Lithuanian Non-Jews} quickly gathered near the synagogue; some of them shrugged their shoulders, being afraid to voice their protest or to show it by the look on their faces. Others looked intently at how the Gothic style roof, the wooden walls, the interior carved decorations were being torn down, and some more active spectators hurried to take parts of those decorations home. After the synagogue had been destroyed, the Jews were ordered to dance and sing. Soon thereafter, the small building situated near the wooden synagogue that had been used as a poultry slaughterhouse was also destroyed. While tearing this building down and cleaning the plates full of blood (which the Germans, apparently, used for some other purposes later on), the Jews dirtied themselves with the blood of the poultry and feathers stuck to their garments. After this work the Jews were ordered to march in formation to the Nemunas River in order to clean up. Arriving by the river, a new order was given: to wade waist deep into the water and then to wash. People who tried to resist were kicked, beaten and pushed into the water by force. The Lithuanians did the beating, while the Germans took photographs. The Jews were cruelly tortured, such as being scalped, and their bodies combed with a sharp iron rake[80].

On the following day, July 26, 1941, this vicious mockery of human suffering continued, and this time the victim chosen was the elderly Jurbarkas Cantor Alperovitz. He was a tall, corpulent, gray-headed man, who had graduated from a conservatory in Germany and composed music. A Lithuanian policeman pulled him out of his house on Butchers Street, tied a brick to his beard and led him through the streets, while the Germans took photographs[81]. Later Cantor Alperovitz was cruelly murdered together with others who remained alive from previous "actions."

On July 27, 1941, 18 Jurbarkas citizens were shot, but it is not clear how many of them were Jews. Policeman P. Bakus confessed that he shot Zilber[82] himself.

On the morning of July 28, 1941, (a Shabbath), an order was given to weed some grass. On the same day at 4 p.m., all Jewish books had to be delivered to the site of the ruined synagogue. Jurbarkas Rabbi Chayim Rubinstein brought his books and writings on a handcart. At 5 o'clock the Torah scrolls were ordered to be brought from the brick synagogue (now a three-story dwelling) and the other smaller synagogues (there were five of them) and put on top of the books already piled up. Petrol was poured over the heap and then ignited. For the religious Jews this was a catastrophe.

On July 29, 1941, another order was proclaimed, "all Jurbarkas Jews were to gather beside the town's library," and warned that "anyone who did not appear would be found in any case (with the help of Lithuanian collaborators, of course) and shot." The Jews gathered and were drawn up three in line. Three elderly men were given the bust of Stalin taken from the library, pictures of the Soviet leaders were put into the hands of the women, and then they were ordered to march through the streets of Jurbarkas. The procession was led by Mykolas Levickas, who was assisted by policemen P. Budvinskas, J. Kilikevicius and others. The procession turned in the direction of Nemunas, where a group of spectators had already gathered, and the spectacle began. The Jews put Stalin's bust on a previously arranged table, while all the others stood around. A policemen ordered Fridman (formerly a well known artist) to read a text abusing and slandering the Jewish nation, after which a bonfire was lit into which the Jews threw all the pictures they had brought as well as Stalin's bust. Again they were ordered to sing and dance, and again the Germans photographed[83] the spectical At the end of July the chief of police P. Mockevicius summoned policemen V. Almonaitis, P. Kairaitis and J. Marcinkus, ordering them to shoot three elderly (50 to 70 years old) Jewish men from the Ghetto. Each of the Jews were given a shovel and then driven in the direction of Smalininkai. At the seventh kilometer along the road leading from Jurbarkas to Smalininkai, the group turned to the right and walked about one kilometer into the heart of the forest, where the policemen forced the men to dig a hole for themselves, about 1.5 m deep. The condemned men were made to stand at the edge of the hole and then the policemen shot at them from a distance of 50 m. Every policemen shot one bullet at his victim. The shovels they left in the forest. They did not bother to take the clothes of these elderly men, as they were dressed[84] rather poorly.

The protocol of J. Grybas' investigation was similar. Not only in this, but also in other investigation protocols it could be clearly evident, that the investigator was more interested in the fate of Soviet activists than in the Jews (inspite of the fact that they were also Soviet citizens). J. Grybas hid from the occupation authorities in a forest not far from Jurbarkas, and four times he witnessed the policemen drive Jews to be shot in large groups of about 100 people. After the words: " I secretly crawled near those places and saw how Jews were shot", the investigator stopped J. Grybas and changed the subject, asking about events after the war, not going into the details of who had shot, or when and where the shooting occurred[85].

2.3 Events in August 1941

August, actually Tuesday, August 1, 1941, started with an "action" of elderly women, children and the newborn, the younger and healthy women still being kept back for work. The arrested women were driven into the yard of the elementary school "Talmud-Torah" and in the evening they were ordered to stand in line two-by-two. It was difficult to obey the German order because children got in the way everywhere, and pushing started, with beating and shouting. The pits had been readied beforehand and the shooting took place at night (at the seventh kilometer on the road between Jurbarkas and Smalininkai). There was great panic, the laughing and crying of women who had gone crazy was heard. Not all the women were killed, as some fell into the pit alive or were only wounded. Policemen split the heads of the small children on trees in order to save bullets.

The events of August became known from the file of policeman P. Kresciunas: "At 2 o'clock at night two carts arrived near the Ghetto, and we dragged about 20 Jews into the carts. We drove them six to seven kilometers in the direction of Smalininkai near the village of Kalnenai, having told them that they were going to work in Germany. Then some of us drove the Jews into the forest, whereas the others stayed on the road to guard. After 10 minutes shots were heard. V.Ausiukaitis arrived and ordered us four men to go into the forest. Four to five Jews were still alive and we were ordered to shoot them. If we did not participate in the shooting, he would tell the others about it. I (Kresciunas), P. Greceiunas, B. Angeleika and S. Sibaitis did the shooting. Whether I killed my Jew I don't know, as it was dark. We, the four of us, returned to Jurbarkas on one cart and the others remained in the forest. After a few days V. Ausiukaitis called me, ordering me to proceed to the police station, where V. Ausiukaitis, S. Gylys, P. Bakus, M. and R. Levickai, P. Greiciunas, S. Sibaitis, B. Angeleika, Narvydas, K. Kilikevicius, Rimkus and three Germans were already present. Everyone got a rifle, and we were told to accompany the remaining twelve Jews. Again we went into the same forest and again we four watched on the road. After 10 to 15 minutes shots were heard..."[86]

In a document from August 21, 1941, in which the chief of the Raseiniai district was informed of the number of Jewish residents within the boundaries of Jurbarkas, these data were given: " Number of Jews - 684; working on the road - 64"[87] . The list of people in the liberal professions dated August 7, 1941, included these Jews: Mrs. Miryam Kopelov (dentist), Miss Gita Zaveliansky (midwife)[88] . The list of specialist workers from August 28, 1941 included Yerachmiel Shmulovitz (tailor) and Shepsel Maister (tailor)[89].

2.4. Events in September 1941

The date of the fourth "action" was September 8, 1941. This time younger working women and hidden children who had been betrayed by local people were shot. Again the women were driven into the yard of the "Talmud-Torah", the women's Ghetto. On the afternoon of September 8, 1941, the building was surrounded by Lithuanian and German policemen. The waiting women were to be driven to "work", but in fact their journey ended at the seventh kilometer, near Kalnenai. Their torment was the same: "The women were ordered to beat one other, to kick and bite, to tear their hair. Questions of "why?"or "because of what?" were answered by automatic shooting or beating"[90].

In Chayim Jofe's material this "action" was mentioned as the last one, but documents of the Central Archives showed that "on September 12, 1941 there were still 272 Jews in Jurbarkas, 73 of them working"[91].

In a list of specialist workers living in Jurbarkas on September 30, 1941 no Jew is mentioned.[92] In a letter from the mayor of the town to the Lithuanian

Statistics Office in Kaunas dated October 6, 1941, he declared: "On the first October of this year there were no more Jews within the borders of the town of Jurbarkas, and such is the situation today"[93].

In the encyclopedia[94] published in Israel, the sequence of events were as follows:

In the "action" of July 3, 1941, 322 people were shot in the Jewish cemetery.

On July 27, 1941, at the fifteenth kilometer along the Jurbarkas-Raseiniai road, 45 Jewish men were shot. Together with them, Jews from neighboring small towns were murdered.

On August 1, 1941, 105 women were shot.

On September 4, 1941, 520 Jews - wives, children and other relatives of the 322 men killed on July 3, 1941 - were arrested and shot.

On the night of September 7, 1941 women and children were shot. The location was a small forest near the seventh kilometer on the Jurbarkas-Smalininkai road.

A week later, about September 14, 1941, the last 50 Jews were shot.

2.5. The Jewish Ghetto in Jurbarkas

On August 27, 1941 the mayor of Jurbarkas, J. Gepneris received an order confirming the orders issued by the mayors and district heads, according to which the Jews had to be transferred into camps and led to work everyday[95]. The same order also stated that this had to be carried out by August 30, 1941. By this date a written report of events had to be sent to the State Commissar, also stating the number of Jews involved[96]. During the same month, a meeting of all mayors and heads of districts in Siauliai took place, where the Jewish problem was discussed. Information was read out by district commissar Gebeke himself. A Ghetto was to be established in every town, where the Jews would be watched until they would be shot[97].

The Jurbarkas Ghetto (we can name it so only conditionally) existed long before these orders were published. Mykolas Levickas affirms in his testimony that "after the first shootings in June, mass arrests were carried out by a group of the police and the auxiliary police. The arrested Jewish men were transferred into the Ghetto (...) The mass murders started in July. I think that there were two Ghettoes, both in Dariaus and Gireno St., being guarded by police and auxiliary police"[98]. Some more information about the Ghetto can be gathered from P. Kairaitis' file: " Policemen J. Marcinkus and J. Jokubaitis guarded the Ghetto. We would stay on duty for eight hours, after which we would be relieved by the other policemen J. Jakaitis, P. Budvinskas and K. Almonaitis (...) The Jews with their children and the elderly were placed in the Ghetto, which was a building surrounded by barbed wire (...). There the Jews lived under prison conditions. Nutrition was bad, consisting of cabbage soup and a little bread. They were driven to work under guard and had to clean rubbish from the houses and the streets and do other most disgusting and difficult work, with food being scarce. M. Urbonas, the deputy chief of police, distinguished himself by beating them (...). Those involved in the shooting of Jews were M. Urbonas, K. Almonaitis, P. Budvinskas, J. Jakaitis and J. Marcinkus. After the shooting was over, they would take the more valuable items, such as dresses and footwear, for themselves, and on returning to Jurbarkas, also would take appropriate domestic utensils of murdered Jews"[99].

It is worth noting, that the Jurbarkas Ghetto was not a specially fenced off area in the town where Jews were to be settled, in order to be taken a few at a time to be shot. As I mentioned before, the mass murder of Jurbarkas Jews started before the so-called Ghetto was established. Finally, Gestapo agent Grigalavicius arrived and ruled that a Ghetto was not needed, but that it was important to expedite the extermination of all the town's Jews[100]. However, the arrested were kept in some special buildings, called Ghettoes, since it was more convenient to supervise these people there, to organize their work and to drive them from there to be shot.

3. The Fate of the Jewish Survivors of Jurbarkas in Lithuania after the Events of June-September 1941

There were several ways for Jews to survive, such as to hide in a village with Lithuanian acquaintances, to escape to the USSR[101], to join the underground or to become a Soviet partisan. A few survived, because they had not been killed along with all Jurbarkas Jews, or arrived in the Kaunas Ghetto and later in the concentration camps in Estonia and Poland, where they stayed till the end of the war[102].

Why did so few of Jurbarkas Jews survive? They were living near the German-USSR border and should have realised what was in store for them, what the Second World War would mean for the Jewish people, but it caught them by surprise. As I mentioned before, the German Army was already in Jurbarkas at 8 o'clock in the morning of June 22, 1941. It was then too late to escape. True, a few left Jurbarkas in time, some to Kaunas early in the morning with the last steamship, others, young people with bicycles to Raseiniai, from there through Siauliai to Riga and on into the heart of Russia, but very few survived. The sister of Chayim Jofe, Perl Jofe-Skirstemunsky with her little son Ice-Leibele, who had just undergone a heart operation, returned to Jurbarkas on a barge on June 22, 1941, where her husband, her two other children, her mother and her brother's family awaited her and ...their death.

Could the Jews have resisted? There were no organizations of any military character in Jurbarkas, which could have provided arms and lead a fight. There were, of course, healthy strong men, and also men, who had served in the Lithuanian army and were familiar with weapons. But there were also sick old men and women, children and babies. People were scattered, the situation seemed to be hopeless for most. In their minds the thought was: "Maybe if we do nothing - nothing will be done to us" or "Whatever will happen to all, will happen to us." The Jews relied upon God's providence, and prayers to God were heard even at the mass murder trenches before the shooting and during the vicious mockeries[103].

Jews saved by Lithuanians:

Leizer Michailovsky was hidden and saved by Juozas Totoraitis and his wife Antanina Totoraitiene-Galinaityte from Geisiu village, in the small district of Jurbarkas[104].

Leib Meigel and his wife Chaite were hidden and saved by Pranas and Veronika Leksaiciai from Auolyno village, the small district of Jurbarkas.

Chana Sviler-Segal was hidden and saved by Vincas Stankevicius.

Chayim Leib Tatz and Dvora Tatz-Peisachov were hidden and saved by Lithuanian peasants (their names could not be found).

Rachile Jamin was hidden and saved by Jonas Sadauskas from Veliuonos[105].

Gita Abramson-Bereznitzky was in the Kaunas Ghetto from August 1941, and a member of the anti-fascist partisan organization from 1942 till August 1944. She was hidden by Marijona Leseiskiene in Vilijampole.

David Levin saved his life by hiding in the house of Polikardas Macijauskas where a special shelter with an exit to the field was built[106].

The Lithuanians Marijona Ambutaitiene and Juozas Domkus[107] gave asylum to Jews.

Hiding Jews was very dangerous both for Jews and for Lithuanians. The head of the Raseiniai district declared in an order: " Persons who are found disobeying the existing strict orders against the Jews, such as hiding them, maintaining them or helping them by any means whatever, are committing a serious crime. I order all residents of the Raseiniai district in whose neighborhood Jews are hiding, no matter what sex or age, to take measures to detain them and to deliver them to the nearest police station. Should, after the announcement of this order, people be noticed to have any contact with Jews, they will be delivered to the German military authorities. If Jews perform terror or sabotage acts, all people in the area where the accused Jews hid, will be held responsible (Raseiniai, August 29, 1941)[108].

There were peasants in the surroundings of Jurbarkas who risked helping Jews. In the summer of 1942 the Jurbarkas police was informed that a 23 to 24 year old Jewish girl, Feja Naividel, was hiding in the village Geisiai, at the place of Petras Stankaitis. Policemen P. Kairaitis, J. Marcinkus and P. Budvinskas went to arrest her. Feja Naividel was shot, but P. Stankaitis was left alive[109]. The fate of J. Blazys, who hid the Jewish girl Mika Lubin on his farm, was different. Mika Lubin had survived the "action" of the women on September 8, 1941. At first some woman sheltered her after finding her in the forest, and later Mika hid with an acquaintance, farmer K. Blazys. In the spring 1943, after a neighbor informed the police, both were arrested and shot[110].

Most painful was the fate of Nisan Zundelovitz. He was a man who would carry various goods needed in the villages on his shoulders and there barter them for agricultural products. Zundelovitz had many acquaintances in the villages, but for some reason he did not go to them to hide. "People related that he hid on an island which divided the Nemunas into two branches, and which was covered with brush and thicket. There he died of starvation." According to another version, the Germans caught and shot him[111].

Conclusions

During the German-USSR {campaign of World War II} war, the Genocide {of the Jews} carried out by the Germans and their Lithuanian collaborators in Jurbarkas accounted for about 1,924 Jewish victims.[112]

During German rule in this country, Lithuanian cooperation with the occupying power could only be called collaboration. The fate of Jews, in general, did not depend on the will of the Lithuanians, {that was the will of the Nazis,} but the suffering and the pain {did depend on the Lithuanians}. Only the first "action" was carried out by Germans. Thereafter, those who did the shooting were Lithuanians only.

Worthy of great honor and remembrance are those Lithuanians, who saved Jurbarkas Jews, risking their own and their relatives' lives. Obviously not all the saviors are known.

We did not succeed in finding all of Jurbarkas's Jewish survivors after World War II (we depend on Chayim Jofe's number mentioned, i.e. 76). This BA thesis is the beginning of an inquiry into the Holocaust in the Lithuanian provinces.

Bibliography: List of Sources and Literature

1.Documents from Archives.

1.1 Lithuanian State Central Archives (LCVA).

Instructions to village heads in the Siauliai district// F.1753. Ap.3. B.12. L.1.

A list of those exiled to Soviet Russia// F.1753. Ap.3. B.3. L.217.

A letter from the Mayor of Jurbarkas to the Lithuanian Statistics Office// F.1753. Ap.3. B.13. L.148.

A letter from the Mayor of Jurbarkas to the Commissioner of the Department for Victims in Raseiniai// F.1753. Ap.3. B.24. L.222.

A letter from the Mayor of Jurbarkas to the Raseiniai District Committee concerning the number of the town's residents// F.1753. Ap.3. B.13. L.4.

A letter by the Mayor of Jurbarkas to the chief of the Raseiniai district concerning the number and composition of the town's residents// F.1753. Ap.3. B.13. L.28.

A letter from the Mayor of Jurbarkas to the chief of the Raseiniai district concerning the population survey // F.1753. Ap.3. B.13. L.10.

A letter from the Mayor of Jurbarkas to the chief of the Raseiniai district concerning the number of the town's residents// F.1753. Ap.3. B.13. L.58.

A letter from the Mayor of Jurbarkas to the chief of the Raseiniai district concerning people who were killed during skirmishes between Germans and Russians// F.1753. Ap.3. B.24. L.3.

List of specialist workers working within the boundaries of Jurbarkas// F.1753. Ap.3. B.13. L.18.

List of specialist artists living within the boundaries of Jurbarkas// F.1753. Ap.3. B.13. L.73.

List of persons in the liberal professions living within the boundaries of Jurbarkas// F.1753. Ap.3. B.13. L.13.

An order by the Chief of the Raseiniai district// F.1753. Ap.3. B.4. L.26

An order by the Siauliai Land commissioner to District Chiefs and Mayors// F.1753. Ap.3. B.4. L.27.

1.2.1 Lithuanian Special Archives (LYA).

1.2.2 File Numbers of the Accused.

85/3. Jurgis Gepneris

5582/3. Aleksandras Dravenikas

7314/3. Pranas Bakus

8231. Jonas Bogdanskis

11039/3. Pranas Kresciunas

14142/3. Mykolas Levickas

16816. Pranas Kairaitis

1.2.3 Titles (Names) of Documents.

The protocol of the investigation of P. Bakus. 1947 05 16// B.7314/3. L.75.

The protocol of the investigation of J. Bogdanskis. 1944 10 18 // B. 8231. L.12.

The protocol of the investigation of witness S. Dravenkiene. 1946 08 20// B.5582/3. L.23.

The protocol of the investigation of J. Gepneris. 1945 08 22// B. 85/3. L.16.

The protocol of the investigation of J. Gepneris. J.Gepneris. 1945 08 23// B.85/3. L.19.

The protocol of the investigation of witness J. Grybas. 1947 11 14// B.11039/3. L.43-44.

The protocol of the investigation of P. Kairaitis. 1948 01 25// B. 16816. L.38.

The protocol of the investigation of P. Kairaitis. 1947 08 23// B. 16816. L.53.

The protocol of the investigation concerning the confrontation of P. Kairaitis with witness J. Keturauskas. 1948 06 21// B. 16816. L.69-70.

The protocol of the investigation of P. Kresciunas. 1947 11 01 // B. 11039/3. L.22-23.

The protocol of the investigation of witness A. Leonavicius. 1944 10 17 // B. 8231. L.24.

The protocol of the investigation of M. Levickas. 1948 02 20 //LYA B. 14142/3. L. 146.

The protocol of the investigation of M. Levickas. 1948 11 10 // B. 14142/3. L. 12.

The protocol of the investigation of M. Levickas. 1948 11 24 // B.14142/3. L.47-48.

The protocol of the investigation of witness P. Mikutatis. 1948 04 14 // B. 16816. L.77.

The protocol of the investigation of witness P. Mikutatis. 1948 05 20 // B. 16816 L.67.

The protocol of the investigation of witness P. Mikutatis. 1948 11 23 // B. 16816. L.46.

The protocol of the investigation of witness Narjauskaite. 1948 01 09 // B. 9007/3. L.24.

The protocol of the investigation of witness Petrukaitiene. 1948 01 04 // B. 4039/3. L.46.

1.3 The Archives of the Lithuanian State Jewish Museum (LVZMA)

The material of Chayim Jofe.

2. Collections of Documents.

The mass murders in Lithuania 1941-1944. Vilnius;

Mintis, 1965 , part 1. Page 347. 1973, part 2. Page 423.

3. Personal archives.

Of Chayim Jofe.

4. Articles.

Chayim Jofe. Antanina // sviesa. 1990 12 04.

Chayim Jofe. Mika // Vastieciu Laikrastis 1990 04 26/ 05 03.

Chayim Jofe. Niskutis // sviesa 1990 10 11.

Chayim Jofe Rachile // sviesa 1990 08 23.

T.Suravinas. The tragedy of Jurbarkas's citizens // Tarybu Lietuva 1944 10 14.

5. Books.

J.Balsaitis, A.Pirockinas, A.Skandunas. A history of the schools from the middle of the 16th century to the beginning of the 20th century // Jurbarkas. Vilnius; 1996. P. 448.

V.Brandisauskas. The fight for the restoration of Lithuanian independence (o6 1940- 09 1941). Thesis for a doctorate in the Humanities, Faculty of History. Vilnius; The Institute of Lithuanian History, 1995. P.16.

The Hitlerite murderers in Kretinga. Vilnius; The State Publishing House of Political and Scientific Literature, 1960. P.159.

Chayim Jofe. Jewish life and death // Jurbarkas. Vilnius; 1996. P.174

The murdered accuse. Vilnius; The State Publishing House of Political and Scientific Literature, 1963. P.208.

Blood infiltrated into the sands of Dzukija, Vilnius; The State Publishing House of Political and Scientific Literature, 1960. P.71.

The Lithuanians Encyclopedia. Boston; The Publishing House of the Lithuanians Encyclopedia, 1957. T.10. P.544.

Populated places in Lithuania. The first population survey of Lithuania in 1923. Kaunas; Ministry of Finance, The Central Statistics Bureau, 1925. P.735.

The Genocide of Lithuania's citizens. Vilnius; The Inquiry Center for Oppression in Lithuania, 1992. T.1.: 1939-1941. P.803.

J.Malinauskas. Health observance in Jurbarkas until 1940 // Jurbarkas. 1996. P.448.

Traces of death beside the Nevezys. Vilnius; The State Publishing House of Political and Scientific Literature, 1960. P.80.

A.Piroe kinas. Victims of the occupation // Jurbarkas, 1996. P.448.

A.Stravinskas. Vocations of Jurbarkas's citizens (from the 19th to the first half of the 20th century), Jurbarkas, 1996. P.448.

The Exiles of Lithuania 1941-1951. Vilnius; Ministry of Interior Issues, 1993. Book 1. P.549.

Documents accuse. V.Gintaras, 1970. P.80.

Encyclopedia of the Jewish Communities in Lithuania (Hebrew), Jerusalem, Yad Vashem 1996. P.748.

Appendix Number 1

Survivors of Jurbarkas's Jews who spent the years 1941-1944 outside of Lithuania.

Jurbarkas Jews, soldiers of the 16th Lithuanian infantry division.

- Shmuel Baron
- Yankel Beiman
- Chanan Berkover
- Josel Berkover
- Yudel Fleisher
- Chayim Jofe
- Bliuma Josefer
- Zalman Kaplan
- Chone Levin
- Hertzel Magidovitz
- Reuven Magidovitz
- Shmuel Mazur
- Moshe Most[113]
- Michael Rizman
- Sholem Rizman
- Reuven Rozenberg[114]
- Baruch Portnoi
- Meir Veinberg

Jurbarkas Jews - Soviet partisans.

1. Yankel Holtzman
2. Moshe Magidovitz

Jurbarkas Jews who survived the hell of German concentration camps.

Bela Abramson
Yankel Gutshtein
Michael Gutshtein
Mere Gutshtein
Moshe Gutshtein[115]
Chane-Mere Most

Leah Most
Pesia Mazur
Tzipa Zeider
Basia Zeider
Dobe Most

Appendix Number 2

Jurbarkas Jews living in Lithuania

In Kaunas: Zelda Krom, Dobe Rozenberg-Most, Judith Mackevitz-Patz

In Vilnius: Chana Kuritzky-Simno, Zalman Kaplan, Asher Mejerovitz, Seroginda Lantzman

In Klaipeda: Zalman Rikler

Appendix Number 3

A list of persons, who participated in torturing and shooting Jurbarkas Jews[117]

1. Kazys Almonaitis, son of Pranas, born 1910 in the village of Klisiu, Jurbarkas sub-district. Served in the police[118] from 25th of June 1941. Sentenced B.1414/3//LYA.

2. Bronius Angeleika, born 1907. Served in the police from 1941.

3. Vincas Ausiukaitis, born about 1900. Chief of Jurbarkas partisans (anti-Soviet and anti-Jewish, previously a hairdresser).

4. Pranas Bakus, son of Antanas, born 1917 in the village of Klisiu, Jurbarkas sub-district. Served in the Jurbarkas police from the 3rd of July 1941 until April 1942, and later enlisted in the German army. A partisan in the surroundings of Jurbarkas in 1945 . Sentenced: B.7314/3 //LYA.

5. Jonas Bogdanskis, son of Jonas, born 1907 in Jurbarkas. Served in the police from August 1941. Enlisted in the German army at the end of 1941. Guarded the Kaunas Ghetto as a policeman in 1942 and served in the German police till 1944. Sentenced: B. 8231 //LYA.

6. Aleksandras Drevinskis (Dravenikas), son of Konstantinas, born 1893. Served as a translator for the Germans from 23rd of June 1941 (worked previously as a bricklayer). Sentenced: B.5582/3 //LYA.

7. Glaviatskis, born about 1913. Served in the police from 1941 and was transferred to Kaunas in 1942, where he guarded the Ghetto.

8. The brothers Gylis: Stasys, born 1914 in the village of Siaudine, Raseiniai district, Kiduliai sub-district. Did not serve in the police.

9. Together with his brother Juozas owned a watch workshop.

10. Pranas Greiciunas, son of Jurgis, born in Klisiu. Jurbarkas sub-district. Served in the police from 1941.

11. Jonas Jakaitis, born about 1894 in the village of Silenu, Jurbarkas sub-district. Served in the police from 1941.

12. Jonas Jokubaitis, son of Antanas, born 1919. Served in the police from 1941. Sentenced: B.36950/3 //LYA.

13. Jonas Jurksaitis, son of Jonas. The interrogator of the Jurbarkas police station.

14. Pranas Kairaitis, son of Jonas, born 1912. Served in the police from August 1941 until 1944 (before which, during the Lithuanian Republic, he had served in the Siauliai police). Sentenced: B. 16816 //LYA.

15. Kazimieras Kilikevicius, son of Jonas, born 1900. The Sergeant Major of the Jurbarkas police (earlier, during the Lithuanian Republic, he had served in the Jurbarkas police).

16. Pranas Krisciunas (Kresciunas), son of Kazimieras, born 1916 in Jurbarkas. Served in the police from the 24th of June 1941 until 1943. Sentenced: B.11039/3 //LYA.

17. Juozas Levickas, son of Matas, born about 1915 in Jurbarkas. Began to work in the office of the Jurbarkas police station in June 1941.

18. Mykolas Levickas, son of Matas, born 1909 in Jurbarkas. A former army officer in the Lithuanian Republic. Taught military training in the Jurbarkas high school. Served as Chief of the Jurbarkas police station from the 24th of June 1941 until the middle of July 1941. After quitting this position he directed the branch of the Lithuanian Nationalist party in the town. Sentenced: B.14142/3 //LYA.

19. Romualdas Levickas, son of Matas, born about 1903 in Jurbarkas. Vocation - driver. Enlisted in the German army in 1943, was released during that year because of illness, returned to Jurbarkas and started to serve in the police.

20. Juozas Marcinkus (Martinkus), son of Jonas, born 1916 in the village of Buzuliu, Ariogala sub-district. Served in the police from August 1941 until 1942. Sentenced: B. 16089 //LYA.

21. Povilas Mockevicius, born 1903. Served in the police from June 1941. Was promoted to the position of Chief of Jurbarkas police as from the middle of July 1941 and served until 1944 (had previously served as a policemen in Jurbarkas, until 1939).

22. Vincas Muleiko (Muleika), son of Jurgis, born 1890. Served in the police from 1941. Sentenced: B.29250/3 //LYA.

23. Juozas Petraitis, born 1912 in the village of Montvilu, sub-district of Jurbarkas. Did not serve in the police. Owned a watch workshop.

24. Aleksas Petravicius. Graduated from the Jurbarkas high school in 1941.

25. Pranas Putvinskas (Budvinskas), son of Stasys, born about 1900 in Jurbarkas. Served in the Jurbarkas police until 1939. Worked as a guard in a timber store 1939-1941. Served in the police from June 1941.

26. Stasys Sibaitis, born 1910 in the village of Kalnenu, sub-district of Jurbarkas. Served in the police from June 1941.

27. Antanas Simkus, son of Jurgis, born 1917 in Skirsnemune, Jurbarkas sub-district. He did not serve in the police, but worked as a telephone fitter.

28. Mykolas Urbonas, born 1915. Deputy Chief of Jurbarkas police as from the 25th of June 1941.

29. Aleksandras Vakselis, high school pupil.

30. Leonas Vakselis, high school pupil.

31. Zebrovskis (he and Karstenis), born about 1895. A nobleman of Polish nationality and a member of the Gestapo. He arrived in Jurbarkas from Tilzit.

Appendix Number 4

A Partial List of Jews Murdered in Jurbarkas[119]

From information compiled by Chayim Jofe with corrections

Abbreviations: husb=husband, daug=daughter, sist=sister, wom=woman, fath=father, mot=mother brot=brother, grma=grand-mother, grpa=grand-father

No.	NAME	RELATE	OCCUPATION	No.	NAME	RELATE	OCCUPATION
1.	Abramson Motel	husb	photographer	14.	Altman Shmuel	son	------
2.	Abramson Pese	wife	housewife	15.	Altman Avraham	son	employee
3.	Abramovitz Zusel	husb	loader	16.	Altman Hirsh	son	employee
4.	Abramovitz Zlate	wife	housewife	17.	Altman Fania	daug	pupil
5.	Abramovitz David	son	loader	18.	Altman Chiene	"	"
6.	Abramovitz Berl	son	loader	19.	Altman Chume-Mere	"	dress maker
7.	Abramovitz Shimon	son	militiaman	20.	Aizenshtat Hilel	husb	steambt owner
8.	Abramovitz Israel	son	singer	21.	Aizenshtat Mina	wife	housewife
9.	Abramovitz Sara	daug	dress maker	22.	Aizenshtat Moshe	husb	steambt ownr
10.	Abramovitz Nechama	daug	dress maker	23.	Aizenshtat Grunia	wife	housewife
11.	Alperovitz Moshe	------	cantor	24.	Apriyasky Chiene	wom	small shop
12.	Altman Riva	wom	housewife	25.	Apriyasky Shefe	daug	dress maker
13.	Altman Natan	son	forwarder	26.	Apriyasky Sheine	"	"

27. Aranovsky Motel	husb	small shop	
28. Aranovsky Chana	wife	"	
29. Aranovsky Riva	daug	dress maker	
30. Arnshtein Monik [124]	----	cashier	
31. ArnshteinYudel [124]	brot	electrician	
32. Ars Chayim	husb	small shop	
33. Ars Sara	daug	pupil	
34. Ars Emka	"	"	
35. Averbach Yankel	fath	tailor	
36. Averbach Gita	daug	------	
37. Baron Moshe	husb	grave digger	
38. Baron Pese	wife	housewife	
39. Baron Roza	daug	pupil	
40. Bas Sholem	husb	watchmaker	
41. Bas Rocha	wife	housewife	
42. Beder Zelda	mot	"	
43. Beder Henia	daug	employee	
44. Beder Mina	daug	"	
45. Beder Leah	"	pupil	
46. Beder Dina	"	"	
47. Beder Motel	husb	invalid	
48. Beder Chaya	wife	housewife	
49. Beder Mina	daug	dress maker	
50. Beder Meir	son	hair dresser	
51. Beder Percel	wife	housewife	
52. Beder Icik	son	baby	
53. Beiman Icik-David	husb	small shop	
54. Beiman Chaya	wife	housewife	
55. Beiman Mira	daug	pupil	
56. Beiman Yankel	son	pupil	
57. Beiman Reuven	"	"	
58. Beiman Riva	grma	retired	
59. Beilis Yakov	husb	book keeper	
60. Beilis Chiene		small shop	
61. Beilis Sara	daug	pupil	
62. Beilis Chana	"	"	
63. Beilis Josel	son	"	
64. Berelovitz Zusman	husb	employee	
65. Berelovitz Leah	wife	cook	
66. Berelovitz Zita	daug	pupil	
67. Berelovitz Meir	son	"	
68. Berkover Riva	mot	housewife	
69. Berkover Leizer	brot	small shop	
70. Berkover Feiga	daug	employee	
71. Berkover Chana	"	dress maker	
72. Berkover Chaya	"	housewife	
73. Berkover Sheine	"	pupil	
74. Berkover Yudel	------	shop	
75. Berkover Aba	brot	"	
76. Berkover Etel		employee	
77. Berkover Sheine	"	dress maker	
78. Berkover Shimon	fath	brick layer	
79. Berkover Yente	daug	employee	
80. Berkover Rikel(Rachel)	"	dress maker	
81. Bernshtein Shmerl	fath	bank director	
82. Bernshtein Zlata	wife	housewife [123]	

83. Bernshtein Mina	daug	baby [123]	
84. Bernshtein Sara		small shop [123]	
85. Berzaner Motel	husb	hotel owner	
86. Berzaner Itel	wife	"	
87. Berzaner Raizale [122]	daug	pupil	
88. Bresky Chone-Yankel		invalid	
89. Bresky Roche		small shop	
90. Bresky Yankel	brot	bathhouse heater	
91. Bresky Mina	wife	housewife	
92. Bresky Etel		dress maker	
93. Bregovsky Liova	husb	pharmacist	
94. Bregovsky Sonia	wife	"	
95. Bregovsky Hirsh	son	pupil	
96. Brun Henia	wom	housewife	
97. Brun Boria	son	student	
98. Brun David	son	pupil	
99. Brun Chana	daug	dress maker	
100. Brun Grunia	daug	employee	
101. Brun Ana	daug	"	
102. Budraicky Motel	husb	loader	
103. Budraicky Mina	wife	housewife	
104. Budraicjy Faivel	son	tailor	
105. Cintkovsky Aron	husb	teacher	
106. Cintkovsky Mika	wife		housewife
107. Tchertok David	husb	tailor	
108. Tchertok Mere	wife	housewife	
109. Tchertok Velvel	brot	hair dresser	
110. Tchechanovsky Leizer	husb	teacher	
111. Tchechanovsky Lina	wife	housewife	
112. Danilevitz H.Reuven	fath	employee	
113. Danilevitz Zalman	son	"	
114. Danilevitz Gershon	"	"	
115. Dimant Rachel	------	dress maker	
116. Dimant Liba		housewife	
117. Dratvin Shmuel	fath	coachman	
118. Dratvin Zalman	son	employee	
119. Dratvin Sara	wife	housewife	
120. Dratvin Rachel		dress maker	
121. Dratvin Riva	"	"	
122. Dratvin Mere	"	"	
123. Es Leizer-Hirsh	husb	small shop	
124. Es Braine	wife	housewife	
125. Es Esther	daug	pupil	
126. Es Josel	son	pupil	
127. Es Reuven	"	"	
128. Es Josel	fath	------	
129. Es Yankel	son	------	
130. Es Etel	daug	employee	
131. Es Hana	"	pupil	
132. Es Mina	"	dress maker	
133. Es Riva	mot	housewife	
134. Es Nechemia	son	butcher	
135. Es Faivel	"	"	
136. Es Beinish	"	hair dresser	
137. Elyashov Chayim	fath	tailor	
138. Elyashov Moshe	son	"	

139.	Elyashov Taube	mot	small shop
140.	Elyashov Itke	daug	"
141.	Elyashov Braine	"	dress maker
142.	Elyashov Yekutiel	son	tailor
143.	Elyashevitz Meir	husb	small shop
144.	Elyashevitz Taube	wife	housewife
145.	Elyashevitz Icik	son	small shop
146.	Elyashevitz Yona (Yeine)"		watchmaker
147.	Elyashevitz Leah-Golde	daug	book keeper
148.	Epelbaum Israel	fath	small shop
149.	Epelbaum Icik	son	mechanic
150.	Epelbaum Chaya	daug	pupil
151.	Es Daniel	husb	small shop
152.	Es Mina	wife	housewife
153.	Es Orke	son	small shop
154.	Es Basia	daug	dress maker
155.	Es Golde	"	pupil
156.	Es Moshe	husb	butcher
157.	Es Gita	wife	housewife
158.	Es Hirsh	son	butcher
159.	Es Shmuel	"	"
160.	Es Chayim	"	"
161.	Es Mina	daug	employee
162.	Es Chiene	"	dress maker
163.	Es Sara	"	pupil
164.	Fainberg Eliyas	brot	power statn ownr
165.	Fainberg Sholem	"	flour mill owner
166.	Fainberg Meir	"	sawmill owner
167.	Fainberg Malvina		housewife
168.	Fainberg Shmuel	------	small trader
169.	Fainberg Rachel		housewife
170.	Fainberg Sonia	"	employee
171.	Fain Gitel	mot	housewife
172.	Fain Nechemia	son	small shop
173.	Fain Mere	daug	"
174.	Fainshtein Leib-Chone	husb	watchmaker
175.	Fainshtein Chana	wife	housewife
176.	Feldman Moshe	husb	small shop
177.	Feldman Leah	wife	housewife
178.	Feldman Yankel	son	musician
179.	Feldman Sheine	daug	dress maker
180.	Fidler Motel	husb	hair dresser
181.	Fidler Mere	wife	gardener
182.	Fidler David	son	pupil
183.	Fidler Jankel	"	"
184.	Fisher Chanan	husb	musician
185.	Fisher Chava	wife	housewife
186.	Fisher Josel	son	small shop
187.	Fisher "	"	
188.	Fisher Yankel	husb	glazier
189.	Fisher Vilentzik Braine	wife	------
190.	Frank Malka		housewife
191.	Fridland Kalman	husb	small shop
192.	Fridland Braine	wife	housewife
193.	Fridland Esther	daug	dress maker
194.	Fin Gershon	------	pharmacist
195.	Flier Elias	husb	"
196.	Flier Riva	wife	"
197.	Flier Mira	daug	pupil
198.	Fridman Yitzhak	husb	hotel owner
199.	Fridman Libe	wife	"
200.	Fridman David	son	pupil
201.	Frakt Yudel	fath	brick layer
202.	Frakt Leib	son	photographer
203.	Frakt Yankel	"	hair dresser
204.	Frank Icik	fath	small shop
205.	Frank Yudel	son	------
206.	Galiner Natan	------	laborer
207.	Geselkovitz Icik	husb	cinema owner
208.	Geselkovitz Riva	wife	housewife
209.	Geselkovitz Sheine	daug	pupil
210.	Geselkovita Konia	"	"
211.	Geselkovitz Nehemia		butcher
212.	Gitelman Zalman	husb	employee
213.	Gitelman Mere	wife	hatter
214.	Gitelman Dora	daug	baby
215.	Gitelman Hirsh	husb	employee
216.	Gitelman Braine	wife	housewife
217.	Gitelman Leizer	son	4 years old
218.	Gitelman Baruch	"	baby
219.	Glazer Zalman	-----	dispatcher
220.	Glazer Heshel	brot	"
221.	Glazer Sender	"	"
222.	Glazer-Kravetz Sonia		housewife
223.	Golde Yakov	husb	wholesaler
224.	Golde Musia	wife	housewife
225.	Golde Leib	son	pupil
226.	Golde Taibe	daug	"
227.	Gitelzon Kopl	-----	small shop
228.	Gitelzon Meir	brot	"
229.	Gitelzon Gita		housewife
230.	Gitelzon Fruma	"	employee
231.	Gitelzon Braine	"	dress maker
232.	Goldshtein Chayim	-----	employee
233.	Gorshon Dora	mot	housewife
234.	Gorshon Leib	son	teacher
235.	Gorshon Mina	daug	employee
236.	Grayevsky Leib	husb	small shop
237.	Grayevsky Mina	wife	small shop
238.	Gut Motel	-----	teacher
239.	Gutshtein Michael	-----	employee
240.	Gutshtein Pesach	brot	"
241.	Gutshtein Reuven	"	coachman
242.	Holerman Elijas	fath	small shop
243.	Holerman Moshe	son	pupil
244.	Hein Boris	-----	engineer
245.	Chosid Leizer	husb	brick layer
246.	Chosid Mere	wife	housewife
247.	Chosid Chaya-Beile	daug	dress maker
248.	Chosid Leah	"	pupil
249.	Ingel Yudel	-----	employee
250.	Ivensky Yankel	husb	"

251.	Ivensky Golde	wife	housewife
252.	Ivensky Avraham	son	---
253.	Yapu Avraham	husb	small shop
254.	Yapu Stira	wife	"
255.	Yapu Hilel	-----	baker
256.	Yapu Chana	-----	"
257.	Yasvonsky Hirsh	fath	small shop
258.	Yasvonsky Mira	daug	pupil
259.	Jofe Roza	mot	housewife
260.	Jofe Chatzkel	son	glazier
261.	Jofe Bela	wife	housewife
262.	Jofe Icik-Leib	son	------
263.	Jofe Chayim	husb	small shop
264.	Jofe Riva	wife	housewife
265.	Jofe Leib	son	pupil
266.	Jofe Mina	daug	"
267.	Jozefer Shlomo	husb	joiner
268.	Jozefer Dina	wife	dress maker
269.	Jozefer Leib	son	student
270.	Jozefer Meir	"	pupil
271.	Jozelit Tzadok	husb	small shop
272.	Jozelit Mere	wife	"
273.	Katzev Chayim	husb	baker
274.	Katzev Bela	wife	"
275.	Katzev Sheine	daug	pupil
276.	Karlinsky Josef	husb	doctor
277.	Karlinsky Sonia	wife	housewife
278.	Karlinsky Judith	daug	student
279.	Kaplan Moshe	fath	cinema owner
280.	Kaplan Josel	son	small shop
281.	Kaplan Sarah	daug	dress maker
282.	Kaplan Leah	"	"
283.	Karabelnik David	husb	steamshp ownr
284.	Karabelnik Mina	wife	housewife
285.	Karabelnik Leib	son	steamshp ownr
286.	Karabelnik Tcherne	daug	employee
287.	Karabelnik Riva	"	"
288.	Kaplan Aba	husb	coachman
289.	Kaplan Feige	wife	housewife
290.	Kaplan Chayim-Ber	-----	loader
291.	Kagan Benyamin	man	small shop
292.	Kagan Dora		"
293.	Kagan Esther	"	"
294.	Kagan Hinde	"	dress maker
295.	Kaplan Leib	-----	small shop
296.	Kaplan Moshe	husb	butcher
297.	Kaplan Etel	wife	housewife
298.	Kaplan Yankel	son	butcher
299.	Kobelkovsky Leizer	-----	tailor
300.	Kobelkovsky Gershon	--	employee
301.	Kobelkovsky Motel	husb	tailor
302.	Kobelkovsky Mere	wife	housewife
303.	Kobelkovsky Chayim	son	laborer
304.	Kobelkovsky Chaya	daug	dress maker
305.	Kobelkovsky Velvel	fath	small shop
306.	Kobelkovsky Freide	daug	employee

307.	Kobelkovsky Chone (Elchanan)	son	small shop
308.	Kobelkovsky Leizer	"	"
309.	Kobelkovsky Motel	"	pupil
310.	Kobelkovsky Leah	------	housewife
311.	Kobelkovsky Chayim	husb	shoemaker
312.	Kobelkovsky Rachel	wife	housewife
313.	Kobelkovsky Moshe	son	shoemaker
314.	Kobelkovsky Motel	"	employee
315.	Kobelkovsky Hinde	daug	dress maker
316.	Kobelkovsky Feige	"	"
317.	Kobelkovsky Icik	husb	shoemaker
318.	Kobelkovsky Leah	wife	housewife
319.	Kobelkovsky Benyamin	son	hair dresser
320.	Kobelkovsky Chiene	mot	small shop
321.	Kobelkovsky Mendel	son	tailor
322.	Kopelovitz Ita	mot	housewife
323.	Kopelovitz Icik	son	hair dresser
324.	Kopelovitz Shaya	"	"
325.	Kopelovitz Leib	"	"
326.	Kopelov Zalman	husb	dentist
327.	Kopelov Ira	wife	housewife
328.	Kopelov Rachel	daug	baby
329.	Kobelkovsky Tzemach	husb	tailor
330.	Kobelkovsky Chaya	wife	housewife
331.	Kobelkovsky Bela	daug	small shop
332.	Kobelkovsky Malka	"	"
333.	Kobelkovsky Chaya (?)	"	pupil
334.	Kopelionsky Avraham	husb	small shop
335.	Kopelionsky Riva	wife	housewife
336.	Kopelionsky Motel	son	technician
337.	Kopelionsky Berel	"	pupil
338.	Krait Fruma	mot	baker
339.	Krait Nachum	son	"
340.	Krelitz Leib	husb	"
341.	Krelitz Tzila	wife	housewife
342.	Krelitz Miryam	daug	baby
343.	Krelitz Moshe	husb	baker
344.	Krelitz Gita	wife	housewife
345.	Krelitz Mina	daug	baby
346.	Krelitz Leah [120]		dress maker
347.	Krupinsky Zelig	fath	rope maker
348.	Krupinsky Pinchas	son	"
349.	Krupinsky Yudel	"	"
350.	Krupinsky Mira	daug	dress maker
351.	Krupinsky Leah	mot	housewife
352.	Kuselevitz Yudel	husb	small shop
353.	Kuselevitz Riva	wife	housewife
354.	Kuselevitz Berel	son	pupil
355.	Kuselevitz Mina	daug	"
356.	Kushner Aba	husb	hair dresser
357.	Kushner Ela	wife	housewife
358.	Kushner Chava		dress maker
359.	Lam Josel	husb	shop owner
360.	Lam Feige	wife	"
361.	Leiptziger Icik	husb	painter
362.	Leiptziger Chaya	wife	dress maker

363. Latush Golde	-----	housewife	
364. Levin Vulf	husb	employee	
365. Levin Golde	wife	small shop	
369. Levin Frade	wife	housewife	
370. Levin Shimshon	son	4 years old	
371. Levin Gavriel	son	2 years old	
372. Levin Shlomo	husb	coachman	
373. Levin Chaya	wife	housewife	
374. Levin Michael	son	employee	
375. Levin Yankel	husb	coachman	
376. Levin Mere-Leah	wife	housewife	
377. Levin Motel	son	pupil	
378. Levin Sarah	daug	"	
379. Levinson Gavriel	fath	employee	
380. Levinson Tuvia	son	laborer	
381. Levinberg Israel	husb	steamship owner	
382. Levinberg Leah	wife	housewife	
383. Levinberg Shlomo	son	steamship owner	
384. Lebiush Aron	husb	small shop	
385. Lebiush Mina	wife	housewife	
386. Lebiush Icik	son	employee	
387. Lebiush Chana	daug	dress maker	
388. Lebiush Gita	"	pupil	
389. Levitan Zusel	husb	small shop	
390. Levitan Golde	wife	housewife	
391. Lubin Shmuel	husb	small shop	
392. Lubin Grunia	wife	housewife	
393. Lubin Gavriel	husb	gardener	
394. Lubin Rachel	wife	housewife	
395. Lubin Berel	son	hairdresser	
396. Magidovitz Avraham	husb	small shop	
397. Magidovitz Chana	wife	housewife[125]	
398. Magidovitz Hinde	daug	pupil	
399. Magidovitz Hirsh	son	"	
400. Machat Noach	-----	employee	
401. Machat Leah		hatter	
402. Maister Shabtai	-----	tailor	
403. Maister Yente		dress maker	
404. Margolis	husb	furniture fact ownr	
405. Margolis Rachel	wife	housewife	
406. Margolis	daug	student	
407. Markir Moshe-Leizer	fath	synagogue supervisor	
408. Markir Meir	son	"	
409. Markir Yente	daug	dress maker	
410. Magidovitz Sholem	-----	coachman	
411. Marger Shiye	husb	bakery owner	
412. Marger Chaya-Golde	wife	housewife	
413. Marger Benyamin	son	tailor	
414. Marger Mendel-Faivel	"	courier	
415. Marger Ore-Shmerel	"	mentally defective	
416. Marger Gita	daug	dressmaker	
417. Mazur Motel-Leib	husb	tailor	
418. Mazur Leah	wife	housewife	
419. Mazur Gershon	son	tailor	
420. Mazur Leib	"	employee	
421. Meirovitz Yekel	husb	small shop	

366. Levin Leib	son	tailor	
367. Levin Hilel	"	pupil	
368. Levin Yekutiel	son	photographer	
422. Meirovitz Etele	wife	housewife	
423. Meirovitz Shlomo	son	musician	
424. Meirovitz Reuven	"	pupil	
425. Meirovitz Elke	daug	mentally defective	
426. Meirovitz Leah	"	dress maker	
427. Mer Yankel	-----	butcher	
428. Mer Boncik	brot	"	
429. Mer Chaya	mot	housewife	
430. Mer Yente	daug	dress maker	
431. Melnicky Daniel	-----	small shop	
432. Michailovsky Baruch	---	"	
433. Michailovsky Shmuel	bro	small shop	
434. Michailovsky Mere	"		
435. Mincer Yankel	husb	"	
436. Mincer Shlame	wife	housewife	
437. Miasnik Berel	husb	butcher	
438. Miasnik Riva	wife	housewife	
439. Miasnik Mere	daug	pupil	
440. Miasnik Eliyahu	husb	butcher	
441. Miasnik Leah	wife	housewife	
442. Miasnik Josel	husb	butcher	
443. Miasnik Leah	wife	housewife	
444. Michelzon Motel	husb	employee	
445. Michelzon Mina	wife	housewife	
446. Michelzon Leib	son	pupil	
447. Most Motel	husb	small shop	
448. Most Bracha	wife	housewife	
449. Most Dodik	son	pupil	
450. Most Faivel	husb	dispatcher	
451. Most Dobe	wife	housewife	
452. Most Tzila	daug	baby	
453. Most Hilel	-----	book keeper	
454. Mushes Zalman	husb	painter	
455. Mushes Pesia	wife	housewife	
456. Mushes Reuven	son	10 years old	
457. Mushes Pesach	"	5 years old	
458. Miler Aba	husb	gardener	
459. Miler Sheine	wife	housewife	
460. Miler Riva	daug	dress maker	
461. Naividel Rachel	mot	housewife	
462. Naividel Fruma	daug	dress maker	
463. Naividel Shlomo	son	pupil	
464. Naividel Reuven	"	bicycle technician	
465. Naividel Fania	wife	housewife	
466. Naividel Chaya	daug	pupil	
467. Nochimzon Leib	husb	small shop	
468. Nochimzon Sarah	wife	housewife	
469. Nochimzon Klara	daug	dress maker	
470. Nochimzon Chana	"	employee	
471. Neviasky Reuven	husb	small shop	
472. Neviasky Gita	wife	housewife	
473. Neviasky Dodik	son	pupil	
474. Olshvanger Reuven	husb	wholesaler	

475.	Olshvanger Perel	wife	housewife
476.	Orimian Elias	------	steamship owner
477.	Patz Fishel	husb	wholesaler
478.	Patz Pese-Hinde	wife	housewife
479.	Patz Betzalel	son	pupil
480.	Patz Elias	------	5 years old
481.	Pazerinsky Pinchas	------	hair dresser
482.	Pazerinsky Moshe	brot	employee
483.	Pazerinsky Zalman	"	pupil
484.	Pazerinsky Libe		dress maker
485.	Pazerinsky Chana	"	"
486.	Pazerinsky Esther	"	employee
487.	Peisachzon Icik	husb	small shop
488.	Peisachzon Liuba	wife	housewife
489.	Peisachzon Leizer	son	small shop
490.	Peisachzon Yechiel	"	"
491.	Peisachzon Reizel	daug	pupil
492.	Per Chayim	husb	gardener
493.	Per Zlate	wife	"
494.	Per Chayim	------	butcher
495.	Per David	------	loader
496.	Per Tzadok	brot	"
497.	Per Yente		dress maker
498.	Per Etel	"	"
499.	Perlman Motel	------	small shop
500.	Polak Shlomo	husb	"
501.	Polak Leah	wife	housewife
502.	Polak Joselson		pupil
503.	Polak Leib		"
504.	Polak Motel	"	"
505.	Polak Tuvia	husb	restaurant owner
506.	Polak Cherne	wife	housewife
507.	Polak Mira	daug	pupil
508.	Polak Liuta	"	"
509.	Polak Sarah	"	"
510.	Polak Koka	"	"
511.	Polak Avraham	husb	employee
512.	Polak Chiene-Etel	wife	housewife
513.	Polak Leib	son	pupil
514.	Portnoy Bela	mot	housewife
515.	Portnoy Chayim-Ber	son	laborer
516.	Portnoy Hinde	mot	housewife
517.	Portnoy Icik	son	pupil
518.	Portnoy Hirsh	"	6 years old
519.	Portnoy Leah	------	housewife
520.	Portnoy Chana	------	"
521.	Portnoy Vulf	------	loader
522.	Portnoy Bunim-David	husb	"
523.	Portnoy Simona	wife	housewife
524.	Portnoy Chayim-Icik	son	driver
525.	Pres Leib	husb	------
526.	Pres Rachel	wife	invalid
527.	Pres Taube	daug	employee
528.	Pres Elke	"	dress maker
529.	Pres Hinde	"	employee
530.	Puchert Yankel	fath	tailor

531.	Puchert Yona	son	tailor
532.	Puchert Manke	"	employee
533.	Puchert Sarah	daug	dress maker
534.	Pulerevitz Motel	fath	factory owner
535.	Pulerevitz Reuven	son	"
536.	Pulerevitz Golde	daug	housewife
537.	Pulerevitz Zlate	"	pupil
538.	Pulerevitz Chaya	"	dress maker
539.	Pulerevitz Leah	"	"
540.	Pulerevitz Shmuel	------	electrician
541.	Pulerevitz Icik	brot	cinemadoorkeeper
542.	Purve Motel	husb	small shop
543.	Purve Gita	wife	housewife
544.	Pulerevitz Zelig	husb	employee
545.	Pulerevitz Alte	wife	housewife
546.	Pulerevitz Yechiel	son	mechanic
547.	Rabinovitz Yudel	------	pupil
548.	Raichman Boris	husb	doctor
549.	Raichman Basia	wife	housewife
550.	Raichman Brone	daug	baby
551.	Ravel Leah	------	small shop
552.	Rizman Shmerel	husb	woolcomb mechanic
553.	Rizman Pese	wife	housewife
554.	Rizman Yudel	son	tailor
555.	Rizman Daniel	"	"
556.	Rizman David	"	watchmaker
557.	Rizman Motel	"	employee
558.	Rizman Zelde	daug	dress maker
559.	Rizman Yankel	son	book keeper
560.	Rizman Bela	wife	housewife
561.	Rochtzo Icik	------	employee
562.	Rochtzo Israel	brot	"
563.	Rochtzo Shimon	husb	small shop
564.	Rochtzo Braine	wife	housewife
565.	Rochtzo Beinish	------	synagog superviser
566.	Rozenberg Chayim-David	husb	small shop
567.	Rozenberg Miryam	wife	housewife
568.	Rozin Hilel	husb	baker
569.	Rozin Bela	wife	"
570.	Rudansky Aba	husb	employee
571.	Rudansky Mina	wife	small shop
572.	Rudansky Chayim	son	employee
573.	Rudansky Judith	wife	housewife
574.	Rabinovitz Mira	mot	"
575.	Rabinovitz Eizel (?)	son	employee
576.	Rabinovitz Masha	daug	pupil
577.	Sigar Chayim	husb	teacher
578.	Sigar Riva	wife	housewife
579.	Sigar Yakov	son	4 years old
580.	Skirsnemunsky David	husb	small shop
581.	Skirsnemunsky Perel	wife	housewife
582.	Skirsnemunsky Leib	son	12 years old
583.	Skirsnemunsky Pinele	"	8 years old
584.	Skirsnemunsky Mutele	daug	3 years old
585.	Skirsnemunsky Hilel	husb	small shop
586.	Skirsnemunsky Masha	wife	housewife

587. Skirsnemunsky M.-Leib husb baker
588. Skirsnemunsky Riva wife   "
589. Skirsnemunsky Leib (?) son   7 years old
590. Skirsnemunsky Hirsh "   5 years old
591. Skirsnemunsky Motel "   4 years old
592. Soloveitzik Aron   husb   small shop
593. Soloveitzik Tzipe   wife   housewife
594. Soloveitzik Esther   daug   small child
595. Shapiro Asne   mot   housewife
596. Shapiro Mendel   son   employee
597. Shapiro Sh.-Reuven "   "
598. Shapiro-Berkover Tzivia wife housewife
599. Shmulovitz Leah   ------   "
600. Shmulovitz Motel   husb   shoemaker
601. Shmulovitz Chaya   wife   housewife
602. Shmulovitz Feige   daug   employee
603. Shmulovitz Nechama "   dress maker
604. Shmulovitz Bentzi   son   shoemaker
605. Shimonov Alter   husb   wholesaler
606. Shimonov Mere   wife   housewife
607. Shimonov Edis (?)   son   pupil
608. Shmulovitz Motel   husb   butcher
609. Shmulovitz Hinde   wife   housewife
610. Shmulovitz Avraham husb butcher
611. Shmulovitz Chana-Eida wife housewife
612. Shmulovitz Mina   daug   4 years old
613. Shmulovitz Perel   "   2 years old
614. Shlomovitz Aron   husb   slaughterer
615. Shlomovitz Feige   wife   housewife
616. Shlomovitz Alter   son   student
617. Shlomovitz Miryam daug   employee
618. Shtern Vulf   husb   coachman
619. Shtern Roza   wife   housewife
620. Shtern Noach   son   handyman
621. Shtern Alter   "   employee
622. Shtern Judith   wife   "
623. Shachnovitz Shlomo husb   cantor
624. Shachnovitz Leah   wife   housewife
625. Shachnovitz Chayim son   employee
626. Shachnovitz Icik   "   "
627. Shachnovitz Mina   daug   pupil
628. Shimne Alter-Leib   husb   small shop
629. Shimne Mere   wife   housewife
630. Shimne Meir   son   employee
631. Shmulovitz Moshe   husb   coachman
632. Shmulovitz Etel   wife   housewife
633. Shmulovitz Mira   daug   artist
634. Shmulovitz Avraham son   pupil
635. Shmulovitz Yerachmiel husb tailor
636. Shmulovitz Feige   wife   housewife
637. Shmulovitz Hirsh   son   tailor
638. Shtok Leizer   husb   employee
639. Shtok Leah   wife   housewife
640. Shtok Aba   son   small shop
641. Shtok Musia   daug dress maker
642. Telzak Avraham   husb   butcher
643. Telzak Chiene   wife   housewife
644. Zarkin Hilel   ------   butcher
645. Zarkin Yankel   brot   "
646. Zarkin Chayim   "   pupil
647. Zarkin Feige   dress maker
648. Zachar Base   mot   baker
649. Zachar Henke   daug   "
650. Zachar Josel   son   teacher
651. Zachar Baruch   "   "
652. Zeider Osher   ------   small shop
653. Zarnitzky Reuven   husb   hatter
654. Zarnitzky Zlata   wife   housewife
655. Zarnitzky Israel-Moshe son hatter
656. Zarnitzky Sonia   wife   housewife
657. Zilber Israel   husb   pensioner
658. Zilber Chaya   wife   "
659. Zilber Aba   husb   small shop
660. Zilber Sheine   wife   housewife
661. Zilber Hinde   daug   employee
662. Zilber Josel   son   small shop
663. Zilber Taube   wife   housewife
664. Ziman Vulf   husb   small shop
665. Ziman Ange   wife housewife
666. Ziman Eva   daug pupil
667. Zundelovitz Nisan   ------ small shop
668. Zundelovitz Bunke   housewife
669. Vales Hene   mot   housewife
670. Vales Yankel   son   pupil
671. Vales Shimon   "   5 years old
672. Vales Dora   daug   baby
673. Vitko Malka   mot   small shop
674. Vitko Josel   son   pupil
675. Vitko Esther   daug   "
676. Vladislavovsky Chone husb small shop
677. Vladislavovsky Leah wife housewife
678. Vladislavovsky Shlomo son musician
679. Verblovsky Ortchik   ------ employee
680. Vainshtein Gavriel   husb   "
681. Vainshtein Mina   wife housewife
682. Vainshtein Sarah   daug pupil
683. Vainshtein Greta   "   "
684. Veitzman Avraham   ------ baker
685. Veitzman Riva   "
686. Veitzman Chana   "   "
687. Veitzman Tile   "   small shop
688. Vainberg Moshe   husb   "
689. Vainberg Riva   wife   housewife
690. Verblovsky Yoche (Yocheved) ----   "
691. Es Esther (Eliashevitz) wife of Es Faivel [121]

[119] The list of Chayim Jofe, available in LVZMA

[120] Leah Krelitz immigrated to Mexico in 1937, hence survived the war (Max Sherman-Krelitz, Leah's son)

[121] Note: Based on a letter from Rachel Ess Greenstein dated 2/15/97

[122] Note: Original list contained name Muti (Miriam, who was brought to the US in the late 1930s). It was the sister Raizale who was murdered. Based on an email from Diana Berzaner Tobin dated 10/5/2000.

[123] Note: Shmerl Bernstein`s (Bernshtein) wife was Chava (Eva), their children were Yetta (daughter) and Wolf (Zeev) (son). The names that appear in the list may be the wife and children of another Bernstein who did not belong to our family, or the given names were in error. Shmerl`s wife and children did not survive, they were killed all together during the liquidation of Kovno ghetto (at the beginning of the war Shmerl and his family escaped from Yurburg to Kovno). Also Sara, Shmerl and Boris's sister, did not have a shop. Sarah was killed in Raseiniai where she lived after her marriage in 1938 with advocate Isaac Friedland. She never had a shop in Yurburg (this information is likely in error). This information was received from Shmerl`s nephew - son of Shmerl's brother Boris Bernstein, Zeev (Wolf) Bernstein, Nathania, Israel. (10/27/2000).

[124] Note: Originally spelled Arshstein in translation of Joseph Rosin, likely should have been Arnshtein, according to Roy Thacker, an Arnstein family member. Also there was a sister Dora Arnshtein, who likely was also murdered, because nothing was found out about her survival after the war. Monik was likely the name associated with a brother Moritz.

[125] Survived and lives in Israel. See testimony in Yizkor book.

Footnotes

(LCVA) : The Central Lithuanian State Archives

(LYA): S pecial Archives

(LVZMA) : The Lithuanian State Jewish Museum Archives

3 Documents Accuse, Vilnius 1970

4 The Murdered Accuse, Vilnius 1963

5 The Mass Murders in Lithuania 1941-1944. A collection of documents. Part 1, Vilnius 1965; Part 2, Vilnius 1973

6 Traces of Death Deside the Nevezys, Vilnius 1960

7 The Hitlerite Murderers in Kretinga, Vilnius 1960

8 Blood Infiltrates the Sands of Dzukija, Vilnius 1960

9 Mass Murders in Lithuania 1941-1944. Part 2, page 26

11 Warriors Without Arms, Vilnius 1967

12 Jurbarkas, Vilnius 1996

13 Pinkas haKehilot Lita. Jerusalem, 1996, pages 324-329

14 The son of the sculptor V. Grybas, a historian, at this time the manager of the Memorial Museum of V. Grybas in Jurbarkas (living at Tulpiu St. 13, Jurbarkas)

15 The scientific secretary of the Lithuanian State Jewish Museum

16 Employee of the newspaper "Lithuanian Jerusalem"

17 Exiled Jew from Jurbarkas on June 14, 1941 (now living in Vilnius)

18 Chayim Jofe. Jewish life and death, Jurbarkas. Vilnius. 1996, page 174

19 The populated places in Lithuania. The first census of the population of Lithuania in 1923. Kaunas 1925, page 195

20 A. Stravinskas. The vocations of Jurbarkas citizens (from 19th to first half of the 20th century)

21 Pinkas haKehiloth. Lita. Jerusalem 1996. Page 327

22 Ibid.

24 Chayim Jofe's material

25 Chayim Jofe. The life and death of the Jews of Jurbarkas. Page 176

26 Pinkas haKehiloth. Lita. Page 327

27 Ibid.

28 Pinkas haKehiloth, page 327

29 Chayim Jofe's material

30 J. Malinauskas, Health observance in Jurbarkas till 1940, Jurbarkas. Page 326

31 Ibid, Malinauskas.

32 Except for these three schools, Jewish children also studied in the Lithuanian high school "Saule" in Jurbarkas. Zalman Kaplan and Jozefer finished this school in 1939.

33 J.Balsaitis, A. Pirockinas, A. Skandunas, The history of the schools from the middle of the 16th century till the beginning of the 20th century. Jurbarkas, page 248

35 The mayor was then J. Gepneris

36 In 1923, after the liquidation of Jewish Autonomy, there remained in Lithuania only Jewish religious communities, and it was not obligatory for all Jurbarkas's Jews to belong to the religious community.

37 Pinkas haKehiloth. Lita. Page 328

38 The director of this association was Fridman

39 Chayim Jofe's material

40 There were more. In this list there are only about one third of Jurbarkas Jews who were shot, to which one must add all those, who escaped to Russia at the beginning of the war.

41 It is not known how many Jews were functionaries in the Soviet institutions because the archives of those years are not available.

42 Lithuanian State Central Archives (LCVA) F.1753. Ap3 .L.217

43 The genocide of the citizens of Lithuania, 1939-1941. Vilnius 1992

43 The genocide of the citizens of Lithuania, 1939-1941. Vilnius 1992

44 The Lithuanian exiles of the years 1941-1952, First book. Vilnius 1993

45 A.Pirockinas. The victims of the occupation, Jurbarkas. Page 191

46 Ibid.

47 The Lithuanians Encyclopedia, Boston, 1957, T.10. page 117

48 LSCA. F.1753. Ap.3. B.13. L.28

49 Encyclopedia of the Jewish communities in Lithuania (Hebrew). Jerusalem 1996 Page 327

50 V.Brandisauskas. The Fight for the restoration of Lithuanian independence (06.1940-09.1941) Vilnius 1995. Page 11

51 LCVA. F.1753. Ap 3. B.12. L.1

52 The protocol of Gepneris' investigation. 1945 o8 22// LYA. B.85/3. L16

53 LCVA, F.1753. Ap.3. B.24. L3.

54 LCVA, F.1753. Ap.3. B.24. L.222

55 Chayim Jofe's brother.

56 Chayim Jofe's material. The story of the late Leib Meigel.

57 The protocol of Mykolas Levickas' investigation. 1948 02 20//LYA B.14142/3. L.146

58 The protocol of the investigation of witness J. Keturauskas confronting P. Kairaitis. 1948 06 21// LYA. B. 16816. L.69-70

59 The protocol of the investigation of the witness P. Mikutaitis. 1948 04 14//LYA. B. 16816. L. 77

60 The protocol of the investigation of J. Bogdanskis. 1944 10 18// LYA. B. -8231. L.12

60 The protocol of the investigation of J. Bogdanskis. 1944 10 18// LYA. B. 8231. L.12

61 Chayim Jofe's material. The story of the late Leib Meigel. His house stood in the vicinity of the mayor's house in German St. On the morning of July 1, 1941, the mayor met Leib (Leibukas - so he amiably called his neighbor) in the street and alerted him to take his wife and run, because tomorrow would be too late.

62 Chayim Jofe's material. Mykolas Levickas gave another number - 100// The protocol of the investigation of Mykolas Levickas 1948 11 10// LYA. B.14142/3. L.12.

63 The protocol of the witness J.Mikutaitis' investigation. 1948 05 20//LYA. B. 16816. L.67

64 The protocol of the witness S.Dravenkiene's investigation. 1946 08 20//LYA. B. 5582/3. L.23

65 The protocol of the witness Petrukaitiene's investigation 1948 01 04//LYA. B.4039/3. L.46

66 The protocol of the witness J.Mikutaitis' investigation 1948 11 23//LYA. B. 16816. L.46

67 The protocol of the witness Narjauskaite's investigation. 1948 01 09//LYA. B.9007/3. L.24

68 Chayim Jofe's material. The story of Dobe Most-Rozenberg (living in Kaunas, Asigalio St. 21-6)

69 T. Suravinas. The tragedy of the Jurbarkas citizens// Tarybu Lietuva. 1944 10 14

70 Chayim Jofe. Mika// Valstieciu laikrastis (Farmers newspaper) 1990 04 26

71 Chayim Jofe's material. The story of A.Vales

72 Among those murdered on July 3, 1941 was also her father Narjauskas.

73 The protocol of the witness Narjaukaite's investigation 1947 01 09//LYA. B.9007/3. L.24

74 A.Leonavicius took part as a witness in the trial of policeman J.Bogdanskis. 'They, policemen J.Bogdanskis and Stasys Strancikas, arrested me. On July 3, 1941 together with about 300 people I was driven to the Jewish cemetery to be shot. I escaped and survived'. The protocol of the witness A. Leonavicius' investigation. 1944 10 17 //LYA. B. 8231. L.24

75 After the war partisans shot P. Striaukas and A. Leonavicius to death.

76 After the war A. Vales emigrated to Israel.

77 Chayim Jofe. Antanina// sviesa. 1990 12 04

78 .Chayim Jofe's material. The story of A.Vales.

79 LCVA. F.1753. Ap.3. B.13. L.4

80 T. Suravinas. The tragedy of the Jurbarkas citizens// Tarybu Lietuva. 1944 10 14

81 Chayim Jofe's material. The story of L. Meigel.

82 The protocol of the investigation of P. Bakus. 1947 05 16 //LYA. B.7314/3. L.75

83 Chayim Jofe's material.

84 The protocol of the investigation of P. Kairaitis. 1948 01 25 // LYA. B. 16816. L.38

85 The protocol of the investigation of J. Grybas. 1947 11 14 // LYA. B. 11039/3. L.43-44

86 The protocol of the investigation of P.Kresciunas. 1947 11 01 //LYA. B. 11039/3. L.22-23

87 LCVA. F 1753. Ap 3. B 13. L.10

88 Ibid. L.13

89 Ibid. L.18

90 Chayim Jofe. Mika// Valstieciu laikrastis. 1990 05 03

91 LCVA. F. 1753. Ap. 3. B.13. L. 58

92 Ibid. L.73

93 Ibid. L.148

94 Encyclopedia of the Jewish Communities in Lithuania (Hebrew) page. 328

95 LCVA. F.1753. Ap.3. B.4. L.27

96 Ibid.

97 The protocol of the investigation of J. Gepneris. 1945 08 23//LYA. B. 85/3. L. 19

98 The protocol of investigation of Mykolas Levickas. 1948 11 24//LYA. B.14142/3. L.47-48

99 The protocol of the confrontation of P. Kairaitis with the witness J. Keturauskas. 1948 06 21 //LYA. B. 16816. L.69-70

100 The protocol of the investigation of J. Gepneris. 1945 08 23//LYA. B.85/3. L.20

101 So it happened that Soviet Russia and other Soviet Republics became a refuge for Jews during World War II.

102 This was also the fate of Dobe Most-Rozenberg

103 Chayim Jofe's material.

104 Chayim Jofe. Antanina//sviesa. 1990 12 04

105 Chayim Jofe. Rachile// sviesa 1990 08 23

106 S.Rozentalis. Macijauskas // Ir be ginklo kariai (Fighters without arms). P.145-147

107 Chayim Jofe's material, existing in LVZMA

108 LCVA. F.1753. Ap. 3. B. 4. L. 26

109 The protocol of the investigation of P. Kairaitis. 1947 08 23 //LYA. B. 16816. L.53

110 Chayim Jofe. Mika// Valstieciu Laikrastis. 1990 04 26/ 05 03

111 Chayim Jofe. Niskutis // sviesa. 1990 10 11.

112 This conclusion is hypothetical: if 2,000 Jews resided in Jurbarkas before the war, of whom 76 survived (according to Chayim Jofe), then 1,924 perished.

113 Was killed on the front.

114 Died in 1997.

115 Emigrated to the USA.

117 The list is not complete, and further inquiry is necessary.

118 All the policemen mentioned in the list served in Jurbarkas.

MY LIFE, MY ENVIRONMENT, MY EPOCH

PASSAGES FROM ZE'EV BERNSTEIN`S AUTOBIOGRAPHICAL BOOK

By Dr. Ze'ev Bernstein (Nathania, Israel, 2000)

These passages are taken from the chapter "My Roots," based mostly on the author's father's, Boris Bernstein's (1895-1978) descriptions, as he told them to his children.

In the end of the nineteenth and the beginning of the twentieth century Yurburg was a little town in Lithuania with a population of about 2,000 to 3,000 people. Until it obtained its independence in 1918, Lithuania was a part of the Russian Empire and it was officially part of the "Province of Kovno" (Kovenskaya Guberniya).

Until 1917, when the Tsar`s regime was overthrown ("the February Revolution"), the highest representative of the central government in Yurburg was Prince Vasilshchikov, a relative of the Tsar, who conferred on him the rank of Prince and gave him a magnificent castle with a big park in the center of the town as well as all the lands in and around Yurburg. In the 1930s, after the Vasilshchikov family had lost all its riches, the prince`s son, who still called himself "prince," lived in Kovno in poverty and begged alms from the former "Yurbrikers." From time to time he used to come to our house and ask my father "for five litas." Every time his begging was accompanied by the words: "This time I will bring you the money back without fail."

In the beginning of the twentieth century Yurburg was a typical "shtetl," as they were depicted in the Jewish literature of the previous century, e.g. in the works of Sholem-Aleichem, Mendale Moicher Sforim, Yehuda-Leib Peretz, Peretz Smolenskin etc. The houses of Yurburg were mostly one-floor wood houses, most of the streets were not paved, and some of them were cobbled. There was no water main, and fresh water had to be drawn from wells. There was no sewage either. The "conveniences" - a small outhouse over a deep hole and a gap in the floor - were outside the houses.

Most of Yurburg`s inhabitants were poor Jews, mostly craftsmen or storekeepers. There were also woodcutters, water-carriers, laundresses etc. among the Jewish population of Yurburg. A special "class" were the town`s beggars: the shtetl and its environment were divided into "zones," every beggar (sometimes whole families) "worked" in his zone, and God forbid if a beggar were to "invade" another beggar`s territory!

One prominent person was the shtetl`s coachman, Bentse der Furman, owner and "operator" of the single means of conveyance of Yurburg.

The Jewish character of Yurburg was seen everywhere. As every "shtetl," Yurburg had its rabbi, its Dayan (religious judge), shochatim (butchers), chazonim (cantors), gaboim (managers of synagogues), shamoshim (attendants ot synagogues), maggidim (preachers) etc. There were three chadorim ("cheders," religious elementary schools) in Yurburg and the names of the melamdim (teachers) teaching in them (including their nicknames) were Shmuel-Yankl der Frishtik (Shmuel-Yankl the Breakfast), Zelig Tseebale (Zelig the Onion) and Hayim-Nossin der Krok (Hayim-Nossin with the slit in the pants). In Yurburg, like every other shtetl, every Jew had a nickname, mostly based on some distinctive characteristic - external or inner, and sometimes the surrounding people even did not know their fellows` surnames, but only their nicknames. Concerning the three "melamdim," it is not difficult to guess the origin of Hayim-Nossin`s nickname while those of his fellow-teachers are not clear (at least to me).

Among the "shamoshim" there was one called Ber der Soldat (Ber the soldier) who was always standing "at attention" during the prayer for the welfare of the Tsar. Asked for the reason of his strange behavior, he used to explain: "For 25 years I was eating the Tsar`s bread. Doesn`t he deserve that I stand "at attention" for him during 5 minutes a week?" The reason of this reverence was, that as a boy Ber was kidnapped by the Tsar`s kidnappers and forced to serve 25 years as a soldier: he was a so-called "cantonist."

Every week, at the beginning of the Shabbes, one of the shamoshim used to go all around the shtetl`s streets, knock at the windows and proclaim loudly and with a steady melody: "In shul arain!" (Come to the synagogue). Every Shabbes and holiday a delegation of Yurburg`s dignitaries used to pick up the shtetl`s rabbi from his house and lead him with songs through the shtetl`s streets to the synagogue.

There were two synagogues in Yurburg. One of them, called by the local Jews "Beis Medresh", was a massive brick building. The other, called "Di Groisse Shul" (the Big Synagogue) was a tall wooden structure built in 1790 and extended and renovated in 1870. Due to its architectural forms and especially to its inner design, which included artistic carving, it was one of the most magnificent and beautiful synagogues in Lithuania, and the "Yurbrikers" were proud of it.

When Lithuania was occupied by the Germans (1941), the Big Synagogue was destroyed and burned down by the local Lithuanians and the Germans. The "Beis Hamedresh" was turned into a storehouse.

Dr. Ze'ev Bernstein is a retired professor of linguistics at the Tel Aviv University. His father, Boris, was the head of the Kommertz Bank in Kovno.

In the Kovno Ghetto
THE HORRIBLE DAYS
The Story of Gita Abramson Bereznitzky
As told to and translated by Regina Borenstein Naividel

Below is the story of how Gita Abramson Bereznitzky (Gita's grandfather was Shmuel Naividel) survived the war, trapped in Kovno at the start of the war and living and surviving in the Kovno Ghetto until it was finally liberated. Part of her story she wrote down in Yiddish and read it to Regina Borenstein Naividel on Friday, November 16, 1994. Regina also asked her for additional details. Regina taped her while reading and questioning, and then translated her story.

Gita and Regina were both very moved while listening to her story. Again, it is only miraculous that she survuved.

How I saved myself from the Kovno Ghetto at the time of the destruction of the ghetto. It was in the last days of the liquidation of the Kovno Ghetto in July 1944. I am Gita Abramson Bereznitzky, born on August 8, 1919, in the town Yurburg, Lithuania.

Gita's Parents: Pesha Rochel (Niavidel) and Natan David Abramson (Town Photographer)

In the beginning of June 1941 I had come to Kovno from Shaulai for an operation. The war broke out while I was still in the Jewish Hospital of Kovno. I was able to walk again, so I went to my sister Bela, who then lived in Kovno on Vilnaer Street. We realized that we could not escape, and therefore we stayed in Kovno. We moved into the Ghetto in August 1941. I remained in the Ghetto from August 1941 until July 1944, from the beginning to the end, that is, from the time when it was established until the destruction of the Kovno Ghetto.   In the Ghetto I was recruited to the illegal anti-fascist partisan organization, led by the writer Chaim Yelin (who was ultimately captured by the Gestapo and died in their hands, possibly by suicide - according to Avraham Tory in his book <u>Surviving the Holocaust - The Kovno Ghetto Diary</u> page 500). As a member of the organization I obeyed every command. Since I was fair-haired, and looked like a non-Jew, I became a courier, a person who could easily pass in and out of the Ghetto without wearing the yellow star. Among those things that I did, I would go to the home of a non-Jewish woman in our organization, Mania Lishinzkene, a Lithuanian. She also was a courier and lived in Slabotke Viliampole, at 14 Ragutsha Street. She had a flat, where the responsible leaders of government and Ghetto organizations would meet, along with partisans and secret weapon dealers. At the end of June 1944, I was living at 8 Brolu Street in the Ghetto. This is the place where the fence was located (the border of the Ghetto) - on one side was Brolu street, and on the other side, outside the Ghetto, was a cemetery. Here it was easy to pass, but in order to pass, someone had to watch. Pesach Shatel and Joshke Mikles would watch when I would pass. Our friends Dima Gelpern (he still lives in Vilna), Lucy Zimmerman, Rochel Padeson lived together with me. It was right next to the Catholic cemetery. We were separated from the cemetery by a barbed wire fence, through which I would pass to go into the city without wearing the yellow star.

Mania Lishinzkene and Gita Abramson

Before the liquidation of the Ghetto, we, the surviving members of the organization, stayed in the Ghetto in a hiding place. In this hiding place, Dima Gelpern, (who now lives in Vilna), Pesach Shate (died) and Nina Finkelstein (died), Dr. Brauns with his family, myself and others stayed together. On July 13, 1944 the Germans discovered our hiding place. They ordered all of us to leave and to stand up in lines of four people in a row, and told us that we would be led to work. While standing in the row, I decided I would escape given the first opportunity. Each of us had one bottle of water, and a loaf of bread, but I gave this away. I didn't take it so that I could run more quickly. While we were being led through the Ghetto, I recognized Mania Lishinzke standing on the other side of the street. She also recognized me, and shouted to me: "Genia" (and she motioned to me with her hand). I had from the beginning decided that I had to risk an escape. While we were led through Panjeru Street and near a big garden, I quickly left the row and started to run. While running, I heard a shot, and at that moment I threw myself into a field of tall potato plants. I quickly threw away my coat with the yellow star, got up and continued to run. While I was running, a young Lithuanian ran after me and told me to stop. I thought that this was my end. He came running up to me and asked me whether I knew a woman named Sara and where she was. I answered him that I did not know her and continued running. In this moment, I saw that Nina Finkestein was running with me, and both of us turned in the direction to Mania's house. Mania was waited for us at her door, so that she could take us immediately to her hiding place, which was under the steps leading to her house. All this happened on July 13, 1944. In the same night, Lucy Zimmerman came to us; she had run from Alexot. All of us were very happy to have escaped and to be together. We slept over night and the next morning, one of us saw two German soldiers through the window. We crept into the hiding place, but Lucy went out through the door. (She looked Jewish). She crept through the fence into Mania's garden and hurt her foot. Later, she went to the Ghetto and saw that the Ghetto was burning. All this we heard only later. While there, the Russian collaborators recognized her. She was a very good looking, dark-haired, Jewish looking woman. Her foot was bleeding. They approached her and asked her for her documents, but unfortunately, she did not have any documents. She pointed to the house and told them that she lived there. When they came back to the house, Lucy asked Mania for the document, and said that Mania was her sister. "Mania, you are my sister" she cried, "give me the passport, help me." We were lying in the hiding place, and heard all that was being said above our heads. Mania called in one of the soldiers and offered him money, but he said that the older one was the commander and if he would take money, he also would agree. Unfortunately, when the second one entered the house, and heard that she offered him money, he shouted at her and said " you are a Jew too and you have to come with us." Mania also looked Jewish. Mania with her little son, Lucy and the soldiers left to the Ghetto. They were already standing against the wall waiting to be shot, when a Lithuanian neighbor of Mania's came after them and swore that she was not Jewish. Then, a German approached her and asked her for her passport. Mania answered that it was in her house in the cupboard. The German soldiers, Mania with the child and Lucy came back from the Ghetto to the house. The door of the cupboard was pulled open and Mania showed the Germans her passport. The Germans said to her: "Sorry, dear lady." Afterwards they left with Lucy to go back to the Ghetto. Lucy was shot afterwards. Lucy had called: "Mania, you are my sister. Give me the passport." Until today, I can hear these words in my ears, but nobody could help her. This was the end of the second day after the escape.

We heard through the floor what Mania said to herself: " Poor Lucy, such a good woman, what a tragedy." Afterwards, Mania opened one of the planks and told me to come out. She told me: "Genia, I have to talk to you. You see that my house is being watched, so you will have to leave." We stayed overnight and the next day she contacted friends in the city and one of them Mikolas Mustekin (this was his pseudonym) gave us an address in Kovno at 4 Lukshe Street, and the name of someone named Mattas. We did not know who Mattas was. The next day Mania dressed us up and brought us to Mattas using a different route. We arrived at a flat on the second floor. The owners of the flat had left for the country and gave it to their comrade Mattas, who carried a walking stick and wore blue glasses pretending to be blind. He greeted us and was very friendly to us. He cooked small flour dumplings for us. Mania and her son Vitas brought us food and cigarettes. Mania was like a mother to us, and her children were like our brothers and sisters. The oldest son Tadas and Vitas, the middle one treated us very well, without getting anything in return. All this was seemed quite natural for them, when in fact, they continually risked their lives for us.

A few days before the liberation of Kovno, which occurred on July 27, 1944, our dear friend Mattas did not come home to spend the night. We were very afraid and concerned and could not understand what had happened. The lock of the outer door was not in order, and so it was easy to enter the flat. Our window on the second floor was exactly opposite the gate of the courtyard. Nina and I decided that one of us would sleep and the other one would watch to see who would enter through the gate. When I was watching, I saw that Germans soldiers entered the courtyard. This was early in the morning. They knocked on the windows and called: "Get up, come out to work." I woke up Nina and we decided to creep into the attic, which could be locked with a key. We agreed that if they found us, we would say that we had escaped from Vilna, from the Russians. Then we waited in silence. Suddenly we heard a woman at the door say: "You, old man, don't have to be afraid. They are only looking for people who can work." To the Germans she said: "There is only an old man living here, and he is not at home." It was our luck that they left. From the anxiety I had very strong stomach cramps. I crept out of the attic and on my belly crept to the toilet. When I left the toilet I noted the sofa in the front room. I lifted the seat and saw that it contained a chest that was empty except for some soft potatoes. I told this to Nina and we decided that we had to hide in the chest in the sofa, and wait until dark until the siege ended. That is what we did. While we lay in the sofa, I put a soft potato between the lid of the chest and the seat, so that we would have air to breathe. We could not stop thinking about what might have happened to Mattas. Maybe he betrayed us? Later we heard a woman come to the flat looking for the old man. She spoke as if to herself: "Don't be afraid, the Germans have already left." I saw her feet through the opening. I cannot recall how long we were in the chest. Suddenly we heard the old man Mattas entering the flat with his stick. He went to the parrot, which was in a cage and noticed that the plaid cloth, which was on the sofa, was in a different position than before. He opened the sofa and saw us. What happiness that he had found us! With tears in his eyes he repeatedly said: "My dear girls, my good children." He told us that that night when he was coming home, he was called to work on the streets. He played a bit, pointing at his blue glasses and saying that he was totally blind and therefore could only walk with the stick and could not work. Thus, they let him go home. He was sure that they had already found us and taken us away. How happy he was to find us! The same day Mania's son Vitas came to us and brought us food. We asked him to have Mania take us back to her house and that is what happened. She again came to us, dressed us up and brought us to the river. Tadas brought us to the other side of the river, one at a time with a small boat. We could not pass the Slabotka Bridge, because one had to show documents, which we did not have. When we came to Mania, we met a Jewish man who was also hiding there. Mania had found him in a public toilet and taken him in to her house. She called him the "shitty one", because he was full of dirt when she found him. On July 31 at night Mania went out to the street and noted that it was totally quiet. Suddenly she noticed the Red Army. She started to call and we all left the house. We all run to the Soviet soldiers on the street and out of joy kissed and hugged them, not knowing what else to do. It is impossible to describe our joy. This we will always remember and tell that only because of them were we save.

I will never forget our dear "mother" Mania Lishinzke and her children who lived 14 Raguchal Street. Mania died on August 20, 1956, from an abscess. We attended her funeral, and accompanied her to her final resting-place.

(Regina asked Gita about the time before the war)

"I was in the Shomer HaZair (Young Watchman - a Zionist organization). I studied at the Gymnasium (secular high school) in Yurburg and I showed you the picture of my class. My best friend in Yurburg was Nuna Chaimovitch. In the Gymnasium we would dance together. I was the girl and she was the "Kozak". In Yurburg we spent a lot of time with the family. Meyerelie Naividel, my mother's first cousin, (and grandfather of your husband Benny Naividel) would come every Friday to our house. Also our friends from school would come - our house was always open and friendly. On Friday my mother would always prepare grey peas. It was a tradition. We would talk then and sing together."

"I was very active in several youth organizations. Then, in 1938 I went to Kovno. Before that I had worked in the Jewish Bank in Yurburg, with Sundelovitch. Afterwards he left for Kovno - there was a factory "Guma", and he was the main bookkeeper there. When he left, he asked me also to come. I worked there from 1938 and in 1940 I was sent to Shavel (Shaulai) in a department of Guma. I worked in this department. Later, the Soviets came and I was transferred from the department in Guma to the "Prokturatur", where I worked in the secretarial department. I worked there until I left for Kovno in June 1941 for my operation. I was there when the war started. My sister Bela lived in Kovno. I went to live with her. We left her flat and since it was late we went to a cellar on the street and were sitting there. Then, we asked ourselves what we were waiting for and so we left the cellar and went back to the flat, because I was still very weak. Shortly afterwards, the cellar was burned down. While sitting in her flat we were afraid, since I was an activist. My mother sent us a letter through somebody - my father was not alive any more by then. On July third the best Jewish men of Yurburg were gathered and murdered. My mother was still alive. She wrote that the "little one" should watch out, since she knew about my activities. Afterwards, my mother was also murdered. When the Ghetto was opened, Bela and I went there and found a place to stay at 5 Ershvuko Street, and we lived there. My sister and I worked. I worked on the airport and in the brigade. Bela married. Together with her husband Yosef Kaplan, she was taken to Alexot and from there to the concentration camp in Stutthof (they now live in Israel). I stayed in the Ghetto, in the organization. A lot of people left to join the partisans, but I was told that they needed me in the Ghetto, because I was fair-haired and could easily leave the Ghetto and act as a courier. "

"After the war I remained in Kovno and worked in the orphanage as a bookkeeper. In the beginning I was again called to work in the Prokuratur. There I worked as a secretary. They paid very little. In the Jewish orphanage I would get food as well, therefore I returned to work there. I did not have anything. Afterwards I left to live in Vilna. There I worked in a department of the Ministry of Health. Josef and I met at the end of 1946 and we were married so thereafter. In 1947 my son Aaron (Alik) was born. After my marriage and the birth of my son, I worked in various places as a bookkeeper. I also worked in a furniture department. I worked until I was 57 years old. On June 28, 1990 we came to live in Israel. "

Gita had written on Oct. 15, 1994, "During the war I was in the Kovno Ghetto together with my sister Bella. We went through an awful lot. Bella was also in the Stuthoff Concentration camp. I escaped from the Kovno Ghetto on July 13, 1944, the day they liquidated the Ghetto in Kovno. I was lucky enough, with the help of a Lithuanian woman, to hid out because I don't really look Jewish. After my sister Bella was freed from the camp, we both resided in Vilna. .... Bella and I with our families are now residing in Israel for the last four years."

Gita Abramson Bereznizky lived with her husband Yosef in Kiron. Their son Aaron (Alik), a psychologist, lives with his family in Kfar Sava, Israel. They immigrated to Israel from Vilna in 1990, along with Gita's sister, Bella Abramson Kaplan.

Gita Abramson Bereznitzky died in August 2000, in Tel Aviv, Israel.

Documents of Her Life

Courtesy of her Nephew Ashley Levinsohn

Ashley Levinsohn reports that his Aunt Hadassa Heussinger (nee Levinsohn) died in December 1999 in Rehovot, Israel. Among her possessions the family found many papers and certificates including her high school graduation certificate and her student identification and also many photographs. These documents reflect the major events in her life.

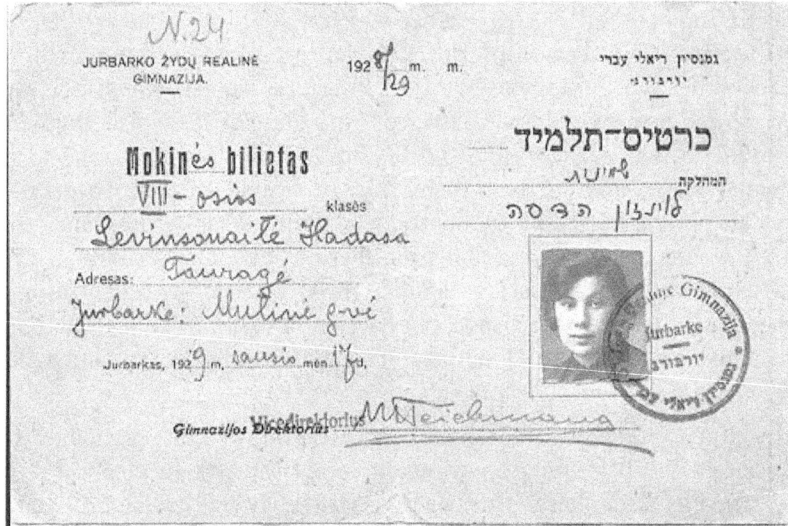

Student Identification Card for the Yurburg Gymnasium

7th Class (Mahlaka) 28th November 1927. Written on the back "Hadassa Levinsohn 7th Class in memory of the day we did not attend the Gymnasium because of the famous 'Soldaritet' dated 6 Jan 28.

Certificate from the Reali Hebrew Gynmasium of Kovno for Hadassah Levinsohn

Third Graduating Class of the Hebrew Gynasium (High School) of Yurburg, 1929

Hadassa Heussinger (nee Levinsohn, aunt of Ashley Levinsohn) is pictured second from the top second from the left.

Bottom row, left to right: Meir Leviosh, Golomowitz, Kaplan, S. Hasklelovitz, Picture of School, L. Shtock, N. Ess, Rachel Laviosh, Leviteh.

Second row from bottom, left to right: G. Kovlakovskit, R. Petrokanskit, H. Baron, J Dambo, Tzikovski, A Altman, T. Haimowitz, Moskowitz.

Third row, left to right: B. Feinberg, H. Levinsohn, Navossitis, Dr. Rotshtein, Y. Lerman, D. Pinkus, Mendlewitz, Bluma Heskelovitz.

Top row, left to right: Weinberg, Colombus, A. Liptziger, Headmaster Engineer D. Chen, Deputy Headmaster Y. Tuchman, H. Lintofski, H. Shachnovitz, Y. Zachar

Exit Permit from Lithuania of Hadassah Levinsohn - Nov. 12, 1933

Hadassah made aliyah to Palestine.

No. 113029/5.   IDENTITY CARD

Name of holder ____ HADASSA
HEUSINGER

Signature
holder _Hadasa Heusinger_

Place of residence _Rehovoth_
Weizman Street
Place of business ____
Occupation _House-wife_
Race _Jewish_
Height _5_ feet _7_ inches
Colour of eyes _brown_
Colour of hair _brown_
Build _normal_ Age _31_
Special peculiarities ____
Signature
issuing officer ____
Appointment ____
Place _Tel-Aviv_ Date _28.7.41_

GOVERNMENT OF PALESTINE

IDENTITY CARD

GPP. 6845—50,000—29-10-38 873/S.

Palestine Identity Card of Hadassah Levinsohn Heusinger

Hadassah Levinsohn Heusinger died in Dec. 1999 in Rehovot, Israel.

Naividel - Krelitz - Eliashevitz Families

**By Joel Alpert, Son of Lee Golda Ellis Alpert,
Grandson of Harry Ellis (Hillel Eliashevitz) and Celia Krelitz Ellis,
Great-grandson of Miriam Naividel Eliashevitz and Leah Naividel Krelitz,
Great-great-grandson of Hillel Naividel**

I am a grandchild of Yurburg. I was born in Madison, Wisconsin in the United States in 1944. My maternal grandparents immigrated from Yurburg to the United States on August 4, 1903; they were Harry Ellis (Hillel Eliashevitz) and Celia (Bat-Sheva) Krelitz and they were first cousins, both grandchildren of Hillel Naividel of Yurburg. Consequently, my "recollections" of Yurburg are from an entirely different perspective than those presented in the original Hebrew-Yiddish Yurburg Yizkor Book.

I was fortunate to have sat with my grandfather, Harry Ellis in 1968 and had a discussion about the "family in the old country." Based upon notes and a family tree that my sister, Niki Alpert (McCurry), and I drew up that day, I created a rather large computerized family tree in the early 1990s. It was large because my grandparents had 15 siblings between them and, in addition, my grandfather knew his aunts and uncles and their families well. After reassembling the family on the computer, I then continued to try to find out more about their town, Yurburg. It was during my search that I found the Yurburg Yizkor Book.

When I was growing up, I never heard of any family left in Yurburg, or of anybody in the family who fell victim during the Shoah. I always thought that my family was spared. Only on that day in 1968, when my grandfather mentioned that he and my grandmother each coincidentally had brothers by the name of Meyer, who had remained in Yurburg, and they each had "large families who were lost," only on that day did I learn the truth. Later, as I dug deeper to discover more about our "lost" family, I found out more. Ultimately, I found our Mexican relatives who still had letters written before the war, begging for papers to help them escape their horrible fate (presented in another article later in this book).

It should be noted that the name Krelitz is likely derived from the shtetl of Korelichi (Karelitz) in Beylorussia, 101 km SW of Minsk (n.b. Dov Levin).

I found out that Hillel Naividel had five children from his first wife: Shemuel Naividel; Shalom Naividel; Sarah Beyle who married her step-brother Yitskhak Rosin; Mary (Miriam) who married Shelomoh Elyashevitz (Eliashevitz); Leah who married Cecil Krelitz and Hana Rochel, who married Yankel Bass (I present these facts as best I have been able to figure out). There is a family story, likely true, that Hillel immigrated to New York, probably in the 1860s, earned money to bring his wife to America, but she found the place unacceptable, and they returned to Yurburg. Forty years later, many of their Krelitz and Elyashevitz (Eliashevitz), grandchildren made the same trip and stayed. They settled first in Altoona, Pennsylvania, then in Northern Minnesota, some as merchants on the Messabi Iron Range, and finally in Minneapolis, Milwaukee and Detroit. Some of Hillel's grandchildren, who by a twist of fate did not leave in time, were murdered together with their families in Yurburg and other towns.

Shelomoh and Leah Elyashevitz (Eliashevitz) had 7 children, 6 of whom immigrated to the United States. Cecil and Leah Krelitz had 10 children, 7 of whom immigrated to the United States.

Krelitz family in Yurburg - 1920s

Same photo is on the back cover of this book.

[Photo on the web that was found by Max Sherman -Krelitz]

Top Row from left: Lieb Krelitz, his father Meir Krelitz, Lieb Zarnitsky, his son, Max Zarnitsky, Aaron Abramson, his father Yosef Abramson, his brother-in-law.

Bottom Row from left: Rivka Krelitz (daughter of Meir), Elka Krelitz Zarnitsky, Masha Krelitz Abramson, sister of Joseph Abramson. Meyer, Elka and Masha Krelitz were siblings to Ben, Bill, Celia, Chereva and Rae Krelitz who immigrated to America.

Only Max Zarnitsky and Aaron Abramson survived the Shoah.

Hillel's second wife was Elka Rosin, and they had one daughter, Pesha, who married Avraham Meyer Zapolsky, also from Yurburg or Sudarg. They settled in Detroit. One of Elka's sons from her first marriage Yitshak Rosin married Sarah Beyle Naividel, his stepsister.

On a trip to Israel in 1994, I was fortunate to talk to Shimon Shimonov in Tel Aviv (one of the people contributed to the creation of the Yurburg Yizkor Book), and mentioned the Naividel name. He led me to Benny Naividel, son of Mordehai Naividel (later we determined that he was a descendant of Shalom Naividel, one of Hillel's sons). Initially, Benny and I could not make the family connection. I had mentioned that my Great-Great Grandfather was Hillel Naividel, and Benny responded that his uncle was also named Hillel Naividel. We realized that there must be a connection. Then I recalled that Jack Cossid had mentioned that there were two Naividel brothers who were attorneys, Mota and Lushka. Benny said that his father Mordechai was called Mota, and his uncle Hillel's was called Lushka. Finally, we made the connection realizing that Benny's grandfather was Meyer, and he was listed on our family tree. Benny's wife, Regina researched the Yurburg connections in Israel and found many descendants of Shemuel Naividel in Israel, including Gita Abramson Bereznitsky and her sister Bela Abramson Kaplan, who had immigrated to Israel from Lithuania in 1990. Benny was born in Lithuania after the war; his father, Mordehai was a "Prisoner of Zion" of the Soviets. The family immigrated to Israel in the late 1970s. The family connections had been severed when my grandparents left Yurburg in 1903 shortly before Mordehai was born, and we had no group memory of this branch of the family.

We knew that Meyer Krelitz, my grandmother's brother, who remained in Yurburg, had two daughters that survived because they immigrated to Mexico in the 1920s and 1930s. Our contact with them had been lost. I had placed a notice on the Internet along with a 1920s family photo from Yurburg, shown above, with a note that I was searching for that Mexican Krelitz family. In 1995, Max Sherman-Krelitz, son of one of those daughters, spotted my note on the web. His mother had been so distraught by loosing everyone from her family, except her one sister, that she could not bring herself to discuss any family with her children. Max and his sister Esther knew nothing of the large Krelitz family in the US, until he spotted the 1920 photo with an identical image of his grandfather Meyer, as the one which hung in his home in Mexico City. We have now established contact and visited both in Milwaukee and in Mexico City. Max's story appears later in this book.

Based upon the expanded family tree, family reunions were organized and held in Minneapolis in 1998 with 85 people attending, in Detroit in 2000 with 135 people, and in Milwaukee in 2002 with 100 people. There was also a reunion held in Israel in 1998 with about 20 people attending. These reunions included not only descendents of Aaron Naividel, Moshe Krelitz but also Elka Rosin and Naftali Fainberg (Feinberg). All these Yurburg families had multiple marriages between them. It was these families that donated generously to the translation effort of this Yizkor book and we express our sincere gratitude to all of them.

While in Vilna, Zalman Kaplan, a Yurbriker, found us, having been informed by Duba Most Rosenberg. After spending hours with us, telling us stories of our ancestors and cousins, whom he personally knew, he left us saying that we were the first group of Yurburgers that he ever met since the war and that "when he leaves this world, and joins all his family and friends in the next world, he'll be able to tell them that he met a group of Yurburg descendants looking for their roots and their town." We were all in tears.

Krelitz family in the United States - 1930s

Ben, Bill, Celia, Cheriva, and Rae Krelitz

Meyer Elyashevitz family in 1902. All murdered in the Shoah

Yurburg descendants with Zalman Kaplan in Vilna Jewish Museum in May 2001

Zalman telling Itzhak Zarnitsky of Zalman's memories of Itzhak's grandparents in Yurburg

**Headstones of Leah Naividel Krelitz and Sarah Beyle Naividel Rosin
(sisters) in the Yurburg Jewish Cemetery**

Through the connections formed in these families and at the reunions, and with the publishing of this book in English, the spirit and memory of Yurburg will be carried forth into the future.

Boston, Massachusetts, USA   January 8, 2002

Itzhak Zarnitsky and Joel Alpert

Leah Krelitz great-grandsons at her grave in May 2001

(Probably the first descendants to visit her grave since the Shoah)

Portrait of Leah Naividel Krelitz

**Great-Grandmother of Yitzhak Zarnitsky and Joel Alpert, above at her
headstone in the Yurburg Jewish Cemetery**

HOME ON THE RANGE

The Mesabi Iron Range

**By S. Aaron Laden,
Son of Bernard Laden,
Grandson of Sarah Ellis Ladin,
Great-grandson of Miriam Naividel Eliashevitz,
Great-great-grandson of Hillel Naividel**

July, 2000

INTRODUCTION

The early decades of the twentieth century witnessed the migration of portions of the Eliashevitz and Krelitz families of Yurburg, Lithuania and the eventual settling of that family in the midwestern United States cities of Detroit, Milwaukee, Minneapolis, and Chicago. The reasons that the migrants came to America, and the unfortunate consequences for those who didn't, are amply documented elsewhere in this book.

It was a youthful and vigorous family that made the voyage. A less energetic family likely could not have made the transition to a new life in a strange new land. And strange it was. The odyssey took nearly thirty years in a land of red rocks, towering virgin forests, deep ice and snow, and rib-cracking cold. The inhabitants of that land spoke many strange tongues, they had curiously straight yellow-white hair, they ate forbidden foods, and they had many curious customs. The land was called "Mesabi," an Ojibwa Indian word for "giant," and it proved to be a giant transition for the descendants of Hillel Naividel from Yurburg, Lithuania.

Open Pit Mine on the Mesabi Iron Range - Virginia Minnesota

THE MESABI IRON RANGE

The Mesabi Iron Range in northern Minnesota was opened in 1892 to harvest a vast expanse of rich hematite ore. It is the largest of three iron ranges in Minnesota and, in its heyday, accounted for one-quarter of the world's production of iron ore.

The range is perhaps 70 miles long and 40 miles wide running east to west. The mines were enormous open pits of red hematite ore. The ore was piled into rail cars and shipped 60 miles to Duluth. The ore was placed on ships eastward bound to provide the iron ore for the steel mills of Gary, Indiana and Pittsburgh, Pennsylvania.

A great spiral of railroad tracks descending into the abyss ringed the walls of each pit. During the warmer months, when the mines could be worked, dynamite charges were set to blast the ore free. Huge steamshovels scooped up the ore and piled it into rail cars to be shipped downhill sixty miles to the port in Duluth, Minnesota. There the hoppers were discharged from specially constructed ore piers onto ships bound to the east through the Great Lakes for the blast furnaces of Gary, Indiana and Pittsburgh, Pennsylvania. As mines were worked out, new mines were opened at other points along the range, and new mining camps sprang up. Some of these camps were destined to become incorporated towns, and some have persisted to this very day. The mine at Hibbing, Minnesota was so successful that, as the pit expanded, it ran headlong into the town itself. The entire town was moved to make way for the mine.

The mines were operated by huge concerns like the United States Steel Corporation. They needed a robust work force for an arduous and dangerous job in a remote wilderness previously populated only by Indians and wild beasts. They recruited young men mainly from Scandinavia and the Balkans. The population of the camps was said to be 90% male. They worked long shifts separated from their families for months or years. Naturally, paydays could be wild and boisterous occasions that were often good for business.

Among the early settlers on the range were a small number of Jewish merchants who came to fill the miners' needs for food, clothing, and household goods. Among these men and women were those with names like Ellis (Eliashevitz in Yurburg), Ladin, Loceff, Lippman (Naividel in Yurburg), Bernstein, and Bankman, all Litvaks, and many from Yurburg, Lithuania. With the nearest large city sixty impassable miles away, the miners depended upon the local merchants for their supplies. Without these businesses, the miners would have been at the mercy of the steel companies for both livelihood and provisions.

Today the land that comprises the range is a band of low hills of elevation 300-500 feet that is pitted by huge crater-like mines and studded with mountains and mesas of rubble tailings. At least one of the worked-out mines (Kinney) has been reclaimed as a recreational lake, though on a visit in July 1998, no actual people were observed recreating there. Originally covered with white pine virgin forest, the timber has been substantially cleared for mines, roads, towns, construction, and not least, for firewood to heat homes and to power trains and steam shovels.

THE FAMILY THAT TAMED THE RANGE

Mary Naividel Eliashevitz and two grandchildren

Mary died Nov. 14, 1934, at age 85 and is buried in Detroit in Chesed Shalom Cemetery on Gratiot Ave., Mt. Clemens, MI. (outside Detroit).

Six sons and daughters of Mary Naividel Eliashevitz (all from Yurburg) and their nuclear families formed the core of the Naividel descendents who came to live on the range. Ultimately, only one son, Meyer, and his family remained to live out their days in Europe. Mary was preceded by several of her children. Others who lived on the range were cousins, the Lippmans (Naividel in Yurburg), the Bankmans, and Ben Craine (Yurburg). A picture of Mary Naividel Eliashevitz is seen at above with two of her grandchildren (photo probably taken in 1920).

George Krelitz

The vanguard of the Naividel descendents in America was George Krelitz who opened a business in Altoona, Pennsylvania. Altoona was an important stopover on the way to the iron country.

Photo of the Krelitz-Lippman Store

Sam and Rae (Krelitz) Ellis with Ben Craine

The first to arrive on the range was Sam Ellis who immigrated in 1897, stopping in Williamsburg, PA in the "general store business" from 1897-99 and in Altoona where he worked at the Guarantee Clothing Company from 1899-1901. He then opened the Ellis Haberdashery Company in Duluth, Minnesota.

Broadway Department Store on the Range:
Sam Ellis and Ben Craine in front left and center

Bill Krelitz, Sam Ellis and Celia Ellis on the left

Inset from above - "The Naividel Mafia on the Range"

Sam Ellis became the first of the Naividel family living on the range to become a naturalized United States Citizen in 1902 (1920 U.S. Census) and the first Naividel to live on the range when he moved to Eveleth, Minnesota in 1903 and opened a general store. Harry Ellis (Hillel Eliashevitz in Yurburg), Celia Krelitz, and Rae Krelitz (all grandchildren of Hillel Naividel of Yurburg) arrived in New York on August 4, 1903 on the liner *Kronprinz Wilhelm*, having departed from Bremen, Germany. Family lore tells of Hillel Naividel immigrating to New York (likely in the 1860s) and returning when his wife, upon arrival decided that the American life was not religious enough.

Although Harry did not reside in Minnesota until 1905 (Naturalization petition, 12/3/1914), Rae apparently proceeded directly to Eveleth where she and Sam were married.

Sam was listed as residing in Gilbert, Minnesota on a May 23,1911 when he witnessed a Petition for Naturalization filed by his brother Harry Ellis. He was subsequently recorded as living in Eveleth, Minnesota on November 18, 1911 when he signed as a character witness on Benjamin Craine's Petition for Naturalization.

A birth certificate for a female "Baby Ellis" born alive on July 27, 1916 shows Sam and Rae living in Eveleth, in a house they owned. Their son Myron Ellis was born in Minnesota in 1918 (1920 Census). At the time of the 1920 Census, Sam and Rae were living with Lillian Golda, Rosalin, and Shalby in Eveleth. The family thereafter remained continuously in Eveleth until moving to Milwaukee in 1928.

Harry Ellis (Hillel Eliashevitz) and Celia (Bat Sheva Krelitz) Ellis
[Maternal grandparents of Joel Alpert, Editor of this volume.]

On February 5,1905, Harry Ellis became a resident of Eveleth, Minnesota (Petition for Naturalization, 5/23/1911). Harry and Celia were married in 1913, and the following year. One year later, their first son, George Ellis was born.

United States Citizenship was granted to Harry and Celia in 1916. Their first daughter Leah Golda (Lee) was born in 1917 (named after Leah Naividel Krelitz, her grandmother). [Leah Golda Ellis was the mother of Joel Alpert, Editior of this volume.] Sholem (Sidney) Ellis was born on the range in 1920 followed by Helen R. (Babe) Ellis in 1924. The family departed the range for Milwaukee in 1927. It is interesting to note that on most of the birth certificates, Yiddish and Hebrew names were used.

The Fair Store, business of Harry and Sam Ellis in Eveleth, Minnesota

The picture is a recent image, taken about 1995. The Fair Store operated by Sam and Harry Ellis in Eveleth (photo by Howard Bern).

Sarah Ellis and Morris Ladin

Bernard Laden, 17 years old

Sarah Reva Eliaschevitz was known to have been on the range since around July 1, 1906, her wedding She married Morris Ladin of Chisholm, Minnesota, a 1901 immigrant from Sveksna, Lithuania which was some 30 miles from Sarah's hometown of Yurburg. Sarah probably emigrated around 1902 (Bernard Laden, personal communication, 2000). Morris was a door-to-door peddler of dress goods and supplies. Ready-made clothes were not yet available on the range. (Sally Ladin Bell. *The Ladin Family: Pioneers of Chisholm, Minnesota*, Self-published, 1983.)

"Sarah Elias" of "Mt. Iron" (Mountain Iron, Minnesota on the map) was married in "Mt. Iron" according to her Marriage Certificate. A year later, their first child Sadie was born in Chisholm. Sadie was the first of the native born "Mesabi rangers" in the family, having been born on the iron range. A forest fire destroyed the town of Chisholm on September 8, 1908. More than eighty percent of the buildings were consumed.

1908 is likely the year that Sarah became a United States citizen since a woman's citizenship was the same as her husband, and Morris is thought to have become a citizen in that year. The family soon thereafter moved to Kinney, Minnesota where a new mine was opening. Morris purchased the second lot sold in the town, the corner of Main and Maple Streets where he opened a dry goods store. The family lived behind the store on Maple Street. The family was known to reside in Kinney as early as 1910 when Morris was elected a trustee of the town.

Laden Store, with Morris Laden and his four children, 1914, Kinney, MN

Sarah's second child, Jeannette, was born in Minneapolis in 1909, but her two younger children, Lillian (1911) and Bernard (1913) were both born in Kinney, a distinction that few can claim. The children with Morris are lined up in the photo above, left to right: Jeannette, Sadie, Lillian, and Bernard. Kinney was not so much a town as it was a mining camp. Notice the incline on Main Street as it slopes down to the mine. Bernard sledded this street in winter.

The family fortunes rose and fell with the economic activity of the mine, and the family moved to the neighboring town of Buhl in 1924. 1928 saw a move to Grand Rapids, Minnesota at the headwaters of the Mississippi River, then Virginia, Minnesota in 1930, and finally Milwaukee, Wisconsin in 1931.

During 1931-32, Bernard Laden lived with the Ben Bankman family (cousins from Yurburg) in Virginia as he completed his studies at Virginia Junior College, before he too, moved to Milwaukee to continue his education and be with the rest of the family.

Jenny Ellis and Max Loceff

Jenny Ellis arrived in America with her sister Fanny and her mother Miriam (Mary) in 1907.) Two of her children were native Mesabi rangers.

Sanford was born in 1912 in Chisholm and Reva in 1914. The family lived above their store across the street from The Fair Store (pictured above), Sam and Harry Ellis's clothing store. They moved to Minneapolis in 1921.

Fanny arrived in America in 1907. She and Max Bernstein (also from Yurburg) were married in 1910 and their four sons were all born on the range: Sanford in 1912, Howard in 1915, Leslie in 1920, and James in 1922. They owned and operated a butcher shop, in Eveleth. Fanny became a naturalized United States Citizen in 1925, the same year that she and her sons moved to Detroit.

Mary Ellis and Fanny Ellis Bernstein with offspring

Reuven was the last of Mary Naividel Eliaschevitz' children to immigrate to the United States and to the iron range. Reuven arrived on the *Kronprinz Wilhelm* from Bremen on May 28, 1913 like his brother and sisters-in-law ten years earlier.

Various documents uncovered during the 1998 visit to the Iron Range Research Center in Chisholm show an impressive range of spellings for both Rueven's first and last names. His signatures reflect the same bewildering array of spellings. Eliashiewitz, Eliashewitz, Elisajewicz all appear. Rubin and Reuvin are predominating, but his name even appears as Robert on a birth certificate for Meyer.

Reuven married Alta Feinberg (also from Yurburg) in Europe and they had four children all born in Yurburg: Solomon born 1907, Abraham (Max) 1909, Milton (Robert) 1911, and Jacob (Joe) in 1913. The family remained in Yurburg when Reuven came to the United States in 1913. World War I intervened, and it was not until after 1920 that Reuven was able to bring them to America. A naturalization petition dated July 24, 1920 showed Chia Faiga (Alta) and four sons all still in Yurburg.

At last, Reuven's family arrived sometime in 1920 or early 1921. Reuven and Alta's fifth son, Meyer, was born in Eveleth on November 2, 1921. Reuven's occupation was listed as "dry goods merchant." Reuven's name was erroneously listed as "Robert" Ellis on the birth certificate. Meyer was good-naturedly welcomed by the family and hence was known as "Mr. America" as the only one of Reuven and Alta's children born in the new land and after a protracted struggle to emigrate. Reuven and Alta are pictured below with children and grandchildren.

Other Family Members on the Range

Brothers Sam and Henry Lippman (the name was Naividel in Yurburg and somehow was changed to Lippman upon entering the United States)) and their sister Ethel lived on the range. Sam and Henry both appear as witnesses on naturalization papers (Sam on Harry Ellis' petition, 5/23/1911 and again 12/3/1914; Henry on Reuvin Ellis' petition, 7/24/1920). Each is listed as "merchant" living in Virginia, Minnesota.

Ethel Lippman became Ben Bankman's bride and the mother of Julius (1907), Pearl (1913), Jack (1914), and Sam (1916). Ben Bankman also signed as a witness for Reuven Ellis' naturalization petition of July 20, 1920 and listed himself as a "merchant" residing in Virginia, Minnesota. Bernard Laden, son of Sarah Eliashevitz, remembers the Bankman children all as brilliant students. He lived with the Bankman family in Virginia during 1931-32, his final year at Virginia Junior College (now Mesabi Community College)(personal communication, 2000). Others who apparently lived on the range included Ben Lippman who reportedly ran a clothing store in Hibbing (account of Rosalin Ellis Krelitz).

Documents show that Ben Craine came to the United States on the ship *Grosser Carfirst* on March 1, 1905. He sailed from Bremen, Germany on February 17, 1905 and disembarked at the Port of New York. He took up residence in Minnesota on February 5, 1907. On May 23, 1911, Ben petitioned for citizenship when living in Virginia, MN. He listed his occupation as "clerk." On March 16, 1912, Benjamin Craine was "admitted to become a citizen of the United States of America," having renounced allegiance to "foreign prince, potentate, state, or soveignty, and particularly to Nicholas II the Emperor of all the Russias." A notice from the U.S. Department of Labor, Bureau of Naturalization dated May 2, 1927 indicates Ben Craine's address as 246 Alexandrine Street, E., Detroit, Michigan.

As of 1998, the only known relative still residing on the Mesabi Range was Sam Bankman, retired physicist, living in Virginia.

Life on the Mesabi Iron Range

The Ellis family and their relatives from Yurburg practiced Orthodox Judaism. They spoke Yiddish at home. Yiddish was not, however, the language of the mines, the schools, or the general community. Bernard Laden recounts that his oldest sister Sadie had to repeat kindergarten for lack of English language skills (personal communication, 2000).

Keeping kosher was considered an important obligation, but it was a practical feat of endurance and devotion. Several *shochet* (ritual slaughterers) lived on the range in the larger towns. Bernard Laden tells of having to carry a live chicken purchased at a farmers market a mile or two to the streetcar station. He took the chicken on the streetcar to the *shochet* in Eveleth or Virginia to be properly dispatched, after which he returned home with the blessed chicken parts.

Sam Ellis was an important member of the Jewish community in Eveleth, having served as president and secretary of the congregation. Eveleth had established the first of four synagogues on the range in 1900, though all of the Jewish communities were small and struggling. The congregation met in homes until eventually purchasing and converting a church for worship. The most impressive physical structure was the brick synagogue built in 1909 in Virginia, which is on the National Register of Historic Places and still exists. A rabbi was even harder to come by. There was a regular rabbi in Virginia from 1909-1915, but rabbis were employed only from time to time thereafter. The Jewish population of the range was counted as 800 in the 1910 census, including 121 in Virginia and 145 in Eveleth. The other two synagogues were located in Hibbing and Chisholm. It was not until the 1950's that a Jewish cemetery was consecrated at Virginia. The synagogue in Virginia was still in operation as of 1991 (Marilyn Chiat "Entrepreneurs and Immigrants: Life on the Industrial Frontier of Northeastern Minnesota" Iron Range Resources and Rehabilitation Board, 1991).

The mining companies and lumber companies played major political and economic roles in the communities. There was sometimes tension between the miners and their union organizers and the mine owners. Jewish merchants sometimes found themselves in the awkward position of sympathizing with the miners but not wanting to arouse the anger of the mine bosses (Marilyn Chiat). Bernard Laden commented that on election days, the miners were told to report to work on the following day if the Republican candidate won (unpublished written recollections). On the other hand, the mining companies were the economic lifeblood of the range. Not only did they provide employment for the merchants' customers, but they also paid the bulk of local taxes. The tax base supported an outstanding public school system. The new Hibbing High School built in 1923 cost a million dollars and had an indoor swimming pool. Virginia, in 1913, had the largest residential steam heating system in the world - steam heat pumped into private residences. This was a significant advantage over a wood-burning stove. (www.virginia-mn.com/history.html)

Leisure time was in short supply. Bernard Laden commented that he was not aware of any. Available time was spent on business, child-rearing, household chores, and religious observance. For children, there was baseball in the street in Kinney during the month or two of summer. Other summer amusements included chopping wood for the winter. In winter, there was chopping the ice off of the woodpile, and carrying wood into the house and carrying ashes out. Snow had to be shoveled and the fire tended. Winter was also the season for ice skating and sledding. Bernard Laden talks of sledding down Main Street in Kinney with no concern for traffic. There was none. Cars had to be propped up on blocks and all fluids drained for the winter. It was too cold and icy to operate a car. Morris Ladin had one of the first cars in the town of Kinney and Sarah Ladin had one of the first washing machines.

Family visits took place on Sundays when the stores were closed. Travel between towns was difficult and time consuming. Traveling was undertaken with trepidation. Automobile suspensions and tires were unyielding, and trips were punishing for the traveleres. Trips of seventy-five miles took all day, and to complete such a trip without a blowout was a remarkable occurrence that was repeatedly remarked upon. Starting a car could be a dangerous enterprise with the manual cranks that could snap back when the engine fired. Many arms were broken in the successful attempt.

Homes were plain wooden structures. The Ladin home in Kinney was a four-room house behind the store on Maple Street. It had a bathroom added on and was the first in town to have indoor plumbing. Other homes had outhouses. The house was illuminated by solitary unshielded incandescent bulbs hanging from each ceiling. A wood-burning stove supplied heat and cooking facilities.

Moving Away

What became of the hard but picturesque life on the range? Why did these families who arrived with so much enthusiasm and against such odds decide to pick up and leave in the late 1920s? Did the great depression arrive early on the range? Perhaps it did. Even in the good years, maintaining a store in these small towns was a risky proposition. The mines began to play out their easy pickings of rich hematite ore, and it was not until the 1950's that a commercially feasible means of processing the lower grade taconite ore was developed (aided by state tax concessions begun in 1964). Morris Ladin suffered a series of financial setbacks triggering a series of moves from town to town in the 1920s. The other Ellis families had all left the range by 1928.

Was it because the children of the iron range pioneers were reaching their teenage years and early twenties and their parents realized that there were few social prospects for eligible young Jews? Was it because the immigrant generation had worked to make a better life for their children, and the better life was in the bustling cities of the Midwest? These questions remain unanswered.

Reuven Ellis and Alta Feinberg Family in Detroit

A 1998 VISIT TO THE RANGE

Following the 1998 Niavidel Family Reunion of these close knit Yurburg families in Minneapolis, I went with my sister Shirley Laden Marcus and my brother Ben Laden to visit the Mesabi range to see it with my own eyes and to attempt to make sense of a lifetime of tales of forty degrees below zero winter days and open pit mines. Apparently, others independently had the same idea. Joel Alpert (son of Leah Ellis Alpert), his sister Niki Alpert McCurry, and her husband Alan McCurry also made the trip.

On Sunday afternoon following the reunion, Shirley, Ben, and I drove up to the range and found a hotel room near Eveleth. On Monday morning we made a beeline for Virginia where my father had lived in 1930-2 while attending Virginia Junior College. In July, Virginia was a tired but substantial little town. Much of the commerce of the area has shifted to strip malls and warehouse shopping stores along U.S. 169, the main highway through the range. A giant loon floats on the lake downtown. On the shore is an old train station that has been converted to a bank building.

We walked around the town and came across the public library where we whiled away a couple of hours reading about the history of the region and checking old city directories without intending to do any serious research. We did find Harry Ellis and Sam Ellis in a 1920 directory showing their Jones Street addresses. There is probably a quite a bit more about the family that might be discovered there.

Ellis Clan in Detroit in the early 1930s: Alta, Mary, Harry, Celia, Reuven Ellis, Jennie (Ellis) and Max Loceff

As we walked back to the car we came to the main thoroughfare and were preparing to cross the street, but for some reason, we kept to the left and walked past the Hotel Coates. As we did so, Ben spied a familiar figure in the hotel dining room. It was Joel Alpert whom we had not expected to see for another two years at the next family reunion. Inside, we found that Joel, Niki, and Alan were holding forth with Sam Bankman, the sole remaining Naividel relative living on the range. Sam had been a physicist working at Los Alamos during World War II, but had returned years ago to Virginia to run the family clothing business. Sam Bankman took us to see the Jewish cemetery in Virginia. We were not aware of any Naividel descendents buried there, and we didn't see any. The family had moved from the iron range before there were any deaths in the family (to our knowledge).

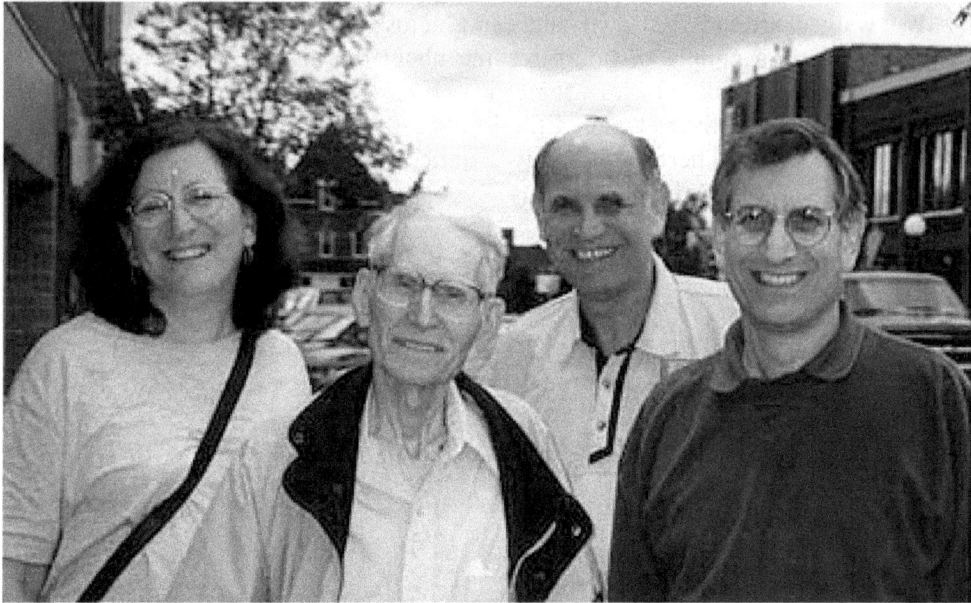

Shirley Laden Marcus, Sam Bankman, Ben and Sam Laden in Virginia, Minnesota (1998)

From Virginia, we all went on to Kinney, my father's birthplace. He had described to me how to identify the lot where the store was located. He said, "Start at the mine at the end of Main Street, and go two blocks. You'll see it on the corner." He had not been there in sixty-five years, but we had no difficulty in identifying the site on the corner of Main and Maple. Where the "Ladin's Store" once stood, there is now a simple garage. It is diagonally across the street from the firehouse that still stands but appears closed except for some town offices upstairs. There once was a theater on another of the corners at this intersection, but it is now gone. A boarded-up hulk of a brick storefront is directly across Main from the store site, and a stamp-sized post office stands next to it. This intersection was clearly the center of gravity of the Town of Kinney. There were only one or two other intersections to choose from. As we milled about the street marveling at the sights, we were the only people about. There were no other cars. The curtains in a mobile home across the street were pushed furtively aside and then closed. We ventured down toward the mine where a couple of one-story corrugated steel buildings housed a St. Louis County office building and the Kinney Public Library. Across the street from the library was the town's only business establishment, a bar.

In the library, we found some townspeople, two friendly men probably in their early seventies, who were pleased to tell us about the town. One was a Serb who had come to Kinney as a youngster shortly after my father left. He told of boom days at the mine when the town boasted of five grocery stores and five brothels. In an impromptu ceremony, he accepted from us on behalf of the Town of Kinney a copy of the photo of the "Laddin's Store" to be placed in the town archives.

We walked down to the mine which was long ago played out. It has now been reclaimed as a recreational lake and has the look of a pristine sylvan lake perhaps a third of a mile across and ringed by a pine forest. The town is not visible from the lake.

From Kinney, we continued on to Buhl, a forgotten backwater town, little larger than Kinney itself. From Buhl we proceeded to Chisholm where we visited the Ironworld Discovery Center which is something like a theme park where you can ride an old railroad around an open pit mine. It is also the site of the Iron Range Research Center which offers a small but very interesting library set up to allow genealogical research on iron range families. The staff was quite helpful, and we all spent a couple of hours there locating the documents that went into the preparation of this article. These included census lists, naturalization papers, voter registration records, newspaper accounts, and others. Ironworld has a wonderful website located at http://www.ironworld.com/index.html. As it had been a full day, we parted ways with Joel, Niki, and Alan. The following day, Shirley, Ben, and I continued our range tour in Grand Rapids. Grand Rapids, Minnesota is probably not the Grand Rapids, Michigan that you have heard of.

Grand Rapids, Minnesota is probably not actually part of the range, either. It is too far west, but Morris and Sarah Ladin moved their family there in 1928, and my father attended high school there.

In Grand Rapids, we found a nicely refurbished Central School that housed a few shops and a very small historical library. There we found a 1929 Grand Rapids High School Yearbook, "The Pine Needles," which featured a couple of pictures of Bernard Ladin including one of him in the orchestra. We found the old high school which had years ago been converted to a junior high school, and we walked across the bridge spanning the Mississippi River (quite small and narrow at this point close to its source) which my father says he crossed on bicycle. Our plan was to put together a package of brochures, memorabilia, and other jetsam from the trip and to mail them to my father with a hand-stamped "Kinney, Minnesota" postmark. We managed to get this package together and then raced to reach Kinney before the post office closed. Alas, we missed the four o'clock closing by ten minutes (though we were never sure that it was ever really open at all). We mailed it, instead, from Virginia.

We returned to tour Eveleth. Eveleth contains a Hockey Hall of Fame and sports the world's largest hockey stick and hockey puck located on a corner lot downtown. We located the site of "The Fair Store" and photographed the brick sidewall with the name painted on the side.

Eveleth, like other towns on the range, has seen more prosperous times. There were several empty storefronts downtown, The yards were well tended, and there were colorful annual flowers on display and banners hung from porches. Some people are still finding the great Mesabi Range a good place to live. The trip for us was truly a walk through our own history one that was filled with reminiscences and fond memories told to us by our elders.

Fannie Ellis Bernstein Rubinstein

Born: Frieda Rochel Eliashevitz

Grand-daughter of Hillel Naividel

Born October 14, 1891, in Yurburg, Lithuania   **Died**
June 13, 1987 in Milwaukee, Wisconsin

The following was written by Leslie Bern, son of Fannie Eliashevitz Bern Rubenstein, based upon conversations with Fannie. It was shown to her, and she made corrections two weeks before her death in June 1987.

THE END OF AN ERA

Fannie, Aunt Fannie, Grandma, Granny Fannie, Bobbe Fannie - all endearing terms for a great, grand woman - Fannie Rubinstein. She was a mother of four boys, grandmother to eleven grandchildren, great grandmother to thirty-two great grandchildren. She was the "god-mother" of a very large family - the consultant - the advisor - the judge - and she had a great deal of influence on many, many people. She was the one her children turned to, to discuss as well as argue about their way of life. She was the confidant of her grandchildren who came seeking advice - talk things over - - very personal discussion even their parents wouldn't be consulted about. She had the knack of making you discuss situations and problems you wouldn't think of revealing to anyone.

A whole city, Rochester, Minnesota, knew her as Aunt Fannie. She was a friend to everyone - gentile or Jew. She was the first Jewish woman from Rochester to become an Eastern Star. She was a walker-- walked miles for as many years as anybody can remember. She befriended the man, woman, or child on the street--always open for conversation. She was a woman libber-- years before the women's rights movement even began. She had a memory for people--where they came from, who their relatives were, and what kind of work they did. She remembered in detail the streets, the people and the countryside of where she was born.

Fannie-Freda Rochel Eliashevitz was born in Yurburg (Yurberik), Kovno (Kaunas) in 1890, in what was then known as Lithuania (then part of Russia). She was one of seven children. Her family was in the grain business and milled flour. She loved to tell stories about her father Solomon, who crossed into Germany and into Russia to sell their grains. The family was well off, considering the times and the community in which they lived, but stories of the golden opportunities in America were to affect all their lives. Solomon was only forty-five when he passed away, and the oldest son Reuven decided to go to America. Other children Sam, Harry and Sarah went shortly after. In 1907, Fannie, sister Jenny and mother Miriam sailed for America.

Jenny and Fannie Eliashevitz

Fannie Ellis and Max Bernstein Altoona, Pennsylvania was the first stop for the new immigrants, as some of the family, the Lippmans [really Naividel, but the name was changed to Lippman upon entry into the United States], who were cousins, had come there first. But they were all destined to go west, to the state of Minnesota, to the Iron Range (North of Minneapolis near Eveleth). The Ellis clan, and many of the relatives were to make their homes in the small communities of "the Range." From the carts in Altoona, the brothers Harry and Sam sought their fortune by opening up department stores in Eveleth and Chisolm, Minnesota. Cousins and other "mishpocha" (family) opened general stores, ladies' stores in Ely, Virginia and Hibbing as well. The open-pit iron-mine workers, the Swedes and the Norwegians, were good customers and the families prospered.

Time passed, and Fannie met Max Bernstein (also from Yurburg), and fell in love. They were married in Virginia, Minnesota on April 17, 1910. They had four boys, Sanford, Howard, Leslie and James - *Sholom, Chamasha, Shmuel Lipeh and Yonah*. Max was a cattle buyer, but wasn't the kind of provider or father Fannie envisioned her husband should be. Differences in their life styles and goals in life, it was inevitable that there would be a separation.

In 1925, Fannie, determined to start a new life, packed up her belongings, took her four boys, ages two to twelve, and headed for Minneapolis. Many of the families were leaving the Iron Range, because they too had married and had children and headed for the big cities to bring up their children in a more Jewish atmosphere. In Minneapolis, Fannie somehow managed to open up a small department store and lived in the back of the building. Those were hard years, difficult to succeed in business, especially under her circumstances. Her sister Jenny, who had married Max Loceff was also in Minneapolis and moved to Detroit, Michigan [where many Yurburikers settled: Feinberg, Zapolsky, Craine, and Ellis families]. Fannie decided to follow the Loceffs. So in 1927, she again packed her boys and moved to Detroit. She, as well as the oldest son, Sanford, worked long, hard hours in a department store. Howard worked in a men's store. Fannie was restless; felt there was no future for her family there and decided again to move on.

In 1928, her brothers Harry and Sam opened a large ready-to-wear store on 13th and Vliet in Milwaukee, Wisconsin. Shortly after, Sam decided to leave the business, and Harry asked Fannie, as well as Sanford the oldest son to come to Milwaukee to work for him. So Fannie and her four sons headed for Milwaukee in 1929.

The Great Depression came along, and everyone was fighting to make a living. Fannie and her two boys were working, struggling to make ends meet, and yet provide a nice home for her family. Harry decided to open a chain of millinery (woman's hat) stores, so Fannie, enterprising as ever, ventured out again in the business world on her own and opened a ladies' ready-to-wear store on Green Bay Avenue. She then opened another store on Mitchell Street in the early 1930's.

As difficult as conditions were they always lived in a nice home, surrounded by a large family. Many were the family gatherings at the homes, on the beaches, and at the lakes west of Milwaukee (Oconomowoc and Pewaukee). The cousins had their card parties and their picnics--a very close knit family. But the depression took its toll, and many businesses were forced to close. Fannie had her problems as well. The stores went out of business, but it wasn't long after that she opened a department store on 24th and Vliet Street.

Her sister Jenny became very sick and had gone to the Mayo Clinic in Rochester, Minnesota for an operation. Fannie went to visit her and while there, Jenny asked Fannie to visit with someone they knew when they lived in Minneapolis, Isaac Rubinstein. He was now a widower and in the furniture business and had five children, the youngest twelve years old. Fannie met Isaac and then went home to Milwaukee. Shortly thereafter, Isaac came to Milwaukee and it was not long after, on July 28,1934, that they were married.

In the fall of 1934, Fannie took her two youngest sons and moved to Rochester. There she helped raise the youngest of the two families. Many were the large gatherings, and parties that the families looked forward to attending. Fannie was very active in the many communal organizations. The highlight of all her involvements was helping found the Bnai Israel Synagogue and Center in Rochester, which serves thousands of Jews from all over the world each year.

World War II came along, and three of her sons went to serve in the army. Many were the tense moments and anxieties that she endured for four years. Many were the bandages she made and the boxes of honey cake that she mailed to her two youngest boys, James and Leslie, in the South Pacific. The war ended and God was good to her and sent her boys home safe and sound.

After the war was over, Howard settled in Milwaukee. Sanford went to Winona, Minnesota (on the Wisconsin river, near LaCrosse Wisconsin), Jim had gone to Detroit, and Leslie went to Owatonna, Minnesota. But after a short while, all the boys ended up in Milwaukee -- all married and lived good lives.

Isaac passed away in August of 1950 and by the spring of 1952 Fannie decided to move to Milwaukee to be near her boys. She lived on Prospect Avenue, reacquainted herself with friends from years ago-- made new friends and was very happy in her new life style.

There were many events in her lifetime not related here, such as one of the happiest days in her life in April 1925 when she became an American Citizen. Perhaps some day we'll try to recollect many more of the happenings and record them for future references for our children.

Fannie lived to the age of 96, a very full life. There were happy times, sad times and hard times. Many, many people were influenced by her actions, her judgments, her thoughts, and her wisdom. And one thing for sure is that Fannie, Aunt Fannie, Grandma, Granny Fannie, Bobbe Fannie will not be forgotten. She passed away on June 13, 1987.

Fannie's brother Harry Ellis (Hillel Eliashevitz) in his store on the Mesabi Iron Range in Northern Minnesota

Sarah Eliashevitz Laden

Grand-daughter of Hillel Naividel

Born 1885 in Yurburg, Lithuania   **Died**
August 21, 1950 in Fairfax, South Carolina

By her son Bernard Laden

My mother's name, in Lithuania, about 1900 was Sarah Reva Eljsevicious, which was a name that was misspelled and mispronounced from its inception. As we knew it, the pronunciation was Elyasevitz.

In the first decade of the twentieth century, it took at least two weeks to cross the Atlantic Ocean. As we learn from history books, most of the Jews who came here were horribly crowded together in what was called "steerage." This is in the hold, the bottom of the ship, where freight is carried.

Ellis Island, in New York harbor, was the port of entry for immigrants, where they were processed, questioned, separated, classified, and scared to death, but eventually were accepted as legal aliens.

In a day at Ellis Island, my mother became an American. She emerged as Sarah Reva Ellis, to match the names of her brothers, Sam and Harry Ellis, who preceded her here, and proceeded to Altoona, Pennsylvania to stay with relatives.

Like most immigrants at that time, she knew about as much English as I do Hindi. Educational opportunities were very limited for most Europeans, especially women. My mother was literate in Yiddish. She read and wrote Yiddish, but she had to come here to learn English. She didn't earn any college degrees, but she got along quite well in our culture.

My maternal grandfather was Solomon, the baker from Yurburg. He died young, in his early 40s, leaving a widow with seven children, a bakery and an exporting business. They bought grain from the local farmers and sold it to the Germans who came up the Nieman River.

Eventually, my grandmother, Mary, came to America, as did six of her children. I remember her living with us in Kinney, Minnesota when I was very young.

My mother never knew much about the "life styles of the rich and famous." Going to the moon would be like "Out of this World" to her.

My mother was an unpretentious woman, completely devoted to her family. She was a hard worker; keeping house, caring for her four children, and helping my father in the store. She was sincere and straightforward. You couldn't find a better cook and baker. Home was not a place of contention. My parents had a harmonious relationship; neither drank hard liquor, smoked or gambled. They worked together for the good of the family.

Date of birth calculated from age 65 at time of death.

Sarah Eliashevitz Laden and Morris Laden

Mary Naividel Eliashevitz (Ellis)

**Mother of Sarah and Fannie, Jenny, Harry, Sam, Reuven, Meyer
Eliashevitz**

Max Zarnitsky

Great-Grandson of Hillel Naividel

Chief Land Appraiser of Israel

Born 1898 in Yurburg, Lithuania   Died 1980 in Tel Aviv, Israel

Max and Bella Zarnitsky

Max was born and raised in Yurburg, Lithuania. He was a Zionist and upon graduating high school, he was ready to immigrate to Palestine, but upon consultation with the Zionist group, he was told that he must have a profession to be helpful there. He was told that they were building a new country and a civil engineering degree would be very valuable. He left Yurburg in 1921 and went to earn an engineering degree in Germany. He had been sent an entry permit to the United States by either his uncle Harry Ellis or his uncle Bill Krelitz. Upon graduation in 1925 he made alyiah to Palestine instead of going to the United States. He sent the entry permit to his brother George (Zerry), who did come to US and settle in Detroit. Max settled initially in Jerusalem and worked in an architecture office there.   In his early years there, he designed some of the first new housing in Jerusalem outside the old city, in Neve Yakov. The British destroyed this neighborhood and the land became part of Jordanian Jerusalem in 1948. Today there is an Israeli army camp built on the spot.

In the 1930s Max designed at least two apartment buildings in the new "Bauhaus" style in Tel Aviv. These buildings still exist. His cousin Ezra Kapshud, also a civil engineer, who was born and raised in Israel, said that Max is considered the "Father of the profession of land appraisal in Israel."

Max Zarnitsky in 1927 in Palestine

Yitzhak Zarnitsky, Max's son, relates that Max's first job in Eretz Yisrael was for the archetecture engineering firm Heker and Yelin in Jerusalem as chief engineer in charge of building the Neve-Yaakov neighborhood of Jerusalem between 1925 and 1926. This photograph is in front of the Hotel San Remo that still exists on Hayarkon and Alenby Street in Tel Aviv.

He married Bella Labok, originally from Moscow, and raised two sons, Yossie (Yosef) and Yitzhak, who both became successful civil engineers. Max designed several apartment buildings in Tel Aviv in the Bauhaus tradition and eventually became the Chief Surveyor in Israel. In that capacity he traveled to US in 1950s, and visited family in Milwaukee and elsewhere. His home was always open to any family members who came to visit Israel. His home in the 1950's was across from the Mann Theatre in Tel Aviv on Marmorik Street. He and Bella eventually moved to northern part of Tel Aviv, at 10 Biltmore Street.

Max always served as an inspiration to his family all over the world. Bella and Max always welcomed any family members who came to visit or live in Israel. They were warm and wonderful people.

Nossun (Norman) Kizell

Born in 1900 in Yurburg, Lithuania

Died in 1973 in Ottawa, Canada

By his daughter Gita Kizell Pearl

Nossun Kizell, son of Moshe Tuvia Kizell and Rochel Laya Feinberg, one of seven daughters of Rafael Feinberg, son of Naftali, was born in Yurburg on April 14, 1900. Moshe Tuvia and his two brothers came from Finland (which I only learned of this past year!).

The Kizell family owned a bakery in Yurburg, so although they were not wealthy, they always had bread to eat.

My father's recollections of Yurburg were pleasant and he had acomfortable childhood there. He bragged of having "nickel ice skates," quite a status symbol compared to the "wire hangers" that his brother Hertz had (as related by Hertz's daughter Greta Kizell Florence).

I assume his house had two stories as he said that he kept his "collection of pistols" (for target practice only) upstairs. He liked school, attending a "cheder" where he learned to read and write Yiddish and Hebrew. He also learned secular subjects. He often recited a Russian poem, which began with the words "buryam gloyit." He never knew in which language the secular subjects would be taught that year, so he ended up speaking Russian, Polish and Lithuanian in addition to Hebrew and Yiddish. He said that in the first grade he was the best in the class in Mathematics, justified by being the quickest to answer the question, "How much is one million take away one?" Nonetheless, his favorite memory about cheder was the last day of the "z'man" (semester), when he threw all his schoolbooks into the bakery oven in his house.

Nossun was always a good sleeper and he told us of the time that his mother said "let him sleep a little longer" even as a fire was threatening their house. This may have been the "Great Fire of 1906."

On his 12th birthday, the news of the sinking of the Titanic reached Yurburg. My father claimed that this was the first news item that he personally remembers from beyond his "shtetl world."

In 1925, at age 25, Nossun Kizell came to Canada to join his three older brothers and one sister in Ottawa, Ontario, Canada. There he became Norman, worked by day, and went to night school where he learned to read and write English correctly, albeit with some idiosyncracies. When he wrote, there never seemed to be spaces between the words, or even any other blank space on the page. We still don't know whether he was trying to emulate Torah script, or just trying getting the most out of each page of paper. He walked to and from work to save the weekly 25-cent streetcar fare allowance he was given by his older brothers. He learned enough spoken French to direct his workers. I often heard him introduce himself as "Ici Monsieur Normand Kizell marchand depe aux quiparle" (Here speaks Mr. Norman Kizell the hide dealer), when calling the butcher and trappers that he was planning to visit on his next "week on the road." On such trips, our biggest worry was that the Mack truck would break down and we would have to get him in the Packard. His biggest worry was that he would be caught with deerskins out-of-season or overweight at the weighing station. At age fifty-six, he was able to retire from his very successful hides and fur business. At this time he began a new career in real estate, which was similarly successful. He bought, sold and managed properties in and around Ottawa. This included carrying with him (at all times) a peach basket full of keys as he visited the tenants to collect monthly rent and to atttend to complaints personally. At the end of the day, he would water his trees with pails of water (not a hose), hammer straight loose nails he had collected. His office had a large map of the local counties, with his parcels (pronounced "possels") shaded in. He was proud of his physical strength - in the early years he would balance and carry around a ladder with his teeth. Later on, he would challenge his daughters' suitors to brick-lifting contests. (My eventual husband was reputedly the first to decline the contest.)

Back to 1935 - my father was single, good looking and "economically promising," but he did not want to marry a "higa" (someone "born in America"). He travelled back to Lithuania on an extended visit to look for a bride. Although his parents and most of the children were already in Canada, his two sisters, Chiene and Gittel, and his brother Dovid still remained in Yurburg. During his visit, he met, courted and married Sonia Gitkin of Shavel (Siauliai, the second largest city in Lithuania at that time). They honeymooned in Paris and sailed back to Ottawa on the "Lusitania."

His greatest pleasure for the second part of his life was driving his wife, children and grandchildren, his many siblings and their families and many guests, for boat rides on his Peterborough outboard and Criscraft inboard motor boats at his summer cottage located just outside of Ottawa (in what is now called Nepean).

One of these guests stands out in my mind. In the summer of 1952 (approx.) we received a lone guest from Israel - Max Zarnitzky, whose family "lived in the same house" as the Kizells in Yurburg. Helen Kizell Beiles, my father's youngest sister, who was born in Yurburg and who now lives in Montreal, confirms that the homes of the Zarnitsky and Kizell families did in fact share a common wall. Max had left Yurburg for Palestine in 1925 with Sam Kizell, Nossun's brother. Sam was not up for the task of building the country - in which his role was to pick up stones in the field, so he joined the Kizell family in Canada, and continued his active role as a Zionist in Ottawa. Max stayed in Palestine married, had two sons, Yossi and Itzhak, and went on to become known as the "father of land surveying" in Israel. When Max returned to Israel from his visit in the 50's, he had his older son Yossi write to me as a pen-pal, and so the friendship between the Kizell and Zarnitsky families continued to the next generation and more. On one of my first trips to Israel with my husband (about 1967), Max and Bella Zarnitsky reciprocated my parents' hospitality. We stayed a night or two with them in their apartment on Biltmore Street in Tel Aviv and they took us to a Habimah Theatre production of Arthur Miller's "The Price." They had two pairs of seats and they insisted that my husband and I sit in the better seats in front, while they took the pair in the back of the balcony. When my daughter Gina Pearl Gotlieb (Ra'anana) made aliyah to Israel, she stayed with Itzhak and his wife Nava for two months. A few years later, the bris of Gina's son Erez was held in Itzhak and Nava's garden. Nowadays, when we or either Zarnitskys' introduce ourselves to others, we do so not just as friends, but always mention that our fathers were "landsmen" in Yurburg.

In addition to being a devoted family man, Norman Kizell's two other principal values were his good name in the community and his acts of *tzedakah*. He founded and funded the Ottawa Hebrew Free Loan Association. Sonia Kizell was a founding member of the Ottawa Newcomers Committee, a ladies group that welcomed and integrated new residents to the Jewish community.

Together with Helen Kizell Beiles, Sonia founded the Rachel Leah Kizell Chapter of Mizrachi, (in memory of Rochel Leah Feinberg Kizell who died in Ottawa in 1941). The chapter is still active to this day.

Norman Kizell passed away in October 1973 (12 Heshvan). Never one to leave all his eggs in one basket, he left funds for ten yeshivas to say Kaddish for him. He had lived to enjoy the birth of his nine grandchildren. Norman's widow Sonia passed away in 2003.

Norman and Sonia descendant include three daughters, nine grandchildren and nine great-grandchildren.

Montreal, Quebec

Jack Cossid (Yankel Chossid)

Born in Yurburg, January 13, 1917

Yankel Chossid was born in Yurburg in January 1917 to a family with several brothers and sisters. His father, Eliezer, was a building contractor. His mother died when Yankel was very young and his father remarried. The couple then had a daughter and twin sons. Yankel grew up in Yurburg, attending the Talmud Torah School and Hebrew gymnasium in Yurburg. As a young adult he worked in the Komertz Bank in Yurburg owned by the Bernstein family. In that position Jack learned much about the business dealings in the town. By the time Jack left Yurburg at age 20, he knew virtually every Jew in the town.

In the summer of 1937, Yankel left Yurburg to immigrate to America with the help of his older brother Hyman, who had already immigrated to Chicago. On August 1, 1937 Yankel left Kovno, Lithuania by train to go to Hamburg, Germany. He left Hamburg on August 4, on the SS Harding and sailed for New York, arriving there on August 14, 1937. From this point on Yankel Chossid became Jack Cossid. The next day he arrived by train in Chicago and was met by his brother Hyman.

Hyman had left Yurburg in 1921 at age 16 along with his sister Sylvia, age 14. Hyman became a buyer for Goldblatt Brothers, a large Chicago department store. Jack accompanied Hyman on one of his buying trips to New York. On that trip Jack met Linda, an office worker at business contact in New York. Jack was immediately smitten by Linda, a sweet shy young lady from Brooklyn. In spite of Linda's reluctance to be courted, Jack persisted and the couple grew close in the week Jack was in New York. They then corresponded and eventually Jack returned to New York, and they were married on July 22, 1945.

When the war broke out, Jack joined the US Army. He served as a quartermaster and then as a translator (making use of his knowledge of german, Lithuanian, Yiddish and Hebrew) at the Prisoners of War camp at Camp Grant in Rockford, Illinois. He had five people reporting to him. In Jack's home a portrait of Linda is displayed, in her wedding gown, drawn by one of the German prisoners.

After the war Jack learned that the whole family left behind in Yurburg was murdered, including his father, stepmother (whom Jack always referred to as his mother, since she was the only mother he ever knew, as his birth-mother died when Jack was very young), a half-sister and twin half brothers; in fact, virtually every Jew who had remained in Yurburg has been murdered by their Lithuanian neighbors.

The Eliezer Cossid Family in Yurburg (about 1925)

Jack Cossid in center bottom row

Only one sister, Dorothy, who had been living Kovno, survived the concentration camps, having lost her husband and a young daughter. She eventually remarried and settled in Milwaukee, Wisconsin (died in early 2003).

Jack has a scrapbook and photo album of Yurburg, including a newspaper article about an award to his father, who was a building contractor and builder in Yurburg. Jack was told that his father was murdered at the site of the Jewish cemetery, and his body thrown down the well that still exists there to this day. Over the years, Jack, like other Holocaust survivors, has always searched for information about the Holocaust in his town. He has accumulated a wealth of information, remembering minute details of the town he had left, a town that no longer exists for Jews.

Jack and Linda created a dry cleaning business in Chicago and raised two daughters, Gail and Benay. Linda passed away in May 2001. Jack now has four grown granddaughters. He volunteers at Jewish Centers often giving courses in Yiddish and on current events. He gladly speaks to anyone who wants to know about Yurburg or their relatives in Yurburg.

Above left: Jack Cossid on the right and and his brother Fievel Chossid in his uniform from the Lithuanian Army. Fievel spent 18 months in the army (1931 or 1932).

Above right: Jack's twin helf-brothers Moshe-Heshelah and Zalman-Heshka. Hitler killed them and Jack's half-sister, sister Basalah.

From the right, Jack Cossid, his sister Dorothy and brother-in law-Peisach Millstein. Photo taken in Kovno on July 30, 1937, one week before Jack left to immigrate to the United States.

Left: Jack Cossid's sister Dorothy and their cousin Sarah Rizman in Lithuanian Park in Yurburg on October 30, 1934. Sarah immigrated to Israel and passed away in 1990 or 1991.

Right: Eliezer Chosid (Jack Cossid's father) about 56 years old, and was taken a few months before Jack left for the United States.

As related in other parts of this book, it was the editor of this book, Joel Alpert who found Jack in 1994, while searching for information on family who had remained in Yurburg. Jack knew them all, the Eliashevitz and Krelitz and Naividel families. Joel's mother's first cousin, Moshe Krelitz was Jack's mentor and a very good friend. Joel had not known about Moshe Krelitz, and he learned much of his own family from Jack. Joel also discovered long lost Krelitz family in Mexico City, Max Sherman-Krelitz (nephew of Moshe). Max's mother Leah had immigrated from Yurburg to Mexico in 1938 and was known to Jack in Yurburg. After his mother's death, Max had discovered a leather briefcase containing over forty handwritten letters in Yiddish from Moshe Krelitz, his sisters and brother, and several friends. These letters were written between 1938 and 1941. The letters did not have much meaning to Max and his sister Esther, mainly because their mother Leah Sherman-Krelitz found it was too painful to talk about her Yurburg family. The trauma of learning that they had all been killed was too overwhelming and she mostly kept her grief deeply inside. Even though Max and Esther read Yiddish, it was too difficult to decipher the letters, furthermore, they did not know much about the tragedy described in such heart-wrenching words in the letters. Joel obtained copies of the letters from Max and sent them to Jack. With Linda's help, he translated the letters into English (see the section by Max Sherman and the translated letters that follow). Now with family background provided by Joel and the clear translation provided by Jack and Linda, many of the mysteries of their family's past began to unravel for both Max and Esther. It was painful for Jack to read letters written by his dear friends nearly 60 years after their murder. It is through these letters that Jack learned more about the destiny of his hometown and even about his own cousins who perished along with the others during the tragedy of the war. Jack said that after this experience he no longer believed that there might be anything impossible in this world.

Due in part to our newly gained knowledge of Yurburg and to the stories about families left behind told by Jack, we began to organize a trip to Lithuania (discussed in an article in this appendix by Fania Hilelson Jivotovsky). A group of Naividel and Krelitz family members traveled to Yurburg, and so began the long road to discovery of our fascinating past, and of the people who were once part of our family and our history.

Jack would have wanted to participate in the trip, but Linda, his dear wife was gravely ill. She passed away the day the group landed in Lithuania in May 2001.

For nearly ten years now, Joel has been referring people seeking information about lost family members from Yurburg to Jack. Painful as it is for Jack to remember his friends and family, who perished in the war, he takes joy being able to tell the callers about their family from Yurburg

The American descendents of Yurburg are indebted to Jack for sharing his memories of Yurburg. Jack will always be our true friend and our beloved Landsman!

Joel Alpert, Boston, Massachusetts   **February 10, 2003**

IŠ ĮMONIŲ GYVENIMO

Jurbarko tinkoriai—stachanoviečiai

Brigadieriai: iš kairės — Chosidas Leizeris, Keturauskas Damijonas ir Fraktas Judelis.

Liūdnas, nebegyvas liko mūsų miestelis po didžiojo gaisro. Sudegė 300 su viršum namų, sudegė ir malūnas bei elektros stotis. Tačiau jurbarkiečiai, kupini pasitikėjimo socializmo laimėjimais, nenusiminė. Šiomis dienomis pradėta statyti sudegusi elektros stotis. Darbo griebtasi su dideliu užsidegimu. Darbą organizavo Jurbarko profesinės sąjungos skyrius, ir per vieną savaitę buvo atremontuotą elektros stoties patalpa. Ypatingai čia pasižymėjo tinkuotojų brigadininkai: Damijonas Keturauskas, Leizeris Chosidas, ir Judelis Fraktas. Per vieną darbo dieną, dirbdami po 10 val., brigadininkai aptinkavo 600 m² sienų. Seniau, dirbdami su pagelbininku nuo ryto iki vėlaus vakaro, tie patys tinkuotojai aptinkuodavo tik 60—70 m².

Taigi, darbo našumas pakeltas per 300%!

J. Ch.

This newspaper article (about 1940) was sent to Jack Cossid after he had lived in the United States for four years. It is from a newspaper from " Yurburg. " Jack Cossid's father Leizer Chosid is on the left with two partners receiving an award in the town of Yurburg for having helped rebuilt it.

Corporal Jack Cossid, a proud member of the U. S. Army in World War II. Jack got married and was promoted to the rank of Sergeant.

```
                            Friday May 25, 1945

 Was at the office and Dobre Rochco, with 2 other women walked in,
 she discribed seeng Chaije Beilkes grave. I was crying awfuly, but later
 woke up..

 Was in Jurbarkas, and went to see and find out where my father was,
 met his patner  Judel x while sitting on Ruve Olswange's steps, I asked
 him where is my father he replied he is no more there.
 later I dreamed that I did see the father, he discribed me how every one
 was killed by the nazis, and that no one is left, I asked him about every
 one induavidualy, but he only discribed about the Muter only, but wouldn't
 tell me how the nazis down it, he said I just can't tell you, and kept
 repeating how wonderful she was .....more people came in the house...and
 tried to tell me that other families lost more than we did, I remember
 that some one told me, that Judl der Melamed lost 18 people in the family..
```

Above is a note written by Jack while in the U.S. Army in 1945 about a dream he had the night before.

Benjamin Heshel Craine

Born Oct. 20, 1887 in Yurburg, Lithuania

Immigrated to the US on Feb. 17 1905

Died May 1943, Detroit, Michigan

By his son Benjamin H. Craine

Ben Craine, Photographer of 1927 Yurburg film

My father, Benjamin Heshel Craine, after whom I am named, came to the United States in the early 1900s. At the time, he immigrated to Minnesota, later moving to Detroit. In 1919, he opened a portrait photography business that grew to be the largest, most highly recognized, and respected portrait studio in Michigan. Under his guidance, the studios counted among its clients, the entire Ford family, starting with Henry, Sr; the Dodge family, the Buicks, many of the Detroit Tigers, and most of the other prominent families in the area. Late in life, in his early 50s, he married for the first time. My mother was twenty years younger, and she came to work in the business. Soon afterward, she became pregnant; then, he was diagnosed with cancer. When he died, my mother was six months pregnant, and she was left with a very large business [at the time, the studios employed around sixty people, including many of my father's extended family including many from Yurburg].

Unfortunately, since she had been married for only a short time, there were those family members that felt he should not have willed the business to my mother, and they attempted to take it away from her. All of the responsibilities, including me, managing the business, and the necessity to defend her ownership of Craine's Studios, made her a very strong woman. As a result of this family rift, I grew up knowing few of the Craine family. My mother remarried when I was five, and, together, she and my stepfather ran the business. Growing up, on the weekends, I often helped in the business. After graduating from University, I returned to Michigan and began to work full time at the Studios.

I must point out that my mother always spoke of my father with reverence. I also knew that many of the people working at Craine's Studios worked there with my father, and, from them, I came to know that he was a great man, leaving me a wonderful legacy. Nevertheless, in spite of the fact that my mother did not want to take away from my relationship with my stepfather, I still knew little of my birth father. At our main office, we had a locked cabinet that contained a variety of items, including a stack of 16mm films on the bottom shelf. From time to time I would ask my mother about the films, and she would say, "They were your father's; leave them be." For whatever reason, I respected that request.

It was some years later, and we sold the Studios to a large, national, company, for whom I went to work. Shortly thereafter, we moved our headquarters, and we had to dispose of the locked cabinet. Although my mother had retired and was living in Florida, her request with regard to the films to, ". . . leave them be," continued to resonate. I moved the films to a shelf at home in our basement. There, they sat for another year or two. One rainy day, I went downstairs, took the films, a 16mm projector, and a screen, and I began to view them. Frankly, I knew little of what I was seeing. I did recognize some people in the films who had been working at the Studios, and it was clear that some of the movies were taken in Europe. Still, I could not recognize or identify anything other than those people who I knew from work. Then, in one scene from Europe, I saw my father pictured with two older people, and I was both shocked and overwhelmed. I stopped the movie, rewound it, and called my wife, Vicki downstairs. I replayed the film, and I said to her, "Look, those people must be my grandparents." Since I look a lot like my father, it was easy to see the strong family resemblance that transmitted from my grandfather to my father to me. Frankly, I had never seen photographs of any Craine family members, so this was quite overwhelming. Not knowing most of the people in the movies, and remaining faithful to my mother, once again I returned the films to the shelf to ". . . leave them be."

Though I have said that I remained apart from almost all of the Craine family, from time to time I did hear from my mother about members of the family with whom she had stayed in touch; these were all more distant cousins who had not taken sides many years ago when my father died. I did not know how most of them were related, but there was one set of Craine cousins with whom we maintained a relationship. Max Craine had run the Frame Shop for Craine's Studios when my father was alive. Later, he went into business on his own, and, still later, his son, Joe, joined him in the framing business. When I came into the business, we began purchasing some frames from Max and Joe, and I was pleased to develop a relationship with some of the Craine family. Also, since at the Studios we produced many High School yearbooks, one year I had the pleasure of working with a student yearbook editor, Sandee Tobin, who it later turned out to be another cousin. [These pieces of the puzzle are relevant; bear with me.]

After viewing the films for the first time, another year passed, and Max died.

My wife, Vicki, and I made a condolence call to his family. Standing there in the middle of the mourners, all of a sudden, we both noticed four elderly women moving toward me, looking at me, frankly, as if they had seen a ghost. They came up, took my hands, looked them over, and said, "You must be Ben." The four women were Max's sisters, and all of them had worked at the Studios years before. Growing up, they lived in Altoona, Pennsylvania. When their father died, my father moved them to Detroit, gave all of them jobs in the business, and became a surrogate father to them; I never knew of that connection. I mentioned the films to them, and the eldest sister knew about each of the reels. In 1927, my father had filmed family in Detroit and Altoona, and then traveled to Lithuania, where he showed the movies to his family there. He filmed the family in Lithuania, and brought the films back to the United States so he could share them with the family here.

I asked the sisters if they would like to see the films, and they said they would. The next day, I took the reels and had them transferred to video, then invited them to my house. Of course, the movies were silent, and that was fine. I connected a microphone to the VCR, then to the eldest sister, and we all watched the movies together. The sisters were delighted and full of information. As we watched, they talked, and they identified many of the people in the films. They also told meaningful stories about those pictured, and, unfortunately, some of those stories included identifying family members who perished in the Holocaust. These were movies taken in 1927 in the town of Yurburg, Lithuania, showing people picnicking, boating down a picturesque river that ran through town, generally having a wonderful time, and even getting married in the town's old wooden synagogue, also later destroyed in the Holocaust. From the National Center for Jewish Film, I later came to learn that there is precious little original film footage available that shows people living happily in such a European shtetl. So, now I had a treasured film in which we had identified many family members, none of whom I had known or was likely to know. This film has been seen by several family members who never knew their grandparents, yet they saw them moving through the steets of Yurburg in the film; these were very powerful moments for them. The film is now achived at the National Center for Jewish Film at Brandeis University, so it can be a source of research and provide authentic film footage for filmmakers.

Remembering the student yearbook editor who was a cousin, after making the video, time passed, and a while later I got a call from Sandee; she had heard about the video, and she wanted to get a copy for her mother (Diana Berzaner Tobin, who had been brought to Detroit by her mother Itel in 1939 - Itel returned to Yurburg to bring her other daughter and husband back to Detroit, but they were all caught when the war started and were murdered). I was happy to make one for her. She was thrilled, and her mother was thrilled.

Time passed, and the original video with the narration sat in a drawer. Then, one day my wife, Vicki, took a call from a man who asked if I was the Ben Craine from the photography studios. She said that I was. He said that he had seen a copy of the video when visiting relatives in Florida and that he, too, was related. In fact the copy he saw was a copy made from the copy that I made for Sandee, the yearbook editor. His name, Joel Alpert, and we spoke. He explained that he lives in Boston and had been collecting information about the family, that, in fact, he had created a family tree and family history. I made a better copy of the film for Joel, and, when we later met in Boston, he gave me a book filled with information about this huge family, about which I knew very little. When Joel and his wife, Nancy, came to our hotel, we arranged to meet in the lobby. So that we would recognize each other, we designated a specific location.

When we met, Vicki said we did not have to worry about a specific meeting point because Joel and I look so much alike. As we talked, and as Joel continued his research, it was through Joel that learned that my father had immigrated to Minnesota, something I did not know. Joel also discovered that my father and his father signed each other's naturalization papers. Even stranger, Joel and I are exactly one year apart in age, sharing the same birthday, as were his grandfather and my father, who witnessed each others' naturalization papers. From Joel, I also learned that the video was now housed in two Holocaust Memorial centers.

As time passed, and we continued to correspond, another cousin, Ruth Ellis Stromer (grand-daughter of Reuven Eliashevitz, mentioned in the article above, "Home on the Iron Range") had the vision to begin organizing a family reunion. I agreed to help and to participate. As we began to plan, I had the opportunity to communicate with other family members, none of whom I had ever known. Our first reunion took place in Minneapolis. At the reunion, I had countless people come up to me to tell me stories how about my father had helped them get started. He had been a pivotal person in the family, providing employment for family members needing an opportunity to get back on their feet; making sure that family groups stopped in Detroit so that they could have family portraits taken at Craine's Studios; generally being someone any family member could turn to for help or advice. Quite a proud legacy for me, learning more about my birth father, a man who I never knew and about whom I knew very little. At the reunion, I introduced the film, telling this same story.

We have held three family reunions, ranging in size from 80 attendees to 120 attendees. The films, the video, have acted as a catalyst to gather people, all with ancestors who lived in the little town of Yurburg, Lithuania, extended family who now travel to our reunions coming from all over the United States, Canada, Mexico, and Israel. I am glad that I had the curiosity to save the films and the opportunity to find a member of the family who could help us learn about the people in the films. I am glad to have a cousin who is willing to spend literally thousands of hours collecting data and ensuring that our family stays connected. I am glad to have found, after so many years, such a large, warm, and welcoming family.

Ben H. Craine   April 26, 2003   Detroit, Michigan

Mordehai (Moti, Motl) Naividel

Born Nov. 11, 1903 in Yurburg
Died March 31, 1993 in Israel

Moti was born on November 26, 1903 in Yurburg, Lithuania. He had a younger brother, Ilusha (Hillel).

His mother died when he was a little child, probably right after the birth of Ilusha. His father remarried, and Moti and Ilusha were raised by their Aunt Polly. Moti attended the Hebrew Gymnasium in Lithuania. Here he obtained his knowledge of the Hebrew language. Moti studied law in Kaunas and became an attorney of the law.

In 1936 his aunt Polly became seriously ill and in order to find a proper treatment, Moti took her to Berlin. Unfortunately, the treatment did not succeed, and Polly passed away during her stay in Berlin. Moti cared to bury her at the Jewish cemetery in Weissensee, Berlin.

Moti Naividel (on the right) with Cheka Karabelnik, her three sisters and her parents - [not in original book]

Moti was married to Cheka Karabelnik probably in 1939 or 1940. They had one daughter, Elinka. Until the Russian army invasion of Lithuania in 1940, Moti and Illusha had a law office in Kaunas (Kovno). However, Moti and his family lived in Yurburg. After the Russian invasion, Moti and his brother, as well as all other private enterprises, had to close their business. Lithuania became a Soviet Socialist Republic and both brothers were offered high-ranking positions in the law administration of the Lithuanian government. Moti served as legal advisor the government and Illusha was appointed as judge in the Supreme Court.

On the day of the German invasion into Lithuania (in June 1941) Moti and his brother with his family were in Kaunas, while Moti's wife and child were in Yurburg. Moti could not return to Yurburg, and he and and Illusha with Illusha's family succeeded in fleeing Kaunas. However, tragically, Cheka and Elinka were murdered by the Nazis in Yurburg.

Cheka and Elinka Naividel   **Hillel Naividel**

Moti, Illusha and his family fled to Uzbekistan, where they spent the whole period of the war. As far as is known, both brothers worked in their profession. They shared a very small room together with other people. With the end of the war, they came back to Lithuania. Moti decided that he wanted to immigrate to Palestine. However, this was of course not possible, since Lithuania was under Soviet government, and the Soviet regime did not allow any emigration to Palestine. As a result of the situation, Moti participated in the "hijacking" of a Soviet airplane. He was a member of a group of about 100 people, who were willing to take this severe risk in order to go to Palestine. Unfortunately, it later turned out that the whole operation a fake and was organized by the KGB, in order to uncover the "Zionist elements" in Lithuania. Moti was sent to prison without any legal trial. He spent 8 years in Stalin's camps in Siberia. Moti used to tell that in the first night during his imprisonment, his hair turned totally white. Moti was imprisoned together with criminal prisoners. This was intended by the system, which sought to weaken the moral of the political prisoners. Luckily, Moti got a jot in the hospital of the camp. Most of the other prisoners were working under very difficult conditions in physically hard work, for example in the coal mines, building the railway etc. On the other hand, due to his work, he was subject to threats by other prisoners, who demanded that he provides them with drugs etc. In 1953, when Stalin died, Moti was released, as were millions of other prisoners. He was forbidden to return to Lithuania for a certain period (2 or 5 years). Moti succeeded in contacting his brother, who arranged his immediate return to Lithuania. In the beginning he had to hide, and only after a certain period all the papers for Moti's return became legal and he could start working. He then joined the largest Lithuanian metal plant as a legal advisor. Here, Moti worked for the next 20 years until his retirement in 1975. In 1954 Moti met Bella Rud, an opera singer and cousin of the husband of Moti's cousin Gita Abramsohn Bereznizky. They were married in 1955. In 1958 Bella gave birth to her only son, Benny.

Днепропетровский институт – 1955 год.

Moti together with his co-worker in the metal factory in 1955.

Moti is the first on the left in the upper row

During the last four years in Lithuania, already retired, Moti worked in the legal department of a toy factory.

Moti and his family made "Aliya" to Israel in May 1979. Moti and Bella settled in Kfar Saba and thereafter moved to Beer Sheva, while Benny joined Kibbutz Gaaton in order to learn Hebrew.

Even after his Aliya, at the age of 76 years, Moti remained was active – he gave legal advice to newcomers and to people who had to fill out forms in order to get compensation from the German government. Moti always loved to read and had great knowledge of literature. He translated Ingmar Bergman's "pictures of a married life" into Lithuanian language. However, this was never published. Moti died on March 31, 1993.

Benny and Regina Naividel   Kiryat HaSavionim, Israel

February, 2003

The Mexican Connection

Max Sherman-Krelitz's Story

On December 22, 1996, being on vacation I started to search the Internet for some information about my mother's place of birth. I had searched several times previously for the town known to me by the name of Jurbarkas, Lithuania. On those previous occasions, when I had searched on the Lithuanian server, I had found only the town's geographic location and some brief references, but nothing was mentioned on the fact that in the near future more information would be included about Jurbarkas. On that occasion I used the Altavista search engine and it also mentioned Yurburg under the Yiddish name by which it was known to me, and to my surprise I found a whole page about Yurburg. I found the heading: "What happened to the Jews from Yurburg," and as an example: "What happened to the Krelitz family." This is my mother's family name! So with much excitement I started to download more information and found a photo in which my grandfather Meyer (Max) Krelitz appeared, the connection was so slow that it took what seemed like hours to appear in full. In these pictures I immediately recognized my grandfather because my mother had a similar picture of him that used to hang in the den of our house. There were also a couple of pictures of her brothers Liebl and Moishe Krelitz, who I also recognized from photos (I had never met them). Of course, I was very excited and crying, in a very emotional state of mind. A person named Joel Alpert, who was totally unknown to me, placed the material on the Internet. Further, on this page it was mentioned that there was a branch of the family in Mexico (where I live) but that all contact was lost. Based upon my own experience, I believed that they (the American side) felt the Mexican branch had very little interest, if any at all, in maintaining family connection. So I was very surprised to note that the page included a request to reconnect to the American family

I immediately called my sister Esther and could not really communicate to her my feeling of the moment. Afterwards, I called a first cousin (son of my mother's sister Riva who was still alive) by the name of Elias Guttman Krelitz, and he told me that he had received a letter from Joel Alpert whom he didn't know personally but knew he was the grandson of Tante Shile (his mother's Aunt Celia) and while considering how to answer, had lost the letter and hadn't answered it. At this moment I will pause to clarify the story.

On several occassions my cousin and I had spoken about creating a family tree but, as it often happens, we had deferred it for sometime "in the future." He had much more knowledge about the family for several reasons. In my case I had tried to talk with my mother about her past, and she always said there was nothing to talk about, nothing to say because all her family members other than her sister had stayed in Yurburg and were all murdered in the Holocaust. I was told that she had an uncle in United States by the name of William or Bill (Velvl) Krelitz but that he had passed away, and also a cousin, George Zerry

(Zarnitsky) who lived in Detroit with whom she had occasionaly been in touch through the mail, mostly updates on news about weddings or bar mitzvahs and the like.

Here it is important to clarify some history which, I found out later, and which now explains the situation. My mother was the youngest of four brothers and three sisters, with a 17 year span between the oldest sister Riva (who immigrated to Mexico) and herself. Therefore, when my mother was born in 1917, my grandfather's brothers and sisters had already left for America by 1904, and even if she had cousins, uncles and aunts, for her they were very distant (being far away and with little comunication with them). Even though she might have seen some photos of them, basically her family consisted of the closest ones she had met in Yurburg. She had also mentioned that on her mother's side there was the Kapulsky family with whom they had not had a very good relationship. The Kapulskys had very little interest (if at all) in her branch of the family because they where very wealthy people in Europe in those days, although my grandfather and grandmother were not in bad shape economically, they were not in the same league, and for that reason they felt ignored. Also my mother lost her mother at very young age (3 years old) and as a result, the family ties with the Kapulskys were very tenuous.

I, by inference, and with a childish sympathy towards my mother, made the mistake to assume that it worked the same way with both sides of her family, and if some of the relatives existed, they probably had no interest to be in contact with her. Consequently, I thought, there would be even less interest in maintaining contact with me and my sister. Therefore, I grew up in a very small family not knowing of the large Krelitz family in the United States (seven aunts and uncles of my mother) and feeling that the subject of family was a forbidden topic.

In 1979 my mother made a trip to Israel and Europe with her sister Riva, and she mentioned she had visited with the Kapulsky family, who were very cold toward them. She also mentioned she had visited a cousin by the name of Dovid Leibke Abramshon who had a wife and two daughters, and they had a very warm reunion. However, I am not sure if they knew each other from Yurburg or not.

It is also very important for me to mention that my mom, who was a widow for many years, married again and then went back to Israel with her new husband and found out that her cousins Dovid Leibke Abramsohn and Max Zarnitzky had passed away, consequently even these relatives were gone.

When my mother had married again, my sister and I decided that because she married at an older age, there was the chance of her becoming a widow again, so we decided that we would keep her apartment, so that if she were widowed again, she would have a place to come back to. Unfortunately, that was not the case, as she passed away before him.

When my mother died in 1983, my sister and I went to her apartment and we found a leather briefcase, which she had brought from Yurburg. In it we found some family photos from Yurburg, which we had never seen before, and a set of letters she had received from her family in Yurburg, written in Yiddish between 1937 and 1941. I am fluent in Yiddish but cannot read Yiddish in script form. For sentimental reasons I decided to keep these letters even though it was not very clear to me who wrote them, or what contents of the letters were. I kept the letters even though my mother's practice was not to hoard, but rather get rid of things. The fact that she herself kept these letters made them very special to me.

Now, going back to my newly discovered family I traced through the Internet, I remember, I called my son Abraham (who lived in Houston). I was in a state of shock to have found family in the United States. Abraham immediately established contact with Joel Alpert and informed him about us. Joel was as surprised as we were, because he didn't know about our existence.

From there on a very close relationship developed, and we now have a record of E-mails and letters we have exchanged. In June 1997, my son Abraham and I made a trip to Milwaukee to meet many of our Krelitz cousins.

Linda and Jack Cossid and Max Sherman-Krelitz in Milwaukee in June 1997 at the Krelitz Mini-Reunion

There is also another story about how I was contacted by Chana Magidovitch who survived the Holocaust and was a witness to the massacres in Yurburg [her testimony of the murders in Yurburg appear in Chapter 6.]

Krelitz Mini-Reunion in Milwaukee, Wisconsin in June 1997

Chana Magidovitz's contact:

I can't recall the exact date, but after my mother remarried, one night I received a call, when I was half asleep, from a person who identified herself as Chana Magidovitz. She said that she was a close friend of my mother's from her hometown and wanted to find her because she hadn't seen my mother since the time my mother left for Mexico in 1937. She had found out that I was the son of Leike (Leah) Krelitz and she contacted me so that she could get in touch with my mother. Somebody had told Chana that my mother wasn't living in Mexico City any longer. By this time I was fully awake and I did not want to miss the chance to ask Chana about those from the town who had survived the Holocaust, since Chana herself was a survivor. Chana told me she survived because she had joined the Partisan Group. After the war she lived in the communist world and when she could leave she had done so, and was now traveling with her husband and speaking about the Holocaust in the Jewish communities. When she came to Mexico she asked the people that worked for the Jewish community about my mother. The advice she got was to contact me.

Chana told me that nobody else from the town had survived; I still hear her words: "they were buried alive and the earth shuddered for a couple of days from the movement of the bodies buried alive." Those words still overwhelm me. My uncles and cousins were among the people who were buried alive; my own flesh and blood were among the people she was talking about. Needless to say, after that I was so upset that I couldn't sleep well for some time. It had been some time since I had spoken Yiddish, and even though it might have been difficult, it was also very easy because, in spite of the fact, that I didn't know Chana personally, I felt close to her because after some many years she still remembered and was looking for my mother. I told her my mother was living in Miami Beach, Florida with her new husband and gave her the phone number. She said she was going to the United States and would for sure give her a call and try to see her. I know, she called because next day I called my mother and mentioned that Chana had called, but gave no details about our conversation (as I write these lines, memories still come to my mind of my mom and me as a five year old child going to the Red Cross to find out about survivors in the family or going to some other place where somebody would let us know about survivors from the Holocaust). Afterwards, when we spoke again my mother mentioned that Chana had called, and confirmed the news she always hoped would not be true.

I can only add that a couple of days after Chana's call, my mother, had a stroke and was hospitalized in Miami. We had always assumed the stroke was not related to Chana's call. However, today we are not so sure. Having partially recovered, my mother came back to Mexico where a couple of weeks later she passed away.

Max Sherman-Kreliz   Mexico City   June 2000

Image of the Yurburg Shul provided by the Vilna Jewish Museum

Shabbas Dinner with Leib, Feiga…, …, …, Leah, and Moshe Krelitz
Yurburg - Both photos taken in 1937 or before

Leah and Moshe Krelitz canoeing in the Nieman at Yurburg
Moshe made the canoe according to Jack Cossid

Excerpts from the Yurburg letters, written from 1939 to 1941, by Moishe, Leibel, Rochel and Feige Krelitz and others

Letters translated by Jack and Linda Cossid and Max and Rosi Sherman

January 30, 1939   Yurburg

Dear Sister Leike, (from Moishe)

How are you? Are you having a good time? I did everything I could to send you some pictures of our Estherle, but they came out too dark because I took them inside our house, and that's why they are not any good. But now I am sending you some new pictures. She is even prettier in person. She is five months old now and she seems to be a very intelligent child.

You ask me if I can make a living. I can answer you that I could make a very good living, but the **business climate is getting very bad, particularly for businesses owned by Jews.   Most of the people of Yurburg say that *we need to get out of Lithuania*, to any other place, because Lithuania is now the worst place in Europe for Jews to live, particularly if there is war, and if Hitler's decrees are enforced in Lithuania** as we presume that they would be.

Leike, what do you think of our planning to leave Lithuania? Do you think we could emigrate to Mexico? Do you think I could make a living with my skills? So now you don't need to be upset because you are not in Lithuania and don't even consider returning because everyone here will tell you that you are crazy to return. Things are very unsettled here in Europe, Leike.

Iztke Kopelovitz requests that you give his cousin a letter that he is enclosing in this letter.   Tatke Lubin's mother passed away, also Zalman der glaze. Feigele Magidowitz sends her regards to you.   Also Leizinke (Leizar) Peisachson says hello to you.   Also my wife Dvora (Dora) and Esther send their love.

Be Well, (signed) Your Brother,

Moishe Krelitz

Moishe, Dora and Esther Krelitz

**Moshe, Feige, Dora, Itzhak Shaye (Feige's husband's last name unknown)
and Leah**

Esther and Moishe Krelitz about 1940

No Date (probably in 1939 - another letter from then reads very much like this one.)

No Beginning (probably from Leibel, but could be from Feige or Rochel)

….See to it that Moishe gets papers so he should be able to come to you. Things are not good here with us. The whole city's businesses are in the hands of the gentiles. The time is now. Later may be too late.

Dear Sister, what you asked us about Itel Berzaner, She's going to America after Passover with her daughter Miriam and Diana. She's going as a tourist and what you asked about a fur coat, has to cost about 800 Lit. Moishe has a very fine little girl. We were there yesterday. **Moishe said he wrote to you about everything. He wants to sell half of his brick building. His business is very bad because he is dealing with the Gentile Lithuanians.**

Malkele, Raizel's daughter got married to Zalman Berke Glazer -------He bought his own truck. He died accidently. The driver pushed him against the wall and he got killed and Chaika was left a widow. It is very sad. Leiska (Eliezer) is coming home after Purim from the Army. If you are traveling to America for the Exhibit [possibly the 1939 World's Fair], try to see the machine that talks like a human being. Here they call it ageilom (golim?, meaning robot in Yiddish). We read about it in our newspaper and also about the exhibit.

Have a happy trip. Try to see our Father's brother, Velvel (Bill Krelitz)

No signature

Dear Sister Leikele, (from Rochel)   No Date

How are you? You wrote and told me that you are getting used to the life there and that you got a job with Shmuel. I'm very happy you also told me that you're going to an exhibit in America and that you'll be able to see everybody. **Perhaps you can tell Uncle Velvel (William Krelitz) that he should send us immigration papers. That's all we're asking him to do. We would sell everything and we could bring some money with us. I'm sure you know that my husband Gershon is not a lazy person. I talked to Moishe and Leibel while I was in Yurbrick. They told me to write to you about it. Maybe this is a place for them in Mexico but the first thing would be good if you could bring Moishe. He can't make a living here. He has a very good trade. He would do well in a big country, but not in Yurbrick. The competition is difficult here and he can't make a living here. They sold the brick building for 16,000 Lit (about $1600 - probably worth $35,000 in 1997) which Moishe could bring with him**. He could go to work right away because he's got a trade.

Dear Leikele, answer right away because Moishe's situation is very bad and because, after all, he is our brother. We tried to get him a job but we were not successful. We were told that they are laying off people. He told

me that he would go there with his wife and beautiful child. What else can I tell you? I'm sure you know what's going on here in Europe. It's in all the newspapers.

They arrested Moishe Eisenstadt in Smolninken. That's where he lived but he was able to escape. They also arrested Moishe the doctor and he had a nervous breakdown and they had to take him to an insane asylum. Mrs. Weinstein told this to me. I must tell you that the situation here in Lithuania is very bad. There are signs all over saying "Don't buy anything from Jews." Every stinking farmer tells us that we are only guests here and there are pogroms in many cities and that is the truth.

No signature.

Dear Leah, (from Feiga)   No date (from Yurburg)

The general situation is very bad. I have a fur coat, but I haven't worn it yet. I was in Kovno (big city nearby). The outlook is not good. I'm sure that you read it in the newspapers. Let's hope that things will turn out for the best. I will answer you when I get your letter. I have a lot to tell you. I wish you the best.

Your friend,

Feiga   Best regards from all your friends.

March 28, 1939   Yurburg

Dear Sister-in-law Leikele, (from Dora, Moishe's wife)

How are you? Are you having a good time? You are in a big world; it's not like in Yurbrick. Here the girls are complaining that it's very lonely. Now the situation in general is very quiet. **We have a lot of refugees from Memel and Smoleninken (two nearby towns, near the German border).** Leizer Peischson was in town on furlough. He was supposed to be released from the Army but they're holding the soldiers back because the situation is unstable. ....

The economic situation in Yurburick is very bad and all the merchants are complaining that they can't make any money. Therefore nobody spends any money. I believe that Moishe wrote to you about everything, therefore I am ending my letter. It is Erev-Passover and I did not do a thing yet. My daughter is a real mensch. She wants me to play with her. She looks beautiful. She got heavier. If the weather will be good, we will take pictures and send them to you.

Be well. Regards to your sister, brother-in-law and nephews,

Dora

No date (from Yurburg)

Leikele, (from Moishe)

Please write and tell me if the trade of a watchmaker is of value there. I know a little bit of the trade but I could learn more in a very short time. I have a guy who is a watchmaker working for me. I hired him so that I could learn the trade. I am a goldsmith and a silversmith and I know those trades well. You won't have to be ashamed of me. I already wrote you about everything. I am waiting for your answer.

Be well and have a good time.

Wishes to you, from your brother, *Moishe*

March 28 (Jack believes it's 1939) (from Lithuania, likely not from Yurburg)

Dear Sister Leah, (from Fanny also called Feiga)

I received your letter and I am aggravated about your plans to come back to Yurbrick. Postpone the trip temporarily. The situation in Lithuania is very bad. A war can break out any day. Germany has already invaded Austria and now Hitler is after Poland and Lithuania. You cannot imagine what we are going through. I am sure a war will break out. Wait until perhaps the Russians come in. I'm sure you'll have a better time there with your sister and spend Passover with her. What is your hurry to come back? Perhaps you can better yourself and go to America to the relatives. Make that trip. I'm sure they will give you money for the travel expenses. By doing that you will have a good time and forget your problems. When you write to me, tell me details about everything.

Your sister Fannie

The children are all, thank G-d all well

Regards from Aserlen. She asks me all the time when Aunt Leah is coming back. I'm waiting impatiently for your letter.

P.S. Everybody is buying gas masks for Passover

March 27, 1939   April 12, 1939   April 18, 1939

Dear Sister Leah, (from Rochel)

You will be surprised that I am writing to you now. Last year you send me a letter and told me that you will write and tell me everything about you and your health. Now, not waiting for your answer, I am writing to you again. **My writing to you now is about the actual Jewish situation in Germany, that you already know. But now it became closer to us. Hitler already entered Memel and is frightening the Jews. Lots of Jewish people could not get out because they did not have any help from anybody. Others barely escaped and need to leave everything behind. They just took their children and ran away. In just one word, there is a big panic. Lots of refugees came** to Tovrik, Yurburg and Kovno and we can not describe the sadness of the situation of these Jews. Here as you know in a small town, we know with our fingers all the poyerim (goyim) wait until Hitler will come, and then they will be against us. Mainly they have "pointed their eyes" toward the ones that are wealthy. Immediately they take the Jewish businesses. The newspapers are writing that the future of our Jewish people will be tragic in a very short time.   Hitler will establish a decree against Jews in Lithuania, that now the panhandle is in their hands (that means he made an ultimatum to Lithuania). You now can imagine how Lithuania is "standing over hen foot" (a Yiddish proverb which means is trembling). In just one word, dearest sister and brother-in-law, the only thing we just want is to be SAVED and that they will not take us before our time from our children. We do not want our children to be orphans like the German children. I do not need to describe you in detail what's happening here. You already know the same news from the newspapers. *My request to you is that you send us papers as soon as possible to be able to get out of here.* About money, you do not need to worry, now there is still time to sell our businesses. Now we can also obtain a loan from our house. Yes, it is really sorrowful that we must give away our businesses so well established and having taken so much work and with a such a good name, but what can we do, the only thing that we want is just to be SAVED FROM DEATH. See my dearest and hurry and do everything possible to try to save us and take us out from the jaws of the lions. My oldest son Yosele says to me, "Mama, write to aunt Leyken a letter and she will save us from death. She knows us so well." There is such sadness from the kids when they listen to the predictions of what will happen. We all have intense feelings of fear and anger because we know that the death is waiting for us. And what can be worse than suffering alive? They are being cruel. IN JUST ONE WORD SAVE US AND HAVE PITY FOR US AND FOR OUR CHILDREN. See urgently what can you do and answer us as soon as possible, because we want to know if we should ask for a loan on our house. I finish my writing to you.

Be well. Your loving sister, sister-in-law and aunt Rochel

Gershon and the children send regards to all of you. I anxiously await your immediately answer with good and happy news.

Just a few words about today news: Please you must urgently get us papers, we do not care if they will be either for the city or another place.

Dear Sister Leike: See to it that they will send us papers as soon as possible. Leike: Please write to me. Do not wait to receive a letter from us.

Be well and regards from your sister

Rochel

Answer right away when you receive our letter.

No date

Dear Leikele, (from Rochel?)

When you go with your friend to America, write and tell us right away. A lot of people are leaving Kovno.

There are now refugees here from Smolininken and Memel. Dear Leikele, imagine what we have to do, we had to make a collection for them. They came without anything. Everything was taken from them. You should see the condition that Shlame came in with her children. It a good thing that she has a few Lits. Yisrael eats at our house. They are in a pitiful situation.

All the rich people in Yurbrick are sitting and eating because they have the money. Those who don't have anything, get help from public aid. How long that will last, nobody knows. In the meantime things are not good. We would borrow but nobody has any money.

Dear Leikele, tell us how you are and how you spend your time. Also tell us about your friend, and do you think you'll get marrried soon. Beile's mother asked us the same thing. Feige and Yakov send their regards. Feige looks very well. Leibel and Rochel came to visit us, and they also went to Shauvel.

Best regards and kisses to everybody,

Yours, *Rochel* (?)   Please answer.

No date (- but after 1940) (Probably from Rochel, or maybe Fanny - Feige)

Dear Sister Leah,

How are you? How is your health? How do you keep busy? Write a few words. My only wish is to see you. Regards to dearest Beila and I wish her all the best. She should get a good man, who is a good-hearted person. I am ending my letter and hope that I get a speedy answer from you. **Save us from Hell. Make out papers for us because if you don't do it now, later will be too late.** We hope you will be able to do.

I'm thanking you in advance.   I'm sure I don't have to tell you the rest you know yourself. Best regards from my husband and children. Have a happy Passover. **It will be a sad Passover for us because we live in a dark world. We want to be rescued otherwise we'll go under.** Leah, I hope you'll be a good mother to your son.

March 25, (1941) (date not clear)

Dear Sister (from Feiga)

My letter would have been in you hands but I neglected to send it to you. I did not get a chance to see your son's picture. You should raise him in good health. Hope you'll be very proud of him. If it isn't too hard, write us a longer letter. Rochel received a letter. She's getting rid of everything.

Be well. Kiss your son from everybody. Our Esther is learning to write and so will be writing a letter to you. After Passover she will go to school.

Your sister, Feiga

This was the last letter received. On June 22, 1941 the Nazis invaded Lithuania, and Yurburg was one of the first towns overrun because it was across the Nieman River from Prussia. Within three months, all the Jews of Yurburg were murdered.

Krelitz Family: Feige, Rochel, Moshe, Leah and Feige's Husband
Only Leah Krelitz survived. All others were murdered.

Moshe Krelitz's Brick Building on Kovno Street in May 2001
Identified by Duba Most Rosenberg

Standing: Eliezer and Hillel Bass
Sitting: Rachel Portnoy Bass - Shalom Bass
At least Rachel and Shalom were murdered in the Shoah
Photo courtesy of Bilha Bass Lerental

Sudarg

By Fania Hilelson Jivotovsky

Great-Great Grand-daughter of Elka Rosin

The small town of Sudarg is known to have come to existence during the second half of the sixteenth century. The quiet sleepy Lithuanian town can be found in the southwest of Lithuania, on the left bank of the Nieman River about 5.4 miles down-river from Yurburg.

The town of Sudarg, with its earthly scent of the forest, drawn out green pastures sprinkled with yellow dandelions in summer, with grasshoppers spinning around and sparrows joining in to sing the tune of other living creatures, is a town where peace seems to be the very essence of existence. But, like other Lithuanian towns, it hides a dark history of our past.

History books tell us that Jews began to settle in Sudarg at the end of the eighteenth or at the beginning of the nineteenth century. In 1923, there was a small Jewish community of about 273 people living peacefully in the quiet boroughs of the town. Jews ran a few bakeries, grocery stores, two taverns, and a pharmacy and had their own two Jewish tailors and a butcher.

My father told me that the Jews of Sudarg also had their own synagogue called "Di Shul", decorated inside with spectacular wood engravings. This synagogue was used for prayers in summer, while in winter people would walk to the other synagogue, the "Beth-Midrash," which was heated by a furnace.

The tightly knit community nurtured its spirit of landsmanship, and the kinship of the people helped to weather all storms in bad times.

Young Jewish people began to leave Sudarg in the twenties and thirties, mainly to Kovno or abroad, looking for a better life and bigger opportunities. Many young people from Sudarg immigrated to El Paso and Dallas, Texas and Albuquerque and other parts of New Mexico and New York City and raised families in safe countries.

My father Gershon Hilelson was born in Sudarg in 1913. He attended the "Heder", where together with other children he learned to read and write, and studied biblical scriptures and Hebrew. Later the few Jewish children of Sudarg either studied in the Lithuanian school or moved to Yurburg to attend high school, and my father went to Yurburg and stayed with relatives while attending school.

He used to tell us about the green meadows and the forests of Sudarg, the river Nieman, and about the town of Yurburg nearby. He considered himself both a Sudarger and Yurburger, and anybody who was from these two places was family. "He is a Yurburger," meant *"he is my own, he is my family"*.

My father took my brother and me as children to Sudarg in 1961. This must have been the first time he returned to Sudarg after the war. I remember the pained, tormented look on his face as he looked at familiar streets. I remember, a local farmer recognized my father and ran towards him "Berchik has arrived! Berchik is here!" He grabbed my father's hand and shook it enthusiastically, but father looked pale and somber. I will never forget my father's voice as he kept repeating on our way back, "God, oh God, what happened to them all?"

Out of a family of nine children he would be the only survivor living in Lithuania. His mother, sister, brothers – all perished in the summer of 1941, when they were rounded up and shot together with other Sudarg Jews. The whole community of Sudarg perished in one day - a destiny so similar to countless other towns of Lithuania.

After the War, the few remaining Jews of Sudarg would not go back to live in their ancestral town, and today, Sudarg is but one more vanished community. A small and forgotten town.

My father carried both the pain and the spirit of his family and his community.

I remember when I was a student at Vilnius University, my parents were trying to find a place for me stay; the university was two hours away from where we lived. The problem was solved in the spirit of the communities of Yurburg and Sudarg.

> "You will stay with the Breskys" – my father said. "They are family".

> "Who are the Breskys? How are we related?" - I asked

> "It is a long story"- my father answered, "they are "kreivim," our own."

I stayed with the Breskys, who were wonderful warm people for two years, but nobody could ever explain what the relation was. It took me about 40 years to figure out the connection, and having attended our family reunion of the interconnected Naividel, Krelitz, Eliashevitz, Rosin and Feinberg families of Yurburg, in 1998, I finally understood how we were related to the Breskys:

> Shulama Bresky was the daughter of Itzhak Rosin, the son of Elka Rosin, Hilel Naividel's second wife. She was my grandmother's Mina's first cousin. Shulama Bresky was also a Yurburger, so that made her twice my family!

As I was growing up, I heard the names of Naividel, Zapolsky, Abramson, Krelitz and others, but I never knew that many years later these names would evoke the same emotions in me as they did in my father – these are Yurburgers, therefore they are my family.

And somewhere far away from the small towns of Sudarg and Yurburg, the spirit of these communities lives on…

Fania Hilelson Jivotovsky   Montreal, Canada   January 2003

Pesach 1932

Left to right: (1-2-3-4-5) Unidentified members of the Eliashevitz family,
(child) Itzhak Bresky, Israel Bresky, Bella Bresky, Shlayma Bresky
unidentified members of the Eliashevitz family.

Top: Pesha Leah Danziger, Natan David and Pesha Rachel Abramson
Bottom: Bella Abrasmon, Mira Danziger Aharonov, and Gita Abramson
[Photos courtesy of Gita Abramson Bereznitzky]

Three Eliashevitz children: Jeine and Itzhak Eliashevitz
Elka on left, Jeine in middle, right unknown.

"The Large Family Lost in the Shoah"

Leah(?) and Shlayma(?) Eliashevitz - Unsure of names
The whole Eliashevitz family was murdered in the Shoah
[Photos courtesy of Gita Abramson Bereznitzky]

Standing: Israel Appelboim - Izhak Appelboim

Sitting: Chaike Appelboim, Pesha Rosen Appelboim, Israel Appelboim's sister, Bilha Bass

Pesha, Chaike, Israel and Itzhak were all murdered in the Shoah

Photo courtesy of Bilha Bass Lerental

Shlayma Rosen Breseky - Hillel Rosen - Masha Rosen Bass

Hillel Rosen was murdered in the Shoah

Photos courtesy of Bilha Bass Lerental

Standing - one Elijashevitz daughter - Masha Rosen Bass
Sitting - Eliezer Bass - Bilha Bass

In Israel in about 1960 - from left Dovid Leib Abramson, Max Zarnizky,
brother of Pnina Wolpe, Nomi Lerental (standing), ? , Pnina Wolpe, Bella
Zarnizky, Leizer Bass, Ruven Lerental

Photos courtesy of Bilha Bass Lerental

Hadassa Eliashevitz   Bella Abramson

Feiga Jaswonski, Ruth Goldberg, Gita Abramson (around 1932)
[Photos courtesy of Gita Abramson Bereznitzky]

A Journey to My Past

By Fania Hilelson Jivotovsky

In Memoriam

Today I remember with love all the people in my family
who have gone to everlasting life,
and I honor the memory of the departed.
As the light of the candle I light burns pure and clear,
so may the thought of their goodness shine in my heart
and strengthen me,
and may I live out the eternal values, which keep their influence alive

The memory of the righteous is as a blessing...

(Prayer for the Yahrzeit, from the book of Jewish Prayers)

Part I

Our plane is taking off in half an hour, and I look at the passengers checking in at the Lithuanian Airlines flight 247 leaving Amsterdam for Vilnius, the Lithuanian capital. I watch a tall slender Lithuanian woman board the plane, then a man with glasses who looks like a professor, chatting in Lithuanian to his companion. On the plane a stewardess asks me in accented English if she can help me with my carry-on luggage. I answer in Lithuanian - "aciu, thank you, I am fine".

The plane takes off and I begin to feel as if I am in Lithuania already. I hear the announcements in Lithuanian and see faces that somehow begin to look familiar. Lunch is served, and I watch a flight attendant take a back window seat as she begins to eat slowly, with an appetite and oblivious of her passengers. Suddenly I feel tense. I have a flashback and remember my Mother and how hard she worked to stock up on preserves in summer because fruits and vegetables were scarce in winter. In the early fall Father would bring home a borrowed small hand-run gadget that would shred cabbage. In about two days a barrel would be filled, sprinkled with cranberries on top, and left to ferment to a champagne-like perfection until winter, enough to last for five long months. Then there would be cans of pickles and jam preserves, the result of tedious labor. I wonder if they still do that in Lithuania.

I have a window seat next to my husband's. Our fellow passenger is a young Lithuanian coming back from the United States. He tells us he went to Florida to earn some cash. He will stay in Lithuania a few months and will go back to America where, he says, cash comes easy.

Thirty years ago I took a train from Vilnius to Vienna, via Warsaw, my first trip to the outside world. The next day I reached my destination - Tel Aviv where I would stay for six years before moving to Canada.

The plane begins to descend. Through the window I see small neat squares of luscious green fields, valleys and hills. The land below looks rich and fertile.

Part II

We take a cab to the hotel where we are about to meet our group - eleven other travelers, Shtetel Shleppers, who are ready to travel with me through the back roads of Lithuania. Though we are not closely related, our roots can be traced back to one big family in Yurberik. I am the only one who has lived in Lithuania and speaks the language

We meet our group in the lobby of the hotel. I look forward to spending some time with the people in the group and getting to know them - Esther and Brenda, Gary and Mark, and our family-encyclopedia-wizard Joel, and all the others who came with us.

We also have a tour guide Chaim Bargman who looks like a character found in the books of Sholom Aleikhem, Bashevis Singer or Babel. He could be Tevie der Milhiker, or Curly of the Three Stooges. Or may be even a defiant Trotsky? In my head Chaim does not quite fit the image of a smooth-talking and well-groomed tour guide. I ignore his funny accent and faulty grammar, and forgive him the spots on his windbreaker and baseball cap, the two inseparable accessories in his attire. For, above all, Chaim looks to me like he is a Jew with a mission. His baseball cap has two embroidered words in Hebrew - "Moreh Derekh", Teacher of the Way.

The next morning we are on our tour bus in Vilnius. I take the window seat and look at the streets that once were familiar. I don't recognize where I am. Then it dawns on me - this is Basanaviciaus street. My friend Genya used to live here, this is where we walked after classes at the University.

Suddenly sadness engulfs me. I realize I will not find anybody I used to know. A town without the people who once lived here is like a town without a name. I remember the faces I used to see on these streets and recognize in a crowd. Without the people who were part of it, it is a strange place, like the one I never visited. Years have gone by, and we have all left. Childhood friends, relatives are now scattered all over the world.

Unlike the generation before us, we left in time, and built new lives. Why then do I still feel so sad?

We go to Subaciaus street, and I see a few blocks of apartment buildings. This time I recognize the place. This is where the Goldsteins used to live. Chaim, our tour guide, explains that before the war this was the Baron de Hirsh Housing Project converted to a Jewish prison camp by the Germans during the War. I am flabbergasted by the discovery that I never knew that this apartment complex on Subaciaus street was a Jewish prison camp.

Behind the apartment building, in the middle of a small square we find a monument. We light a candle and say the words of Kaddish for those who perished in this camp.

Chaim Bargman, "Guide of the Way" in the Lithuanian Park in May 2001. Palace of the Russian Prince is in background. Photo not in original Yizkor book - Photo courtesy of Dr. Leon Menzer.

Part III

Our next visit is the old city. We go to the Vilnius State University and enter old and damp hallways of my Alma Mater. Posters at the entrance and the narrow halls mark its 500th anniversary.

Slowly my memories take me back to my once carefree existence in Lithuania when I was a student. Where I was, if you wanted to fit in, you had to read the likes of Kafka, Nitche and John Updike or Sallinger's "Catcher in the Rye".

I remember poetry readings in dimly lit, smoke-filled student cafes, and evenings with bards, and guitar players, and groupies humming along to the sound of a weeping saxophone or a guitar until the wee hours of the morning. If you had seven kopecs to pay for black coffee, you were in for a treat. Sipping bitter coffee in between chains of cool Bulgarian BT cigarettes, you could engage into endless discussions on the purpose of existence and the meaning of life, and chat with bohemian dissidents who frequented the cafes. To add a simple sophistication and an air of nonchalance, you would don a beret pulled to one side, or would puff imported cigarettes with long filters. There was nothing to compete for with other students, and the only rat race you could find was "who managed to get hold of the latest issue of Solzhenitzin's book published by Samizdat?" Those were simple times filled with dreams of a future in distant lands.

Back in the hallways of my Alma Mater, I stop to skip through dozens of announcements on the billboards and come across a curious notice about a program offered by the school. The program is called "Stateless Cultures", and it includes studies of the Yiddish language. A visiting American Professor Dovid Katz teaches the course. This truly amazes me. Yiddish was never permitted in any educational institutions in the Soviet Union. It is now a disappearing language, and I hold on to the idiomatic, expressive vernacular I still remember.

We walk outside and go to a narrow street just behind the small University campus. This was the street once called "Jewish", and it was home to many families. The street had a different name when I lived here. Today it got back its original name. I am puzzled and I try to figure out, why I did not know any of this when I lived here. And why didn't anybody tell me that during the war the Jewish Ghetto of Vilnius was just around the corner?

Only at the end of the trip I would find my answers to all these questions that kept haunting me all through this trip.

Part IV

Religious affiliation is no longer forbidden in Lithuania, and there is a dwindling Jewish Community in the city. Out of a community of 120,000 before the war, only 3,000 Jews remain in Vilnius today. Many of the families are not of Lithuanian descent, having moved here in the last few years from Russia, where life is still tough.

The Lithuanian Capital now boasts a Jewish Community Center. Our next stop is there.

We enter a shabby building carrying architectural remains of Stalin's epoch with its signs of exuberance - high ceilings, big windows and large rooms. The Director of the Community Center, Mr. Levinson greets us. I recognize him; he is the father of Natasha, an old friend of mine, now living in Toronto. I am afraid he will think I am a ghost, but I approach him asking in Russian:

"Mr. Levinson, do you remember me? I used to live around the corner, remember me?

He looks at me and says - "I am so sorry, dear, did you really? I can't remember, I am an old guy".

I tell him I occasionally speak to his daughter in Toronto. Levinson warms up and shakes his head. "So many years went by."

We walk into another hall where walls are decorated with hundreds of photographs. These are photographs of Jewish soldiers who fought the Germans in the 16th Lithuanian Division. I remember my father used to say that the 16th Lithuanian Division should have been called "the Lithuanian-Jewish Division". The hyphenated semantics presented no interest to me at that time. I was more interested in D. Lawrence's "Lady Chaterleys Lover" and the Voice of America on my short-wave radio. I would only come to understand the importance of these semantics to War Veterans later in my life.

My father's photograph is not there. He and his brother Leib were soldiers serving in the 16th Division. Leib lost his life in 1943. I think the Jewish Community just did not have Leib's photograph because he perished early in the war. What about my father's photograph?

Chaim tells me I should send my father's photograph to the Jewish Community Center of Lithuania when I return home to Canada. I remember that we had one remaining small passport-size picture of Leib with an inscription in tiny Yiddish letters on the back of the photograph. I make a note to send the photographs of both my father and Leib to be put up on this wall.

On an adjacent wall there is a huge plaque with many names. That's the list of fallen soldiers. I read through hundreds of names carefully inscribed in alphabetical order, with a date next to each name. I get to the letter "H" and I read, "Leib Hilelson, Killed in Action, 1943, Battle near Oryol". I read the name over and over again, and touch the engraved letters with the tip of my fingers. This is Leib, my father's brother? Though Leib's photograph is missing, his name is here. I feel a lump in my throat. For the first time, I actually see a place where the memory of Leib Hilelson can be honored. He never even had a burial place. I feel so grateful to have found his name on this memorial wall, one among hundreds of other names.

Then, I think of all the other relatives we lost - uncles, aunts, cousins, grandmothers and grandfathers. We have to find the places where we can light a candle and say Kaddish for them - something I never did when I lived in Lithuania.

Throughout our 10-day journey through the back roads of Lithuania we found these places where white monuments would mark common graves and memorial plaques would state numbers, not names. The inscriptions would often be in the Hebrew of Yiddish languages seemingly undergoing a late revival in this part of the world.

We found many small towns that once hosted vibrant Jewish communities where nothing but old Jewish cemeteries remained, overgrown with impenetrable thick weeds, and broken gravestones and even those could disappear overnight.

Chaim knew of all the 250 Jewish mass massacre sites in Lithuania and the history of every small town where Jews lived. All of Lithuania was Chaim's backyard. A keeper of the collective memory of Lithuanian Jews and a scholar in his own right, Chaim was eager to impart his knowledge to anybody who would listen. He told us many heroic and tragic stories my generation hardly ever knew, although our history books were filled with dates and battles the glorious Soviet Army won in World War II.

Leib Arieh Hilelson, 1911-1943   Mother and Father, Lithuania, 1967

Chaim's stories were from the era where stories would never end, and today many people are going back to Lithuania to hear and find out more.

Sometimes I would wonder - if Chaim, who knew of all these forgotten places, if he left Lithuania tomorrow, who would know where to find these cemeteries and mass murder sites? Who will preserve the memory of our lost relatives and who will guard their resting places?

The poignancy of those moments would often overcome me, as I would remember that Lithuania was like hundreds of other places in Europe where Jewish Communities once lived and then vanished. My generation, actually, helped this happen by choosing to leave. Should it not be up to us to preserve the memory of what now seems to be our ephemeral past?

Like other countries, Lithuania today, is just one big and sad museum, a showcase of a vanished culture, which so greatly enriched us. This culture left its lasting imprint on us, the Jews, called "Litvaks."

I carry it with me, this special sense of Yiddishkeit, the Lithuanian kind. When I came back to revisit that part of my identity and find its roots, I did not find it Lithuania.

I found it in me instead.

Part V

Ponar looks like a country place in the outskirts of Vilnius. We leave our bus and walk through the densely wooded area with winding pathways. We hear the wind as it softly runs through summer leaves barely touching them. Birds are twirling and chirping above in their summer dance, and ever so friendly. There is a soft smell of pine and cedar trees. It is serene and peaceful.

We walk to the small Museum of Ponar. We find a Lithuanian employee inside. He shows us a map where arrows point to geographic locations of Shtetls where Jews once lived. The arrows, actually, mark places where large numbers of Jews were killed.

I find Yurberik on the map, then skip through a dozen of other shtetls I come across a town called Solok in the East of Lithuania. That is my mother's shtetl. When we lived in Lithuania, I remember, my mother would make an annual trip to Solok in summer on Memorial Day. But she would never take me, or my brother along. Not even one photograph of her family could be found after the war. I have never seen a picture of my grandmother from Solok. When I was a child I would imagine my smiling grandmother I have never met, with gray hair, kind blue eyes and an apron. She would softly pat me on my cheek and tell my brother and me the wonderful tales of her past....

Chaim tells us the story of Ponar, and, as I look at the winding paths, this place begins to look somber and ominous. I remember lyrics from a Jewish Ghetto song "Never say you walk the road of no return". Prisoners sang that song as they walked these paths and never returned...

Ponar is the place where all hell broke loose in 1943. It was the killing ground of Jews from Lithuania, Poland and Germany. From the Ghettos and Labor Camps Jews were transported here to be killed in the thousands. They were made to dig their own graves, stripped naked and shot into the freshly dug pits.

We say Kaddish and light candles at every monument in Ponar. I am overwhelmed with emotion and wipe off tears that welled up in my eyes. Others cry too.

Part VI

Dobba Rosenberg is a Yurburger. She never left Lithuania and lives with her son in Kovno. She is a robust 75-year-old who speaks this Lithuanian Yiddish, which I love to hear so much. Chaim arranged to bring her along at our request. He knows her well because both live in Kovno where the few remaining Jewish families know each other.

Dobba joins us on our trip to Yurburg and walks us through the famous Kovner Street. She shows us the Tel Aviv Park, the gymnasium, Mituva River and the Nieman. She recognizes every stone and every crack in the sidewalk of Kovner Street.

She walks us past the houses of the Krelitzes, the Eliasheviches and the Zarnitskys, who were all members of our extended family, and tells us their stories. The story of Yurburg comes to life again through Dobba.

Doba calls us to follow on Kovno Steet in Yurburg

(Left to right) Fania, Yitzkhak Zarnitsky, Lottye Brodsky, Nava Zarnitsky, Doba Most Rosenberg, Chaim Bargman and Joel Alpert walking through the Streets of Yurburg.

Doba brought us to this rock, which was where they always used to bring visitors to Yurburg to have their photos taken -Memories of Happy times of the past! Doba was most happy to bring us here!

Noon time in Yurburg

It is noontime in Yurberik. Kovner Street is deserted and there are almost no passersby. I approach one older man on the street and can't help but ask him in Lithuanian.

"Excuse me, can you tell me, where the old Jewish gymnasium of Yurburg used to be?"

He does not know. I feel a sense of defiance and continue:

"Are there any Jews in Yurburg today?"

"None", he says,

"Where are all the Jews that once lived here?"

He looks at me, thinks for a minute and retorts:

"There was one broad, but she is dead"

I want to ask him if it is better here without the Jews, but I know the answer. Today Yurburg is a ghost town, with empty streets and locked-up shops; it is one of the poorest towns in Lithuania.

Doba Most Rosenberg at the Site of the Mass Massacre of the Jews at the Yurburg's Jewish Cemetery

Doba, remembering our past

Part VII

We are back on the bus. I remember that my father told me that there are about nine kilometers from Yurburg to Sudarg. He must have walked this road a hundred times, or rode in a cart pulled by a horse. He loved Sudarg, the town of his childhood and youth. Like Dobba, he remembered the vast green fields, the Mituva River and the Nieman.

We stop near a farmer's house, and he comes out to greet us. His name is Gintas Damusis. The old Jewish cemetery of Sudarg is right in his back yard. We take pieces of chalk and start going from stone to stone. We brush the old inscriptions with white or yellow chalk until we can read the names. Somebody calls out - here, out here!

I go there and approach a stone. I gaze at it and wonder how the stone could have remained so intact. I lean over to read the name and it says: **" Dov ben Dov ROSIN, died 1/8/1921 at the age of 63."**

Fania at Her Great-Grandfather's grave in Sudarg
Dov ben Dov ROSIN, died 1/8/1921 at age 63

Devorah Leah bat Shabtai ROSIN, died 3/29/1929

Fania's Great-Grandmother

My great grandfather Berchik? Next to him is the stone of Leah Rosin, his wife.

I touch the stone with my hand to brush off old dust. We take a picture of me next to Berchik's stone. Somebody brings a memorial candle. Everybody gathers around me, and we say together:

"Yidgadal ve Yidkadash Shmei Raba "

Words from the Book of Jewish Prayers come to my mind, and I repeat them silently

"Offer me no tribute of tears, nor monuments of sorrow. Do not weep for me. Instead live for me. Show your love by walking the Way in devotion to commandment, faith, and people".

Gintas Damusis, the farmer, hangs around and watches, the unexpected visitors to his back yard. He is amazed; he does not often see a bunch of foreigners in his back yard, perusing inscriptions on broken stones. I tell him that here in Sudarg, in his back yard, I found my roots, carved in stone.

Suddenly he asks me for my address and makes me a promise. He says he will fix these two stones and plant flowers. Later, in September, back in Montreal I will get a letter from Sudarg with photographs of the two gravestones with red flowers in full bloom. Gintas Damusis kept his promise, and I saved his letter:

Dear Fania,

I want to let you know that I am taking care of the burial places of the two people that are dear to you. I know what it means to lose somebody you love. Don't you ever worry dear Fania. Just let me know when I should light the candle and I will light it for your people. I light candles every year for my own too. I recently lost a son; his grave is not far from here. I will honor the anniversary of you people as I honor my son's

> *Sincerely,*
> *Gintas Damusis*

Devorah Leah Rosin's Grave and Berthik's grave after treatment by Gintas Damusi.   Photo by Gintas Damusis, October 2001

Part VIII

My thoughts take me back to the story of our ancestors, and here is how I think the story might have gone.

It happened in Yurburg in the middle of the 19th century. Jewish families of Yurburg were poor and pious, and raised many children, as many as God would give.

One young Jewish family by the name Naividel is hit by a devastating tragedy when unexpectedly Hilel Naividel's wife dies. Hillel Naividel, heart-broken about his loss, is left to care for his five children alone. He does his best to feed and cloth his children, and struggles with his daily chores.

Somewhere in the other end of town Elka Rosin is also left to grieve for a husband she just lost. Her two sons Berchik and Yitshak are too young to help her around the house and cannot yet support themselves.

Both families grieve separately. A long time would elapse before Hillel Naividel would notice Elka, still young and attractive, and what a neat housekeeper! One evening he puts on his long Shabbat coat and his hat, and knocks on her door.

When he comes out, he is smiling. There will soon be a wedding. Hillel Naividel will marry Elka Rosin.

Together they will care for their reconstructed family of seven children. There will be no end to their joy when Elka gives birth to one more child, a girl named Pesha.

The descendants of these eight children of the Naividel and Rosin family will find their destinies in various continents of the globe and in different countries.

Many will perish during the tragedy of the war.

Those who will live will try to preserve the memory of a family that began in the middle of the 19th century in a Lithuanian town called Yurburg.

In 2001 twelve descendants of the Naividel-Rosin Family would go back to visit the town where Elka and Hilel fell in love and married.

There, in the back yard of a Lithuanian farmer I would find the gravestone of my great grandfather Berchik Rosin, who was Elka's son

One hundred and fifty of us would gather at family reunions every two years.

At the reunions we will celebrate life, and remember how it all began - in Lithuania, in a small town called Yurburg.

Part IX

Our next stop is at the house of an old man in Sudarg. Joel, my husband Misha and I enter a very tidy home. It is neat as a pin. We meet an old clean-shaven man who sits at a kitchen table and watches Joel who came in with his video camera rolling.

I take out my old pictures of Sudarg and ask the old man.

- Do you remember any of these people?

I point at my father on the picture in his Sudarg years. The old man takes a look, squinting and straining his eyes. He puts his glasses on and looks again. What happens then is the most riveting moment of the trip.

"This is Gershke", he says, pointing at my father. "And this is his brother Yitske (short for Gershon and Yitshak). They were both Berchik's (the grandchildren of Berchik). They were tall and handsome fellows with black curly hair, I remember them".

I feel a lump in my throat and can hardly say a word.

The old man adds: *"As kids we all played together, we were all friends. My best friend was Danilke Zapolsky, a Jewish boy".*

I look at the old man and can't get rid of a persistent thought - was he really a friend of the Jews? Or was he a foe? He looks to me like he was a friend.

He stops for a moment and looks at the pictures again.

Second row: Goldberg with his daughter Leah, father, Yitskhak First row: Elka Goldberg, father's sister, Mina Rosin (my grandmother) and Leah Hilelson (Yitskhak's wife)

" *I was taken to Berlin as a slave laborer, and when I returned to town, all the Jews were gone, not one was left.*" They killed everybody, even the little girl, Goldberg's kid, you know, Gershke's niece?

I know the story and shudder remembering it, but continue listening.

"Berchik's Yitske jumped the train when the Nazis were taking him to the camps. He lived in the forest for some months. He made it through the war".

Part X

As the old man talks, the story of Yitshak and Leah, his wife comes back to me. I remember finding Leah's picture among old photos in our family album. I asked my father who this beautiful woman was, he told me that it was his brother's Yitshak's wife. It was Mother who told me their story.

Yitskak and Leah were married before the war. Their son was just a little boy when the war broke out. Leah and Yitshak were trapped in Kovno on the first day of the war. They were forced to move to the Ghetto together with their little son and Leah's mother.

Leah was a beautiful slender woman with blue eyes and blonde hair. She could sometimes sneak out of the Ghetto gates into the town unrecognized. She would be able to bring back food in exchange for jewelry and small belongings.

One afternoon, as Leah was walking on the street, a Lithuanian Officer began to yell obscenities pointing his finger straight at her. He called her a *kike* and *a dirty Jew*. As Leah tried to flee, the Lithuanian Officer pulled out a gun and shot her. Leah died on the spot.

Leah's mother began to spend days and nights with the little boy, her grandson. The dark day of the Children's Action came to the Ghetto and the planned execution of the Ghetto children was about to begin. All children had to leave their parents and line up at the Ghetto gate. Leah's mother held the boy tightly in her arms on the morning of the Action. She would not let go off the boy even when ordered to step aside. The Nazi Officer smirked seeing her age, then relented and told her to come along.

Among heart-wrenching cries of other children and parents, the grandmother comforted the boy in her arms, as she too went with him to the killing ground. A frail grandmother hugging a little boy disappeared in the foggy mist of that infamous morning, along thousands of others.

Yitshak carried on alone, grieving for Leah and their son. Then one day younger and stronger men were rounded up in the Ghetto and ordered on trains heading for labor camps to Shtudhoff. The train was running along the Lithuanian railway. At dusk Yitshak whispered a prayer and jumped from a running train into a ravine near a forest, rolling over several times. He survived the jump and crawled to the forest. Protected by darkness with his bare hands and sturdy sticks he dug a hole in the ground, choosing leafier branches to cover the hole. He hid in his makeshift shelter when the first rays of light broke. When night fell again he could see thousands of stars twinkling in shades of blue, and yellow white. He knew then he would survive. Yitshak climbed out of the hole to look for food in a forest lit only by the moon and the bright stars. He ate wild berries and licked morning dew from leaves. One moment he heard voices and barking dogs. He jumped back into the hole. Squatting low, he stopped breathing, waited, and danger passed. One night he ventured out further than usual reaching a farm. He waited until a farmer showed up in the early hours of the morning and called out.

The Lithuanian farmer brought food and water. From then on he would leave a jug of water and bread for Yitshak. Once the farmer did not show up for three days. Yitshak starved. Then the farmer showed up again. "It was too dangerous the days before", the Lithuanian farmer said, "The Germans were too close".

Before winter Yitshak joined the Army.

He survived the war, and life triumphed over death. He married again and had a son David. They all went to Israel in 1953. David lives in Israel with his family.

For the first time, as I remember Yitshak's story, I begin to wonder if anybody knows the name of the Lithuanian farmer whose kindness saved a person.

Yitskhak, the first days after the war, 1945.

Part XI

Our host continues to look at the pictures. I hear him say: "I don't know what happened to Gershke. I think he died in Kaunas".

No, not so.

My father survived the war too. He went to Israel, where he spent the best years of his life. He worked in a Tel Aviv Bank, and at his happy moments he would say with pride. - " I, one of the Berchiks became an Israeli Banker".

Father's story was special because it had an ending from the Torah.

"You shall take your brother's widow"(Be Rashit, Leh Leha ve Ishuv, p. 88.)

Gershon Hilelson (Gershke) was born in Sudarg in 1913 in a family of nine children. At that time there was not much for young people to do in the small town like Yurburg or Sudarg. Everybody was dreaming of moving to Palestine or other countries.

In 1921 three brothers and a sister managed to get visas to go to America and they settled in Albuquerque, New Mexico.

Gershke, the youngest, was only eight years old when his older brothers left in 1921. Other brothers and sisters stayed behind, hoping some day to go to America too. But for them, it would be too late.

Gershke and his older brother Leib Hilelson settled in Kovno before the war. Leib just got married to Tzilia when the war broke out. On June 21, 1941 at 4:00 o'clock in the morning Tzilia woke up in a panic. Sirens and loudspeakers were announcing the beginning of the war, and the German planes were hovering all over the city. There was mayhem outside, and people were running towards the train station. With an instinct for survival, Tzilia urged both brothers to run and catch the first train out. Nazi planes were already bombing the city as they ran to the train station and caught the last train out. The train was bombed repeatedly and was forced to stop in Latvia. Many passengers continued the journey by foot. They ran through fields and forests, hungry, scared and desperate. They met local peasants on the way who told them that German planes returned to Germany, and it was safe to go back to Kovno. Leib, Gershke and Tzilia turned around to go back. They met other stranded Jewish families on the way and were told not to go back to Kovno. Leib, Gershon and Tzilia managed to hop on another train and then they were forced to get off. They ran again through fields and forests. They were on the run for two long and hungry weeks, until they finally reached a village in Uzbekistan.

The three registered with local authorities and were sent to live on a collective farm. Even though there was hunger, lice, anti-Semitism and other plagues, the Nazis were far away.

Soon both brothers were called to serve at the 16th Division of the Lithuanian army, with the largest Jewish contingent. There was talk that race was the reason why soldiers of the 16th Division were poorly armed, yet sent to fight the toughest battles.

The fatal battle took place near the Russian town of Oryol in Russia in 1943. Both Leib and Gershon were in the front lines. Gershon was seriously wounded. Leib, who was a military paramedic, ran to help his brother; he wanted to get Gershon out of the battle zone. While running to save Gershon, Leib was hit by a sniper. He was dying in front of Gershon's eyes, and Gershon was unable to help. Gershon lost consciousness and when he came to, he was in a military hospital where he would remain confined to bed for six months. Although he recovered, shrapnel stuck in his leg, left him with a permanent limp. Overwhelmed by guilt, Gershon grieved for the brother he adored. He would remain haunted by this moment of the war for as long as he lived.

Tzilia was unaware of the fate of the two brothers. One morning, as she was walking in the village street a Jewish woman took her aside and told her - " Tzilia, I heard bad news".

She lowered her head and then said almost in a whisper, not looking at Tzilia.

"Your husband died in the battle near Oryol"

Tzilia was inconsolable.

"Where is Gershon?" she asked after a while, still sobbing

Nobody knew.

Six months later, still weak, Gershon returned to the village where Tzilia lived. He came back to marry his brother's widow and take her back to Lithuania.

The Torah says, **" You shall take your brother's widow "**

Both survived the war and returned to Lithuania.

My twin brother and I were born a few years after the war, when both Tzilia and Gershon returned to Kovno. Father never spoke about this. Mother did when we were 22 years old.

My twin brother on the left and our parents, 1952

Part XII

I ask the old man from Sudarg if he remembers where the Berchiks lived. He tells us that they used to live in the house up the hill. We say good-bye to our host and drive up the hill. Gintas Damusis points out the house.

I take out an old photograph and see that this is the same house Even the doorframe remained the same. But it is not my father's house. This is where Elka Goldberg, my father's sister used to live. The old man referred to the little six-year-old Leah Goldberg, daughter of Elka. I remember the chilling story passed down in the family.

"We are like a breath, our days are like a fleeting shadow.

We are like new-grown grass

In the morning it flourishes and sprouts afresh,

In the evening it is cut down and withers

So teach us to number our days

That we may get us a heart of wisdom" (Psalm 144)

The house in Sudarg where the Goldberg's lived, now it is the house of elderly farmers.

Little Leah in Sudarg (1940)

Little Leah was only six years old when the war started. In the summer of 1941 a sixteen-year-old Lithuanian neighbor, passing by the house saw little Leah outside. He grabbed her by her feet and threw her violently into a tree as her mother watched. A six-year-old child died in the hands of an overzealous local murderer.

That summer of 1941 in the months of August all the remaining Jews of Sudarg perished, mostly in the hands of their neighbors.

We go to the forest and after a short walk find a white stone - the monument to Sudarg Jews. This is the Mass Massacre Site.

Jolanta, a local woman with a young son, tells us that neighborhood school children are brought here twice a year on a field trip, Part of the field trip includes clean up of the place. She explains that this is how authorities keep up face and save money.

I am afraid that we will run short of memorial candles. We lit so many along the way, but Joel and Nancy brought enough.

We say Kaddish one more time but still not our last.

Jolanta, the local woman says there is one more place to visit in this forest. We walk for about half an hour, but she can't find the place.

In September she will send me a photograph of another white monument she found in the woods.

I read her letter and I am touched beyond words.

The sign on the monument reads, "In this place Hitler's murderers and their local helpers slaughtered 48 Jews men, women and children on 8/12/1941."

Dear Ms. Fania,

You came all the way from Canada to find a monument, and I felt so bad I could not help you find it. I went to look for the monument after you left. I took a picture for you when I found it and I am sending you one. I hope you will accept my apologies that I could not find the monument when you were there.

Jolanta.

I am grateful for the kindness of strangers we meet on our way in these forgotten Lithuanian places.

The photograph Jolanta Gedviliene sent me is the monument for 40 women and 16 children from Sudarg who were shot by the Nazi occupants and their local helpers on August 11, 1941.

I do not know where the Hilelsons and the Goldbergs were murdered, but it must be at one of these two places.

This picture was sent by Jolanta, after she found the monument.

Part XIII

My father never wanted to go back to Sudarg; He wanted to get further away from it. Thirty years after the war, he was finally able to leave and go to Israel. He never looked back, and, if he did, it was only in his dreams when in his shtetl Sudarg everybody was still alive.

We leave Sudarg and Yurburg. We are back in the old city of Kovno, and Chaim shows us where the Jewish Ghetto used to be. I can't believe him, I am so perplexed. I was here a hundred times when I lived in Kovno, and I never knew this was the place.

There are so many things I did not know when I lived in Lithuania. Why didn't I know? I ask Joel.

Joel who was born in Madison, Wisconsin and raised in Milwaukee tells me that in his family nobody spoke about the Holocaust.

Holocaust was not a subject to be discussed in Jewish families in America or Lithuania. Perhaps, that was the way to protect the children from the memories and the horrors of the past. To be able to continue their lives the survivors tried not to think about it, but the silent beast always lurked close by. And we, the children, knew it was there.

So that was the answer I was searching.

What matters now is that Joel and I know more now. So does Brenda, Mark, Nancy and all the others who went with us on this journey.

Our trip is coming to an end. Time to say good-bye to Chaim. We shake his hand and wave to our "Teacher of the Way". We are all grateful to him for helping us find the places of our common past along the forgotten back roads of Lithuania. Mission accomplished? No, Chaim Bargman will stay behind to guard the remaining Jewish cemeteries of Lithuania and tell the next group of travelers' stories of the past. Our ancestors will be a part of that story.

We are back on the plane. We will take a connecting flight to Amsterdam.

The stewardess makes the announcements in Lithuanian, but this time I do not follow.

I listen to music and try to figure out in how many hours I will be back home in Montreal.

Part XIV

Every two years we attend a family reunion along with other 150 people. I remember when I first heard Joel Alpert's name four years ago, I did not know who he was. Joel Alpert seemed to me a whiz that managed to figure out our intricate family connections, design complex family trees, and remember all the names along the way. His was the name of a genius.

I wrote to Josef Rosin, my father's first cousin in Israel, to ask how we were related to Joel Alpert.

" We are not", replied Joseph bluntly.

I was very disappointed. Still, I continued to search through multiple family branches to figure out, perhaps, a distant connection? It was, indeed, remote - through remarriage of the Hillel Naividel to the Elka Rosin four or five generations earlier-

At the first family reunion it was even more confusing. Who is who? How do I figure out the family ties binding me to these nice cousins who flew in from many different corners of the North America, Mexico and Israel to the family reunion?

Each time I spoke to a cousin, I tried to figure where she would have to be placed on the family tree. I heard other cousins asking the same question "So how are we related?"

Finally I found my answer:

We have a common past through the lives of our ancestors. This life started in a small Lithuanian town called Yurburg over a century ago. No Jewish family in Yurburg or surroundings shtetls and towns would remain untouched by exodus, war and loss.

By a twist of fate or the wisdom of our grandparents some of us were born in safe haven. The reunion is a tribute to the ancestors who had the wisdom to know better and leave in time. The reunion is also homage to the memory of the others, who, by fluke of fate, did not make their journey to safety.

I thought about our family. I began to understand that the history of our family epitomizes a larger Jewish history. Our family is but a small part, a microcosm of the bigger Jewish world. This larger world was as uprooted, filled with loss as ours, and the final victory of life triumphed in the larger world, as it did in our family. .

The reunion is then a tribute to our lost folks, no matter from which branch of the family they were. I am sure our ancestors would have liked to see us today, heirs to their wisdom at such a big reunion, celebrating life, with a cheer "LeHaim", and to all of us.

Fania Hilelson Jivotovsky   Montreal, Canada   June 2002

Rosin Family at the Yurburg Family Reunion in Detroit June 2000.
Fania at lower left.

Naividel Family at the Yurburg Family Reunion in Detroit June 2000.

Feinberg Family at the Yurburg Family Reunion in Detroit June 2000.

Craine Family at the Yurburg Family Reunion in Detroit June, 2000

Krelitz Family at the Yurburg Family Reunion in Detroit June, 2000

The first Yurburg family reunion was held in Minneapolis, Minnesota during July 1998, with 85 attending. The second was held in Detroit, Michigan in July 2000, with 135 attending, and pictured above; shortly afterward a reunion was held in Israel, attended by about 20 Israeli cousins from the same families. A third reunion was held in July 2002 in Milwaukee, Wisconsin, with 100 people attending. The next one is tentatively planned for the summer of 2005, possibly in Montreal, Canada.

Naividel - Rosin - Yurburg Family Reunion in Israel in 2000.
These families were gathered at these reunions because many were members of several family groups and hence were all cousins in one way or another.

The Jewish Cemetery in Yurburg

By Joel Alpert and Fania Hilelson Jivotovsky

"Show me your cemeteries, and I will tell you what kind of people you have."   Benjamin Franklin (1706 - 1790)

For most of us any cemetery is a somber and a sad place to visit. It is the "city of the silent," where we seek out that very special stone that carries the name of the person we still love, and recapture our treasured moments and images with that person. We shed a tear and place a flower or a marble on the carved granite, and whisper a prayer before we leave.

In front of the stone of a loved one, we face our own mortality. There and then, we are better able to sort out what is really important in the big scheme of things, before we too depart one day.

Other cemeteries might be less personal to us, yet they remain fascinating places with a unique tranquility and history, where a name carved in stone becomes eternal and carries the spirit of somebody's life and a memento of achievements of the common everyday person who lived and worked, and contributed to the creation of a better place for those that followed.

But not all cemeteries are sources of community pride and not all societies promote an attitude of reverence and respect, and encourage preservation of these unique resources for future generations to appreciate and learn from. If a society fails to deal with this issue not only will genealogical and historical past be distorted, but also this society will potentially lose its civility. Along the way the ability to record the true course of its human history will also be lost.

On our trip to Yurburg in May of 2001, we found the "Old Jewish Cemetery of Yurburg", which remains a forgotten but unique memorial to a centuries old Jewish community that perished in the hands of the Nazis and their willing Lithuanian collaborators.

The cemetery sits on a hill about a kilometer to the east of the town, overlooking the Nieman River in a beautiful and idyllic setting of the Lithuanian countryside. Amazingly, this cemetery, unlike the other sites we have visited, remains in relatively good condition, with the grass not too high, and the view of the headstones and graves still unobstructed by the bushes and trees overgrowing the monuments that remain. Some headstones still stand proudly upright, while others, worn out by relentless passage of time or vandalism, are lying on the ground.

The Nazis overran the Jewish community of Yurburg on the very first day of the German invasion of Lithuania, on June 22, 1941. This is the only institution of the Jewish community of Yurburg remaining today, six decades after the murder of all the Jewish residents.

The Yurburg Cemetery in May 2001 [Photo by Dr. Leon Menzer]

It is now well known that that the old Jewish cemetery of Yurburg became one of the massacre sites of the Jews of Yurburg. Today, in this cemetery, we can find a memorial engraved in stone and long rows of gravel marking the site where Jews were forced to dig their own graves into which they fell after they were brutally massacred.

But things are slowly beginning to change. In 1990, the current Yurburg community, now all non-Jews undertook to clean up the cemetery. Dobba Most Rosenberg, a 72 year old former Yurburger, who still lives in Lithuania, accompanied us on the trip to Yurburg in May 2001; she told us of an effort to engrave a new stone in memory of the Yurburg Jews who perished in the war. A proper inscription on the monument will place Jews at the beginning of the citation, because most of the victims of the massacres were Jews. The old memorial inscription bearly mentions that the Jews were the majority of the victims. Gladly, we gave money to the Jewish community in Vilna to help them accomplish this task.

In 1995, Donald Levinsohn of Maple Shade New Jersey commissioned a Lithuanian to photograph the headstones of the Old Jewish Cemetery of Yurburg. Donald then sent the photos to Joel Alpert who translated the legible inscriptions. Of the 325 photos, Joel could read the first names and the family names of about half of them, and first names on most of the remainder (see the "List of headstones" below, revised by Max Michelson of Natick, Massachusetts).

One late night as Joel was translating these head stones, he realized in amazement that he had found his own great-grandmother's head stone. "Leah (Naividel) Krelitz, daughter of Hillel" was what he read. Joel relates that the date of her death, as indicated on the head stone was 1904 and confirms the family story. "My grandmother, Celia Krelitz, was faced with a painful and most difficult decision of her life - to stay with her mother who had fallen ill, or leave before borders would close tightly. Celia Krelitz chose the ultimate sacrifice that would have repercussions for generations to come - with a pained heart she left her mother she knew she would never see again. Thanks to her sacrifice, a generation of her descendants could live in safe haven. Celia accompanied her sister Rachel and her cousin Hillel Eliashevitz (Harry Ellis), whom she would marry a few short years later, and went to America in 1903." Leah did have a son Meyer Krelitz, and two daughters, Elka Krelitz Zarnitsky and Masha Krelitz Abramsohn, who remained behind with her in Yurburg.

In May 2001, Joel Alpert, Brenda Freshman, and Itzhak Zarnitsky, all descendants of Leah Krelitz had made a trip to Lithuania and visited her grave in the Old Jewish Cemetery of Yurburg. It was most likely the first time in 60 years since the Shoah that anyone in the family had visited the gravesite.

On that trip in 2001, we visited numerous other Jewish cemeteries. In Rassein, we could only find a plaque on a low stone wall overlooking an empty field that indicated the site of the old Jewish cemetery. In Kibart we found the Jewish cemetery surrounded by a fence with many standing headstones, all overgrown with trees, weeds and thick bushes growing right out of the graves. But the mausoleum marking the grave of our cousin's Josef Rosin's grandfather could still be easily identified, in spite of continuous vandalism endured over the years.

In Sudarg, just a few kilometers to the west of Yurburg, behind a farmer's house, we found a fenced off field behind a farm house with a sign telling that this was the site of the Old Sudarg Jewish cemetery. With only a handful of headstones visible, finding an old stone of an ancestor in an old forgotten graveyard of Lithuania was tantamount to a sheer miracle. Said Fania: "two standing headstones of my great grandparents had an emotional impact on me that is difficult to convey. Splendidly preserved and imprinted for eternity in a dusty stone of Sudarg, these were my roots, the ones I came to reclaim. To learn about the past was an enriching experience for me and it became a journey of self awareness and understanding."

What many of us have learned is that, it is important to preserve and visit these forgotten places of our past. Our ancestors, they too made this world a better one for us to live. Some of them paved the way for others to find better lives, and sacrificed their own along the way.

By visiting these forgotten Jewish cemeteries of our ancestors in blood-soaked Lithuania and paying tribute to our past, we accept all of life – with the joys and the sorrows, the love and the loss, as we remember….

March, 2003, Montreal and Boston

The Yurburg Cemetery

Headstones of Yakov Naividel and Rafael Feinberg

New Memorial Plaques that now Memorialize the Jewish Victims

Not in original Yizkor book - Courtesy of Dr. Leon Menzer - June 2003

Close up of New Memorial Plaques that Memorialize the Jewish Victims

Not in original Yizkor book - Courtesy of Dr. Leon Menzer - June 2003

These plaques read in Lithuanian on the left and in Yiddish on the right:

"Here, on the third of July 1941, the Nazis and their local collaborators murdered more than 300 Jews and several tens of Lithuanians and Russians. In 1941 the entire Yurburg Jewish community was liquidated - more than 2000 people."

LIST OF PHOTOS OF HEADSTONES

Commissioned by Donald Levinsohn. Translations by Joel Alpert with corrections by Max Michelson. Material owned by Donald Levinsohn and Joel Alpert, may be used for genealogical purposes only.

#	LAST NAME	FIRST NAME	FATHER'S NAME	FATHER'S LAST	Death Year
135	Abramson	Abraham-Zalman	Chaim Yehuda	Abramson	1860
290	Abramson	M			
117	Abramson	Rachel	Shmuel		1902
43	Alperovitz	Aharon	Hashitz Yitzhak Dvd		1915
177	Anazavitz?	Sarah Leah	Yosef		
230	Anshel	Eliahu	Shraga	Anshel	1910
57	Apriaski	Yitzhak	Ychzka	Apriaski	1897
109	Arenyai?	Sarah Hinda	Mier		
12	Arnstein	Eliahu	Yehuda	Arnstein	1921
241	Azafavitz	Yisrael	Tzvi Hersh	Azafavitz	1890?
227	Azaftitz	Eliezer Kitka	Tzvi Hersh	Azafavitz	1864
10	Barski	Moshe	Sharmyahu	Breski	1895
251	Barski	Yacov Meir	Yehuda	Barski	
19	Beckman	Matatyahu	Moshe	Beckman	1932
148	Beralmitz	Sarah Frieda			
147	Beralover	Hanah	Manat		1913
229	Berkover	Shalmad Tzvi	Yehuda	Berkover	1928
75	Berman	Chaia	Yitzhak	Berman	1925
142	Berman	Chaisa Hanah	Shmuel		
314	Bernstain	Jetta		Gittelmann	1929
315	Bernstein	Wolf			1937?
36	Bernstein	Yenta Kreena		Gitelman	1929
14	Bluma	Mrt.? (daughter)	Meir	Alperovitz	1930
34	Boraski	Rueven	Yehuda Lev		1882
35	Chabdon	Shalom	Yisrael		1889
5	Chosid	Shnaier Zalman	Aharon	Chosid	1922
232	Dramveen?	Pnina Malka	Dovid	Perlman	1919
268	Epshtein HaLevi	Asher	Avraham Yitzhak	Epshtein	
58	Epshtein	Yakov	Moshe	Epshtein	1901
61	Ess	Dov	Nachman Mordechai	Ess	1939
154	Ess	Rachel Elka	Aharon	Ess	1868
190	Ess	Yosef	Avraham HaCohen	Ess	1906?
305	F(e)inberg	Nachum Yacov	Moshe Menachum	Feinberg	1917
179	Feenah	Devorah	Dovar		
303	Feinberg	Chaie Taube	Benjamin (Born 1850)	Jacobsohn	1923
21	Feinberg	Hanah Malka	Yeheskal Mordechai	Karmi? Born 1886	1933
174	Feinberg	Rafael	Naftali Hertz		1885
140	Feinberg	Rena Malka			1933
84	Feinberg	Sarah	Yacov Asher		1921
6	Feinberg	Shlama Lev	Nachum Yacov	Feinberg	1912
52	Feinberg	Yoel	Shlomo-Zalkind		1887
6	Feinberg	Yosef Dov	Nachum Yacov	Feinberg	1912
302	Fidler	Dawid			1927
72	Fidler	Dovid Leb	Tzvi	Fidler	1927
64	Fidler	E. M.		Born 1850	1940
60	Freeman	Gita	Kappel	Freeman	1936

222	Galvshar	Yehuda	Akehlim	Galvshar	
96	Glazer	Ezriel-Yakov	Zalman-Dov		1930
25	Hacohen?	Leib	Yisrael Hakohen	Hacohen?	1915
26	Hacohen?	Yehuda Leib	Eliahu Hakohen	Hacohen	1923
267	Hertz	Asher			
73	Heselkbein	Yehuda Leb	Yehoshua	Heselovitz	1932
85	Heselovitz	Avraham	Baruch	Heselovitz	1912
76	Heselovitz	Sheina	Yitzhak		1915
316	Ivenski	Ita Raina			
326	Ivensky	Chloine? Zelik			
309	Jablonski	Melik?			1936
318	Jablonsky	Shloma	Tzvi		1911
139	Joelsohn	Sophie	Dovid Abraham	Zundelevitz	1913
321	Joffe	I. L.			1917
328	Joselit	Chaim			1923
16	Kagan	Rachael Batia	Nachum Yakov		1931
134	Karabelnik	Yonah	Yisrael Natan		1935
137	Katz	Shayna	Yacov		1865
224	Kavakalaska	Yosef Yakov	Ykutial	Kavakalaska	1906
103	Kobelkowski	Chaia Bacha	Nachum-Mordechai		1906
68	Kobelkowski	Hanah Frieda	Nachum Mordechai		1913
13	Kolisar	Pinchas	Eliezer	Kolisar	1927
28	Kopelov	Guttman Lev	Zvi	Kopelov	1917
93	Kopelovitz	Nemal? Shoham	Nathan Lieb		1921?
94	Kopelovitz	Nemal? Shoham	Nathan Lieb		1921?
327	Kopelow	Scheitel	David	Feinberg	1926
265	Krelitz	Leah	Hillel	Naividel	1904
30	Kushlevitz	Hana	Yitzhak	Hacohen?	1921
71	Kushner	Elihu	Avraham	Kushner	1923
310	Landau				
161	Lashitz	Mina	Numyhi?		1864
253	Latushitz	Mordechai	Shlyma	Latushitz	1909
277	Lau?	Rachel Leah			1921
252	Lavzinov	Yitzhak	Natan	Lavzinov	1866
145	Leivin	Yisrael Dovid			1934
156	Levin	Chasha	Eliezer	Levin	1934
67	Levin	Chasha			
80	Levin	Pesha	Moshe		1915
225	Levin	Yacov Dovid			1906
152	Levin?	Yisrael Dovid	Moshe	Levin?	
159	Levinson	Devorah	Eliakum		1864?
1	Levinson	Israel	Moshe Halevi	Levinson	1887
4	Levinson	Raiza	Yisrael	Levinson	1913
3	Levinson	Sarah	Dober Hacohen		1865
2	Levinson	Yitzhak	Moshe Halevi	Levinson	1867
171	Levishitz?	Solzdison	Alez?		1904
226	Levitan	Chaim Tzvi	Avraham	Levitan	1872
160	Levitan	Sarah Feiga			
160	Levitan	Zalman			
304	Liubin	Jakir			1933
259	Menev?	Menachem	Yosef	Zar? Tanase?	
317	Michalauskienes	Rive		Born 1876	1936
44	Michelovsky	Devora Rivka	Eliezer	Michelovsky	1936
69	Michves	Ruven	Noah		1931
32	Mintzer	Avraham	Yakov	Mintzer	1929

100	Mishkin-Stenzer	Avraham	Eliahu		1907?
208	Modar?	Hillel	Benjamin	Blass	1910
17	Most	Israel Yitzhak	Mordechai	Most	1919
213	Naividel	Shmuel	Yacov	Naividel	1910
306	Ormian	ME			1938
23	Palavin	Meir Shrage	Yakov	Palavin	1917
207	Poledevitz	Yakov	Yitzhak	Poledevitz	1864
54	Pollak	Hinda Tzerla	Yehoshua		
27	Pulerevitz	Chai Reesa	Yakov	Pulerevitz	1913
88	Pulerevitz	Hersh	Yisrael		1880
27	Pulerevitz	Rivka	Yakov	Pulerevitz	1915
97	Pulerevitz	Yosef	Aharon		1888?
38	Rabinovitz	Chai Sarah	Zadok		
92	Rabinovitz	Hinda Rachel	Chaim	Rabinovitz	1910
324	Rabinovitz	Maks?			
35	Rabinovitz	Miriam	Yoel HaCohen	Rabinovitz	
38	Rabinovitz	Yehuda			1913
250	Razkeal?				
24	Rickler	Chiena Rachel	Note? Halevi		1935
29	Rickler	Rachael		Lewinson	1934
108	Rifkin?	Beer	Yitzhak		1890?
319	Rochca	Henna Rivka	Shmuel-Bentzion		1919
323	Rochco	Moshe Menachem	Shraga		1915?
90	Rozen	Sarah Beylah	Hillel	Rozen	1924
301	Sack	Salomon	Shmuel?	Sack	1806?
307	Schmulovitz	Scheine Malke			1934
89	Shachnovitz	Yitzhak	Aharon		1912
79	Shapira	Eliezer	Yehuda Hacohen		1914
20	Shapira	Miriam Rivka	Yosef	(Shapira)	1916
70	Shapira	Shraga	Menachem HaCohen	Shapira	1917
170	Sheftelboim	Miriam	Dovid		1852
125	Shenftron ?		Eli		
124	Shmulovitz	Shayna Tochel?	Yacov		
209	Shov-zatzal?	Teshe Leah			
45	Shraga	Mordechai	Yosef Yitzhak		
116	Shraga?	Chaia	Noah		1884
329	Simonov	Olga	Yoel		1907
320	Singermann	Sore Pesche	Yehuda		1915
247	Sobil	Yakov Dovid	Eliezer	Sobil	1899
308	Sundelowitz	Dora Dvora	Yitzhak Leb		1903
311	Sundelowitz				1900
244	Taibman	Yisrael	Chaim	Taibman	
33	Taumim	Chaia	Mordechai		1936
9	Tompavski	Rivka	Mordechai Tov		1880
312	Urbach	Schmuel	Yehuda ?		1901
243	Vaiborski	Lev	Yon Raud ?	Vaiborski	1902
95	Valdislevski	Tooba	Eliezer		1939?
158	Veber	Yacov Yaka	Moshe	Vachan	1925
62	Veelenzek	Blooma	Moshe		1913
15	Verbelovski	Gershon	Yehuda	Verbelovski	1921

7	Verbelovski	Haim	Avraham Akiva	Verbelovski	1912
14	Verbelovski	Sarah	Dov Baer		1936
313	Verblauskas	Chaimas			1912
149	Weizman	Blooma	Tzvi		1935
8	Yablonsky	Miriam Devora	Moshe Yonah		1936
18	Yaffach	Yitzhak Lev	Chaim Zeev	Yaffach	1917
146	Yankelovitz	Benzion	Noah	Yankelovitz	1909
276	Yazelit	Yakov Dovid	Tsadok	Yazelit	
101	Yazepovitz	Dov Baer	Tzvi		1911
162	Yerkmeaheum	Chana Hinda	Rachmiel	Alexandrovitch	1889
256	Yoselit ?	Mariasha	Avraham v Gvia		1936
99	Zachvald ?				
322	Zak	Raizel-Miriam	Aizik		
163	Zalabartski	Yisrael Yosef	Tzvi HaLevi		1883
260	Zalkind	Shmuel Nachum			
151	Zapolsky	Shayna Beylah	Menachem Mendel		1940?
228	Zaratzeer	Avraham Yitzhak	Leib	Zaratzeer	1865
65	Zeedar	Chaia Yenta	Shmuel? Dovid		1930
153	Zundel	Yehuda Leib	Crenta?		1865
37	Zundelavitz	Shamri Tovia	Zalkind Zeev		1925
140	Zundelevitz	Gisha Misha?			1931
22	Zundelevitz	Hitzla	Dov	Bernstein	1922
212		Aharon	Tzvi	Bal Lavar	
216		Amra?	Avraham	Varabalovski	
234		Asher Dovid			
237		Avital	Molchar	Ardnutz	1863
279		Avitar		Zel??	
112		Avraham			
41		Basha		Dan	1915
136		Batia?	Moshe		1865
46		BatSheva	Yona		
121		Beylah	Yehuda?		1887
115		Blume	Yitzhak		
126		Chai Micla	Abraham Aba	Hacohen	1885
143		Chaia Bailah	Yitzhak HaLevi		
111		Chaia Yichbad?	Avarahm		1879?
50		Chana ?	Shlomo		
165		Chasia	Yakov		1924
199		Chaya	Moshe HaCohen		1882
201		Cheana-Rikle	Hillel	Yabo	1865
31		Devora	Aharon Yosef		
47		Devorah	Yisrael		
86		Devorah	Moshe		1887
129		Devorah	Yitzhak		1879
175		Devorah			1891
278		Dinah	Yitzhak HaCohen		
186		Dov Baer	Aharon	Kalitz (Born 1854)	1922
261		Dovid			
77		Dvora ?	Dovid Avraham		1841?
119		Eisar	Chaim		1904
78		Eliezer	Moshe		1902?
281		Elka			
105		Ephriam	Shlayma		
274		Esther	Eliahu	Feller	
180		Esther	Yisrael? Yitzhak	Sharasharski	
195		Esther	Moshe		
257		Esther Rivka	Yitzhak	Konamski	
40		Eta		Yakov	1876
132		Eta Malka	Natan Nata	Levi	
63		Etel	Nachum	HaLevi	

138		Fiega	Shloma		1885
150		Frieda	Dovar		1900
223		Frumme-Friede	Nachum		1861
11		Gala Raisa	Zvi Zarin		1909
235		Genia	Yehuda		1910?
39		Hanah	Shlomo		
91		Hanah	Aharon?		1895
155		Hanah	Mohard?		
168		Havatula Mulka	Yitzhak		
263		Itta-Dvora	Moshe	Dachdelach	
130		Leah			
102		Leib	Noah-Zvi HaCohen		
164		Liba			
48		Libe-Malke	Yitzhak		1882
106		Malka			1869
220		Mattityahu	Yitzak Halevi		1900
86		Meir	Duber ?		
289		Menachem	Yacov Haled?	Levamal	1884
287		Menachem			
55		Michal	Zeev	HaLevi	
231		Miriam	Dov	Azafavitz	1872?
275		Miriam	Shmuel	Belski	1900
273		Miriam Rivka	Yakov		
182		Moshe	Simcha	Komstone?	
144		Motala	Nochum		
185		Motti-Tzvi	Simcha	Kochman?	
56		Nachman			
81		Nachum	Eliahu		1845?
239		Pesha			1861
167		Pesia	Avraham		1911
42		Rachel			
280		Rachel	Yitzhak		
144		Rachel Rivka	Yehoshua		1864
131		Reesha	Meir		
297		Rivka	Dovid		1932
87		Rivka Rose	Avraham		1869
245		Sarah		Benhol	1890
74		Sarah	Naftali Hertz		
120		Sarah	Yitzhak		1880?
110		Sarah	Yechiel		
296		Sarah ?	Halenel ?	Bosazar ?	
82		Sarah Rachel	Simcha		
66		Sarah Rochla	Simcha		
221		Shalom Levi Chiad	Tovia	Herdnariu?	
201		Shayna		Shapira	
242		Shimshon Dovid	Pinchas		1919
59		Shlomo-Zelik	Pinchas		
107		Shmari	Zvi?-Mordechai		1886
255		Taiba	Machor	Tinchov	
254		Tamar Tzadok	Afraim		
85		Toiba Leah	Nachman		1925

98		Toomba?	Hershal?		
214		Tova Dafra	Moshe-Yitzchak		
293		Tzvi			1879
83		Yehezkel-Wulf	Yakov HaChazzan		1848
197		Yehoshua	Avraham		
166		Yehuda Shalom	Shaul Ha Cohen		
291		Yehuda Shalom	Avraham		1864
258		Yisrael			
325		Yisrael	Yosef		
285		Yitzhak	Dovar	Daztan	1909
53		Yitzhak	Hamoleg		
127		Yitzhak	Adriel?		
169		Yitzhak Chain	Aharon		
176		Yomhada?	Eliezer	Tomazvitz	
178		Yosef			
270		Yosel	Moshe		
203		Yosl			
283				Avalanska	1932
208			Avraham	Karza?	1910
173			Sfula	Mulish	
272			Yakov	Polerevitz	
114			Tzfee	Rosenfeld	1885?
49					
51			Tzvi		1883
104			Yisrael		1881
118					1883
123					1882?
128					1914
133			Avaraham		
157					
181					
191					
198			Moshe-Eli		1904?
211			Pinchas		1885
222			Alimard??		
233					
236			Mordechai		
238					
246					1861
248					1902
249					1861
266					1865
271			Avraham		
278					
294					1893
299					1910

Model of the Yurburg Shul in El Paso

By Joel Alpert

View Right Side of the Model of the Old Wooden Synagogue of Yurburg

There existed in El Paso a Holocaust museum of 3000 square feet built through the energies of Henry Kellen, a Holocaust survivor from Lithuania. This building burned down due to an electrical fire on Oct. 1, 2001. Undetered, Henry decided to convert the disaster into an opportunity to build an even larger Holocaust Museum and is now (2003) in the process of erecting a 30,000 square foot structure, with the generous financial help of the Mexican Jewish community and on land donated by the Mesa Group of El Paso. It will be located near the downtown close to the entrance to the I-10 freeway. The architect will be a young Mexican Jew.

As part of this new museum, Henry Kellen has asked that Hank Scherr build a model replica of the Yurburg Shul (Old Wooden Synagogue) for placement into the museum. Henry had visited that shul in 1935 and fondly recalls it and wanted it memorialized through this model.

Shown above and below are views of that model already built by Hank Scherr.

Front and Back View of the Model of the Wooden Synagogue of Yurburg

Left Side View of the Model of the Old Wooden Synagogue of Yurburg

Map and Property Records of 1907

From the Kaunas Regional Archives
Fond I-51, Inventory 5, File #63
List of Real Estate Owners of Yurburg
From Town of Jurbarkas, Uyezd of Raseiniai, Gubernia of Kaunas

1. See plot number identification on map following the list for the corresponding record numbers.

2. Note that the spellings of the names may differ from accepted English spellings due to different transliteration convention.

Surname	Given Name	Plot #
ABELSON	Abel	250
ABRAMSON	Itsyk	99
ABRAMSON	Izrael	101
ABRAMSON	no name	102
ABRAMSON	no name	194
ABRAMSON	Zusel	174
ADLER	Ette	356
ALEKSANDROVICH	Iosel	240
ALPEROVICH	David	82
ANTSEL	Ilia	248
ARSHTEYN	Ilia	345
ARSHTEYN	Yankel	245
AYZENSHTADT	Chaim	187
BEKER	Leyzer	159
BEKKER	Orel	24
BERENSHTEYN	Berel	165
BERENSHTEYN	Ekhil	207
BERENSHTEYN	no name	162
BERMAN	Abel	147
BERMAN	Berel	180
BERMAN	Itsyk	185
BERMAN	Movsha	116
BEYMAN	Kreyna	83
BEYMAN	Rocha	65
BLUMENTAL	Shmuel	164
BORKOVER	Ionel	16
BORKOVER	Slon (??)	177
BRESKY	no name	160
BRESKY	Roza	263
BRESKY	Shmaya	152
CHERTOK	Chaya Mera	25
DANILEVICH	Chaim	87
DAVIDOVICH	Piner (?)	171
DAVIDZON	Shaim	127
DEVAL	Orel	360
DVINAYTSKY	Abram	90
DVINAYTSKY	David	251
ELIASHEVICH	Leyzer	89
EPSHTEYN	Freyda	117
EPSHTEYN	Sura	182
ERSH / ERIN (?)	Girsh	79
ESS	Etla (?)	92
ESS	Irsh	80
ESS	Movsha	148
ESS	Tevel	62
ESS	Yankel	93
FEYNBERG	David	67
FEYNBERG	Gabriel	68
FEYNBERG	Leyzer	121
FEYNBERG	Leyzer	136
FEYNBERG	Mordkhel	257

FEYNBERG	Sora	122		KABLUKOVSKY	Rochel	173
FEYNBERG	Zelik	123		KABLUKOVSKY	Zelik	91
FIN	Girsh	253		KABLUKOVSKY	Zelik	94
FINBERG	Nokhim	367		KANTER	Bentsel	190
FLEKS	Anna	233		KAPLAN	Abel	85
FRIDLAND	Kalman	276		KAPLAN	Abel	138
FRIDLER	David	338		KAPLAN	Abel	140
FRIDMAN	Leyba	354		KAPLAN	Nosel	20
GACRALSKY	Honel	280		KAPLAN	Orel	224
GAMLER	Leyb	184		KAPRIAS	Sora	28
GERMAN	Oisel	74		KIZEL	Movsha	111
GERSHELEVICH	Girsh	95		KIZEL	Movsha	151
GESELEVICH	Abram	110		KIZEL	Movsha	157
GESELKEVICH	Leyb	66		KOMEL	Mordkhel	249
GESELZON	Kushel	124		KOMEL	Mordkhel	260
GESHENFELD	Mikhel	384		KRECHMEN	no name	149
GEYNSHEYNFELD	Mikhel	361		KRELITZ	Meyer	161
GEYSHENFELD	Mikhel	178		KRELITZ	Meyer	163
GLAZER	Benjamin	355		KRUPINSKY	Iudel	113
GLAZER	Girsh	189		KURLIANDSKY	Mikhel	398
GLAZER	Girsh	234		KUSHELEVICH	Berel	129
GOLDSHTEYN	Iokhel	88		KUSHELEVICH	Leyzer	369
GOLDSHTEYN	Joseph	199		KUSHEVSKY	Abram	175
GOLDSHTEYN	Mendel	145		KUSHNER	Eliash	6
GRIMFERD	no name	100		LATYSHEVICH	Mordkhel	382
GRINBERG	Mordkhel	254		LEVIN	Beyla	373
GUTOVSKY	Chaya	77		LEVIN	Notel	78
IOZEFER	Shlema	351		LEVINSON	Chana	352
IOZELIT	Abram	31		LEVINSON	Leyb	132
IOZELIT	Robert	115		LEVINSON	Leyba	153
IOZELIT	Robert	125		LEVINSON	Reyza	188
IOZELIT	Robert	128		LEVITAN	Mordkhel	58
IOZELIT	Tsodyk	139		LEVITAN	Sora	232
IOZELIT	Tsodyk	141		LIBOVSKY	Abel	181
Jewish School		186		LIBOVSKY	Leyzer	375
Jewish Synagogue		109		LIBOVSKY	Leyzer	385
Jewish Synagogue		119		LIUBOVSKY	Sholem	349
Jewish Synagogue		120		MARKEL	Shmuel	179
KABLUKOVSKY	Abram	130		MASHLEVICH	Wulf	103
KABLUKOVSKY	no name	370		MASTER	Chaim	104

MAZUR	Iosel	48		ROKTSOV	Abram	108
MAZUR	Iosel	53		ROKTSOV	Movsha	107
MAZUR	Orel	98		ROVAL	Orel	365
MEYBIZNER	Itsyk	54		ROZEN	Itsyk	144
MEYEROVICH	Iosel	183		ROZENFELD	Orel	86
MEYEROVICH	Leyb	158		ROZENSHTOK	Gersh	168
MEYEROVICH	Leyzer	244		SHAKHNOVICH	Iudel	112
MEYEROVICH	Rykler (?)	126		SHMEREL	Zundel	118
MEYEROVICH	Shmuel	137		SHNEYDER	Shlioma	146
MIASNIK	Girsh	96		SHRAYDER	Eder	267
MIKHALOVSKY	Chaim	357		SHTOK	Leyb	143
MIKHELSON	Eliash	8		SHUVAL	Aron	358
MIKHELSON	Shulem	97		SOBOLEVSKY	Osip	172
MINTSER	Abram	377		SOLTS	Boris	237
MINTSER	Shaya	60		SOMASHEVICH	Isaac	242
MOSKOVICH	Mordkhel	73		TEPLIR / TEPMER (?)	Albert	262
NAYVIDEL	Feyga	134		TEPLIR / TEPMER (?)	Albert	264
NAYVIDEL	Feyga	150		TEPLIR / TEPMER (?)	Rudel	281
NAYVIDEL	Feyga	156		VERBALOVSKY	Iler	383
NAYVIDEL	Meyer	191		VERBALOVSKY	Sora	161
NAYVIDEL	Sholem	348		VILENCHIK	Rakhmiel	364
ONSHVONGER	Izrael	131		VOLK	Chaim	255
PANE	Chaim	135		WULF	Meyer	159
PATVENTS	Mikhel	332		YABLONSKY	David	266
PER	Itsyk	176		YANKELEVICH	Chaim	105
PITSILEVICH / GITSELEVICH (?)	Iosel	241		ZARNTSKY	Leyba	154
POLIAK	Sheyer	72		ZENDELEVICH	Chana	19
POLOVICH	David	258		ZENDELEVICH	Uga (?)	261
POLOVIN	David	81		ZHEBROVSKY	A.	18
POZHARINSKY	Itsyk	372		ZONDELEVICH	Wolf	193
PRES	Itsyk	344		ZUNDEL	Leyb	106
PUKARD	Mortkhel	61				
PUKHER	Zelman	166				
PULIAREVICH	Chaim	169				
PULIAREVICH	Notel	170				
PULIAREVICH	Yankel	167				
RABINOVICH	Isaac	29				
RABINOVICH	Iudel	252				
RABINOVICH	Max	371				
RACHEL	Chaya	155				

Yurburg Town Map Properties – 1

German Street

Rasein Street

1907

Following is new material added in the third printing.

Restoration of the Jewish Cemetery in Yurburg

By Joel Alpert

My wife, Nancy Lefkowitz, and I, traveled to western Lithuania in June 2007 to take part in an unusual project that resulted in the restoration of the Jewish cemetery of Yurburg (Jurbarkas in Lithuanian), the hometown of my maternal grandparents.

This adventure had its genesis back in 2001 when, after visiting Yurburg with a group of cousins, we stopped in Vilnius (Vilna). There we were approached by Zalman Kaplan, an 80 year-old survivor from Yurburg, now living in Vilnius, with the request to rebuild the decaying fence around the Yurburg cemetery. Miraculously, in contrast to most Jewish cemeteries in Lithuania, which sadly have been turned into parking lots, soccer fields, or, at best, empty fields nearly devoid of headstones, the stones having been carried off and used in construction, this Jewish Cemetery in Yurburg still had over 300 identifiable headstones.

Zalman Kaplan
In Vilna

We could not refuse such a request. My cousins and I decided to create a not-for-profit organization to raising funds to finance the building of the new fence. Thus, the "Friends of the Jewish Cemetery of Yurburg, Inc." was founded in 2005, and in the fall of 2006, with the organizational help of the Jewish community of Kaunas (Kovno), a new entrance to the cemetery was erected. This was the first step in refurbishing the cemetery.

The next development was completely unexpected. Unbeknownst to me, Dartmouth College Hillel runs a unique program called "Project Preservation" that brings Dartmouth students to Eastern Europe to work on Jewish cemeteries that are in varying states of disrepair. The program has been in place for the past five years.

New entrance to the Yurburg Jewish Cemetery constructed in fall of 2006

Rabbi Edward Boraz of Dartmouth Hillel was searching the Internet for a cemetery for the 2007 project. After finding our Yurburg cemetery project, Rabbi Boraz contacted me. As a result of the extensive research that had been posted about the town of Yurburg, as well as the cemetery's need for ongoing repair, Yurburg was an ideal site to meet the needs of the students and their project. In addition, my 2003 publication of this English translation of the Memorial Book of the Jewish Community of Yurburg, Lithuania, originally written in Hebrew, could serve as the textbook on the Yurburg Jewish community for the students participating in the project.

In June 2007, Dartmouth Hillel brought nearly two dozen students, both Jewish and non-Jewish, to carry out the hands-on labor to restore the cemetery. The Dartmouth students completed the work initiated by the "Friends of the Jewish Cemetery of Yurburg, Inc." by erecting a new fence, over 700 feet in length, along the decaying pre-war fence around the perimeter of the cemetery. The students also dug up numerous headstones that had fallen over and been slowly covered over by earth and grass. Every headstone was photographed, and the wording on each is being translated and cataloged. A map of the tombstone locations ws drawn up in order to assist future visitors in locating their family members' headstones. A catalogue of the identified headstones along with links to pictures of the headstones and their translation is available at:

https://kehilalinks.jewishgen.org/yurburg/CemFiles/Project%20Preservation%202007%20-%20Yurburg,%20Lithuania%20__%20Names-1a.html

A map of the cemetery is on:
https://kehilalinks.jewishgen.org/yurburg/CemFiles/MAP.html

Something else was accomplished: a change in the relationship with the town. In May 2005, the Friends of the Yurburg Jewish Cemetery had proposed to the Jurbarkas town council the possible restoration of the Jewish cemetery, but our plan met with a rather cool reception. It seems that the council had heard other American Jews promise to do work in the town but with poor follow up.

New fence alongside the pre-war fence

This time, however, the response was remarkably different. A leader of the Dartmouth students, Evan Konwiser, visited Yurburg's high school a few days before the other Dartmouth students arrived. There, the English teacher, Asta Akutaitiene, recruited 10 high-school students for the cemetery project. These students worked alongside the Dartmouth students in erecting the fence and in digging up and cleaning the long-buried headstones. Upon seeing the American students working with the local students, the town authorities became cooperative and supportive.

We had felt that it would be very important to involve the townspeople for another reason. Once the Dartmouth students completed their work and left, it would rest with the town to assist in maintaining the improved condition of the cemetery, as there is no Jewish resident left in Yurburg to oversee the cemetery. (The 1,887 Jewish residents recorded in the 1923 census constituted 43% of the town population. During World War II, the Nazis and their Lithuanian helpers slaughtered 94% of the Jewish population in Lithuania.)

Lithuanian high school students having just excavated a long buried headstone with their Engish teacher

While working at the cemetery, we encountered a mystery: there were newly re-painted inscriptions on some of the old headstones. Who was doing this, and why? We discovered that a 34-year-old local Jurbarkas woman, Rita Vaiva, has been repainting the inscriptions for the past three years. She explained that growing up in the town as a young teenager, she would come out to the cemetery after school to read and contemplate because the cemetery and its grounds were quiet and beautiful. After a time, she wondered about the place. Who was buried here? What were these people's lives about?

Eventually she decided to go to Vilnius to study Hebrew so that she could understand what the headstones said. (Rita even pointed out to us misspellings and malformed Hebrew letters!) After work, Rita goes to the cemetery to carry out her mission. Soft-spoken, sensitive, and committed, she told us her story and was happy to see others so interested in her adopted cemetery. The American group was moved by

Rita's story and by her ongoing devotion and dedication to this old, abandoned Jewish cemetery.

For more about RiVa Vaiva read "Preserving the Past of the Jurbarkas Jews" a translation from the Regional Lithuanian Weekly Newspaper "Sviesa (Light)" at https://kehilalinks.jewishgen.org/yurburg/Rita.html

RiVa Vaiva reinscribing a headstone at the Yurburg Jewish Cemetery

One of the highlights of the work in Yurburg for me came when I located the headstone and grave of my great-grandmother (in addition to the graves of several other relatives). My joy at this discovery and the history of those relatives, which I shared with the Dartmouth students, added meaning to their work. The headstones, they realized, belonged to actual families, and these families had histories. The Dartmouth students recognized that this journey to Yurburg and their work had resulted in a dream-come-true for me, and they were proud to share in it. In addition, the Jewish students among them understood that it was their heritage, too.

Just before we all left, I went over to my great-grandmother's grave and, following Jewish tradition, placed a small stone on the headstone as a sign that I had paid my respects at her grave. Two of the Dartmouth students did likewise. I was deeply moved.

Headstone of Leah Naividel Krelitz, great-grandmother of Joel Alpert at the Yurburg Jewish Cemetery

The now-restored cemetery will serve as a memorial to honor the Jews who lived and died in Yurburg when the town was vibrant and played an important role in enhancing and enriching Jewish culture. The bond that was made between the local high school students and the Dartmouth college students in their connection to the vanished Jewish community serves as a sign of hope for the future.

For more pictures taken during the restoration go to: https://kehilalinks.jewishgen.org/yurburg/CemFiles/Project%20Prese rvation%202007%20-%20Yurburg,%20Lithuania%20__%20Photos.htm

Below are additional pictures taken at the cemetery in 2007.

Rabbi Edward Boraz translating headstone with RiVa Vaiva to the right

Headstones reinscribed by RiVa Vaiva

More Headstones reinscribed by RiVA

Below is a list of 185 photographed and translated headstones that can be found on
https://kehilalinks.jewishgen.org/yurburg/CemFiles/Project%20Preservation%202007%20-%20Yurburg,%20Lithuania%20__%20Names-1a.html

Last Name	First Name
[Gutman] Lev	Kapalow
[Washlin][B18]	Chaim Tzvi son of Abraham
Abrahamson	Isaac
Abrahmson	Dobre Zlate
Alperovitz	Aaron son of Isaac David
Alperovitz	Bluma
Anschel	Eliyahu
Aronson	Sarah Hindah
Arstein	Eliyahu
Azapowitz	Miriam daughter of Dov
Azapowitz[B1]	Yisrael
Bainas[A1]	Sarah Rachel
Bakbag	Hayah
Balcher	Aaron the son Tzvi
Bambag	Hayah
Behrman	Hayah
Behrman	Hasyah
Behrman	Rachel
Benzion[A2]	Shmuel
Berkawar[A3]	Shlomo Tzvi
Berkovar	Betzallel
Berkowar	Hannah
Bernstein	Wolf
Bernstein[G1]	Yenteh Kreinah
Bernstein[B2]	Hetzelah
Berolovitz	Sarah Freida
Borski	Moses

Borski	Reuven
Borek	Tzadok
Chaimowski	Ruchama
Chaiken[F1]	Dubar the son Of R Yitzcak
Choas[A4]	Reuven
Chosid	Shneer Zalman
Chosid	Aaron
Egonska	Eliyahu
Eisenberg	Yisrael Moseh The son of Dov Yitzchak
Elbaum	Israel Mordechai
Epstein	Jacob
Evonoski	Etah Rainah
Feinberg	Sarah
Feinberg	Shlomo Lev
Feinberg	Sarah Mina daughter of Yosef Dov
Feinberg	Henneh Malkah
Feinberg[B3]	David
Feinberg[B4]	Rafael
Feinberg[B5]	Joel Zalkin
Fiedler	A.M. (1940)
Fiedler	David Dov (1927)
Finberg	Nachum Yaakov
Freeman	Risa Gita
Galbartzki	Yisrael Yosef Halevi
Galgishar	Judah
Gitelman	Yenteh Kreinah
Haselkovitz	Shanah
Haslkovitz	Judah Halev son of Joshua Hesel
Jablonsky	Davd Shlomo son of Zvi
Joelsohn[F2]	Sophie daughter Of David Avraham
Joselit	Faige Yente daughter of Chaim
Joselit	Jacob David son of Zakoknah
Kabalkavski	Hannah Freida
Kabalkovski	Hayah Bakbag (or Mambag) daughter of Nachum Mordechai
Kabelkovski	Shmuel son of Shlomo
Kapalow	Shaitl daughter of David

Kaplan	Rachel Leah daughter of Eliyahu
Kaplan	Joseph son of Shimon Nachman
Karabalnik	Jonah son of Yisrael Natan
Karabalnik	Yisrael Natan
Karabalnik[F3]	Riklah daughter of David and wife of Jonah
Kerem (or Krom)	Rachel daughter of Moshe
Kogan	Rache Batyah daughter of Nachum Yaakov
Kolisar	Pinchas son of Eleazer
Koshalovitz	
Kosolovitch	Menachem Mendel son of Aaron Yehuda
Krelitz	Leah Krelitz daughter of Hillel [Naividel]
Krom[6]	Rachel daughter of Moshe the Kohen
Kushner	Eliyahu son of Avraham
Latushavitz	Mordechai son of Shlomo
Levine	Israel David son of Moshe
Levine[B7]	Pesha daughter of Moshe
Levine[B8]	Yehudit daughter of Avraham
Levinsohn	Pesiah daughter of Avraham and wife of David
Leviton	Sarah Mina daughter of Yosef
Leviton	Tzvi Zalman son of Shlomo Meir
Levitz	Hashah Daughter of Eliezer
Levitz	Eliezer
Lewin[B9]	Yehudit daughter of Avraham
Lewinson	Deborah daughter of Elykum
Lewinson (may not be Lewinson)	Hasyah daughter of Yakov
Lewinson	Yitzhak son of Moshe HaLevi HaKohen
Lewinson	Sarah daughter of Dubar
Lewinson	Raisah the Daughter of Israel
Lincoln[F4] (or Linkeen)	Yakir son of Israel David
Lotaman	Menachem son of Yakov
Lovine[B10]	Peshah daughter of Moshe
Lovitz	Hashah daughter of Eliezer
Lovitz	Elizer
Lovitz[B11]	Dov Ber son of Judah
Unreadable [H1]	Mariashah daughter Of R. Josef

Most	Yisrael Yitzhak son of Mordechai
Michalovska	Divorah Rivkah daughter of Chaim
Mintzer	Avraham son of Yaakov
Mintzer	Sarah daughter of Avraham
Mintzer	Sarah daughter of Avraham
Mintzer	Avraham[F5]
Naividel	Shmuel son of Yakov
Nerunah	Rachel Nirunah daugher of Yitzhak
No Number	Orman Sleiman
Palman	Tzvi Yehudah son of Tzvi
Palvin	Meier Shraga son of Yakov
Paretz[2]	Sarah the daughter of Naphtali
Pearlman	Faigah Malkah pf Rotwine daughter of David
Polaravitz	Hirisah daughter of Yakov
Polaravitz	Rivkah daughter of Yakov
Polaravitz	Yakov
Polarawitz	Yakov son of Yitzhak
Polarawitz	Yosef son of Aaron
Pollack	Ruuach[B13]
Pollack	Hindah Tzirlah daughter of Joshua
Pollack[H3]	[Achtat daughter Of [Yisrael]
Rabinowitz	Hindah Rachel daughter of Chaim HaCohen
Rabinowitz	Dov Ber son of Josef
Rabinowitz	Haye Sarah wife of Judah and daughter of Zadok
Rabinowitz	Yitzchak [G2] son of Judah
Rachtzah	Henna Rivka daughter of Shmuel Benzion
Rachtzah	Moses Menachem [A5] son of Shraga
Rachtzah	Sarah Rachel daughter of Benyamin Rainas
Rachtzah	Shagra son of Avraham
Rachtzah	Riklah Hannah
Ramah	Faigah
Rikler (born Lewinson)	Kaina Rachel
Rikler[G3]	Rahel
Rosen	Isaac son of Dov Ber
Rosen	Sarah Balah daughter of Hillel [Naividel]

Rosenfeld	Aaron sson of Chaim
Rotwein[B15]	Faigah Malkah daughter of David Pearlman
Salanter	R Yitzchak
Saltz	Dov Ber son of Aharon
Saron	Gilah Raizah daughter of Tzvi Saron
Shaitovitz	[ ] son of Dov
Shamashowitz	Miriam Hedah daughter of Eliezar
Shapira	Eleazer son of Yehuda HaKohen
Shapirik	Yitzchak son of Yechezkel
Shapiro	Shraga son of Meachem HaKohen
Shapiro	Miriam Rivkah daughter of Yosef
Shashowitz	Eliezer
Shebach[C1]	Hayyah Sarah, daughter of Shimon HaLevi
Shevi[B16]	Israel son of Sherirah Shevi
Singermann	Sarah Pesche daughter of Yehuda
Smolovitz	Shainah Malkah daughter of Yaakov
Sondelowitz	Devorah daighter of Judah Lev (Yitzhak Lev)
Sondelowitz	David son of Z'rusmah [?]
Sondelowitz[B17]	Hitzlah daughter of Dov Bernstein
Sondelowitz[F7]	Siphrah Joelsohn daughter of David Abraham
Sondolowitz	Shomrei Tuvyah son of Zalkind Zev
Sondolowitz	Sisah Mushah {requires translation}
Soundelowitz	Judah Lev [not readable}
Taditz [G4]	Tzviyah daughter of Naptali
Tas[F8] or As	Dov son of Nachum Mordechai
Tumim[F9]	Hayah
Urbach	Shmuel son of Yechezkel
Waldislavivaski*	Toivah daughter of Eliezer
Walim	Yechezkel son of Yaakov HaKohen
Weitzman	Blumah
Welantzik	Avraham Wilantzik
Werbelovski	Gershon son of Yehuda
Werbelovski	Sarah daughter of Dov Ber
Werbelowski	Ida daughter of Avraham
Werbilovski	Chaim son of Avraham Akivah

Wilnar[B19]	Shalom son of Yisrael HaKohen
Wolnar	Shalom son of Yisrael HaKohen
Yablonski	Miriam Devorah
Yafo	Yaakov son of Yehuda
Yafo	Yitzchak Lev son of Chaim Zev
Yafo (Yapo)	Hannah Riklah daughter of Hillel
Yalowitz	Avraham [son of Baruch] and Tovah Leah [daughter of Nachash]
Yankelowitz	Ben Zion son of Noach
Yatzchantan	Leibah daughter of Avraham
Yazapovine[B20]	Dov Ber son of Tzvi
Zalkin	Yoel son of Shlomo
Zalkinber[g][B21]	David
Zapolski	Shaynah Baylah daughter of Manachem Mendel
Zarnitzky[A6]	Abraham Isaac son of Lev
Zidar	Hayah Yenteh

Synagogue Square Memorial
Dedicated to the Memory of the Jewish Community of Jurbarkas

Jurbarkas is home to an extraordinary memorial, opened to the public on July 19, 2019. It has become a symbol of hope that Litvak history will become inseparable from Lithuanian national history, culture and heritage.

The Synagogue Square Memorial was a multinational effort, connecting descendants of the Yurburg community from Israel, the USA, South Africa, UK, Russia and Canada as well as philanthropists from Lithuania, Germany and Israel.

This project was initiated by the Jurbarkas township and the regional municipality led by the town mayor Skirmantas Mockevicius in 2016.

The first step was naming the corner square at Kaunas and Krantas streets - *The Synagogue Square*, following the suggestion of the ambassador of the State of Israel to the Republic of Lithuania, Mr. Amir Maimon.

This location was part of the central Synagogue complex of Yurburg, next to the entrance to the Great Wooden Synagogue and the Stone Beis Midrash. This square used to be the town's regular market place and a central gathering place for the Jewish community of Yurburg.

Next, the concept for the memorial was developed: inspired by the Neman river, which was the key resource that attracted Litvaks to settle in Jurbarkas, this river of stone blocks carries over 1800 surnames in Yiddish and Latin scripts, of all Jewish residents of Georgenburg-Jurbarkas-Yurberik, ever registered in this town from late 18th century till 1940. This could be considered as a real life *Yizkor* (memorial) to the whole community, one of a kind in Lithuania.

Alongside the Jewish community members, the memorial includes names of dozens of Righteous Among the Nations from the Yurburg vicinity - becoming the first ever memorial to those who saved Jews during the Holocaust in Lithuania."

Jurbarkas is known as one of the Lithuanian towns where all crimes - murders and looting - was either initiated or executed by local residents. Therefore it is quite symbolic that 75 years after the darkest period of this town's history, this would be the place to acknowledge the heroism of those who chose to remain humane and true to their neighbors, while risking their lives and the lives of their loved ones.

The central element of *The Synagogue Square Memorial* carries a sculptural image of the destroyed Wooden Synagogue, the stones carry parts of the *"Avinu Malkeinu"* prayer as well as the Catholic equivalent – "Our Holy Father" in Lithuanian.

This project was completed with great support of four major non-profit organizations

- Outset Contemporary Art Fund, the Israeli chapter
- Good Will Foundation (Lithuania)
- Kuriam Jurbarkui Association, created by local residents to fundraise in Jurbarkas and Lithuania
- The Friends of Yurburg Jewish Cemetery, which is dedicated to restoring and caring for the cemetery and fostering the memory of the destroyed Jewish communiity of Yurburg

The work on this memorial, including the fundraising campaign, idea and concept development, detailed planning, project coordination, historical research, sculptural stonework and installation works were done by three members of a Yurburger family:

- Sculptor David Zundelovitch
- Art-director Gregory Zundelovitch
- Architect Anna Zundelovitch

In memory of the Zundeliovich, Dimant, Bregovsky and Levitan families and the incredible Jewish Community of Yurburg.

May their memories be for a blessing.

First Press Conference - Project Presentation in Jurbarkas.
From Left to right:
H.E. Ambassador Amir Maimon and his assistant Liana Jagniatinsky
Mayor of Jurbarkas regional municipality Mr. Skirmantas Mockevicius
Head of the Jewish Community in Lithuania Mrs. Faina Kukliansky
Authors of the Synagogue Square Memorial Project:
   David, Anna and Gregory Zundelovitch

Mayor Skirmantas Mockevicius and Sculptor David Zundelovitch

Sculptor David Zundelovitch presenting details of the memorial sculpture to Jurbarkas mayor Skirmantas Mockevicius and head architect of Jurbarkas regional municipality, arch. Grazina Gadliauskiene

Sculpture Representation of the Famous Wooden Synagogue

Synagogue Square Memorial On-Site Visualization

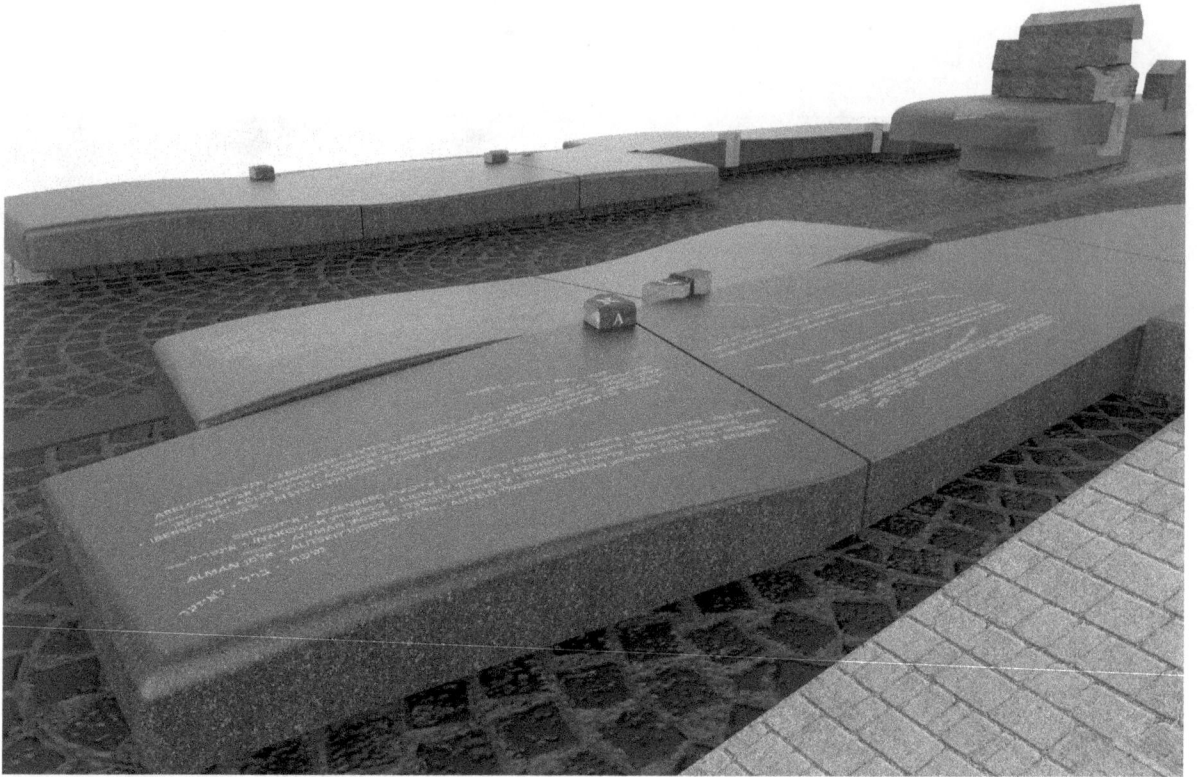

View of the Memorial Stones with Yurburg Family Names

Central axis of memorial composition - Shiny granite strip directed towards Jerusalem

Following are family histories of the Zundeliovich Families

Bregovsky family

The Bregovsky brothers Markus (Mordekhay) and Itzhak moved from Jonava to Jurbarkas around the 1880-s and established a pharmacy in town. They became a known and respectful family, with almost every family member involved in the pharmaceutical business.

Their house, next to the stone pharmacy (which is operating to this day), was on German street, now called Donelaicio street.

Markus was married to Fanny (Feiga) Dlugatch, who moved to Lithuania following her husband. They had three children - sons Savva and Nikolay and a daughter Vera. Nikolay grew to be one of the Jewish community leaders, a pharmacist like his father, he invested in education and supported Zionist youth movements active in Yurburg. Nikolay was executed on July 3rd, 1941, during the first 'action'. His wife, Eugenia was staying at that time in Kaunas, with their son Max (Markus). Many Jews assumed that since Kaunas was annexed by the Soviet Union, the war won't reach them.

Eugenia and Max were killed during the liquidation of Kaunas ghetto in summer 1944.

Vera, the youngest daughter, married her childhood friend, Simon Zundelovich, who's brother Gregory was an apprentice at her father's pharmacy. They moved from Jurbarkas to Kaunas in the late 1930'es following Simon's work as general accountant of Guma factory. They had a son, David Zundelovich born in Jurbarkas in 1923.

Vera survived the horrors of Kaunas ghetto. Witnessing the murders of her son, nephew and sister-in-law, as well as the news of the killings of her brother, cousins and family remaining in Jurbarkas, turned her into a quiet and very close lady. She lived thanks to her husband Simon. They passed away within a month from each other in 1971, in Vilnius Lithuania.

Levitan Family

The Levitan Family lived for quite a few generations in Jurbarkas. Zalman-Hirsh Levitan son, Meyer-Zusman was one of the elected Jewish community leaders, serving as a town council member and deputy to the mayor. The family lived in a large house on Kalishu (Alexandr) street. Meyer-Zusman married Rebecca-Beile Kobelkovsky and they had two sons. First born, Yekutiel (Kushel) married Dora Girshovich from Siauliai. They spent their first years as a married couple in Jurbarkas, raising their daughter Mina. Just around 1939 the young couple moved to Kaunas, but as news of Jewish persecution in Germany and Poland reached Lithuania, Yekutiel returned to Jurbarkas to encourage his parents and brother to leave. Zusman Levitan refused his son's request, but made sure Yekutiel and Dora manage to leave to Belarus and get evacuated to Central Asia. Dora and Yekutiel had two younger children, who passed away while they were in Central Asia. They returned with Mina to Vilnius.

Mina Levitan studied art and textile design in Vilnius Art Academy and grew to be one of the most progressive and creative gobelen artist in USSR, known and respected for her incredible monumental works for various public buildings, all around the world. Her art works can be found in museums and private collections in Lithuania, Russia, Israel, USA, the Netherlands, France and elsewhere. In 2008, Mina Levitan received a recognition Order - Merit of Lithuania, Knight's Cross, from the President of the Republic of Lithuania. Mina Levitan-Babenskiene lives in Vilnius, Lithuania. She has a son, two granddaughters and a grandson.

Zusman-Meyer Levitan, his wife Rebecca and younger son remained in Jurbarkas when the Nazis invaded Lithuania. Their son was executed during the first 'action' on July 3rd, 1941. Zusman and Rebecca managed to escape the first massacres, hiding with neighbors and friends. Eventually someone exposed them and they were caught. While being led to their death, Zusman begged their convoy, whom he knew since childhood as he was Yekutiel's friend, to spare the long walk and kill them. The convoy granted their wish and their burial place is unknown.

Zundelovitch family

Sundelowitz - Zundeliovich – זונדעליאוויץ

Starting from the very first census records there has always been a record of Zundel \ Zundeliovitch \ Sundelowitz family in Yurburg. Male members of the family were mostly tradesmen, both first and second guild members, which allowed them to move quite freely around the Russian Empire and settle in Russia's largest cities - Moscow and St. Petersburg. However, Yurburg always remained their "hometown" and there are numerous records of Zundelovitch merchants using passports issued in Jurbarkas around the Empire. By the end of the 19th century members of the family began immigrating to the New World countries settling in South Africa, United Kingdom, United States, and Australia.

By 1910 there were two Zundelovitch\Sundelowitz families living in Yurburg. The family of Shimrey-Tuviah Zundeliovitch, who waselected Jewish Community leader and representative at the city council (buried in Jurbarkas Jewish Cemetery), and family of David-Eliash Zundeliovich.

David-Eliash Zundeliovich was a first guild merchant, he started his business ventures as tax and customs officer at the border service set in Jurbarkas and later became one of the main timber merchants in the region, dividing his life between St. Petersburg and Jurbarkas. He married Rozalia Dimant, whom he was introduced to by relatives in St. Petersburg, as she was also from a respected Litvak family. David-Eliash and Rozalia had 5 children, daughters Xenia and Sofia and son Simon Zundeliovich were born in St. Petersburg and the two younger children daughter Lidia and son Gregory (Hirsh) Zundeliovich were born in Jurbarkas. They rented a stone house on Robert Jozelit lot on Kaunas street, just next to the market place and town's major synagogues.

In 1914, following a sudden death of David Eliash Zundeliovich in St. Petersburg and the news of the World War I front line reaching Prussia, Rozalia and her children moved to St.

Petersburg and remained there with her relatives until the winter of 1918.

While in Russia, Simon completed the Royal Cadet college, and Gregory, who was trained as a pharmacy apprentice from the age of 9 (he worked at Bregovsky pharmacy), intended to study medicine.

The family returned to Jurbarkas for a few years but as Lidia married Joseph Sokolowsky (representative of Columbia Records and His Masters Voice records) and moved to Kaunas, other siblings also spread out with only Simon Zundeliovich remaining in Jurbarkas with his wife, Vera Bregovsky, and her relatives, working at the Jewish bank as senior accountant.

Gregory Zundeliovich completed his bachelor degree in Sorbonne university, Paris, and masters degree in pharmaceutical sciences in Strasbourg university. He returned to Lithuania in the early 30'es and soon enough opened his own pharmacy in Klaipeda. There he married Bertha (Beile) Gurfinkel from Palanga. In 1938, after seeing Hitler speaking to public in Klaipeda, he decided to join his relatives and the whole family was united again in Kaunas.

In 1940, when Soviet forces took over Kaunas, Lidia's husband was arrested and her family (Joseph, Lidia and their children) were sentenced to labour camps in Siberia. Joseph never returned from that journey. The remaining family members were trapped in Kaunas ghetto. They managed to survive until the very last days of the ghetto. Refusing to separate and being sent to concentration camps the family remained for two nights in a burning house, where Simon and their neighbor Hirsh Tzadok, left a note to whoever finds the message to avenge their death.

Gregory, Simon and his wife Vera Bregovsky managed to escape the burning ghetto and survived. The rest of the family members did not survive.

Lidia and her children, Asia and Faivush, survived the Stalinistic labour camps and returned to Lithuania in late 1960's. Shortly after their family made Aliyah fulfilling her husbands last will to move and live in Israel.

Gregory Zundeliovich remarried in 1949. He called his son David, after his own father David-Elias, and nephew David who was murdered in the Kaunas ghetto.

David studied art from childhood and became a sculptor. His works often relate to the Jewish history of Europe and the origins of Jewish spirituality in Israel.

In 2016, David was requested to create a memorial dedicated to his father's family community - the Jewish Community of Jurbarkas. His older children, Greg and Anna joined the project and together they created a unique memorial at the Synagogue Square in Jurbarkas, completed and opened to public in July 2019.

While being introduced to the location selected for the memorial, they discovered it would be located just next to the stone house where David's father, Gregory was born.

INDEX

Please note that the lists on page 725, 733 and 747 were not included in the index due to technical difficulties.

Also please keep in mind when using the index that different translators used different spellings and the transliteration of names is not consistent. So please search for family names under all possible spellings.

Israel, 9, 10, 12, 13, 15, 16, 17, 19, 20,
22, 23, 33, 34, 35, 37, 38, 48, 49, 59,
63, 64, 65, 66, 67, 68, 82, 83, 89, 91,
92, 97, 99, 109, 131, 133, 134, 136,
138, 139, 140, 142, 145, 147, 152,
157, 158, 163, 169, 171, 175, 180,
181, 184, 186, 189, 190, 191, 192,
193, 196, 197, 199, 200, 202, 203,
205, 206, 207, 209, 211, 212, 213,
214, 215, 216, 218, 219, 220, 221,
222, 223, 224, 226, 227, 228, 230,
231, 232, 233, 234, 235, 236, 237,
238, 240, 242, 243, 244, 246, 247,
248, 249, 253, 254, 255, 256, 257,
259, 260, 261, 263, 264, 266, 267,
268, 272, 273, 274, 275, 277, 279,
280, 281, 285, 289, 290, 292, 294,
295, 297, 300, 301, 302, 303, 306,
307, 308, 309, 310, 312, 333, 334,
340, 341, 344, 346, 347, 348, 353,
355, 356, 357, 358, 359, 360, 361,
362, 365, 366, 367, 368, 379, 385,
386, 395, 398, 399, 400, 402, 403,
404, 416, 426, 433, 444, 455, 457,
464, 465, 484, 485, 492, 494, 495,
496, 497, 498, 500, 502, 506, 508,
510, 512, 513, 516, 517, 518, 544,
549, 550, 551, 552, 553, 554, 557,
569, 571, 574, 577, 580, 582, 589,
597, 599, 601, 602, 603, 604, 606,
608, 615, 616, 620, 623, 646, 650,
651, 653, 658, 665, 666, 668, 670,
687, 689, 690, 709, 710, 716, 717,
719
Ivanski, 524
Ivensky, 599, 600

J

Jabotinsky, 142
Jaffe, 11
Jaffe Fine, 11
Jakaitis, 589, 596
Jamin, 591
Jarovski, 524
Jasunski, 534
Jasvonski, 524, 535
Jofe, 17, 335, 337, 575, 581, 582, 585,
588, 590, 592, 594, 595, 597, 600,
603, 604, 605, 606, 607
Joffe, 549
Josefer, 595
Josefovitz, 546, 547
Joselevitch, 545
Joselevitz, 521

Joselzon, 579
Jozefer, 579, 580, 600, 605
Jozefovitz, 527
Jozelit, 600
Juozas, 591, 596, 597
Jurburk, 576
Jurgenburg, 558
Jurksaitis, 596

K

Kabilkovsky[28], 578
Kadmon, 527
Kagan, 535, 545, 600
Kagansky, 579
Kairaitis, 583, 584, 587, 589, 591, 593,
596, 606, 607
Kalinski, 546
Kalisher, 143
Kaliski, 546
Kalnienai, 430, 437, 442
Kaluga, 60, 300
Kalyani, 423
Kamai, 298
Kamel, 334, 336
Kameri, 140, 295
Kaminskas, 453
Kamzon, 5, 47, 49, 50, 137, 567
Kandel, 207
Kansky-Shaltofer, 138
Kanter, 527
Kantor, 207, 536, 548
Kaplan, 9, 23, 103, 137, 170, 229, 251,
328, 334, 340, 349, 374, 417, 430,
443, 496, 522, 523, 525, 539, 540,
541, 542, 549, 551, 552, 576, 578,
581, 595, 600, 605, 615, 618, 623,
624, 625
Kapulsky, 207, 216, 292, 670
Karabelnik, 6, 21, 51, 64, 94, 96, 147,
171, 221, 228, 229, 239, 240, 276,
299, 307, 400, 401, 429, 498, 500,
523, 538, 545, 546, 583, 584, 600,
666
Karabelnik[25], 577
Karlebach, 278, 279, 280
Karlinksy, 104, 459
Karlinski, 443
Karlinsky, 428, 436, 578, 580, 584, 600
Karsten, 440
Karstenis, 597
Karstenis[52], 583
Kasif, 297, 524
Kassif, 7, 249
Kastel, 339

782   APPENDIX – Material Not in Original Yizkor Book